To Derek Ingram Hill O.K.S.

in commemoration

of the seventieth anniversary

of his entry into the King's School

from the Senior and Junior Schools

with our warm affection and prayers

John PH Lackway
Senior Chaplain

Canterbury

21st September '93

BARCHESTER

BARCHESTER

English Cathedral Life
in the Nineteenth Century

PHILIP BARRETT

First published in Great Britain 1993
Society for Promoting Christian Knowledge
Holy Trinity Church
Marylebone Road
London NW1 4DU

British Library Cataloguing-in-Publication Data

A catalogue record for this book is available from the British Library

ISBN 0–281–04667–0

Typeset by Ponting–Green Publishing Services, Chesham, Bucks
Printed in Great Britain by
Mackays of Chatham plc, Chatham, Kent

Contents

❈

Abbreviations

❃

ABDC	Act Book of the dean and chapter
ABVC	Act Book of the vicars choral
CCF	Church Commissioners' files
CCR	*Church Congress Report*
CM	Chapter Minutes
Chadwick, *York*	W. O. Chadwick, 'From 1822 until 1916', in G. E. Aylmer and R. Cant, eds, *A History of York Minster* (Oxford 1977), pp. 272–312
CRO	County Record Office
CT	*Church Times*
DRO	Diocesan Record Office
EHR	*English Historical Review*
FHCAR	*Friends of Hereford Cathedral Annual Report*
Greenhalgh, *Wells*	D. M. Greenhalgh, 'The Nineteenth Century and After', in L. S. Colchester, ed., *Wells Cathedral: A History* (Shepton Mallett 1982)
Hansard, P. D.	Hansard's Parliamentary Debates
HCA	Hereford Cathedral archives
HCL	Hereford Cathedral Library
HMC	Historic Manuscripts Commission
HT	*Hereford Times*
JEH	*Journal of Ecclesiastical History*
LPL	Lambeth Palace Library
MBVC	Minute book of the vicars choral
MT	*Musical Times*
NCL	Norwich Cathedral Library
Peel, *Memoirs*	Lord Mahon and E. Cardwell, eds, *Memoirs of Sir Robert Peel* (London 1856–7), 2 vols
PHPR	Pusey House Pamphlet Room
PP	Parliamentary papers
SDG	*Salisbury Diocesan Gazette*
TAMS	*Transactions of the Ancient Monuments Society*
TLCAS	*Transactions of the Lancashire and Cheshire Antiquarian Society*
Trefoil	A. C. Benson, *The Trefoil* (London 1923)
TWAS	*Transactions of the Worcestershire Archaeological Society*
TWNFC	*Transactions of the Woolhope Naturalists' Field Club*
VCH	*Victoria County History*
Walcott, *Traditions*	M. E. C. Walcott, *Traditions and Customs of Cathedrals* (London 1872)
Win.CA	Winchester Cathedral archives
Worc. C. Mss.	Worcester Cathedral manuscripts
Worc. C. Add. Mss.	Worcester Cathedral additional manuscripts
WSCRO	West Sussex County Record Office
YML	York Minster Library

List of Plates

❊

Photographic acknowledgements

Chichester Cathedral Trust/John Crook: 19
The Church Commissioners for England and the Lord Bishop of Salisbury/John Crook: 25
The Dean and Chapter of Exeter Cathedral/ University of Exeter: 11
Hampshire Record Office: 29
Clive Haynes: 22
The Dean and Chapter of Hereford Cathedral: 5, 12, 15, 18, 23
National Portrait Gallery, London: 2, 3, 4, 6, 9, 16, 17, 28
The British Architectural Library, RIBA, London/Geremy Butler photography: 21
Royal Institution of Cornwall: 20
The Dean and Chapter of Salisbury Cathedral/John Crook: 1, 24
The Pilgrims' School, Winchester/John Crook: 14
The Dean and Chapter of Winchester Cathedral: 7, 8, 26, 27, cover
The Dean and Chapter of Worcester Cathedral/ John Thoumine: 10, 13

I am also grateful to the following for their personal help in obtaining illustrations: John Crook, Miss Suzanne Eward, John Hardacre, Miss Sarah Lewin, Canon Iain MacKenzie, Captain H. B. Parker RN, R. D. Penhallurick, Miss Joan Williams, Dr Marshall Wilson.

Acknowledgements

❋

The research on which this book has been based was begun in 1969 while I was a student at Cuddesdon College, Oxford. I am very grateful to Lord Runcie of Cuddesdon, who was then principal of the college, for allowing and encouraging me to begin this work while I was still being trained for the Church's ministry.

I have been fortunate in being able to visit many splendid and gracious libraries and record offices during the course of my research. In particular, I should like to thank the staffs of the Bodleian Library, Oxford; Bristol City Record Office; the Church Commissioners Record Office; Dorset County Library; Exeter Cathedral Library; Gloucester Cathedral Library; Gloucestershire County Record Office; Hampshire County Library; Hampshire Record Office; Hereford Cathedral Library; Hereford and Worcester County Library; Lambeth Palace Library; Leicester University Library; Norfolk and Norwich County Record Office; Norwich Cathedral Library; Peterborough Cathedral Library; Pusey House, Oxford; Salisbury Cathedral Library; Southampton University Library; Wells Cathedral Library; West Sussex County Record Office; Winchester Cathedral Library; Worcester Cathedral Library and York Minster Library.

There are many individuals, both living and departed, to whom I owe a special debt for their help and assistance: Mr D. A. Armstrong, The Very Reverend Trevor Beeson, Dr G. F. A. Best, Canon Colin Beswick, Dr E. G. W. Bill, Canon Paul Britton, Dr C. K. F. Brown, Canon Frederick Bussby, Dr Owen Chadwick, Mr L. S. Colchester, The Right Reverend Peter Coleman, Mr Michael Craze, Miss Elisabeth Dimont, Mrs Audrey Erskine, Miss Suzanne Eward, Canon Arthur Gribble, Mr John Hardacre, Canon Peter Hinchliff, Mr C. L. Hodgetts, Miss Meryl Jancey, Mrs Bridget Johnston, The Reverend Adrian Leak, Miss Felicity Magowan, Dr David Marcombe, Canon Philip Martin, Mr F. C. Morgan, Miss Penelope Morgan, Dr Geoffrey Rowell, Mr Arthur Sabine, Miss Pamela Stewart, Mrs Barbara Carpenter Turner, Canon David Welander, Miss Joan Williams and Miss Pamela Woollard.

The early stages of the research were aided by a grant from the Cleaver Trustees, whose help I acknowledge with much gratitude. Part of Chapters 7 and 8 originally appeared in an article in the *Journal of Ecclesiastical History* in January 1974, and I am grateful to the Syndics of Cambridge University Press for their permission to reproduce some material from

ACKNOWLEDGEMENTS

that article in this book. I am also grateful to the Council of the Friends of Hereford Cathedral and to the Department of Adult Education of Nottingham University for permission to include material from various articles written by me and originally published by them. I am most grateful to the dean and chapter of each of the cathedrals mentioned in the bibliography of this book for enabling me to consult their records.

Several institutions and individuals have assisted me by providing the illustrations for this book, and their help is acknowledged on p. viii. To Miss Eilene Hassall I owe a very great and special debt for all her sterling assistance in the typing and retyping of much of the manuscript. I am also very grateful to Judith Longman and her colleagues at SPCK for all their help and assistance.

My greatest debt is more personal. As an undergraduate at Oxford, I had the great good fortune to be a pupil of Dr Eric Kemp, now Bishop of Chichester. His example, teaching, encouragement and friendship have been a major influence in my life, and he has patiently watched over this project for more than twenty years. I therefore dedicate this book to him, on the seventeenth anniversary of his enthronement, with my affection and gratitude.

Philip Barrett
Otterbourne Rectory,
25 October 1991

INTRODUCTION

❉

'T he work of cathedrals, like all other work,' Dean Lake of Durham
told the Church Congress in 1872, 'must be the work of living men;
it is we ourselves who must put life into it.'[1] The purpose of this book
is to describe the life of English cathedrals in the nineteenth century
and to show how this was founded on the work of a multitude of men
and women.

It is a study based on three strongly held convictions. First, that
cathedrals are a vital and essential element in the life of the Church of
England. Second, that a proper understanding of their distinctive opportunities and problems can be gained only by studying the way in which
they have developed, especially during the last 200 years. Third, that the
various duties for which cathedral chapters are responsible need to be
held in balance. Thus the cathedral fabric must be maintained, the music
and worship properly ordered, the library cared for, the mission of the
cathedral extended, the vergers properly motivated, the close kept tidy,
visitors welcomed, and the necessary funds to do all of this and more must
be raised. It is the interplay between these responsibilities and the
individuals responsible for them that gives cathedral life much of its
distinctive character.

I hope to follow this account of cathedral life in the nineteenth century
with a further study, in about ten years' time, of developments since 1900.
The remarkable resurgence of cathedrals during the last thirty years has
its roots in the reforms of the nineteenth century, but many contemporary
problems (not least financial ones) can also be traced back to that time.

Cathedrals are, indeed, powerful witnesses to the historic continuity of
the Church. They acquire their particular atmosphere through their daily
use by a particular group of people: the dean and chapter and other
persons appointed by them to fulfil the functions for which the cathedrals
were founded. The corporate responsibilities of the dean and chapter have
traditionally centred on the maintenance of the cathedral and its daily
round of worship. The elaborate liturgies of the Middle Ages were
replaced by simpler forms at the Reformation, but the tradition of sung
worship was maintained with at least two daily choral services, and the
number of said services gradually increased during the nineteenth century. The dean and chapter appointed and controlled all who assisted in
the worship of the cathedral, especially the organist, lay clerks, choristers,

junior clergy and vergers. They were also responsible for keeping in good repair the fabric of the cathedral itself and its ancillary buildings and other property in the close. Another local responsibility was the cathedral library, which might be (as for example, at Canterbury, York and Durham) of considerable size. The dean and chapter were also responsible for the administration of various local charities and charitable institutions, such as St Ethelbert's Hospital at Hereford, the College of Matrons at Salisbury, or Bishop Morley's College at Winchester. To enable them to discharge all these duties, they were endowed with estates. The chapter acts of all cathedrals up to the middle of the nineteenth century indicate that the chief concern of any dean and chapter was the administration of their property. The renewal of leases, the finding and appointment of tenants, the periodic inspection of the capitular estates, the repair of farm buildings, the constant concern to obtain the maximum profit from the property in question – these are the subjects that dominated the attention of a typical dean and chapter between the Reformation and the early nineteenth century. But it is important to realize that there were and are different kinds of cathedrals, each with their own characteristic constitution and tradition.

In the Middle Ages, there were two kinds of cathedrals in England. The first group consisted of nine secular cathedrals (St Paul's, Chichester, Salisbury, Wells, Exeter, Hereford, Lichfield, Lincoln and York), staffed by canons.[2] Their day-to-day life was based on customs which, in many cases, survived the Reformation. Their statutes were originally attempts by various medieval bishops to supply the defects of unwritten custom by promulgating a statute after discussion with the dean and chapter.[3] Codes of statutes, or individual statutes, were, however, amplified by the issuing of injunctions by bishops after their visitation of their cathedrals, and in the sixteenth century the injunctions by diocesan bishops were supplemented by royal or metropolitical injunctions to cathedral chapters.[4] Lincoln Cathedral followed the *Novum Registrum* of Bishop Alnwick, dating back to 1440, but this was only a draft set of statutes that had become hallowed by centuries of unofficial observance.[5] New codes of statutes were issued to Wells and Hereford Cathedrals in the reign of Elizabeth I and those of Hereford were further amended following Archbishop Laud's metropolitical visitation in the 1630s.[6]

The second group of cathedrals in medieval England were monasteries that also served as cathedrals. There were eight of these: Canterbury, Durham, Winchester, Rochester, Carlisle, Worcester, Norwich and Ely.[7] These were re-founded by Henry VIII, together with six former monasteries (Gloucester, Chester, Bristol, Peterborough, Oxford and Westminster) that became cathedrals. Westminster Abbey's short life as a cathedral lasted only until it became a monastery again in 1556. The cathedrals founded or re-founded by Henry VIII are both known collectively as cathedrals of the new foundation, as opposed to the surviving secular cathedrals known as cathedrals of the old foundation. All the new foundation cathedrals received statutes under an Act of Parliament of 1540,[8] but these were not issued under the Great Seal, as specified in the Act. In other words, they were only draft statutes for trial use. Under a fresh Act of Parliament in the reign of Philip and Mary, new statutes for Durham were issued.[9] The Henrician act was repealed shortly afterwards, with a proviso that the foundations should nevertheless continue.[10] New statutes for each cathedral were drafted in 1572, but not authorized. Even the statutes given to cathedrals such as Canterbury and Winchester in the reign of Charles I or those given by Charles II to Ely and Worcester were of doubtful validity, since they were not confirmed by Parliament. Matters came to a head at Carlisle in 1707 and a new Act of Parliament[11] said that in all the cathedrals founded by Henry VIII the statutes under which they had been operating in the reign of Charles II should 'be taken and adjudged to be good and valid in law, and be taken and adjudged to be the statutes of the said churches respectively'.[12]

The old and new foundations were alike in that their chapters were headed by a dean, but there were important constitutional differences between them. In the old foundation cathedrals the rest of the chapter was generally formed by a small group of residentiary canons (usually four or five) elected out of the larger number of prebendaries. In the new foundation cathedrals there was a larger group of residentiary prebendaries (varying between four at Carlisle and twelve at Westminster, Canterbury, Winchester and Durham), but no other non-residentiary body before the 1840 Cathedrals Act enabled them to style their residentiary prebendaries as canons and to have a larger body of honorary canons. In addition to the dean, there were three other dignitaries – the precentor, chancellor and treasurer – in old foundation cathedrals, but often they were not residentiaries and seldom attended their cathedrals. C. A. Belli was appointed Precentor of St Paul's Cathedral in March 1819 and died in January 1886 aged ninety-four, still in office. When he attended the Thanksgiving Service for the Prince of Wales in 1872, the dean's verger refused him access to his own stall; Belli visited the cathedral so rarely that he did not recognize him.[13]

A similar distinction should be made between the junior clergy of old foundation and new foundation cathedrals. In the late Middle Ages, those at old foundation cathedrals were incorporated into colleges of vicars choral, with their own buildings, endowments, rights and privileges. As a result, they formed a distinct corporation within the life of the cathedral and were often involved in disputes with the dean and chapter.[14] The junior clergy at new foundation cathedrals, on the other hand, were not gathered into a separate corporation. The Henrician statutes envisaged that they should still have a common table, but they depended absolutely on the dean and chapter to maintain them. On the other hand, the senior minor canon at a new foundation cathedral had a much greater control over the worship of the cathedral than any vicar choral in an old foundation cathedral, since he was given the duties of precentor.

Between the reign of Henry VIII and the end of the eighteenth century, English cathedrals enjoyed varying fortunes.[15] In Edward VI's reign they were subject to several royal injunctions which gave them a more Protestant ethos. Chantries were dissolved and statues and other images defaced. English services were introduced and vestments removed. When Mary succeeded to the throne, those cathedral clergy who had married were ejected and Catholic worship was revived. At the accession of Elizabeth, the wives and children of cathedral clergy were forbidden to live in the cathedral precincts, though the bishops were unsympathetic to this injunction. Puritans disliked cathedrals.[16] Preaching became more important, but their choirs flourished.[17] They become centres of education and learning.

Cathedrals were greatly influenced in the early seventeenth century by William Laud. Dean of Gloucester from 1616 to 1621, he reformed his own cathedral and, in 1634, after he had become Archbishop of Canterbury, he undertook an extensive metropolitical visitation of all cathedrals.[18] Some glimpses of life at Winchester may be gleaned from Dean Young's diary,[19] while in 1635 the descriptions of various cathedrals by Lieutenant Nowell Hammond and his companions give a fascinating account of cathedrals on the eve of the Civil War.[20]

Cathedral life, as it had been known for centuries, was destroyed during the period of the Civil War and Commonwealth. Many cathedrals were badly damaged by parliamentary soldiers,[21] Lichfield and Peterborough perhaps suffering the worst.[22] The Root and Branch Bill, introduced in 1641 but later abandoned, proposed the abolition of deans and chapters as well as bishops. Various ordinances during the next few years achieved this aim, and for the rest of the period of the Commonwealth, with their lawful clergy dispersed, their traditional services abolished, their estates confiscated, their fabrics often damaged or in decay, cathedrals were in a poor state, their only religious use being that of preaching-houses.

When Charles II was restored to the throne in 1660, cathedral life was also restored.[23] Many cathedrals were repaired. Lichfield, desolate and ruined in 1660, was rededicated in 1669. Old St Paul's was lost in the Great Fire of London in 1666, but Sir Christopher Wren's new baroque cathedral symbolized the confidence and ambition of the revived Church. Much research still needs to be carried out on cathedral life between the late seventeenth century and the end of the eighteenth century,[24] but there are two dominant impressions that have survived. The first is of the high level of scholarship among many cathedral clergy of the time. The Morley Library at Winchester and the Wren Library at Lincoln are evocative symbols of the importance placed on learning by chapters in the late seventeenth century.[25] Secondly, many cathedral clergy owed their advancement to royal or political patronage, and were often expected to exercise considerable influence on behalf of their patrons.[26] Many of them were both gentlemen and scholars, loyal to the established order of Church and State, playing their part in contemporary politics, maintaining the ordered round of worship in their cathedrals, often combining their stalls with a variety of other preferments. They were often educated, urbane, civilized men, whose considerable gifts have yet to be fully appreciated.

This settled way of life continued into the early years of the nineteenth century. But there was a growing demand for reform in both Church and State and in the 1830s a series of measures, culminating in the Dean and Chapter or Cathedrals Act of 1840, affected cathedrals radically. Their staffs and endowments were reduced and the enforced changes highlighted the need for those who worked in cathedrals to become more active and more faithful in discharging their duties. From the 1830s to the 1870s it is possible to see gradual changes taking place. Many extensive programmes of restoration were undertaken, but perhaps the most important change was the way in which most chapters commuted their estates in return for an agreed grant from the Ecclesiastical Commissioners, later being re-endowed with different estates which were supposed to give them a guaranteed income. In the last thirty years of the century there were some notable examples of vigorous cathedral life, especially at St Paul's and Worcester. New dioceses and cathedrals were being founded and the place and value of cathedrals in the life of the Church was widely recognized.

The process of reforming cathedrals, begun in the 1830s, was continued in various ways during the rest of the century.[27] Two Royal Commissions on cathedrals were appointed. The first lasted from 1852 to 1855 and the second from 1879 to 1885. Neither resulted in any specific legislation, but the reports of these commissions helped to make cathedrals more aware of their duties and responsibilities and are an invaluable quarry of material for historians. Archbishop Tait made several contributions to the debate about cathedral reform and issued two questionnaires, in 1869 and 1872, which also provided much useful information.

At the beginning of the nineteenth century there were twenty-two cathedrals in England. By 1900 there were thirty, as new dioceses had been founded at Ripon, Manchester, St Albans, Truro, Liverpool, Newcastle, Southwell and Wakefield. When Ripon and Manchester were created in 1836 and 1847, they were the first new dioceses for 300 years. In both dioceses there were suitably grand churches available to become cathedrals, but both had parochial responsibilities which therefore provided (from force of circumstances) new models of cathedral life and work.[28]

The see of Ripon was established by an Order in Council in 1836. James Webber, who was Dean of Ripon from 1828 to 1847, destroyed many interesting features of the Minster and discontinued some interesting customs, such as the Rogation Day procession and the distribution of apples among the congregation by the choristers on Candlemas Day.[29] A choral tradition was established only with difficulty. Nearly fifty years after the foundation of the cathedral it was still in a precarious state.[30]

The dual role of Manchester as both a cathedral and a parish church caused difficulties, but a succession of good deans helped to improve its liturgical life and pastoral influence. A good deal of restoration to the building was carried out and efforts were made to transform the jet-black building with a rather dirty interior into something more fitting. The Sunday services were mainly parochial in nature, but the daily services were more typical of cathedral worship. The ritual of the cathedral was an object of complaints in 1884, when the reredos was said to be 'only suitable for a Chinese joss-house'.[31]

The diocese of St Albans, founded in 1877, had a ready-made cathedral available in its ancient abbey, though its early history as a cathedral was dominated by the ill-judged restoration of Lord Grimthorpe.[32] At the diocesan conference in 1879 there were calls for the establishment of daily services and a model cathedral.[33] There was no dean and chapter and the substantial parochial responsibilities remained in the hands of the rector. The choir was voluntary and the daily offices were said. In 1899 a petition was sent to the Queen asking for the foundation of a dean and chapter. Letters Patent were issued and the first dean was appointed in 1900.[34]

The foundation of the diocese of Truro and the appointment of E.W. Benson as its first bishop was a momentous event in the history of English cathedrals in the nineteenth century. Benson had a deep love of cathedrals and an extensive knowledge of their history and constitutions. His boundless energy and enthusiasm was exactly what was needed to inspire the construction of the first new cathedral in England since Sir Christopher Wren's rebuilding of St Paul's in the seventeenth century. Benson was enthroned by the Bishop of Exeter in St Mary's Church, Truro, on 1 May 1877, with much pomp and ceremony.[35] But this church was far too small for a permanent cathedral. A new site was impossible since the Act of Parliament creating the see had specified this church as the cathedral. A committee was established under the chairmanship of Lord Mount Edgcumbe, the Lord Lieutenant, to consider what should be done.[36] A competition was held and J.L.Pearson's plans were accepted in August 1879. Benson was delighted and thought that his new cathedral would rank among the noblest in the land 'for grace, for religiousness, for simplicity'.[37] The foundation stone was laid on 20 May 1880 by the Prince of Wales, an occasion marked by huge crowds, triumphal arches and much bunting.[38] The old church began to be demolished in October 1880 and a large wooden building was erected to serve as the pro-cathedral until the first part of the construction work was completed.[39] This temporary building cost £430, seated 400, and was very cold in winter and too hot in the summer.[40] Benson tried to be at one of the services each Sunday, but felt that the interests of the growing cathedral and its ancient parish were divergent. His views found expression in the Truro Bishopric and Chapter Acts Amendment Act of 1887.[41] The statutes that he devised for Truro were modelled on those of Lincoln, and provided forms of service for the admission and installation of all members of the foundation. Although based on ancient precedents, Benson's statutes were specially adapted for the needs of the new diocese. One of the novel provisions was for a canon missioner, while the residentiary canons were given definite duties and required to keep eight months' residence. Benson secured for himself and his successors an important part in the affairs of the cathedral and also ensured that the honorary canons had a real voice in its deliberations.[42] The first eight honorary canons were installed in January 1878, but the residentiary chapter was not legally formed until the Act of 1887, which also provided for the rector of the parish to hold the office of subdean, the deanery being held by the bishop himself.[43] The endowment of the new cathedral was a continuing problem. The 1876 Act had precluded the Ecclesiastical Commissioners from endowing either the bishopric or the dean and chapter. Some progress had been made with the 1878 and 1887 Acts, but a further Bill introduced in 1887 by Lord Mount Edgcumbe was opposed by Earl Stanhope on behalf of the Ecclesiastical Commissioners and also by Lord Grimthorpe, who disliked chapters anyway. The Bill was thrown out in committee and the finances of the cathedral were therefore dependent on precarious local support.[44]

The consecration of the first part of the new cathedral took place in 1887. It was preceded by quiet days throughout Cornwall and processional litanies in the streets of Truro. A substantial portion of the cathedral had been completed, including the quire, transepts, St Mary's Aisle and two bays of the nave. Lists of guests were carefully drawn up and nineteen bishops attended the ceremony. Afterwards 500 people attended a civic banquet. The cathedral choir was augmented by choristers from eight other cathedrals and St Peter's, Eaton Square, London.[45] The sum of £120,000 had been raised for the erection and adornment of the first part of the cathedral and another £40,000 was collected by the end of the century.[46] Forms of daily prayer to be used by the workmen at the beginning and close of each day's work were drawn up by Benson, though later they were replaced by a weekly service. The largest number at work at the cathedral was 110 men. A rest room was provided for them and the public was asked to give magazines.[47] The furnishing of the new cathedral was paid for by the ladies of the diocese and the Community of the Epiphany supervised the cleaning, the flower arranging and the care of the sacristy.[48] At first, cathedral and parish responsibilities seemed to be in conflict, but the 1887 Act recognized St Mary's Aisle as the parochial church and gave it 'full parochial rights and privileges without interference by the capitular body'.[49] Work on the incomplete cathedral restarted in 1897 and was completed six years later.[50]

The dioceses of Liverpool, Newcastle, Southwell and Wakefield were formed in quick sucession between 1880 and 1888. At Liverpool, St Peter's Church became the pro-cathedral in 1880, but little progress was made until after the appointment of Bishop Chavasse in 1900, when the site for the present cathedral was chosen.[51] When the diocese of Newcastle was created in 1882, the large parish church of St Nicholas became the cathedral. There was no proper chapter at first and the honorary canons undertook some duties at the cathedral.[52] An Act of Parliament made provision for canons residentiary and £20,000 was given in 1900 for their endowment.[53] Southwell had an ideal building for a cathedral in its ancient minster. This became the cathedral of the new diocese in 1884. The non-residentiary canons of Lichfield and Lincoln who lived in the new diocese were able to transfer to the new chapter, and new honorary canons were appointed from Nottinghamshire and Derbyshire. The complete chapter numbered twenty-four honorary canons, in accordance with an Order in Council of 26 June 1884. It met for the first time on 16 December 1885. Definite duties were assigned to some of the honorary canons, but Bishop Ridding was installed as dean and the rector of the parish became the subdean.[54] This arrangement continued until the 1930s, though Bishop Ridding, who at first was puzzled by his 'cathedral in a village', drew up some regulations for it in 1887.[55]

Wakefield was the last cathedral to be founded during the nineteenth century. Here again there was a suitable parish church that was turned into a cathedral in 1888. The first bishop, William Walsham How, was enthroned by the Archbishop of York.[56] Ten years later his successor, Bishop Eden, stressed the need for an adequate cathedral, but here, as elsewhere, it took time for this to develop.[57]

This book is based on a wealth of available evidence, both published and unpublished. The primary sources for this investigation into the life of cathedrals during the nineteenth century are the chapter Act Books. They give a detailed picture of the actual working of cathedral government throughout the century. In addition, several chapters kept minutes of their meetings. In some cases, such as Hereford, these are rough notes written out later more fully in the Act Book. At Wells, however, the chapter Minute Books give the fuller picture of chapter meetings, while the Act Books record only the more formal and important decisions. The term 'Act Book' has been used throughout this book, even though at some cathedrals a slightly different term was used. Although some chapter Act Books of medieval and later times have been published, no Act Books for the nineteenth century have so far appeared in print. In addition to these books, there are substantial financial records for most cathedrals, as well as miscellaneous bundles of documents relating to various aspects of cathedral life. There are surprisingly few valuable collections of the private papers of cathedral dignitaries, but the extensive records of the two Cathedrals Commissions and the Ecclesiastical Commissioners have produced much important material.

As a comprehensive investigation of nineteenth century cathedral life would take a lifetime to complete, the research for this account has been concentrated on nine cathedrals in the south and west of England (Bristol, Chichester, Exeter, Gloucester, Hereford, Salisbury, Wells, Winchester and Worcester), though the work of other scholars has enabled material relating to the nineteenth century from each cathedral in England to be included. There are few references either to Westminster Abbey or to St George's Chapel, Windsor. These two great collegiate churches are royal peculiars and, although in their capitular organization and style of worship they share many affinities with cathedrals, they lack any diocesan reponsibilities. In the same way, the unique foundation of Christ Church, Oxford, both as the cathedral church of the diocese and as a college of the university, means that it is really *sui generis* and cannot easily be compared with other cathedrals.

The history of cathedrals as institutions as well as buildings seems to be attracting increasing attention from scholars. York Minster and Wells Cathedral were the subjects of extensive composite studies some years ago, and it is understood that further volumes on Canterbury, Lincoln and Rochester Cathedrals are in preparation. Canon Frederick Bussby's account of Winchester Cathedral, Canon David Welander's massive study of Gloucester, and more limited books on Durham and Canterbury by C. J. Stranks and Derek Ingram Hill, have also appeared in recent years. Peter Moore's unpublished survey of cathedral worship from the Reformation ended in the nineteenth century, but a more recent thesis by P. V. Coghlan has concentrated on the worship in the cathedrals of Ely, Norwich, Peterborough, St Albans and St Paul's from 1815 to 1914. Two other recent books include S. E. Lehmberg's study of cathedrals in the Tudor era, and a collection of essays on cathedrals since 1540 edited by David Marcombe and Charles Knighton. Many other recent studies of more limited aspects of nineteenth century cathedral life are listed in the bibliography.

The history of thirty institutions over a period of up to a hundred years in most cases is so vast a subject that some of the following chapters should be regarded only as introductory studies. There is ample scope for further research into subjects such as the restoration of cathedral fabrics in the nineteenth century, the administration of capitular estates, the finances of cathedrals, and the relationship between cathedral chapters and the Ecclesiastical Commissioners.

Those who delve into the history of cathedrals often find that the terminology is confusing. Sometimes this is simply a matter of spelling, since one encounters both 'virger' and 'verger' and 'bedesman' and 'beadsman'. The original documents of individual cathedrals are not always consistent, but 'verger' and 'beadsmen' are used in this book (although spelling has been left as in the original for direct quotes from source material). A more important ambiguity concerns the word 'prebendary'. This term was used for the members of chapters of new foundation cathedrals until 1840, after which they were styled 'canons residentiary'. In old foundation cathedrals, though, throughout the century the resident members of the chapter were known as canons and the term 'prebendary' was generally confined to those who were non-resident – apart from at Lincoln, Salisbury and Chichester, where the term 'canon' was preferred from about the middle of the century onwards.

This book is based on material presented in a thesis for the degree of Bachelor of Divinity submitted to the University of Oxford in 1989. It has been extensively rewritten, but the reader who wants further information may like to consult the copy of the thesis now deposited in the Bodleian Library at Oxford.

The life of English cathedrals in the nineteenth century experienced profound changes, but it is clear that it was a great age for cathedrals. The novels of such authors as Anthony Trollope, Victor Whitechurch and Hugh Walpole can give us only glimpses of cathedral life. We need to know the facts. It is hoped that this book will give the reader an accurate impression of what the life of Barchester was really like.

1

ENGLISH CATHEDRAL LIFE
IN THE EARLY NINETEENTH
CENTURY

❋

William Cobbett visited Winchester Cathedral on Sunday, 30 October 1825 and attended matins. He was not impressed with the experience and wrote:

> The 'service' was now begun. There is a *dean* and God knows how many *prebends* belonging to this *immensely rich* bishopric and chapter: and there were at this 'service' *two or three men* and *five or six boys* in white surplices, with a congregation of *fifteen women and four men*! Gracious God! ...it beggars one's *feelings* to attempt to find *words* whereby to express them upon such a subject and such an occasion.[1]

In the following year Cobbett visited Salisbury Cathedral and again attended a service:

> Yesterday morning I went into the Cathedral at Salisbury about seven o'clock. When I got into the nave of the church and was looking up and admiring the columns and the roof I heard a sort of *humming* in some place which appeared to be in the transept of the building.... I at last turned in at a doorway to my left, where I found a priest and his congregation assembled. It was a parson of some sort, with a white covering on him, and five women and four men: when I arrived there were five couple of us. I joined the congregation until they came to the Litany; and then, being monstrously hungry, I did not think myself bound to stay any longer.[2]

Although Cobbett was a very prejudiced observer, indignant at those who enjoyed the wealth of cathedral endowments at the expense of 'half-starved labourers', his views reflect a contemporary opinion of cathedrals which saw little to commend and, indeed, much to criticize in their life. There are three elements in his criticisms which were fairly common at the time. First, a clear anger directed at the wealth of cathedrals; second, a regret at finding such small congregations in such large buildings, and the implication that cathedrals were spiritually moribund; and thirdly, a lofty, rather worldly approach which recognized the artistic merit of the

1

architecture, but which saw little beyond a curiosity value in the life and worship of cathedrals. It is remarkable how these themes contributed together to the reforms of the 1830s and have continued to warp the popular estimation and understanding of cathedrals ever since. But Cobbett's impressions are those of a journalist, addicted to sensational comments and intemperate expressions. If we are to discover the truth about cathedrals in the early nineteenth century, then we must investigate them more fully and more carefully.

Cobbett's first concern when he visited Salisbury was to look about the nave and admire the architecture. We must therefore examine first the state of the actual cathedral buildings in the early nineteenth century. With the exception of St Paul's, built at the end of the seventeenth century, all the cathedrals in England were at least three hundred years old in 1800 and many had stood for six or seven centuries. They were the largest buildings in the country to have remained in continuous use for so long a time, and it is hardly surprising that many of them were in a very poor physical condition.

The architect E. W. Garbett, in describing the state of Winchester Cathedral in 1809, said:

...the transept was in great dilapidation, some of the northern part being used as a common workshop and depot for the coarsest materials; the windows were unglazed; many of the staircases and galleries choaked [sic] up with accumulations of rubbish of every description.[3]

A similar account of Hereford Cathedral in the following year by F. E. Gretton indicates a good deal of neglect:

...in the Cathedral were to be seen broken pavements, monuments uncared for, the grand Norman pillars buried in coats of whitewash. In the choir, the stalls were surmounted by galleries, both painted a yellowish-gray.... The Minster Yard was an untidy and uncared-for place.[4]

In 1832 the dean and chapter of Hereford told the Ecclesiastical Revenues Commission that

the fabric of the Church is kept in as good and sound state as the operation of time will permit, though the eastern transept, the Cloysters [sic] and some of the windows are much damaged by age and there have been (but not recently) serious sets or rents in some parts of the building.[5]

Nevertheless, many cathedrals had been extensively renovated and repaired in the late eighteenth and early nineteenth centuries. In some cases this was both necessary and timely. Hereford, after the fall of the western tower in 1786 and the consequent destruction of much of the nave, was repaired by James Wyatt. Elsewhere, however, Wyatt was more of a vandal than a restorer; he did extensive work at Lichfield between 1788 and 1795, but not without attracting criticism of his rearrangement of the quire,[6] while at Salisbury he removed many of the internal screens remaining from the Middle Ages, destroyed two chantry chapels and much of the stained glass, and repositioned several ancient tombs.[7] James Essex was another architect who did important, if regrettable, work at Ely and elsewhere, though here too Wyatt wreaked a certain amount of havoc.[8]

The spiritual condition of cathedrals in the early nineteenth century also varied. Matins and evensong were sung daily throughout the year, generally at 10 a.m. and 4 p.m., and in addition there was an early said service.[9] Holy Communion, however, was rarely celebrated. At Worcester in the early nineteenth century there were several Sundays each year when there was no celebration of communion 'for want of communicants'.[10] In 1827 there was no communion service on thirty-eight Sundays, including a long period between 5 August and 7 October.[11] Choral celebrations of the eucharist had virtually ceased. The only place where they were still held seems to have been at Durham, where

> great sublimity is still maintained on these occasions from the very impressive and devout assistance the service acquired by the addition of the organ and the voices of the choir, which never fail to infuse into the souls of the communicants a real sense of the benefits they receive.[12]

Sermons, however, were much appreciated. Thomas Rennell, who was Dean of Winchester from 1805 to 1840, was highly regarded as a preacher by William Pitt the Younger, who called him the 'Demosthenes of the pulpit'. But Sydney Smith described him in the *Edinburgh Review* in 1802 as 'a ponderous limner'.[13] Smith's own preaching certainly caused a great impression, both at Bristol Cathedral, where he became a prebendary in 1828, and later at St Paul's Cathedral. A contemporary account of his sermon on 5 November 1828 records:

> Although we went to the Cathedral long before doors were open, we found a crowd already established there; and when the doors *were* opened, it was a rush like entering the pit of a theatre on the night of a new play.... As he walked up the aisle to the altar, I always thought of Cardinal Wolsey, there was an air of...proud dignity.[14]

There are more detailed comments on his preaching style after Smith had become a canon of St Paul's. In 1834 an evening sermon there was reported to be 'very good; manner impressive, voice sonorous and agreeable, *rather* familiar but not offensively so, language simple and unadorned, sermon clever and illustrative'.[15]

An American visitor, George Ticknor, was also impressed with Sydney Smith's preaching, describing a sermon that he heard as 'by far the best sermon I ever heard in Great Britain'.[16]

The charitable responsibilities of English cathedrals have a tradition that goes back through many centuries. Several chapters, or individual members of them, took this side of their work very seriously in the early nineteenth century. One of the most notable in this respect was Frederick Iremonger, a prebendary of Winchester Cathedral. His premature death in 1820 at the age of thirty-nine caused acute shock throughout the diocese, not least among schoolchildren, in whom he had taken a particular interest. The *Hampshire Chronicle* commented: 'Wherever there was poverty, affliction or disease, there was Frederick Iremonger.'[17] At Hereford, Canon John Napleton was known as 'a discriminating and liberal benefactor of the poor': 'He always considered it best to relieve the Poor by giving them employment, by supplying them with small sums unknown to the parish officers, and by procuring them medical aid during illness.'[18]

In 1816 the vicars choral at Hereford, possibly enouraged by Napleton's example, gave 10 guineas to a fund to relieve the 'labouring poor' of the city, 'owing to the great scarcity and distress of the present time'.[19] The dean and chapter of Canterbury gave £10 'as a gratuity towards providing Flannel Wastecoats [sic] for the Canterbury Volunteers' in 1803 and 100 guineas 'for the sufferers in the British Army under the command of Lord Wellington at Waterloo' in 1815.[20] In 1801 the dean and chapter of Worcester gave 20 guineas towards the establishment of a Sunday School for poor children in the city.[21] A few months earlier they contributed towards a fund for the widows and orphans of sailors who died in the battle of Copenhagen.[22] Two years later they gave £100 to the county subscription for clothing the Loyal Volunteers, and £50 to the similar city subscription, and £50 to the poor in 1816.[23] At Winchester in 1809 the chapter sold 1,000 bushels of coal to the poor at half-price, gave £20 to poor relief, and sent the chapter clerk to ask the mayor to call a public meeting to consider 'a proper mode of relieving the poor inhabitants of the said city and suburbs at this inclement season'.[24] In the following year the dean and chapter of Salisbury gave £50 to the Society for Clergy Orphans,[25] while in 1833 the dean and chapter of Winchester gave £125 to distressed Irish clergy.[26] Many similar expressions of charitable concern may be found among chapter acts in the early years of the century.

If cathedrals were a centre of charity at this time, they were also a place of learning and scholarship. In a pamphlet published in 1833, E. B. Pusey devoted many pages to proving the long history of cathedral scholarship[27] and complained that: 'the only remaining provision for what every portion of the Church of Christ has thought necessary for its well-being, a learned and studious clergy, is our Cathedral Institutions. And shall we, in such times, destroy these?'[28]

Winchester Cathedral again provides two good examples of cathedral clergy who were well known for their scholarly labours in the early years of the century. Although he was only dean for a year, from 1804 to 1805,

Robert Holmes has left an enduring reputation for his prodigious learning in his great collection of the Greek manuscripts of the Old Testament. The Bodleian Library contains no less than 164 volumes of manuscript collations that he wrote in preparation for this work.[29] Only five years after Holmes's death, George Nott was appointed a prebendary of Winchester at the age of forty-three. For the next thirty years he was to be a major figure in the life of the cathedral. He had already held the appointments of Fellow of All Souls and Bampton Lecturer at Oxford. He edited the works of Henry Howard, Earl of Surrey, and Sir Thomas Wyatt the Elder, published a translation of the *Book of Common Prayer* into Italian as well as other books in that language, and amassed a huge library of over 12,000 books.[30]

Cathedrals in the early nineteenth century were therefore not quite so moribund as William Cobbett believed. Admittedly the few examples quoted are outstanding rather than typical, but it is clear that in many cases deans and chapters took their responsibilities seriously. Nevertheless, there were many individuals on cathedral chapters who brought nothing but notoriety to the close. The chief abuses in the cathedral system were non-residence, pluralism, nepotism and general worldliness.

Probably the most flagrant example of non-residence was that of the daft Earl of Bridgewater, who was a prebendary of Durham for forty-nine years until his death in 1829. He lived, however, in the Rue St Honoré in Paris, collecting manuscripts and pairs of boots, fathering several illegitimate daughters, and stocking his garden with rabbits and his house with dogs, two of whom were specially favoured by being dressed in yellow coats and silver collars and fed by lackeys at his table.[31] Dean Powys of Canterbury was seldom seen in his cathedral between 1797 and 1809, though it is said that 'he spent Lent in Canterbury to hear the minor canons preach',[32] while the redoubtable Maria Hackett severely rebuked the dean and chapter of St Paul's in March 1813:

> The Dean's attendance for the last ten months has not amounted to so many days. I believe Dr. Weston has not been in the Cathedral since July. Dr. Wellesley... rarely favours them with his presence above thirty days in the year.[33]

Prebendary Fountain of Worcester was not able to take his turn of residence because of ill-health for the first fourteen years of the century. In 1806 the chapter reminded him of the 'ruinous state' of his prebendal house; two years later, since he had taken no action, the house was repaired by the chapter and the cost deducted from Fountain's stipend and dividend.[34]

Cathedral stalls were often held in plurality with other preferments. Nearly forty years later it was alleged that in 1829 the deaneries of St Paul's, Durham, Wells and Rochester were all held by various diocesan bishops, who also occupied canonries at St Paul's, Durham, Christ Church, Oxford and Westminster Abbey. Two canonries at Durham were also held by bishops.[35] E. B. Pusey complained that in 1836 the bishoprics of Bristol, Carlisle, Chester, Exeter, Gloucester, Hereford, Llandaff, Oxford, Rochester and St David's were all combined with cathedral preferment.[36] George Pelham, who was bishop successively of Bristol, Exeter and Lincoln, managed to retain a stall at Chichester Cathedral for over twenty years from 1806 to 1827.[37] Though pluralism often meant that the bishops in question rarely appeared in their cathedral stalls, George Murray, who was Bishop of Rochester and Dean of Worcester from 1828 to 1845, was (at least initially) very regular in his attendance at meetings of the chapter at Worcester. Installed on 13 April 1828, he attended every meeting until 23 June in the following year.[38] In 1840, the prebendaries of York Minster included four deans (Lichfield, Wells, Norwich and Gloucester), two residentiary canons of other cathedrals (Exeter and Carlisle), one canon of Christ Church, Oxford, two prebendaries of other cathedrals (Exeter and Durham) and incumbents from parishes as far distant as the Isle of Wight and Kent.[39] At Bristol Cathedral in 1832 the dean and all the canons also had livings, some as far away as Norfolk and Wales.[40] Dean John Lamb combined the deanery of Bristol with the mastership of Corpus Christi College, Cambridge, and the living of Olveston, driving in from there to attend services at the cathedral. Lord William Somerset, who was a canon of Bristol from 1822 to 1851, held no less than six livings, three of which he never visited. His combined income from all his ecclesiastical preferments came to over £3,000 a year.[41] This was exceeded by George Pretyman, a canon of Winchester from 1825 to 1859. In addition to his Winchester canonry, he was also Chancellor of Lincoln Cathedral and Prebendary of Biggleswade, and incumbent of three parishes. He spent three months of each year at Winchester, another three months at Lincoln, and divided the rest of his time between his various livings.[42] The canons of Canterbury in the early nineteenth century were all well provided with additional livings.[43] Walker King, who was Bishop of Rochester from 1809 to 1827, was a canon of Wells Cathedral and Westminster Abbey and also held the benefice of Burnham-on-Sea.[44] In 1812 John Fisher, whose uncle was Bishop of Salisbury, became a prebendary of the cathedral a month after his ordination as a deacon. Within a few months he had also been given a living that was worth £250 a year, but he employed a curate to maintain the parish as he preferred to live at the palace and fulfil the role of domestic chaplain to his uncle.[45] This general habit of combining cathedral stalls with other work was a considerable abuse, and only added to the widespread feeling against cathedrals in the early years of the century.

In many cases, of course, pluralism was compounded with nepotism and to have a bishop as a relative was a useful means of ecclesiastical advancement. The 1832 edition of *The Extraordinary Black Book* revealed that the two sons and one son-in-law of Bowyer Edward Sparke, who was Bishop of Ely from 1812 to 1836, had annual incomes of £4,500, £4,000 and £3,700 respectively (though the bishop himself had an income of £27,742).[46] When Bishop Brownlow North of Winchester died in 1820, the chapter of his cathedral was something of a family club, since two sons, two sons-in-law and three more distant relatives all held stalls there.[47] Richard Beadon, who was Bishop of Bath and Wells from 1802 to 1824, made one of his relatives precentor of the cathedral and another chancellor. His successor, G. H. Law, made one of his sons Archdeacon of Wells and canon of the cathedral, while another was appointed treasurer. The latter also enjoyed a prebend of Chester (as did his brother-in-law), where Law had previously been bishop.[48] George Pretyman's two stalls at Lincoln and Winchester can be explained by the fact that his father, George Pretyman Tomline, was successively bishop of both those sees. His brother, Richard Pretyman Tomline, was precentor of Lincoln, warden of the Mere Hospital, and incumbent of four livings. By 1837 his income from fines and the sale of timber exceeded £14,000.[49]

George Pretyman is a good example of one of the most telling criticisms of cathedrals in the early nineteenth century: that of worldliness. Although he survived until the 1850s, and was by then something of a relic of a bygone age, he still gave great dinners at Winchester and equipped his servants with yellow livery.[50] At Lincoln, where he was chancellor, he was said to appear at services 'in top boots and white cord breeches' and 'was said to hurry from a cathedral service to Doncaster where he would appear on the course with book and pencil'. At the 1834 Lincoln races he was rumoured to have lost £7,000.[51] Dr Nelson, a brother of Admiral Lord Nelson, was a canon of Canterbury from 1803 to 1838. He was described as 'a rough man, fitted to be a country squire, rather short and stout, who wore a long black frock coat nearly to his ankles, Hessian boots and a large shovel hat'. From time to time he would take a newspaper with him into his stall at weekday services, but his deafness prevented him realizing that others present were aware of the rustling of the pages.[52] Many cathedral closes were well known for their social life in the early nineteenth century. In 1808 Thomas Wait, the chapter butler at Carlisle Cathedral, listed the contents of the pantry in the fratry, which contained eight wine decanters, one pint decanter for brandy, forty-one best wine glasses, fifteen ale glasses and twelve silver spoons.[53] Dining in each other's houses in the close was clearly taken very seriously at Salisbury in the early years of the century. John Fisher wrote to John Constable in 1822: 'So belly devoted are the good people here that they look upon it as a sort of *duty* imposed on the Canons-in-residence, to dine out or give a dinner every day as punctually as he goes to Church.'[54] It was still a feature of the life of Durham when J. B. Dykes became a minor canon there in 1849.[55] The Three Choirs Festival, held annually in turn at Gloucester, Hereford and

Worcester Cathedrals, was as much a social as a musical occasion, and something of the atmosphere of its social side may be gained from the following account of the Festival Ball in *Berrow's Worcester Journal*:

> The Ball at the College Hall on Friday evening was one of the most brilliant assemblages ever seen in this neighbourhood; nearly seven hundred persons were present and the dresses of the ladies were superb, displaying a profusion of costly jewellery. Weippert's excellent band was in attendance and gallopades, waltzes and quadrilles were the order of the evening. Towards 12 the company began to adjourn to the Chapter Room, where a most sumptuous supper was prepared...
>
> After partaking of this repast, the company returned to the Hall, where dancing was kept up till between five and six in the morning. On Wednesday and Thursday evenings the Dean and Prebendaries liberally entertained 350 guests with a sumptuous supper in the Chapter Room.[56]

Dinner parties at Hereford, however, occurred only rarely. F. E. Gretton recalled that they were generally at 5 p.m. rather than the usual hour of 3 p.m.:

> The favourite gatherings were at six o'clock; tea and cards, with negus and cakes handed about during the evening; departure before tea. Sometimes the party ended with a supper – some substantial and mostly hot dish at the head, various kickshaws down the table. To these parties the matrons came in sedan-chairs. The younger damsels walked with a lantern borne before them... [57]

Despite all these abuses, difficulties and distractions, however, the daily life of cathedrals still continued. For the average canon in the early years of the century, two preoccupations would have dominated everything else: the corporate responsibility of the dean and chapter for their capitular property, and the regular choral worship of the cathedral. At Worcester in 1800, apart from admitting a chorister, inspecting the accounts of St Oswald's Hospital, presenting two incumbents to livings, giving a guinea each to the beadsmen and vergers as a Christmas bonus, re-electing the subdean, receiver-general and treasurer, and receiving a medical certificate from an absent prebendary, the only matters discussed by the chapter related to their property.[58] At this time it was common for chapters to lease nearly all their property, whether a farm, a tenement or tithes, for a number of years. A small annual rent was paid to the chapter for each property rented, but the leases were renewable every seven years and the bulk of the income from property came from substantial fines paid when a lease was renewed.[59] Contact between the chapter and their tenants was maintained through an agent,[60] though cathedral clergy often took a lively interest in their estates and tenants.[61] At the June audit each year the dean and chapter of Worcester fixed the price of wheat on the capitular estates, while the price of barley was determined earlier in the year.[62] In November the Audit Dinner was held. This could be quite expensive; in 1808, £34 was spent on 'wine, brandy and etc.', while for 1820 a complete list of expenses has survived, totalling over £112.[63] At Winchester, Audit Dinners were held on three consecutive days – the Thursday, Friday and Saturday in the week preceding 25 November, the day of the November audit and general chapter meeting. One of the canons, who occupied the position of receiver, and who was thus the member of the chapter responsible for the administration of the capitular estates and the funds that they had produced, entertained successively 'the gentlemen of the Close', the minor canons and the farmers. The menus for these dinners have survived and they provide a fascinating (and possibly unique) insight into capitular diets in the nineteenth century. The festivities began at noon on the Thursday, when a hot leg of mutton was sent down for the cathedral servants. At six in the evening, however, the canons sat down to a feast that always included a whole sirloin of beef and a calf's head, but with a great deal more besides. The 1839 dinner, for example, included cod fish, boiled turkey, patties and mutton cutlets, gurkin pork and champagne, curry, tongue, rissolles and sauterne, the great roast sirloin, white soup, three partridges, raspberry cream, stewed pears, jelly orange, rice shapes, mince pies, plum pudding and pheasant. 'The plum puddings', a note with the menu adds, 'are the rich puddings that are called the pound puddings; besides those for the parlour two very large ones are made every day for the hall for the servants of the church who dine there the three days, and the clerks'. In 1840 the first day's dinner showed some variation, and the menu included stewed pigeons, sweet breads, 'champagne handed round', apple jelly and sponge. Whatever was left over, the servants could have for their suppers and for a cold lunch on the next two days. On the Friday it was the turn of the minor canons to sit down to a sumptuous meal; while on the Saturday at 3 p.m. the farmers were regaled with a more country-style menu, which included three boiled fowls, vegetables (not specified), goose, pig's face, two ducks and two pheasants. The apple and gooseberry pies seem to have been too much for them in 1839, while a note against the 1840 menu tells us that an attempt to cut down to two boiled fowls had been insufficient to meet the demand. Finally, on the Saturday evening, the cathedral servants were issued with punch. The cost of the food in 1840 amounted to £12 10s 1½d but, with the addition of coal, candles, breakages, wine and tips, the total came to £26 10s. Between ten and twenty people sat down to dinner each day.[64]

The general condition of cathedral choirs in the early nineteenth century was poor. At Winchester, George William Chard needed frequent reminders to attend to his duties. In particular he was told

to instruct the choristers regularly and systematically in their duty and teach them by note, and that he be particularly impressed with the necessity of instructing them to make the responses and etc. in a decent uniform manner and not at the highest pitch of their voices as at present, which resembles a street cry rather than a religious rite.

Chard continued to be neglectful, only taking choristers' practices fourteen times between 1 December 1817 and the same date in 1818 and including an absence of more than three consecutive months. He was frequently absent on Sundays and was threatened with dismissal.[65] But Chard had only half his mind on his music. He was more interested in hunting.[66]

Probably the best-known organist in England at the beginning of the century was Thomas Attwood at St Paul's Cathedral. A protégé of the Prince of Wales and a pupil of Mozart, he was appointed to St Paul's in 1796 at the age of thirty and remained there until his death in 1838. He befriended and encouraged Mendelssohn, but the standard of the cathedral choir in his day left much to be desired. Maria Hackett gives the impression in her diary that there was no pre-service practice and that Attwood's preparation for services was lax. Her journal for 6 September 1834 records that

> in the psalms the organ accompaniment was so rapid that it was scarcely possible for the choir to keep up with it.... In the Creed and Lord's Prayer all parties seemed to be running races to try who should first reach the Amen. An anthem by Boyce was appointed, but the leading bass voices being, as usual, absent, a prolonged discussion took place, and an anthem by Greene was finally substituted.

A few days earlier, on 31 August 1834, it had been decided to alter the Jubilate from *Boyce in A* to another setting. This led to much whispering and shuffling of music books by the choir. No one had told the organist and he began to play the original setting: 'Another interchange of messages was required, another search for music took place, and the hymn was half over before the organist and choir came to a right understanding.'

On 22 September a discussion of ten or twelve minutes' length took place about changing the anthem and Miss Hackett added: 'During the last few weeks I have noticed more blunders and substitution of music than in all the other cathedrals I have visited throughout England.'[67] She was tireless in her concern to improve the educational facilities for choristers, which were certainly at a low ebb at the beginning of the century. At St Paul's in 1813 she found one boy who after seven years in the choir 'could neither play a bar of music nor read at sight'.[68] When Ralph Banks was appointed organist of Rochester Cathedral in 1790 after some years at Durham, he found that only one lay clerk attended each week. Two services – *Aldrich in G* and *Rogers in D* – and seven anthems had been used in rotation on Sundays for the past twelve years.[69] When Sir Charles Anderson attended a service at Lincoln on the eve of Whitsunday 1830, he found only the officiating vicar choral and ten choristers: there was no one besides himself in the congregation.[70]

By the time of the great Reform Bill of 1832 it was widely apparent that cathedrals, no less than Parliament itself, needed to be reformed. That they were served by men of piety as well as worldliness, learning as well as ignorance, and devotion as well as slackness, was not doubted. But few could deny that their considerable wealth was hampering the urgent need of the Church to develop its missionary and pastoral work in the rapidly growing urban areas of the country. Both investigation and reform were needed. For cathedrals as well as for the country as a whole, 1832 was a momentous year and marked the beginning of the end of the old order in the cathedrals of England.

2

CHURCH REFORM
AND CATHEDRALS

❖

The clamour for church reform, which reached its peak in the 1830s, had its origins in the late eighteenth century. Bishop Richard Watson told Archbishop Cornwallis in 1783 that a fairer distribution of ecclesiastical revenues was needed. Another influential advocate of reform was Richard Yates, the chaplain of Chelsea Hospital.[1] In the early nineteenth century some measures were passed, including the Non-Residence Act of 1803, the Curates Act of 1813 and the Church Building Act of 1818, but more far-reaching reforms were still needed.[2]

By 1830 there was a growing demand for parliamentary reform. The Church's initial opposition to this led to a demand that the Church should also be drastically reformed.[3] The government that Lord Grey formed at the end of 1830 included not only Whigs but also several Canningite Tories who saw the need for parliamentary reform. When a Reform Bill was introduced in 1831, it was rejected in the House of Lords. Only two bishops voted in favour of the Bill and six abstained, while Archbishop Howley and twenty other bishops voted against it.

The bishops swiftly became the focus for popular anger and there were ugly scenes in different parts of England. The worst trouble was at Bristol, where a mob attacked the Mansion House, the city gaol, and the bishop's palace, wrecking the furniture and setting it on fire. The chapter-house of the cathedral was ransacked and many books and documents burnt. The cathedral itself was spared only by the brave action of William Phillips, the sixty-one-year-old sub-sacrist, who closed the cloister door and defended it with an iron bar.[4]

During the winter of 1831–2, attempts were made both by Grey and William IV to persuade the bishops to change their minds. Grey introduced a fresh Bill in December 1831 that included some minor changes without losing its major thrust. It was passed by the Commons and survived its second reading in the Lords in April 1832 by nine votes. On 7 May 1832, however, the Lords carried a wrecking amendment. Grey asked the king to create enough peers to carry the Bill and resigned when he refused.

William turned to Wellington and asked him to form a ministry to carry 'the Bill, the whole Bill, and nothing but the Bill'. There were further ugly incidents in England against the bishops, the peers, and even the king and queen. Wellington failed to persuade the Tories to support him and abandoned the task. The king therefore had to return to Grey and could persuade him to resume office only by giving a written promise to create sufficient peers to carry the Reform Bill in the House of Lords. When this threat became known, the opposition in the Lords subsided; not a single bishop voted against the third reading of the Bill on 4 June 1832. When Archbishop Howley visited Canterbury in August, however, for his primary visitation, he was faced with an unruly mob who pelted his carriage and broke its windows. The established Church, with its bishops and its cathedrals, had its back to the wall as a result of the widespread hostility and unpopularity it had attracted through its opposition to the Reform Act.[5]

This unpopularity was caused not only by political considerations. There was a great deal of criticism of the Church on financial grounds. Between 1820 and 1823 a Utilitarian journalist by the name of John Wade had published a series of pamphlets entitled *The Black Book*, in which he gave details of the income of the clergy and other members of what a later generation called 'the establishment'. By 1831 he had sold 14,000 copies. In 1831 he published a new and revised edition under the name of *The Extraordinary Black Book*, and further editions appeared in 1832 and 1835. Although many of his figures were wrong, Wade showed clearly the massive amount of wealth unequally enjoyed in the Church. Sir Samuel Whalley described the Church as 'one universal system of fraud and robbery'.[6] The question of a reformed Parliament had raised the question of a reformed Church. Men began to demand that church endowments, pluralities and non-residence must be investigated without delay. Archbishop Howley introduced two Bills in 1831, but they were not sufficient to stem the cry for reform. *The Times* said that the 'establishment of the Church of England is now in serious peril'.[7]

The attack on the Church was fanned by Radicals and Utilitarians such as Hume and Bentham. They would have dismantled the Church, with its bishops, cathedrals and endowments. But the Church was in no less danger from those who were its most ardent defenders. A blind, unyielding conservatism that refused to recognize the beam in its own eye would have led inevitably to the destruction of the Church of England. Yet the Church itself had no power to help itself; the convocations remained in suspension and there was no formal machinery for the making of decisions. If the Church was to survive, only the government could act.[8] When Hume suggested an official enquiry he managed to unite the conservatives and moderates, for an investigation of accurate facts and statistics would be an effective reply to the wilder pamphleteers while the moderates saw that a commission should lead to reform. On 23 June 1832 Lord Grey issued the names of the Church Revenues Commission and charged it with the task of a complete investigation of the Church's finances. This marked the beginning of the reform of the Church.[9]

The appointment of the Commission could only delay the inevitable changes that would have to be made; it could not prevent them. Indeed, in the sense that later reforms were based upon the findings of this Commission, it facilitated them. Pamphlets continued to be published suggesting various changes. The most influential was *A Plan of Church Reform* by Robert Eden, better known as Lord Henley. Henley was a barrister, a master in chancery, and an expert on bankruptcy. He was the brother-in-law of Sir Robert Peel and was removed from public office in 1840 as a result of mental incapacity. Henley's proposals sprang from two general principles – to separate the Church of England from its involvement with the State and to turn cathedrals into parish churches. His scheme therefore envisaged the bishops being turned out of the House of Lords and being appointed by a commission of senior bishops and laity. Their income would be equalized and translations from see to see prohibited. All stipends in the Church would be linked with pastoral duties, canonries suppressed, and cathedrals converted into parish churches. Henley saw that these measures could be effected only by the establishment of a permanent board of commissioners, which would administer church property with a consistency and competence that individual clerical landlords could not always emulate.[10]

If the call for the reform of the Church of England was insistent, the demand for the reform of the Irish Church was urgent. There was continuous agitation and violence. Even *The Times* could not defend the provision of four archbishops and eighteen bishops for the Protestant minority. The Bill to reorganize the Irish Church was published in February 1833. Radicals, moderates and Catholics were overjoyed, but the Tories were enraged. Five months later John Keble preached the Assize Sermon at Oxford and denounced the government for 'National Apostasy' in seeking to reorganize the Irish Church. Thus the Oxford Movement was born.

The Irish Church Bill once again threatened a clash between the Lords and the Commons. Wellington suggested that if its more extreme provisions were dropped this danger could be averted. The Catholics and radicals were angry, but the emasculated Bill was safely passed. By the summer of 1834, in the aftermath of the Irish reforms, Lord Grey's government was falling apart. Lord Melbourne briefly succeeded Grey, but the king soon dismissed him and sent for Wellington. Wellington told the king that the new Prime Minister must be in the Commons and so Peel was summoned from Italy and asked to form a minority government.[11] Parliament was dissolved and an increased number of Tories was returned at the ensuing election.

Peel's policies at the election in December 1834 were set out in the address to his constituents at Tamworth known as the Tamworth Manifesto. In this document he stated his support for the great Reform Act of

1832 and indicated that he was in favour of a redistribution of ecclesiastical revenues:

> if, by an improved distribution of the revenues of the Church, its just influence can be extended, and the true interests of the Established religion promoted, all other considerations should be made subordinate to the advancement of objects of such paramount importance.[12]

Thus Peel committed himself to reforming the Church of England and this began a process that has had lasting effects. Yet it appears that he did not have a preconceived plan.[13] Early in 1835 he had interviews with Archbishop Howley and others.[14] A month later the names of the Ecclesiastical Duties and Revenues Commission were announced. They included both archbishops, and the Bishops of London, Lincoln and Gloucester. Peel himself, with two Cabinet ministers and four others, represented the laity. As long ago as December 1832 Blomfield had advocated a commission of clergy and laity 'to consider what measures should be adopted in the way of Church reform'.[15] Peel's commission was asked not only to bring about 'the more equal distribution of Episcopal Duties' and the prevention of commendams, but also to set forward the increased efficiency of cathedral and collegiate churches and the 'best mode of providing for the Cure of Souls'.[16]

Peel's objectives were clearly based on his brother-in-law's plan published nearly three years earlier.[17] The commissioners wasted no time. Their first report was published in March 1835, only six weeks after their first meeting. It was based on the newly collected statistics provided by Grey's commission of inquiry and proposed a reconstruction of episcopal boundaries and incomes. The cathedrals were not touched, but none doubted that they were next in line. Only three weeks later, however, Peel's government was defeated three times and he resigned. The Whigs, led by Lord Melbourne, returned to power. Nevertheless, Peel had initiated an irreversible reform of the Church which was supported by both the Tories and the Whigs.[18]

Melbourne renewed the Commission on taking office and replaced its lay members with Whigs. His nominees were not so interested in the business of the Commission as the Tories had been, and so the bishops came to have the dominant place in its affairs. The Commission certainly pressed on with its work, with Blomfield as its leading member. Archbishop Vernon Harcourt's comment has often been quoted, but nevertheless shows clearly how the other members regarded him as indispensable: 'Till Blomfield comes, we all sit and mend our pens, and talk about the weather.'[19] The second report of the Commission, published in March 1836, proposed a radical reconstruction of capitular establishments and revenues in order to provide new churches and clergy for the teeming industrial cities. The second report was made possible by the final report of Lord Grey's commission of inquiry, published in June 1835.[20] It was also aided by an enquiry that the Commission had promoted in 1835 among bishops and cathedrals of the old foundation who were not represented on the Commission, asking their views about the best way of applying sinecure prebends and offices to the improvement of spiritual instruction.[21] The second report proposed the abolition of all non-residentiary canonries in cathedrals, the limitation of residentiary canonries to four in each cathedral, and the appropriation of the separate estates of deans and canons of old foundation cathedrals. About £130,000 per annum was thought to be available from the endowments of nearly 400 prebends and their share in corporate revenues. Other provisions included a reduction in the number of minor canons or vicars choral.[22] The commissioners hoped to use this money to build more churches in urban areas and to augment poor livings – they estimated that there were 3,528 worth less than £150 a year.[23] In this report they said that they had begun their deliberations with the premise that if cathedral endowments were larger than necessary, they would use the surplus to endow poor benefices.[24] Their instructions, so far as cathedrals were concerned, had been to consider their state 'with a view to the suggestion of such measures as may render them conducive to the efficiency of the Established Church'. They were now

> prepared to recommend such measures as will, in our opinion, leave a sufficient provision for the proper performance of the services of the churches, for the continual reparation and maintenance of the Fabrics, and for the other objects contemplated by the Founders; and at the same time allow the application of a considerable portion of their revenue to the purpose of making additional provision for the Cure of Souls in Parishes where such assistance is most required.[25]

The third report, which appeared in May 1836, proposed that the Commission should become permanent, while the fourth report, published a month later, outlined various changes in benefices. A fifth report was prepared in draft, but not signed, owing to the death of William IV.

The first piece of legislation based on these proposals was the Ecclesiastical Commissioners Act of 1836.[26] This abolished the practice of holding livings *in commendam* with sees, made episcopal incomes more equal, authorized two new bishoprics at Manchester and Ripon and several new archdeaconries, united the see of Gloucester with that of Bristol, swept away the last vestiges of secular jurisdiction from the sees of York, Durham and Ely, and established the commissioners as a permanent body with power to lay schemes before the king as Orders in Council. Two other Bills were framed at the same time, and eventually became legislation in the Pluralities and Residence Act of 1838,[27] and the Ecclesiastical Commissioners Act (usually known as the Cathedrals Act) of 1840.[28] The proposals eventually enacted in 1840 were the object of intense pressure from cathedral dignitaries and others between 1836 and 1840.

The letters and petitions sent to the commissioners as a result of the proposals included in their second report were collected and printed.[29] Many chapters were very alarmed, but they were forced to think about the purpose and life of their cathedrals and how adequately they were fulfilling their responsibilities. Their old way of life would certainly be threatened if the commissioners' proposals were enacted. The dean and chapter of Bristol told the commissioners that their proposals might be regarded by the world 'as the deliberate opinion of the highest authorities both in church and state, that cathedral bodies are no longer deserving of the respect which has been hitherto assigned them'.[30] The dean and chapter of Canterbury were particularly concerned about the proposal to reduce the number of residentiary canons in each cathedral to four:

> The joint residence of two prebendaries at the least is often essential to secure the constant attendance of one. For illness and accidental causes sometimes make absence a matter of necessity; we ourselves have had at the same time four prebendaries of whom three were more than seventy years old, two of them more than eighty, and one so much an invalid that he was seldom equal to his duty; what would have been said of our 'efficiency' if our number had been limited to those four?[31]

The dean and chapter of Bristol were full of complaints:

> there is...no notice taken of ancient constitution of cathedral bodies, and no exposition offered of their high duties and utility; there is no attempt made to restore them to their intended efficiency, and no effort adventured to undeceive the public mind as to any supposed inherent defect in their nature.[32]

They were particularly concerned about the plan to reduce the number of minor canons or vicars choral: 'the confinement of a small number of these officials to an almost unremitted repetition of routine duty will tend to diminish their devotional feelings, and in the same proportion mar the effect of their services'.[33]

Some of the prebendaries of Chester worked out that if the commissioners' proposals were enacted they would have to reside for three months instead of two. This would make serious demands on the revenues that they obtained from their stalls which are

> even now quite inadequate to cover the expenditure incurred in the repairs of our prebendal houses, in travelling, and the removing of our families, in our decent maintenance whilst in residence, and in the contributions expected from us to the public charities of the cathedral

city; and they are manifestly more inadequate still to the keeping of such hospitality as might otherwise be deemed befitting our station.

They feared that a lower standard of living would render them 'liable to suffer contempt'.[34] The dean and chapter of Durham, despite their enormous wealth, also objected to the proposals, which they said 'must go far to destroy the influence and usefulness of cathedral establishments, and to render them unfit to accomplish the objects for which they are to be preserved'.[35]

One of their number, Dr Smith, pointed out that if canonical houses were alienated, 'this would be productive of great inconvenience to the members of the chapter, and might lead to the introduction of very objectionable inhabitants'.[36] At Ely it was feared that '...should the proposed reduction take place it would most seriously impair the dignity, solemnity, and efficiency of those religious offices which were ordained by their founder'.

In addition to their task of supporting the bishop and assisting him at ordinations, their work included

maintaining an influence over the cathedral city and its neighbourhood by the example of a body of men dedicated to the service of God, the patronage of schools and charities, the exercise of hospitality, the management of the corporate property, and the fulfilment of those trusts with which the chapter revenues are charged for the spiritual benefit of the city and the neighbourhood.[37]

The dean and chapter of Norwich declared their opposition to the second report, describing it as 'an act of direct spoliation, not only unjust but ill-timed and inexpedient – a dangerous example to rash and ill-principled men'.[38]

Dean Pellew of Norwich took advantage of the situation to state his opposition to intoning: 'The practice of singing the prayers, that relic of popery, so opposed to the spirit of Protestantism and to the simplicity of the English character, will I earnestly trust be abolished.'[39] He also complained that the cathedral choir at Norwich depended on the addition of two supernumeraries, since the lay clerks were 'so unequal to their duties'. There was no provision for pensions and, until recently, three out of eight lay clerks were no longer useful singers.[40]

The dean and chapter of Winchester submitted a weighty memorandum which clearly indicated their understanding of the life and work of their cathedral:

We do not make light of our daily services of prayer and praise...neither would we depreciate the value of our Sunday services, nor detract from the benefits derived from them by the large and attentive congregations on that holy day; nor yet, again, would we overlook the advantage which has been derived in cathedral towns from the support afforded by the members of the chapters, both individually and collectively, to the various local charities, which cannot but suffer in proportion to the diminution of the number of residentiaries.

They also stated that cathedrals were also useful for 'the aid which they give to the theological learning of the country and in the opportunities which they afford for its public development'.[41]

The dean and chapter of Lincoln were openly hostile: 'Fifty-two dignities, or nearly so, abstracted at once from our magnificent foundation we cannot but contemplate as an act nearly allied to sacrilege.'[42] In particular, they were very concerned at the amount of patronage they would lose: '37 advowsons will be found, amid the wreck of prebends, 19 will be taken from our dean, 9 from our precentor, chancellor and subdean, and 31 from our body corporate'. In short, and especially in regard to the proposals affecting minor corporations: 'we find a contempt for the rights of property, a defiance of the respect due to the memory of our founders, and an open avowal of indifference to the constitution of choral establishments, which fill us with unfeigned astonishment and sorrow'.[43]

There was an ambivalent response from Hereford. On 2 January 1837, Theophilus Lane, the chapter clerk, wrote to the archbishop and the Ecclesiastical Commissioners on behalf of the chapter, protesting against

> the violation of our statutes in the future mode of our appointment, the reduction of our number – and the alienation of our ecclesiastical patronage as well as the proposed dismemberment of the College of Vicars Choral – measures which we presume to think altogether inconsistent with the confessedly important object of maintaining the Cathedral establishment in a state of respectability and efficiency.

But Dean Merewether dissented from this view in a letter of 30 January 1837 and regretted 'the present state of opposition between the Ecclesiastical Commission and Cathedral Bodies as most unconstitutional and most detrimental to the Church'.[44] The only chapters that refrained from submitting objections were those of Chichester, Gloucester and Peterborough.

These individual protests sent to the Ecclesiastical Commissioners were to some extent the result of an organized policy. Through the initiative of the dean and chapter of Canterbury, a meeting was held at St Paul's in July 1836, attended by representatives of cathedral chapters. The following day Pusey printed a petition which he circulated to the canon-in-residence at each cathedral to be used if they wished to protest about the suggestions of the commissioners.[45] The dean and chapter of Salisbury were keen supporters of this plan to present a unified defence against the proposals.

They sent two canons to the meeting in London, and contributed £30 'towards the expence [sic] attending the defence of cathedral bodies'.[46] They told the commissioners:

> ...we are deeply impressed with the value of the Cathedral establishments to the cause of true religion – by maintaining a well-ordered gradation in our ecclesiastical institutions, by providing a suitable reward for solid learning and distinguished professional character, by supplying champions against every heresy, by giving a tone to the morals, and setting an example of propriety of conduct to all classes of the community, by supporting the various charities and assisting the local pecuniary resources of the respective Cathedral towns – lastly, by rendering essential aid to the Bishop in the performance of his various duties.[47]

The chapters continued to argue their case with every means at their disposal. One of their leading advocates was J. H. Spry, vice-dean of Canterbury. Spry's own views were set out in a pamphlet he published in 1838:

> The question is one of principle, not of detail: it involves the rights of property; the liberties, immunities, and privileges of the Church; the independence of her Prelates; the functions of her clergy; the security of her revenues; the validity of testamentary bequests; the sanctity of oaths.[48]

In February 1838 Spry and another prebendary of Canterbury, Dr Russell, held a meeting in London, with two prebendaries of Ely (one of whom was William Selwyn) and Archdeacon Jones of St Paul's. As a result of this meeting, Spry wrote to every chapter in England, suggesting that they should brief counsel to appeal to the House of Commons and the House of Lords on their behalf. Sir William Follett MP was suggested as a suitable counsel, though he would have to find a deputy to appear at the Bar of the Commons. The dean and chapter of Hereford readily supported this plan.[49]

Many prominent churchmen also criticized the commissioners' proposals in both published and unpublished writings. The most celebrated of these controversialists was Sydney Smith, by this time a canon of St Paul's and a well-known figure in London political and literary society. In three open letters to Archdeacon Singleton in 1838–9, his colourful opinions were vividly expressed. He believed that the commissioners should not appropriate the revenues of individual cathedrals since this would be a breach of trust with those who long ago had endowed each individual cathedral:

> The people of Kent cannot see why their Kentish Estates, given to the Cathedral of Canterbury, are to augment livings in Cornwall. The

citizens of London see some of their Ministers starving in the city, and the profits of the extinguished Prebends sent into Northumberland.[50]

Further, he claimed, the proposed redistribution of cathedral revenues would not materially assist incumbents. It would amount only to £5 12s 6½d per incumbent per annum.[51] But Smith described the chapters' published objections to the proposals as 'abominable trash and nonsense'.[52] William Selwyn, a canon of Ely, was also critical of the attitude taken by the chapters and bombarded Gladstone with a series of letters about the commissioners' proposals and the role of cathedrals. It all stemmed, he believed, from the mistaken view that parishes alone were important.[53] Having effectively drawn attention to the way in which bishops would be restricted in their government of their dioceses by the commissioners' proposals about the union of benefices,[54] he published a further pamphlet about cathedrals.[55] His brother, G. A. Selwyn (later a distinguished bishop in New Zealand and afterwards at Lichfield), certainly took a high view of them:

> I feel convinced that if the holy intentions of the Founders were carried into full effect, not a single Prebendary could be spared. This is a point which has scarcely been sufficiently considered.[56]

Selwyn was particularly keen about the suitability of cathedrals as a setting for ordinations:

> ...might not the solemn ceremony of ordination be made still more striking, if the Bishop were to be attended at the altar by the whole body of his cathedral clergy? Would not the heart of the Deacon burn within him, while he was receiving on his knees the blessing from the hands of his spiritual Father in Christ, surrounded by the Elders of the English Church?[57]

There were many values needed in cathedral clergy, not least piety, learning and hospitality. The value of cathedrals as educational institutions could be developed considerably, both for children and students as well as for the further training of diocesan clergy. But the heart of the work of a cathedral was its worship.[58] Because they were open to the public each day they were ideal for private prayer, but, he realized, the utilitarian spirit of the age was against them.[59]

One of the most weighty criticisms of the Ecclesiastical Commissioners' proposals was published in the *British Critic* in 1838.[60] Complaining that 'the whole process is amputation', the author said:

> The Commissioners seem to have borrowed a hint from the treacherous act of Medea, when she cut in pieces the aged king, limb from limb, and seethed him and boiled up his flesh, in order to restore him to the freshness and vigour of youth.[61]

The chief charges were a lack of proper enquiry into the local conditions and responsibilities of each cathedral and the dominance of utilitarianism;[62] the author goes on to say:

> The recommendations for the suppression of stalls which, by the terms of the Commission, they were not empowered to make, was founded on the entire neglect of inquiry, which was the very professed object of their appointment.[63]

If the commissioners had taken more trouble to enquire into and consider the ways in which the best cathedrals were run, they might have brought forward very different conclusions:

> Exeter, which is among the most efficient and well-conducted cathedrals in the Church, attests that it owes that efficiency to the *constant* residence of two or more of its prebendaries, as opposed to the modern lax system, which in consequence of these preferments being held with distant cures, too often, but not uniformly prevails, that one only should reside at once. This modern innovation the Commission took as its standard.[64]

Utilitarianism was a principle that could not be applied to cathedrals. To attempt to do so would not only damage them, but threaten their very existence.[65]

A. J. B. Beresford Hope, in an article written in the *Christian Remembrancer* in 1855, pointed out that in the legislation of 1836–40:

> not a single regulation was introduced to improve the Cathedral service; not an additional sermon was provided for, though in half our cathedrals there is only one on the Sunday; nothing was done for the improvement of the fabrics; nothing for the management of the Chapter property; nothing, above all, for the revival of its functions as the Bishop's Council, or for restoring in any shape its ancient connexion with diocesan administration.[66]

A further critic of the Ecclesiastical Commission was Henry Manning, who produced two pamphlets on the subject.[67] Manning had no time for the commission at all: 'I cannot remember having met any one who has not expressed his regret and alarm at the very existence of the Ecclesiastical Commission.'[68] He was also totally opposed to the Church being reorganized by the State, and condemned the Ecclesiastical Commission as '*a virtual extinction of the polity of the Church* and an open assumption of the principle that all legislative authority, ecclesiastical as well as civil, is derived from the secular power'.[69]

Manning clearly regarded cathedrals as not only possible centres of learning, but as the spiritual heart of each diocese, where the chapter's chief responsibility would be 'to pray without ceasing and by the frequent ministration of the eucharist, to keep up a standing and holy memory and witness of Christ's holy sacrifice'.[70]

The opposition to the work of the Ecclesiastical Commission, though strong, was not sufficient to deter its members from their chosen path of reform. They answered their critics staunchly and cogently. John Kaye, Bishop of Lincoln, said that he 'had formed no adequate conception of the destitution of the manufacturing districts and of the large towns, until the facts, detailed in our second Report, were brought under my notice'.[71]

Henry Monk, Bishop of Gloucester and Bristol, explained that there was no other source of money available to remedy spiritual destitution except cathedral revenue:

...when I regarded the frightful deficiency of spiritual instruction under which such numbers of my countrymen were suffering; when it was clear that no earthly resource was available except what might be spared from cathedral appointments, it became a question, not of predilection or of taste, but of duty to the sacred cause of Christ's Church.[72]

The Ecclesiastical Commission could never have come into being without the support of Archbishop Howley. Between 1832 and 1836 he changed his mind about the necessity for, and extent of, the reform of the Church. Particularly after the death in 1836 of Van Mildert, Bishop of Durham, Howley gave strong support to Peel, Melbourne and Blomfield.[73]

It was Blomfield who was the decisive figure. His vigour and unassailable determination carried all before him. He set out his arguments in his Charge of 1838;[74] but it was his famous speech in the House of Lords on 30 July 1840 that clinched the matter:

I traverse the streets of this crowded city with deep and solemn thoughts of the spiritual condition of its inhabitants. I pass the magnificent church which crowns the metropolis, and is consecrated to the noblest of objects, the glory of God, and I ask of myself, in what degree it answers that object. I see there a dean, and three residentiaries, with incomes amounting in the aggregate to between £10,000 and £12,000 a year. I see, too, connected with the Cathedral 29 clergymen whose offices are all but sinecures, with an annual income of about £12,000 at the present moment, and likely to be very much larger after the lapse of a few years. I proceed a mile or two to the E. and N. E. and find myself in the midst of an immense population in the most wretched state of destitution and neglect, artizans, mechanics, labourers, beggars, thieves, to the number of at least 300,000. I find there, upon the average, about one church and one clergyman for every 8,000 or 10,000 souls; in some districts a much smaller amount of spiritual provision; in one parish, for instance, only one church and one clergyman for 40,000 people. I naturally look back to the vast endowments of St. Paul's, a part of them drawn from these very districts, and consider whether some portion of them may not be applied to remedy, or alleviate, these enormous evils. No, I am told, you may not touch St. Paul's. It is an ancient corporation which must be maintained in its integrity. Not a stall can be spared.[75]

As a result of Blomfield's powerful advocacy, the Act generally known as the Cathedrals Act, but officially as the Ecclesiastical Commissioners Act, became law on 11 August 1840. It limited the number of canons in each cathedral to four, with the exception of Canterbury, Durham and Ely (six each) and Winchester (five). The period of residence was fixed for deans at eight months in each year and three months a year for canons. Canonries above the fixed number were to be suspended gradually as they became vacant, but some canonries were annexed to professorships at Oxford, Ely and Durham. Non-residentiary prebends were disendowed, but twenty-four honorary canonries were founded in new foundation cathedrals. The deans of old foundation cathedrals and three canons of St Paul's Cathedral were to be appointed by the Crown by means of Letters Patent (thereby abolishing elective deaneries), but canons of old foundation cathedrals were to be appointed by the bishop 'so soon as every person who was a member of the respective chapters of such churches at the passing of this Act shall cease to be such a member'. Canonries were founded at Manchester and Ripon, and the separate patronage of members of chapters was vested in the bishop. Each cathedral should have a maximum of six minor canons (appointed by the chapter) and a minimum of two. The profits of suspended canonries were to be paid to the commissioners and their estates vested in them. The separate estates of deaneries, canonries, dignities and non-residentiary prebends that were not suppressed were to be vested in the commissioners or transferred (in the case of some old foundation cathedrals) to form the corporate funds of the chapter. The income of the Dean of Durham was fixed at £3,000 per annum; the Deans of St Paul's, Westminster and Manchester were to get £2,000 per annum; the canons of these institutions were to get £1,000 per annum. All other deans in England were to get £1,000 and each canon £500. The commissioners were to set up a common fund for suppressed stalls out of which they were to make additional provision for 'necessitous parishes' by means of Orders in Council. Finally, the Ecclesiastical Commissioners were enlarged to include all diocesan bishops and a small number of deans.[76]

The Act was a triumph for the policies of Peel and Blomfield. Cathedrals of both old and new foundations were stripped of much of their ancient endowments for the benefit of parishes. The arguments advanced on behalf of cathedrals as centres of learning were conceded up to a point by the establishment of a few professorial canonries, but at a stroke the cathedrals of England had been cut down to size (though in some cases their reduction in personnel took several years to achieve). Ever since 1840, arguments have arisen as to whether this drastic pruning helped cathedrals or whether they are still suffering from the shock. Their role had been questioned and limited, but they were allowed to survive. Without the intervention of the government, it may be doubted whether this would have been the case.

The parochial system was henceforth to be the main area of the Church's life. The reforms of Peel and Blomfield thus laid the foundation for the substantial growth in the power and influence of the Victorian Church, but they presupposed a pattern of church life and organization that may not always be appropriate. By weakening the cathedrals they have bequeathed to us a long list of problems, but their reforms did break up soil that for far too long had been lying fallow. Their ploughing led to the growth into new life of some important seeds.[77] It is to the various elements of that distinctive kind of life that we must now turn.

3

THE ENVIRONMENT OF
THE CATHEDRAL:
THE CLOSE

❄

A lthough hundreds of books have been written about the history and architecture of cathedral churches in England, the precincts of cathedrals and their complicated topography and social history have been studied less often.[1] The precincts of those foundations that were formerly monasteries naturally reflect their conventual origins. Their adaptation as newly founded or refounded cathedrals at the Reformation led to the establishment of dwellings for the canons, minor canons and other members of the foundation among, or on the site of the former monastic buildings. The nine secular foundations, however, have a continuous history which straddled the Reformation. No such adaptation of their buildings was necessary, and the precincts of these cathedrals usually include several canonical houses of great antiquity, as well as collegiate buildings for the vicars choral. Both secular and monastic cathedrals preferred to keep their enclosures distinct and separate from the city that surrounded them. Great gatehouses can still be seen at Norwich, Ely, Worcester and Canterbury among monastic cathedrals, and at Salisbury, Wells and Lincoln among secular foundations. The need for such privacy was brought about not simply by a desire for isolation from the world in order to lead a life of contemplation and silence, but through the very real dangers threatening cathedral staffs in the Middle Ages if they had unenclosed churchyards. There are several examples of massive walls being built round cathedral precincts in the late thirteenth century,[2] and the close at Hereford continued to be a dangerous place throughout the medieval period.[3]

Indeed, misbehaviour in cathedral closes was a recurrent problem for many chapters in the nineteenth century. In 1800 the dean and chapter of Hereford ordered that four men were to be appointed constables for the cathedral precincts annually and sworn in by the magistrates.[4] In 1802 two of the 'pensioners' or beadsmen of Bristol were employed as constables to preserve good order in the neighbourhood of the cathedral on Sundays.[5]

The close at Salisbury formed a separate liberty (which was the term actually used at Wells) and three of the canons acted as justices of the peace within its boundaries.[6] At Exeter the commercial life of the city overlapped into the close, which caused certain difficulties. In 1800 the dean and chapter protested at coaches being left outside the door of an inn in the close and in 1819 they were indignant that a coffee house in the close called Molt's Coffee House was open during the times of services in the cathedral, not only on Sundays but also on Christmas Day and Good Friday. They asked the chapter clerk to take up the matter with their tenant.[7] When William Rench was appointed close constable at Exeter some three years later, his duties were 'to keep the peace and prevent nuisances and annoyances by fireworks or otherwise within the Close'.[8] Canon Hobart of Hereford complained in 1826 of 'the riot and disorder existing nightly in the Cathedral churchyard'.[9] At Exeter, after the questions of jurisdiction and security in the close had been reviewed, two vergers, the dogwhipper and the man who looked after the Treasury ground were sworn in as special constables.[10] At Hereford, the city beadle was employed at the direction of the chapter during the time of the daily services and during the early prayers on saints' days and Sundays to prevent misbehaviour in the cathedral churchyard.[11]

When Jacob Nash was appointed at Chichester in 1845 at £12 per annum, his duties were not only to prevent trespassers in the churchyard and the area contained within the cloisters known as Paradise, but he was also expected to see to the mowing of the grass and the proper pruning of the trees.[12]

A more serious and particular problem occurred at Wells in 1858 when it was discovered that the statues on the west front were being damaged by boys flinging stones at them. William Priest, who was supposed to keep order among the children who played on the green in front of the cathedral, was plainly unequal to the task; the dean and chapter therefore resolved to find a replacement who could 'devote his whole time during daylight to the care of the Green and the precincts of the Cathedral'.[13] Rochester did not need to appoint a precinct warden until 1861,[14] but in the same year the Dean of Hereford was authorized by his chapter to arrange with the mayor for a policeman to patrol the close from six o'clock until eleven o'clock or midnight each evening.[15] A similar arrangement made at Chichester fourteen years later did not prevent the east window from being damaged by a glass marble fired from a catapult; George Triggs, one of the bell-ringers, was accordingly employed as a temporary watchman.[16] By 1881 the services of the police were also requested in the close at Salisbury, especially on Sundays when the dean and chapter objected to members of the public 'laying at full length on the grass, sitting on the steps of the porch, or on the walls of the churchyard' and other disorderly or indecent behaviour.[17] A more serious threat was taken seriously at Norwich in 1883 when Dean Goulburn consulted the chief constable 'on the best mode of protecting the cathedral against dynamite and other explosives'.[18] A similar threat was made at Winchester in 1885, where the chapter authorized the dean to arrange 'for locking the gates and etc. leading to the east end of the Cathedral in consequence of the injury done by dynamite explosions in London'.[19]

At Worcester the parts of the environs of the cathedral most liable to abuse were the terraces between the River Severn and the west front of the cathedral. In 1892 the dean and chapter ordered that these should be kept closed except between 12.45 p.m. and 2 p.m. each day.[20] Four years later there was 'constant disorder' in college precincts to the east of the cathedral and the police were informed.[21]

The most comprehensive list of duties of a close constable in the late nineteenth century is to be found at Hereford, where in February 1885 the dean and chapter defined the duties of a new constable for the cathedral precincts after he was sworn in by the city magistrates as a special constable:

> To attend in the Cathedral Close every evening from dusk to 11.30 throughout the year and keep order there and prevent prostitutes and other improper characters loitering in the Close.
>
> To assist in blowing the organ at the Cathedral morning and evening services throughout the year except on Sunday evenings and on the evening when the special services are held in the Cathedral when a substitute will be provided.
>
> When on duty in the Cathedral Close his beat will be from the Broad Street gates round the Cathedral, through the College Cloisters, by the School, the Deanery and on the north side of the Close to Broad Street, giving an eye to Harley Court to prevent improper characters resorting there.[22]

In the early years of the century cathedral precincts were often in a most neglected state. The area known as Paradise at Chichester was said to be in a state of disorder in the 1820s.[23] At Bishop Carr's visitation in 1825, the prebendaries told him that 'the churchyard and cloisters are so much frequented with idle children and others that they are seldom so clean as they would otherwise be'.[24] Sixty years later, however, the nuisance was still causing irritation. On 7 May 1886 a petition from some thirty local residents was presented to the dean and chapter, complaining about the 'very disgraceful' condition of the cloisters:

> Pieces of paper are constantly dropped on the paths or thrown among the grave stones and these remain for days. Orange peel, ginger beer bottles, old bones and tin canisters may also often be seen strewn about. The Cloisters are a playground and resort for the idlest and dirtiest boys in the city, with most annoying and disgusting results. We humbly submit that watch and guard be kept over the Precincts and that all refuse [be] removed daily.[25]

This had clearly been a problem for some time, as in 1857 the dean and chapter had informed the police at Chichester that only the choristers were allowed to play in Canon Lane.[26] The cleanliness of the cathedral precincts was the responsibility of the chapter verger. He was paid £5 annually 'for pruning the ivy when required and keeping clean the precincts of the Cathedral (excepting the Paradise and churchyard)'.[27] The dean and chapter were certainly not unaware of the problems to which the petition drew their attention; in the summer of the previous year they had asked the Chapter Clerk

> to request the Mayor to cause a police supervision in the Cathedral Yard during the pleasure of the Dean and Chapter, with a view to preventing the children and others from making a playground there, and the Chapter Clerk is further directed to have a suitable notice board erected stating that the Police have orders to prevent games and disorderly behaviour in the Cathedral Yard.[28]

Another nuisance was the use of the close for beating carpets. This was prohibited (together with hanging out clothes to dry in public areas) at Worcester in 1843,[29] at Wells in 1861,[30] at Winchester in 1883,[31] and at Chichester (in the meadow behind the deanery and the Residentiary) in 1885.[32] In 1809 the dean and chapter of Winchester decided that the grazing of cattle in the churchyard was causing a nuisance and ordered that in future only sheep were to be allowed this privilege.[33] Sheep were the only animals allowed to graze in the close at Salisbury.[34]

In the early years of the century, several closes were equipped with gas lamps. At Winchester in 1806 they were to be lit daily from the first day in September until the end of April.[35] A City Lighting Act at Exeter provided for ten lamps to be lit in the close there, but the chapter were in the habit of providing twenty lamps and resolved to continue this policy on the introduction of gas.[36] Gas was installed in College Green at Worcester in 1824,[37] while at Gloucester, Mr Spinney (the lamp-lighter) was responsible for lighting eighteen lamps each night in the close for a salary of £90 per annum.[38]

There is certainly evidence to show that chapters took seriously the amenities of the close and their responsibility for maintaining them in good order. Gas pipes were laid in the close at Exeter in 1837,[39] while at Hereford a careful investigation of trees in the close revealed that though the roots of many of them were decayed it was thought that they could safely be allowed to remain.[40] Later in the century, the town council was asked to water the walks in the close at Hereford.[41] In March 1851 the chapter decided to spend up to £200 in laying out the close, and at the end of the year the commissioners under the Hereford Improvement Act wrote to express their pleasure in the great improvement in the close: 'improvements which the Commissioners feel are as much a Credit to the

City as they are satisfactory to the Inhabitants'.[42] The dean and chapter of Wells were informed in 1844 that the gardener recently appointed to keep the green in order had lost the donkey that he had purchased for £4 to pull the mowing machine. They made good his loss but said that he should in future bear the cost of a pony or donkey himself. He quickly bought a new donkey for £6 and the chapter paid him £2 towards the cost of keeping the animal during the winter.[43]

The close at Exeter suffered to some extent from being a public thoroughfare. In 1830 the chapter considered that one effect of a proposed new road in the city would be to bring lime carts and timber wagons through the close; in this case they would have to exercise their right to shut the close as a thoroughfare at night.[44] They removed some posts in the close,[45] but resisted a suggestion of a road that would enable carriages to come through the close from Broad Gate to Southernhay.[46] When the improvement commissioners objected to an iron railing at New Cut, the dean and chapter replied that they

> are most desirous that in this and every other alteration they have made in the public ways through the Close, the public convenience should not be diminished. In fact they have improved the roads in various instances at a very considerable expence.[47]

In 1835 they petitioned the House of Lords against the Municipal Corporations Bill in order to preserve the liberty of the close.[48]

At York the liberty of the close gradually faded out in the middle of the century and a road immediately adjacent to the south side of the Minster brought the life of the city up to its very walls. Before that there were gates across the road at the west end of the Minster. At least once a year these were closed and the dean and chapter's policeman stopped all heavy carts and wagons and turned them back. In 1870 a deputation from the city tried to persuade the chapter to permit a permanent right of carriage way through the Minster Yard, but this was not granted until 1891 when the corporation offered to make and maintain a new road through the Yard.[49] In 1856 at Salisbury an objection was raised to the Board of Health's rate for lighting and repairing the roads of the close as an enfringement of the liberty of the close.[50]

One of the best-known contemporary descriptions of a cathedral close in the nineteenth century occurs in the diary of Francis Kilvert. Visiting Worcester on the occasion of his aunt's funeral in 1870, he writes:

> We passed along an irregular quadrangle formed by the N. [sic] side of the Cathedral on one hand and houses on the other sides. A carriage drive swept round an iron-railed grass enclosure within which were some ancient elms with almost all their limbs lopped or broken off. This was the Cathedral Close or College Green. Most of the houses were red

brick, some stuccoed white, all irregular and unlike each other. 'There', said the girl with the baby, 'that is Miss Kilvert's house, the last house, red brick with white blinds down'. It was a curious looking house in an inner recess of the Close, red brick, white window frames, a conical roof with tiles, and a small front. In the middle of this inner recess was a smaller open grass plot. The Close may be pretty in summer, but it looked bare and dreary in December.[51]

The houses in a typical cathedral close were mainly the dwellings of the dean and canons, minor canons and other servants of the cathedral. Often one or more of the houses would be used as a school for the choristers or others. In most of the old foundation cathedral closes there were separate collegiate buildings of the college of vicars choral. In the early years of the century, canonical houses were often in a dilapidated condition. This was because their occupants generally had a variety of other preferments and rarely visited their cathedrals. Prebendary Fountain's house at Worcester was said to be in a 'ruinous state' in 1806.[52] When Sydney Smith became a canon of St Paul's in 1831 he did not live in his canonical house, which remained empty until 1839 when he let it to Minor Canon Barham.[53] Forty years later H. W. Beadon told a story about a newly appointed canon who had let his canonical house, which was 'unfit for residence', and was residing in 'a salubrious suburb'.[54] Beadon adds that 'the Deanery at Bristol was sold and pulled down some years ago, for a public improvement, but has not been rebuilt. Three canonical houses out of four have been for many years unfit for residence.'[55] The precentor and the minor canons of Gloucester were in an even worse predicament in 1813, for there were simply no houses near the cathedral available for them.[56]

In 1842 the dean and chapter of Worcester decided to pull down the old deanery on the south side of the cathedral and to purchase instead the building now known as the Old Palace which lay to the north, provided that the great hall of the new deanery could be regarded as the audit room and be made available to the canons.[57] The old deanery was said to be injurious to the cathedral 'and in other respects objectionable as a Residence'. When it was demolished, two canonical houses were also pulled down.[58] At Exeter the canons paid 'ancient rent' to the dean and chapter for the houses that they occupied.[59] An Act of Parliament[60] allowed chapters to dispose of houses that were not required, subject to the consent of the visitor and the ecclesiastical commissioners. The minor canons of Winchester were in a difficult position, as they had no houses in addition to their stipends and found that the cost of renting accommodation in the city was heavy: 'we believe it would be difficult to find other instances similar to that of Winchester where houses exist in the Cathedral Close, rented by strangers, the minor canons having neither houses nor compensation in lieu thereof.'[61] Ten years later the dean and chapter of Winchester asked the surveyor to report on the state of each house annually at the Lady Day Chapter.[62]

Towards the end of the century an increasing sense of responsibility towards canonical houses may be detected in the record of various chapters. This is best demonstrated at Bristol, where the dean and chapter decided to adopt as their rule one of the provisions of the 1883 draft statutes which had been drawn up by the cathedral commissioners:

> We will that every canon newly appointed shall have such prebendal house as the Dean and Chapter shall assign to him; we further give to the Dean and Chapter authority to permit an exchange of prebendal houses or of a house not prebendal for one that is. We direct that no canon shall be empowered to let his house except with the permission of the Dean and Chapter. It will be understood that dilapidations will have to be received and paid for on transference as though the houses had become vacant in the usual course. If also there is any mortgage due on account of a house, the interest will have to be paid by the canon to whom the house is assigned.
>
> The Dean reported that two prebendal houses, viz. 'Canon's' House, late the residence of Canon Girdlestone, and the house ordinarily called the 'Abbot's Lodge', at present in the hands of the Venerable Canon Norris, had been repaired by funds received from Queen Anne's Bounty under mortgage of those several houses, but that the Chapter has no official record of the transactions and recommended that the consent of the Chapter be obtained before any funds should be borrowed on the security of the dividends of any canon for purpose of alteration or repair, and that the plans and deed of mortgage be handed over to the Chapter for security.[63]

There was still some hostility, however, against unnecessary or extravagant improvements. When the dean and chapter of Wells were asked to install a bathroom in the organist's house, they said that they considered this 'a modern luxury' and would pay only half the cost.[64] In fact, they had been dissatisfied for some time with the large sums that the surveyor had recommended should be spent on their houses, and the organist's bathroom had 'brought this feeling to a decisive point'. As a result, they changed their surveyors.[65]

At York, Ripon, Chester, Chichester and Bristol for at least part of the century, there was only one house available for the canon-in-residence, and this was occupied in turn by each of the four residentiaries.[66] At Manchester three canons' houses had been demolished in a road improvement scheme and the remaining two were let as shops. Two canonical houses at Chichester were permanently occupied by the principal of the theological college and the senior canon, leaving the other canons to fend for themselves in finding suitable lodgings in the city during their months of residence.[67] When Charles Kingsley was appointed a canon of Chester in 1869, his wife wrote:

> It enables us to remain at Eversley and to have a nice change once a year without giving dear Charles very heavy work.... There is a very good furnished house, which the four canons inhabit by turns, which does not sound comfortable but it will save us a great outlay of furnishing, which would have absorbed a year's income, so we are well satisfied.[68]

One of the other canons of Chester at this time was George Moberly, later Bishop of Salisbury, and one of his daughters has left an amusing description of the shared house:

> This is a large house – a great boon to us: it is comfortable, but the furniture is very old, much of it of the last century. The Canons share one house, so they can seldom meet – or rather, their families cannot. Each one has a cupboard in which the goods of the different Canons are kept, and the choosing of a new carpet should require a Chapter meeting.[69]

There are few firm statistics of the population of various closes. The population at Chichester in 1801 was 187, but this probably included the houses (now shops) in South Street, north of the entrance to Canon Lane, as well as those on the north side of the cathedral.[70] The shops in South Street were created in 1825, thus ruining the former appearance of Vicars' Close.[71] Alterations in the close at Chester about the same time were also contentious. Prebendary J. T. Law built some new houses on the site of his old stables, but Dean Copleston disapproved of them, saying that all the neighbours regarded them as a nuisance:

> ...the houses being of an inferior order and likely to introduce a low population within the precincts of the Church. They were besides objectionable, as darkening the School windows, confining the air, hiding the ancient architecture of the Abbey and carrying back their office within a few feet of the School window.

Dean Copleston also asserted that Law had broken the provisions of his lease, which stated that the stables should be maintained and kept in a state of repair, as he had in fact pulled them down. Law stoutly defended his actions:

> I consider the Archdeacon's stables, *blocking up* the East Window of the School as a *much greater* nuisance. Perhaps you would begin by having them removed? Again, the house immediately opposite the Deanery, I mean Mr. Rowland's surgery, etc., and also the house to your right as you go along the passage from the Deanery to the Cathedral surely are worse. They too should be previously removed.

Law was suspended by Bishop Blomfield in 1827, but he refused to resign, despite being severely criticized by Dean Copleston.[72]

The cathedral close and its houses may not have been a subject that has attracted much attention from historians, but as the environment that surrounded the cathedral itself and as the arena where much of the life of the cathedral was lived out, it certainly merits our attention. Although many of the surviving records of nineteenth-century cathedral life inevitably reflect its more formal aspects, such as worship and chapter meetings, the more informal encounters between those who make up the life of a cathedral are no less important in giving character and direction to that way of life. Mandell Creighton's habit in Worcester in the 1880s of chatting with his brother canons after matins or on summer evenings overlooking the River Severn[73] was a significant element in the achievement of a happy and successful chapter. The precincts of a cathedral, and the residences of the various members of the foundation, are no less the arena of the life of a cathedral than the great church itself.

4

THE OFFICE AND WORK

OF A DEAN

❊

T he principal house in each close was that of the dean,[1] and as the head of the cathedral body he held the pre-eminent place in the social life of the cathedral, as well as in its day-to-day work. Particularly in the early years of the century there were several non-resident deans. When Dean Gretton was installed at Hereford in 1809, he broke a tradition of mainly non-resident deans which stretched back over a period of more than thirty years.[2] Newton Ogle, who was Dean of Winchester till 1804, had been an absentee dean for many years, as he found his 'golden prebend' at Durham more attractive than his decanal responsibilities.[3] Dean Cockburn of York, after his stormy career there, retired to his Somerset rectory and rarely returned to live in his 'new' deanery, even though he had built it himself. The house gradually fell into disrepair and was hired out to wealthy race-goers or hunters.[4] Another dean who lived in seclusion towards the end of the century was Dean Elliott of Bristol. He had married a divorced woman and was absent from cathedral services for a period of at least ten years.[5] Of course, there were sometimes substantial reasons for deans to be absent from their deaneries. While the deanery at Salisbury was being repaired in 1811, the dean lodged with the close porter.[6] But a resident dean did make a great difference – John Jebb reported in 1852 that Canterbury and Ely had sprung to new life since their respective deans had become resident.[7]

Until the Cathedrals Act of 1840, deans of old foundation cathedrals were elected by their chapters, though (as in the case of bishops) this was more a matter of form, following the receipt of a *congé d'élire* and a nomination from the Crown.[8] In new foundation cathedrals, however, deans were (and are) appointed directly by Letters Patent. The alteration in the mode of appointing deans to cathedrals of the old foundation came about as a result of a *cause célèbre* at Exeter in 1839. Following the death of the late dean, Whittingdon Langdon, the chapter received Letters Patent from the Crown granting the deanery to Lord Wriothesley Russell. The chapter objected to this unlawful proceeding and discussed the matter with Lord Melbourne, the Prime Minister. The chapter were firm that the deanery of Exeter was elective and that they could elect only one of the residentiary canons of the cathedral.[9] In April, further Letters Patent arrived in Exeter, granting the deanery to Thomas Grylls, one of the prebendaries. He was not, however, a residentiary canon and recent legislation had suspended the appointment of additional canons. Melbourne's next step was to introduce a Bill into the House of Lords enabling the Crown to appoint to old foundation deaneries. The chapter upheld their right to elect a new dean and asked why the Crown could not select one of the residentiary canons. Melbourne agreed to postpone the third reading of the Bill until the general chapter had considered it.[10]

It now became clear that both parties had become entrenched in their opinions. Melbourne's Bill was passed on 4 June. On 14 June the chapter clerk delivered Royal Letters recommendatory under the Sign Manual and Privy Seal (a form not used since the reign of Charles II), recommending Grylls to the chapter and commanding them to elect him. Thomas Lowe, the president of the chapter, wrote immediately to Melbourne to say that the chapter would not agree to this, and on 27 June the chapter took the law into their own hands and elected Lowe himself as the new dean. This election was confirmed by Bishop Phillpotts on 1 August and Lowe was installed the next day.[11] The matter would have ended with Lowe's installation had not Grylls, the Crown's second nominee, brought a case in the Court of the Queen's Bench on 23 April 1840 against the president and chapter of Exeter Cathedral. The attorney-general appeared for the Crown and Sir William Follett represented the chapter.[12] Judgment was given on 24 June in favour of the chapter by Lord Denman.[13] The government had the last word, however, for the 1840 Cathedrals Act transferred the appointment of old foundation deaneries to the Crown.[14] A further provision that deans of old foundation cathedrals need not already have been prebendaries of the cathedral was passed shortly afterwards.[15] Dean Ellicott was the first Dean of Exeter to be appointed by Letters Patent in 1861.[16]

From time to time, though, there were still grumbles about the appointment of deans. When Dean Duncombe was appointed to York in 1858, a question was even asked in the House of Commons by a member who thought a parish priest should have been appointed.[17] When Dean Cowie of Manchester was appointed to Exeter in 1884, however, the *Guardian* hailed the appointment of one who was 'not merely the scholar, but... the man who has a distinct and decided conviction of the historical continuity of the Church'.[18]

In 1891 H. W. Massingham compared Lord Salisbury's decanal appointments with those of Gladstone. He described Gladstone's deans as excellent:

Dr Payne Smith of Canterbury, Dr Lake of Durham, Dr Kitchin of Winchester, Dr Plumptre of Wells, Dr Henderson of Carlisle, Dr Cowie of Exeter, a Senior Wrangler and the Prolocutor of Convocation, are all men of ability in some way, who have made some mark as writers or as men of light and learning. Of Dean Merivale, the historian of Rome under the Empire; of Dean Burgon, who with all his crabbedness and rigidity of outlook was a writer of singular charm; and of the great Dean Church there is no need to speak.

Massingham was less happy with the deans chosen by Salisbury, and criticized his recent appointments to St Paul's, Wells, Chichester, Gloucester, Manchester, Norwich, Rochester and Worcester:

None of these gentlemen are men of the least eminence either in theology or in literature, and more than one of the nominations is tainted with a suspicion of party influence or of private intrigue. Three are Dublin men of not the smallest academic or literary distinction. The new Dean of St. Paul's (Gregory) is an active organiser, but he has achieved no literary success, and is in no sense a leader of thought either in the Church or out of it. Dean Hole has written a charming book on roses and is a preacher of some merit. Dean Spence is a respectable scholar and a vigorous pulpiteer.[19]

As cathedrals came to be more in the public eye during the course of the century, so men began to discuss the value of the work done by deans. Dean Burgon of Chichester (an unhappy dean) lamented the unreality of his position in 1877: 'My *ministerial* work *here* is a kind of unreal shadow; – a lesson read – an occasional sermon preached – I don't know to whom. That is all!'[20] But Harvey Goodwin, the energetic Dean of Ely, despised such a negative view of decanal work. Goodwin's biographer says that 'He had no wish for *otium cum dignitate*, nor for the traditional shelf to which it is erroneously supposed Deans are consigned.'[21] However, Goodwin did dislike having to deal with petty disputes and complaints.[22] Nevertheless, some deans found difficulty in adjusting to their new life and work. A. C. Tait remarked in the House of Lords in 1861 that when he was Dean of Carlisle, he spent some years trying to find out what his duties were.[23] Dean Alford of Canterbury wrote in 1871 that the office of dean 'is, in many of our cathedrals, practically useless; the dean, while nominally the head of the cathedral body, is almost without employment, and absolutely without power to act'.[24] Dean Pigou of Chichester was similarly bewildered at first, but found his feet after two months.[25]

During a debate in the House of Commons in 1850, Sir B. Hall complained that deans and canons were 'useless offices' and a waste of money. Sir John Russell said that 'they were heads of the chapters and he thought they were of great use in a cathedral town, for the general purpose of carrying on the business of the Cathedral and assisting in the spiritual business of the diocese'. Mr Hume, however, asked whether there was any necessity to have deans at all, since he thought that they performed no real or essential position in the Church. They should be abolished, and their income given to the hard-working parochial clergy. Mr W. P. Wood, however, felt that

> two and frequently three services a day on Sundays, with perhaps two sermons, and services on other days of the week, and perhaps the super-added supervision of endowed schools, were labours or duties of an onerous kind.[26]

Bishop Maltby of Durham said in 1853 that he thought deans spent too many months in residence. They should take charge of a parish, even a distant one, and so increase their usefulness.[27] Bishop Pepys of Worcester, though, thought that one of the difficulties of being a dean was being

> interrupted either by the gossiping visiting, which always prevails to so great a degree in a cathedral town, or by the less important questions, whether A or B had the better bass or tenor voice, or what anthem should be sung by the choir on any particular day.[28]

R. C. Trench said that it all depended on the man: 'a deanery being very much what a man will make it – nothing if a man be nothing, very much if a man be much and disposed to make much of it'.[29]

Before long Hume's cry of 'do away with deans' was taken up in a pamphlet with that title by Edward Stuart, the incumbent of St Mary Magdalene's Church, Munster Square.[30] This view was shared by Henry Alford, Dean of Canterbury, who believed that bishops should be deans of their own cathedrals.[31] When E. W. Benson became the first Bishop of Truro in 1877, he put this idea into practice and appointed himself dean of his pro-cathedral. Perhaps the weightiest suggestion in this direction came from A. C. Tait. In a speech to the House of Lords as Bishop of London, he proposed that deans should be made suffragan bishops in order to make them 'more distinctly useful'.[32]

Dean Harvey Goodwin was one of the outstanding deans of the century. In Howson's collection of essays[33] he wrote the chapter entitled 'Recollections of a Dean', which includes much valuable reflection on his work at Ely. It was, he said, very much a public office. His daily routine was well known and his time was often frittered away.[34] Goodwin placed first in the duties of a dean his attendance at the daily services of the cathedral:

> ...there can be no manner of doubt that the daily office of the Cathedral is the Dean's prime occupation. My own opinion is that, when at home, he should never be absent from a single service unless compelled by infirmity.... It is a considerable advantage to a dean to have some knowledge of and taste for music: this enables him to take his own proper part in the choral service, and also to speak with some kind of

authority when the music of the service is bad: moreover the conscious-
ness that the Dean can appreciate their efforts will almost infallibly have
its effect upon the whole choral body.[35]

When Tait was appointed Dean of Carlisle in 1849,[36] Samuel Waldegrave,
a canon of Salisbury, told him:

> ...if a man has judgment and courage, a Dean might prove an invaluable
> person in a Cathedral town. Not only might he take the lead in the
> works of mercy and in the business of education, but he might also be
> the foremost man in preaching the Gospel to the people.[37]

The experience and wisdom of deans was, to some extent, handed down
and shared. When Burgon was appointed to Chichester, he stayed two
nights with Dean Goulburn of Norwich 'to learn Dean-craft', in the same
way as Goulburn had himself visited Dean Hook at Chichester when he
took up his duties.[38]

These theoretical reflections on the duties and activities of a dean can be
compared with what we know of their lives and achievements. Fortunately, a few glimpses have been given of the daily life of some deans
(either by themselves or others). A. C. Tait was installed as Dean of Carlisle
in January 1850. He spent a month there after his installation, attending
the services regularly, examining the choristers and the pupils of the
Central School, visiting the infirmary, inspecting the capitular accounts,
and taking careful note of the advice and information given to him by
Canon Harcourt.[39] Some idea of his regular routine may be glimpsed from
the entry in his diary for 10 May 1850:

> Rose 7.30. Dressed a few minutes after eight. Private reading till 8.45.
> Prayers at 8.45. Breakfast till 10. Cathedral till 11. Sermon till 2. School
> till quarter to 3. Letters till 4. Walked and rode till 6.30. Dinner till 8. Sat
> in study and dining-room reading Neander's *Julian* – talking and
> sleeping a little till prayers.[40]

In August 1850 he noted that 'The duties of this place are very great.
There is a vast amount of sin and misery around – and little means of
alleviating it.'[41] Yet he was reasonably content:

> The happiness I enjoy here in this quiet life with my family is very
> great.... The duties of this place – the duty of preparing for Sunday – of
> preaching – of superintending the schools – of relieving the poor – of
> prosecuting my own studies – what others could be more agreeable –
> what others better suited to be a preparation for Heaven than these may
> be if followed in a Christian spirit.[42]

A few days later he added: 'My occupations in this place, though they
cannot be called laborious, are incessant – and my time easily runs away.'[43]

Before long, though, he was depressed by the 'deadness' of Carlisle and asked, 'Why is so little progress being made in this town?'[44] Yet he kept busy. On 4 June he listed his occupations on that day as 'teaching the young, speaking God's truth in the congregation, administering the Holy Communion, first in Church and then to the sick, teaching the factory girls, teaching the choristers, visiting a dying man'.[45]

The teaching he did at the Central School, the Adult School and in his two Bible classes continued to give him 'opportunities of usefulness' and in December 1854 he lamented that he had not had time to visit any poor or sick person because he had been so fully occupied with the Church of England Institute, the educational committee, the relief committee, the Schoolmasters' Association, the night school, the grammar school, the Central School and the Sunday classes. A note a few weeks later shows that he was busy preparing soldiers for a confirmation service.[46] In the autumn of 1855 Lady Wake spent a whole Sunday with Tait at Carlisle:

> Besides the two services in the Cathedral, at one of which he preached, he found time for a most touching meeting in his night school-room with a number of old people and invalids who were not able for a Cathedral service....Later in the day there was a similar gathering of young women, most of them mothers, to whom he spoke so earnestly that they evidently hung upon his words. Later still there was a children's class examined by him, and quite late in the evening, when, exceedingly fatigued, I thought the duties of the day entirely over, I found a most interesting gathering of young men in the Dean's study, to whom he gave instructions more like that given to the Sixth Form at Rugby ....It was a bright scene that enlivened the old Deanery. Cheerful young voices sounded merrily as we gathered in the mornings in the picturesque old drawing-room to obey the solemn injunction that had been carved centuries before on the ceiling, 'That here prayer should every day be made.[47]

Soon Tait's life at Carlisle was clouded by the death of most of his children,[48] but the cathedral was 'crowded to excess' for his farewell sermon in October 1865.[49]

Dean Goulburn gives a similar, if understated, account of his own daily activity:

> I find but scant time for reading when at work here. Perhaps you will say, as many do, 'What can a dean have to do except the going to church?' I fear I must say 'Little enough (except on General Chapter weeks) which he *need* do, but a good deal which he *may*'. I have always some (small) literary work in hand. The Bishop supplies me with plenty of preaching [the Dean only preached as of official right on the great festival days] ....my correspondence, among which are usually cases of

conscience which cannot be rapidly answered, is rather heavy; and the twice-a-day service, much as I enjoy it, lays a heavy embargo on my time.[50]

At Chichester, Dean Burgon worked relentlessly: 'I begin my studies at an early hour every morning; work on all day; and seldom or never go to rest until every other candle is extinguished within the Cathedral precinct.'[51] W. J. Butler kept similar long hours at Lincoln:

Up at six every morning, he set to work at once. Working-men, who knew his early hours, would come to him then with demands on his counsel or help. After his breakfast at 8.30 till ten he would be busy with correspondence.... He would then robe and go to the Cathedral for matins, walking with a quick, firm step across the choir, but never omitting a brief but reverent inclination to the altar as he passed. On entering the vestry he would go to the end of the table and after a few whispered words of necessary business, he would cover his face with his hand and remain standing in that position till the hour sounded.[52]

There is insufficient space to include more than a few accounts of some of the more outstanding or notorious of Victorian deans. The following studies attempt to show how men of varied ability and interests affected the life of their cathedrals and left behind a reputation that has endured.

John Merewether became Dean of Hereford in 1832 at the age of thirty-five.[53] A son of an old Wiltshire family, he was educated at Queen's College, Oxford. Four years after his ordination, in 1819, he was given the parish of Hampton in Middlesex. The Duchess of Clarence (later Queen Adelaide) began to worship at his church and he became known to the Duke (afterwards King William IV). He was appointed chaplain to the Duchess and was clearly on intimate terms with the Clarences. When Clarence succeeded to the throne in 1830 he ordered that Merewether should always be invited to administer the chalice to him when he received communion. For the next few years, then, Merewether spent each Easter and Christmas at Court and became a Deputy Clerk of the Closet in 1832. When Lord Grey, the Prime Minister, elevated his brother, the Honourable Edward Grey, from the deanery to the bishopric of Hereford in May 1832, the King personally suggested that Merewether should succeed him.

So it must have been a very self-satisfied man in his mid-thirties who arrived at Hereford as the new dean in the summer of 1832. He brought with him a plate worth 200 guineas which his parishioners at Hampton had given him as a parting-gift, the fulsome declarations of their gratitude for his ministry, and the evident favour of both the monarch and his prime minister. He may well have thought that he was destined for even greater things, as he indicated in a pamphlet entitled *A Statement of Circumstances*

41

Relating to the Late King's Wishes in Respect of the Dean of Hereford, which he published after William IV's death. But only one further preferment came his way: a country parish a few miles outside of the city of Hereford.

Merewether's first action was his best. On the day of his installation on 16 June 1832, the chapter decided to dispense with the services of their elderly and infirm organist, Dr John Clarke-Whitfeld, and in the following month Merewether appointed as his successor the youthful Samuel Sebastian Wesley, destined to be the most famous cathedral organist in England. Merewether knew Wesley already; he had been his organist at Hampton.[54]

The Reform Bill was finally passed that summer and Merewether was keenly aware of the poor reputation of the Church in the eyes of the public. He found much that was wrong at Hereford and he was determined to reform the cathedral and improve its ways:

> When I first came to the Deanery of Hereford I found the Cathedral Service on the Sabbath a disgrace, a blot to the Church – from the insufficiency, the coldness, and the meagreness of its choral performances, and I have endeavoured to succeed to some extent in rectifying its deficiencies...[55]

Merewether was a man of great energy and perseverance, which first expressed itself in 1834 when he attempted to make the vicars choral more regular in their attendance at cathedral services. He fined them when they were absent, and sent letter after letter urging them to attend to their duties. Even Canon Hobart was faced with a demand for a fine when he missed evensong on one occasion. In 1835 Bishop Grey held a visitation of the cathedral and his injunctions generally supported Merewether's policy of enforcing the members of the foundation to attend to their duties more carefully.[56]

In 1837 Merewether began a long feud with the chapter which revolved around the custody and use of the chapter seal. Merewether objected to the chapter using it in his absence, but the canons were becoming increasingly irritated at his frequent absences and clearly the business of the chapter had to be continued. The canons appealed to Bishop Grey, which caused 'indignation and disgust' to Merewether. He poured out his heart to Grey. Having described his view of the worship at the cathedral when he arrived in Hereford,[57] he continued:

> I found that not one Prebendary in ten preached in his statutable turn – and called upon them all to conform to the statutes and have rescued the credit of that body from the stigma which attached to it in consequence, and recovered to the Cathedral Church a decent congregation. Is it because I was not content with the plain reading of the Morning Service by one vicar which *no residentiary ever attended* and the evening

chaunting by *two only* on that sacred day, but have pressed the re-establishment of both in their regular and proper mode, and have myself assisted by reading the lessons at those services? Is it because by my own example in not omitting any one preaching turn which the statutes assign to me, I have put to shame those who formerly delegated to a regularly paid substitute those duties and are even now rarely to be seen ascending the pulpit steps, and if reluctantly compliant with the requisition are easily diverted from the accomplishment by the more important avocations of a secular engagement or an invitation to dinner? Is it because I not only have declined to take payment for residing instead of one of the body, but required him to reside himself and refused to permit a continuance of that unstatutable practice? Is it because by my efforts and perseverance the Chaunts, the Choral Services and the Anthems in the morning *and* evening daily service have been restored whereas when I first came amongst them they had been content with having only on Wednesdays and Fridays a chaunt through the psalms and services, and to suffer the evening service of every day of the week to be hurried through *without an anthem* and only one monotonous chaunt throughout the psalms.... Is it, my Lord, because I have discouraged the divisions of fines and the sealing of leases whenever the fines, however paltry, could be grasped in defiance of the statutes and have solicited attendance at Chapter for the *transaction of business* too often in vain when no dividends were expected, have pressed the appointments of choristers and others for the sake of the service to be done to the Church and not only for patronage sake? ....Is it because I have reminded some members of the body that both they and their families have largely, very largely, benefited by its profits, have advocated the performance of duty before the indulgence of luxury, and the necessary demands of the Church before the gratification of family requirements?

Seldom can a dean have expressed himself more strongly to his diocesan. The canons, not unnaturally, were furious when they heard about this letter. They sent a joint reply and each canon wrote separately to the bishop. Canon Matthews's letter was so long that it occupies more than forty pages in the Act Book. The row over the custody of the seal continued, but Bishop Grey died before it could be resolved. The controversy was still raging when the documents for the election of Bishop Musgrave were issued, but eventually Merewether gave way, only to continue his feud with the canons over various other matters.

Merewether has three other claims to fame. It was he who took emergency action in 1841 to prevent the cathedral from collapsing, all the canons being away at the time the danger became apparent. This led to an extensive restoration of the cathedral[58] and its interior reordering.

Secondly, Merewether is remembered in the field of archaeology; his most famous excavation was of Silbury Hill.[59] Thirdly, he appeared in the margin of national history in 1847 when he played a key role in the attempt to prevent Renn Dickson Hampden, the Regius Professor of Divinity at Oxford, from being appointed Bishop of Hereford. Merewether tried to persuade the general chapter to refuse to elect Hampden, and told Lord John Russell, the Prime Minister, that he would not vote for him. Russell's reply, written on Christmas Day 1847, has become famous.[60] Merewether failed to carry the general chapter with him, but he maintained his opposition to the end, refusing to attend the enthronement and sending a protest to the chapter clerk.

Merewether was a reforming dean who was ahead of his time. He was right in many of the principles that he tried to introduce at Hereford, but his ambition and tactlessness cost him the support of his chapter and in the end he gives the impression of being a pathetic figure. Nevertheless, his achievements were considerable and his reputation depends more on them than on his character.

Throughout the time that John Merewether was Dean of Hereford, the Dean of York was William Cockburn.[61] Born in 1773, he was appointed to York in 1823. His brother-in-law was Robert Peel. At first he seems to have been a successful dean. His first sermon was described as 'a display of eloquence seldom equalled', his early months were dominated by plans to improve the area surrounding the Minster, and he enthusiastically supported the great musical festivals in 1823, 1825 and 1828. The last of these was particularly splendid and everything augured well for a harmonious relationship between the Minster and the city.

In February 1829, however, the Minster was severely damaged by fire, but this disaster was met by a determined and generous response, so that the quire was reopened for services in little more than three years after its destruction. There was considerable disagreement about the position of the pulpitum and organ.[62] Although there had been a generous response to the rebuilding appeal, the dean and chapter were already in debt and the cost of rebuilding the quire increased their debt still further. In May 1840 there was a second fire that destroyed the nave. This time the public response was not so generous and so the dean and chapter sank still further into debt. The canons were critical of the dean's 'unbusinesslike nonchalance'. Canon William Vernon Harcourt was the dean's most vehement critic. He told Cockburn in 1836 that his actions would bring 'ruin and disgrace' on the Minster.[63]

The second fire brought to light the condition of the fabric fund, which was in a state of complete chaos. In 1841 Canon Harcourt persuaded his father, the archbishop, to undertake a visitation of the Minster. It was the first visitation since the reign of George I. Public interest was intense and Cockburn was furious. He believed himself to be under attack by the chapter and refused to acknowledge the court's jurisdiction.[64] After the visitation had been proceeding steadily for a few weeks, Cockburn was suddenly accused by Canon Dixon of selling livings in the patronage of the dean and chapter. Cockburn had certainly been behaving in a dangerous way in the late 1830s when York, along with all the other cathedrals, was threatened by the proposed legislation that was enacted in 1840:

> When I found that the bishops were plotting to gain possession of all our preferments, I offered the next presentation of every living I had for sale, which was then a legal transaction, and requiring no concealment...[65]

He even wrote letters to this effect in the local newspapers.

The accusation of simony brought Cockburn back to York from his country living in Somerset. He stormed into the court, interrupted Dr Phillimore, who was presiding as the archbishop's commissary, and created such uproar that Phillimore declared him in contempt of court and guilty of simony. He accordingly deprived him of the deanery and this sentence was confirmed by the archbishop. Cockburn immediately appealed to the court of Queen's Bench, who found in his favour and restored him to the deanery. In fact, Cockburn had not sold livings, only the advowson, the right to present to vacant livings. He had been very foolish and high-handed, but he was not a criminal.[66] Although the citizens of York were, on the whole, pleased that Cockburn was still the dean and presented him with a silver bowl, the acrimony in the chapter continued and the Minster suffered as a result. He entered into protracted and complicated correspondence with the Ecclesiastical Commissioners about commuting his estates, and lived mainly in Somerset.

By the 1850s, despite its restored nave, York Minster was a sad place. James Raine wrote of it at that time:

> We well remember being among the worshippers on a Sunday, chilled to the very bone with piercing damp; pigeons were flying about the choir during the service; and there were only six communicants, including the officiating clergy.[67]

By the time Cockburn died in April 1858, aged eighty-four, he was a relic of another age. Of all the deans of Victorian England he was the most notorious.

Despite their angular nature, both Merewether and Cockburn received extensive public support for the restoration of their respective cathedrals. The most expensive Victorian restoration was at Worcester, coinciding almost exactly with Dean John Peel's period of office. Peel was a brother of Sir Robert Peel and came to Worcester in 1845 from Canterbury, where he had been a prebendary.[68] At Canterbury he was known for his impressive and eloquent preaching as well as for his generosity.[69] Peel swiftly became very popular at Worcester. He had a prodigious memory: it was said that he could read a column in *The Times* and afterwards repeat it word for word.[70] He knew by heart all the collects, epistles and gospels for the year.[71] His sermons were delivered with much pathos, and he sometimes wept at the most pathetic parts. One Christmas Day he was so overcome by the words of his text, 'They laid him in a manger because there was no room for him in the inn', that he could scarcely continue.[72] He spent only three months each year in the city; he was also Rector of Stone and lived at Waverley House near Kidderminster. His local popularity was demonstrated whenever he drove out in his carriage, which was always followed by two spotted dogs. James Smith, a lay clerk, said: 'I have many times seen him pass through the High Street in his open carriage, bowing on either side to the people who saluted him bareheaded. More respect could not have been given to Royalty.'[73]

Peel was the first dean to live in the large building to the north of the cathedral which had formerly been the bishop's palace. He was very hospitable and gave frequent parties and concerts there, often inviting the lay clerks of the cathedral to sing glees.[74] Mrs Limoelan, daughter of the cathedral organist W. H. Done, said in her reminiscences:

> It was a lesson in courteous manners to see Dean Peel come down the stairs leading from the Dining Room in the Deanery into the Hall, at some great function, smiling and greeting his guests, who had assembled for the evening party, saying some kindly word to each and all from the greatest to the least. He spoke almost in a whisper and so did Mrs Peel. He much disliked loud voices. He always stood near the piano when singing and playing was going on, enjoying simple songs the most, and was very easily moved by *Home, sweet home, Robin Adair, Cherry Ripe* and such like songs.... The Hall (as it was then called) looked very handsome with its furniture of oak and crimson velvet, and lighted by wax candles.[75]

Dean Peel suffered terribly from gout, his hands being badly distorted. This was no doubt aggravated by his fondness for port. It was said that 'he could drink a couple of bottles after dinner without any noticeable effect'.[76] Peel was very popular with the boys of the King's School and the choristers; he encouraged them to call at the deanery, visited their homes, and gave sovereigns to the best singers. Mrs Limoelan said: 'He was most kind to us young people. He gave us some white Bantum fowls and some white fantailed pigeons which were the joy of our hearts.'[77]

During the winter, when it was extremely cold in the cathedral, a stone hotwater bottle would be placed in his stall. Whenever he was conducted by a verger from the deanery to the cathedral for services, he was liable to be encountered by poor old women to whom he gave money. On one such occasion both the dean and the verger fell over and lay flat on their backs until they were rescued.[78]

John Peel was not an outstanding dean, but this stout, smiling and large-featured man achieved much through his easy popularity, gracious hospitality and devoted attention to the restoration of Worcester Cathedral, which he lived long enough to see completed in 1874. In many ways he is one of the most typical of Victorian deans.[79]

If John Peel was one of the most typical of Victorian deans, then the Honourable Augustus Duncombe, Dean of York from 1858 to 1880, was one of the greatest. He was chosen by Lord Derby, not for his experience, nor even because he had special gifts that would be best employed in such a position, but simply because he was rich. Disraeli openly admitted in the House of Commons that 'whatever the other recommendations of Mr Duncombe for the office, he certainly had the advantage of possessing ample means'.[80]

When Duncombe came to York he could scarcely have been encouraged by what he found. Not only was the deanery dilapidated, but the Minster was cold and cheerless and his own appointment had been questioned and criticized. For two years he received no stipend while official arguments about it continued. When he finally received it, he gave £2,000 to improve the songmen's salaries.

Duncombe was forty-three and at the height of his powers. Constantly resident, he gradually became all-powerful within the Minster. Four years after his appointment, the precentor (who was also Dean of Gloucester and rarely came to York) died and Duncombe persuaded Archbishop Longley to appoint him to this office in addition to the deanery. The chancellor died only two years after Duncombe came to York and he took over many of the duties of this dignity as well. Not until Archbishop Thomson was appointed did Duncombe encounter substantial opposition. Thomson said:

> The truth is... the duties of dean, precentor and chancellor were all centred in one person.... These duties comprehend nearly all that the Minster has to do.... This democratic constitution has been turned into an absolute monarchy.[81]

Duncombe was certainly not without good advice on the necessary reforms in the Minster. The *Yorkshireman* muttered in 1858: 'Too long has vergerdom sat like a dark dragon at the porch of God's house in the obscure watch for sixpences.'[82] The nave was 'without life or meaning', 'a hollow shell', 'a scandal to the city and diocese'.[83] The new dean threw himself into the work of reform; he restored the exterior of the chapter-house from his own pocket, double-glazed some of the windows to protect them, and cleared away unsightly buildings in the vicinity of the Minster and restored the south transept. He ensured that the vergers had fixed salaries, increased the number of choristers from ten to fourteen and found a new school building for them; he improved the songmen's salaries, appointed E. G. Monk as organist after years of the Camidge family, and encouraged the rebuilding of the organ. In 1863 he installed a new organ in the north aisle of the nave; and brought in Gurney stoves and introduced gas lights into the nave, starting services there. There was a choral festival in 1863 while in 1866 the Church Congress came to York. Duncombe spoke about 'Cathedrals – their Work and Influence' and Dean Hook referred to him as a model dean.[84] Duncombe had begun choral celebrations of the Holy Communion and every weekday of the Congress between 400 and 700 people attended one of these. The annual number of communicants in the Minster rose from 1,614 in 1863 to 2,645 only five years later. He introduced an extra early celebration once a month in 1868; this became weekly in 1873. New robes were provided for the choristers, and outstanding men were persuaded to join the chapter. A series of disputes with Archbishop Thomson clouded his latter years, but he met these with dignity.[85] James Raine's memoir of him, published a few months after his death in 1880, claims:

> At the present day there is no cathedral church in the country in better order and it is mainly to the late Dean that this marvellous change is due....No one connected with the Cathedral has ever had so much influence in the city and county as the late Dean.[86]

In his twenty-two years as dean he had transformed the Minster and made a real centre of Christian worship and witness.[87]

William Charles Lake was Dean of Durham from 1869 to 1894. Impressions of him vary. He was thought to be aloof and austere by many who could not penetrate his shy grandeur.[88] Once he rebuked Minor Canon Greenwell for attending a service in thick laced boots. Greenwell complained to Archdeacon Bland who told him that Lake was 'possessed by three imps: he is imperious, he is impetuous, and he is impertinent'.[89] On the other hand, Miss Oakley recalled his dignity and courtesy:

> The Dean of Durham was the greatest figure of my childish world. I remember once wondering what was the difference between King and Dean....When the stately figure of Dean Lake passed up the long nave of Durham Cathedral at the end of the procession of schoolboys, choir, minor canons and major canons, to the sound of the solemn voluntary, the pitch of human greatness was reached for me....After the service, outside the Cathedral, he used to hold, as it seemed to me, a little court. I have a keenly vivid impression of the Dean's tall form, his white head and black velvet skull-cap, the flowing surplice and scarlet hood, greeting on the College Green with fine, old-world courtesy his friends, and among them the older children who came up to him.[91]

Yet despite his proud bearing, none doubted his energy and vigour, and his broad sympathy for both the ecclesiastical and educational aspects of his work. For Lake was *ex officio* warden of the university and did much to establish it as a sure foundation. He founded the Newcastle School of Science as a branch of the university (which later developed into a university in its own right). He restored both the cathedral and the chapter-house, despite the opposition of Bishop Baring, improved the services and greatly enlarged the cathedral's sphere of influence in the city. He insisted that the choir should enter the cathedral for services in procession, instead of straggling in one by one, buttoning up their surplices as they walked up the nave.[92] A long and stately procession of the whole cathedral foundation at the commencement of the services made a marked impression and the importance of the eucharist was emphasized with an early celebration each Sunday and a choral celebration monthly.

Yet Lake lacked confidence in his work, as he confided to Tait: 'I really cannot see my way through this Cathedral millstone at all, except that I more and more incline to *residence* in some shape being absolutely necessary...' [93] When Bishop Baring was succeeded by Lightfoot in 1879, Lake's opportunity came, and he designed a splendid enthronement service.[94] Lake's name does not immediately come to mind when one thinks of Victorian deans, but he undoubtedly did a good job at Durham in difficult circumstances, and his own dignified bearing and manner were reflected in the added dignity that he gave to the cathedral and its services.

John William Burgon, however, was one of the least successful and certainly among the unhappiest of Victorian deans. After a long career at Oxford, where he was well known as a valiant champion of lost causes and unfashionable opinions, he was appointed to Chichester by Disraeli in 1876 in succession to W. F. Hook. The cathedral that he inherited had recently been rebuilt after the collapse of the spire and central tower in 1861, and although Hook had been less effective as a dean than as Vicar of Leeds, it was by no means a dead cathedral. Burgon, however, was temperamentally unsuited to the work to which he had been appointed. A life-long bachelor, his crabbed relations with his colleagues began to go wrong even before he arrived in the deanery. It seemed to his canons that he was treating them like curates and they came to a single mind for the first time in their opposition to him. He tried to discover the extent of his responsibilities in the statutes and charters of the cathedral, but the chapter knew more about them and outwitted him.[95] His particular adversary was Dr Swainson; Burgon said that he was 'insufferable'. There was much to be done. Burgon was distressed at the poor state of the bell-tower, the gateway in Canon Lane, the north-west tower of the cathedral and the cloisters and the library, but instead of attending to their repair, again and again he was engaged in defending the integrity of his office against the assaults of Swainson.[96] He relieved his feelings in the extensive reply he made to the cathedral commissioners.[97] He was overworked, poor, and he was snubbed by his colleagues.[98] As far as his income was concerned, his stipend of £1,000 a year was totally inadequate for him to live in his large deanery: 'I never knew the sense of being really poor until I came hither.... I find myself utterly unable to make both ends nearly meet in this place.'[99] Burgon claimed that he was the poorest member of the chapter, but what really grieved him was the way in which he had been treated by Swainson. The first serious disagreement had been over the repositioning of the nave chairs in August 1878, when Swainson had countermanded Burgon's attempt to replace them in their original position, insulting and humiliating him before the vergers.[100] Burgon read a formal address and protest at the chapter meeting on 10 October and told Swainson he would report him to the Visitor 'for his irregular and oppressive conduct'. But the other canons supported Swainson and refused to allow Burgon's protest to be entered in the Act Book. The dean therefore said he would print it.[101]

The matter was compounded by a personal quarrel between Burgon and a female voluntary helper in the cathedral. Burgon was a misogynist and had spoken vehemently against the education of women at Oxford. It is therefore no surprise that in a case of this nature his pastoral sense was totally inept. The woman in question was in the habit of

a certain unauthorised practice of her own which had the effect of distracting my attention every Sunday morning whilst celebrating at the early Sacrament, and even of interfering with my private devotions. She persevered...I expostulated....To my surprise the lady now set me at defiance and informed me in writing that 'she should lay my note before the Chapter'.

Burgon then changed his request to an order, that she should 'desist from annoying me in this unwarrantable manner'.[102] But he had reckoned without his canons, one of whom wrote to him denying that he had any right to give orders in the cathedral. Burgon was beside himself with rage: 'When the chief of a great and time-honoured institution has to contend with a female servant for his very existence and finds a Residentiary concealed behind her skirts – the end has come.'[103] But the end had not come. A further blow to Burgon's pride occurred in November, when he returned to the city after a week's absence and found the churchyard

reduced to a state of utter confusion. The Canon-in-Residence *proprio motu* – without authority – had taken to felling and lopping the trees in every direction, desiring (as he said) 'to get the business done before the Dean returned'.

Four days later Burgon discovered by accident that the altar in the Lady Chapel had been 'draped in a new and singular manner'. Then he saw that the stall of the late treasurer had been hung with purple, while the canon who was responsible for all this was covering the Lady Chapel windows with green paint.[104] When Burgon brought up these matters at a chapter meeting, the canon said that he would never consult the dean, who concluded sadly:

> The patience of the present Dean is at all events exhausted.... It has already had the effect of darkening and embittering his daily life. To live in a state of perpetual feud with one's brethren is unbearable.[105]

In an inter-leaved copy of this pamphlet in the Bodleian Library, Burgon added in his own hand:

> I finished my remarks on the Wednesday night – sitting up for the purpose till three in the morning of New Year's Day. At nine o'clock I gave it to the printers.... In after years, anyone reading the ensuing remarks will see the very difficult position I have had to maintain in this place and will be made aware that the author of all the present trouble has been Dr Swainson... he has made it the business of his life to testify jealousy for my office and impatience of the very title I bear.[106]

Burgon's poor relations with his chapter did not entirely prevent him from doing some good work at Chichester. He started Bible classes and gave Sunday evening lectures at Bishop Otter College. He also continued with his patristic studies and his enthusiasm for coins. His study was crammed with books, rubbings and pencil sketches. He was very fond of birds, feeding those who came into his garden with hemp-seed every day, and also fond of children. He once broke away from a procession in the cloisters to play with a boy who was trying to amuse himself with a ball.[107] Relationships in the close improved when Dr Crosse was appointed to the chapter in 1882; Mrs Crosse has left a delightful vignette of Burgon:

> No Dean ever loved his Cathedral more and few indeed have ever been so constant in their attendance at the services. Day by day, a few moments before the bell ceased, the little garden door of the private walk leading from his study used to open, and the tall bent figure, clothed in cassock, surplice, hood, stole and college cap, preceded by his verger, would pass out, crossing St. Richard's Walk to the cloistered entrance of the Cathedral. He was generally interrupted by a perambulator and a small group of children drawn up with a sure hope of being noticed. The Dean would never pass a child without a word.[108]

Burgon, for all his interest in children and scholarly work, is an unattractive figure. Although he mellowed with age, the reverberations of the conflicts with his chapter must have echoed for years at Chichester and must certainly have impeded the work and influence of the cathedral. A good dean is one who can work harmoniously with his chapter.

One such good dean, indeed the greatest of all Victorian deans, was Richard William Church, Dean of St Paul's from 1871 until his death in 1890.[109] Church had been a great figure at Oxford earlier in the century. Keble and Newman were at the height of their influence during his undergraduate years. He became a fellow of Oriel in 1838 and soon came to know Newman intimately. Church stood by Newman during his gradual withdrawal from university life and it fell to him to protect Newman in February 1845 when an attempt was made to persuade the university to censure Newman's teaching in Tract 90. Church and his fellow proctor vetoed the proceedings which came to an abrupt end. Seven years later, Church was ordained priest and left Oxford for the country rectory of Whatley in Somerset, where he and his wife settled down to a quiet life, removed from the excitement of university politics. After his death, many of the sermons that he preached at Whatley were published under the title *Village Sermons*. They have a purity and simplicity that render them very readable over one hundred years later. Church's spirituality and broad sympathies were assisted by his extensive foreign travels. He was especially influenced by a visit to La Grande Chartreuse in 1862.[110]

Eventually Church was persuaded by Gladstone to exchange his secluded life in Somerset for the very public and crowded ministry of Dean of St Paul's. By this time, Wren's great cathedral had become something of a byword for slovenliness and neglect. It was cold, dirty and lifeless, but its great days were just beginning. Robert Gregory, Henry Parry Liddon and J. B. Lightfoot had recently been appointed to the chapter. Liddon and Lightfoot both held university chairs, but fulfilled the duties of their residence punctiliously. Gregory succeeded Church as dean, Liddon predeceased him by only three months, while when Lightfoot was appointed Bishop of Durham he was succeeded by Henry Scott Holland. From 1879 to 1884, the great historian W. H. Stubbs was a canon of St Paul's. The chapter at St Paul's for these twenty years was therefore exceptionally able. With Liddon's preaching, Lightfoot's gifts as a counsellor and lecturer, and Gregory's sure-footed reconstruction of the cathedral's finances, Church's chapter transformed St Paul's. He presided over it with great grace and tact.[111]

It is a measure of Church's greatness that he took up his new work with humility and foreboding.[112] Nevertheless, although very apprehensive, he was clear that St. Paul's needed to be aroused and to fulfil its role as 'the great central church of London'.[113] He outlined his purpose as dean very clearly:

> It is to set St Paul's in order, as the great English Cathedral, before the eyes of the country ...I have three things before me: (1) To make a bargain with the Ecclesiastical Commission about the whole future revenues of St Paul's, and get from them what will be necessary for the

works and wants, material and other, of the *reformed* Cathedral. (2) To carry on the architectural restoration, for which a quarter of a million is the sum demanded. (3) To fight and reduce to order a refractory and difficult staff of singing men, etc., strong in their charters and inherited abuses. I don't mean that all this is to be done single-handed, but the responsibility will fall on the Dean.[114]

Church was certainly unhappy during his first year at St Paul's, but he gradually achieved his object of turning it into a model cathedral. He continued with his scholarly work, which embraced Anselm, Dante and Pascal, and completed his authoritative account of the Oxford Movement shortly before his death. Hensley Henson said that he had 'the unearthly refinement of a scholar-saint'.[115] There are many Victorian deans who were distinguished scholars, but in none of these was there such a perfect blend of scholar, priest and judge. Church's singular purity and nobility of mind and soul not only transmitted itself to his chapter and so influenced the reforms that they introduced at St Paul's, but it gave to the Church of England the quintessence of a dean, whose greatness lingers after him.

It is clear from these vignettes that an essential part of the work of a dean was the development of a harmonious relationship with his chapter. Merewether and Burgon, despite their own personal qualities and achievements, never managed to understand this. Dean Church, on the other hand, understood this instinctively and this contributed in no small measure to his success at St Paul's. The collegiality of the dean and his chapter was emphasized at Hereford by the dean also being a residentiary canon, although he was not allowed to hold any of the elective offices of the chapter.[116] This did not prevent the difference of opinion between Merewether and his canons over the custody of the chapter seal. At Wells in 1839 Dean Goodenough personally ratified all the acts of the chapter which had been made during his illness and absence for the previous eighteen months.[117] Harvey Goodwin, one of the best Victorian deans, was well known for his smooth relationship with his chapter:

His relations with the chapter were from the first always harmonious. They found him strong-willed, a little brusque – this in part perhaps the result of his own shyness...but they recognised that he was an excellent chairman of their meetings, a first-rate man of business, clear-sighted, prudent, hard-working...[118]

Goodwin himself commented:

I always took care to make myself thoroughly acquainted with all the business that came before us; and as no one of the canons ever did this, and as I had generally formed an opinion and they had not, I found almost invariably that the majority eventually came round to my way of thinking.[119]

Another dean who developed a harmonious relationship with his chapter was E. M. Goulburn. When he went to Norwich in 1866, the four residentiary canons received him cordially and supported him throughout his twenty-three years as dean.[120] Canon J. M. Nisbet wrote to the Ecclesiastical Commissioners in 1879 on behalf of his brother canons, placing on record 'our deep sense of the substantial benefits that have been conferred on the cathedral by the liberality of the present dean out of his private means'.[121]

One of the most important aspects of a dean's work is the interest he takes and the support that he gives to the music of his cathedral. The negative attitude of Dean Gaisford was blamed for the poor state of the choir at Christ Church, Oxford. The choristers were unruly and inefficient and the lay clerks, recruited from worn-out scouts and bedmakers, were scarcely competent for their duties.[122] Gaisford's successor, H. G. Liddell, improved the services and once ordered an unsatisfactory alto lay clerk to sing bass.[123] Harvey Goodwin established his musical reputation at Ely when he sang the service 'with the inflections' at his installation; he often attended choir practices, singing tenor 'with intelligence and effect'.[124] He introduced Helmore's *Psalter Noted* and used himself to sing the final part of the Litany.[125] Dean Alford of Canterbury had a pleasant baritone voice. Not only did he sing the service instead of a minor canon on the *Precum* days, he also sang his part in the canticles and anthems and compiled a new hymn-book with the assistance of the precentor.[126] Dean Yorke of Worcester, however, was most unpopular on account of the 'Mock' Festival of 1875. The elaborate choral and orchestral concerts, for so long a feature of the Three Choirs Festival, were replaced by grand services. The hoteliers and tradesmen of Worcester were furious, for their livelihood was threatened. Ribald posters and black flags were displayed in the city and the dean was burnt in effigy.[127] Dean Forrest, however, invited the Worcester lay clerks to audit dinners and made no secret of his love for music.[128] But Dean Randall of Chichester was unpopular in the city because of his dislike of music. Not only did the citizens send him 'a monster petition' asking for the music of the cathedral to be left alone, they also left him in no doubt of the offence he had caused by refusing to stand during a performance of the Hallelujah chorus.[129]

Not every dean could be expected to be musical. Many of them were gifted and industrious in other ways. Although Trollope claimed that many deans were chosen for their taste in literature rather than any real vocation for their position, it is clear that many of them were men of wide and useful influence.[130] Dean Close arranged night schools and Bible classes at Carlisle,[131] while Dean Bowers and his successors at Manchester gave an annual dinner to the poor on Christmas Day.[132] Hospitality of another kind was provided at Norwich in 1884 where it was the custom for Her Majesty's Judges to be entertained to a state banquet at the deanery, complete with robes and trumpets.[133] Dean Lefroy of Norwich was very well known in his cathedral city. He was a familiar figure at every civic function, and was usually asked to make a speech. Education, medical charities and freemasonry were his special interests.[134] Dean Farrar of Canterbury instituted an annual meeting of deans, the first of which took place at Canterbury.[135] The Dean of Christ Church, Oxford, was in a unique position: the head of a cathedral chapter as well as that of a college of the university. Dean Gaisford spelt out the heavy responsibilities of this dual appointment in 1854:

> The head of this large society cannot be absent even for a few days during term time, without great inconvenience. From the morning services at 7 or 8 a.m. to the evening service at 9 he is liable to be called on for direction or advice daily....In a word, a dean of Christ Church must devote himself entirely to the government of his college, and his share in the public concerns of the university.[136]

Dean Plumptre of Wells, who was appointed in 1881, was an expert on Dante and the biographer of Bishop Ken. He took a great interest in the Cathedral School and left £2,000 for old choristers in his will. When he died after only ten years in office, the chapter recorded their deep sorrow.[137]

Dean Hole of Rochester was well known throughout England as an evangelist, and has left behind an enduring reputation in the horticultural world as an expert rose grower.[138] Another dean who was famed as a gardener was Dean Garnier, who resigned in 1872 at the age of ninety-six after thirty-two years as Dean of Winchester. Known as 'the good old dean', he never refused anyone who asked him for money, and his garden at Bishopstoke, where he was vicar for sixty-two years, was quite famous.[139]

Many deans, of course, were well known as scholars, such as the Greek lexicographers Liddell (of Christ Church) and Scott (of Rochester).[140] Other well-known Greek scholars were Blakesley of Lincoln[141] and Alford of Canterbury,[142] while Kitchin of Winchester was a capable historian.[143] W. J. Butler of Lincoln took a great interest in educational affairs in his cathedral city, especially the School of Art, and retained close links with the Wantage sisters.[144]

Butler is a good example of a late Victorian dean. He had won his reputation as a hard-working parish priest, gained useful cathedral experience at Worcester where he was a canon for five years, and continued to work hard at Lincoln until his unexpected death. By the end of the nineteenth century, deans were expected to be vigorous as well as studious. St Paul's had shown what a cathedral could be, and men expected the same transformation to take place in provincial closes as well. If the public expectation of deans was greater in 1900 than it was in

1800, then that achievement was the result of the successful and influential ministries of great men such as Harvey Goodwin, Edward Goulburn, Augustus Duncombe, W. J. Butler, W. C. Lake and E. H. Plumptre, and above all Richard Church. It was their vision and their leadership that transformed Victorian cathedrals, revived their spiritual life, and equipped them for the tasks that were to face them in the twentieth century.

5

CANONS AND
CAPITULAR GOVERNMENT

✸

In theory, a cathedral is a collegiate religious community, whose members are bound to live in accordance with the rules laid down in the cathedral statutes. Both its worship and its system of government are corporate, and although some members of the chapter have specific responsibilities, the more important decisions affecting the life of the cathedral as a whole are taken by the whole chapter.

The constitutional position of the nine cathedrals of the old foundation at the beginning of the nineteenth century had scarcely changed since the Middle Ages. At each of them there were between twenty-four and fifty-eight prebendal stalls. Most of the clergy who occupied them were non-resident, but a small group elected from (but not by) the larger body was in close residence at the cathedral, and, with the dean, formed the administrative chapter. In cathedrals of the new foundation, however, there was a varying number of prebendaries besides the dean.[1] They were in residence for a month at a time.

How, then, were men appointed to be canons?[2] Usually they were the unfettered choice of the bishop of the diocese or the Crown, though sometimes this choice was restricted. At Chichester, for example, the Wiccamical prebends of Bursalis, Exceit, Windham and Bargham were confined by Bishop Sherburne's sixteenth-century statutes to alumni of Winchester College and New College, Oxford.[3] The statutes of Hereford Cathedral clearly stated the bishop's right to appoint prebendaries.[4] From the whole body of prebendaries a certain number in old foundation cathedrals were elected as residentiary canons. This was certainly the case at Salisbury in 1803, where a new residentiary was obliged to pay an entrance fine of 100 marks and 100 shillings.[5] At Chichester, the elections of residentiaries were controlled by the Duke of Richmond and Gordon and the Duke of Newcastle. In 1832 Bishop Maltby made a new statute to curb this custom, despite the vigorous protest of three residentiary canons. When George Wells, prebendary of Exceit, was elected by a meeting of the general chapter under the new statute in March 1832, they considered the whole process null and void and themselves elected George Shiffner, prebendary of Eartham. After a legal case in the Court of King's Bench in 1835, Shiffner was confirmed in office and held the canonry until his death. Bishop Otter extracted an assurance from Arch-deacon Webber in 1838 that he would not 'consider himself bound by any pledge...in the choice of candidates'. The other residentiaries had also agreed to this policy.[6]

Under the terms of the 1840 Act, the appointment to residentiary canonries at Chichester, York, Hereford, Exeter, Salisbury and Wells was transferred to the bishop of the diocese, but because of an ambiguity in the wording of the Act, elections continued to be held for some years afterwards. The last election at Chichester was in 1870, and was almost farcical. It was carried out in great haste. Canon Hutchinson was in feeble health and, should he die before a successor to Canon Pilkington could be elected, the appointment would pass to the bishop under the terms of the 1840 Act. A chapter meeting was hastily arranged at Canon Hutchinson's house. However, the votes were evenly divided, and as the dean had no casting vote the chapter disbanded without making a decision. A fortnight later the chapter met again and this time a majority of the canons (but not the dean) voted in favour of Prebendary Parrington – Canon Hutchinson having been persuaded to change his mind. Canon Swainson dashed to Bishop Otter College in a hired cab and brought Parrington to Canon Lane. Canon Hutchinson was lying full-length on a sofa in the dining-room of the house known as The Residentiary, too ill to sit up. The chapter there and then elected and admitted Parrington to his canonry. As he was already a prebendary he was not installed, though the next canon, A. R. Ashwell, who was appointed by the bishop, was installed as he was not already a prebendary.[7] At York, the appointment of residentiary canons from among the prebendaries was in the power of the dean.[8] The 1840 Act did not become fully operational there until the death of Archdeacon Charles Musgrave in 1875.[9] The non-residentiary canons of York, however, were recognized as full members of the chapter,[10] though there was confusion about the distinction between the residentiary and non-residentiary canons. When Canon Thorold of York was appointed Bishop of Rochester in 1877, following the translation of Bishop Claughton to the new see of St Albans, the right to appoint his successor therefore passed to the Crown. As there was no emolument still attached to the prebendal stall, Archbishop Thomson considered that he had the right of appointment to this stall and collated a new non-residentiary canon. After he had been admitted by the chapter, the Crown presented Canon Fleming, Vicar of St Michael's, Chester Square, 'to the place and dignity of a canon residentiary'. This created a problem, as no one could be admitted as a canon unless he already held a prebendal stall. As the archbishop had filled the vacant prebendal stall, there was no stall available. The chapter was therefore locked in a battle with the Crown on one side and the archbishop on the other. As far as the Crown was concerned, the difficulty over Fleming's appointment was being used by the dean and chapter and the archbishop as a means of furthering their long-standing quarrel. Fleming travelled to York and tried to vote at chapter meetings, but some members of the chapter objected. In 1879 Fleming at last established his right to vote at chapter meetings. Two year later the archbishop appointed him as succentor, and in 1883 he became precentor and prebendary of Driffield.[11]

At Hereford a prebendal stall was always reserved for the penitentiary, following a decree of the Fourth Lateran Council in 1215.[12] According to the seventeenth century statutes of the cathedral, no prebendary at Hereford could be 'promoted to the greater residence' unless, in addition to his degree, he was also 'a learned and diligent preacher'. He must also hold, or be likely to hold, a canonical house and have an income (from either private or ecclesiastical sources) of not less than £40 per annum. A prebendary who wished to be admitted to the greater residence also had to preach four Latin and four English sermons (each an hour long) within the space of two months. The English sermons were preached in the cathedral 'before the people congregated by the bell' and the Latin sermons were preached in the chapter-house 'before all the Canons and Prebendaries and Ministers of the same Church being then at home'.[13]

Prebendaries were put in possession of their prebend by a ceremony of installation. This was quite a complex affair and varied in detail from cathedral to cathedral. At Hereford, a prebendary-designate, dressed in his canonical habit, presented himself with the bishop's mandate to the dean and chapter in the chapter-house. The chapter then led him in procession to the cathedral to the accompaniment of Psalm 51. Here he was installed in the quire in his allotted stall 'and as he kneels there the accustomed prayer shall be said over him'. He was then brought back to the chapter-house and assigned a stall there. The dean invested him with the spiritualities of the cathedral by presenting him with a copy of the Scriptures and with the temporalities by means of a loaf of bread. He then took the capitular oath on the Gospels and was given the kiss of peace by all the present members of the chapter.[14] At Salisbury, in the early years of the nineteenth century, vicars choral were often installed as proxies of new prebendaries.[15] H. W. Pullen castigated the prebendal installations at Salisbury around 1870 in his pamphlet *Mediaeval Mummery*:

> At the commencement of morning service, while three minor canons, the choristers, and the lay clerks are taking their accustomed places in the choir, the Dean, Canons and Prebendaries, together with those about to be installed, repair to the Chapter House, where a Service is performed, comprising detached portions of mediaeval Latin, relieved by intervals of agreeable conversation in the mother tongue. As soon as the chanting of the psalms has begun, two minor canons leave the Choir for the Chapter House, where they are instructed by the Dean or

'President of the Chapter' to instal [sic] the newly-appointed Prebend-aries into their respective seats in due form. This they proceed to do, conducting each prebendary into the Choir, standing over him as he takes possession of his stall and pronouncing some mystical words in a language understanded of nobody at all, inasmuch as the Psalms are being sung and the organ is playing its full accompaniment throughout the ceremony.... Further, on the return of the minor canons and prebendaries to the Chapter House after the installation, some more mediaeval Latin and some more scraps of agreeable conversation ensue, while the minor canon on duty reads the first lesson in the Choir; after which the service is deliberately suspended until the Dean and Prebend-aries are ready to assume their accustomed seats.[16]

Before the reforms of the Ecclesiastical Commissioners, every prebendary enjoyed an income derived from his stall. It is quite possible that all the stalls and titles might have been lost in the course of these reforms, but an amendment proposed by Bishop Denison of Salisbury in the House of Lords in 1837 secured their retention when their endowments were alienated.[17] Three endowed prebendaries survived at Salisbury until 1881. These prebendal incomes varied considerably. The Ecclesiastical Revenues Commission published details in 1835.[18] At Chichester, for example, the best-endowed prebend was that of Wightring (Wittering) with an income of £46 per annum and the least-endowed prebend was Eartham with an income of £2 per annum. The annual income was only part of the story, though. Leases occasionally were renewed and fines were charged. The prebend of Sutton was worth only £18 per annum, but £900 had been received in fines during the three years ending 1831. The dean and residentiary canons were entitled to divide the general net income of the cathedral between themselves. At Chichester, the average amount was £3,721.[19] The best-endowed new foundation cathedral was Durham. Four of the twelve stalls had an income of over £1,000 a year and the income of the poorest stall was £395. The duties, of course, were heavier, and each canon of Durham was supposed to take a month's residence at the cathedral, whereas the only duties of the non-resident prebendaries of old foundation cathedrals were to preach once or twice a year in the cathedral pulpit. The average net income of the dean and chapter of Durham was £27,933. The dean and twelve canons had over £20,000 to divide among themselves, plus various stipends and allowances amounting to over £5,000.[20] Durham was an exception. At most new foundation cathedrals the income of the dean was approximately £100 and that of each canon was £20. In addition they usually had about £5,000 to divide between themselves, though the average net income at Gloucester was £3,897 and at Chester only £634.

The amount an individual canon received might vary widely from year to year, depending on the number of fines for the renewal of leases that became due in any year. W. K. Hamilton pointed out the difficulties of this system: 'I received in 1844 £970 14s and from October 1851 to April 1853 I only received £169 1s 2d.'[21] Following the creation of Manchester Cathedral in 1845, the stipends of the canons there were equalized by a special Act of Parliament.[22] In 1852 the amount divided among members of chapters was £160,713, out of a gross revenue of £313,005.[23] The cathedral commissioners noted in 1854 that the annual incomes of the members of some chapters still varied considerably – from £1,033 to £210 at Ely, and from £163 to £1,033 at Salisbury.[24] The Agricultural Depression later in the century helped to keep canons poorer than they were supposed to be. The four canons of York Minster were supposed to receive £500, but their income was only about £370.[25] In 1888 the income of each residentiary at Salisbury had fallen to under £250.[26]

In order to qualify for a full share in the capitular income of a cathedral, a canon had to be resident at the cathedral for several months each year. At Hereford in 1800 the dean and five residentiaries were each in residence for two months in the year,[27] but at Wells in the same year it was noted that the dean would be in residence 'as he pleases'.[28] It was possible for a canon or prebendary to obtain a medical certificate for non-residence. Prebendary Fountain of Worcester obtained one annually for fourteen consecutive years in the early years of the century.[29] Another way of obtaining permission for non-residence was by means of a royal dispensation, as in the case of Prebendary Stillingfleet of Worcester who obtained one in 1808 'by reason of his great age and manifold infirmities'.[30] A new residentiary at Hereford was supposed to be resident for forty successive days to complete his first residence, and he was not allowed to leave the city during that time without special leave from the chapter. In 1801, however, Canon Russell obtained permission to 'ride out' frequently from Hereford on account of his health.[31] An attempt was made in 1802 to ensure that the subdean and treasurer at Gloucester should keep proper terms of residence.[32] At Bristol a system of forfeits was introduced 'in case the Dean or any Prebendary be absent on any account whatever during the whole of his Residence'.[33] Strict residence was also enjoined at Winchester in 1807,[34] and four years later the vice-dean was forced to pay 2s for missing two days of his residence.[35] In 1819 the dean and chapter of Worcester reaffirmed the binding nature of a late seventeenth-century order in respect of residence.

Yet the system continued to be abused. No canon attended services at St Paul's during the whole of the first fortnight of January 1829.[37] Canon Hobart of Hereford was fined 5s by Dean Merewether in 1834 for his absence from services during his period of residence.[38] At Bristol in the same year the dean and chapter decided to impose a fine of £15 a week if the dean or any of the prebendaries neglected any part of their residence, unless they produced a royal dispensation.[39] The Dean of Bristol was unhappy with the custom whereby he was expected to keep a term of residence without any of the prebendaries being present. He claimed that this practice was unstatutable and unknown at other new foundation cathedrals.[40] The dean and chapter of Ely told the Ecclesiastical Commissioners in 1837 that according to the statutes one canon had to be present at the daily services.[41] The dean and chapter of Exeter attributed 'the high and acknowledged efficiency of their whole establishment' to the constant residence of at least two canons and the daily presence of one, throughout the year.[42]

The 1840 Act made important new requirements about residence. Henceforth, all deans had to be in residence for eight months in each year, and canons were required to do three months' residence.[43] Until 1845 the Dean of Ely kept an extra fifty days' residence each year as an extra canon.[44] In about 1850 the dean and chapter of Canterbury arranged that the canon treasurer should be resident throughout the year to supervise the cathedral workmen.[45] At Wells the custom was for a newly elected residentiary not to commence his residence either in the year in which he was elected or in the following year. After the reduction in the number of residentiaries caused by the 1840 Act, this placed an extra burden on the remaining residentiaries, and in 1852 the dean and chapter decided that a new canon should occupy the same months of residence as his predecessor without any interval.[46] In 1855 the Cathedral Commission recommended, but not unanimously, that each dean and canon should be resident for nine months in every year.[47] W. K. Hamilton had told the Commission in the previous year that the canons of Salisbury were irregular in their attendance. The old custom was for two canons who were in residence to share the duty between them, on either a daily or a weekly basis, but he had declined to enter into any such arrangement. The result was that there was only a double residence when he was in residence.[48] The *Guardian* complained in 1864 that the months of residence for residentiary canons were inadequate:

> Still the scandal remains, that a Canon 'Residentiary' may be non-resident three-quarters of the year.... The canon who has completed the laborious duties of the capitular residence is allowed to refresh himself in London, or at the sea-side for another quarter of the year before he betakes himself to the living of which he has the spiritual charge. The consequence is that he is neither an efficient canon nor a successful parish priest.[49]

Dean Goulburn disagreed and welcomed the 'wholesome influence' and 'agreeable social variety' that a canon who retained his living could bring to a cathedral city. A canonry also offered opportunities for study and writing to a theologically gifted canon.[50] Canon Harvey said much the same in the Convocation of Canterbury in 1881:

I can state from my own experience that my duties as a parochial clergyman have not been interfered with by having work to do in the Cathedral. Coming into residence at the Cathedral is a change and I do not think that a parochial clergyman needs any holiday, especially if he has cathedral work to perform during a part of the year. [51]

In reply to the archbishops' questionnaire in 1872, the dean and chapter of Exeter said that they should have an increased number of canons so that more of them could attend the daily services.[52] Benjamin Harrison, Archdeacon of Maidstone and a residentiary canon of Canterbury Cathedral, told the cathedral commissioners in 1880 that during the previous thirty years the chapter there had changed from being pluralists, only resident in the precincts for part of the year, to being full-time cathedral clergy, resident throughout the year.[53] Harrison explained in 1881 that residence meant being present in a canonical stall, not merely sleeping in a house in the precincts for the required number of nights.[54] George Trevor, a non-residentiary canon of York, said that residence was the whole key to cathedral reform: 'All Cathedral reform is summed up in the single word "residence". Get the men in their places and the duties will arrange themselves.'[55]

The 1840 Act highlighted a problem that had existed before, but that became more acute after the reduction in the number of residentiary canons. This was the question of deputizing. At Chichester in 1828 it was agreed that a residentiary could deputize for one of his colleagues in the case of illness.[56] At Worcester in 1830 the subdean was paid an extra £10 and was expected to reside for an extra month in addition to his ordinary residence.[57] Under the terms of an Order in Council dated 11 August 1841, the canons of Worcester were allowed to deputize for an absent canon at the rate of £50 a month.[58] Similar provisions were made at Gloucester and Winchester.[59] At Bristol a more cumbersome procedure was adopted.[60] At Winchester in 1863 it was arranged that the canons should help each other out if one of them was unable to perform all or part of his residence because of sickness.[61] If there were no dignitaries present at Wells, a prebendary was allowed to read the lessons in their place.[62] Prebendaries could also deputize for canons in cases of illness.[63] An ill canon at Winchester had to pay £10 a week to another residentiary canon or honorary canon who took his residence for him,[64] but at Bristol the dean was empowered to arrange a deputy for an absent canon, paying him out of the capitular funds.[65] The canon missioner at Gloucester, however, was not allowed to deputize for absent residentiaries.[66]

The provisions made by the 1840 Act for the foundation of honorary canons in new foundation cathedrals was implemented by an Order in Council on 23 May 1844. This applied to all the new foundation cathedrals except Christ Church, Oxford.[67] It was also provided that an honorary canon could deputize for an absent residentiary canon and must fulfil an annual preaching turn if a list of these were compiled. Canon Seymour, an honorary canon of Worcester, said at the Norwich Church Congress of 1865 that, although he had been an honorary canon for nineteen years, he had preached in the cathedral on only four occasions, three times at the bishop's invitation and once at the request of the dean and chapter. He said that he believed that at Peterborough and Norwich the honorary canons took the afternoon sermon for six months in the year.[68] In 1873 the dean and chapter of Worcester provided a special place for the honorary canons to keep their robes in order that they might attend cathedral services more frequently.[69] When Newcastle Cathedral was founded in 1882 there was no money for residentiary canons and the honorary canons had to fulfil some of their duties for the first five years.[70] Dean Scott of Rochester pointed out in 1880 that the honorary canons there grumbled about having to pay between £9 and £10 in legal fees at their installation.[71] The honorary canons were employed as substitutes for ill canons at Worcester, sometimes for three or four months in the year.[72] Canon Edward Payne, however, who in 1869 was appointed an honorary canon of Christ Church, Oxford, had only a slight connection with the place:

> I have been applied to by the Dean and Chapter for a subscription towards the restoration of the Cathedral; and I have been twice invited by that body to a semi-public dinner, which apparently had in it more of the nature of a college gaudy than of a Cathedral festival. The asked-for subscription I gave; the invitations I declined. This constitutes the whole intercourse which I have had with the Dean and Chapter of Christ Church since my appointment.[73]

The honorary canons of Canterbury included the metropolitan of Canada and a bishop from the West Indies,[74] while at Truro they met together at least three times a year and acted as the bishop's council.[75]

Although the 1840 Act led to a great reduction in the number of residentiary canons, in various ways their numbers began to grow again later in the century. The 1840 Act itself established a fourth canonry at Lincoln, to be held by an archdeacon.[76] The Cathedrals Amendment Act 1873[77] enabled some suspended canonries to be restored, as at St Paul's,[78] Gloucester[79] and Canterbury.[80] At the newer cathedrals, too, canons began to be appointed. The first canons of Truro were installed in January 1878. Although they were honorary at first, they were given definite offices – chancellor, missioner, president of the chapter, and treasurer.[81] Four years later, however, despite the opposition of Lord Grimthorpe, plans were drawn up to appoint canons at St Albans.[82] The diocese of Southwell was created in 1884 and non-residentiary canons of Lichfield and Lincoln who were resident in the new diocese were given the opportunity of transferring to the new chapter. Five new Nottinghamshire canons were appointed in 1885 and five from Derbyshire in the following year.[83]

What was the work of canons? What duties did they have, apart from their attendance at cathedral services and chapter meetings? Were they busy or idle? Pusey certainly thought that they had insufficient leisure.[84] W. K. Hamilton disapproved of residentiary canons combining parochial appointments with their canonries. He anticipated the plans of E. W. Benson by suggesting that canonries should be linked to diocesan appointments – such as archdeacon, diocesan missioner, or director of education.[85]

For much of the century it was unusual for the dignitaries of old foundation cathedrals (precentor, chancellor and treasurer) to hold residentiary canonries in addition to their dignities. Ouseley, for example, who was precentor of Hereford from 1853 until his death in 1889, did not become a residentiary canon until 1886.[86] C. A. Belli, the precentor of St Paul's from 1819 to 1886, was not a canon and rarely visited the cathedral.[87] W. K. Hamilton at Salisbury, though, was a model canon precentor. He chose the music to be sung at services with great care and took a close interest in the choristers and lay vicars. Wearing a cassock all day, he revived discontinued services, visited the training college, rearranged the cathedral archives and often preached.[88] Precentor Venables of Lincoln was 'a learned and accomplished musician' and his stall was piled high with music books. He had a close knowledge of the cathedral choir and staff, and spent his Saturdays taking groups round the cathedral.[89] The Precentor of York was also Dean of Gloucester and visited York rarely. Later Dean Duncombe held the office of precentor in addition to the deanery, and a similar doubling of functions occurred at both Salisbury and Exeter.[90] As late as 1881, however, Archdeacon Emery said in the Convocation of Canterbury: 'Do not we hear even now that there are Precentors of certain Old Foundation Cathedrals who do not know one note from another?'[91]

The Cathedrals Commission reported in 1854 that many archdeacons also held canonries. They also suggested that one canon in each cathedral should be given the spiritual charge of a district attached to the cathedral. Another could be given a poor endowed city benefice, while further canonries could be linked to the presidency of the theological college, the superintendence of the cathedral grammar school, and the inspectorship of diocesan schools.[92] Every third year at Hereford the residentiary canons elected among themselves a senior and junior claviger, a master of the fabric and a master of the library.[93] Although much progress was made at St Paul's, the canons there included Liddon and Lightfoot, who both held professorships. Gregory was the only full-time canon between 1871 and 1884, when H. S. Holland succeeded William Stubbs.[94] Other professors who combined their chairs with canonries included Creighton at Worcester and Westcott at Peterborough. Dean Johnson told the cathedral commissioners in 1880 that the canons of Wells were not idle during their period of residence:

> The canon who has just gone out of residence in Wells has preached 20 times during his residence, visited every body, attended chapter meetings, assisted the bishop in all diocesan work which occurred during his residence and is now taking charge of a large population moderately endowed.[95]

Archbishop Thomson of York, however, said that up till 1879 the canon who attended quarterly meetings found there was no business, apart from the occasional exercise of patronage. He had tried to find out what the duties of the canons were, but had received only negative replies.[96] Bishop Bickersteth of Exeter, determined to make his cathedral more obviously the centre of church life and work in the diocese, assigned definite diocesan responsibilities to each of his four residentiary canons. One was responsible for education, a second for deepening the spiritual life of the diocese, a third was responsible for links with overseas missions, while the fourth canon was given the duty of cultivating pastoral theology.[97] When Bishop Magee of Peterborough suggested in 1882 that special duties should be attached to the canonries there, the chapter resisted the proposal as 'unnecessary and undesirable'.[98]

Disendowed prebendaries still retained some cathedral duties. At Hereford they were invited twice a year to the general chapter meeting and could share in electing a chapter proctor, though at Wells and Chichester they were not allowed to do this. Opportunities for prebendaries to preach in cathedrals varied, but at Exeter they regularly preached on Sunday afternoons; they were given £4 and the use of a furnished house in the close.[99] At various cathedrals they were expected to attend on certain formal occasions.[100] At Chichester the four Wiccamical prebends and two others were exempted from disendowment and remained so until 1936 when the income from these stalls was pooled to endow the Prebend of Bursalis as a residentiary canonry.[101]

Further light on the duties of canons may be shed if we look at some individual canons of the nineteenth century. Some worked hard; others were lazy. Some achieved great things for the Church; others were more noted for their eccentricities. But through this kaleidoscope of canons we may glimpse some insights into the day-to-day life of an essential constituent in the life of cathedrals during the century.

In the early nineteenth century many canons were noted for their worldliness. In 1838 Sir Charles Anderson described the Subdean of Lincoln, Thomas Manners Sutton, as: 'one who like most of that name loves the loaves and fishes in the literal sense, who devour a jowl of salmon with their eyes before it is cut, yet a *good-natured* fellow'.[102] Probably the best-known canon of this time was Sydney Smith. He became a prebendary of Bristol in 1828 and told Lady Holland that he had 'an extremely comfortable prebendal house, seven-stall stable, room for four carriages'.[103] When he became a canon of St Paul's he was much better placed to continue his social life, but he did not neglect his work at the cathedral. Dean Milman respected his 'sound judgement, knowledge of business, and activity of mind'.[104] Smith was concerned about the music and the welfare of the choristers. He saw that efficient fire-fighting equipment was placed in St Paul's and insured the cathedral properly. He installed a stove in the library and saw that the books were carefully repaired. He clambered about the roofs and towers, gave directions for monuments to be cleaned, and demanded competitive tenders for all work done to the cathedral. He was diligent and efficient in his handling of the financial affairs of the cathedral and in his dealings with C. R. Cockerell, the surveyor. Christopher Hodgson, the chapter clerk, said that Sydney Smith 'was one of the most strictly honest men he ever met in business'.[105]

At Norwich, Adam Sedgwick became a canon in 1834. He brought his own servants, but engaged two extra maidservants. He purchased his predecessor's furniture and wine, and gradually settled into the routine of preaching and attending cathedral services regularly: 'We have also to give certain dinners of ceremony to the officers of the Cathedral. Giving and receiving dinners constitutes a formidable service in a city like this.'[106] He moved to a new house a few years later, which he found 'quite charming':

> I have one very good bed-room fit for a married couple; and three spare beds for bachelors... I have a capital housekeeper who provides and cooks for me...a housemaid, and a young lass to help her. My own servant comes and acts as my butler and waiter and *factotum*; and I have an assistant and occasional waiter to rub down my horse. Such is my establishment.[107]

Sedgwick described his household in 1844:

> John, my old *factotum*, is grave and solemn; my groom is a lout; but he is virtuous as well as dull. But Mrs Barnes! the perfect image of a Canonical house-keeper – grave and respectful in manner – voluble in tongue – neat in dress – tall in person, and skilled in the lore of old receipts for table-comforts and practised in the use of them.... My cook makes mutton-broth and plain pudding to a marvel and my housemaid airs sheets well, and makes blazing fires.[108]

At first he would rise very early for prayers with his servants by candlelight, before breakfasting at eight. Later his routine altered, and he wrote in 1844:

I rise early (often between five and six) and do *all my work* in the mornings, often before anyone is stirring.... At nine I meet my servants – quarter past, breakfast – at ten, morning service at the Cathedral – after service, odds and ends – callings and shoppings and I know not what – lunch at one – then a scamper on horseback (when I have time) with my niece.... Cathedral service again at four – dinner at six.[109]

A generation later, E. W. Benson became canon chancellor of Lincoln. He and his family lived very simply in the chancery without either horse or carriage, and only maidservants in the household. Benson conducted family services in the private chapel in his house and frequently walked about the garden, wearing his cassock and preparing his sermons. He founded the Scholae Cancellarii, held a Bible Class for Lincoln mechanics, started a system of night schools in the City, and gave Lent lectures in the chapter-house.[110]

The canons at Winchester in the early 1870s were elderly and eccentric. One suffered from the delusion that his nose was coming off and fixed it to his cheeks with black sticking-plaster, 'which gave him the appearance of a venerable tiger'. Another, who preached in lavender kid-gloves, had a regular rota of sermons, punctuated by an unvaried sequence of familiar anecdotes.[111] Worcester had a fair number of quaint canons. The Honourable John Fortescue was subdean. He was a tall man and wore 'immense starched collars and tie':

In the Cathedral he always seemed to look untidy; he wore an extremely large starched surplice, immense black scarf, tied at the neck with tape to keep it in place, bands that were generally awry, black gloves that did not come within an inch of his finger ends; when he preached he used to wag his hand which made the end flop up and down.

He took regular walks with his wife and family and could often be seen in his beautiful garden, spade in hand, pulling up weeds and tending his roses.[112] Canon Benson of Worcester was very deaf: 'When he preached someone in the organ gallery had to hold up a handkerchief to let him know the voluntary had ceased.' He did not attend chapter meetings on account of his deafness and opposed the new reredos in the cathedral.[113] J. R. Wood was aristocratic in appearance and was a canon of Worcester for forty-six years. A royal chaplain and former tutor to the Duke of Cambridge, he was a favourite of Queen Adelaide, who often drove to see him from her home at Witley. He had courtly manners, such as walking backwards towards the door when leaving a room.[114] Sir Gilbert Lewis, Bart., was an easy-going man, good-tempered and courteous, kindly and generous, with a lively sense of humour. He spent little time at Worcester, preferring to live in one of his many other homes.[115] Canon Melville used 'unusually long words and sentences in his sermons', but 'was a most graceful skater on the ice'.[116] Canon Seymour preached only once and became so feeble that he could not walk, and had to be wheeled to the cathedral lying on his back 'on a kind of hand-barrow'.[117]

The next generation of canons at Worcester included such outstanding men as Barry, Butler, Creighton and Knox-Little. John Randall, a lay clerk at Worcester, described Barry as 'a man of conspicuous ability and talent', while another lay clerk, James Smith, recalled his 'commanding presence' and 'masterful disposition'.[118] He was Principal of King's College, London, and later Archbishop of Sydney. W. J. Butler had been Vicar of Wantage for over thirty years when he came to Worcester; he stayed for five years before becoming Dean of Lincoln. Randall remembered him as being 'strong-minded', hard-working and 'a born leader'. His greatest work in Worcester was to found the Alice Ottley School. He was also largely responsible for the re-foundation of a separate choir school. He knew all about the vergers and beadsmen and ran a communicants' class for the servants of the canons.[119] At Worcester he was largely responsible for an increase in the number of communion services.[120]

Mandell Creighton succeeded Butler. His reputation attracted 'an immense crowd' to hear his first sermon in 1885.[121] He loved showing parties around the cathedral and instituted lectures in the chapter-house. When Knox-Little was in residence he generally walked up to the Creightons' house every evening to smoke a pipe, or else asked the Creightons

> to go and spend the warm summer nights on his charming terrace overhanging the Severn. Then questions of every kind – art, literature, religion and politics – were discussed to the accompaniment of much tobacco smoke, and the two canons, so dissimilar in temperament and in many of their opinions, learnt from the first to love and respect one another.

After matins, Creighton and Melville often walked up and down College Green, 'discussing educational or political questions, interspersed with many jokes and much laughter'.[122] In the afternoon he would go for a country walk, often having a desperate race to get back for evensong. Creighton arranged for the ground to the west of the cathedral to be laid out and opened to the public in 1889. During the 1887 Three Choirs Festival, the Creightons were very hospitable and entertained about sixty people to lunch and tea every day.[123]

Apart from Worcester, the only chapter in England that included so many able men in the late nineteenth century was St Paul's. In Robert Gregory, Henry Parry Liddon, J. B. Lightfoot, William Stubbs and Henry Scott Holland, St Paul's could boast a distinguished administrator, two brilliant preachers, a great theologian and a leading historian. Dean Church brought his own incomparable personal gifts and welded the chapter into a united team. Much of the credit for this is due to Gladstone who appointed Gregory, Liddon, Lightfoot and Church.[124] W. H. Hutton praised Gregory's work at St Paul's:

> He was the wise steward who made provision for the needs of all; and chiefly, he was concerned with the details of Cathedral management. He made it his business to know everything that had to be done and everyone who had to do it. He recognized the importance of details in preparing the harmonious whole. He was a master of finance. But it was the religious side of the whole work which appealed to him above all and guided him in everything.[125]

Liddon's chief contribution was his preaching.[126] He would spend his mornings writing letters, and in the afternoon he often walked along the Embankment with his sister, who lived with him in Amen Court. But on Saturdays, when he was in residence, he would forgo his usual walk in order to take visiting parties of men around the cathedral. His biographer, J. O. Johnston, speaks of his great interest in St Paul's:

> The Cathedral was, of course, the centre of all his work. There was no part of its life in which he did not take the warmest interest. Not only important Chapter business, and great questions about the music, the Services, and the more worthy decoration of the building, but every question of arrangement and order, and any detail about choir boys and vergers always commanded his interests.[127]

When the twelve new bells were installed in the north-west tower in 1878, Liddon spent hours there, watching with great interest all the details of the work.[128]

As well as his incomparable preaching, Liddon also did much to develop the pastoral work of the cathedral and raise its liturgical standards.[129] Liddon's conservatism was balanced by the energy and vision of Scott Holland. Soon after his appointment to St Paul's in 1884, Holland wrote:

> It is so noble to look up at the great Dome – and know that it beats,now, like a great Heart – in London – a home for all who watch after God. To help to make it as a *heart*, a Christian *heart*, to great London – this is one's prayer.[130]

His house in Amen Court became 'a centre of literary and social propaganda'[131] and for much of his twenty-six years as a canon of St Paul's he was also precentor. He loved the choir and the choral services:

> Just at Easter I feel the heart of St Paul's beating – all the rush and flow and glory of the choir: and the trumpet-stops: and the *shout* we give on 'Now above the sky He's KING'. There's nothing like it in all the world.

And the great church is flooded with people all day long: and we never stop: and there is all one splendour.[132]

J. B. Lightfoot spent only eight years at St Paul's, from 1871 to 1879, combining this with his professorship at Cambridge. His transparent goodness, great learning and robust common sense were widely appreciated and gave a sense of stability to the chapter.[133]

Worcester and St Paul's were unusual in having several notable canons in their chapters at the same time. The contribution of individual canons at some other cathedrals also deserves recognition. Canon John Napleton at Hereford at the beginning of the century was a strict disciplinarian, setting a scrupulous example in his own attention to duty. He was very business-like and in effect ran the cathedral.[134] William Welfitt was a canon of Canterbury for forty-seven years and was remembered as 'a shining example of clerical piety in a slack age', because he was resident for nine months each year and attended the daily services regularly.[135] At Wells, the outstanding canon for many years was H. W. Barnard. He was well known as an industrious county magistrate, a governor of the Blue School, a visitor to the County Asylum and a supporter of the local savings bank.[136] Canon Hawkins of Rochester was better known as Provost of Oriel College, Oxford, but he remained a canon of Rochester until his death, at the age of ninety-one, in 1882. Known as 'the East Wind' because of his cold and restrained manner, he was nevertheless a valued member of the chapter. Dean Burgon praised 'his habits of business and his *appetite for work*, joined to his lofty integrity and soundness of judgment'.[137]

H. W. Burrows was another distinguished canon of Rochester, though he was not appointed until he was sixty-five. Boys from the training-ship *Worcester* and local army officers were invited to his home, and he was both eager to entertain parties of visitors to the cathedral and resolute in his weekly visits to the local Infectious Hospital.[138] John Wordsworth, later Bishop of Salisbury, was also a canon of Rochester, combining this with the Oriel Professorship of Divinity at Oxford. He spent his vacations at Rochester, holding classes for the dockyard 'mateys' and taking an active part in the life of the cathedral and the city.[139] Another bishop who had a previous appointment as a canon was B. F. Westcott. He became a canon of Peterborough in 1869, and instituted early morning lectures in a side chapel, promoted devotional gatherings of the parochial clergy, stressed the need for nave services and successfully formed a large voluntary choir. He took a lively interest in the choir and the music of the cathedral and declared that his policy was to make the cathedral 'a centre of popular religious energy and feeling'.[140] He was very fond of going into the cathedral at night.[141]

C. M. Church spent most of his life and ministry at Wells. He was a student at the theological college in 1849–50, returning as a member of staff in 1854. He became a prebendary in the following year and was principal of the college from 1866 to 1880. Subdean of the cathedral from 1861, he became a canon, librarian, and master of the fabric until his death in 1915.[142]

Vernon Harcourt was an able canon of York, but he was also rash and insensitive. He lost all patience with Dean Cockburn, and persuaded his aged father, the archbishop, to conduct a formal visitation of the Minster which only exacerbated the difficult situation there in the 1840s. Vernon Harcourt's other claim to fame (besides being a model parish priest) was that he became president of the British Association for the Advancement of Science.[143]

Then there was Canon Lord Saye and Sele who gave sumptuous dinners and soirées in his house at Hereford. He was 'kind, genial and charitable, hospitable to a fault...with a good deal of humour and, it must be admitted, a good deal of amusing eccentricity'.[144] He often went to sleep during sermons in the cathedral, covering his face with a handkerchief saturated in eau-de-cologne and snoring heavily.[145]

Archdeacon Kaye of Lincoln was another rather quaint character. A. C. Benson described him as

a small, precise-looking man, his shoulders much bowed, bald, with a long, sharply-pointed chin, a small, rather prim mouth, and with an expression strangely compounded of amiability and acuteness. He had the most courteous and deferential manner and accompanied his remarks, which were few, cautious and precisely phrased, with a constant succession of little bows, like a pigeon patrolling a lawn.[146]

Canon Wray of Manchester was another survivor from a past generation and claimed to remember the days before Bonaparte. He had a great devotion to the liturgical observance of the anniversary of the Gunpowder Plot on 5 November, but disliked hymns, evening services and extempore preaching. He used to preach his own sermons over and over again. Generous and hospitable to neighbouring curates, he always arrived at the cathedral in some style, driving there in a carriage and pair, and attended by footmen in dark blue livery. On arrival at the chapter-house he would bow to the dean and address him as 'Sir', using his full hand to shake hands with the canons, but only two fingers with minor canons and one finger with a curate. Yet he was regular and diligent in his duties and gave weekly lessons in the Sunday School. He gave a Christmas dinner of beef and plum pudding to the elderly, while on Good Friday he distributed hot cross buns to schoolchildren. In his will he left money for eight poor men and women who attended the cathedral to buy new worsted stockings each year. He claimed to have conducted more christenings and weddings than any other clergyman in the Church of England.[147]

A. P. Stanley, who was briefly a canon of Canterbury, valued the opportunities it gave him of 'rest, seclusion and the tranquil opportunity for independent research and studious leisure'. He preached twice every Sunday of his month of residence, once in the cathedral and once in one of the city churches, and 'attracted unusual congregations by the life and freshness of his sermons'. He used his house at Canterbury to entertain a wide variety of guests from all over England.[148]

The reputation of cathedral chapters naturally varied. The Salisbury chapter was in a poor state in 1823, and the artist John Constable referred to the 'many imbeciles' there: 'a Dean dead – Cox, blind – Jacobs, old – Price, dead – and Hume an idiot'.[149] The chapter at Exeter in 1839 was strongly Tory.[150] A local newspaper at Lincoln in 1856 said that complaints about the uselessness and inefficiency of the chapter could no longer be justified, though five years later the city clergy still thought that they were 'lifeless and idle'.[151] A. P. Stanley said in 1853 of his colleagues at Canterbury:

> On the whole I end this audit with a better opinion of my brethren than ever before. They look at everything in a totally different light from what I should; but I think they show a real desire to do justice according to the views of their own generation and are certainly very good-humoured.[152]

The York chapter in Dean Duncombe's time included several notable canons.[153] Some chapters, such as that of Chichester in Dean Burgon's time, were quarrelsome. At Hereford, early in the century, Canons Morgan and Napleton kept up a deadly feud,[154] and the atmosphere at Bristol was little better.[155] At York, too, there were frigid relations between the canons in Dean Cockburn's time.[156] But towards the end of the century there was a better atmosphere at Chichester under Dean Pigou,[157] and Canon Butler told the Convocation of Canterbury in 1881 that this was generally the case.[158] Dean Lefroy's reforming ideas at Norwich were given a cool reception by his canons, but gradually they showed a greater willingness to co-operate with his experiments.[159] At Wells in 1900 the dean was requested to send 'a joint message of love and sympathy' to two of the canons who were dangerously ill.[160]

At some cathedrals the custom of a corporate capitular dinner was still maintained. Sydney Smith approved of this annual custom at St Paul's. He was also pleased to discover that during his months of residence he was responsible for giving a dinner each Sunday to the minor canons and (lay) vicars choral. Before long, however, Smith found that this was too much trouble and in 1843 the college of vicars choral agreed to forgo their weekly dinners in return for an additional £15 added to their stipends.[161]

Durham also maintained the custom of a residence dinner in circumstances that had changed very little since the seventeenth century:

The host still presides in his canonical habit of cassock and gown, and the young scholar still comes in at a certain time to read a portion of the Psalter, after which the residentiary addresses him with *Tu autem*, to which he responds *Domine, miserere nostri*, a remnant of the old Office of the *Benedictio mensae* in which it occurs. The *poculum charitatis* [sic] then makes its round.[162]

At Ely, too, great importance was ascribed to this custom. Dean Merivale recalled:

'Shoulder of mutton' was a great institution at Ely. Twice a year, before the grand audit, the canons and their wives dined together at the deanery, on which occasion *all* the ladies were treated as visitors, and while the dean took his place at one end of the table his wife yielded hers to the chapter clerk, who dispensed the stewed eels and roast shoulder, which always formed the principal dishes – a reminiscence, no doubt, of the time when rents were paid in kind and eels were plentiful in the Fen rivers. Canon Selwyn, who was a great authority on the old customs, never allowed the slightest deviation from the established usage, nor failed to revive the old jokes about 'cold shoulder', etc., etc., with fresh enjoyment each year. 'Black teapots' followed next morning, i.e. breakfast, also at the deanery, at which every person was served with a small black pot in which to make his own tea according to his own taste, the vergers carrying round kettles of boiling water to fill them up. Tradition said that this was the invention of a certain bachelor dean who found the whims and fancies of his eight canons more than he could cope with.[163]

The most important corporate activity of the canons (apart from their regular worship together in the cathedral) was attendance at chapter meetings. In addition to the regular meetings of the administrative chapter composed of the dean and residentiary canons, there were also occasional meetings of all the canons and prebendaries who composed the general or greater chapter.[164] At the Pentecostal meeting of the chapter at Salisbury on 11 June 1813, most of the prebendaries attended and heard the dean declare that its purpose was to take 'into full consideration the present state of the Cathedral Church'.[165] No further annual Pentecostal chapters were held at Salisbury until 1888.[166] The general chapter of Chichester met only rarely in the early years of the century; the meeting in 1819 was the first for five years.[167] A general chapter was summoned at Worcester in 1824.[168] At York the non-residentiary canons enjoyed the unique privilege of being full members of the chapter, though they were virtually excluded from normal meetings since the citations were fixed to the door of the chapter-house and only those who happened to see them would know about the meetings.[169] The general chapters at Bristol in June and November appear to have lasted for two days each.[170] At Gloucester it was decided to hold general chapter meetings on the first Wednesday in January and in July and the second Thursday in January.[171] When G. A. Selwyn was bishop, the greater chapter of Lichfield met twice each year,[172] but the meetings at Hereford were poorly attended.[173] Meetings of the greater chapter of Chichester were held in the bishop's dining room or in the vicars' hall, although in 1876, after prayers had been read by the dean in the robing-room of the cathedral, the meeting was adjourned to the library. Only two meetings were held between 1879 and 1893.[174] The dean and chapter of Worcester held a joint meeting with the honorary canons in 1889,[175] and the Sarum Pentecostal Chapter of 1899 called for greater legislative freedom for the Church of England and supported Bishop Wordsworth's resolution in favour of the establishment of a general synod to include a house of laymen.[176] When the first meeting of the greater chapter of Winchester Cathedral was held in 1892, the bishop said that he regarded this body as his council and suggested that it met twice a year in the spring and the autumn; discussions would avoid the subject of the cathedral itself.[177]

At most cathedrals the dean and chapter held a monthly meeting. This was certainly the case at Worcester in 1826 and at Winchester in 1874.[178] In other cathedrals a weekly chapter was the rule; at Exeter the weekly Saturday chapter had a long tradition[179] and at about the same time the dean and chapter of Winchester were holding weekly chapters on the question of land tax.[180] Weekly chapters were held at Hereford in about 1841, chiefly through the energy of Dean Merewether.[181] The revival of the weekly Saturday chapter at St Paul's was one of the main reasons why that cathedral became more efficiently and effectively governed.[182] In the later years of the century some cathedrals began to augment the formal meetings of the chapter with more frequent informal meetings. Weekly meetings of this kind were begun at Wells in 1874 and at Salisbury (before or after the official meetings) in 1878, becoming established as a monthly custom there four years later. At Worcester in 1882 the dean and chapter began to hold informal meetings once a fortnight.[183] The dean and chapter of Wells noted in 1841 that, according to an Act of Parliament, chapter meetings due to be held on Sundays would have legal effect only if they were transferred to another day.[184] At Gloucester a standing order was passed in 1891 prohibiting meetings at the same time as any services in the cathedral.[185] At Chichester, in the early years of the century, the dean and chapter usually met four times a year – on 20 January, 1 May, 1 August and 20 October – but the meetings were kept open if the business could not be completed on the same day.[186] In 1865 the October chapter was permanently transferred to November.[187] In some new foundation cathedrals, half-yearly special chapters were held, usually about 23 June and on a day towards the end of November.[188] Tait found these meetings wearisome at Carlisle, and in 1853 he wrote:

We have had our Chapter since my last memorandum. These are always to me painful meetings. I cannot feel that the Cathedral fulfils its work.... And perhaps I speak at times too warmly at these meetings, thereby causing irritation...[189]

Additional chapter meetings were sometimes held, as at Gloucester in 1867[190] and Bristol in 1869.[191]

If there was still a suitable chapter-house, the statutory meetings of the chapter were held in it, but at Hereford the chapter-house was in ruins and the library (then in the Lady Chapel) was generally used instead.[192] The deanery was the venue for a meeting at Gloucester in 1824,[193] and at Bristol also the meetings were held in the dean's house after the riots of 1831 had damaged the chapter-house.[194] At Wells, though, meetings were held in Mr Parfitt's house.[195] The dean and chapter of Worcester occasionally met as far afield as Canon Barry's house at King's College, London,[196] while the Chichester meetings adjourned to a more convenient place, such as the chapter clerk's office.[197] When Canon Sedgwick lay dying at Cambridge in 1873, the dean and chapter of Norwich had a chapter meeting in his rooms, but 'the excitement proved too much for him'.[198]

Until the Ecclesiastical Commissioners enabled the chapters to commute their estates in the 1850s and 1860s, much of the business conducted at chapter meetings was concerned with the administration of capitular estates. This was certainly the case at Worcester in 1800.[199] Thirty years later the picture had scarcely changed.[200] A. P. Stanley, later to become Dean of Westminster, has left an interesting account of a chapter meeting held at Canterbury on 26 November 1851 while he was a canon there:

Behold the date! Now the second day. A conversation in Chinese (as far as relates to me) going on between the Dean, Dr Spry and the sixmillenarian C— on leases and tithes at one end of a long table. The aged M— wrapt in the *Times*, the infirm D— wrapt in vacancy; the auditor warming himself by the fire; Archdeacon Harrison really doing business; Lord Charles Thynne and A. P. S. writing letters as fast as the pen can carry us – which possibility is the redeeming feature of the whole affair and really prevents it from being so intolerable as it would otherwise be.[201]

Dean Goulburn recorded the subjects discussed and decisions made at chapter meetings at Norwich in 1867. On 22 April he wrote:

A long chapter meeting here at Canon Robinson's house, in which we discussed the proposition of the Commissioners, the division of the services consequent on the introduction of the weekly communion, the throwing open of the Church, the better education of the choristers and other subjects from 10.30 to 3.15.

On 4 June his diary contained the following entry:

> The audit began after morning church and did not end until 4.30 p.m. –
> Sedgwick, Robinson, Heaviside present:
> 1. We ratified our acceptance of the terms of the Ecclesiastical Commission.
> 2. Settled the services to be in summer at 8 and 5; in winter at 9 and 4.
> 3. Made a slight increase in the stipends both of subsacrists and vergers, and agreed to throw the Church open from service to service.
> 4. Arranged that Alden should have the offer of the vacant lay clerk's house.
> 5. Decided to give £5 to the Dean of Ely's musical scheme.
> 6. Decided to accept Barnard and Bishop's scheme for warming the Church.
> 7. An increase of pay to the choristers and lay clerks for the extra service on Sunday.
> 8. Decided to take the Norman chamber as a choristers' school room.
> 9. Decided to open another *grille* in the Cloister opposite to the existing one.
> 10. Question of more efficiently cleaning the Church postponed till we should know more of Scott's plans.[202]

In 1890 the dean and chapter of Worcester met thirteen times, including the June and November audits. There were usually at least three members of the chapter present, and often more (the maximum was five), but the business transacted had little similarity to that of earlier epochs. In January they admitted a beadsman, appointed one incumbent, a new precentor and sacrist, confirmed the appointment of a new custos and elected a new chorister. In March they objected to a public urinal and voted £50 to help fight a proposed new sewage works. In May they approved the accounts, talked about repairs to chapter property, thanked the bishop for his gifts to the library, made one presentation, and agreed to a new brass memorial tablet in the cathedral. In June they were absorbed by choir holidays, and discussed the services during the approaching Three Choirs Festival and the possibility of instrumental music on certain days. No more substantial work was done until the November audit. The list of preaching turns was then agreed, and other subjects discussed included special offertories, a day of missionary intercession, financial statements submitted by the receiver-general and the treasurer, the precentor's report, the inventory of church goods, the voluntary choir, the library, the surveyor's report, fire extinguishers, the retirement of the bishop, a course of theological lectures, and various other small matters.[203] In 1900 the dean and chapter of Winchester decided to devote their meetings 'chiefly to spiritual and charitable interests, not taken up as hitherto with discussions on leases, bargains and percentages'.[204]

Naturally it was important to establish rules of procedure at chapter meetings, though sometimes there could be disputes about the way in which decisions were made. In 1805 Dean Lukin of Wells objected to the rest of the chapter electing a new canon residentiary in his absence and unsuccessfully tried to break up the chapter meeting.[205] At Winchester, a full attendance on the last day of chapter meetings was particularly desired, 'when the business transacted shall be revised and the booke [*sic*] signed in the presence of not less than six prebendaries and the Dean and Vice Dean'.[206] When only one canon turned up to a chapter meeting at Salisbury in 1811, the meeting was adjourned.[207] At Gloucester where the chapter met on the first Monday of the month immediately after morning service, 'for the better preservation of discipline and for the other interests of the church', it was agreed that the November and midsummer audits should be adjourned until the following January and August respectively, so that the accounts and revenues of the cathedral could be properly considered.[208] But in April 1818 and also in the following January, chapter meetings at Gloucester were cancelled for lack of business.[209] At Salisbury the responsibility for summoning a monthly meeting of the chapter lay with the dean. When special meetings were called, ten days' notice was required to be sent to the parochial as well as the canonical residence of each canon.[210] Proxy voting was common at several cathedrals in the early years of the century and continued at Worcester until 1835.[211] There is no clear evidence as to whether chapter meetings usually began with prayers, though they were certainly enjoined at Chichester in 1864.[212] In 1865 the dean and chapter of Gloucester resolved that draft minutes should be taken of their meetings; important matters were then entered in the Act Book and lesser business was entered in the chapter Minute Book.[213] At Worcester the minutes of meetings were read, confirmed and signed at the next meeting; all chapter orders were 'made out from the minutes and submitted to the Dean for approval before being finally recorded'.[214] Within two years of this act, the dean, subdean and treasurer at Worcester were constituted as a subcommittee of the chapter to consider urgent business and to report to the full chapter.[215] In 1877 the chapter clerk at Chichester wrote to each member of the chapter asking him to submit subjects for the agenda of chapter meetings,[216] and a similar arrangement was made four years later at Gloucester.[217] At Worcester, however, the summoning of chapter meetings seems to have remained the responsibility of the dean. After the meeting, a draft of the minutes was written, which was then copied into the Act Book.[218] At Chichester no matters could be decided at a chapter meeting which had not already been placed on the agenda, and private discussions about chapter business were not permitted.[219] The chapter clerk was required to read out the oath of secrecy enjoined on all members of the chapter at the beginning of each meeting.[220] At Wells, Edmund Goodenough, who was dean from 1831 to

1845, attended 128 meetings out of a possible 155 up to March 1838. After this he rarely attended owing to illness. Canon H. W. Barnard, however, was extremely diligent, attending 505 meetings out of a possible 634. Richard Jenkyns, who was Master of Balliol College, Oxford, as well as being Dean of Wells from 1845 to 1854, attended 151 meetings out of a possible 168.[221]

For the implementation of their decisions, cathedral chapters were dependent on their clerk or agent. Since many deans and chapters owned a considerable amount of property for much of the century, it is not surprising to find that the duties of a chapter clerk were similar to those of the agent on secular estates.[222] Capitular estates, like the smaller secular estates, were generally supervised by a local solicitor, but his income as chapter clerk was considerably less than the agent of a large secular estate.[223] Much of an agent's time would be spent dealing with tenants and their grievances and in collecting rents.[224] He was also responsible for finding new tenants and assessing their suitability. The agent had to put in long hours at his desk, submerged by correspondence, leases and accounts, but equally he was obliged to spend much time out of doors, travelling to the various estates and meeting the tenants.[225] It was, indeed, a highly responsible and busy occupation.[226] Cathedral chapters were very dependent on their agents because of their lack of business experience.[227]

The duties of the chapter clerk were carefully defined at Exeter in 1810 when the great Ralph Barnes was appointed. He was to reorganize and index all the papers of the dean and chapter, also making indexes for the Chapter Registers and Act Books. He was to inspect the manors, estates, houses and timber owned by the chapter, and to attend the weekly chapters in person.[228] At Bristol the chapter clerk might find himself defending the dean and chapter in an action over a disputed plumbing invoice or visiting the House of Lords to deliver a petition for the dean and chapter over the Bristol Harbour Bill.[229] In November 1812 there was a major row at Chester Cathedral over the appointment of a new chapter clerk.[230] There was also a disputed election of a new chapter clerk at Winchester two years later.[231]

The passing of the 1840 Cathedrals Act had a severe effect on chapter clerks, for as the Ecclesiastical Commissioners gradually took over the management of capitular estates from them, so their income from fees was greatly reduced. At York, C. A. Thiselton repeatedly pressed the commissioners for compensation, claiming that he was approaching ruin.[232] The responsibilities of the chapter clerk at Bristol were defined as

> attending on all chapters, preparing and entering minutes in the Minute Book, summoning members to attend, copying out and sending any minute or minutes of chapter with such explanatory letter as may be

79

necessary to any person whom these may concern – apprizing minor canons, clerks, etc., of their election to minor canonries and etc., consulting with lessees as to fines, renewals or the like, either by letter or personally once at least – and the like as occasion may require – also attending on all baronial courts, with the duties similar to those on chapter business and when the profits shall be considerable, the expense of travelling to hold courts to be borne by him.

In all other cases the expence of attendance, consultations, letter writing and the like to be charged on the Dean and Chapter.[233]

Fifteen years later the office of chapter clerk and steward of the manors of Bristol was separated from that of the chapter's solicitor.[234] In 1865 M. E. C. Walcott collected together some details of the duties and pay of the chapter clerks in various cathedrals. At Lichfield the chapter clerk received £230 a year and was also registrar; at Carlisle he was steward and deputy treasurer; at Chester his functions as steward were carried out with the assistance of a bailiff; at Winchester he made out leases, while at Gloucester he acted as legal adviser, steward of the manors and held courts, transacted land business and acted as receiver of rents with the treasurer. At Ripon the chapter clerk was also registrar, attending chapter meetings, and recording the acts of the chapter, paying choir salaries, receiving all rents and profits arising from the renewal of leases and copyholds, and transacted all other matter of business on behalf of the cathedral.[235] At Gloucester the chapter clerk also acted as registrar and as deputy to both the treasurer and receiver-general of the chapter.[236] At Chichester the chapter clerk was obliged to attend a service in the cathedral on chapter days and was allowed the use of the subdean's stall.[237]

W. E. Hughes was appointed chapter clerk at Bristol in 1879 and paid £20 per annum; he was also appointed subtreasurer at a rate of £30 per annum. He was responsible for looking after the minute and account books, maintaining the book of bye-orders and the register, summoning chapter meetings, preparing the agenda, and taking the minutes. He also saw to the correspondence of the dean and chapter and cared for their records. As subtreasurer he was obliged to assist the treasurer in the cathedral accounts, and in the supervision of the condition of the cathedral and precincts. He was to make sure that the roof was inspected weekly, inspecting it himself each month, and giving a report to the chapter once a quarter. He was to report any defect in the building or precincts, and to obtain estimates for any work to be done. He had charge of the cathedral stores and of the firehose, checking that the latter was tested regularly. He was also in charge of the chapter's supply of coal and wood and had to keep locked the gate between Anchor Lane and Lower College Green.[238]

At Winchester the accounts prepared by Mr Comely, the chapter agent, were inaccurate and subject to delay. The dean and chapter therefore decided to appoint a new agent and asked Messrs Clutton to take over the management of their estates on a percentage basis. As there was no longer to be a resident agent, the sums normally paid to the agent were to be paid direct to the receiver's account at the bank.[239]

In 1885 a Bill was promoted in Parliament providing for the remaining capitular estates to be commuted; deans and chapters were to be required to set aside a fabric fund for the maintenance of their cathedrals and to be liable for the repair of their own houses. George Whitcombe, the chapter clerk of Gloucester, convened a meeting in London attended by several chapter clerks. They were concerned about their loss of income if the estates were commuted, and hoped that they would receive compensation. But the Bill never became law.[240]

Chapters were certainly aware of their indebtedness to their clerks, who had often served them for many years. Mr Rogers, the chapter clerk of Bristol, retired in 1838 after fifty-two years in office.[241] When Edmund Davies, the chapter clerk of Wells, died in 1863, the dean and chapter recorded his 'trustworthiness, great ability and unwearied industry'.[242] Perhaps the greatest of Victorian chapter clerks was Ralph Barnes, who held that office at Exeter for no less than sixty-six years. When he died, the dean and chapter acknowledged

> not only the gentle, yet independent urbanity which contributed to the maintenance of that unbroken cordiality which existed between themselves and him, but also the eminent assistance in their acts and deliberations which they received from one whose judgment was equalled by his profound acquaintance with capitular statutes, the importance and significance of cathedral usages and the principles of ecclesiastical law.[243]

R. G. Raper, the chapter clerk at Chichester, even received a knighthood and was solely in charge of the capitular estates.[244] When Mr Macdonald, the chapter clerk at Salisbury, resigned in 1888 after twenty-five years' service, however, he dismissed any delusions about his own contribution to the conduct of capitular business, saying: 'I can never be more than a cipher.'[245] In 1890 when J. H. Knight, the chapter clerk of Hereford, died, the dean and chapter paid tribute to his work over the previous twenty-four years, and set on record

> his scrupulous fidelity, his consistent integrity, his excellent judgment and ability in transacting their business, sometimes under circumstances of great difficulty, and the great skill and patience which he shewed in dealing with the various persons with whom he was brought into contact in its course.

He was, they said, 'ever friendly, ever patient and considerate'.[246]

Cathedral life is not the same as either monastic life or parochial life. It is a survival of canonical life that was well known before the Reformation. The canons are therefore the key to the whole system. The dean, certainly in an old foundation cathedral, was their senior, a *primus inter pares*. The vicars choral were their deputies. The lay clerks and choristers were originally members of their households. It was the canons who formed the chapter and, with the dean, governed every aspect of the cathedral's affairs. There were some canons, as we have seen, who neglected their duties and were lazy or indifferent; but there were others, such as Benson at Lincoln, or Butler at Worcester, or Liddon and Gregory at St Paul's, who took their responsibilities very seriously. By their zeal and devotion to the life and work of their cathedrals they helped to raise both the reputation and the effectiveness of cathedrals in the nineteenth century.

6

THE CATHEDRAL
STAFF

❀

The essence of the cathedral system is the existence of a group of canons forming a corporate body ('the dean and chapter'). This body sustains the daily worship and takes joint decisions about the cathedral, its property and its responsibilities. From the early Middle Ages onwards, the complexities of cathedral organization led to various other officials being recruited to assist the canons. In some cathedrals there were cantarists, formed to serve the numerous chantry chapels; in the cathedrals of the old foundation there were colleges of vicars choral, who were chiefly responsible for the musical parts of the daily services.[1] In the new foundation cathedrals there was a small group of minor canons, and in all cathedrals there were vergers, or sub-sacrists or sextons. In addition, there were beadsmen who assisted the vergers in various ways in the new foundation cathedrals, and all cathedrals were dependent on various kinds of paid workers who assisted with cleaning, tolled the bells, kept order in the close, or acted as porters.

The colleges of vicars choral were the most distinct group of these *ministri inferiores*. They had their own buildings, endowments, rights and privileges and made their own special contribution to the life of their cathedrals. The college at Hereford is a typical example. Incorporated by Richard II in 1395, it received a new charter from Elizabeth I and new statutes from Charles I.[2] The vicars choral occupied a fifteenth-century quadrangle near the cathedral, with their own chapel, library and hall. The hall had been enlarged in the mid-eighteenth century to accommodate concerts held during the Three Choirs Festival and to provide a suitable venue for the meetings of glee clubs, in which the vicars had often taken prominent parts. Originally there were twenty-seven vicars choral at Hereford, but this number had been reduced to twelve in the late sixteenth century. A new vicar choral had to make certain statutory payments. For example, when G. R. Hancock became a probationary vicar choral in 1802 he paid 13s 4d for linen. When he was perpetuated twelve months later he paid 20s for eight bushels of wheat and fourteen bushels of barley.[3] When a new vicar choral was sought in 1836 at Hereford, the advertisement asked for a gentleman in Holy Orders to fill the office of a vicar choral in Hereford Cathedral now vacant. The candidate must possess a good knowledge of Musick and be used to chaunting the Service, singing Anthems and Cathedral Musick – as in Hereford Cathedral these duties devolve entirely on the Vicars Choral, there being no lay singers in that Establishment.[4]

When five vacancies in the college occurred in 1849, advertisements were placed in the London *Times*, the *English Churchman* and the two Hereford papers.[5] No less than seventeen priests applied for a vacancy among the vicars choral at Wells in 1858.[6] A newly elected vicar at Wells was required to take an oath of fidelity to the college.[7] In 1867 the dean and chapter of Hereford resolved to appoint on a temporary basis two assistant vicars choral. They had to be graduates in holy orders, were granted a stipend of £100 per annum, and were given rooms in the college and the use of the college kitchen and garden.[8]

The collegiate atmosphere was sedulously fostered and maintained. According to the sixteenth century statutes at Chichester, no vicar was permitted to enter the hall unless he wore a gown and no dogs were allowed within the college.[9] The head of a college was generally known as the custos (as at Hereford) or the principal (as at Chichester), but there was often an elaborate hierarchy of officers. At Wells, for example, five of the vicars were elected as seniors, two as principals and three as auditors, while one fulfilled the duties of receiver.[10] At Hereford there were two auditors, a librarian, a steward of the buttery, and a steward of the rents.[11] Meals were taken in common, and this custom only ceased at Hereford when the kitchen area of the college was badly damaged by fire in 1828.[12] In 1803 the Hereford vicars decided that any member who ate meat for supper should be charged 6d, and 18d if he brought a guest to dinner. If a college servant dined in the kitchen he was charged one shilling.[13]

Sometimes, of course, the domestic life of the college became strained. In 1809 Matthew Hill, who was steward of the buttery at Hereford, drew £40 from the bank without the knowledge of the other vicars, who found as a result that they were faced with an overdraft of £27. They thereupon made a rule that no sum of money should in future be withdrawn from the bank without their formal approval and a record being made in the college Act Book.[14] Among the college servants were a gardener, whose wages were raised to 13 guineas in 1810, and a scullion who was paid £5 per annum.[15] In the same year a clock was purchased for the college kitchen and twelve silver table spoons, while in 1811 the college also received a present of two silver goblets from Thomas Watkins and a turbot and a lobster which were sent by coach from London by Sir Henry Gwillim.[16] In 1813 a patent steam kitchen was ordered for the college and a few days later it was decided that the college silver was not available for private use.[17] The Hereford vicars did not neglect their charitable duties: in 1810 they gave £2 towards the erection of Nelson's Column on Castle Green and 10 guineas in 1816 to a fund to relieve the 'labouring poor...owing to the great scarcity and distress of the present time'.[18] There were three fires in the college at Hereford in 1820, and a further, more serious, outbreak in 1828, which badly damaged the south-east corner of the quadrangle and claimed the life of John Constable, the college butler.[19]

In 1833 the other vicars were thrown into great consternation when Henry Pearce brought his wife to live with him in the college. They complained to the dean and chapter that this was 'a proceeding so extraordinary, so unprecedented in the annals of the College, and accompanied withal by a total want of courtesy and respect towards his brethren'.[20] Forty years later the dean and chapter told the custos and vicars that they disapproved of married vicars living with their wives and children in the college.[21] In 1875 the college gardener was paid £20 per annum, 'his duties being to keep [the] quadrangle in order, cut ivy, clean out spouts, gutters and etc., plant out flowers, attend to the kitchen garden and keep walks and etc. in proper order'.[22]

At Wells, the vicars were careful to uphold the tradition of an annual service in their chapel on 8 November to commemorate Bishop Ralph of Shrewsbury. They leased their hall to the local freemasons for 12 guineas per annum in 1890.[23]

At most colleges there were twelve vicars in the early nineteenth century, but at York there were only five and at St Paul's the six vicars choral were all laymen. The colleges at Wells and Lichfield also included laymen. Jebb said in 1843 that 'the vicars choral are looked upon as the drudges of the Chapter, as an order of men inferior in caste, though really their equals in ecclesiastical order'.[24]

By 1893 there were five colleges (St Paul's, Hereford, York, Chichester and Lincoln) where all the vicars were in orders – the college at St Paul's being a college of minor canons – and four (Lichfield, Wells, Salisbury and Exeter) where there was a mixture of clergy and laymen. At Hereford and St Paul's there were six ordained vicars; there were five at York, four each at Chichester, Lincoln, Salisbury and Lichfield, and three each at Wells and Exeter.[25] In the early nineteenth century vicars choral often took an active part in the choral singing of cathedral services, as well as intoning the prayers and the litany and reading lessons.[26] At Hereford they were not assisted regularly by any laymen until 1851.[27] Dean Merewether told Lord John Russell in August 1836 that the constitution of the college at Hereford was 'peculiar and different from any other ecclesiastical body in the kingdom', since the vicars constituted

the entire vocal force of the cathedral...by them the chaunting, services and anthems are performed, there being no lay singers in our church – if therefore this body should be dissolved our choral services would be of necessity annihilated.[28]

The dean and chapter of Exeter were insistent in 1815 that two priest vicars must be present at every service,[29] but in 1827 this stipulation was reduced to all Sundays, litany days and other special days.[30] One priest vicar was paid 50 guineas a year to act as a stand-by preacher in case any of the prebendaries failed to keep his preaching-turn.[31] By 1861 at Chichester the priest vicars served 'in course', only one at a time appearing at cathedral services.[32] In 1867 the dean and chapter of Chichester tried to introduce a Sunday evening service, but the priest vicars objected.[33] When some of the vicars choral at Hereford complained about their duties in 1890 they were told that they should 'fulfil their cathedral duties with religious zeal and in no carping and grudging spirit'.[34] Matters came to a head shortly afterwards when Dr Innes was cited in the Court of Arches for neglect of duty, as he had refused to intone the litany.[35] A crisis of a different nature occurred at Exeter nearly thirty years earlier when Mr Corfe, one of the priest vicars, lost his singing voice and it took determined action by the dean and chapter to force his colleagues to undertake the extra work that this caused.[36] One of the saddest cases was that of a priest vicar at Lichfield, who was deprived in 1898 because of his immoral conduct.[37]

At Wells by the closing years of the century there were three priest vicars and eleven lay vicars, and they were paid approximately £120 and £80–90 respectively. Some of the priest vicars looked after small parishes in the neighbourhood; some taught in the Cathedral School or in the theological college. One of them, G. A. Hollis, later became Bishop of Taunton.[38] In the early decades of the century there were some remarkable characters. F. E. Gretton recalled that in 1809 Custos Underwood was still presiding over the college at Hereford:

> ...a good humoured, easy-going veteran in a scratch wig, who, besides his office in the Cathedral, was incumbent of St. John's and St. Nicholas, and chaplain to the gaol. This last involved a week-day service which the Custos was always glad to escape.

Underwood was a well-known local figure as a magistrate, and a prominent freemason. He was also domestic chaplain to Bishop Beauclerk and carried the mitre in procession at his funeral in 1787.[39] The senior vicar, Thomas Kidley, was 'old and quaint, partially palsied', but still fond of a glass of port.[40] A particularly troublesome vicar choral at Hereford was Gilbert Rice Hancock. In November 1807 the custos and vicars complained to the chapter about his 'gross and unprecedented neglect'. They had shown 'the greatest forbearance' to Hancock for nearly three years, but their patience had now run out. Hancock had been continuously absent for over three months without having made any provision for a deputy. On 10 November he was called to attend a chapter meeting, and a week later he wrote to the dean and chapter saying that he had had to leave Hereford to resolve some financial difficulties. The dean and chapter decided that Hancock had been 'grossly negligent of the duties of his place' and suspended him. Early the next year he wrote from Bath, saying that he was ill and had been advised to take the waters. When he refused to return, the dean and chapter dismissed him.[41]

Twenty years later there was a marked drop in the average age of the vicars. The college wrote to the dean and chapter and told them that, 'Nine members of the twelve are young men and the three seniors are not so far advanced in years, but that the youngest of their brethren may have passed much beyond the meridian of life.'[42] In 1848 Dean Merewether told the Ecclesiastical Commissioners that the condition of the remaining eight members of the college meant that 'the choir is now reduced to such a state of disgraceful inefficiency: and it is daily getting worse and worse so that ere long the service must cease'. All eight vicars were either elderly (the oldest, Robert Pearce, was seventy-eight) or in bad health, or resident out of the city.[43] Dean Richard Dawes, when he succeeded Merewether, was of the same opinion. The vicars were, the said, 'from age totally inefficient as regards the choral service and a more deplorable state of things and the more likely to drag down our Cathedral system cannot well be imagined'.[44]

It was quite usual, as it had been in the eighteenth century, for some of the vicars choral to hold office for long periods. When Thomas Kidley of Hereford died in 1813, he had been a vicar choral for forty-nine years.[45] William Cooke retired in 1836 after forty-three years' service.[46] Another long-serving vicar choral was Lewis Maxey. He was a counter-tenor and came from a family of twenty-six children. His voice gradually declined and after he became Rector of Byford, he rarely visited either the cathedral or the college, since he could no longer intone the prayers or sing in tune. He became incurably deaf and very deranged.[47] When William David vacated his stall at Exeter in 1908 he had been custos for forty-one years. His two immediate predecessors had served for fifty-one years and fifty-nine years respectively.[48]

Age and infirmity were a particular problem at York where there were only five vicars choral. At the beginning of the century, two vicars became incapable of duty; a third, 'though an uncommonly strong man and in full vigour of health', lost his voice and the two remaining vicars choral had to be augmented by substitutes, who were admitted as vicars when the incapable vicars choral finally died.[49] At Hereford, in November 1834, Mrs Henry Pearce wrote to Dean Merewether and told him that her sick husband had not received a farthing from the college of vicars choral since the previous April. He was faced with walking to his parish as he could not afford to ride.[50] Richard Garvey, the senior priest vicar at Lincoln, told the Cathedrals Commission in 1854 that he had faithfully served the cathedral for thirty-two years. Having reached the age of sixty-nine, he was 'much enfeebled by a chronic cough' and pleaded that elderly vicars should somehow be released.[51] By 1867 only two vicars choral at Hereford were fit for duty, and one of these was in delicate health.[52] In 1875 a new vicar choral at Hereford caused a controversy between the dean and chapter and the college, for the custos and vicars complained that Alfred Capel had a 'harsh unpleasant voice' and was often out of tune. None of them was willing to join him in intoning the litany.[53] The dean and chapter loftily replied that, 'powers of chanting are not of such primary importance as to determine the choice of the Dean and Chapter in the selection of minor canons'.[54] In 1888 they decided that when one of the college was no longer able to intone, he should pay £50 to the dean and chapter in order that they might engage a substitute.[55]

The problems of having two grades of clergy in the same church led to considerable discussion at Hereford about where the vicars choral should sit in the quire of the cathedral. In 1870 it was decided that they should sit in the second row of stalls, but a year later they were allowed to occupy vacant prebendal stalls. In 1873 it was established that when a vicar choral preached he was to be led to and from the pulpit by the mace-bearer. A few days later the vicars choral received permission to have their own mace.[56] H. W. Pullen, a troublesome minor canon or vicar choral of Salisbury, was sensitive about his seat in the cathedral.[57] The Dean of Salisbury had pointed out to him in the previous year that only at St Paul's, Exeter, Chichester and Hereford were the vicars choral permitted to sit in prebendal stalls, though at Hereford 'they never avail themselves of this permission'.[58]

Vicars choral were often irregular in attending cathedral services. Two vicars were required to attend evening services on Sunday and Christmas Day at Hereford, according to regulations drawn up in 1800, and one vicar was obliged to assist at the altar in the mornings if required by the dean or hebdomadary.[59] From time to time there were defaulters. The difficulties caused by G. R. Hancock have been mentioned above,[60] but in 1819 the dean and chapter noted how infrequently the vicars attended services.[61] Ten years later only one vicar was present at a Sunday evening service and the dean and chapter sent a sharp reminder to the custos.[62] In 1832 the dean and chapter sent a schedule of attendances by the vicars for each year since 1824 to the college. This showed that the slackest member was Henry Pearce, who was present at cathedral services for an average of only seventy-nine days a year. The most regular attender was F. E. Gretton, whose average attendance of 212 days a year showed up the slackness of all but one of his colleagues.[63] Such a record on the part of the college was unlikely to escape the reforming zeal of Dean Merewether, who was appointed to Hereford in 1832. On 19 July 1834 Merewether was appalled to discover that there was not a single vicar choral present at evensong and so he fined each of them 2s 6d.[64] A heated correspondence ensued between Merewether and the succentor; and by November Merewether was fining the vicars choral £1 each for being absent from a service.[65] By 1837 a better spirit seems to have been achieved, for the custos and vicars decided 'that on all State days, Visitation and Assize Days, they will make a point of attending the Cathedral service without reference to the cycle of duty', and hoped that thereby they would avoid further complaints from the dean.[66] Merewether could not claim the entire credit for this improvement. The threatened recommendations of the fourth report of the Ecclesiastical Commissioners prompted James Garbett, the custos, to assert that:

> The College of Vicars is the most compleat [sic] Choral Establishment in the Kingdom, and there being no lay singers, the whole burden of the choir service devolves upon them. As things are at present constituted, you have never less than six in attendance on Anthem days, generally eight, occasionally ten, and sometimes the full compliment [sic] of 12.[67]

But Merewether proudly told Archbishop Howley, when he forwarded this letter from Garbett in August 1836, that 'it seldom happens that a week passes without all the numbers of the College being present at Choir and rarely a day without from five to eight at each service'.[68]

There were also difficulties at York, where no vicar was present at the morning service in the Minster on Easter Day 1849. Thus the dean and chapter ordered that no vicar should be absent from the city for more than a week without permission.[69] A few years later the vicars drew up their own rules for their attendance at the cathedral – each vicar was to be on duty for two weeks out of every five.[70] At Hereford, however, the situation had not improved, for in 1857 the dean and chapter attempted to fine the vicars £2 each for two occasions when they did not attend services. This led to a new cycle of attendance being drawn up which was accepted by the dean and chapter.[71] A further cycle of Sunday attendance ensuring the presence of two members of the college at each service was drawn up in 1867.[72]

At Wells, too, the vicars were notorious for their slack ways. The dean and chapter even consulted the solicitor-general about the best means of compelling the vicars to perform their duties adequately.[73] There was one occasion in September 1876 when all the priest vicars were absent and a further set of rules was drawn up by the dean and chapter.[74] In 1883 the dean and chapter told the cathedral commissioners:

> For some time...the services of the Cathedral suffered greatly from the non-attendance and insubordination of some members of the body of vicars. One member of it absented himself from his place in the choir more than 500 times in one year.[75]

There was a further attempt to regulate the vicars' absences at Wells in 1887.[76] For a while the situation seems to have improved, and in 1888 the vicars choral heard the dean read a letter from Canon Browne, expressing 'his entire satisfaction' with their attendance and conduct,[77] but in 1899 all the vicars were summoned to the chapter-house where they were given a severe reprimand by the dean and two of the canons.[78]

There were still problems at Hereford in 1870.[79] Six years later it was found that one vicar, J. R. G. Taylor, had attended much more frequently than he should have done and that three other vicars had been over-slack.[80] Taylor wanted to be absent after Christmas 1878, but Dean Herbert said that this would set a bad example.[81] By 1895 the dean and chapter said that the cycle of attendances by the vicars choral 'has practically broken down', largely because of the wilful ways of Dr Innes.[82]

Infrequent or irregular attendance was only one of the causes of tension that often existed between a dean and chapter and a college of vicars choral. Until his attention was sidetracked by the Hampden affair, Dean Merewether tried to persuade all the Hereford vicars to resign in return for a pension and the right to attend cathedral services. He wanted the dean and chapter to take over the endowments of the college so that there could be a reasonably efficient choir.[83] At Wells in 1868 a dispute between two of the vicars over a surplice led to a brawl and an 'abundance of abuse and a blow', but the dean and chapter declined to interfere.[84] When one of the vicars choral at Hereford claimed in 1872 that Dean Herbert had been rude to him, the other vicars declined to take their place in the procession until the dean apologized.[85] Their surly attitude continued the next year, when they refused to help pay for the washing of the lay clerks' surplices or the expenses of a voice trial for a new assistant vicar choral.[86] In 1874–5 there was a serious dispute at Wells over the persistent absence of a vicar by the name of Drayton. The college stoutly resisted an attempt by the dean and chapter to appoint an extra vicar. Dr Robert Wallis, the senior priest vicar, wrote on 5 June 1875:

> I, of course, respectfully recognize the Dean and Chapter as rightfully the governing body in the cathedral; and in that capacity I am always ready to submit myself to their control – but surely this does not constitute me in any reasonable sense their *servant*.

The chapter clerk replied ten days later, in a most haughty letter, saying that the dean and chapter

> deprecate communications such as they have now twice received from you...they consider that counsels in the cause of moderation and 'equity' come with a bad grace from the writer of the two letters in question, in which reckless charges are made and motives imputed without any ground to support them.[87]

Four years later two of the vicars were again in trouble with the dean and chapter, mainly through drunkenness, but presumably they were lay vicars.[88] In January 1880 Robert Wallis complained of 'the supercilious and haughty bearing with which their superiority is asserted by the capitular clergy whenever they come into official contact with the priest-vicars'. But another of the priest vicars said that 'the best possible personal relations exist between all Cathedral clergy'.[89]

At Exeter Dean Boyd wanted to suppress the college of vicars choral. He told the Cathedrals Commission in 1879 that 'the existence of such a body was most detrimental to the good government of the Cathedral establishment'.[90] That there was some friction between the dean and chapter and the college seems to have been public knowledge in 1888.[91]

As independent corporations, the colleges of vicars choral owned lands and leased them to tenants. Just like the chapters, they held regular meetings to renew leases and superintend their corporate revenues. In 1800 the vicars choral at Hereford decided on a new way to renew their leases,[92] and seven years later they fixed the price of a seven-year lease on land as two years' value, with one year being the price for houses.[93] Some idea of the processes involved at Salisbury can be gained from a note made in the vicars' account book in 1802: 'The Town rents all except the Angell are receiv'd by the Rent Gatherer....This account is given to the Procurator at the end of the year who enters it into the book and passes it to the vicars with his own account.' The total amount received by the Salisbury vicars between 1831 and 1867 was £29,092 4s 4½d. The average amount per annum from fines on the renewal of leases was £786 5s 6d, with a further average annual amount of £453 9s 6d from reserved rents, redeemed land tax and pensions. The average annual outgoings amounted to £248 12s 2d. This meant that the average income divided between the four vicars was £991 2s 10d, or £247 15s 8d each. The highest individual fine was £5,589 from the sale of a lease in 1837.[94] From time to time it was necessary for vicars choral to inspect their properties. In 1802, for example, two of the vicars at Wells were asked to inspect some college property at Cheddar.[95] At Hereford the interest on the timber money was divided equally among the members of the college, but the custom with the timber money itself, as with fines, was for it to be divided after the annual reserved rents chargeable on the property which was sold to produce it had been deducted.[96] As reserved rents were difficult to collect, the college at Hereford resolved in 1822 to appoint a professional agent, Jonathan Gough, as deputy collector of rents. He was to come to College Hall on the first Monday in October and April each year to receive the rents.[97] The dean and chapter of Exeter were concerned about the college's mismanagement of its leases in 1832 and asked their chapter clerk, Ralph Barnes, to investigate the situation. The chapter generously agreed to match each £50 that the vicars raised in order to pay off the college's debts. In 1846 the college acknowledged with gratitude the help given by the dean and chapter in discharging a debt that had existed for twenty-five years, but only three years later they needed another £25 from the chapter to wipe out a further deficit.[98] By 1850 the vicars choral at Hereford had also run into financial difficulties. They explained to the dean and chapter that most of their property consisted of houses let for twenty-nine years at a time. Many of these leases had not been renewed and the reserved rents were inconsiderable. Where the leases had been renewed, the fines had been reduced, 'in consequence of the depreciation of house property in Hereford'. This was also true of twenty-one-year leases reserved for lands owned by the college. Grain rents had also been reduced, and £900 per annum was about the maximum income they could hope for.[99]

In fact, the college's income rose markedly in the early 1850s. The annual amount for each year between 1846 and 1852 shows that the income in 1852 (£1,803 2s 1d, with £1,105 2s 7d coming from fines on the renewal of leases) was almost back to the 1846 figure of £1,820 11s 5d for total income, with £1,154 1s 6d coming from fines.[100] The Exeter vicars had a very varied income from fines in the years up to 1865. The total in any one year varied between nothing and £52 as a minimum figure, with £2,982 and £1,170 being the highest maximum figure. The average over a period of twenty years was £500.[101]

Following the example of several chapters, some of the colleges entered into negotiations in the 1860s with the Ecclesiastical Commissioners over the commutation of their estates. The estates of the vicars choral at Chichester were commuted in 1865[102] and those at York in the following year.[103] When the vicars choral of Wells asked the Ecclesiastical Commissioners to take over their estates in 1852, they declined, but when the subject was reopened in 1866 an agreement was made and the college was guaranteed an income of £880 per annum.[104] The Exeter estates were commuted in 1867 and the Salisbury estates in 1868.[105] The *Guardian* gave details in 1887 of the annual sums paid by the ecclesiastical commissioners to the vicars choral of seven old foundation cathedrals. The Lichfield vicars received £2,160, but at the other end of the scale the college at Chichester was paid only £300. The other colleges at St Paul's, Exeter, Salisbury, Wells and York received £900, £650, £960, £880 and £1,400 respectively.[106] The average annual income of the college at Hereford between 1884 and 1890 was £2,901 and the divisible balance amounted to £1,583.[107]

The formal meetings of the vicars were, of course, serious occasions and fines were imposed for absence from them at Wells unless a 'good and sufficient reason' could be proved.[108] The custos and vicars of Hereford agreed in 1868 to hold a meeting on the first Sunday in every month at 11 a.m.[109] Two years later they framed comprehensive regulations covering the income of each vicar and their respective duties, and in 1871 they attempted to revive their common table in College Hall.[110] Unfortunately the common table lapsed in 1875, never to be revived.[111] At Chichester there was no fixed pattern of meetings before 1875, when it was suggested that they should be held quarterly. Following the death of E. W. Johnson, who had been their clerk for over thirty years, the Chichester vicars appointed George Raper as his successor. The vicars resolved to meet annually in his office in West Street on St Thomas' Day and empowered him to summon extra meetings as required.[112] The clerk to the vicars at Salisbury was made responsible in 1864 for keeping the minutes and bringing the minute book to each meeting.[113]

In 1865 the dean and chapter of Hereford held a formal visitation of the college and each vicar had to appear before the chapter. Articles of enquiry were issued about the choral foundation in general, about the lay clerks, and about the choristers and their education. The college took legal advice before answering these questions and a committee, chaired by Sir Frederick Ouseley, examined the relations between the dean and chapter and the college. This led to the short-lived revival in the life of the college noted above.[114] Bishop Hervey conducted a formal visitation of the college at Wells in 1872 following a disputed election, and further visitations were held in 1875 and 1888. On this last occasion he reminded the college that they shared with the dean and chapter in 'the promotion of God's glory and the edification of his Church, by reverent, devout and comely services'. Strife and faction were to be avoided, and the vicars ought

> to aim at a life out of church in thorough harmony with your work in the church; to look upon the Dean and Canons as, what they really are, your best friends and counsellors, and to live in thorough peace and kindness towards one another as members of one College and as companions in the house of God.[115]

The cordial relationship with the diocesan was underlined in 1894 when Bishop Kennion arrived at the palace. The vicars welcomed him with an elaborate ceremony.[116]

Vicars choral often combined their cathedral duties with other pastoral responsibilities. At Hereford in the early years of the century, several of the vicars held country livings which resulted in them being absent from the cathedral on Sunday mornings.[117] At Lincoln also the vicars often held small parishes outside the city, but did not reside in them.[118] Until 1855 one of the vicars choral at Chichester was also Master of St James' Hospital.[119] At Salisbury one of the vicars was appointed vicar of the close. A note, dated 1817, in the back of an index to leases states:

> The Close Vicar is a peculiar place given by the Dean and Chapter to one of the Vicars as they please, though it has been the custom to offer it to the senior – his Duty is to read morning service at 6 o'clock in summer and at 7 in the winter; to bury all in the church or churchyard, to baptize

the children of the Close, to marry all that are married in the Cathedral and to pray with the sick of the Close and liberty thereof, for which he has for his trouble a yearly salary paid by the clerk of the works £2, the offering at the sacrament on Easter Day and the Sunday following, the Easter Dues which he gathers from house to house and the Clerk has 3d each of each shilling which is so gathered. The Dean and each canon do pay as their Easter Dues though they are not here at the time, each 5s, now 10s 6d.

It is the custom for the Godfathers and Godmothers to make an offering to the Close Vicar at the baptizing any child and also to the clerk...as also at the churching any woman he receives her offering.[120]

One of the vicars choral at old foundation cathedrals generally held the office of succentor and was thus responsible for the day-to-day worship of the cathedral. Theoretically he was the deputy of the precentor, but as this dignitary was often non-resident in the first half of the century, the succentor thus became quite important. Sydney Smith criticized the succentor of St Paul's in the 1830s for choosing difficult music for the choir.[121] When a new succentor was appointed at Chichester in 1868 he was instructed

> to advise the Dean and Canon-in-Residence on the Combination paper prepared by the Choir Master...to visit the Choir School, to superintend the order and behaviour of the boys in the Cathedral and to be present at the choir practices.[122]

He was later asked to supervise the arrangement of music in the choir stalls by the choristers before services.[123] One of the most outstanding succentors of the late nineteenth century was W. Sparrow Simpson, succentor of St Paul's from 1876 to 1885. He worked closely with Stainer, sharing with him the choice of music to be sung, and insisting on as wide a range as possible. He attended the weekly choir rehearsals and communicated his own enthusiasm and vigour to the members of the choir. He compiled a collection of cathedral statutes, and attended more cathedral services than any other of the clergy.[124] At Chichester the succentor was to supervise the choristers 'both morally and in the Cathedral', but was not allowed to possess keys to the Cathedral.[125] At Exeter the succentor was expected to attend the practices of the Sunday evening choir.[126]

At two old foundation cathedrals, St Paul's and Hereford, the vicars choral were known as minor canons, though at Hereford only two (formerly four) of the vicars were so termed.[127] The senior minor canon at St Paul's was known as the warden and the next in seniority were known as 'cardinals'. They usually held city benefices in addition to their minor canonries, and the average age of the twelve who were in office in 1831 was forty-one years. Several of them were composers and three were doctors of divinity.[128] One of the most celebrated of the minor canons at St Paul's was R. H. Barham, a diligent parish priest who was a friend of Sir Walter Scott, a member of the Garrick Club, and on intimate terms with the literary and noble society of London. He did much good work in the cathedral library.[129] In 1834 there was a clash between the minor canons of St Paul's and Sydney Smith.[130] They often left the quire-stalls on a Sunday morning just before the communion service began.[131] Indeed, their infrequent attendance was becoming a scandal. Edward Taylor wrote in 1845:

> Let any person walk into St Paul's, morning or afternoon, and satisfy himself whether twelve minor canons are there, assisting in the performance of the anthem and service for the day. He must have better fortune than has fallen to our lot for some years past if [he] ever find one.[132]

Another dispute, which began in 1850 and lasted for some four years, concerned the appointment of new minor canons. In the past, the college of minor canons would select and present two candidates to the dean and chapter, who would then make the final choice. The chapter now claimed that since the 1840 Act they had the sole right to appoint new minor canons, but eventually the old method was resumed.[133]

The 1840 Act limited the number of minor canons to six, but by 1872 there were still several long-serving members of the college who clung to their offices. It was clear that separate legislation was needed to regulate the affairs of the college, and thus the St Paul's Cathedral, London, Minor Canonries Act was passed in 1875.[134] This stipulated that only alternate vacancies in the college were to be filled until the numbers were reduced to the required level. Apart from existing holders, the freehold of the minor canons was abolished, but there were provisions for a minimum income and for pensions. No future minor canon was permitted to hold a benefice with his minor canonry, the separate estates of the minor canons were taken over by the Ecclesiastical Commissioners, and the corporate property of the college was commuted for £2,000 per annum. Long-serving minor canons were still a feature of the cathedral long after this Act was passed – Minor Canon Coward, who died in 1911, had been a minor canon for sixty-five years and warden of the college from 1858 to 1909.

In 1876 the dean and chapter ordered that new minor canons must not only be well qualified musically, but also able to teach, lecture and undertake whatever work they were asked to do.[135] The dean and chapter were particularly anxious to develop the mission of the cathedral to the young clerks and warehousemen who worked near the cathedral. William Russell and H. C. Shuttleworth, the first two minor canons appointed under the new system, were successful in carrying out this work.[136] They immediately organized special classes, lectures and guilds, conducted parties of young men around the cathedral, and even made contact with some nurses from St Bartholomew's Hospital.[137]

In the new foundation cathedrals, the number of minor canons varied, and in the early part of the century it even increased at Bristol, where in 1824 the numbers were brought up to six.[138] The dean and chapter of Bristol were very critical of the proposal of the Ecclesiastical Commission to reduce the number of minor canons in each cathedral and told Archbishop Howley in 1837:

> The confinement of a small number of these officials to an almost unremitted repetition of routine duty will tend to diminish their devotional feelings and in the same proportion mar the effect of their services.[139]

The 1840 Act limited the number of minor canons at most cathedrals to between two and six.[140] This took some time to come into effect, and in 1843 there were still eight minor canons at Durham, Norwich, Worcester and Christ Church, Oxford, six at Canterbury, Winchester, Bristol, Carlisle, Chester and Rochester, but four at Ely, Gloucester and Peterborough.[141] There were still six minor canons at Durham as late as the 1880s. Dean Lake told the Cathedrals Commission:

> I have found them a most effective and attentive body of clergymen in the Cathedral. But...I cannot think it necessary or desirable that there should be as many as six minor canons each paid £300 a year.[142]

Earlier in the century, however, the minor canons often lived in fairly reduced circumstances. The minor canons of Winchester asked the dean and chapter for an increased stipend in 1807, 'the necessary expenses of life having become enormously exorbitant', but their request was refused.[143] Five years later, though, their stipend was increased to £200 each.[144] The Worcester minor canons were much worse off: in 1824 their salaries were *raised* to £60 per annum, including corn rent.[145] It is clear that they continued to feel aggrieved.[146] A national picture emerges in 1835 as a result of the enquiries of the Ecclesiastical Duties and Revenues Commission. At Bristol the six minor canons were not provided with houses and were paid only £40, apart from the precentor who had an additional £20 plus funeral fees, so that he could expect £80 per annum. The minor canons at Canterbury were paid £80 per annum, and each was given a house. At Carlisle one of the six minor canons had extra responsibilities as lecturer at St Cuthbert's and could expect to receive £100 per annum, but some of the others could expect no more than a basic £8 per annum, plus £20 from tithes and some extra tithe money from St Cuthbert's. Two of the minor canons at Chester were provided with houses, but the income of each of them was only £15 per annum, plus £48 each from a legacy. The eight minor canons of Durham had annual incomes that ranged between £148 6s 9d and £168 6s 9d. Three of the minor canons of Gloucester were paid £50 per annum and one £90, though two of them had additional allowances as under-schoolmaster and librarian. The four minor canons at Peterborough were little better off, with only £52 per annum, though the precentor (who also held the office of sacrist and librarian) was also provided with a house, unlike his colleagues. The six minor canons of Rochester were even poorer, with a basic salary of only £30. At Winchester three of the six minor canons were paid £85 14s. The precentor and epistoler were paid an extra £12 each. The eight minor canons at Worcester had a basic salary of £34, with extra allowances for the precentor (£14 15s), schoolmaster (£39 19s 6d), sacrist and librarian (£4 each) and undermaster (£28 1s 5d).[147] The Ecclesiastical Commissioners said that the smallness of these salaries had led to the custom of minor canons also holding livings. They felt that their numbers should be reduced and their salaries increased so that they could concentrate on their cathedral duties.[148] The 1840 Act, as we have seen above, reduced the number of minor canons and gave them a salary of £150 per annum.[149] The dean and chapter of Gloucester at once fell into line and reduced their minor canons to three at £150 per annum each, stipulating that they were not to hold attached benefices.[150] At Worcester the scheme for fixing the number of minor canons at four at £150 each was not drawn up until 1854.[151] At first this was to include corn rents, but it was soon found easier to make a cash payment of £20 per annum in lieu of corn rents.[152] But the Worcester minor canons still felt they were underpaid. In 1868 an application by two of them for more money was turned down by the dean and chapter, and similar requests were refused in 1870 and 1874.[153] At Norwich in 1865 the third minor canon was paid £200 per annum, with a house; a fourth minor canon appointed in the same year was paid £150, plus a house.[154] Dean Alford of Canterbury said in 1869 that the minor canons there were paid £227 10s with a good house.[155] When the dean and chapter of Gloucester were in financial difficulties in 1887, all salaries of their employees were cut by 10 per cent. The minor canons pointed out that they were not being paid their rightful salary anyway, but if they could be paid the full amount they would willingly return 10 per cent of it. By July 1888 the crisis had blown over.[156]

A house provided by the dean and chapter could sometimes be a mixed blessing, as G. Willoughby Barrett, Precentor of Norwich, explained to the cathedral commissioners in 1884:

When I took possession of this house in March 1877 I found it in so bad a state that I was obliged to spend nearly £30 in labour alone before I could inhabit it, and for this I got no compensation. Constant repairs, owing to the age of the house, have been necessary from time to time since then.[157]

In 1864, houses were provided for minor canons at Canterbury, Durham, Ely, Bristol, Norwich, Peterborough and Rochester, but not at Winchester, Carlisle, Chester or Gloucester.[158] The Winchester minor canons found this a heavy burden, especially as some of the houses in the close had been let by the dean and chapter.[159]

Probably one of the hardest-working minor canons was J. M. Elvy at Manchester. The minor canons of Manchester undertook all the parochial work of a large parish and, as senior vicar, Elvy presided at the vestry meeting and was greatly involved with many local charities, schools and other organizations.[160] In most cases, the routine work of minor canons was confined to officiating at the daily services of the cathedral, a duty that was generally shared out fairly between them. At the beginning of the century at Norwich, as at some old foundation cathedrals such as Hereford, the eight minor canons were also responsible for providing the lower voices in the cathedral choir and thus attended the services daily:

> Well do I remember the delight with which I used to listen to the service in Norwich Cathedral, when the minor canons, eight in number, filed off to their stalls, Precentor Millard at the head, whose admirable style and correct taste as a singer I have never heard surpassed; Browne's majestic tenor; Whittingham's sweet alto and Hansell's sonorous bass....Walker's silvery tones and admirable recitation found their way into every corner of the huge building.[161]

A minor canon of Gloucester got into trouble in 1806 for refusing to sing an anthem and using disrespectful language.[162] At Bristol in 1806 two minor canons were required to be present at the morning and evening services on Sundays.[163] There was a similar rule at Gloucester.[164] By the middle of the century each of the three minor canons at Bristol officiated for a week in turn, overlapping on Sundays. All three were to be present at a communion service, if required by the canon-in-residence.[165] When a new minor canon was appointed at Rochester about the same time, he was told that he had to attend the morning and evening services on Sundays, saints' days and certain other days, and to officiate for two weeks out of every six.[166] When two new minor canons were appointed at Winchester in 1858, they were told to divide the duties between them for two weeks in each month, the remaining weeks being shared by the other three minor canons who had been there longer.[167] T. G. Livingstone, a minor canon of Carlisle, complained in 1865 that he had received no additional pay in spite of having to undertake extra duties, and claimed that his case was 'unique in degree of hardship among the Cathedrals of England'.[168] At Worcester also, two minor canons were required on Sundays and holy days and they were not to leave the city without permission. There were continuing difficulties about this in the 1870s and on several occasions they neglected their duties. There was even a kind of honorary minor canon who deputized for them on an 'informal understanding...sanctioned by the late Dean'.[169] A seven-week cycle was introduced in 1876, but Precentor Wheeler told the dean that this was 'incongenial' and unnecessary.[170]

From 1881 the dean and chapter required two minor canons to be present at each of the daily services. One of them officiated until the end of the third collect, when the other one took over. At the same time a scheme was drawn up to ensure that three minor canons were always resident at the same time, but although two minor canons were required on Sunday mornings, only one was needed on Sunday afternoons and evenings.[171] At Winchester one of the minor canons was expected to read the epistle at communion services in the absence of a canon.[172] The dean and chapter of Gloucester required two of their minor canons to be resident constantly, but the same minor canon was not allowed to take all the services in the cathedral on any one day.[173] When a new minor canon was appointed at Peterborough in 1883, he was told that he was expected

> to be present on all Sundays and Holy Days at all the services, also twice on weekdays except but for one week in three he may be absent from the Sunday or ordinary weekday service according to arrangement with the other minor canons.[174]

Two minor canons were required at Peterborough to be present for each celebration of the holy communion.[175] When the dean and chapter of Bristol changed the time of the Sunday evening service in February 1888, the minor canons objected as they had already undertaken extra duties in the city, but they agreed to cover the duties at this service on a voluntary basis.[176] George Carroll, a minor canon of Worcester, was persistently absent and neglectful of his duty in 1889. Eventually he was dismissed.[177] At Winchester in 1890 the dean and chapter required two minor canons to come to the Sunday morning service, but otherwise left their duties to be sorted out among themselves.[178] Precentor Woodward of Worcester told J. H. Hooper, the chapter clerk, in November 1896 that he printed the names of the two minor canons on duty at the foot of each scheme and also wrote them at the foot of the weekly list of celebrants.[179]

Minor canons were allowed to preach and to celebrate from time to time, though their opportunities to do so were rather limited. The minor canons of Bristol were responsible for the sermon on Sunday afternoons.[180] At St Paul's, one of the minor canons was appointed to a divinity lectureship in 1853. He preached on saints' days and holidays throughout the year, as well as on Wednesdays and Fridays in Lent in the absence of the duty canon.[181] The dean and chapter of Winchester were careful to see that a minor canon was not out of pocket if he were displaced from the pulpit.[182] The minor canons of Worcester preached in rotation at the evening service on the first Sunday in the month.[183] Robert Rake, the

Precentor of Canterbury, complained to Archbishop Tait in 1872 that his opportunities to preach were extremely limited. In eighteen years he had preached only twice a year on weekdays in Lent. Rake was equally upset that he was allowed to celebrate the eucharist so rarely, the only opportunities being 'when one or other of the residents in the Cathedral precincts has been sick (and the number is always very small) during the three years in which I happened to be sacrist'.[184]

At Worcester Cathedral there was a dispute between Precentor Woodward and Sacrist Melville about which of them was responsible for acting as celebrant at the 8 a.m. Sunday service in the absence of any member of the chapter.[185] A fairer system was begun at Winchester, following Bishop Davidson's visitation in 1900. On the last Sunday in each month the minor canon in course was responsible for the 8 a.m. celebration in the Lady Chapel.[186] Before this their opportunities to celebrate had been severely limited. One of the minor canons, C. H. Thompson, told Davidson that he had celebrated only three times in the previous five years.[187]

There was often considerable competition among clergy for minor canonries. There were four candidates for a vacant post at Canterbury in 1810. Each took turns at singing the Te Deum and an anthem, and chanted a service.[188] When a new minor canon was appointed at Gloucester in 1835, the candidates likewise had to chant a service.[189] Both Gloucester and Durham stated that their minor canons must be musically qualified.[190] In 1862 at Winchester there was some disagreement as to whether two new minor canons were obliged to take the customary oaths, but in the end they did so.[191] No satisfactory candidate could be found at Worcester in 1875 and the vacant post was readvertised.[192] Three years later the existing minor canons at Winchester were each consulted for their opinions on the merits of the candidate for a vacancy.[193] At Gloucester the dean and chapter stipulated that any new minor canon must be a graduate of Oxford or Cambridge Universities, though the rule was later relaxed to include graduates of other universities.[194]

Some minor canons and vicars choral were great characters and were often renowned for their musical abilities. Dr Troutbeck at Manchester had a beautiful voice which attracted many people to the cathedral, but another minor canon by the name of Johnson was well known for his habit of covering his face with his surplice sleeve during the lessons to conceal his eating of biscuits and toast.[195] At Canterbury a minor canon by the name of Rouch held office for forty-one years from 1827 to 1868. He had a feeble voice, but could still hold a note. When he was appointed, the clergy and lay clerks did not process to their stalls, only the choristers did so. Rouch refused to the last to walk in procession.[196] A. C. Benson has left a lively description of the vicars choral of Lincoln in the early 1870s:

Mr Gibney was the senior, a small, dignified man with high collars, like a Victorian statesman. Perhaps he had once possessed a singing voice, but he was an elderly man and his intoning of the prayers consisted of a start on the right note, a rapid decline into a more conversational tone, with gallant attempts at intervals to regain the original pitch.

Associated with many public and charitable activities, he died after falling through a skylight at the School of Art.

> Then there was Mr Hutton, a fair-haired, round-faced man with spectacles...Mr Mansell was a remarkably handsome figure, with a head of dark, curling hair, a little grizzled, black whiskers and soft eyes of a velvety darkness – he had a rich melodious voice, somewhat husky, but of great sweetness; and lastly Mr Harvey, an upright, clean-shaven priest, with an expression of great force and energy....Mr Gibney was succeeded by Mr Maddison, an old pupil of my father's at Rugby with a delicate-looking intelligent face and charming manners, who was often at the Chancery. He was a great antiquarian.[197]

Minor Canon Greenwell of Durham was very fond of fly-fishing, but did great work sorting out the library and archives.[198] Richard Cattley at Worcester was well known and popular, and had a good singing voice.[199] Dean Goulburn said in 1872 that contemporary minor canons included 'men of high cultivation, great erudition and fervent piety'.[200]

A correspondent in the *Guardian* in 1881 said that there were 117 minor canons in England. Two of them had served for fifty-three years, being appointed in 1827, three more before 1840, six between 1841 and 1850, sixteen between 1851 and 1860, and nineteen from 1861 to 1870. In other words, forty-six had been in office for over ten years and twenty-seven had been in office for twenty years or more.[201]

The senior minor canon at each new foundation cathedral held the office of precentor. His duties were laid down by the cathedral statutes. In the Winchester statutes, for example, it was stated that:

> It shall be his duty decently to conduct those who chant in the church, to lead the rest with his voice, and to be in a manner the Chief, lest any discord arise in the singing; to rouse the careless to sing, and soberly to rebuke and allay disturbances and running to and fro in the Choir. As touching the business of the choir, all the minor canons and clerks shall obey him; and the rest that enter the choir to sing ought readily to obey whatever he shall appoint to be said or sung.

He was also to note the absence of members of the chapter as well as of members of the choir and to report the same to the dean and chapter each fortnight, and to have charge of the music books.[202] In 1815 the Precentor of Winchester was reminded by the chapter to be more diligent in the performance of his duties.[203] At Bristol he was responsible for all funerals and burials in the cathedral and churchyard, retaining the fees from these services. He was to attend every service on a Sunday and to be ready to preach in the absence of the canon-in-residence, for which his salary was increased from £60 to £80 per annum.[204] At Gloucester the precentor was instructed to examine the choristers' proficiency in music and make a report to the dean and chapter.[205] Whenever the precentor and his deputy were absent from services at Winchester, the dean and chapter decreed that

> the senior bass voice present shall in such case take the lead; and in *all* cases when the services are sung without the organ, the Chapter will invariably hold the senior bass present responsible for the commencement of Venite, psalms, services and anthems as it is impossible for the precentor or his deputy to undertake this and also to officiate as minor canon.[206]

At Worcester the precentor was required to be present at not less than three services in the cathedral each week, in addition to his weeks in course.[207] His duties were confirmed by the dean and chapter in 1876 in terms very similar to those quoted above from the Winchester statutes.[208] In 1877 the dean and chapter made a printed summary of these duties when they were appointing a new precentor. They included the general direction of the music of the services, attendance at all services on Sundays and festivals, and at least once a day on other days during his nine months of residence. The precentor was to note any unauthorized absence or case of misconduct among the lay clerks and choristers, reporting grave offences to the dean and chapter and musical errors to the organist. The members of the choir were to be in his spiritual charge, and he was responsible for the religious instruction of the choristers, including their preparation for confirmation. He was to 'superintend' choir practices and arrange additional rehearsals where necessary, 'being careful to sustain the authority of the organist and choirmaster as actual teacher'. He was also to inspect the music of the choir regularly, replacing worn copies and adding new music. He was to make all the necessary arrangements at the cathedral when Her Majesty's Judges or the mayor and corporation attended. He was responsible for drawing up the weekly scheme of music with the organist and providing sufficient copies thereof. He was to draw up the rota of attendance by the other minor canons, to assist the dean and canon-in-residence at communion and ante-communion services, and to read the lesson in the absence of the dean or canon-in-residence. He was also to perform the duties of sacrist, and was entitled to a salary of £230 per annum 'with a good house, rent free, in the immediate neighbourhood of the Cathedral'.[209] Each year the Precentor of Worcester presented an annual report to the dean and chapter and in November 1883 he was requested to include in future reports a list of the music sung during the previous year.[210] Stephen Phillips, the Precentor of Peterborough, told the Cathedrals Commission in 1884 that in addition to his duties as a minor canon he was responsible for

> the arrangement of the music, the supervision of the choir and of the vergers, the management and training of the voluntary choir, the responsibilities of the special services, the pastoral charge and surplice duties of the precincts.[211]

At Bristol, E. H. Fellowes installed a speaking-tube between his stall and the organ loft so that he could communicate with the organist.[212]

In 1892, during the dispute with the organist George Riseley, the Dean of Bristol wrote to several other cathedrals asking for details of the duties of their precentors in relation to the cathedral and especially the organist. He also asked whether the organist was at liberty to vary the precentor's choice of music and whether the precentor attended any choir practices. The Worcester reply stated that the precentor there was responsible for all special services, for the general direction of the music of all services, exercising authority over everyone who took part, including the organist. He also attended 'the weekly *full practice* of the Choir. Here he conducts the practice – the organist presiding at the organ'.[213] At Chester, though, he did not attend choir practices, except the last one before a performance. At Durham there was occasional friction between the precentor and the organist, who was 'far superior in musical knowledge to the precentor'. The music was never changed from the printed scheme, and although the organist trained the choristers for an hour daily, the precentor presided at the Saturday morning full practice. At Ripon the precentor had the general supervision of the choir and music, but his duties were not so definite as in some of the older cathedrals. The Precentor of Peterborough asserted that he had never considered it his duty to attend choir practices. At Norwich the precentor chose the music to be sung, presided at all full rehearsals, conducted auditions, and ensured that the choristers were neat and tidy before services, also giving them religious instruction. He also kept a list of attendances at services. At Manchester the precentor presided at full rehearsals, but the musical and secular training of the boys was in the hands of two of the lay clerks. The precentors of both Canterbury and Rochester also presided at full rehearsals, and at the latter cathedral the organist was regarded merely as the accompanist. At Winchester, though, the organist presided, but the precentor was required to be present and allowed to make 'such comments as he thinks necessary' at rehearsals.[214]

One of the best known of Victorian precentors was J. B. Dykes of Durham. Appointed precentor very shortly after his arrival in Durham in 1849, he was paid the generous salary of £340 per annum. His daily routine gives a good idea of the life of a mid-nineteenth-century precentor. Awake at 6.30 a.m., he tried to be downstairs before 7.30 a.m. so that he could have an hour's quiet reading before breakfast at 8.30 a.m. After breakfast, a little piano practice filled in the time before matins at the cathedral. After the service he either went into the town or returned to his home where he would read until 2.30 p.m. In the middle of his studying he would eat some bread and butter and drink a glass of sherry. Then he would go out for 'a good, brisk walk', returning in time to read through the lessons appointed for evensong, and go to the cathedral in time for evensong. On his way back from the cathedral he might look in at the newsroom, and then he had dinner. After dinner, if he did not have any evening engagements, he would do a lot of instrumental and vocal practising until tea. After tea, he would do a little general reading, concluding with some of Keble's poems and his Greek New Testament between 11 p.m. and midnight.[215] In addition to his cathedral duties, Dykes undertook regular pastoral visiting in St Oswald's parish as well as being pastorally responsible for the members of the choir and their families.[216]

Peter Hansell, the Precentor of Norwich, was also father-in-law to the organist, Zechariah Buck. He was said to be

a clergyman of the old school, who wore his hair powdered, and was always very neat in his attire – black dress-coat, with velvet collar, black vest, pantaloons, and Hessian boots; he was a strict disciplinarian, a thoroughly good musician, possessed a sonorous bass voice and was particularly fond of glee-singing.[217]

S. S. Wesley described the Precentor of Winchester in 1849 as

a very sensible man, a most kind man, an excellent preacher and Parish Priest, and he has done much for the Music of this Cathedral by selecting good serious things for performance, in controlling the Choir and in resisting the very erroneous views of the canons and Dean.[218]

Kendrick Pyne described Precentor Wray of Winchester as 'an unusually zealous officer' who took charge of choir practices and 'had the temerity, in the presence of Wesley, to conduct the rehearsals. It was indeed a wonderful sight to see him directing affairs, Wesley grimly standing by his side'.[219]

Worcester Cathedral was served by three very competent precentors in the closing decades of the century: T. L. Wheeler, E. Vine Hall and H. H. Woodward. Wheeler, who was secretary of the Three Choirs Festival Committee for many years, 'was a little man with a fine head, with a quantity of beautiful white hair, which was dressed with a curl on his forehead'.[220] James Smith, one of the lay clerks, recalled him as 'a short chubby man of a most amiable disposition, a splendid reader and a good preacher and had a strong sense of humour'.[221] He was quite well off and used to drive down to the cathedral for services (he was also Rector of St Martin's) in a carriage and pair.[222]

Vine Hall was 'a big fat man with lank hair and a large pale face, without any sign of a beard...he had a clear, high-pitched voice – was a mild preacher and a fair musician'. James Smith added that, 'he was generally at loggerheads with someone, and at the rehearsals of the Choir he had an unfortunate habit of making everyone uncomfortable, and antagonistic by his remarks'.[223]

Woodward was 'lean and thin-faced – a good musician and a strict disciplinarian...he always superintended the rehearsals, the organist rehearsing his part with the choir at the organ'.[224]

But precentors sometimes incurred criticism. Edward Taylor complained in 1845 that they were often ignorant.[225] Precentor Caley was rebuked by the Dean of Bristol in 1853 for sending an inaccurate letter to the Ecclesiastical Commissioners without his knowledge, 'an act lacking both courtesy and candour on your part'. He was further reminded that, 'as minor canon and precentor you hold a very subordinate office in the Cathedral'.[226]

In 1879 there was a lively correspondence between the precentor and organist at Winchester Cathedral about their respective responsibilities, but the matter was settled over the dinner table.[227] The following winter the precentor of Winchester forgot to attend the greater chapter meeting.[228] Vine Hall at Worcester was also somewhat erratic in his attendance,[229] though he felt he had done a good job as precentor:

> I found the Worcester Choir ten years ago in a deplorable condition....But I set to work; and in a year's time I had the satisfaction of being told by Dr Stainer that he was much pleased with the service, and that he would even carry back some hints to St. Paul's. From that time to the present I have laboured incessantly to keep the choir in an efficient state.[230]

Another minor canon in new foundation cathedrals held the post of sacrist, though sometimes this office was combined with that of precentor. According to the Winchester statutes he had charge of 'the Cathedral, altar, monuments, vestments, books, chalices, vessels and other ornaments'. He was responsible for providing the bread and wine for communion and the wax for candles. He was also to visit any sick person on the foundation and give them the sacrament and receive the offertories given in the cathedral.[231] The sacrists' accounts at Worcester list the amount given in collections and disbursed by the sacrist to poor and needy people. In 1801 there were forty-seven poor persons on his list and they received £5 17s 6d. Extra disbursements were given to debtors and prisoners in the gaol. Preference was always given to beadsmen and their widows. By the end of the century £500 or more was given away, often to various charities as well as to individuals.[232] The sacrist of Bristol Cathedral was specially required to be present at each Eucharist and to take charge of any special services.[233] In 1877 the dean and chapter of Worcester drew up details of the sacrist's work and had them printed. He was required to be present, either in person or by deputy, at every Eucharist and to prepare (with the help of the sub-sacrist) vessels and the elements that were needed.[234] In 1891, 1894 and 1898, lists of plate and other altar furniture were drawn up at Worcester. H. Clifford, in his report in 1892, advised that the large Charles II flagons and other altar silver should not be allowed to remain on the altar overnight, but should be locked in a safe each evening. This was the custom at Truro. The previous year he had asked permission to assume overall responsibility for the altar flowers, which had not been arranged well.[235] In 1894 Clifford drew attention to the poor condition of many of the prayer books in the cathedral and suggested that there should be extra kneelers in the nave.[236]

All cathedrals in the nineteenth century, as today, were reliant on a group of vergers and sub-sacrists. In some cathedrals there were only two of them – as at Rochester or Ely – but at Durham there were as many as ten.[237] In 1804, James Price, one of the lay vicars of Chichester, resigned and was appointed chapter verger and bell ringer, also holding the offices of gatekeeper, bailiff of the manor of Canon Gate and precular.[238] One of the vergers at Hereford was paid £5 for dusting the books in the library in 1822.[239] When a new verger was appointed at Bristol in 1827, he was required 'to attend personally as virger at all times of divine service in the Cathedral and to obey the orders of the Dean and Prebendaries'.[240] The duty verger at Exeter was required to see that the cathedral doors were locked each night.[241] When none of the three vergers at Wells was present at a eucharist in 1832, they were firmly instructed by the dean and chapter not to depart before the end of the service, one remaining in the quire and one in the nave.[242] At Gloucester in 1858 the vergers were asked to keep the cathedral, churchyard, cloisters and precincts clear, acting as constables for the precincts. They were also to wind up the chimes, look after the library and practising room, and do any other work that the dean or canon-in-residence might require.[243] The junior verger attended the early morning service, and both vergers were present at all the other services, one in the quire and one in the nave. Only one verger was needed in the cathedral between 12 noon and 2 p.m., but at other times they were both needed whenever the cathedral was open. They were to receive and guide visitors round the building, a fee being required only for the quire, chapter house, cloisters and tower. Other duties included those of church and belfry sexton, custodian of plate, and the care of the library.[244] At Winchester the vergers were helped by sub-sacrists. They were respon-sible for the daily covering and uncovering of the altar. The senior sub-sacrist was responsible for all the arrangements for the early morning celebration, with the assistance of the junior sub-sacrist at the midday celebration. The senior sub-sacrist also presented the service register to the dean and canon for signature after each service, drew up statements of the quarterly and monthly monies due to the lay vicars and others, and of the monies placed in offertory boxes, and the fees from the college. The junior sub-sacrist found the lessons and the music to be sung for the precentor, minor canons and lay vicars at each service. He changed the weekly schemes (or bills) of services, presented the new ones for signature, and took them to the printers. He gave necessary assistance to the senior sub-sacrist, especially at special services such as confirmations.[245] At Worcester Cathedral the head verger was known as the custos, and was responsible for finding seats for the congregation.[246] His salary was £100 per annum (later increased to £120) and he was in charge of the whole interior of the cathedral, with authority over the sub-sacrist, vergers, beadsmen 'and others who are employed in cleaning, warming and repairing the Cathedral'.[247] He was later allowed to have a free afternoon on Sundays and one weekday in addition to his summer holiday, but was required to submit a monthly report on the beadsmen's absences.[248] In 1895 the custos was given authority over the porters, clerk of the works, and towerkeeper and was 'expected to devote all his time to the work and interests of the Cathedral'.[249] The sub-sacrist at Bristol was required in 1884 to maintain reverence and order in the cathedral at all times, taking note of the interior condition of the building, ordering all fresh supplies of necessary goods, and supervising the work of the pensioners.[250] Isaac Trott, who held the post for many years, was in the habit of showing favouritism in reserving seats for the congregation, and incurred the displeasure of the sacrist.[251] One of the most detailed and comprehensive surviving accounts of the duties of vergers and others on the cathedral staff may be found at Chichester. There were six men employed, four as vergers and two in other capacities. H. H. Moore was paid £42 10s per annum plus £3 formerly paid by the treasurer. He had to be in daily attendance on the cathedral every alternate week and was responsible for cleaning the nave and nave aisles. J. F. Darbyshire was the dean's and canons' verger and sacristan and was paid £60 per annum plus £8 for acting as bishop's verger. His responsibilities were similar to those of Moore, but he was supposed to sweep and dust the whole of the cathedral. He was also responsible for the arrangements for all eucharists. G. Payne was in attendance on the dean during services every other week and for both services on Sundays. He also took charge of the communion plate and all collections. He was clerk of the cathedral and prepared the bread and wine for all eucharists. He was also responsible for reminding the prebendaries of their preaching turns. For these duties, he was paid £43 per annum. Charles Benford attended the canon-in-residence at both daily services on alternate weeks. He attended the 8 a.m. celebration on Thursdays and saints' days on the same basis. For the rest of each day he patrolled the cloisters and precincts, remaining in the cathedral during services on alternate weeks, and was paid £50 per annum. Between October and May he attended to the cathedral stoves and was paid a further £5 15s as custodian of the precincts and stoves. James Evans was paid 10s for looking after the stoves in the library and singing school, but his main work, for which he received £29 10s, was to toll the bell for all services, to assist the organ blower and to clean the cloisters, Canon Lane and St Richard's Walk. Finally, there was W. Spurlock, the organ-blower, who was paid £17.[252] A third verger was appointed at £75 per annum in 1899 at Salisbury to relieve some of the pressure on the others, to keep order during services, and to enable the cathedral to remain open to visitors for a longer time, especially in the spring and autumn. Additional duties included lighting the gas in the quire, keeping the canons' vestry clean, keeping the library books clean, and assisting in showing visitors over the quire.[253] In 1900 the duties of the vergers at Chichester were to attend the daily offices, to escort the dean and canon-in-residence from their houses to the cathedral, to walk in procession between the priest vicar and the members of the chapter, and to remain for services alternately. Each verger was to have a full day off each week and an annual holiday.[254] Vergers naturally found themselves given various miscellaneous duties. The dean's verger at St Paul's was Deputy Surveyor of the Fabric, charged with making weekly inspections of the building and making running repairs.[255] Verger Green's particular responsibility as sub-sacrist at St Paul's was the care of the altar vessels.[256] One of the vergers at Ely brewed ale for the dean and chapter, but he had to give way when the grammar school was enlarged.[257] The Ely vergers also waited at table on official occasions when requested to do so by members of the chapter. One of the vergers looked after the communion plate and another supervised the utensils and crockery of the dean and chapter.[258]

At several cathedrals the vergers were specifically responsible for welcoming visitors and acting as guides. The sacrist or principal verger at Wells was ordered in 1873 to 'show the Cathedral without charge or fee at such hours and subject to such regulations as the Dean and Chapter may prescribe'. Notices were issued asking visitors who wished to see the quire, Lady Chapel, chapter-house and tower to give 6d to the fabric fund and write their names in the visitors' book. During the summer a verger was available for this duty from 10 a.m. to 4 p.m.[259] A similar system was brought into operation at Winchester in 1874.[260] The *Guardian* included a considerable correspondence about it in 1888. One letter complained of difficulties encountered at Winchester, Truro and Gloucester.[261] Another correspondent said that, 'neither at Lincoln nor at Worcester can you get beyond the nave of the Cathedral without the inevitable verger in attendance'.[262] At Winchester the vergers were not allowed to receive gratuities from visitors. A notice was displayed in the cathedral warning visitors of this, and a box was provided in which they could put money which was used to increase the vergers' stipends, to pay for incidental expenses involved in inserting new statues into the Great Screen, and to augment the fabric fund.[263] Dean Goodwin firmly believed in the importance of good vergers and the help they could give to visitors.[264] But an American visitor complained about a stupid verger at Lichfield in 1856,[265] and their failings were also noted at Canterbury[266] and Christ Church, Oxford.[267]

Cathedral vergers were normally provided with gowns to wear in the cathedral by the dean and chapter, as at Bristol in 1801,[268] but when a verger at Wells Cathedral called Misselbrook procured his own gown he received a caution.[269] At Worcester the vergers received an annual payment of £4 for clothes.[270] The dean and chapter of St Paul's provided purple gowns for their vergers from 1871,[271] while at Chichester the vergers were ordered to wear cassocks when on duty in the cathedral.[272] At Peterborough, both the sextons and vergers wore gowns, and the sextons carried white wands.[273]

Among the vergers, as among other cathedral employees, there were occasional disciplinary difficulties. A verger at Exeter in 1809 was reprimanded for incivility towards one of the cathedral clergy.[274] Fifteen years later the Exeter vergers were in trouble for accepting bribes to secure seats for members of the congregation.[275] At Norwich in 1830, John Howes, a sub-sacrist, was admonished for 'demanding money for admitting persons to seats in the cathedral'. He was also in trouble for failing to clean and prepare the consistory court and for neglecting to put the altar in order.[276] George Crupper, a verger at Winchester, was strongly reprimanded and fined 10s for using coarse language to a visitor at the cathedral,[277] and James Dennett was accused of using 'improper language' at Winchester in 1862 while showing two ladies to their seats before a service.[278] The head verger of Wells Cathedral was reprimanded for incivility in 1873.[279] One of the vergers at St Paul's was a persistent drunkard and was eventually dismissed.[280] When a verger named Leef became not only elderly but also unfit for duty, the dean and chapter of St Paul's found that there were serious legal difficulties involved in forcing him to retire.[281] At Bristol, Dean Pigou invited the vergers to tea on Sundays, so that they should not need to return home between services. They were all ex-servicemen with a good sense of discipline.[282]

Only a few nineteenth-century vergers have left much of a name behind them, such as Verger Green of St Paul's, whose careful notes about events in the cathedral offer a valuable glimpse into its daily life. At Chichester, however, Charles Crocker, who was verger from 1845 until his death in 1861, was well known as a poet and as the author of the cathedral guide book.[283] One of the longest-serving vergers was William Miles, who spent nearly all his life in the service of Rochester Cathedral. He was a chorister from 1826 to 1834 and five of his sons were also choristers. From 1839 to

1844 he was a lay clerk, and then he assumed the various posts of sexton, sub-sacrist, porter, barber and organ-blower until, three years later, he was appointed head verger. He held that office until his retirement in 1900 at the age of eighty-four.[284] The head verger of Lincoln in the 1870s was a man called Logsdail. A. C. Benson says that he was

> a man regarded by everyone with extraordinary respect and affection. He had a rugged-looking head, with a beard and thick hair and walked in the procession carrying his little silver mace with an unconscious air of dignity and distinction. He was very learned in the antiquities of the Cathedral.[285]

Another verger of distinction was William Bond, who was verger at Winchester Cathedral from 1868 to 1913 (apart from a brief interval of two years). When he retired, at the age of eighty-two, he became assistant librarian. The *Hampshire Observer* described him in 1916 as 'one of the oldest and most highly esteemed residents of Winchester'.[286]

Various cathedrals also employed sextons. At Hereford, they were required in 1800 to keep order in the cathedral when a service was being held in the north transept, which they were expected to keep clean – in addition to cleaning duties in the rest of the cathedral. They each received 20s pew rents from the pews in the north transept, which was fitted up for use by the parish of St John the Baptist.[287] In 1809 both the sextons were required to attend all the services, one sitting in the quire and one in the nave.[288]

There was certainly a sexton at Worcester.[289] Henry Holding Moore was appointed as sexton at Chichester in 1868 to undertake cleaning and stoking duties,[290] and the second sexton at Hereford was required to assist in lighting and extinguishing the gas lights in the cathedral.[291] At St Paul's Cathedral a group of wandsmen was appointed in 1861 to help the vergers keep order at the Sunday evening services. In 1879 their constitution was revised and two years later they were supplied with official bronze badges.[292]

Since the time of Henry VIII, there had been a group of beadsmen at new foundation cathedrals. Varying in number between six and twelve, they were variously known as almsmen or poor men or pensioners as well as beadsmen (or bedesmen). Their appointment was in the hands of the Crown. At Winchester, for example, there were to be 'twelve poor old men, poverty stricken, and distressed by want, broken by war, or maimed, or otherwise enfeebled and reduced to want and wretchedness'. They were required by statute to attend the daily services, to keep the cathedral clean, to assist in kindling and extinguishing lights, and ringing the bells. They were provided by the dean and chapter with gowns with a red silk rose on the left shoulder, which they had to wear at services and out of doors.[293] At Worcester in 1824 their stipends were augmented by £1 per annum in return for additional duties as organ-blower.[294] At Norwich their salary was increased from £8 to £10 per annum in 1818. By 1887 it had reached £17 per annum. In 1898 they received 6 guineas at the Christmas charitable distribution, to be divided among them for bread and coal.[295] In 1854 the cathedral commissioners said that in the majority of new foundation cathedrals the beadsmen's stipends had not been sufficiently increased and were insufficient to maintain them.[296] When the dean and chapter of Worcester increased the stipends of the ten beadsmen from 14 guineas to £16 a month, eight of them refused to accept the increase 'on the score of its insufficiency'.[297] In 1888 the Worcester beadsmen were given a monthly course of spiritual instruction by the precentor.[298] By 1900 the twelve beadsmen at Winchester had been reduced to six. In addition to their sweeping, weeding and cleaning duties, they took turns to sit by the iron gate leading into the south transept and supervised the admission of visitors to the eastern part of the cathedral.[299] At Worcester they sat inside the gate of the north porch and admitted visitors, or stood there on Sundays to receive the alms of the congregation who left before the sermon.[300] At Norwich they helped in the general cleaning and tidying of the church, tolled the bell, and guarded the doors at services.[301] As might be expected, there were several occasions when various beadsmen were in trouble for drunkenness, assault, theft, receiving tips or neglect of duty.[302] No wonder that Dean Perowne of Peterborough regarded them as 'an unmitigated evil'.[303] At Norwich, however, their contribution to the daily life of the cathedral was highly valued.[304]

Porters were employed to guard the gates of the close at several cathedrals,[305] though drunkenness and neglect of duty was a recurring problem at Worcester.[306] At both Winchester and Worcester they were responsible for posting and delivering letters in the close.[307] At Salisbury the under-porter was paid 5s a quarter by the vicars choral for opening the close gates for them at night.[308] William Boucher told Archdeacon Macdonald in 1833 that the porter acted as verger to the dean.[309] At Exeter, where dogs in the cloisters were regarded as a nuisance, a dog-whipper was appointed by the dean and chapter. He was required to attend the daily early service in a gown and act as clerk. Keys, the eccentric old verger at Christ Church, Oxford, also acted as dog-whipper, since dogs frequently accompanied their undergraduate masters to cathedral services.[310]

Many cathedrals maintained bands of ringers, or individuals who helped to chime the bells for services, such as 'poor old blind Phil' who daily climbed the tower at Hereford by himself to ring the six o'clock morning bell and the curfew bell.[311] In 1827, as a result of their 'irregular conduct and ill behaviour', the dean and chapter of Gloucester drew up new rules for their ringers which stated when the bells were to be rung. The ringers refused to accept these regulations and resigned, but after seven months they returned to the tower.[312] The two ringers at Durham were not only responsible for ringing the bells, but had to maintain the clock, open and close the doors of the cathedral daily, and search the building after the doors were shut. Altogether there were eight ringers with a stipend of £47. The four ringers at Canterbury were paid £20 per annum and the three ringers at Winchester received £24 a year.[313] In 1866 the dean and chapter of Wells confirmed that there were four special ringing days each year, for which they bore the expense: the Queen's birthday, the Queen's Accession Day, the Prince of Wales's birthday and Innocents' Day.[314] At the bishop's enthronement in January 1870, the Wells ringers wanted to be paid £10 for ringing the bells, but the dean and chapter thought that this was exorbitant and would not give them more than £5.[315] The pay of the Hereford ringers was increased to £2 per annum each in 1866, with an additional £1 for the 'foreman'.[316] In 1877 the dean and chapter of Hereford ordered that a bell should continue to be tolled twelve hours after the death of a canon; it should also be tolled for fifteen minutes each evening until the day of the funeral. It was to be tolled for an hour during the funeral and a muffled peal was to be rung in the evening of the same day.[317] At Worcester it was decided in 1900 that the bell should be tolled on the death of the Queen or any member of the royal family, the Archbishop of Canterbury, the bishop, the dean and the canons, and their wives and children, the minor canons and the Mayor of Worcester.[318]

The ringers at Chichester were troublesome. In 1878 they were all dismissed and a new band was recruited and constituted as a guild with strict regulations drawn up by the dean and chapter.[319] This move was evidently a success, as a few months later the dean and chapter visited the belfry and recorded 'their entire satisfaction'.[320] In addition to their ringing duties, they were also constituted as an honorary fire brigade to the cathedral.[321] Ten years later, however, the guild was dissolved and reformed, with new rules.[322] The number of ringers was fixed at ten, including a foreman, leader and deputy leader. The duties of the foreman were to ring the curfew, to ring for funerals, and to look after the bells, belfry and ringing chamber.[323] It was particularly stressed that the bells should not be rung during the week of the Goodwood races unless there was a wedding or other important event at the cathedral.[324]

E. Vine Hall, the Precentor of Worcester, suggested in 1884 that only two of the bells should be chimed for the daily services, reserving the use of all the bells for Sundays and holy days.[325] By 1895 there were thirteen qualified ringers at Worcester. They had a practice night on alternate Monday evenings and rang on Sunday mornings before the service, and on various other special occasions. A short office was said by them before they began to ring and they were well behaved.[326] At Winchester the ringers practised on Wednesday evenings at 7 p.m. At least eight bells were rung each Sunday before the services, and ten bells on special occasions. There was muffled ringing on New Year's Eve and during Lent.[327]

Cathedral ringers sometimes incurred the wrath of the dean and chapter. In 1807 the deputy bell toller at Exeter was reprimanded 'for permitting a foot race in the tower during divine service', and six months later the bell toller was in trouble for allowing boys into the tower.[328] In 1835 a ringer at Winchester was accused of using 'disrespectful and offensive language' to a member of the chapter,[329] and another one was reprimanded for a similar offence towards a visitor in 1856.[330] The ringers at Wells were criticized by the dean and chapter in 1872 for careless ringing.[331] They were also inclined to leave open the nave doors on practice nights.[332] Stephen Slade, the clock-winder at Wells, was found unsatisfactory and liable to intoxication, which led to his dismissal in 1888.[333]

The arrival of a new or recast bell was often the occasion for considerable celebrations. When Great Tom was recast and brought back to Lincoln in the reign of George IV there was a great procession through the city streets, 'with bells ringing and a band of music'. It was put on a truck and wheeled into the nave, surmounted by a little chimney-sweep.[334] A new ring of bells was installed at St Paul's in 1878 and the installation of Great Paul in 1882 took three days.[335] When the chapter at Wells wanted to install a new clock and bells in 1883, they borrowed £300 from Dean Plumptre.[336] There was a special towerkeeper at Worcester who was paid £40 in addition to his salary as one of the porters. He was responsible for winding the clock and chimes, which he found a laborious and time-consuming duty.[337] He was not allowed to be absent when the cathedral was open to the public and, in addition to the maintenance of the clock, chimes and bells and the cleaning of the tower, he was required to accompany all visitors to the tower; to be present whenever the bells were rung, and have authority over the ringers; and to be responsible for lighting and extinguishing the gas lighting in the tower.[338]

Although vergers, beadsmen and others included cleaning among their duties, cleaning a cathedral could often lead to a considerable upheaval, as at Exeter in 1830, when the services in the quire were transferred to the Lady Chapel for an entire week.[339] When a prayer book was found to be missing from one of the galleries at Wells in 1883, the dean and chapter ordered that Mrs Francis, the cleaner, should not be allowed to bring anyone with her when she came to clean the cathedral.[340] Salisbury Cathedral employed a woman to help with the dusting, and two female cleaners were appointed at St Paul's in 1869.[341] Ann Andrews, a char-woman, was paid 5s a week at Exeter to clean the chapter-house and singing school room.[342] Some women were employed at 11s a week at Gloucester to clean the sacristy, chapter room and library, as well as the cathedral itself.[343] The men who cleaned the sacrarium and altar steps at

Salisbury were issued with special slippers.[344] At Chester in 1879 the cathedral staff included one 'engine-man' and two labourers.[345] At Wells it was decided in 1880 that a thorough internal cleaning of the cathedral should take place twice a year – during the week after the stoves were extinguished in the spring and in the week before they were lit in the autumn. Harry Smart was engaged just over a year later to clean the cathedral, to kill the bats, and to remove weeds from the exterior of the building.[346] At Chichester the annual cleaning was discontinued in 1890; thereafter, only the stalls and floors were dusted regularly.[347] In 1898 Mrs Vick, the cleaner, was instructed to clean only the matting and chairs and pavement of the nave.[348]

Another valuable member of the cathedral staff was the clerk of the works. Joseph Watkins was appointed clerk of the works at Worcester in 1876, and ordered to make a monthly report on the fabric.[349] In 1879 the dean and chapter of Salisbury wrote to five other cathedrals for details of the duties and rates of pay of the clerk of the works, but only two replies were received. At Exeter the position was honorary, but at Gloucester the clerk of the works was paid £100 per annum. The Salisbury chapter therefore decided to offer £3 10s per week for this post.[350]

Few cathedrals had developed elaborate ceremonial before the end of the century, but there were altar servers at Worcester in 1899.[351] Manchester and Ripon were parish churches and their churchwardens had certain rights. At Ripon the churchwardens and sidesmen were appointed by the dean and chapter, while at Manchester they had a monthly meeting in the overseer's office.[352]

It will thus be seen that within the hierarchy of each cathedral there was a multitude of men (and indeed a few women), both ordained and lay, who worked under the direction of the dean and chapter and assisted them in the day-to-day running of the cathedral. Some were appointed by statute and others recruited as various needs arose. Many of them were unusual characters, but they all had their own distinctive contribution to make to the life of cathedrals in the nineteenth century.

7

CATHEDRAL WORSHIP
IN THE NINETEENTH
CENTURY

❁

'The principal feature of a Cathedral', said Harvey Goodwin, 'is the maintenance of a daily service upon a grand scale.'[1] In the same essay he quoted some words of Dean Goulburn, who said that the chief work of cathedral clergy was 'the keeping up, and attending upon, and striving (each one in his place) to raise to the highest point of perfection the daily church services of the house of God'.[2]

One of the features of the Sunday pattern of services in cathedrals in the early nineteenth century was a long morning service, consisting of matins, litany and ante-communion. At Worcester in 1825, though, the chapter decided to restore the practice of a divided morning service.[3] In the following year they resolved to discontinue the early service on a Sunday, and to leave out from matins the prayers for Parliament, for all sorts and conditions of men, and the general thanksgiving, but to add an anthem after the third collect and to introduce a psalm between the communion service and the sermon.[4]

It is not until the 1850s that a national picture of the Sunday pattern of worship in cathedrals emerges in the research carried out by the Cathedrals Commission. The commissioners found that there were two choral services on Sundays in each cathedral in England and Wales (except Llandaff). At half of them there were two sermons each Sunday and one in the remainder. The sermons were generally preached in the quire, but at Ely one sermon was preached in the quire and one in the octagon. In addition, Durham had an evening service (including a sermon) in the galilee. A divided morning service was the custom at Worcester, Salisbury and Hereford. At Winchester, both the morning and the afternoon services were divided, so that there were four choral services each Sunday. Holy communion was celebrated weekly in twelve cathedrals, and monthly in seventeen, while in one cathedral it was celebrated twice a month.[5] At Salisbury in 1851 a weekly communion service at 8 a.m. was begun, allowing a short interval after the conclusion of the early morning said prayers, which began at 7 a.m.[6] In 1850 the dean and chapter of Hereford received a petition from the mayor and 140 citizens asking for services on

Sunday mornings to be at a later hour 'so as to ensure a larger congregation of the inhabitants'.[7] In the following year, the dean and chapter of Hereford decided to bring forward evensong by two hours, from 5 p.m. to 3 p.m., while at Exeter in 1858 evensong on Sundays was transferred to the nave as soon as the necessary matting and furniture had been obtained.[8] Dean Goulburn introduced a divided morning service at Norwich in 1867, but found on Easter Day that year that there was too short an interval between the two services.[9] By 1872 the pattern of services on Sundays at St Paul's was as follows: 8 a.m. holy communion (in the North Chapel); 10.30 a.m. morning prayer with choral celebration and sermon; 3.15 p.m. litany, with anthem, sermon and hymn; 7 p.m. evening prayer, with hymn and sermon. In the following year the choral eucharist was moved to 9.30 a.m. and morning prayer with litany and sermon commenced at 11 a.m.[10] It appears, however, that the original pattern was restored, but with a long and dull sermon frequently lasting forty minutes from a prebendary, so that the service often lasted from 10.30 a.m. until after 1 p.m.[11] In 1886 the dean and chapter of Salisbury resolved to have at 10.30 a.m. matins and the litany, followed by a sermon, offertory and hymn. There would then be a pause, during which the bell would be rung before the eucharist, which was choral on the first Sunday of the month, but plain at other times. The 8 a.m. celebration was to be choral on the third Sunday of the month.[12] In 1887 at Worcester the chapter decided to terminate Sunday matins after the third collect, the anthem serving as an introit to the eucharist and the litany continuing to be said in the afternoon.[13]

The cathedral commissioners found in 1854 that seven cathedrals still continued to have early morning prayers on weekdays, in accordance with various sixteenth century injunctions, in addition to a mid-morning choral matins. At Exeter the time of this early service was frequently altered; in 1811 the chapter established 7 a.m. as its time from the beginning of March until the beginning of November, and 8 a.m. during the winter months; early prayers on Sundays were to be said at 9 a.m. 'for the accommodation of the military stationed in the city'.[14] Severe weather in January 1814 caused them to be suspended for a fortnight.[15] The early service was still said as late as 1865[16] and 1891, even though there might be just one person in the congregation.[17]

At Gloucester, the early service was ordered to be said between 1 April and 1 November in 1843.[18] It was held in the Lady Chapel.[19] In 1865 early prayers on Sundays were discontinued in favour of an early celebration during the summer months, except on those Sundays when there was a later celebration.[20] As late as 1870, however, the dean and chapter of Gloucester were still making new arrangements for the times of the daily early prayers.[21] The early service was said, at least on Sundays and holy days, early in the century at Hereford.[22] When Bishop Grey conducted a visitation of the cathedral in 1835 he found that no early prayers had been said during the winter in the memory of any member of the college of vicars choral, while the prayers were discontinued in the summer at the instance of the bishop and dean.[23] Grey ordered that the service should be reintroduced, and said at 7 a.m. in the summer and 8 a.m. in the winter: 'on Sundays and other holy days the choir service with chanting and services and anthem with the organ accompanyment [sic] be fully and duly performed at the hour of 8 in the mornings throughout the year'. Dean Merewether accordingly ordered the custos and vicars to say morning prayer in the north transept of the cathedral daily from 3 August 1835, the early Sunday services being recommenced the previous day.[24]

The early prayers were discontinued at Norwich in 1814,[25] but they were revived at Salisbury in 1847 by W. K. Hamilton, who told the Cathedrals Commission that the first lesson was always omitted at services there, following an injunction of Elizabeth I.[26] They were finally abandoned on Sundays in 1875 because so few attended. The early celebration that had been introduced in 1849 had proved to be more popular.[27] Early prayers were still being said at York in 1818, but they had been discontinued at Wells by 1839.[28] There is evidence that they were said, at least in the early years of the century, at Lincoln, Winchester, Worcester, St Paul's and Durham.[29]

Choral eucharists were rarely sung in English cathedrals in the early nineteenth century. The only example of a fully choral eucharist was at Durham in 1802.[30] John Jebb, writing in 1843, says that the full communion service was to be found only at Durham, Worcester and York. At Durham the service was celebrated 'with the utmost solemnity'.[31] The *Parish Choir* adds:

...there is no music except on the first Sunday in the month when the whole choir remain, the adults communicating. The non-communicants retire after the sermon; the choir then move within the rails of the Sacrarium, where desks were placed for them, I believe, by Bishop Cosin. A voluntary is played during the administration.[32]

In some other cathedrals, such as St Paul's and Canterbury, the custom was to sing the Sanctus as an introit at the beginning of the service.[33] By 1872, choral eucharists were also celebrated at Ely, Chichester, Chester, Exeter, Hereford, Peterborough and Salisbury.[34] The service at Exeter seems to have persisted throughout the Hanoverian era at least once a month and on great festivals, and included a curious custom:

...there were two altar rails at Exeter – one near the Holy Table, the other at some distance. Within these rails the communicants were assembled and the Sacred Elements administered to each by the officiating priests going round to them. At the *Gloria in excelsis*, the ten chorister boys, who alone appear to have remained, were arranged outside the outermost of these rails....After the service the boys closed the procession of clergy, each party filing off to their respective vestries. But, when the Bishop was present, the boys preceded, and arranged themselves in a line on their knees in the south aisle, to receive the Bishop's blessing as he passed on his way out of the Cathedral to the palace.

Bumpus adds that this custom was still in use in 1906 on Christmas Day, Easter Day and Whitsunday.[35] Choral eucharists on great festivals were sanctioned at Winchester in 1864,[36] and Dean Duncombe introduced one at York during the 1866 Church Congress. The Sanctus and Gloria in excelsis were sung on the first Sunday of each month and on great festivals, an introit being added in 1869. In 1874, E. G. Monk, the organist, arranged Merbecke's setting of the eucharist and this enabled a choral celebration to have a permanent place in the life of the Minster.[37] James Smith, a lay clerk at Worcester from 1864, records that in his early days there was only a monthly eucharist, the exhortation being said the previous Sunday. A full choral eucharist, including the singing of the Sanctus and Gloria in excelsis was celebrated only three or four times a year. When this service became more frequent, the Benedictus and Agnus Dei were added, until eventually there was a choral celebration every Sunday.[38] The precentor was in favour of the 8 a.m. choral eucharists:

> We now get a dignified and unbroken rendering of the office. On the old plan, the solemnity of a choral Eucharist was disturbed by the withdrawal of a large part of the congregation, first before the sermon and secondly after the Church Militant Prayer, leaving a few old fashioned people behind, to whom the music was not helpful.[39]

In the following year he said that the early time had its difficulties:

> ...music worthy of the Cathedral could not be sung properly at that early hour. Accordingly the Chapter appointed this service to be sung after Mattins on the last Sunday of the month. Since the change of hour, music of a more elaborate character has been very efficiently rendered.[40]

Precentor Woodward said in his report for 1896 that he saw no objection to a weekly sung eucharist, 'provided the Sunday morning service begins at 10.30 instead of eleven. 10.30 was in former days the hour fixed; and it would enable the lay clerks who live at a distance to get home in good time for early dinner'.[41] The dean and chapter accordingly altered the time of matins so that they could have a weekly sung eucharist.[42]

A weekly sung Eucharist was introduced at St Paul's on Easter Day 1873. The previous custom had been for the choir to leave after the sermon. The singing of settings of the Nicene Creed at eucharists at St Paul's was revived in 1842 and at Gloucester in 1873.[43] At the services at St Paul's, the celebrant stood at the north side facing south and the two minor canons who had just sung the Litany went to the south side – for there was plenty of room for the two – and faced north. When the time came for the Epistle, one stepped forward and read it, after which he went back and the other came forward and read the Gospel from precisely the same spot.[44]

Choral eucharists on saints' days were started in 1880.[45] The dean and chapter of Salisbury resolved in 1886 to ask the duty vicar choral to celebrate the monthly sung eucharist,[46] while at Wells the singing of the choir for the Kyries, Gloria in excelsis and Sanctus at the early celebration on Easter Day in the same year gave such satisfaction that the chapter decided to repeat the experiment on Whitsunday.[47] There were sung eucharists five times a year at Peterborough in 1889.[48] One or more of the offertory sentences was sung at the choral eucharist at Chichester on Sundays from 1890.[49] In 1892 the following parts of the service were ordered to be sung there: introit, Kyrie, responses before and after the Gospel, creed, offertory sentence 'with or without a hymn', Sursum corda, preface, Sanctus, Lord's prayer, Gloria in excelsis, with a sevenfold amen after the blessing on greater festivals.[50]

One important feature of Sunday worship in cathedrals in the later part of the century was a Sunday evening congregational service.[51] Early examples include Durham in 1837[52] and Wells in 1841.[53] Although a sermon at Sunday evensong was introduced at Norwich in 1833, it was not till much later in the century that Sunday evening services were established there.[54] Experimental services were held at St Paul's during the Great Exhibition in 1851 and again in 1858, following pressure from Bishop Tait. On Advent Sunday 1858 a service at St Paul's caused such a sensation that Ludgate Hill was completely blocked by a great crowd who wished to attend. Some 2,500 chairs were brought in and the floor was covered with matting, which was not removed until 1877. At least 10,000 people failed to get inside the cathedral. The experiment lasted only a few months, but was repeated every winter.[55] The popularity of these services at St Paul's led to their introduction elsewhere. From January 1873 they were held every Sunday throughout the year, with a special Sunday evening choir.[56] They became nationally famous. Between 2,000 and 6,000 people flocked to hear H. P. Liddon's sermons.[57] There was talk of introducing nave services at Bristol in 1863,[58] but nothing was done until Canon Percival's appointment in 1882. He had a pulpit made at his own expense, defying Dean Elliott, and the nave was crowded during his months of residence, but his brother canons did not agree with him and did not continue the services during their periods of residence.[59] In 1888 popular Sunday evening services were held in Advent and Lent,[60] but it was Dean Pigou who made them really popular.[61]

An evening service was instituted at Ripon in 1858 for the poor people of the parish, and an assistant curate engaged to minister to them.[62] In the summer of the same year similar services were begun at Rochester,[63] but they later lapsed, only to be revived in 1885 as a result of pressure by John Wordsworth.[64] Sunday evening services were introduced at both York and Hereford in 1863. The great attraction at the latter cathedral was that it had just been reopened after a restoration lasting more than twenty years. They were fully choral, but 'exceedingly popular'. The crowd waiting at the north door for the doors to be opened was said to be 'not unlike that at the pit door of a theatre'.[65] Dean Duncombe was responsible for the introduction of Sunday evening services at York. They swiftly became most popular, sometimes attracting a congregation of two or three thousand people. At first they were held in the afternoon, but Duncombe transferred them to the evening in 1866, 'to induce the working classes more especially to attend divine worship'. The services were congregational in character, but the singing was encouraged by a voluntary choir. The responses were said, the psalms and canticles were sung to chants, and two hymns were sung. The sermons were always delivered by eminent preachers. Duncombe claimed that nearly all the congregation never went to any other church, but others disagreed. Archdeacon Hay believed that they drew worshippers from the parish churches, and Canon George Trevor, a city incumbent from 1847 to 1867, said that the transformation of services in the cathedral – from being cold, dull and lifeless when he arrived, to being flourishing and crowded twenty years later – had emptied his church. He felt that he was 'thoroughly beaten' and thus accepted a country living.[66] In 1878 the *Guardian* praised the success of Sunday evening services at St Paul's, Chester, Worcester, Westminster Abbey, York and Gloucester.[67] At Canterbury, Dean Alford introduced a Sunday afternoon sermon in spite of the opposition of the chapter. He therefore had to undertake the duty himself, but the quire was packed from end to end. Later, Dean Payne-Smith introduced a service and sermon on Sunday evenings. In order to pacify complaints from local churches, part of the collection was sent to them.[68]

Dean Pigou's success with a Sunday evening service at Bristol may be contrasted with his experience at Chichester, where there were doubts about such a service because of the effect on the city churches.[69] Another problem at Chichester was the opposition of the priest vicars, who declined to take part in this service in case it overtaxed their strength.[70] Nevertheless, an evening service with a sermon was introduced at Chichester during Advent 1881 and continued until Trinity Sunday the following year, resuming in Advent 1882.[71] A further attempt was made in 1890, when the subject was considered at a special meeting between the dean and chapter and the incumbents of the city churches, which was chaired by the bishop.[72]

Dean Lake introduced afternoon sermons in Advent and Lent at Durham,[73] and Canon Tinling proposed that there should be Sunday evening services at Gloucester during Lent 1870. The chapter declined to continue them after the end of Lent – except on Easter Day and Whitsunday if Tinling felt that there should be such a service on those days.[74] A fresh attempt was made in 1878 when Canons Tinling and Evans presented a joint report to the chapter. They recommended that there should be an evening service at 7 p.m. on each of the Sundays in Advent and Lent and also on Easter Day. At a later chapter meeting payments for attendance at these services were sanctioned.[75] A few years later, the dean and chapter were still willing for Tinling to hold courses of services, provided they were not liable to any expenses as a result of them.[76]

Harvey Goodwin seized the opportunity given at Ely when the Lady Chapel was closed for cleaning to transfer the Sunday evening services to the Octagon. There was an immediate and large increase in the congregation, despite the smallness of the city.[77] On St Etheldreda's Day in 1878, a special evening service was held, attended by 2,500 people, of whom 500 could not find seats. The scarlet uniforms of the soldiers who attended made an effective contrast with the white surplices of the choir and the King's scholars. All the official bodies of the little city were represented, including the schools and benefit clubs. Even the nonconformist ministers and their congregations were there. The cathedral was abundantly lit and the short and simple service, sung by the augmented cathedral choir, clearly had a great effect. After the sermon, the precentor conducted part of a cantata; he wore a surplice and stood in the pulpit.[78]

Dean Butler introduced a Sunday evening service at Lincoln. He had experienced such a service during his time at Worcester and was determined to have one at Lincoln. He therefore undertook to cover its cost himself, though fortunately the collections defrayed the greater part of this. He preached at it only once a month and expected the canon-in-residence to preach the majority of the sermons. Although the parish churches were affected at first, Butler refused to accept this as a reason for the cathedral to be closed when so many people might be attracted by a bright musical service in the nave. When he or the bishop preached, the nave was packed, especially with working men and women.[79]

At Manchester, Sunday evening services were started in 1857 by one of the minor canons, despite the opposition of the canons. When the congregation outgrew the Derby Chapel, the services were transferred to the nave. Bishop Prince Lee never preached at them, and the canons would not attend. Guest preachers were not invited and the only semblance of official support was given by Dean Bowers. When the cathedral clergy tried to start pastoral visits to the congregation 'it appeared that one reason for the crowds at the Cathedral was that they wished to escape the pestering of the parochial clergy'. By 1884, the cost of these services was causing difficulties.[80]

At Norwich, Dean Lefroy initiated the Sunday evening services and became a household name in the city. In March 1890 a contemporary wrote:

> Dean Lefroy has literally taken Norwich by storm. Entering the Cathedral on Sunday night just after the Mission Service in the Nave had commenced, I found a crowded congregation,...the fact that on three nights in Lent, Sundays, Wednesdays and Fridays, he is able to utilise the Nave of the Cathedral is a wonderful testimony to the influence he has already obtained over the citizens of Norwich. On Wednesday evenings in Lent the Dean gives an address in the course of a service of sacred music for the people, while on Friday evenings he is preaching another course of sermons in the Nave.

These services were very popular among nonconformists, many of whom would go on to the cathedral to listen to Dean Lefroy after attending a service in their own chapel.[81] Lefroy had to overcome opposition to these services at Norwich, and at Winchester the dean and chapter refused to have them in case the parish churches of the city were affected.[82]

B. F. Westcott, during his brief time as a canon of Peterborough, managed to start nave services there on Sunday evenings in Advent and Lent. He formed a large voluntary choir to sing at them, while in the summer there were special services for various special groups, such as volunteers, railwaymen, Oddfellows and Sunday School teachers.[83] Sunday evening services for working men were begun at Wells in August 1886. On the first occasion there was a large congregation in the nave and nave aisles. More came on the next two Sundays and the sermon at the third of these services lasted nearly an hour. After such an encouraging start, they became a regular feature every year in August, with the bishop and the cathedral dignitaries sharing the preaching.[84] The service began at 8 p.m. and included the litany, three hymns and a sermon.[85]

Canon Barry began Sunday evening services at Worcester and founded a voluntary choir to sing at them. The large congregation, and the effect caused by the gas lighting of the cathedral, evoked many comments. No walking about was permitted and the custos had orders to check any irreverence.[86] In 1882 there was a serious dispute between the precentor, E. Vine Hall, and Minor Canon Richard Cattley about the taking of the collection at these services.[87] Canon Barry's services were a revival and an extension of an experiment that had been carried out in the 1850s when a series of special sermons on Sunday afternoons had been introduced at Worcester:

> There were Benches arranged in the Nave for the Members of the Cathedral and Choir, and a thousand chairs for the congregation: and

when the usual afternoon service was terminated in the Choir, nearly all the persons who had been present in the Choir moved into the Nave, where they found a large number of additional persons already assembled. A Psalm was sung – a plain Sermon was then preached – the sermon ended, the Choir and congregation sang the Evening hymn before the blessing was given.... The congregations were large and orderly, always exceeding a thousand persons – and amounted on the 18 of July, when the Bishop of Oxford preached, to probably double that number.[88]

Congregational services on a Sunday evening were therefore an important element in the life of many cathedrals in the late nineteenth century. In many cases (such as Worcester, Exeter and York) they have survived long into the present century. At other cathedrals (such as Winchester and Chichester), where they were not successfully introduced in Victorian times, such a service has not become a regular feature of the life of the cathedral. Yet the movement in favour of these services was by no means universally supported. Their introduction was generally achieved by the enthusiasm of a single member of the chapter, often (but not always) the dean. There was opposition to them from within the chapter (as at Bristol, Gloucester and Canterbury) and they were often a cause of controversy. The *Church Times* regretted the tendency to turn cathedrals into 'huge parish churches with popular Evensong and then to think that all has been done'.[89] Yet these services certainly caught the imagination of the public, and helped to make cathedrals more popular than they had been for centuries. At a time of rigid social distinctions, many deans and chapters could show that the worship offered in their cathedrals enabled people from differing social backgrounds to take part, and that cathedrals were participating in the evangelistic work of the Church in an important and effective way.

Cathedrals also responded to the needs of the times by introducing special services (often of a musical or devotional character) during particular seasons in the Church's year, and by arranging services specially constructed for important occasions or for various bodies in the community. At first the movement was in an opposite direction, and some interesting survivals from the past were lost – such as the custom at Exeter Cathedral of the organist and choristers attending early morning prayers on Christmas Day and singing Psalm 150 at the beginning of the service from the Minstrels' Gallery.[90] Ely seems to have been one of the first cathedrals to introduce special seasonal services; on Wednesday evenings in Advent and Lent in the 1860s simple unaccompanied services were held, later including Haydn's *Seven Last Words* and Spohr's *Last Judgement*.[91] Details of the arrangements at Canterbury for Christmas 1873 may be gleaned from the *Guardian*:

On Christmas Eve at 8 p.m. (Evensong having taken place at 3 p.m.), there was a very solemn and affecting service. It consisted of the 150th Psalm, the Magnificat, two appropriate lessons, the Lord's Prayer, the Advent and Christmas Day collects, and then a short address, most earnest and touching, from the Dean. This was followed by the first part of the *Messiah*, the Lady Day and last Epiphany collects, a hymn and the blessing. The choir was crowded; all classes and all callings were there, mixed together, and the behaviour of the people was very reverent. Many stood throughout the oratorio.[92]

Christmas and Easter were marked in novel ways at St Paul's in 1868–9. At Christmas 1868 the sacrist decorated the quire, while at Epiphany 1869 a star was placed on the altar. At Easter 1869 a crimson velvet 'reredos' was erected on the altar, with the text 'He is risen', surrounded by hothouse flowers that cost £20.[93] By 1878 there were special services on weeknight evenings during Advent and Lent at Lincoln, Norwich and Bristol, and the special musical services at Canterbury and Lincoln on the eves of Christmas and Easter Day were becoming well known. Many cathedrals included performances of Bach's Passion Music in their services during Holy Week.[94] At Worcester in 1880 there were special services each evening in Holy Week, attended by large and devout congregations mainly drawn from the middle and lower classes. On Good Friday, the cathedral was thronged from end to end. On the first four days, Bach's Passion Music (either from the *St Matthew Passion* or from the *St John Passion*) was sung. The cathedral choir was augmented to 100 voices by members of the Philharmonic Society. Each evening the canon-in-residence gave a short address before the music, while on Good Friday the Passion Music from the *Messiah* was sung. The same formula was in use at Norwich on Good Friday 1880, with the addition of a small orchestra.[95] It attracted an enormous congregation of between seven and eight thousand people which filled both nave and quire. At Lincoln Cathedral the services during Holy Week were unaccompanied, with additional addresses each day in the Morning Chapel at 7.45 a.m. and after evensong. On Easter Even, part two of the *Messiah* was sung by an augmented choir to an immense and reverent congregation, while the services on Easter Day were enriched by Bishop Wordsworth wearing a crimson velvet cope with a brilliant jewelled morse when he celebrated the eucharist. Durham Cathedral had sermons at evensong throughout Holy Week. On Maundy Thursday afternoon a selection from Spohr's *Calvary* was sung to a very large congregation. Increased attendance at the services had been a marked feature of recent Holy Weeks there.[96] Canon Knox-Little was responsible for the introduction of a Three Hours' Service at Worcester. The communion table and cross were draped in crêpe and at the end of the service a bell was tolled, as for a funeral.[97] A novel pattern of worship on

Good Friday was introduced at Wells in 1884. At 8 a.m. there was an address on the first word from the cross, and part of the communion service was read. Matins and ante-communion was sung at 11 a.m, with addresses on the second and third words, while from 1.30 p.m. to 3 p.m. there were addresses on the next three words, interspersed with portions of the litany. Finally, evensong was sung at 4 p.m. with a sermon on the last word.[98] St Paul's was thronged with relays of worshippers for successive services on Good Friday 1884, which followed almost without interruption from 8 a.m. to 8 p.m. Nearly 2,000 attended the Three Hours' Service at St Paul's on Good Friday 1885. During Lent, midday unaccompanied services were held, conducted by a minor canon:

> Nothing could have exceeded the beauty and impressiveness of the hymn 'When I survey the wondrous cross' sung as it was without choir or accompaniment by the multitudes who thronged the Cathedral in Holy Week.[99]

In 1884 a revised form of the weekday Advent service at Worcester was introduced (which indicates that it had been started some years previously). The service commenced with a hymn, followed by a sermon, a metrical litany (sung from *Hymns Ancient and Modern*) and three short preces. These were followed by the Lord's Prayer, three collects and the blessing.[100] These services were held on Friday evenings in Advent 1887 and the music on Christmas Day included part of the *Messiah*.[101] In Advent the following year, Spohr's *Last Judgement* was included in the services at Worcester.[102] At Hereford, the Christmas music from the *Messiah* was sung on Christmas Eve 1889, together with eight carols, while on Christmas Day 1893 a further selection from the *Messiah* was sung at 5.30 p.m., with the hymn *Hark the herald angels sing*. During Advent of the same year, the praelector preached at matins on three Tuesdays and on St Thomas' Day, and special services were held at 7.30 p.m. on Thursdays. Evensong on Easter Eve 1893 included the Passion Music from the *Messiah* and the hymn *The Day of Resurrection*.[103] There were sermons at St Paul's on Wednesdays and Fridays in 1884 and 1885, and addresses were also given at a late evening service held either in the crypt or the north-west chapel on Tuesdays and Thursdays. The main burden of these fell on the minor canons. In each Lent there were sixty-one addresses during the forty days of Lent, besides the three regular Sunday sermons.[104] Evensong on Innocents' Day at Chichester in 1890 was made specially appropriate for children to take part.[105] At Winchester in the same year evensong was sung at 8 p.m. on Christmas Eve, but a carol service was introduced in the quire at 4 p.m., the dean giving the address. This pattern was repeated the following year, but in 1893 carols were sung after evensong on Christmas Eve and the next three days. In 1894 they were sung in this way on Christmas Eve and Christmas Day, but two of the canons objected to this practice being repeated for more than two days.[106] In the same year the Festival Choral Society at Worcester assisted in the performance of the appropriate parts of the *Messiah* instead of an anthem on Christmas Day, Good Friday and Ascension Day.[107] Although there are examples of 'oratorio services' at Chester in 1880, Liverpool and Salisbury in 1884, Ely in 1896 and York in 1900, by the end of the century it is possible that the vogue for weekday evening devotional services was waning. The dean and chapter of Salisbury decided in 1898 to discontinue the evening services on Fridays in Advent. Instead, lectures were given by the chancellor at 4 p.m.[108]

In the early nineteenth century the normal round of services was interrupted only rarely by occasions of a special nature. F. E. Witts, a Gloucestershire clergyman, attended the Assize service at Gloucester in August 1826 and found it 'extremely crowded'. The judges, the sheriff, the county magistrates and other gentry made 'a very imposing sight and the Bishop preached an excellent sermon on the Day of Judgement'.[109] But often special services had a rather sombre character, such as the diocesan day of fasting and humiliation which was observed in Wells Cathedral in 1849 during an outbreak of cholera.[110] St Paul's Cathedral was naturally the focus for national religious occasions. Here too the cholera epidemic of 1849 was marked, and a Day of Thanksgiving was held in November when it had ended. Five years later there was a thanksgiving service for a plentiful harvest. Both the Crimean War and the Indian Mutiny were marked by Days of Humiliation and Thanksgiving, while in 1861 vast crowds came to hear the funeral sermons following the death of the Prince Consort. Extensive black hangings, edged with white, were draped in the quire. Bishop Tait preached to a crowded cathedral at the service for the Day of Humiliation for the Cattle Plague in March 1866, but the annual service to commemorate the Fire of London was not held after 1858.[111] Each year the Corporation of the Sons of the Clergy held their annual festival at St Paul's. Stainer considerably developed the musical content of these grand services.[112] The most colossal spectacle at St Paul's, however, was the funeral of the Duke of Wellington in November 1852. Extra galleries enabled 13,000 to be present at the service, and a choir of eighty men and boys, drawn from the choirs of St Paul's, Westminster Abbey and the Chapel Royal, led the singing. The coffin was transferred from the funeral car to the bier nearly an hour after the scheduled timetable.[113]

B. J. Armstrong attended the annual service for the Society for the Propagation of the Gospel at St Paul's in 1854 and was impressed by the huge congregation, though not by the service. This he described as 'a noisy and undevotional affair – more of an oratorio than a service'.[114] He went again in 1872, noted the presence of the archbishop and sixteen other bishops in their scarlet convocation robes, but added: 'Service badly carried out, the music being of the lightest and most secular kind, and the whole thing misarranged.'[115]

But provincial cathedrals also experienced huge crowds. Special trains were provided to take people to a gathering of temperance societies at Peterborough Cathedral in 1855. There were 800 people in the quire and galleries and as many in the nave: the dean and the canon-in-residence could scarcely push their way through to read the lessons. Another large congregation was drawn to Peterborough for the annual festival of a new association to assist the widows and orphans of cathedral organists and lay clerks. A choir of eighty was present, with representatives from many different cathedrals.[116] A. J. B. Beresford Hope told the Church Congress at Norwich in 1865 of three recent occasions when he had seen vast congregations at cathedral services – at the reopening of Lichfield Cathedral, where 'train upon train rolled in', at the enthronement of Archbishop Longley at Canterbury, and at the Church Congress at Manchester in 1863.[117]

St Paul's Day was observed with some emphasis at St Paul's in 1871. W. Sparrow Simpson, one of the minor canons and librarian, presented a new silver gilt chalice and paten at the 8 a.m. service, when there were fifty communicants. The dean preached at evensong, which was attended by the Bishop of London and seventeen prebendaries. This was followed by a chapter dinner, to which the minor canons and lay officials of the chapter were also invited. From 1872 on, St Paul's Day was observed as an annual feast for the whole foundation and the lay vicars choral were also invited to the dinner.[118]

Military services were also held in various cathedrals from time to time. The first service to lay up colours in Winchester Cathedral was in 1871, when the colours of the 101st Royal Bengal Fusiliers were entrusted to the dean and chapter.[119] The Annual Military Sunday at York was first held in 1885.[120] Military services were allowed at Exeter in 1886 on condition that no secular music was included and that the services, which were to begin at 9 a.m., were finished in time for matins at 10.30 a.m.[121] In 1893 the dean and chapter of Winchester negotiated an agreement with the military authorities by which they were to receive £26 per annum for wear and tear on the cathedral by troops attending services.[122] The outbreak of the Boer War at the end of the century led to the establishment of regular services of intercession at Wells, Winchester and elsewhere.[123]

When a diocesan synod was held in the chapter-house at Salisbury in 1872, the dean and chapter held special services in the cathedral for the synodsmen. There was a eucharist at 10 a.m. on the first day of the synod, while at 8 p.m. on the same day a large congregation was present as a long procession of choristers and cathedral clergy processed into the quire singing the hymn, 'Christ is our corner-stone'. Bishop Moberly celebrated the eucharist at 8 a.m. on the following two days and evensong was held immediately following the end of each day's business.[124]

The Lent Assize service at Winchester in 1873 included some novel features. The choir, as well as the clergy, went to the west door before the service to greet the judges and lead them in procession to the quire, singing the anthem 'O how amiable' by Richardson:

The clerical procession was kept distinct from the secular one, the clergy not walking with the judges as formerly. By this arrangement, the talking and levity which formerly characterised these ceremonies was avoided.[125]

When Worcester Cathedral was reopened in 1874 following its extensive restoration, a series of great services was held. The main service on Wednesday, 8 April, began with a processional hymn, followed by Psalm 68 and the rest of the morning prayer, the litany, a choral communion and a sermon by Bishop Philpott. Afterwards the dean and chapter sent their special thanks to the mayor for the 'warm personal interest' he had taken in the reopening festival.[126] Thousands of people from all over Northumberland and County Durham flocked to Durham Cathedral when it was reopened after six years' restoration (though the daily services were never discontinued). The service was thought to be the most impressive religious spectacle north of the Humber for many centuries. Although Bishop Baring refused to take part, nearly all the clergy of the diocese were present and there were 500 communicants at an early celebration of holy communion.[127] Special services were also held to mark the reopening of the quire at Exeter in 1876, the installation of new bells at St Paul's in 1878, and the reopening of the cloisters at Chichester in 1890.[128]

There were special services for the foresters at Gloucester in 1880 and for cyclists at Winchester in 1892.[129] A Harvest Festival service was held annually in the nave of York Minster from 1881.[130] Special arrangements were made in a number of cathedrals when the Church Congress was held in the city. In 1894, following the Exeter Church Congress, the dean and chapter recorded their gratitude to the succentor, organist, choir and voluntary choir for their help at Congress services.[131] Another conference that involved large services was the Lambeth Conference, and some sixty bishops visited Durham for a big service in 1888.[132] Canterbury was the natural home for the opening service in 1888 and also witnessed the consecration of several overseas bishops in the later nineteenth century.[133]

Durham Cathedral had a close relationship with the new university that grew up alongside it. Morning prayers for the university were held in the Chapel of the Nine Altars as early as 1836, though in 1847 they were transferred temporarily to the galilee. The Sunday morning service of the university was cathedral matins; seats were assigned to the officers and undergraduates in the quire and north transept.[134] Civic pomp suffered at the hands of the dean and chapter at Lincoln Cathedral in the 1860s. On one occasion, 'the clergy were not ready for the mayor and corporation, and the sword and the mace had to lie on the ground. The collection was taken in willow pattern soup and dinner plates'.[135] In 1876, following the indignation caused by the 'Mock' Festival at Worcester the previous year, the Mayor of Hereford invited his colleagues in Worcester and Gloucester to attend in state the opening service of the Three Choirs Festival in the cathedral, a practice that has continued ever since.[136]

From time to time the normal round of cathedral services was varied to include the installation of canons and other dignitaries. Adam Sedgwick was offered a Crown canonry at Norwich in 1834. He presented his deed (with the Great Seal affixed) to the dean after the first lesson at matins and was formally installed.[137] Robert Gregory was installed as a canon of St Paul's in December 1868. Every light in the cathedral was extinguished after evensong and everyone turned out of the building (including some of Gregory's own friends). Archdeacon Hale installed him in a chair by the light of a wax taper carried by a verger in a tin kitchen candlestick. Gregory was not impressed. He had nothing but contempt for such a slovenly ceremony, and was determined to make sweeping changes.[138] Less than two years later, when Liddon was installed following the second lesson at evensong, the entire chapter was present and the marked contrast with Gregory's installation was widely noted.[139]

Even the installations of deans were not impressive ceremonies early in the century. Dean Leigh of Hereford was installed by proxy (then the common custom) in 1808,[140] though his successor Dean Gretton was personally installed.[141] By the closing years of the century such a service was rightly regarded as an important occasion. Dean Lefroy was installed at Norwich in 1889 at a fully choral service attended by a large congregation.[142]

The year 1875 saw the baptism of the archdeacon's grandchild at St Paul's, the first such service since 1713, while the wedding of the Lady Mayoress in 1877 was thought to be the first wedding at St Paul's since 1760.[143] Manchester was well known for its numerous baptisms. They were conducted freely on Sundays and festivals, but a small charge was made on other days. J. M. Elvy claimed to have christened no less than 19,000 children during his forty-two years on the cathedral staff, though one of his predecessors saved some time by arranging the infants in a semi-circle, then going round them touching their foreheads with his wet hand which he had previously dipped in the font. On 26 February 1837, 369 children were baptized in a single day.[144] At York, however, christenings were unknown between 1804 and 1883, and there were only forty between that year and 1911.[145] Manchester was equally popular for weddings. Every Sunday in the year and on most weekdays, couples came to be married there, often in droves. On one Christmas morning there were eighty weddings; the signing of the registers lasted until 4 p.m. Even publishing banns of marriage could take a quarter of an hour. Sir Frederick Bridge said:

While morning service was being conducted in the Nave, a number of people were actually being married in the Choir...on certain Sundays in the year the number of weddings was so great that... dozens of couples were married simultaneously.[146]

Elsewhere, cathedrals without any parochial responsibilities gradually became venues for weddings. In 1861 the dean and chapter of Wells asked the bishop to authorize the reading of banns and the conducting of marriages in the cathedral; two years later the dean and chapter of Chichester secured episcopal consent for weddings to be held there.[147] When one of the daughters of Dean Garnier was married at Lincoln Cathedral,

> it failed as a spectacle, the whole place being turned into a bear garden or a badly-ordered playhouse. There was a crowd in the choir and nave, three thousand or more, one fellow walking about whistling, with his hat on.[148]

If, for the majority of cathedrals, baptisms and weddings were rare events, funerals were reasonably frequent and often very impressive occasions. Early in the century the dean and chapter of Bristol, where great delays had been experienced in the payment of funeral fees, drew up new rules for the burial of any corpse in the cathedral or churchyard. The undertaker had to pay the necessary fees before the interment.[149] In 1808 the dean and chapter of Exeter decided that the wives, widows and children of members of the chapter should have free funerals.[150] In 1842, John Hunt, who had succeeded S. S. Wesley as organist of Hereford Cathedral, had the misfortune to fall over a dinner wagon, laden with plates and glasses, which had been left in a dark part of the cloisters after an audit dinner, and died from his injuries. His adopted nephew, one of the choristers, died from shock three days later. Their joint funeral in the Lady Chapel was most pathetic: 'the officers of the Cathedral...were seen leaning against the walls and pillars, sobbing like children'.[151]

Bishop Stanley's funeral at Norwich Cathedral in 1849 was a vast affair, with a crowd of some 20,000 mourners.[152] When the ten-year-old step-daughter of the Precentor of Bristol died in 1864, the *Guardian* printed a full account of her funeral:

> At two o'clock the hearse bearing the coffin, with the attending mourning-carriages, arrived at the entrance of the north transept. Here the whole Cathedral staff were ready, waiting to receive the corpse and attend it to the grave....First came the inferior officers of the Cathedral in their black gowns, wearing white scarfs and white gloves; next came the choir boys and men in their surplices and white gloves, the men wearing across their surplices black silk scarves. Then followed the minor canons, preceding the canon-in-residence, in their robes, with

black silk scarves over their stoles, and white gloves....After the coffin followed, as chief mourners, the Precentor, in his robes, holding by the hand his little stepson, an only brother of the deceased; behind them followed relatives and other mourners and etc...[153]

When Richard Dawes, Dean of Hereford, was buried in 1867, nearly 800 persons gathered in cold, snowy weather outside the deanery. By the time the procession reached the west door, where the clergy and civic processions were waiting, this number had swelled to over 1,100. Spohr's anthem was sung at the graveside, but this was spoilt by the solo chorister, a protégé of the dean, bursting into tears. A muffled peal was rung on the bells, and the pulpit and the lectern were draped in black cloth.[154]

In 1881 the dean and chapter of Chichester ordered that when any dignitary or canon of the cathedral died, a purple mourning frontlet should be hung in his stall and remain there for a month, unless his successor was installed within that period.[155] Ten years later they ordered that the large bell should be tolled, 'according to the ancient custom', when a member of the cathedral foundation died. The Dead March from *Saul* was to be played 'in the presence of the Choir after the service on the Sunday afternoon following'.[156] But by far the best-known description of a Victorian cathedral funeral is Francis Kilvert's account of the service held in Worcester Cathedral in 1870 for his aunt, Maria Kilvert, who was the daughter of a former canon:

One very fat man had constituted himself chiefest mourner of all and walked next to the coffin before my Father and myself. The bearers, blinded by the sweeping pall, could not see where they were going and nearly missed the Cloister arch, but at length we got safe into the narrow dark passage and into the Cloisters....So the clergy and choir came to meet us at the door, then turned and moved up the Cathedral nave chanting in solemn procession, 'I am the Resurrection and the Life saith the Lord'. But meanwhile there was a dreadful struggle at the steps leading up from the Cloisters to the door. The bearers were quite unequal to the task and the coffin seemed crushingly heavy. There was a stamping and a scuffling, a mass of struggling men swaying to and fro, pushing and writhing and wrestling while the coffin sank and rose and sank again. Once or twice I thought the whole mass of men must have been down together with the coffin atop of them and someone killed or maimed at least. But now came the time of the fat chief mourner. Seizing his opportunity he rushed into the strife by an opening large and the rescued coffin rose. At last by a wild effort and tremendous heave the ponderous coffin was borne up the steps and through the door into the Cathedral where the choristers, quite unconscious of the scene and the fearful struggle going on behind, were singing up the nave like a company of angels. In the Choir there was another dreadful struggle to

131

let the coffin down. The bearers were completely overweighted, they bowed and bent and nearly fell and threw the coffin down on the floor. When it was safely deposited we all retired to seats right and left and a verger or beadle, in a black gown and holding a mace, took up his position at the head of the coffin, standing. The psalm was sung nicely to a very beautiful chant. The Dean had the gout and could not appear, so Canon Wood read the lesson well and impressively in a sonorous voice. The Grave Service was intoned by the Sacristan Mr Raisin and sung by the choir, standing on the planking round the vault whilst a crowd of people looked in through the cloister windows.

Afterwards, John Hooper, the chapter clerk, read Miss Kilvert's will back at the house.[157]

The preaching of sermons was naturally an important element in the worship of cathedrals during the nineteenth century and was surrounded by much ceremony at Manchester Cathedral.[158] This was a matter that was officially governed by various provisions in cathedral statutes. The statutes of Hereford Cathedral, revised by Archbishop Laud in 1637, ordered that 'for the banishing of ignorance, the encouragement of piety, and the promotion of Christ's Kingdom', a sermon 'for the space of an hour or thereabouts' should be preached every Sunday and on festival days immediately after the Nicene Creed.[159] The Henrician statutes of Canterbury Cathedral, confirmed by Charles I, also made provision for a sermon each Sunday, so that the dean and each canon were to preach at least four times in every year.[160] The statutes of Winchester Cathedral made similar provisions for the preaching of sermons.[161] In Chichester, the dean and the four residentiary canons selected the festivals on which they would preach.[162] In the same year the dean and chapter of Hereford agreed to nominate a preacher from time to time in place of themselves.[163] If a prebendary failed to keep his preaching turn, then his place was often supplied by a minor canon or vicar choral. At Exeter in 1817 one of the priest vicars was appointed to deputize for any absent prebendaries for a whole year.[164] In 1825 the dean and chapter of Worcester decided that each prebendary (as the canons were then termed) should reside for two consecutive months with 'charge of the pulpit during one of those calendar months'. In the same year they made an order that any member of the chapter who failed to preach in his turn should give 2 guineas to the treasurer to hand on to the preacher. A minor canon was to preach if a canon could not be found.[165] At Hereford, Dean Merewether obtained two wooden frames (which still exist) to be hung on either side of the western entrance to the quire. On one the details of the choral services were given, while the other contained details of the preaching turns and the readers for the week.[166] Earlier in the same month Merewether had instructed the prebendaries to preach themselves and not to rely on deputies.[167] Two guineas was also the rate for a sermon preached by the duty priest vicar at Chichester Cathedral when a prebendary did not fulfil his preaching turn, but when the prebends were disendowed in 1840 it became impossible for these payments to be enforced.[168] The situation was regularized by the dean and chapter in 1841 when they agreed that the dignitaries and prebendaries who had been appointed before the passing of the 1840 Act, together with the archdeacons and the prebendaries of six stalls that were still endowed, should continue to be responsible for their prebendal sermons. The canon-in-residence was normally responsible for preaching in place of the regular preacher.[169] The 1840 Act caused problems elsewhere. In his charge of 1842, Bishop Denison of Salisbury said that the dean and chapter there had set aside £70 per annum so that each unendowed prebendary could receive £5 for fulfilling his preaching turn. Denison himself had invested £650 to help this fund.[170] In November 1846 the dean and chapter of Winchester decided that all morning preaching turns, except those of the dean and archdeacons, should fall to the canon-in-residence, though the dean would be entitled to one Sunday in each of the four months of his residence.[171] At St Paul's in 1843 the prebendaries preached on holy days, and the residentiaries on Sunday evenings. The Sunday morning sermons, which were a relic of the old sermons at St Paul's Cross, were arranged by the Bishop of London. At Exeter the residentiaries preached on Sunday mornings and the prebendaries on Sunday evenings.[172] Until 1850 the Bishop of Norwich had a similar right in his cathedral.[173] At Wells the dean and chapter resolved in 1858 not to exact a fine from any disendowed dignitary or prebendary who failed to fulfil his preaching turn. The dean or canon-in-residence would take his place. If one of the minor canons preached, he was paid 1 guinea.[174] Apparently prebendaries sometimes failed to appear when they were due to preach, and in July 1858 the chapter clerk of Wells was asked to remind them in good time.[175] Prebendary James Coleman explained to the cathedral commissioners in 1883 why comparatively few of the prebendaries of Wells fulfilled their preaching turns:

> Probably the expense of providing for his own Sunday duties in his absence at Wells, of a long and tedious journey, in many instances to and fro, and of an hotel bill, and etc., is the cause of many a prebendary declining a duty for which there is no remuneration.[176]

Dean Johnson of Wells was really not in favour of the system at all:

> A prebendary leaves his incumbency from Saturday to Monday, and is entertained by the Bishop or canon-in-residence during that time, in order to deliver a sermon, which not uncommonly, from the nature of the case, is unsuitable for the occasion. The preaching in the Cathedral is generally admitted to be inferior to that which is common in many of the parishes of the diocese; and prebendaries who address their own

congregations with spirit and effect, not infrequently in the Cathedral disappoint expectations.[177]

Not only were minor canons expected to supply the place of absent prebendaries in many cathedrals; at Winchester their own right to preach could be superseded by the dean or canon-in-residence, though they still received the customary fee.[178] At Worcester, however, they had the right to preach on the first Sunday evening of each month.[179] In some cases the rota of preaching turns was in a hopeless state of confusion. In June 1864 Francis Lear, the Precentor of Salisbury, pointed out to the dean that while some prebendaries had two turns each, the Archdeacon of Dorset and four of the prebendaries had no turn at all. The Archdeacon of Berkshire had been transferred to the diocese of Oxford twenty years previously. The chancellor had no less than twenty-five preaching turns each year. A new list was therefore drawn up and a new statute codifying the amended provisions was confirmed by Bishop W. K. Hamilton in 1865 and entered in the statute book in January 1873.[180] In 1872 the Dean of Salisbury, in reply to the archbishop's questions, sent a copy of the sixteenth-century preaching roll which provided for one sermon on all Sundays and holy days. He added that the canon-in-residence was responsible for the other sermon. The preachers at the special services on Wednesdays and Fridays in Lent were appointed by the bishop with the dean's assent.[181] New provisions were made at Chichester in 1877,[182] while at Gloucester in 1900 a strict rule was agreed by which no canon could devolve his preaching turn on to a clergyman who was not on the foundation without the sanction of the dean. All invitations to visiting preachers were to be issued either by the dean or by the subdean.[183]

The value of the rota of preaching turns in a cathedral was that (theoretically, at least) it enabled each member of the chapter to preach there. The disadvantage of it was that it restricted the number of occasions when those who lived under the shadow of the cathedral could actually preach in it. At Chichester, both Dean Hook and Dean Burgon had fretted that they had no more than three preaching turns a year. If Dean Pigou was not due to preach in Chichester Cathedral on a particular Sunday, he offered to do so in a parish church in the diocese. Pigou invited the bishop to preach on the afternoon of Easter Day as he had no fixed preaching turn.[184] Although the statutes at Ripon Cathedral restricted the dean to preaching only a few times each year, Dean Fremantle followed the example of his two predecessors in preaching every Sunday evening.[185] At Canterbury, Dean Alford found his opportunities to preach very limited and established a Sunday afternoon sermon so that he could preach more often.[186] Hook did the same at Chichester.[187] But Sunday afternoon sermons were not a novelty elsewhere. Jebb recorded in 1843 that they were the custom at Rochester and St Paul's, and at Exeter Cathedral they had continued ever since the Reformation.[188] At Bristol the dean and chapter sold some land in 1818 to enable a new gaol to be built in the city, and used the interest on the money obtained thereby to pay the minor canons to preach on Sunday afternoons.[189] Their responsibility for these sermons was confirmed in 1849.[190] A. C. Tait introduced Sunday afternoon sermons (preached by himself) at Carlisle in 1850.[191] Two years later he wrote in his journal:

> These afternoon sermons are a great interest to me. The people are very attentive. In the morning there seems always to be a deadness. How far does this arise from my so often preaching old sermons in the morning?[192]

Sunday afternoon sermons in Lent were introduced at Gloucester in 1866,[193] and were established at Lincoln by 1869.[194] At Salisbury they were introduced in Dean Pearson's time during the summer months. Previous to this there was only one sermon each Sunday, except on Easter Day and Assize Sunday.[195] It was ordered at Chichester in 1884 that the Sunday afternoon sermon should follow immediately after the third collect, but five years later it was transferred to the end of evensong.[196]

Sermons were also preached on some weekdays in the latter part of the century, though as early as 1835 it was the practice at Hereford to have sermons on all saints' days, state days and every Tuesday throughout the year, as well as on Easter Monday, Whitmonday and every Friday in Lent.[197] Ash Wednesday was marked with a sermon at Chichester in 1866,[198] while at Wells a daily sermon was usual during Passion Week, though it was omitted in 1868.[199] Daily sermons in Holy Week, as well as one each week during the rest of Lent, were begun in Worcester in 1873.[200] Sermons on saints' days were introduced at Wells in 1876[201] and at Chichester in 1878.[202] They were introduced at Worcester on a limited number of days in 1893,[203] and in 1900 a sermon was given there on All Saints' Day at a eucharist.[204] Dean Butler introduced short addresses on saints' days at Lincoln, but these were given in the retro-choir after evensong had finished.[205] There were sermons at the service on Thursday afternoons at Exeter during Advent 1881, while during Lent 1884 a short address was given at noon in the Lady Chapel.[206] At Norwich, however, Dean Goulburn's plan to introduce a series of apologetic sermons broke down through lack of support, though he was remembered for the development of preaching at the cathedral.[207]

Despite the increase in the number of sermons towards the end of the century, it was still the Sunday morning sermon that was held to be of the greatest importance. Before 1852 at Ely only one sermon was preached to the inhabitants of the cathedral precincts and the parishioners of St Mary and Holy Trinity. They assembled and sat on seats in the Octagon, but beforehand there was much 'gossipping perambulation' in the nave.[208] At

Chichester the sermon on Sunday mornings was transferred to a new position following the litany in 1885, but reverted to its proper place during the eucharist in 1889.[209] The sermon on Sunday mornings at Worcester was transferred from the quire to the nave in 1885.[210]

A new scheme of sermons for the year was drawn up at Worcester in 1874 to enable the honorary canons to preach there regularly.[211] At Exeter in 1881 the dean and chapter agreed to a suggestion from Bishop Temple that eminent preachers be invited to preach a course of sermons during the summer months.[212] The planned preaching at St Paul's in 1883 provided for sermons on Sunday mornings and afternoons and on saints' days, and at other ordinary services during Lent. These were generally preached by members of the cathedral staff or other eminent men, with the canon-in-residence always preaching on Sunday afternoons. The sermons on Sunday evenings during Lent were intended to be of a more missionary character.[213] Publicity was obviously a key factor at this time. At Worcester the dean and chapter ordered in 1884 that details of the forthcoming preachers should be circulated to local newspapers.[214]

What was the effect of all those sermons? Were they appreciated? Did they help those who heard them to come to a deeper understanding of the Christian faith? Tait said in 1853 that cathedral sermons were generally considered dull.[215] Twenty years later the picture was changing. Dean Lake said in 1872 that it was vigorous preaching that had 'done most to endear our Cathedrals to the people and to give them real power'.[216] The most famous cathedral preacher, of course, was H. P. Liddon at St Paul's. Sermons of an hour or more were common custom at St Paul's, but Liddon's magnetism held his congregation spell-bound.[217] Such large crowds came to hear him preach during his first month of residence in May 1870 that the sermons were transferred from the quire to the dome. The doors of the cathedral were opened an extra fifteen minutes earlier when Liddon was preaching, and the congregation would fill the quire, dome and both transepts (the nave was free of chairs) and some had to stand.[218] Liddon was certainly a popular preacher, but his gifts were also appreciated by some of his eminent contemporaries. E. W. Benson described his style as 'very beautiful and very eloquent',[219] while William Bright noted 'his power of *vitalising* Scripture events'.[220] Henry Scott Holland spoke of 'the piercing tones of that most beautiful of all voices'[221] and described how 'that voice rang on, like a trumpet, telling of righteousness and temperance and judgment, preaching ever and always, with personal passion of belief, Jesus Christ and Him crucified'.[222]

Worcester was another cathedral where distinguished preaching could be heard, mainly from Mandell Creighton and Knox Little. An 'immense' crowd turned up to hear Creighton's first sermon in September 1885. Knox Little was the most popular preacher on the chapter, but the congregations were always large, 'and it was said that even the factory girls had their favourite preacher among the canons'.[223] One of the lay clerks, John Randall, described Creighton's sermons as 'fluent, learned and charming'; he admired Knox Little's 'great oratorical efforts' and noted that Canon Melville's sermons were 'adorned with elaborate sentences', while he felt that Dean Gott's sermons were 'more searching and delivered with intense earnestness, which arrested your attention and made you think'.[224] Knox Little was popular among nonconformists[225] and women. James Smith, another lay clerk, recalled:

> I suppose the Cathedral was never so crowded, before or since, as when Canon Knox Little preached. He was much given to the signing of the cross, even holding his stole cross'd on his chest when preaching. He used to gesticulate much and shout a word at the top of his voice in a startling manner.[226]

Other notable cathedral preachers included A. P. Stanley, when he was a Canon of Canterbury,[227] Dean Lake of Durham,[228] B. F. Westcott at Peterborough,[229] and E. W. Benson at Lincoln.[230] But Canon Wray of Manchester used to preach the same sermons over and over again,[231] while at Hereford the chapter often fell asleep during sermons.[232] In 1891 the *Guardian* said that cathedral sermons were often below standard.[233] In 1897 the *Chichester Observer* attacked the dean and chapter for reducing the amount of choral music at the services, and complained about Dean Randall's long sermons.[234] The great era of preaching in Victorian cathedrals was beginning to wane.

The celebration of the holy communion was probably the service that changed more than any other during the nineteenth century. As we have already seen,[235] celebrations in the early nineteenth century were infrequent. At Chichester in 1832 there was a celebration on the first Sunday of the month and on great festivals.[236] There was a similar custom at Wells.[237] In 1852 the Cathedrals Commission found that a monthly communion was the rule at Wells, Carlisle, Chester, Ely, Gloucester, Bristol, Hereford, Lincoln, Norwich, Peterborough and Manchester.[238] In Dean Liddell's time at Christ Church a monthly celebration was still the rule.[239] B. J. Armstrong attended a meeting of the English Church Union in Norwich in April 1865, where a petition was drawn up asking Dean Pellew 'to restore the weekly communion in the Cathedral Church, it having degenerated into a monthly one'.[240] The weekly communion at Norwich was in fact discontinued in 1827, but, as at Worcester, there were often Sundays in the early years of the century when there was no celebration for lack of communicants.[241] The weekly celebration at York was reduced to a monthly one in 1824, but restored by Archbishop Vernon Harcourt's injunctions in 1841.[242] Jebb noted in 1843 that there was a weekly celebration at Durham, and that this had recently been restored at Canterbury as well as York.[243] In 1849 the *Guardian* said that there were weekly celebrations at Canterbury, York, Exeter, Winchester, Chichester, Durham, Salisbury, St Paul's, Lichfield, Worcester and Manchester, and added that this was 'an indication of greater religious earnestness in the Cathedrals generally'.[244] A weekly celebration was begun at Christ Church, Oxford, in 1865[245] and at Hereford the following year as a result of pressure from Jebb and Ouseley.[246] The dean and chapter of Bristol refused to introduce a weekly communion, despite a request from Bishop Ellicott.[247]

Celebrations on saints' days were introduced in a number of cathedrals in the closing decades of the century. The celebration on Ascension Day in 1865 was said to be the first on that day at Norwich since 1688 and the large attendance astonished the chapter.[248] Unsuccessful attempts to introduce such a service were made by Jebb at Hereford in 1868[249] and 1869 and Ouseley in 1870.[250]. At Peterborough, however, an early celebration on saints' days was introduced in 1869.[251] Celebrations on saints' days began at St Paul's in 1871[252] and Worcester in 1879.[253] Communion services on ordinary festivals were celebrated in the Lady Chapel at Salisbury in 1880, except during the winter,[254] and most red letter days were marked by such a service at Wells in 1882.[255] Holy communion was celebrated with considerable dignity in St Luke's Chapel at Norwich on St Barnabas' day in 1887. Two of the canons acted as gospeller and epistoler, but there were only six communicants. Even ante-communion services were performed by three clergy.[256] A second celebration on saints' days was introduced at Chichester in 1889.[257] At Winchester, however, such a service was not introduced until 1895.[258] A daily eucharist was begun at St Paul's in January 1877,[259] and Canon Gregory said that it was particularly valued by travellers and others with urgent spiritual needs.[260] The quire and transepts of the new cathedral at Truro were consecrated in November 1887 and a daily celebration was started immediately.[261] It provided a useful opportunity for intercession on behalf of individuals and parishes in the diocese.[262] Dean Randall initiated a daily eucharist at Chichester as soon as he arrived there in 1894, despite opposition from Bishop Durnford.[263] The *Guardian* noted in 1897 that a daily celebration had been started at Lichfield in Advent 1896, and this was the custom at St Paul's, Worcester and Truro.[264] But Salisbury did not have a daily celebration until 1915.[265]

As the influence of the Oxford Movement developed, an increasing emphasis was placed on the value of early morning celebrations. Salisbury Cathedral began to have a eucharist at 8 a.m. every Sunday morning in 1849.[266] A eucharist once a month at 8.30 a.m. was instituted at York in 1868; this was extended to every Sunday in 1873.[267] Early celebrations were introduced at Bristol in 1869.[268] By 1872, Walcott found that there were also early celebrations from time to time at Chichester, Chester, Peterborough, Durham, St Paul's, Lichfield, Hereford, Norwich, Gloucester and Canterbury. On Easter Day 1852, he said there had been celebrations at 5 a.m. and 7 a.m. at Ripon.[269] At the early eucharist for lay helpers at St Paul's in June 1872 there were 320 communicants.[270] An early eucharist (8.15 a.m.) at Canterbury on Christmas Day 1872 was said to be the first 'since the Reformation'.[271] Early celebrations were begun at Winchester and Norwich in 1874,[272] and at Worcester in the summer of 1875.[273] The frequency of early celebrations at Worcester was gradually increased until June 1893, when a daily celebration throughout the year was achieved.[274]

When W. J. Butler left Worcester to become Dean of Lincoln, he instituted an early celebration there on Sundays and Thursdays; the latter service, celebrated by a rota of prebendaries and priest vicars, was held at the Lady Chapel altar and Butler was usually present.[275] The dean or canon-in-residence were responsible for the early services at Wells in 1887, though they could delegate the celebration to another member of the foundation.[276] An early celebration on Thursdays was begun at Salisbury in 1887[277] and at Chichester in 1889.[278] Dean Pigou made an unsuccessful attempt to enlist the support of the priest vicars at this service. A. H. Glennie, the principal, told him that they were unwilling to help as some canons had brusquely displaced them in order to maintain the 'north end' position.[279] Early celebrations were also introduced at Peterborough in 1893 and St Albans in 1894.[280]

Earlier in the century, in the 1840s, a slack attitude on the part of the minor canons of St Paul's had led to a neglect of the eucharist.[281] As a young man, Archbishop Frederick Temple attended St Paul's on a Sunday morning, intending to remain for communion, but a verger came to him and said, 'I hope, sir, you are not intending to remain for the sacrament, as that will give the Minor Canon the trouble of celebrating, which otherwise he will not do.' Thus Temple left the cathedral.[282] Liddon claimed the credit for stopping the vergers from turning non-communicants out of the cathedral, following an incident when a couple of undergraduates were prevented from seeing a friend ordained.[283] Jebb says that the rule of St Paul's was for three senior members of the foundation present to officiate, but at Canterbury two of the prebendaries (canons) were thought a sufficient number.[284] At Wells it was decided in 1861 that a priest vicar must always allow a dignitary or prebendary of the cathedral to take precedence over him in the administration of communion.[285] When B. J. Armstrong visited Norwich Cathedral for the bishop's visitation in 1865, he noted the 'many ritual incongruities which accompanied the celebration'.[286] When Dean Lake arrived at Durham, he soon remedied the impression that the Eucharist was an 'extral spiritual luxury'.[287] A correspondent in the *Guardian* noted that at choral eucharists at Lincoln in 1869, 'the offertory is collected from the congregation by the lay clerks in their surplices'. The bread and wine were brought to the celebrant by a minor canon. After the communion, the assistant clergy consumed the elements and a lay clerk removed the vessels. Sometimes his daughter helped him to do this, though the chapter disapproved.[288] At Chichester in 1892 it was decided to have vestry prayers before and after each choral eucharist. The celebrant carried into the service the vessels at early celebrations, but when the bishop was the celebrant they were carried by someone else. Further provisions included the use of the mixed chalice (mixed at the altar except when the bishop celebrated, when it was mixed at the credence) and the ablutions were taken at the altar, except when the bishop celebrated, when they were taken in the vestry.[289] One of the canons, F. J. Mount, was unhappy at certain current practices at Chichester and protested about 'the saying of the collects in the early portion of the communion service at the south side of the altar; the reading of the Gospel facing eastward; the introduction of the use of the wafer; [and] the pronouncing of the first portion of the final blessing facing eastward'.[290] Prebendary F. G. Bennett also sent a formal protest to the dean and chapter, objecting to a weekly celebration, non-members of the foundation celebrating, the publication of banns of marriage and notices from the pulpit, the singing of a hymn during the offertory, the use of the mixed chalice, the omission of the long exhortation and the intoning of the preface, Lord's Prayer and blessing.[291]

The responsibility for drawing up a list of celebrants each week at Worcester was given to the sacrist, after consultation with the canon-in-residence.[292] In 1896 a dispute arose between Precentor Woodward and the sacrist, W. G. Melville, about the early celebration on Sundays.[293] The dean and chapter also ordered that

> there is no need for more than one minor canon to be present in the sacrarium when members of the Chapter occupy the kneeling-places for Gospeller and Epistler [sic] – the minor canon can then have a small kneeling stool placed for him at the south side (as has often been done). If only one member of the Chapter and three minor canons are present, the former will naturally be celebrant and the three main minor canons can occupy the places of Gospeller and Epistler and one kneeling stool as mentioned above. It will be the duty of the sacrist to inform the Custos when the extra kneeling stool is required.[294]

In the early decades of the century, of course, the celebrant at the eucharist always occupied the north end of the altar. This was certainly still the case at Winchester in 1850, where a strict order of seniority in celebrating was observed.[295] Armstrong noted that the eastward position (as well as coloured altar frontals) was the rule at York in 1880.[296] A few years earlier, Gregory and Liddon had made a stand about using the eastward position at St Paul's, despite the recent judgement of the Privy Council and the disapproval of Bishop Jackson.[297] Dean Pigou adopted the eastward position at Chichester.[298] It was said in 1886 that, apart from

Archdeacon Kaye, all members of the chapter at Lincoln used the eastward position.[299] When J. M. Elvy was first appointed to the staff at Manchester Cathedral he was nearly dismissed for adopting the eastward position, but he lived long enough to see it become the universal custom there.[300]

Altars in the nineteenth century were often covered with a velvet frontal, usually a red one. Instructions were given for the altar at Gloucester to be so covered in 1808 and a 'new velvet' was bought at Bristol in 1828.[301] At Worcester Cathedral in the mid-1850s the altar table stood in front of a perpendicular stone screen. The top of the table was covered by 'a mean red cloth with fringe' and in the centre there was a small stand on which was kept a prayer book bound in crimson velvet with gold plates. Never used, this book was said to have been given to the cathedral by Charles II. Formerly there were two silver gilt candlesticks, but they had long since disappeared.[302] At York in 1867 there were violet, green and crimson frontals.[303] A new communion table was commissioned at Exeter in 1872. This had to be 'of sufficient breadth for the present usage of the Cathedral with two officiating ministers at the south end'.[304] The sacrist's reports at Worcester in the last decade of the century indicate the careful provision of frontals and matching furnishings for the altars there.[305] A violet cloth was given to Peterborough for the altar in 1891.[306] Yet some archaic survivals persisted. At Christ Church, Oxford, the sacrament was taken to communicants where they sat, even in the early years of the present century.[307] At Exeter it was ordered in 1885 that communicants must come up to the altar rails, though the sick and infirm were allowed to receive communion in their places.[308]

When the new cathedral at Truro was opened the ceremonial was noted for its dignity, stateliness, simplicity and reverence. The pattern established at St Paul's was followed closely. From Easter Day 1890 there were two lights at the early celebration (later extended to all celebrations); coloured stoles were worn, the ablutions were taken at the altar, and the Agnus Dei was sung during the communion.[309]

The distinctive cathedral vestment was the cope, as provided for in the canons of 1603. But it was rarely used in the early nineteenth century. When John Carter visited Durham in 1795 he saw some copes that had been used at communion services less than twenty years previously.[310] They may even have been worn as late as 1804.[311] Walcott said in 1872 that copes were preserved at Salisbury, Carlisle, Ely and Westminster,[312] and their use had recently been revived by the Bishops of London, Ripon and Lincoln and the Dean of Ripon. Bishop Bickersteth and Dean McNeile certainly appeared in purple copes one Christmas Day at Ripon.[313] The Purchas Judgement of the Privy Council, which had banned the eastward position of the celebrant, also indicated that he should wear a cope. At St Paul's, Liddon and Gregory said that if the cathedral supplied one for the bishop to use at the ordination on Trinity Sunday, they would be recognizing this Judgement. So Bishop Jackson brought his own violet cope, which was the first time anyone could remember seeing one there.[314] The dean and chapter of Winchester, however, having found out that most cathedrals were not intending to obtain or use copes, also decided not to do so.[315] Bishop Christopher Wordsworth was using a cope for ordinations by 1882.[316] A. C. Benson said that: 'The sight of him going up Lincoln Cathedral in procession in his stiff red velvet cope...seemed to me in those years to sum up in one supreme symbol all that was majestic and pontifical.'[317] Bishop Mandell Creighton wore a cope and mitre for the reopening service at Peterborough Cathedral in 1892.[318] It was not until 1898 that copes were worn regularly (but only on major festivals) at St Paul's or coloured stoles allowed at early celebrations there.[319] Sir Gilbert Lewis, a canon of Worcester, supposed that if he had to wear a cope he would have to wear a surplice over it.[320] Dean Cowie wore an alb and coloured stole at Manchester,[321] but there is no evidence for full eucharistic vestments being worn at any cathedral in the nineteenth century. Dean Goulburn said that he had no intention of wearing a chasuble and alb and regretted the disappearance of preaching gowns.[322]

The heart of cathedral worship, though, then as now, was the daily recitation of matins and evensong by the cathedral choir. Throughout the nineteenth century both matins and evensong were usually sung each day in the middle of the morning and the middle of the afternoon. At Chichester in 1822, for example, it was ordered that morning prayer should be sung at 10 a.m. and evening prayer at 4 p.m., except during November, December and January, when it was moved to 3 p.m.[323] The daily services were rearranged at Exeter during the restoration of the cathedral, with matins being said at 8 a.m. instead of the usual sung matins, and a single choral service each day at noon.[324] When Worcester Cathedral reopened in 1874 after its long restoration, the times of the daily services were fixed at 10.15 a.m. and 4.15 p.m.[325]

The daily cathedral services had both their champions and their critics. Both R. S. Hawker of Morwenstow and Dean Stanley valued their opportunities for intercession and continuous worship.[326] Henry Scott Holland described the policy of the St Paul's chapter under Dean Church, stressing the value both of the daily services and also the eucharist:

It was essential that the worship carried on in the central church of London should be continuous as the life which it was needed to sanctify....And, secondly, the worship must not only have the mark of continuity, but also that of dignity and grace....And, above all, the central Eucharistic Act of the Church's Communion with God must occupy the house which was built to enshrine it....Again this worship, continuous and honourable, must be also on a large scale...its music must be full-voiced, powerful, abundant; it should reach to all parts of the building; it must be capable of drawing multitudes under its spell.[327]

At the beginning of Queen Victoria's reign the standards of the daily choral services were often irreverent, incompetent and slovenly. By contrast, J. C. Cox, writing at the end of the century, emphasized the 'most happy and wonderful contrast in 1897 to what was customary in 1837'.[328] The cathedral commissioners, in their third report, displayed an ambivalent attitude towards the daily services in cathedrals. On the one hand, they praised their 'increasing solemnity' and said:

> We believe that a love for sacred music is on the increase in our larger communities....As the Cathedral Churches are the most appropriate places for the celebration of musical service, we recommend that the Cathedral choirs be maintained in full strength, and if possible, increased in power, especially on the Lord's Day.

But they also complained that

> the music of the choral service is often too elaborate and intricate for an ordinary congregation; and that this is one of the causes which have tended to diminish the Cathedral congregations. While the anthems may properly be such as require skill in music for their due performance, the ordinary chants and services ought, in our judgment, to be of a simpler character, in order that the people may be encouraged to take part in them.[329]

In 1900, in his reply to Bishop Davidson's visitation of Winchester Cathedral, Canon Warburton said that he supposed the prime function of the cathedral was 'to carry on daily public worship in a solemn, dignified and in all respects exemplary form'. At Winchester the services were conducted with 'carefulness and brightness and reverence', though the congregations were very small.[330]

Congregational participation in daily cathedral services has always been a vexed question. In November 1890 the Precentor of Winchester noticed that some members of the choir were in the habit of handing copies of the music during the service to members of the congregation who were sitting behind them. This was a fairly simple matter to deal with, but another member of the congregation used to bring his own music to evensong on Sundays and join in with the choir. The precentor wrote to ask him to desist. As he took no notice, the precentor, after conferring with the dean, sent him a stronger letter and resolved the matter by asking the vergers to ensure that he was shown to a seat well away from the choir.[331] The same problem occurred at Salisbury a few years later, but there the chapter declined to endorse an open letter on the subject from the precentor to members of the cathedral congregation.

Instead the dean wrote to the local newspaper 'explaining that the choir were sometimes disturbed by loud singing in the stalls under the organ'.[332]

Exceptional circumstances sometimes led to the suspension or transferral of the daily services. When a new altar screen was being erected in Exeter in 1818, the quire was closed and the services were discontinued except on Sundays. They were not restarted until over a year later.[333] The services were suspended at Exeter for two days in 1865 'on account of the work on the warming stoves'.[334] The daily services at Peterborough were transferred to a parish church during restoration work in 1830.[335] Extensive repairs to Hereford Cathedral were begun in 1841 and the services were transferred first to College Hall and the College Chapel, and later to All Saints' Church.[336] Meanwhile at Worcester the daily services during the great restoration of the cathedral were held either in the Lady Chapel or at the west end of the nave, where an altar was placed in front of the west door. The congregation mainly faced west to recite the Creed, though some continued to turn east and others did not know which way to turn. One daily service was held at noon while the workmen were at their midday meal, so as to interfere with their work as little as possible.[337] In 1859 the daily services at St Paul's were held in Christ Church, Newgate Street, while major alterations were being carried out,[338] and at Chichester the fall of the spire in 1861 meant that the daily services had to be transferred to St Andrew's Church.[339] The chapter-house at Salisbury was used for some while in 1866 while the cathedral roofs were being releaded.[340] At Wells, however, in 1874 the daily services were read in the Lady Chapel while the cathedral was undergoing its annual cleaning.[341]

Towards the end of the century plain or said services became increasingly common, either on a weekly basis to give the choir a regular rest, or during official choir holidays. The *Parish Choir* noted a said service at Lincoln earlier in the century, but this was because the organ was being cleaned. The lay clerks and choristers were still present, but presumably were not able to sing unaccompanied.[342] At the new Cathedral of Ripon, choral services were only established gradually; in 1865 the services on Wednesdays and Fridays were plain.[343] Around 1870 the services at Canterbury were performed without music on Ash Wednesday and during Holy Week.[344] Wednesday was the plain day at Salisbury in 1883,[345] at Chichester in 1889,[346] and at York in 1891.[347] Lord Alwyne Compton, Bishop of Ely, resisted a plan in 1888 to have a weekly said evensong in his cathedral. The dean and chapter pointed out that no diocesan bishop had tried to prevent this elsewhere.[348] The dean and chapter of Worcester decided to give the choir a week's holiday and had said services during the week following the Three Choirs Festival in 1887.[349] Three years later, during the choristers' holidays, the morning services at Worcester were maintained by the lay clerks while voluntary choristers sang at evensong. The precentor said that the holidays had been welcomed both by the boys and their parents.[350] Weekly services for men's voices only (which enabled the choristers to have a regular day off) were established at Lichfield in 1887 and at Ely in the following year.[351] The lay clerks at Salisbury were given a regular free afternoon in 1877 and those at Ely in 1887.[352] In 1899 choral services at Wells were suspended for the first half of August in order to allow the choristers to have a proper holiday.[353]

Of all the services said or sung in cathedrals, the daily choral services of matins and evensong have probably altered less than any others since the nineteenth century. One important difference is that the penitential intro- duction was intoned, the choir joining in the general confession and the Lord's Prayer. Harmonized confessions were used at York, Ely and St Paul's, and a harmonized version of the general thanksgiving was in use at York by about 1900.[354] The versicles and responses were usually sung to fairly simple music, which included local variations of the ferial responses; more elaborate settings by Tudor and later composers were not used. The psalms were sung to Anglican chants, though pointed psalters appeared only half-way through the century. The canticles and anthem, then as now, provided the main musical part of the worship, and the prayers after the anthem rarely varied from the state prayers provided in the Prayer Book.[355] There is some evidence of anthems having been dropped from the daily services early in the century. Walcott records that there was no anthem at York on Sunday afternoons in Lent;[356] there are various chapter acts in different cathedrals ordering the introduction of an anthem.[357]

This general picture may be substantiated by some relevant detailed information. At Rochester in 1790 the prayers were read, not intoned.[358] In 1807 a minor canon of Worcester by the name of Shapland objected strongly to intoning or 'chaunting' and refused to do it. In his reply the chapter clerk said that the chapter would allow him to employ a substitute, provided he still attended the services himself.[359] In the follow- ing year the dean and subdean of Gloucester caused the services to be chanted on weekdays as well as Sundays and were pleased to receive support from Bishop Huntingford.[360] In 1825 the dean and chapter of Worcester ordered that evening services as well as morning services should be 'chaunted according to the ancient custom of the Cathedral'.[361] In 1838, however, Bishop George Murray, the Dean of Worcester, ordered: 'That for the future the service in the Cathedral shall be read by the priest and the responses chanted by the choir accompanied with the organ.'[362] The intoning of prayers was abandoned at Peterborough in 1830, while the daily services were transferred to a neighbouring church during restora- tion work at the cathedral.[363] A visitor to Durham in 1840 noted that he heard there 'masterly chanting, perhaps unrivalled in the empire',[364] and Thomas Evans, remembered as a savage headmaster of the King's School, Gloucester, between 1841 and 1850, was nevertheless a good intoner: it was said that his words were audible even at the west door while he was intoning in the quire.[365] Jebb noted in 1843 that intoning had been abandoned at Chester, Ely and Christ Church, Oxford, though it had recently been revived at Rochester.[366] At Salisbury and Wells the prayers were sometimes chanted and sometimes read.[367] Jebb was firmly in favour of intoning and spoke enthusiastically of the prevalence of similar customs among South Sea Islanders and North American Indians! He noted that at Durham and Bristol the confession would be sung a semi-tone below the pitch of the rest of the introduction.[368] A higher note was preferred at Winchester and Exeter, but there was no change of pitch at St Paul's and Canterbury. At Winchester and Canterbury the Lord's Prayer was sung a minor third higher than the rest of the introduction, while at Gloucester the cadence at the end of the confession was sung in harmony.[369] The canons sometimes intoned the prayers at Winchester and Dean Garnier imparted much 'life and energy' to the service when he intoned.[370]

In December 1848 the dean and chapter of Bristol created a public scandal when they ordered that the intoning of prayers and versicles should cease. At least one of the minor canons, Eccles Carter, continued to intone the services, and a petition, headed by the Mayor of Bristol, was sent to the dean and chapter, protesting against the alteration. Carter and the other minor canons appealed to Bishop Monk. This had the effect of dividing the chapter, who, on 13 February 1849, rescinded the act of 5 December 1848 which had abolished intoning. Dean Lamb continued to object to it and issued an order on his own authority forbidding the intoning of services in the cathedral. Bishop Monk's judgement upheld the case of the minor canons, annulled the private orders of the dean forbidding intoning, and required the dean and chapter

> to uphold and maintain the celebrations of the Choral Services in the Cathedral Church, according to the usage and practice observed in the said Cathedral Church antecedently to the order made by the Dean and Chapter on the 5th day of December 1848.

Any further proposed changes in the service needed to be submitted to him for confirmation.[371] The *Guardian* commented: 'Never was any would-be innovator more summarily bowled out than has been the Very Revd. The Dean of Bristol. And never, we will add, was such summary extinction more justly provoked and merited.'[372]

Intoning at Durham was in abeyance on Sundays about this time,[373] and at Peterborough also the minor canons were not required to chant.[374] The *Guardian* reported in 1858 that two priest vicars had recently been appointed at Wells without any kind of musical test. Some members of the chapter there were said to want to discontinue intoning the service.[375] In September of the same year the dean and chapter of Wells ordered that the daily services should be intoned 'when practicable'.[376] A corres-pondent in the *Guardian* lamented in 1859 that 'even in the best cathedral choirs the Amens and Suffrages are often shamefully given, whilst they are really the finest parts of the service'.[377] At Christ Church, Oxford, the state prayers were intoned, with the versicle and response for the sovereign being repeated.[378] That there was still some dislike of intoning at Bristol may be seen in 1869, when it was ordered that no intoning should take place, either in the communion service or in the pulpit.[379] When Dean Alford intoned the prayers at Canterbury, his beautiful voice added considerably to the tone of the service.[380] Dean Goulburn was keen to intone the prayers at Norwich and had lessons from Dr Buck, the organist, but his first attempts were not very successful. On 30 March 1867 he wrote in his diary: 'Began monotoning in the Church both morning and afternoon, with the help of the harmonium – in the afternoon quite failed.' Three weeks later on Easter Day he wrote: 'Dr Buck came in and gave me a little trial at singing before the 9 o'clock service – on both occasions I got on *tolerably* well, wavering once or twice, but not at all to my own satisfaction.'[381]

A little earlier at both Ely and Peterborough the right of the members of the chapter to officiate at the daily services was stressed.[382] The dean and canons of Winchester were finally persuaded to give up this 'unedifying' custom in 1897.[383] The dean and chapter of Chichester issued careful regulations in 1891 about which parts of the services were to be sung on a monotone and on the use of Stainer's Amen.[384] Two years previously the chanting of the service at Chichester was described as 'perfunctory to the last degree and characterised by an entire absence of distinct articulation'.[385] By the end of the century there was little opposition to the custom of intoning, providing that it was undertaken by a competent minor canon.

Another part of the weekly round of services that had to be intoned was, of course, the litany. This was normally sung every Wednesday, Friday and Sunday. In 1838 the Dean of Worcester, Bishop George Murray, ordered: 'That on Wednesdays and Fridays the Litany shall be chanted by the priest in a plain chant, and the Responses made by the Choir without the organ.' The Windsor Litany was always to be used on Sundays at 11.15 a.m.[386] Two minor canons were responsible for singing the litany at St Paul's, but at Lincoln two lay vicars performed this role. At Lichfield and Exeter a compromise was in force so that the duty was shared by a priest vicar and a lay vicar.[387] Jebb noted that at Lincoln the litany received an 'irreverent mode of performance' and was 'often sung with a coarseness and want of feeling which totally impairs the effect of the service'.[388] The usual place for the litany to be chanted was from a low desk in the centre of the quire, as at Lincoln, Lichfield, St Paul's, Exeter, Canterbury, York and Christ Church, Oxford.[389] The litany was read, not sung, at York, while at Lichfield the organ accompanied the responses of the choir.[390] A. C. Benson described the Lincoln litany:

147

The two tenor lay clerks left their places and went to a double desk in the centre of the choir; on the floor at that place was a long grey marble slab, with circular ends, on which in old Byzantine capitals was inscribed *Cantate Hic* – it was, I suppose, the place where the mediaeval singing-lectern stood – and the two together sang the litany in unison, down to the Lord's Prayer, when the service was taken up by a minor canon. The setting was Tallis' Festal Litany and I shall never forget the beauty of the *Agnus Dei* with its severe chords of full harmony. The Litany was sung with the same precise deliberation and delicacy as the Psalms and was really a beautiful event in the service.[391]

At Worcester the custom in the 1860s was for the litany to be sung from the minor canons' stalls and not from a central desk. James Smith, a lay clerk, recalled how it was sung there:

Minor Canon Saunders was the picture of the old-fashioned country parson, had an excellent voice and used to sing the Litany very deliberately and well – only he sometimes went so nearly to sleep over it, as to apparently just wake up in time to go on again after we had sung the response.[392]

Dean Goulburn attempted to sing the litany at Norwich in 1867 with unsuccessful consequences: 'I tried the litany at morning service, but was very nervous, in consequence of the organist's omitting to give me the note, as I had asked him to do, and introduced a false note into two of the suffrages.'[393] In December 1868 he broke down while singing the litany.[394] At St Paul's the litany continued to be sung on Christmas Day 1878 when this fell on a Wednesday.[395] The repetition of the litany in the special evening services on Wednesdays and Fridays in Lent at Salisbury led to a reduction in its use on the morning of those days in 1880,[396] while at Hereford the litany was transferred to the afternoon on greater festivals.[397] A new place for singing the litany was found to be necessary in 1889 at Chichester, partly because the faldstool was too far away from the choir, and partly because the voices of the congregation in the responses distracted the officiating priest vicar.[398]

When a new lectionary was authorized in 1871, several cathedrals were quick to use it for their daily services. At Bristol, Chichester, Exeter, Wells and Worcester this change excited little controversy, but at Hereford Canon Jebb objected to its 'revolutionary nature'.[399] In 1843 he criticized canons who read the lessons badly 'by their colloquial tone of voice and rapid articulation' and 'by their position, lolling on their desk, leaning on their elbow, and etc.'.[400] At Lichfield on weekdays the first lesson was read by a lay clerk,[401] while at Winchester a minor canon read the first lesson and a member of the chapter read the second lesson.[402] There was no indication by way of announcement at Canterbury when the end of a lesson was reached.[403] In 1866 the dean and chapter of Gloucester ordered the minor canons to read the lessons from the eagle lectern.[404] In 1873 they were asked to read both lessons at the early morning service.[405] In 1870 it was decided at Wells that a prebendary should read the lessons rather than a priest vicar, if no canon were present.[406] At Hereford, if only one canon or prebendary were present, he was permitted to ask one of the minor canons to read the first lesson.[407] The *Guardian* reported a new regulation at St Paul's in 1898 by which the dean and canons were to read the lessons on major festivals in place of the minor canons.[408]

The chants for the psalms were mainly composed in the late eighteenth and nineteenth centuries. At Exeter in 1830 four copies of Bennett's and Marshall's collection of chants were purchased to increase the repertoire.[409] John Goss published in 1841 a collection of the chants used at St Paul's; other influential collections were published by T. A. Walmisley in 1845 and by Edward Rimbault in 1844.[410] Until pointed psalters were introduced, each lay clerk and chorister made his own attempt to marry the words and the music by employing the 'rule of three and five' (changing notes on the third or fifth syllable from the end of each half-verse). Jebb felt that this encouraged devotional freedom and elasticity and avoided a dull, mechanical performance of the psalms, though it tended to encourage a hurried recitation of the words. The first pointed psalter was produced by Robert Janes, organist of Ely Cathedral, in 1837. An agreed systematic way of pointing the psalms did not appear until the publication of the Cathedral Psalter in 1875.[411] The *Parish Choir* noted that at Durham in the 1840s chants by such composers as Robinson, Hewley, Longdon, Dupuis and Lord Mornington were sung.[412] The custom of singing a metrical psalm after the sermon survived until 1843 at Ely.[413] Gregorian tones for the psalms were rarely sung, though during Harvey Goodwin's time at Ely they were used on Wednesdays and Fridays, with Anglican chants being sung on the other days of the week.[414] H. W. Pullen said that at Salisbury in 1869 the psalms were 'pointed with such a total disregard of emphasis and gabbled in such reckless confusion, that they might as well have been sung in Hebrew'.[415] E. Vine Hall, the Precentor of Worcester, admired the *Cathedral Psalter*: 'The introduction of the Cathedral Psalter has worked very well. The Book is really well done, and I think that in time our chanting will greatly improve.'[416]

Towards the end of the century, an organ play-over of the whole chant, followed by the whole choir singing the first verse of the psalm in harmony, replaced the older practice of 'precenting', in which the bass line of the first quarter of the chant was sung in unison for the first half of the first verse, after it had been played on the organ. Speech rhythm was also introduced as a more effective way of conveying the flow of the words.[417] Sir John Sutton had earlier attacked the way in which the psalms were accompanied in cathedral services in the 1840s:

...attention is continually drawn from the voices by the perpetual changing of stops and clattering of composition pedals, for the modern Cathedral organist scarcely ever accompanies six verses on the same stops, or even the same row of keys, and keeps up a perpetual thundering with the pedals throughout the psalms.[418]

For much of the century cathedral choirs used large part-books (often kept in the choir-stalls), either hand written or printed. These contained canticles and anthems in the repertoire; where they were in score, alto and tenor clefs were used for these parts. In 1771 at Worcester Cathedral there were nine volumes of services and anthems for the trebles, seven for the 'contra-tenors' and for the tenors, and nine for the basses. There were also printed collections of music by William Boyce, Maurice Greene and other composers.[419] A list of the music books at Bristol in 1800 reveals that there were sixty-seven volumes altogether, including ten manuscript volumes of services and anthems in score, and printed collections of music by Croft, Greene, Boyce, Kent, Handel, Beckwith, Langdon and Nares. There were eight manuscript part-books for each voice.[420] These volumes were usually kept in the choir-stalls – this was certainly the case at St Paul's.[421] When new copies of unprinted music were required, they had to be copied out laboriously by hand. In 1836 the subchanter at Hereford was paid £5 6s at a rate of 6d per page for copying out 212 sheets of music.[422] No wonder the music books were guarded so jealously. In 1816 the dean and chapter of Worcester ordered that they were not to be 'taken out of the choir on any pretext whatever'.[423] Forty-five years later the lay clerks had to report each month on their state and whether they were in their proper places at the monthly roll call.[424] As late as 1865[425] these books were still in use. In the same year the dean and chapter ordered that 'no music be purchased or copied without the sanction of the Precentor', who had to put down the details in a special book and mark the music with the cathedral stamp. Not more than £10 could be spent on this each year,[426] but by 1889 up to £26 could be spent.[427] Forty-six additional anthems were printed and added to the books at Exeter in 1821[428] and a further supply of new music was purchased in 1848.[429] Several cathedrals bought copies of Wesley's volume of anthems when it was published in 1853, and they were sung very frequently at Rochester.[430] In the same way, copies (both in parts and score) of music edited by Ouseley were purchased at Chichester in 1858.[431] It was stressed at Exeter that new music must be ordered through the chapter.[432] Additional copies of music were purchased at Worcester in 1876[433] and at Wells in 1899, where there were so few copies that books were noisily passed around during the services.[434] At Bristol a considerable bulk of new music was purchased (mainly from Novellos) between 1823 and 1849.[435] At Ely, Dean Harvey Goodwin authorized the purchase of new printed volumes of music and carefully supervised the care of the music books. Five choristers were appointed book clerks and were responsible for carrying the books into the quire before services and putting them out.[436] One of the lay vicars at Chichester had arranged the music in the stalls, but because he had not done it properly the succentor was asked to arrange for one of the choristers to do it under his supervision.[437]

In the early nineteenth century the music to be sung was usually chosen during the actual service. At Salisbury, for example, at the end of the psalms

> the head boy left his place to inquire of the Dean, or in his absence of the Canon-in-Residence present, what Service and anthem he wished to be sung. Having got an answer he turned towards the boys who were waiting for the information and gave out in a loud whisper the name of the author and the key of the Service chosen; he then passed on under the gates round to and up the Staircase to the Organ loft, to acquaint the Organist, which done, he retraced his steps back to his seat. Sometimes, when the first lesson was a short one, or the Canon took a long time to make up his mind, an awkward pause would ensue, accompanied by a good deal of tumbling about of music books, turning over of leaves, anxious whisperings between Choristers and Singing-Men etc.; but in general all went off smoothly. Sometimes too, but not often, the Organist would play the wrong Anthem or Service, through having mistaken what the head boy had told him.[438]

But Salisbury was by no means the only cathedral where this custom could be found.[439] Although it was less frequent in Worcester by 1839,[440] in 1861 the dean and chapter ordered the choristers to stay in their places during the services,[441] thus robbing a chorister of the chance of returning from the organ-loft and saying to the precentor, 'The Lord hear thee blow, sir'.[442]

Other methods of choosing the music to be sung at services were also defective. At Durham Cathedral in the late 1840s the new dean's 'great taste for noisy and showy music' meant that 'adaptations from the semi-operatic music of Mozart, Haydn and etc.' were in vogue,[443] and about the same time Dean Peel of Worcester was also said to be 'too fond of trashy music'.[444] The *Guardian* sarcastically stated:

> A modern Precentor, deaf to music and ignorant of propriety, leaves these matters to the organist and he leaves the attendance of the singers to be regulated by their convenience and the choice of music by the young ladies who take lessons of him on the pianoforte. The too frequent results are meagre and lazy choirs, irrelevant anthems and trifling unimpressive music.[445]

S. S. Wesley agreed: 'Too much of the music now in use at cathedral worship is as bad, or worse, in its composition as it is in its mode of performance.'[446] It was 'chiefly the production of the organists of past times' and 'much of it excited but little interest now'.[447]

Although a late seventeenth century music list has survived at Durham, the earliest known nineteenth century list is preserved at Hereford Cathedral and dates from the year 1851.[448] It gives details of settings and anthems sung between Monday 11 August and Sunday 24 August. The litany replaced the anthem at matins on Wednesdays and Fridays, and the great bulk of the anthems are by composers of the seventeenth and eighteenth centuries, such as Purcell, Humphries, Croft, Blow, Greene, Nares, Hayes, Clarke, Kent, Tucker, Crotch and others. There are only three Tudor anthems. The services included the contemporary *Goss in E* evening service and some Tudor music (*Patrick in G*, *Gibbons (Short Service)* and *Batten in D)*, but once again the bulk of the music is by composers of the standing of Aldrich, Travers, King, Boyce and lesser-known men. A similar picture may be gained from the lists printed by Bernarr Rainbow.[449] Occasionally a novel piece was included, such as *Worthy is the Lamb* by Corelli at York, or *Jomelli in E flat* (Sanctus and Kyrie) at Peterborough, and most cathedrals had a liberal diet of choruses by Handel, Mozart, Haydn, Beethoven, Mendelssohn and Spohr in their daily repertoire. But a great deal of eighteenth century music was being sung at St Paul's in the 1830s[450] and in the 1880s at Worcester. The oldest surviving music scheme at Worcester (January 1890) still includes such favourites as *King in F*, *Arnold in A*, *Boyce in A* and Purcell's *Rejoice in the Lord*, as well as four Mendelssohn choruses.[451] But times were changing, and Goss, Smart, Stainer and S. S. Wesley are all represented, together with Stanford's newly published service in A major. The favourite composers at York in the last twenty years of the century were Mendelssohn, Handel, Ouseley, Goss, Attwood, Walmisley, Monk and S. S. Wesley, though Tudor music was increasingly sung by 1900.[452] Earlier, Mozart, Haydn and Beethoven were popular.[453] A fascinating volume in the temporary possession of the author lists all the music sung at Ely Cathedral between 1873 and 1885. This was evidently the precentor's note-book, from which he prepared the printed schemes or combination papers. Handel's Chandos Anthems were a feature of the repertoire at Ely.[454] Lists of anthems used at Worcester in the 1880s have survived,[455] but the details of new music sung, as given in the precentor's reports for 1884 and 1887–9, show that apart from home-grown pieces, new compositions were mainly well-tried favourites such as Mendelssohn's *Hear my prayer* rather than contemporary music. From the autumn of 1889 to the end of 1890, no less than 155 anthems and thirty-two services were added to the library (and, of these, fifty-one anthems and six services had been sung), not to mention replacement copies for worn-out music.[456] A catalogue of the choir library at St Paul's was compiled in 1884 by Henry King, one of the vicars choral. Some 230 composers were represented.[457] In Stainer's final year at

St Paul's (1887–8), twenty-six anthems from the seventeenth century were sung; 110 from the eighteenth century, and 365 from the nineteenth century. The favourite composers were Mendelssohn, Gounod, Bach, Handel and Spohr.[458]

At Winchester, the precentor was responsible for the choice of music and he generally managed to resist 'the very erroneous views of the Canons and Dean as occasionally expressed by them at the instigation of *Ladies* and idle people of *distinction*, who visit Cathedrals and ask for pretty, shewy things to be sung'. When S. S. Wesley arrived as organist, 'although the Precentor claimed, and had conceded to him an absolute power here, I found him desirous to consult me in every way. He urged me to always express my views to him and whatever I said was attended to.' But when the precentor was unable to attend cathedral services no difficulty was presented when Wesley took over 'his business in the Music Lists'.[459] However, the precentor's right to choose music was not absolute. A sensible man, like Sparrow Simpson, the succentor of St Paul's, would be in close touch with the organist (in his case, Sir John Stainer).[460] At Worcester the chapter supervised Precentor Vine Hall's schemes, as he was wont to choose seasonably unsuitable anthems.[461] At Chichester in 1893 the dean and chapter instructed the succentor and organist to practise the music of *Eyre in E flat* and to use it for the eucharist on Christmas Day.[462] At Carlisle there was a serious dispute over the choice of music between Dean Close and Precentor T. G. Livingstone.[463] Dean Pigou at Chichester said that he had power to erase music put down on the scheme, but doubted whether he had the right to choose any other music in its place.[464]

Hymns began to be introduced into cathedral services from the middle of the century onwards, though communion hymns had been in use at Durham, Exeter and Gloucester before then. From the beginning of 1870 a hymn replaced the anthem at three morning services and one evensong each week at Worcester.[465] *Hymns Ancient and Modern* came into use in many cathedrals within a few years of its publication. It was introduced at Rochester in 1864, Bristol in 1866, Wells in 1868, Hereford in 1869, Exeter in 1870, St Paul's in 1871, Chichester in 1877 and Worcester in 1882.[466] Precentor Vine Hall was much in favour of unaccompanied hymns, and said in 1882 that 'the use of the organ simply destroys the beautiful effect of the Hymns, and robs them of their delicacy'.[467] A correspondent in the *Guardian* remarked in 1884 that a hymn was becoming customary at cathedral services.[468] In 1897 the dean and chapter of Chichester asked for 'a louder accompaniment to the metrical Litany and hymns at services when the congregation is large, with a view to making the singing more congregational on such occasions'.[469] Yet even in this respect there could be controversy. H. P. Liddon, who preferred congregational hymns to anthems, had what he described as 'a most unpleasant scene' with Fynes

Webber, the Succentor of St Paul's, after evensong on Christmas Day 1875, over his choice of hymns.[470]

The weekly list of the music to be sung at cathedral services was not printed until the late nineteenth century. Before this they were written out by hand. One of the lay vicars was responsible for this at Chichester in 1806,[471] while at Exeter the scheme was drawn up on Saturdays for the ensuing week.[472] At Winchester, 'in order to preserve the more decent and decorous performance of the service in the choir', a list was placed on the chapter table each week by the precentor for the approval of the dean, and ten copies, made by the two senior choristers, were distributed. One was placed on each side of the quire in the prebendal stalls, one in the ladies' stalls, one on each side in the minor canons' stalls and in the seats of the lay vicars and choristers, and one in the organ loft.[473] At Wells the weekly list of music was drawn up by the organist, who had to show it to the dean or his deputy after the services each Friday. Before Sunday morning, copies had to be placed in the vestry of the canons, the vicars choral, and in the prayer book of the dean and each canon who was currently resident.[474] The schemes at Hereford were displayed on a notice-board at the western entrance to the quire.[475] At Gloucester in 1900 the weekly programme of services was prepared by the canon-in-residence and laid on the table in St Paul's Chapel at the end of each week, 'so as to secure responsibility for all services of the following week'.[476] Before this, copies of the music lists were copied out by hand.[477]

One feature of cathedral services that improved very considerably during the century was the orderly procession of the choir and clergy at the beginning of each service. The usual custom in the early years of the century was for members of the choir to take their places informally before the service began.[478] Bristol and Canterbury are usually said to be the only two cathedrals in the early nineteenth century where the custom of a daily processional entry had survived,[479] though sometimes a greater festival was marked elsewhere in this way.[480] But processional entries were revived at Norwich (based on the Canterbury practice) in 1829.[481] Jebb was firmly in favour of the restoration of proper processions.[482] In 1843 the dean and chapter of Worcester made a regulation that at the services on Sundays, Christmas Day, Good Friday and Ascension Day the lay clerks and choristers, together with the schoolmaster and college boys, should meet the dean and canons at the door 'and walk before them in procession to their respective places in the choir'.[483] At Lichfield in the previous year the choristers were ordered 'to assemble at the church door in a body five minutes before the commencement of Morning and Evening Service and there await the approach of the Dean or Canon-in-Residence as the case may be and accompany him into the choir'. The vicars joined the procession from their vestry, but at the end of the service the choir merely dispersed from their places once the rest of the congregation had departed.[484] The custom of entering the quire in procession was revived at Wells on Whitsunday 1847. The organist was asked to play a voluntary before and after the services to cover the processional entry and withdrawal.[485] The clergy at Durham in the late 1840s left their stalls in procession, with the vergers bearing silver maces before them. When they reached the entrance to the quire, they turned round and 'very lowly and solemnly bowed toward the East' before they left the cathedral.[486] It was Dean Lake who organized a proper processional entry for the whole choir at Durham.[487] In 1856 Dean Garnier of Winchester said he was in favour of making the choristers and lay vicars enter the quire in procession on weekdays as well as on Sundays.[488] When Lichfield Cathedral was reopened in 1861, the *Guardian* found much to criticize in the arrangements:

> ...surpliced clergy and choirs mingled with clergy in gowns, unsurpliced choristers, and female singers, to the destruction of all processional order and effect; the bulk of the surpliced clergy followed the Bishop instead of preceding him.[489]

Any lay vicar who was not ready to join the procession at Winchester was liable to a fine of one shilling.[490] Not until 1869 was a regular procession in and out of the quire begun at St Paul's. It was an uphill struggle; Canon Gregory recorded many examples of disorderly processions, as, for example, on 24 August 1869: 'Procession very irregular. One of the choirmen stayed to talk to a friend at gate of north choir aisle, breaking the order, and then made a rush: all straggling and irregular.'[491] When Archbishop Tait was enthroned at Canterbury in the same year, there was a grand procession at the beginning of the service:

> Seven bishops and some 300 clergy met in the Chapter House and, arrayed in surplice and hood, and preceded by the choir of the Cathedral chanting the 121st and 122nd psalms, escorted the Archbishop to his new seat...[492]

Psalms in procession were also a feature of the great service held in connection with the reopening of Worcester Cathedral in 1874.[493]

As processions became more frequent, so queries and disputes often arose as to their correct ordering. In 1878 the dean and chapter of Chichester told the chapter clerk of Ely that the dignitaries of the cathedral took precedence over the archdeacons.[494] Nearly fifty years previously there had been a dispute between Samuel Holland, the precentor, and the dean and chapter at Chichester as to whether the canons should walk in order of their seniority as canons or in the order of seniority of their dignities.[495] In 1859 the dean and chapter of Hereford felt that the vicars choral should not walk behind the capitular mace when entering the quire before services.[496] In 1873 John Goss, the custos of the college of vicars choral at Hereford, reminded the dean and chapter that it had been agreed that the vicars could have their own mace to precede them in processions.[497] It was ordered in 1882 that the priest vicars at Wells should be preceded by a verger in processions.[498] A dispute about the correct order at Chichester in 1889 encouraged A. H. Glennie to tell the chapter clerk about the custom in several other cathedrals. He said that the priest vicars had felt 'great pain and annoyance' at a change in the order which had been made in August of that year:

> It is not the custom for the priest-vicars to precede the vergers at York, Lincoln, Exeter, Salisbury, Wells or St Asaph (cathedrals resembling our own), nor the minor canons to do so in the new foundations of Canterbury, Durham, Winchester, Norwich, Worcester, Rochester, Ely, Manchester, St Albans; at Hereford and Lichfield alone are the priest-vicars by their constitution in any way connected with the choirs.[499]

At Salisbury the subdean and succentor took precedence over the non-residentiary canons by reason of the dignitaries whom they represented.[500] At Chichester the chapter clerk walked between the choristers and the priest vicars, the prebendaries being preceded by two vergers.[501] When the dean and chapter attempted to alter the order of procession at Chichester they met with strong resistance from seventeen of the non-residentiary canons, who claimed that such decisions should be taken only at a meeting of the general chapter.[502] In 1893 the dean and chapter of Worcester arranged that when the Bishop of Coventry (a bishop suffragan in the diocese) attended services in the cathedral, he should walk with the dean or, in his absence, with the senior canon.[503] When both a minor canon and the dean or a canon were present at services, the minor canon was to be preceded by a verger with a staff and the dean or canon by one carrying a verge. Only if the minor canons alone were present should they be preceded by the staff.[504] A processional hymn was introduced in 1892 at Worcester at matins and evensong on saints' days; it was to begin as soon as the procession left the chapter-house.[505] One of the choir carried a processional cross on great festivals in place of the staff usually carried by the custos.[506] In 1897 the processions on saints' days were extended to include the cloisters. On Easter Day and Whitsunday at evensong the procession was led by two trumpeters.[507] James Smith, a lay clerk, disliked processional hymns at Worcester:

> ...at least half of those we get through we neither know the words or the music, and we cannot see either until we arrive in the Choir. And it is very trying to walk up steps and sing at the same time.[508]

Questions of precedence also affected the blessing at the end of a service. This was normally given by the dean or canon-in-residence, except when the bishop of the diocese was present. In 1888 the dean and chapter of St

Paul's laid down strict rules about this custom, though it was not unknown for a visiting bishop to disregard them.[509]

Occasionally a solemn Te Deum was sung. Gounod's setting was sung at St Paul's after the sermon at evensong on the eve of the Feast of the Dedication in 1885. A solemn Te Deum was also sung at St Paul's after the choral eucharist for the Lambeth Conference of 1897. When the new reredos at Bristol was dedicated in 1899, the choir sang a solemn Te Deum in front of it.[510]

Vestry prayers before the service (generally said by a chorister and often in the choristers' vestry) were known at Durham, Hereford and Ely in the 1860s.[511] A vestry prayer before and after each service was introduced at both St Paul's and Norwich in 1872.[512] A prayer at the vestry door after the service was introduced at Chichester in 1876.[513] Vestry prayers before services were introduced at Gloucester in 1881.[514] Silence before services was enjoined in both the canons' vestry and the choir vestry at Chichester in 1891,[515] and vestry prayers with the choir before and after eucharists came into use in the following year.[516]

How large were the congregations at cathedral services? In the nineteenth century, as today, numbers varied considerably and many of the recorded impressions that have survived are inevitably subjective. But there is sufficient evidence to build up something of a picture, even though the circumstances of each cathedral varied widely at different times during the century. York Minster was said in 1800 to have orderly crowds at the services on Sundays and feast days.[517] At St Paul's in July 1824 a crowded congregation attended evensong on Sundays; no seats were available except in the galleries. In 1839 Sydney Smith claimed that he had 'very often' counted 150 people at weekday evensongs, while on Sundays the quire was 'full to suffocation'.[518] Detailed statistics have survived at Worcester Cathedral. In 1847 the number of communicants varied between four and thirty-five on ordinary Sundays, with sixty-three on Easter Day, fifty on Whitsunday and fifty-seven on Christmas Day. By the end of the century at Worcester, on an ordinary Sunday, there were between thirty and forty communicants at the 8 a.m. service and between twenty and thirty at 11.30 a.m. The Easter Day figures reached a peak in 1895 when there were 378 communicants.[519] The services at York in 1847 were 'thinly attended',[520] and less than a dozen were noted at Durham about the same time.[521] In March 1848 a Member of Parliament, Edward Horsman, gave some figures in the House of Commons for the average size of congregations on weekdays in various cathedrals. At Canterbury he found an average of twenty-five at matins and fifty-three at evensong. At York there was an average matins congregation of fifty, but at Durham it varied between four and eleven; evensong there was better attended with a congregation of between twenty-five and thirty-seven. He also gave figures for Peterborough, Wells, Carlisle, Rochester, Oxford and Lincoln,

Peterborough having the smallest congregation with only seven. Sir Robert Inglis also produced some statistics from Canterbury, where the previous autumn the congregation had varied between sixty-two on 19 October and 165 on 1 November, and reported that Christ Church, Oxford, was frequently crowded.[522] In another debate in the Commons on the Ecclesiastical Commission Bill on 15 July 1850, Mr Heywood said that cathedral congregations were declining,[523] but John Jebb reported only two years later that St Paul's and Canterbury both had weekday congregations of over one hundred.[524] There were about thirty communicants at Carlisle on Sunday, 3 February 1850,[525] while on Christmas Day 1853 there were fifty and about twenty-five on Sunday, 1 July 1854.[526] Dean Close told the Royal Commission on Ritual in 1867 that the average number of communicants at the monthly communion service at Carlisle was between forty and fifty.[527] St Paul's was said in 1854 to be 'most respectably attended' on Sunday mornings and thronged with greater numbers than it could cope with in the evening.[528] W. K. Hamilton told the Cathedrals Commission that some twenty to twenty-five people attended the early morning prayers on summer weekdays, but far fewer in the winter. He attributed the small congregations at other services to the attitude of the cathedral clergy, who were often to be seen walking about the close during the times of services, or paying calls, 'their carriage perhaps starting at the very moment the bell is going...'[529] John Camidge, the organist of York Minster, told the commissioners that recent improvements in the choir there had led to crowded congregations; sometimes the quire, which held 2,000, was not big enough to accommodate them all.[530] At Manchester also large congregations were common, and nearly 4,000 were said to attend nearly every Sunday.[531]

The seating arrangements in many cathedrals were very different in the nineteenth century. At Exeter the space between the altar and the stalls was filled with benches facing *away* from the altar. At Bristol a large school sat near the altar, which was fenced off. Scrambles for seats often occurred before services at several cathedrals, and every available space was taken. Two women sat in the archbishop's throne one morning at Canterbury, while the same afternoon their place was taken by two privates of Dragoons. At Exeter, Lichfield, Bristol and Chichester the 'pue-system' was still in use in the middle years of the century and 'pue-openers' controlled the seating and received money for the best seats.[532] In 1813 Archdeacon Hale failed to get a seat at a service in St Paul's as he did not resort to a bribe, and the system caused criticism in 1824 when the recognized bribe was said to be half-a-crown.[533] The quire at St Paul's, although it could hold 900 people, was regularly overcrowded in 1841–2. Not only were the congregation locked in, but many had to stand.[534] The dean and chapter of Bristol gave strict instructions to the sub-sacrist in 1805 not to allow anybody to demand fees for opening pew doors and a notice to this effect was displayed in 1831.[535] In 1867 Mr Trott, the sub-sacrist, was told to reserve stalls and pews at Bristol for regular attendants and clergy. Any vacant places could be filled by 'respectable people' just before a service began.[536] The nave seating at Exeter was removed in 1829, but new chairs and stalls were provided there in 1877.[537] Following the reopening of Worcester Cathedral in 1874, the dean and chapter decided to appropriate seats in the quire for their own families and for those of the bishop, precentor, headmaster, minor canons, chapter clerk, organist and for those families who lived in College Green.[538] Three benches on each side of the nave were reserved for the families of the dean and chapter and other regular members of the congregation for the Sunday evening services.[539] Reserved seats were kept for the servants of the dean and chapter in 1882.[540] Careful directions were drawn up at Hereford about seating in the quire in 1800 and in the nave in 1871.[541] The first four rows of chairs at Chichester were reserved in 1879 until within five minutes of the beginning of services.[542] The mayor and corporation of Wells were allowed to sit in stalls on the north side of the quire provided they were vacant. Extra chairs were supplied if too many councillors attended.[543] The chapter clerk was asked to make a plan of the ladies' stalls in 1868.[544] Only residents in the liberty were assigned stalls and only adults could be admitted to any unassigned stalls.[545] In 1800 the minor canons of Bristol asked whether seats could be kept for their wives,[546] while at Gloucester in 1816 two pews were reserved for the servants of prebendaries.[547] New galleries were erected above the stalls on each side of the quire at Winchester in 1818,[548] but the cumbrous, two-storied galleries in the transepts at Norwich were removed in 1837.[549] Only gentlemen were admitted to the stalls at Lincoln, and the vergers and stall-keepers had strict instructions to remove any trouble-makers.[550]

In Carlisle in 1865 Francis Close complained that, although more than 30,000 people lived in the city and its area, only five or six attended the daily services. Some came just to hear the music while others stood in the transepts or aisles and left during the prayers or before the sermon.[551] At Lincoln also, rather earlier, people stood in the transepts, 'strolling in just in time to hear the anthem and then clattering away with their heavy boots, laughing and talking', though in fact the congregations at Lincoln were growing and at times the seating was insufficient.[552] At Exeter disturbances were caused during services by people walking about, and the dean and chapter made regulations about closing doors and placing the vergers in the nave in an attempt to prevent this.[553] At Chichester too Bishop Carr noted that there was a similar problem in 1825:

...the service of the Church is scandalously interrupted by the indecent and improper behaviour of idle and disorderly persons who are walking about the Ailes [*sic*] and Nave of the Church and making a noise and disturbance particularly on Sunday evenings.[554]

The dean and chapter of Wells ordered in 1862 that the cathedral doors should be closed after the second lesson at each service and kept shut until the conclusion of the service, 'to prevent the noise and interruption during service occasioned by persons waiting in the Nave and aisles and leaving the church after the conclusion of the anthem'.[555] At Salisbury in 1899 it was reported that there was much disorder in the nave during Sunday services: 'a large number of young persons coming in and going out at their pleasure and practically making the Cathedral a lounge'.[556] Irreverent perambulation during the services had been a problem at Salisbury fifty years earlier.[557] In an open letter to Dean Cockburn in 1831, Colonel Cholmley of Howsham complained about behaviour during services at York: 'It is quite disgraceful to see the wanderers and love-makers in every part of the Cathedral; and, when the Anthem is finished, it is like the close of a Theatre.'[558]

By 1865, especially on summer Sunday afternoons, the congregation at Canterbury approached one thousand.[559] At the York Church Congress of 1866, Dean Duncombe spoke of the many visitors who attended the services in the Minster during the summer, and of the 'steady, unfailing and not inconsiderable daily congregation' who came in the winter.[560] When B. F. Westcott first went to Peterborough as a canon in 1869 he was 'cheered by the sight of a large congregation'.[561] Yet in the same year a correspondent in the *Guardian* mentioned a visit to Peterborough when there was no member of chapter or even a minor canon present, and the officiating minister was a young deacon who was a curate at a nearby parish.[562] Another correspondent spoke of an experience at Rochester Cathedral when there was not a single canon present: 'One minor canon who read the prayers, four boys on each side, one lady and myself constituted the whole congregation. Even the vergers left us as soon as the choir were in their places.'[563] At Exeter, however, a better atmosphere prevailed. Another correspondent in the *Guardian* noted a good attendance of clergy at the services there, a 'commendable choir' and large or very large congregations. He was pleased that when one arrived at the cathedral door, 'no hungry verger, no hopping old woman, no sneaking official comes to molest you'.[564] The Norwich chapter said in 1872 that they had

large congregations, as may be witnessed on Sundays and on all special occasions, such as the Advent and Lent services....Even on Saturday afternoons, when many of the inhabitants of the County pour into Norwich, there is always a considerable congregation at the Cathedral.[565]

Canon Sedgwick of Norwich said in 1857:

I preached every Sunday during my three months' Residence of the past year to a very large congregation. And it went on increasing, for every corner of our large Cathedral choir was at length filled, and I had each Sunday of the summer months a congregation of about 1200 persons sitting under me.[566]

There was a large congregation for a special service at Wells in 1872, and the congregation at the daily services was said to average around fifty.[567] Huge congregations attended the services to mark the reopening of Worcester Cathedral in 1874 and every spare space was crammed with extra chairs.[568] Ten years later, however, the services at Worcester were said to be 'poorly attended' except on Sunday evenings, when there was special music.[569] In 1882 Archbishop Tait spoke of 'the large attendance of worshippers at St Paul's',[570] and on Good Friday 1884, 'the Cathedral was literally thronged with relays of worshippers at the services which were going on, almost without interruption from eight in the morning till eight o'clock at night'.[571] There were 545 communicants at St Albans on Easter Day 1899.[572] A chorister at Exeter in the 1890s recalled that there were few worshippers at the daily services, except at evensong on Fridays, which was market day in the city. The Sunday services were well attended, however, and evensong was held in the nave because of the large numbers that came.[573]

The value of cathedral services does not ultimately depend on the size of the congregation. As the corporate acts of worship of the cathedral foundation they should be offered and conducted as perfectly as possible. Yet there is plenty of evidence, from several cathedrals at different times throughout the nineteenth century, that the conduct of the worship left much to be desired.

On Easter Sunday 1808, Christian Ignatius Latrobe went to St Paul's, 'but they sang a parcel of the most clumsy services...I never heard worse'.[574] The music at Ely was at a low ebb when Robert Janes commenced his duties as organist there in 1831 at the age of eighteen. As the versicles and responses were sung to a monotone, he tried to introduce a harmonized setting, but the minor canons objected to a lengthening of the services.[575] In 1837 an anthem at St Paul's was attempted with only two altos and one tenor.[576] Jebb thought that 'the acme of irreverent and careless chanting was to be found at Lincoln' until he went to a service at Gloucester, where 'half the words of the psalms were inaudible: I doubt whether they were uttered at all'.[577] He also recorded that on the day of his ordination at Wells, morning prayer was read through by a vicar choral 'in the most rapid and irreverential manner conceivable'.[578] The services at Christ Church, Oxford, in 1847 were described as 'the most slovenly and irreverent...in any English Cathedral'.[579] Two years later it was said that the service at Bristol was performed 'in a cold and lifeless manner'. At Hereford the service gave an impression of 'disgust and aversion' through its 'irreverent' music and 'evident want of earnest feeling'.[580] Another correspondent in the *Guardian* expressed himself even more strongly in 1848:

There are various opinions as to where the Cathedral service is *best* conducted. Some say at Exeter, others at Canterbury, others at Norwich. There can be no difference of opinion whatever amongst those who have been at the spot where it is worst conducted. It is *worst* conducted in Lincoln Cathedral...the specimen of Cathedral service which I heard in Lincoln Cathedral yesterday was scandalous...

To say that the boys could not sing and the organ could not play and boys and organ could not go together would only half describe it. It was sluggishness and torpor personified. It crawled like a wretched lame insect from beginning to end. Its excessive feebleness was such that it seemed every moment on the point of stopping from mere want of breath. I was surprised that it went on at all. It seemed always at its very last gasp. At no one point in the service did the organ rise to the substance or dignity of a street barrel. The organist – if he was one – was afraid of touching a bass note and one man blowing on a bad flute would have produced quite an equal, or a very similar effect, to that of his playing.[581]

A further correspondent criticized the conduct of the choristers at York Minster:

They were laughing, talking, pinching each other and pulling each other's hair during the greater portion of the divine service. The eldest boy, instead of setting a good example, seemed to be ring-leader in all the mischief.[582]

An American clergyman described the services at York as 'an absolute burlesque of religious worship'.[583] The *Ecclesiologist* included a report of a depressing service at Worcester in 1852 during preparations for the Three Choirs Festival:

The service shortly after commenced, two canons and a reader only present, and another layman and myself the sole occupants of the stalls. In the 'free' seats were seated a few decrepid old men and women, the latter kneeling with their backs to the altar, for the rest of the congregation. But the coldness of the service...all read by one person in one dreary preaching tone – not a sound of music – not a note of organ...all reduced to one level, shallow, cold, formal, dead, pro-testantism....I turned away from the white-washed cathedral, chilled, cold, sorrowful and dead at heart.[584]

A visitor to Carlisle in 1858 was shocked to attend a service conducted by a single lay clerk and the canon-in-residence, attended by a verger, while the rest of the foundation were apparently on holiday. Mandell Creighton said in 1865 that the covering on the altar was not removed during services and that other matters were in need of reform:

> The small boy choristers amuse themselves all the time by squabbling and pinching each other in the middle of a chant, the men are perpetually turning over their music and restoring large folios to their place with a horrid bang in the middle of the lessons, while the precentor sits blinking above, looking down on all this irreverence, which he plainly sees, with an air of abject helplessness.[585]

The *Parish Choir* in an article entitled 'Defects in the Cathedral Service' was sharply critical of many current practices, and especially of the irreverence of choristers and lay clerks and the languour and carelessness of the officiating clergy.[586]

The early morning service at St Paul's came in for some criticism in the 1850s. The minor canons, who were responsible for the service, employed a deputy to conduct it:

> In these grey, slushy, November mornings, splashed with the mud of Watling Street, the officiating priest walks through the Cathedral into a prayer-desk, and then, drawing out a dirty surplice, puts it on in the face of a scanty congregation.[587]

The services at Norwich were described as 'the acme of irreverent and theatrical display',[588] though B. J. Armstrong thought that a service there in 1859 was 'beautifully performed'.[589] An editorial in the *Guardian* in 1859 said that most sung services were 'slovenly, meagre and ineffective', chiefly because the choirs were not sufficiently large.[590] Ten years later the *Musical Times* complained that there was still much to criticize:

> It is only necessary to enter one of these places of worship during service and notice the perfunctory way the work is gone through by clergy and singers alike, from the Dean, who seems to avoid any appearance of being engaged in an act of worship, to the junior chorister, who counts his marbles or engages in a surreptitious conversation on his fingers with his friends opposite.

The article concluded:

> The apathy of the clergy, the inefficiency of the organist and lay clerks, the dry antiquated character of the music, and the utterly lifeless tone of the whole performance, renders a Cathedral service...a matter of disgust to the earnest Christian and a scandal to the whole nation.[591]

At Rochester in 1869 'the responses were given in a feeble, discordant manner',[592] and another visitor, while enjoying the 'beautifully sung anthem' found the service 'so depressing'.[593] James Field accompanied

Charles Dickens on a visit to Rochester, when he 'noted how sleepy and inane were the faces of many of the singers', to whom the cathedral services were 'a sickening monotony of repetition'. Dickens had elsewhere described 'the shivering choristers on a winter morning, huddling in their gowns as they drowsily go to scamper through their work'.[594] The standard of the services at Ripon, Peterborough and Manchester in the early 1870s was said to be 'disgraceful'.[595] The services at Durham Cathedral were popular with visitors, 'but anything more heartless, slovenly or irreverent they could hardly have witnessed in the most neglected church of the diocese'.[596] At St Paul's in the late 1860s and early 1870s chaotic services occurred so frequently before Goss's retirement that they became 'a byword for slovenliness'.[597] At Norwich Dean Goulburn was aware of his own failings in the conduct of services: 'At the second service...I celebrated. Forgot to take the Anthem Book to the Altar; so there was a pause. And in the afternoon made another foolish mistake about the anthem, placing it before the Sermon.'[598] An anonymous minor canon said in 1880 that the choral services in most cathedrals were 'shocking and disgraceful'. He claimed that this was because lay clerks were often too old and there were too few boarding-schools for choristers.[599] The Precentor of Winchester said in 1890 that the services there were often 'tuneless and slovenly'.[600] At Worcester the precentor said that the services were poorly performed and he added a severe criticism of the organist, Ivor Atkins.[601]

It is sad to find examples of slovenly services in the closing years of the century when the life and work of cathedrals was generally improving. They were exceptions and there are certainly other examples of carefully conducted services of considerable devotional beauty and character, showing that at least in some cathedrals at different times during the century a high standard of worship was the aim. Maria Hackett, who was quick to note any defects in the conduct of services, was impressed by what she found at Salisbury in 1830:

> Here at the hour of prayer the Bishop may be seen on his throne, the Dean at the altar, the Canon in his stall; a full and efficient choir assembled before the commencement of the exhortation, and remaining in their places till after the blessing has been pronounced. The service is performed with great solemnity in its most attractive form.[602]

Charles Greville went to a service in St Paul's in 1834, which he clearly enjoyed: 'The service is exceedingly grand, peformed with all the pomp of a Cathedral, and chanted with beautiful voices.'[603] As an undergraduate, W. E. Dickson was much impressed by the quiet dignity and gravity of a service at Ely in 1842,[604] while Jebb spoke highly in the following year of the services at Chester and Canterbury.[605] The *Kentish Observer* agreed with this opinion, saying the daily service at Canterbury was 'a delight to all who are in the habit of attending it'.[606] A visitor to St Paul's in 1851 was pleased with the choir, describing the chanting as 'perfectly smooth, very sweet and the voices excellent'.[607] St Paul's may have fallen into slack ways in the 1860s, but in the previous decade it clearly made a marked impression on one American visitor:

> The effect of the immense vault of the dome, as it first struck my sight, was overpowering – the more so because at that moment, a single burst of the organ and the swell of an Amen from the choir where service was already begun, filled the dome with reverberations, that seemed to come upon me like thunder....Tears gushed from my eyes, and my heart swelled to my throat, as this overwhelming worship was continued. It was all so entirely unexpected. Cold, cheerless, modern, all but Hanoverian, St Paul's – who dreamed of such a worship here! Yet so it was...[608]

A. C. Benson has left a detailed account of Sunday worship at Lincoln when his father, E. W. Benson, was chancellor there. He was particularly impressed by the singing of the psalms, which had 'a deliberation, a purity of intonation, and an almost ultra-refinement of pronunciation such as I have never heard elsewhere'.[609] When T. F. Bumpus attended Worcester Cathedral on a brilliant May morning in 1882, 'the beauty of the architecture was materially enhanced by the music in the distant choir'.[610] The Precentor of Worcester mentioned in his report to the dean and chapter in 1885 that an incumbent in the diocese had recently praised the services for their 'reverence and devotional feeling'.[611] By the 1890s a consistently high standard had been achieved at Worcester,[612] while at Lincoln Bishop Edward King referred to 'the excellence of the Cathedral services', which attracted many clergy, schoolmasters, organists and choir members.[613] In his visitation charge of 1900 at Winchester, Bishop Randall Davidson said: 'Never, I suppose, in its long history has the saying or singing of the public offices in our cathedral church been more reverent, more orderly, more careful, more cultured in their harmonies than it is today.'[614] The evident satisfaction that Davidson reflects in this comment is an appropriate note on which to end this long survey of cathedral worship in the nineteenth century. Much had been achieved. Through the efforts of men like Jebb, Ouseley, W. K. Hamilton, Mackenzie Walcott and Gregory, and their deep devotion to the ideals of cathedral worship, the care and reverence with which it was offered was undoubtedly higher in 1900 than it had been one hundred years earlier.[615]

8

CATHEDRAL CHOIRS
IN THE NINETEENTH
CENTURY

In 1854 the cathedral commissioners printed some interesting details on the comparative sizes of different cathedral choirs and the difficulties that they faced.[1] Carlisle Cathedral had eight men and eight boys, but only four of the men attended daily.[2] Chester boasted six lay clerks and twelve choristers, but only three of the men came every day, and when illness reduced the numbers still further, F. E. Thurland the precentor, found it 'indeed painful to be present at a service so lifeless'.[3] Various rules at Salisbury ensured that there were always four out of six lay vicars and three supernumeraries present each day, but W. K. Hamilton, the precentor, complained that this indicated 'how utterly the musical power of our choir is below what is required for the due celebration of Divine Service'.[4] Exeter managed to have twelve laymen singing on Sundays and six on weekdays, together with ten choristers, but their general efficiency and attendance left Alfred Angel, the organist, rather dissatisfied.[5] At Ely, eight men and an equal number of boys were 'quite unequal to perform choral music in so large a building', but ex-choristers were being recruited as supernumeraries. Robert Janes, the organist, even had a lay clerks' faults chart drawn up, which included 'negligence and refusing to perform the part allotted to him'.[6] R. L. Caley, the Precentor of Bristol, wished to increase the eight choristers to twelve and grumbled at the attendance of only three lay clerks at the daily services.[7] Both J. B. Dykes, the Precentor of Durham, and John Goss, the organist of St Paul's, felt that their choirs were too small.[8] In 1848 C. W. Corfe, the organist of Christ Church, Oxford, abandoned antiphonal singing and placed the whole choir on one side of the aisle.[9] Frederick Gunton, the organist of Chester Cathedral, concluded that there was scarcely a cathedral in the country where the choir was at its proper strength.[10] The commissioners agreed 'that in very few Cathedrals, if any, is the number of the choir sufficient to provide against the casualties of health'.[11]

A few years earlier the *Parish Choir* noted that although the choir at Lincoln was supposed to contain fifteen choristers and eight lay clerks, only two or three men were usually present on weekdays.[12] There were seven lay vicars at Chichester in 1849. Their salaries ranged between £20 and £50 and they included two tailors, two carpenters, one schoolmaster and the town crier.[13] The lay vicars of Salisbury augmented their musical stipends by performing the duties of various other officers in the employ of the dean and chapter, such as altarist of the cathedral, parish clerk of St Thomas's Church, clerk of the close, writing master of the choristers, and church pricker.[14] Later Bishop Hamilton told the Cathedral Commission: 'I see no objection to their being tradesmen – it gives them an influence in the town. One of our most respectable tradesmen is one of our tenors. He is a man most respected.'[15] At Wells the lay vicars included clerks, tradesmen, innkeepers, music teachers and photographers; one was a stonemason and the wife of another kept a small private school.[16] In 1884 the secular occupations of the lay clerks at Winchester included keeping a music shop, acting as clerk in a house of business, teaching singing in parish schools, and acting as schoolmaster to the choristers.[17] One of the Chichester lay vicars was given £10 per annum for setting out the men's music before each service and then replacing it afterwards.[18] There were only six choristers at Bristol in 1850,[19] while a few years later at Manchester there were six boys and four men.[20]

In the 1860s the choir at St Paul's consisted of fourteen boys and ten men.[21] Five of the ten men in 1871 were (lay) vicars choral and five were supernumeraries, but on Friday mornings a very unbalanced choir sang: there were three tenors, but only one bass and one alto. One of each part sat on *cantoris* and sang any verses, while the two remaining basses both sat on *decani*.[22]

In 1880 a meeting of cathedral organists declared that every cathedral choir should have twelve lay clerks and twenty choristers.[23] By this time several cathedral choirs were larger than they had been thirty years earlier. Bristol now had eighteen choristers[24] and Exeter twelve, but the organist, Daniel Wood, thought that this was an insufficient number to balance the fourteen men.[25] In 1883 the choir at St Paul's included eighteen men, who were all communicants and pensionable at the age of sixty, and thirty to forty boys.[26] Manchester Cathedral Choir, however, was still reliant on four singing men, with three supernumeraries.[27]

There were still problems elsewhere. At Chester there were six lay clerks and eight choristers (with six recognized probationers and ten preparatory probationers), but the choristers' school was 'very defective and crippled' through lack of funds, with 'a mean building in a poor condition'. The organist, J. C. Bridge, complained that he had few candidates at voice trials and was 'therefore compelled to accept boys of mean parentage and poor quality of voice. The choir is, therefore, gradually deteriorating'. He felt that with only six men and twelve effective choristers, 'it is absolutely impossible to perform efficiently the music that modern services and anthems require and the general public expect'. The lay clerks agreed with Bridge: 'The number of lay clerks is too small to bear the perpetual and unremitting strain on their physical energies necessary to maintain the high character of the cathedral service.' The problem was exacerbated by the fact that lay clerks at Chester frequently left for better-paid posts in other cathedrals, so that there was a constant succession of young and inexperienced singers joining the choir.[28] C. E. Hey, the Precentor of Bristol, also complained of the difficulty of retaining adequate lay clerks.[29]

At Ely the statutory number of eight choristers had been doubled,[30] while at Norwich there were two altos in addition to the eight foundation choristers and a varying number of supernumeraries.[31] In 1871 a new statute at Hereford Cathedral stipulated that there should be thirteen adults in the choir (six vicars choral in priests' orders and seven lay assistants), eight of whom should be present at each service, with twelve singing boys (eight choristers and four probationers).[32] There were between fourteen and sixteen choristers at Lichfield,[33] while at Exeter there were eight lay vicars, six secondaries and twelve choristers.[34] Dean Stephens told Bishop Davidson in 1900 that he had added eight Sunday men and two full-time choristers to the choir at Winchester at his own expense.[35]

Where improvements could be made there were some notable results. In the 1830s there were eight regular singing men at York Minster. John Camidge, the organist, suspended two of these and engaged eight supernumeraries at £10 per annum each. They sang twice on Sundays and also had to attend one weekly service and the weekly full-choir practice. Ex-choristers were often recruited among the supernumeraries. The improved choir attracted large congregations and often the quire, which could accommodate over 2,000 people, was not large enough to hold all those who wished to be present.[36] But in 1850 Camidge was stricken by paralysis while playing the organ and his duties were taken over by his son.[37] Dean Duncombe did much to improve the choir at York.[38]

Lay clerks and choristers were frequently absent. In 1806 the dean and chapter of Salisbury, noting the frequent unauthorized absences of the lay vicars, introduced an elaborate system of forfeits based on a minimum attendance of 630 attendances by any one lay vicar in any year.[39] In 1809 they decreed that there should always be at least three lay vicars present at services (one of each voice).[40] No lay vicar could be absent on a Sunday unless ill, and in that case he must send a sick note.[41] The lay vicars at Exeter were also slack and often arrived late for services. In 1814 it was decided that those who were not in their places before the beginning of the general confession were to be fined.[42]

In 1837 William Butler, a lay clerk at Bristol, compared his attendances over the last three years with one of his colleagues. In 1835 he was present at 371 services, while his colleague had managed only 292. The following year the figures were 483 and 332 respectively. In the first ten months of 1837 he had been present for 324 services as opposed to his colleague's 169. He further pointed out that he had missed only three Sunday services during this period while his colleague, who had a clerkship in a parish church, had been absent from seventy-two Sunday services.[43]

In November 1816 the dean and chapter of Worcester Cathedral admonished a lay clerk who had moved to Malvern and attended only irregularly.[44] Such entries are by no means uncommon.[45] In the late 1830s there were only one or two lay clerks present at the services on several occasions.[46] When S. S. Wesley's anthem *Blessed be the God and Father* was first sung at Hereford Cathedral on Easter Day 1833, the only adult member of the choir was a single bass – the dean's butler.[47] On one occasion at St Paul's, Handel's *Hallelujah* chorus was chosen for the anthem, but during the service a message was sent to Goss in the organ loft that only one tenor and one bass were present. 'Do your best,' he replied, 'and I will do the rest with the organ.'[48] S. S. Wesley once attended a service at Christ Church, Oxford, and remarked to the organist, Dr Marshall, 'Why, you have only one man in a surplice today, and him I can't hear.' 'No,' said Marshall, 'he is only a beginner.'[49]

When W. K. Hamilton complained about the frequent absence of the lay vicars at Salisbury, he was told: 'Well, sir, I dare say you are right, but you must know that the rule at Salisbury has always been "Let everybody get off everything he can".'[50] A new system of rules for attendance and fines for non-attendance was drawn up for the lay vicars at Salisbury in 1851.[51] In 1852 Francis Gilmour, one of the Salisbury lay vicars, was dismissed because he was so frequently absent. He had missed 104 services in 1847, 45 in 1848, 51 in 1850 and 128 in 1851.[52] In an attempt to stimulate a more regular attendance among the lay clerks at Durham in 1800, the chapter offered them a shilling a day in addition to their stipends if they were present at both services. This custom continued until 1807 on condition that they were present for the whole service.[53] In 1823 the dean and chapter of Hereford asked the vicars choral (who alone provided the lower voices in the choir at that time) to ensure that there was an equal number of altos, tenors and basses on each side of the choir, and asked that more of the vicars choral should attend evensong on Sundays.[54] The dean and chapter of Exeter insisted in 1841 that six probationers or lay vicars must be present for each service; only sudden illness could excuse the lack of a substitute.[55] In 1856 the dean and chapter of Winchester increased the size of the choir and required two of each voice to be present at each service[56] and they further stipulated three years later that any of them who was forced to be absent through illness must provide a deputy.[57] This meant that each lay vicar should be present for 576 services each year, for which he would be paid £72, or 2s 6d per service. New sets of rules were introduced at Winchester in 1887,[58] 1891 and 1897.[59] The choir of

Gloucester Cathedral, however, was a model of regularity.[60] Canon Gregory was greatly displeased with the attendance of the choirmen at St Paul's when he first went there. One November morning he told them that it was disgraceful.[61] Dean Mansel told him:

> These men have had their own way so long under the old régime that it is far easier to lead them than to drive them. They are like spoilt children and have points of dignity which no one but themselves would dream of.[62]

New rules for the lay vicars choral at St Paul's were introduced in 1873.[63] In 1876 the lay vicars of Chichester attended so regularly that no record of their absences was kept.[64]

It was no easy matter to persuade cathedral choirs to practise the music sung at the services. J. B. Dykes complained in 1854 that at Durham he could only arrange choir practices 'by begging it as a personal favour'.[65] But choir practices were not unknown earlier in the century. In 1805 the dean and chapter of Hereford ordered the organist to rehearse the choristers three times a week 'conformably to ancient usage'.[66] The efforts of the dean and chapter of Winchester between 1814 and 1818 to make Dr G. W. Chard more diligent in his attendance at rehearsals have already been mentioned.[67] In 1828 it was decided that the lay clerks of Gloucester should be fined one shilling if they missed the weekly practice.[68] A daily rehearsal for the choristers and secondaries was known at Exeter by 1830.[69] The boys rehearsed from seven until nine each morning.[70] A full choir practice on Saturday mornings was ordered at Wells in 1831,[71] but William Perkins, the organist, was reluctant to arrange rehearsals for the choristers.[72] A new piano for choir practices was purchased in 1858.[73] There were three practices a week at Chichester in 1832.[74] The Norwich choristers, with the training of Dr Zechariah Buck, were famed for the use of the 'shake',[75] while the choristers of St Paul's were reported in 1836 to be practising the psalms before breakfast and had three more hours' practice between 11 a.m. and 2 p.m. each day.[76] New arrangements for rehearsals were made at Winchester in 1840, and the lay vicars were ordered to have a weekly practice under the direction of the precentor.[77] They were to be paid 1s 6d for each practice as they had not rehearsed together for some years, but new lay vicars were not to expect this remuneration.[78] In 1841 Chard was reminded to give the choristers two practices each week.[79] These arrangements were confirmed by the dean and chapter in 1843, when Monday was chosen as the normal day for full rehearsals. Absentees were to be fined and one of the canons or the precentor would normally be present.[80] In 1842 at Worcester the choristers had to practise in the Audit Room after morning service on Thursdays and Saturdays, while the lay clerks' weekly practice was in the same room on Thursdays.[81] S. S. Wesley, when he was organist at Exeter Cathedral, set such store by practices that he once punished two boys for singing at a Glee Club instead of attending a practice.[82] Rehearsals at Exeter in his time were at 6.30 a.m.[83] Later, he became slack in his attendance at rehearsals when he was at Winchester.[84] In 1860 the choristers at Norwich spent an hour with the organist before each service,[85] and in 1868 the lay clerks were given a shilling bonus for attending practices.[86] The full choir met for 229 rehearsals in 1867.[87] In 1869 Precentor T. L. Wheeler of Worcester told the dean and chapter that more frequent rehearsals were required.[88] William Done, the organist, in a letter of the same date, suggested that there should be two practices each week in his house opposite the north door of the cathedral.[89] At Ely, two full weekly practices were established in 1871.[90] When John Stainer became organist at St Paul's, he soon called the vicars choral together for a rehearsal, 'an experience then new to them'. Previously the most they might do would be to 'cast an eye through it [the music] during one of the lessons at a previous service'.[91] An hour's rehearsal each day was ordered for the choristers at Bristol in 1872 and a weekly rehearsal for the full choir was begun in 1877.[92] The arrangements for recruiting and training the choir were in the hands of the precentor,[93] but in 1886 the dean and chapter drew up new instructions for the organist, after the affair of George Riseley, requiring him to be present at four out of six rehearsals of the choir each week; one of these was to be a full practice.[94] There was a weekly rehearsal for the lay clerks at Peterborough in 1875.[95] When C. H. Lloyd succeeded S. S. Wesley as organist of Gloucester Cathedral in 1876, he found that

> the standard of singing in the cathedral choir was at a very low ebb...the training of the choristers was left in the hands of one of the lay clerks. When a full rehearsal of the choir took place, the men made no attempt to sing out but just whispered their parts. This tradition continued for some time after Wesley's death.[96]

A daily practice for the choristers was considered 'essential' by the organist, precentor and succentor of Salisbury in 1877;[97] they asked that the twice-weekly hour-long rehearsals for the lay vicars should be extended when necessary. In 1879 the dean and chapter of Exeter said that a weekly rehearsal of the choir was desirable, but three of the lay vicars were repeatedly absent and 'met the remonstrances of the Chapter with insolence and defiance', though they later apologized.[98] At Hereford there were frequent arguments at practices in the early 1880s.[99] In 1882 Precentor Vine Hall told the dean and chapter at Worcester that the two daily practices for choristers had been reduced to one, with resultant loss of style and delicacy in their singing. They now had less than five hours' practice a week, whereas before they had seven or eight hours. This compared unfavourably with other cathedrals – the choristers at Christ Church, Oxford, were used to between an hour and an hour and a half daily, as were those at Gloucester, where there were practices in both the morning and the afternoon. But the Durham choristers spent no less than twelve to thirteen hours a week in practice, more than two hours each day.[100] Vine Hall repeated his request for more practice time in his reports for 1884 and 1889, and in 1887 he complained that the choristers should be better trained for singing solos. By this time, William Done, the organist, was growing very old and from 1891 on the choristers were trained entirely by the assistant organist, Hugh Blair.[101] When Woodward became precentor, he took charge of the rehearsals, with the organist being relegated to accompanying the choir.[102]

There is a valuable account in the *Guardian* in 1884 of a choristers' practice during Stainer's time at St Paul's.[103] After scales, agility exercises and some instruction in the theory of music, the boys were rehearsed in the settings and anthems for the daily services. Their sight-reading was good, their tone shrill but unforced, and they rarely practised psalms and hymns as they knew them so well. There was one full rehearsal each week. Forty years earlier, a novel technique was employed by John Hopkins, the organist of Rochester Cathedral. He gave each boy a small mirror to hold in his left hand while he beat time with his right hand. The choristers were to look into the mirror as they sang to check that they were opening their mouths properly.[104] At Exeter in the 1890s the choristers had a daily rehearsal in the singing school from 9.30 until 10.30 every morning, except on Mondays and Thursdays when they attended the full practice that followed matins.[105] At Winchester also, at the end of the century, there was a daily practice for the boys and a twice-weekly full rehearsal.[106]

But what was the final result of all this practice? What did the Victorians think of their cathedral choirs? For much of the century they had a low opinion of them. When Dean Markham was appointed to York in 1802, the choir was 'scarcely able to execute the ordinary choruses in the anthems, which were often therefore omitted'.[107] The singing at Lincoln around 1815 was said to be 'below mediocrity'.[108] In the same year the dean and chapter of Winchester noted the 'neglect and inattention observable for some time past in the performance of the public service of the choir'.[109] Three years later they were still concerned about its 'bad state'.[110] The whole choir at Exeter was admonished 'to a more diligent performance of the choir duty, particularly the secondaries to learn their parts'.[111] Later, in 1834, a visitor to Exeter noted that

the antiphonal chanting was excellent and the accentuation perfectly correct. In double chants two verses were alternately sung by each semi-chorus in a major or minor key, according to the subject of the psalm. Each verse occupied, on an average, fifteen seconds.[112]

In 1821 the dean and chapter of Hereford 'observing with much concern the neglected state of the choristers with respect to their choral qualifications', reminded Dr Clarke-Whitfeld, the organist, that his prime duty was in the singing school.[113] At St Paul's in the 1830s Sydney Smith complained that boys with broken voices were being retained and the succentor chose difficult music at short notice.[114] In 1844 he told William Hawes:

> I think the choir of St Paul's is as good as any in England. We have gone on with it for two hundred years; why not be content? You talk of competing with other cathedrals, but cathedrals are not to consider themselves rival Opera Houses. We shall come by and by to act Anthems – it is enough if your music is decent, and does not put us to shame. It is a matter of perfect indifference to me whether Westminster bawls louder than St Paul's. We are there to pray, and the singing is a very subordinate consideration.[115]

John Jebb condemned the choir at St Paul's as 'degenerate' in 1843, along with those of Lincoln and Westminster Abbey.[116] The dean and chapter of Gloucester were dissatisfied with the state of their choir in 1844,[117] and two years later Dean Merewether of Hereford drew the attention of his chapter to the 'very inefficient' state of their choir.[118] In 1848 he told the Ecclesiastical Commissioners that the choir was so bad 'that it is with the utmost difficulty that the service can be performed even...in the most meagre and unsatisfactory manner'. The service had been transferred to All Saints' Church during the restoration of the cathedral, but 'such is the state of the choir that...by the time the Cathedral is fit for being reopened it will be utterly impossible decently to perform a choral service'.[119]

At Winchester in 1857 the dean and chapter were very unhappy with the condition of the choir and asked three of the canons to make a full enquiry.[120] At York, too, the choir was in a bad state. 'The choral music in this Cathedral,' said Canon W. V. Harcourt in 1857, 'is sunk below the level of religious impressiveness'.[121] In 1857 Sir Frederick Ouseley, who was non-resident precentor of Hereford, said that the choir there was the worst he had ever heard. Ouseley described the choristers as 'notoriously and disgracefully inefficient as vocalists and musicians, vulgar and provincial in their address and irreverent in their behaviour...year by year the matter becomes worse and worse'. He said that they should be given proper education and training, and boarded with a clergyman who could take good care of them.[122] Psalm-singing at Norwich was described as 'reckless gabbling' in 1860.[123] A few months earlier an Oxford graduate attended a service there on Christmas Eve: '...a worse service, in many points, I think I never heard, even at Norwich'. The canticles were 'hurried through in the most unseemly manner, with very slight attention either to time or to tune'. As for the psalms, they were chanted without the least attempt, so far as I could perceive, at articulation of the words on the reciting notes. It will be no news to anyone who has attended the Norwich service as frequently as I have, to hear that the lay clerks, during the prayers, were sitting, lolling about, talking and laughing, and that not once or twice only.[124]

John Hullah complained in 1864 that several of the lay clerks at Lichfield sang 'with forced tone and bad intonation'.[125] The vicars choral at Hereford told the dean and chapter in 1865 that the choir was very unsatisfactory. The boys were 'frequently of a low class' and there was a 'great difficulty in obtaining a regular supply of eligible candidates'. The instruction that they received in music was 'barely sufficient to qualify them to take their parts in Divine Service'. The lay clerks were 'men of inferior eduction' and were not paid enough.[126] In 1869 the *Musical Times* said that something must be done to remove the stigma that rested upon cathedral choirs; choristers must be given a better education and lay clerks must be paid more.[127] In the same year a correspondent in the *Guardian* described a service at Lincoln as 'poor and cold, like all the services here'. Part of the service was read by one of the canons, but he was 'perfectly inaudible – a good vigorous bluebottle would have made more sound'. The same correspondent said, 'the choir is very weak, the men almost all worn out, and the organ is often played so *piano* that it is no support to their feeble voices.' But another correspondent defended the choir at Lincoln:

> The excellent training and singing of the boys and their decorous behaviour are so constantly commended by the most competent judges, on casual visits to the Minster, that there is no occasion to defend the organist on that score. If, as many think, he carries his love of *piano* too far in some of the psalms, that is a matter of opinion, and scarcely an occasion for censure of the authorities.[128]

The dean and chapter of Exeter criticized the choir there in 1870 for hurrying in the psalms and responses,[129] and in the same year H. P. Liddon repeatedly reprimanded the choir at St Paul's for their bad behaviour.[130] In 1878 all six lay vicars at Chichester sent a letter to the dean and chapter complaining about the frequent criticisms by Dean Burgon of their singing after cathedral services:

> It is unfair to stigmatize our efforts as 'a disgusting noise' and etc. We take the greatest delight in the services and are conscious that we try our best to sing the music heartily and skilfully.[131]

In 1880 Langdon Colborne, the organist of Hereford Cathedral, with the support of the succentor, criticized many aspects of the choir:

> The general effect of the music, owing to the inability of some and the

carelessness of other members of the choir has of late been deplorably bad....The responses and Amens are seldom, if ever, sung in tune.... Our next complaint is that, at the Saturday and Monday evening practices, when a mistake is pointed out by the organist or subchanter, it is the habit of some members of the choir to raise a dispute and to begin to argue the point.[132]

In 1889 J. H. Mee was appointed Precentor of Chichester and told the dean that the choir had a notorious reputation in the diocese.[133] George Riseley, who had a stormy career as organist of Bristol Cathedral, was urged in 1896 to ensure that the choristers should be more careful in singing the confession, creed and Lord's Prayer.[134] A few months later one of the canons reported that the services 'had been slovenly performed and the boys ill behaved'.[135]

But there were some efforts at improvement. The choir at Canterbury in about 1830 was said to be 'very efficient' and often sang unaccompanied music.[136] S. S. Wesley 'greatly improved' the choir at Exeter during his time there,[137] while the *Parish Choir* said that the choir at Durham had a good reputation: 'The men's voices are of good quality and the boys are well instructed.'[138] Canon Sedgwick praised the choir at Norwich in a letter to the organist, Zechariah Buck, in 1842:

> I think it my duty to tell you how much I have been delighted with the progress made by the younger members of our Choir....Their singing, last Thursday, of Kent's beautiful anthem, *My song shall be of mercy,* was quite faultless and in admirable taste. I never heard it better performed. Nothing but great skill combined with unbounded zeal could have put our Cathedral music in the condition in which it now is.[139]

Under J. M. W. Young's instruction, the choir at Lincoln 'improved wonderfully' during his long tenure of office from 1850 to 1895. He laid special emphasis on the clarity of the psalm-singing and also improved the reverence of the choir.[140] It was claimed that Ely was the best cathedral choir in the mid-1860s,[141] and in 1876 the choristers of Norwich were said to have voices of 'thrilling sweetness'.[142] Standards were clearly improving both in reverence and musical ability.[143] The *Church Times* said in 1876 that 'expressiveness of light and shade' was common in cathedral choirs, while the choir of York Minster was praised for its expressive and controlled psalm-singing.[144] T. L. Wheeler, the precentor of Worcester, said in 1873 that 'the choir has never, in my opinion, been in a more efficient condition'.[145] Five years later his successor, E. Vine Hall, reported 'a great improvement both in the singing and also in the behaviour of the choir during the last few months'.[146] In November 1883 he described a recent performance of a Bach anthem at Worcester as 'little short of perfect'[147] and six years later he reflected that the 'slovenly' services of the late 1870s were a thing of the past: 'Other choirs greatly excel ours in the good voices they possess; but the refined and devotional singing of the Worcester Choir is remarkable'.[148] In 1879 W. Sparrow Simpson, the succentor of St Paul's, praised the choristers there for their 'love for the work and a uniform excellence of conduct and sobriety of demeanour which I have rarely seen equalled', and the men for their 'thoroughly artistic feeling'.[149] At the new cathedral at Truro it was not easy to establish a choral tradition, but the young G. R. Sinclair 'led on the choir until he succeeded in making them fit to render the best cathedral music'.[150] In 1899 J. E. West said that 'the choir of Chester Cathedral has always been noted both for its discipline and musical efficiency'. It was also praised by visiting American musicians.[151]

Although at some cathedrals the precentor was responsible for choir-training, the organist was always a key figure in the musical life of every cathedral.[152] At the beginning of the century there were several inadequate organists. Thomas Pitt was organist of Worcester Cathedral from 1793 to 1806. On one occasion, while he was accompanying a lay clerk by the name of Griffiths, the latter slammed his book in the middle of a service and shouted 'Pitt's wrong, Pitt's wrong'.[153] Some organists at that time disdained to use pedals. Highmore Skeats (senior), who was organist of Canterbury between 1803 and 1831, greatly disliked the 16 ft pedal pipes and would not use them. If anyone expressed a desire to hear them he would call his pupil and say: 'Here, Jones, come and show these *things* off, I never learned to *dance*.'[154] John Amott, who was Wesley's pre-decessor at Gloucester, used the pedals so rarely that he had a board placed over them on which he rested his feet.[155] C. J. Dare was organist of Hereford Cathedral from 1805 until 1818. The dean and chapter com-plained that his predecessor, Miles Coyle, had 'greatly neglected' his duties and reminded Dare that he must regularly teach the choristers.[156] But Dare also had slack ways:

His bibulous propensities earned him rheumatic gout; his gout made him indolent and unlocomotive, consequently it now and then hap-pened that he was behind his time. I think I hear him now crawling upstairs into the organ-loft, which was perched between the nave and the choir, while the Psalms were being chanted; gradually and stealthily he manipulated the keys till all at once he broke into the note of the chant. It was something wonderful and doubtless often saved him a wigging from the residentiary.[157]

By contrast, Charles Clarke was one of the youngest cathedral organists ever to be appointed. Born in Worcester, he was appointed organist of Durham Cathedral in 1811, before his sixteenth birthday. After two years there he returned to Worcester, where for some years the head chorister was his brother.[158] Although G. W. Chard was Mayor of Winchester and had a doctorate in music, his long reign of forty-seven years at the cathedral was a story of slackness and inefficiency.[159] William Perkins, who was organist of Wells from 1820 to 1859, was also mayor of his cathedral city. He was well known locally for putting an end to bull-baiting, but became less and less effective in the cathedral until he was finally asked to resign.[160]

Many organists were paid such low salaries that they were forced to spend much of their time teaching private pupils. The eccentric William Mutlow, organist of Gloucester from 1782 to 1832, combined piano lessons with cooking: 'In the middle of the lesson he would say, "There, go on; I can hear ye, I'm only going to baste the air [hare]"; so he walked into the kitchen, did what he proposed, came back and finished the lesson.'[161] Robert Janes of Ely had a very extensive private practice, extending into Norfolk and Suffolk and earning him a reputed income of over £1000 per annum. He rode long distances through the fens with a pair of lamps attached to his horse's saddle.[162] Shortly after S. S. Wesley became organist of Hereford Cathedral in 1832, he told his father that he was obliged to augment his salary by private teaching.[163]

Wesley, of course, was the most famous cathedral organist of the century. After three years at Hereford, he moved to Exeter. After a spell at Leeds Parish Church, he became organist of Winchester Cathedral in 1849 and finished his career with eleven years at Gloucester.[164] His name lives on today, since many of his anthems and services still find a regular place in the repertoire of cathedral choirs, while some of his tuneful compositions for the organ are deservedly popular. At a time when much church music was written, often indifferent and unmemorable, his highly individual harmonies and impressively structured compositions stand pre-eminent among the efforts of lesser men.[165] His other considerable achievement was his impassioned advocacy of important reforms in the way cathedral music was valued and practised.

In 1844–5 Wesley published by instalments a service in E major. In the preface, dated January 1845, he outlined some of the aspects of cathedral music that he felt were in need of reform.[166] Wesley overstated his case and was taken to task by the *Morning Post* as 'a grumbler and a Radical Reformer'.[167] Wesley's next essay in this field was a pamphlet that he published in 1849 entitled *A Few Words on Cathedral Music and the Musical System of the Church with a Plan of Reform*.[168] He was clear enough in his objective:

> All that is sought to be attained is a correct and decent performance of the Cathedral Services as by law established; and to shew what are the very least means by which that object, at the present time, may be carried into effect.[169]

The suggestions that Wesley made were as follows: there should always

177

be twelve lay clerks singing each day in a cathedral choir, at a stipend of £95 per annum, and three reserve men engaged at a stipend of £52 per annum. They should attend proper rehearsals, and if there was any conflict with their secular employment they should be paid more by the dean and chapter so that they were free to continue singing. The organist should be consulted in the appointment of new lay clerks, and a musical college might well be established at a selected cathedral for the training of lay clerks. Cathedral organists should be of a professional standard and paid between £500 and £800 per annum, as they were 'the *bishops* of their calling'. A commission should be established to exercise some kind of authority in the field of church music, and to administer a common fund for the training of choristers, the provision of music and the restoration of organs.[170]

A third opportunity for Wesley to air his views came in 1853 when the Cathedral Commission invited precentors and organists to consider certain suggestions about the way in which cathedral worship might be improved. Wesley published his reply.[171] In it he stressed the need for twelve lay clerks in each choir, so that a proper contrast could be made between the effect of soloists and choruses. They should be decently paid.[172] He argued that both the music performed in cathedrals and the quality of its peformance left much to be desired.[173] Wesley felt that cathedral music should not be controlled by chapters and that choristers should be better cared for.[174] He was justly critical of chapters, but they were also critical of him. In 1859 the dean and chapter of Winchester admonished him for neglect of duty as he had attended only 397 services out of a possible 780 in the course of a year, frequently leaving the organ in the hands of a fourteen-year-old pupil. He had neglected the training of the choir and had been disrespectful and discourteous.[175]

Why was Wesley, for all his talent and real contribution to cathedral music, such a difficult and insensitive man? Why did he fail to live up to the ideals that he himself so ardently propounded? Of course he was his own worst enemy, but a further reason, not mentioned elsewhere, may be suggested. In 1835 Wesley married the sister of his first dean, John Merewether. Merewether was a passionate, pugilistic man, at variance with his chapter, constantly struggling to improve his cathedral and its affairs, embittered by his lack of preferment. Wesley owed his early advancement to him, and had previously been his organist at Hampton. Was there an element of hero-worship in his relationship with Merewether? As a young man he may have taken him as his role model. The similarity between the two men is striking, and, although the point should not be stretched too far, it is possible that this family and professional link may have been a significant factor in shaping Wesley's life and career.[176]

Another outstanding organist in the nineteenth century was Zechariah

Buck, organist of Norwich Cathedral from 1819 to 1877.[177] Buck's chief claim to fame was as a trainer of choristers, and his choir was famed for the beauty of the boys' tone. Some of his methods were ingenious:

> ...in order that the boys should open their mouths, he resorted to the use of beans, marbles, nuts, acorns, coffee-berries, etc., the nuts proving a decided failure as the boys were always cracking them. At length the excellent idea occurred to the ingenious Doctor to experiment with a neat wooden mouthpiece, in the exact shape of his mouth; and to fit in with the teeth...[178]

He took great care over his solo boys, carefully supervising their diet and giving them phials of port to drink just before they sang their solos.[179] But he made sure that several boys were prepared for each solo, and his choristers were renowned for their ability.[180] One of his most famous choristers and pupils, A. H. Mann, later organist of King's College, Cambridge, recalled that Buck

> would never allow us to actually *sing*, except for a very short time indeed – not more than ten minutes; he might keep us at practice for over two hours (a common occurrence) but he would only let us *sing* for a brief interval and then rest. Secondly, he would never permit us to force our voices under any consideration whatever, while tone, words, and expression were very carefully watched...[181]

When a memorial to Buck was unveiled at Norwich in 1900, the dean said: 'there was not in England his superior as a trainer of boys and as an organiser of a great choir'.[182]

John Goss was a contemporary of Buck who was organist of St Paul's Cathedral from 1838 until 1872. He had studied with his predecessor Thomas Attwood, who was himself a pupil of Mozart. The choir of St Paul's never reached a high standard in his period of office and he is chiefly remembered now as a composer. Many of his compositions have been deservedly forgotten, but a few of them still keep his name alive and represent some of the best traditions of Victorian church music.[183] Unfortunately, towards the end of his time at St Paul's he was clearly failing both as an organist and in his direction of the choir.[184]

Goss was succeeded at St Paul's by John Stainer. Stainer had been a chorister at St Paul's, but later came under the influence of Sir Frederick Ouseley, who appointed him as organist at St Michael's College, Tenbury. Later he became organist of Magdalen College, Oxford. He was a brilliant player and a great choir-trainer. Within five years he had transformed the choir at St Paul's so that it had a national reputation. He widened the repertoire, extended and supported the practice of special performances of oratorios in the cathedral, rebuilt the organ, and altogether made the profession of cathedral organist respected and respectable, both among clergy and professional musicians. By the time he resigned in 1888 he had transformed the music of St Paul's. The *Musical World* said:

> The record of Dr Stainer's work at St Paul's is written in letters of gold on the memories of all those who contrast the Cathedral's services as they now are with what they were twenty years ago. The progress is almost phenomenal.[185]

A very different character was George Riseley, organist of Bristol Cathedral from 1876 until 1898. In 1884 he had a row with the precentor which was investigated by the dean and chapter. On Whitsunday, Riseley declined to perform the precentor's choice of anthem, as he felt his depleted choir could not adequately sing it, and chose an alternative. The chapter expressed their earnest hope that 'good sense and Christian forbearance' would 'heal any irritation that may have arisen', but warned that 'any future act of insubordination or discourtesy will involve his dismissal from his office'. At the same time they asked the precentor to exercise more discretion.[186] In the following year the dean and chapter resolved to dismiss Riseley and gave him three months' notice. Riseley, however, declined to recognize the notice. In November 1885 the chapter declared his office vacant and appointed A. H. Brewer as his successor.[187] Riseley, however, appealed to Bishop Ellicott as Visitor, who found in his favour and ordered the dean and chapter to reinstate him.[188] Brewer's temporary position only lasted three months. The dean and chapter set out very clearly their understanding of the organist's duties,[189] but in April Riseley said that he could not find any organist who was willing to act as his 'sole unpaid deputy'. The chapter said that they were willing to reconsider the question of a deputy organist, but that the other rules they had drawn up must be adhered to.[190] In October 1886 Riseley told the dean and chapter that these rules were unreasonable:

> No such requirements were ever made of my predecessor or of me, and I am quite at a loss to understand why this new departure is now attempted, especially as no complaint of inefficiency has ever been made, nor is it alleged or suggested that I have been slack in attendance or negligent in the performance of my duties.[191]

In January 1887 the dean wrote to Riseley refusing to give way, but the matter was not further developed until 1894 when after various rumblings Riseley was asked to attend the next chapter meeting: 'to shew cause why he should not be punished for disobedience to the first and second instruction of February 1886 and to subsequent Chapter orders'.[192] Riseley again appealed to Bishop Ellicott, but this time he declined to interfere. In January 1895 the dean and chapter told Riseley that he had been 'disobedient to their lawful and reasonable order' and admonished him.[193] Riseley then took the dean and chapter to court, but his appeal was dismissed.[194] The tense relationship continued, this time centring on the precentor's choice of music, which Riseley considered 'unplayable and unsingable'.[195] A further clash occurred over whether or not the precentor should speak to the choristers about the music.[196] In April 1896 Riseley complained that the music chosen was impossible for his weakened choir to sing.[197] In 1897 E. H. Fellowes was appointed precentor. Riseley's attendance at services continued to be erratic and in July 1898 he was again called before the chapter, who admonished and rebuked him.[198] Matters came to a head during the following winter. Fellowes told the chapter of several disputes that he had had with Riseley, and in October the dean and chapter told him that his conduct was 'both contumacious and disrespectful'. Riseley was again summoned to appear before the chapter, but the matter was left in the hands of the chapter clerk, who eventually reported in January 1899 that he had had several interviews with Riseley's brother which had resulted in Riseley agreeing to resign providing he could have a pension for life of £50 per annum.[199] Thus ended one of the bitterest disputes of the nineteenth century between a dean and chapter and a cathedral organist.

William Done was appointed organist of Worcester Cathedral in 1844, having been a chorister and articled pupil under his predecessor, C. E. J. Clarke. He was to be paid a stipend of £50 per annum, and was not allowed to engage a deputy without permission. He or his deputy were obliged to remain in the cathedral until the conclusion of each choral service. He was to rehearse the choristers, and the organ could not be used by any other person without his permission.[200] His daughter, Mrs Limoelan, gave a good description of his work:

> He rose soon after 6 o'clock in the morning, and began his teaching at 7, coming to the Cathedral for morning service, training the boys, or holding a full rehearsal, and then back again to his pupils, again teaching and attending Divine Service in the afternoon. In the evening he was often occupied in training the various choral societies – sometimes his teaching took him into the country.... The organist's income was very small and he could not have brought up his family without private teaching. But for the holidays at Christmas and Midsummer all this work would have been impossible and Festival years increased the strain.[201]

James Smith, one of his lay clerks, described him as 'an excellent musician – a good organist, pianist and teacher – the choristers have never been better trained than they were under him. He was of the old school, solid and good and a gentleman'.[202]

In 1869 Precentor Wheeler said that a better understanding between Done and the lay clerks would improve the services, and suggested that he should be officially recognized as choirmaster.[203] Done himself told the chapter that he was having difficulty in finding and keeping suitable choristers. He agreed that his relationship with the lay clerks should be more carefully defined:

> Ever since I have been in office (now 25 years) I have performed the duties of choirmaster under the Precentor. The attitude the choirmen have lately thought fit to adopt makes it necessary that the extent of my control over them, with regard to the music of the services, should be better understood. The fact of my never having been officially recognised as choirmaster may have led to these difficulties.[204]

In 1874, Done asked the chapter for an increase in salary, pointing out that many other cathedral organists were better paid and often given a house as well. Done contended that his stipend of £130 per annum was scarcely more than half the average figure.[205] Done was eventually appointed choirmaster in 1877.[206] A few months earlier the dean and chapter had expressed their appreciation of the peformances of special Passion music during Lent and made him an *ex gratia* payment of £5.[207] Although his assistant, Hugh Blair, took over his duties in 1889, he continued to hold the office of organist until his death in 1895. Shortly before his death he was given a Lambeth doctorate in music to mark the fiftieth anniversary of his appointment.[208] Precentor Woodward paid tribute to his 'unwearied devotion to duty'.[209]

The closing years of the century saw one more outstanding organist in the person of George Robertson Sinclair. He was a chorister at St Michael's College, Tenbury, and later was a pupil of Dr C. H. Lloyd at Gloucester, and assistant organist there. Appointed organist of Truro Cathedral in 1881 at the age of seventeen, he was able to lay the foundations of a choral tradition in the new cathedral. Bishop Benson kept a firm hand on Sinclair, who frequently went to receive instruction from him and seek his advice: 'In fact...I was a sort of prefect, with the Bishop as head-master.' Sinclair made a name for himself at the consecration of Truro Cathedral in 1887. Representatives of many cathedral choirs took part and a series of diocesan choral festivals was held during the celebrations, with some 4,000 singers from all over Cornwall being conducted by Sinclair during the week. Sinclair designed the fine four-manual Willis organ at Truro and then became organist of Hereford Cathedral in 1889. In making the appointment, the dean and chapter noted the excellent reputation he had gained at Truro.[210] At Hereford, Sinclair raised £2,300 to rebuild the organ and was prominent among those who wished to have a window in the cathedral in memory of Sir Frederick Ouseley. The *Musical Times* said in 1900 that he had a great influence on the musical life of Hereford. He was a close friend of Elgar, who dedicated one of his *Enigma Variations* to him. He was also conductor of many local choral societies and also held the prestigious post of conductor of Birmingham Festival Choral Society, which he was offered in 1900. With his interests in cycling, photography, yachting and freemasonry, besides his famous bulldog Dan, Sinclair was a familiar and much respected figure in Hereford from 1889 until his sudden death in 1917. When he was given a Lambeth doctorate in 1899, he was presented with the robes, which had been paid for by his many friends and admirers, at a 'brilliant function' in the Shirehall at Hereford in November of that year. The *Musical Times* praised his 'urbanity and tact' and the wide range of subscribers to his robes.[211]

Sinclair had as his assistant, both at Truro and at Hereford, Ivor Atkins. After a short spell as organist of Ludlow Parish Church, Atkins succeeded the ill-fated Hugh Blair at Worcester in 1897. Blair had been admonished in December 1896 and finally suspended in July 1897 'for continued neglect of the duties of his office and for general irregularity of life'.[212] The basic problem was drink. In November 1896 Precentor Woodward wrote to Dean Forrest, complaining that Blair was drunk when playing for evensong the previous Christmas Day, 'and this has occurred at intervals ever since'.[213] Woodward was optimistic when Atkins was first appointed. In his report for 1897 he wrote:

> He is undoubtedly an accomplished musician, and is showing every disposition to work cordially with the Precentor. His ability in training the choristers is already making itself felt; and this is largely due to the fact that he is able to maintain order and discipline at the daily practice.[214]

Unfortunately in 1900 Woodward revised his opinion of Atkins and said in his report for that year:

> I feel bound to draw attention to the unsatisfactory results achieved by the organist. There has been no neglect of the boys' practice. The allotted hour is always fully employed. But during his three years' tenure of office there has been a failure to produce even one satisfactory solo singer...
>
> Then with regard to the Choral Services themselves, they are frequently marred as far as the organ is concerned by careless blunders, and ill-judged accompaniments. It is patent to all that the voices are often drowned by the organ, with the result that the lay clerks cease singing and the boys shout. I do not deny that Mr Atkins possesses great facility of execution in the matter of voluntaries and recitals, but his accompaniments are neither artistic, devotional, nor reverent. Moreover, these defects as a trainer and accompanist are unfortunately accentuated by the fact that Mr Atkins fails to make himself a *persona grata* to those of the Body with whom he is brought in contact; while any remonstrance as to short-comings is always met by the answer that he is indifferent to criticism, as he is conscious of doing his duties to the best

of his ability...at the end of three years I see no more signs of efficiency than in his first six months of office. I am obliged therefore to admit that I now agree with those who have so often pronounced him not up to his work.[215]

The dean and chapter considered this report and asked Atkins to resign, but he responded with a very long letter to the chapter. As far as organ-playing was concerned, he felt that this was caused by the poor state of the organ and went on to describe some of the many faults that had developed in it. The criticism of his training of the choristers he felt to be unfair, since

the fault lies in the material....In my three years' work here I cannot recall amongst the boys half a dozen with good, strong, natural voices. Generally they have had bad breaks in their voices and often come with radical defects which I have *hoped* to cure (against my better judgement), but in many cases have been unsuccessful. Too many boys have been taken as probationers (and admitted afterwards) who were not good enough for a parish choir...[216]

Atkins was eventually let off with an admonition 'for constantly making mistakes in the services, for loud accompaniments and for failure in production of voice culture'. Dean Forrest was influenced by Woodward's advice that Atkins's work had improved.[217] Atkins remained at Worcester for another fifty years and proved to be a very distinguished organist.[218]

Organ recitals today are an important and regular part of the work of cathedral organists, but in the nineteenth century they were much rarer. When A. T. Corfe wanted to use the organ and hold a concert in Salisbury Cathedral in aid of the Infirmary Building Fund, he was refused leave by the dean and chapter.[219] E. T. Chipp, who was organist of Ely from 1867 to 1886, would sometimes give private organ recitals on summer evenings in the cathedral.[220] An organ recital was arranged at Wells during the Agricultural Show in 1886,[221] and they were a regular feature on Thursdays after evensong at Worcester in 1896.[222] Some cathedral chapters laid down specific instructions about organ voluntaries. At Hereford in 1800, the organist, Miles Coyle, was required to play a voluntary before matins and evensong on all Sundays and Christmas Day and before matins on all state holidays and days of the bishop's visitation and confirmation when the bishop, dean, hebdomadary or other presiding residentiary entered the quire, and on Assize Days when the judge entered.[223] In 1865 Precentor Wray of Winchester said he thought there should be a voluntary before and after every service, as was customary in many cathedrals.[224] In the previous year Wesley had been asked to play a voluntary before every service on Christmas Day, Easter Day, Ascension Day, Whitsunday and Trinity Sunday: 'The organ to commence playing when the clock strikes and to continue until the clergy have taken their places in the choir.'[225] Voluntaries after services on weekdays were requested at Hereford in 1870.[226] Voluntaries before and after each service were standard practice at Hereford by 1877,[227] and they were also customary at Ripon.[228] A feature of services that has now been dropped from common custom was that of a middle voluntary after the psalms at matins and evensong. S. S. Wesley was celebrated for his extempore voluntaries after the psalms and before the anthem. A long improvisation on the organ before the anthem was a common feature at Sunday evensong at all cathedrals.[229] Jebb notes that a middle voluntary was customary at York and Lichfield and suggested that its purpose was to cover the movement of a reader to the lectern.[230]

Many cathedral organists learnt their profession by serving as articled pupils to the local cathedral organist; the position of assistant or deputy organist varied from cathedral to cathedral and was only recognized with difficulty at some places. An early example of an official assistant was at Winchester, where Chard was allowed to employ one at the same stipend as a lay vicar received.[231] A crisis occurred on Christmas Day 1822 at Exeter when the organist, James Paddon, was absent without providing a deputy.[232] In 1830 the dean and chapter agreed to the appointment of an official assistant for Paddon, mainly to assist him in taking choristers' practices.[233] When John Hunt was appointed to succeed S. S. Wesley at Hereford in 1835, he immediately asked for a deputy to play the organ on two days in each week.[234] The dean and chapter of Wells were so pleased with the deputy organist there in 1846 that they gave him a gratuity of £5 per quarter.[235] In 1865 the dean and chapter of Exeter agreed to pay £10 towards the stipend of an assistant organist who was engaged for one year.[236] George Cooper had been assistant organist at St Paul's from 1838, but he was not paid by the dean and chapter until 1869, when the chapter gave him £20. When he died in 1876 he was succeeded by George Martin and the salary was increased to £100 per annum. Martin took an important part in the music at St Paul's under Stainer's direction, and was in many ways the first modern assistant cathedral organist.[237] S. S. Wesley was allowed to have an official assistant at Gloucester in 1872 under certain conditions,[238] and three years later the dean and chapter of Exeter took over the organist's contribution to his assistant's salary, so that they were to be responsible for paying him a total of £50 per annum.[239] But there were still some cathedrals where the situation was less than satisfactory. George Townshend Smith told the Ecclesiastical Commissioners in 1867 that he was allowed to employ a deputy for two days a week, but he had to pay him himself. He had no articled pupil and it was difficult to take a holiday.[240] At Durham, Philip Armes complained that he had not had a Sunday off-duty between September 1878 and January 1890.[241] In 1887 Precentor Vine Hall said that more use should be made of Hugh Blair, the assistant organist at Worcester.[242] In 1888 the dean and chapter clarified

185

his position and asked that Done should be more specific in the allocation of duties to him.[243] In the event, Blair came to be almost completely responsible for the organist's work until Done's death in 1895.[244] By 1891 he was in full charge of the choristers' rehearsals and in 1892 he was praised for his 'skilful and artistic accompaniments'.[245] An additional assistant was engaged to accompany the weekday morning services.[246] The established position of assistant organist at Worcester may be seen in 1897; when Atkins was appointed organist in that year, the assistant organist was asked to continue in office.[247]

When a new organist was required, he was usually chosen by a competitive trial. The dean and chapter of Durham were pleased in 1811 that they had so many able candidates for the vacant organistship.[248] When Philip Armes was appointed organist of Chichester Cathedral in 1861, 'There were five competitors for the post and Turle was adjudicator. All the candidates played on the same day and afterwards lunched together at the Deanery.' Dean Hook appointed Armes because he had an Oxford degree (the only one of the five) and was highly commended by Ouseley.[249] Eighteen months later he applied for the post at Durham. E. T. Chipp, later organist of Ely, was a fellow-candidate and J. B. Dykes acted as adjudicator. Each of the candidates had to play a solo piece on the organ (Armes was the only candidate who did not play the Hallelujah chorus, a favourite of the dean's maiden sisters), and to extemporize a four-part fugue on a given subject. They also had to play for the two cathedral services and cope with sight-reading two oratorio choruses.[250] When a new organist was appointed at Peterborough in 1870, under the supervision of Edward Hopkins, the organist of the Temple Church, the candidates were required to realize a figured bass at sight as part of the audition.[251] When a successor to D. J. Wood was appointed in 1876, the dean and chapter of Chichester asked Sir Walter Parratt to select a shortlist of six candidates for them.[252] In 1898 the Royal College of Organists formed a special committee under the chairmanship of Sir Frederick Bridge to consider the appointment of cathedral organists. In a letter dated 24 May 1898, they wrote to every dean stressing the importance of the organist's position.[253] When T. T. Noble was appointed to succeed Naylor at York in 1897 there were no less than seventy-nine applicants for the vacant position.[254] When C. F. South was appointed organist of Salisbury in 1884, he was expected to play the organ at all musical services in the cathedral, and not to be absent or delegate his duties to a deputy without permission of the dean or canon-in-residence. He was also responsible for the care of the organ and to ensure that no one else played it, except for his articled pupils, without the specific permission of the dean or canon-in-residence and by arrangement with him. He was also to be choirmaster and to rehearse the choristers, attending all regular practices and any special practices called by the dean, precentor or succentor. He was also to teach the piano and organ to any of the choristers for £5 each, provided that after six lessons the said chorister was seen to be making progress. He was to keep his house in repair, paying all rates and taxes thereon, and not make alterations without the consent of the dean and chapter. The appointment was terminable by three months' notice on either side, and the organist's salary was to be £230 per annum.[255]

During the century, then, there was a marked development in the professional standing and achievements of cathedral organists. By 1900 they were often musicians of considerable local, and indeed national, significance. The appointment of Stainer to St Paul's was the watershed. Despite Wesley's greatness, he was still a mere musician, an employee of the dean and chapter. Stainer, and men of his model such as Sinclair, were professional musicians in their own right and held in esteem by their chapters.

In the end, despite the energy and talent of the organist, the quality of a choir depends on the quality of its members. In the first half of the century, in some old foundation cathedrals (notably Hereford), it was customary for the men's voices to be supplied by clergy who were members of the colleges of vicars choral attached to these cathedrals.[256] This custom was also found in some new foundation cathedrals, such as Norwich where the eight minor canons attended the choral services every day.[257] Difficulties sometimes arose when the choir was partly composed of clergy and partly of laymen. A Wells priest vicar complained that one of the lay vicars (who were mainly carpenters, shoemakers, stone-masons and other respectable tradesmen) had 'rudely assailed' him and 'peremptorily ordered me to answer immediately a question he put to me, reminding me at the same time that I was his junior'.[258]

Nevertheless, there were generally at least six lay clerks in most cathedrals, required to attend a minimum of two services every day in the year.[259] Some of the numbers given in 1854 can be compared with those in 1893.[260] They frequently faced enormous problems: S. S. Wesley told the cathedral commissioners in 1854 that lay clerks were paid 'at the rate of inferior mechanics and day labourers' and asserted that 'at least half the numbers of choir men engaged in trade had once or oftener been bankrupt or compounded with their creditors'.[261] In 1800 a Worcester lay clerk could expect only £20 per annum as his basic stipend, plus a house allowance of £2 per annum and corn rent and wood money off the capitular estates.[262] The dean and chapter of Winchester were quite generous to their lay vicars at the beginning of the century, giving occasional bonuses on top of the basic salary of £30 with augmentations.[263] The salary of the Exeter lay vicars was raised by £40 a term in 1803[264] and in 1818 the dean and chapter of Bristol increased the salary of their singing-men from £21 per annum to £31 8s, provided they attended at least eight services each week.[265] At Peterborough in 1822 one lay clerk was paid only

£10 per annum, but in 1826 the pay of lay clerk William Pheasant was increased from £20 to £26.[266] The salaries at Worcester were raised to £60 per annum (including corn rent) in 1824, with a 6d bonus for each service attended (or £18 5s in a full year).[267] In 1826, £30 was the current annual rate at both Chichester[268] and Winchester Cathedrals.[269] In 1840 the dean and chapter of Winchester paid a long-serving lay vicar £80 per annum.[270] At Canterbury, though, the lay clerks felt that they were so badly treated that they sent a printed account of their grievances to the Prime Minister.[271] In June 1848 they sent a memorial to the dean and chapter complaining about their low stipends, pointing out that they had been increased from £25 per annum to £40 between 1770 and 1810, but had remained at that figure for nearly forty years. At Durham, they said, the lay clerks had an annual salary of £114 12s and the Canterbury lay clerks felt that they should receive a similar amount.[272] Each of the three junior lay vicars at Winchester had their stipends increased to £63 per annum in 1853.[273] Winchester was therefore roughly in the middle of the range of stipends, for in 1854 the cathedral commissioners found that the Durham lay clerks were the best paid in the country, and the poorest were at Christ Church, Oxford, where their annual income was little more than £30 per annum. Most cathedrals paid their lay clerks between £40 and £80 per annum.[274]

The 1850s were a time of inflation. At some cathedrals the dean and chapter recognized this and adjusted stipends accordingly; at Chichester, for example, the dean and chapter raised the salaries of the lay vicars to £55 per annum in 1854 'in consequence of the continued high price of provisions'.[275] Elsewhere, though, lay clerks faced difficulty. In 1852 a new lay clerk at Worcester 'was obliged to borrow money to be able to live... I distinctly remember the difficulty I had to provide myself with food and lodging the first year of my service'.[276] During the 1850s and 1860s there was little improvement in lay clerks' salaries.[277] The *Musical Times* urged in 1869 that the stipends of lay clerks were still not high enough: 'If the lay clerks are paid at the same rate and treated much in the same way as an unskilled labourer, is it a matter for astonishment if they be somewhat rough and uncouth in manner?'[278] When the lay vicars of Salisbury complained about their salaries in 1869, the dean and chapter increased them from £73 per annum to £78,[279] while at Winchester four years later they were given a fixed stipend of £100 per annum with deductions of 2s 6d for every absence, instead of the previous bonuses for attendance.[280] Some figures published in 1876 show that nine out of ten lay clerks at Bristol were paid approximately £60, while those at Chester received £70 and those at Canterbury were paid £79 15s per annum. Three out of four lay clerks at Carlisle were paid £80 and the fourth £50, but at Rochester they were all paid £55. Two of the lay clerks at Lincoln were paid £80 and the other two received £50. The stipends at Chirst Church, Oxford, varied between £40 and £90, and those at Exeter were thought to be between £80 and £100. At Gloucester, however, the rate was only £40, plus 1s 6d for each service attended. The sum of £94 15s was paid to each lay clerk at Manchester. The three cathedrals where generous stipends were paid were Hereford (£100–£120), Durham (£152 16s–£177 16s) and Lichfield (£129 1s 4d–£197 13s 8d).[281] In 1877 some of the lay clerks at Ely were paid £100, while the remainder received £80.[282] At Carlisle in 1880 there was a wide variation in the pay of lay clerks; the highest paid received £120 and the lowest a mere £15 per annum. Five others were paid £80 and one was paid £60 per annum.[283] The stipends of the songmen at York, which ranged between £50 and £100, were thought to be still inadequate,[284] while the lay vicars of Chichester claimed that their remuneration of £60 each per annum meant that they were 'the lowest paid choir in the kingdom'.[285] A survey of the lay clerks at some seventeen cathedrals in 1893 showed that those at Durham were still the highest paid at about £150 per annum each, but at other cathedrals they were paid much less; at Gloucester their stipends had been *reduced* to £60 per annum, 'owing to a large reduction of cathedral income'.[286] Wesley's complaint that lay clerks were badly paid was certainly true, but it is difficult to substantiate his claim of frequent cases of bankruptcy, though there were instances of this at Wells in 1891 and Worcester in 1892.[287]

Dean Harvey Goodwin of Ely (later Bishop of Carlisle) was quite clear about the sort of man a lay clerk should be:

> No amount of trouble and inquiry is wasted which tends to procure really holy and religious men for the occupation of this responsible post. Voice and knowledge of music must not stand for everything. The Dean should be quite satisfied as to the previous history of every applicant and nothing should induce him to admit a doubtful member into the choir. Every Lay Clerk should be a consistent and devout communicant.[288]

But it was not easy to recruit lay clerks. At Exeter a new lay vicar was elected by the others following a voice trial.[289] Often a new lay clerk had to serve a probationary year.[290] In 1881 the dean and chapter of Winchester refused to admit a lay clerk after his year's probation; he had to serve two further periods of six months before he was eventually admitted.[291] There was much embarrassment at Norwich in 1851 when the lay clerks tried to interfere in the appointment of a new lay clerk by coming in a body to the vestry and improperly urging Dean Pellew to select the very man he had already chosen.[292] Rochester found 'great difficulty in finding a duly qualified person' to fill vacancies in the 1850s,[293] and John Young, the organist of Lincoln, said thirty years later: 'we cannot get competent men...men who come have no knowledge of Cathedral music'.[294]

From about 1880 until after the turn of the century, the alto part was sung by boys instead of lay clerks at Peterborough Cathedral.[295] When a bass layclerkship at Worcester was advertised in the *Musical Times* in 1876, however, applications were received from seven singers, including one each from the choirs at St Paul's, Wells and Lichfield Cathedrals.[296] Seven candidates applied for a tenor vacancy at Winchester in 1879. The voice trial included singing with the choir at both daily services, a solo of their own choice, and some sight-reading tests.[297] Precentor Vine Hall was critical of the appointment of a young lay clerk, against his advice, at Worcester in 1884.[298] In the 1890s at least three lay clerks from Southwell Minster moved south to Worcester.[299] The dean and chapter of Chichester were insistent in 1890 that they should be informed of the date of voice trials; new lay vicars could only be appointed at meetings of the chapter.[300] New lay clerks at Norwich had to take a formal oath and subscribe their names at a ceremony in the vestry before being admitted,[301] while at St Paul's a new form of service for the admission of lay clerks and vergers was drawn up in 1880 by Canon Liddon.[302]

The average lay clerk of the nineteenth century did not always match up to the high standard demanded by Harvey Goodwin. Ouseley complained that

> if they kneel down at all, it is not to pray; if they utter with their lips anything beyond what they have to sing, it is too often some common everyday conversation addressed *sotto voce* to their neighbour, or some jokes, at the expense, perhaps, of the officiating clergyman, or some criticism of the music, or of the performance of it...even when a choral celebration of the Holy Eucharist renders their vocal assistance necessary, they then for the most part do not communicate, or if they do, it is in a perfunctory and indevout manner, which is worse than if they had stayed away altogether.[303]

In 1801 William Sharpe, a singing-man at Bristol, was admonished 'on account of the irregularity of his life and negligence of duty'.[304] In about 1830 the lay clerks of Gloucester Cathedral were rather troublesome and were admonished frequently for their quarrelling and bad behaviour.[305] Dean Pellew of Norwich was taken to task by an anonymous correspondent in 1831 for his 'capricious and tyrannical rule' and for keeping the lay clerks standing while he read the statutes to them.[306] Misconduct in the cathedral was the cause of William Topham, a lay clerk at Worcester, being admonished in 1858.[307] A lay vicar of Winchester by the name of Corps was in trouble with the dean and chapter in 1860. He had deliberately taken a different note from that given by a minor canon during the course of a service and later, in the presence of the dean and two of the canons, had spoken of the incident to the minor canon 'in a very rude and unbecoming manner'.[308] In 1864 John Goss, the succentor of Hereford, complained to the chapter there about the 'disrespectful deportment' of James Barnby, one of the lay clerks.[309] William Cooper, a lay clerk at Rochester, was a troublesome character. He was an insolvent petitioner before the County Court. He was admonished by the dean and chapter for indecorous behaviour in the cathedral and was described as an 'unbecoming and inefficient performer of his duties'. He was suspended in 1866 as a result of his insolvency, but ignored this and appeared the following morning in his surplice and took his place in the choir. The dean and chapter then declared him 'contumacious and disobedient' and he was reprimanded by the vice-dean. When his insolvency was quashed by the County Court he was reinstated.[310] A lay clerk of Worcester was admonished in 1870 for striking a chorister,[311] and nine years later Precentor Vine Hall complained to the dean about the behaviour of another lay clerk at Worcester who had inflicted 'very rude and insulting language' on him.[312] D. G. Manning, one of the priest vicars at Wells, told the cathedral commissioners in 1883 that there were 'numerous cases of grossly irreverent conduct' during services.[313]

Strict rules and regulations were drawn up for the lay clerks of Ely in May 1887.[314] At Winchester in 1889 one of the lay clerks, John Phillips, defied the precentor by impertinently refusing to stay to a special rehearsal.[315] In the following year at Chichester there was a complaint about the irreverent behaviour of the lay vicars during services.[316] On Christmas Eve 1894 the Precentor of Winchester reproved a lay clerk by the name of Gardiner for hurrying in the psalms, but the latter retaliated by refusing to sing during the service on Christmas Day. He was accordingly marked as 'absent' and suffered the customary deduction in pay.[317] Two years later Gardiner was admonished by the dean and chapter for not taking his proper part in the singing and for sending an insolent letter to the precentor, after he had remonstrated with him.[218] The Dean of Salisbury complained in 1896 about 'unseemly altercations between certain of the lay vicars within the walls of the Cathedral'.[319] At Winchester, Canon Warburton told Bishop Davidson in 1900 that one of the cathedral clergy should be given the 'cure of souls' of the lay vicars in order 'to elevate their moral and spiritual tone'.[320] On the other hand, there were some places, such as Lichfield and St Paul's, where the lay clerks seem to have developed a commendable *esprit de corps* in the 1880s.[321]

Another problem was the extra-mural musical activities of lay clerks. Victorian chapters strongly disapproved of their singing in such places as public houses, or even visiting them. In 1864 the dean and chapter of Winchester decided that no lay vicar should be admitted unless he had previously promised not to keep a public house.[322] When Gardiner was appointed as a lay vicar at Winchester in 1879, Precentor Crowdy wrote to impress upon him 'the necessity for absolute steadiness and temperate habits', as he had been seen leaving a public house on the day of his audition.[323] In 1883 the Dean of Salisbury complained that three of the singing-men 'were habitually frequenting the Crown Hotel in High Street', and agreed to interview them.[324] The problem was prevalent at Winchester four years later; a lay vicar there was reprimanded and warned 'for frequenting public houses'.[325] Following the death in 1891 of a young lay clerk at Worcester – 'a victim to intemperance' – the dean and chapter forbade them from accepting

> any engagement to sing at concerts held in places where drink is sold...these restrictions were made in the interests of the lay clerks themselves, that is to save them from taking what may very possibly be the first steps to ruin.[326]

In 1896 it was decided to enforce more strongly the rule that lay clerks were not allowed to sing in hotels or public houses.[327] The outstanding example of this attitude was an episode that has come to be known as the Shoreham Gardens saga. In May 1875 the dean and chapter of Chichester considered a courteous request from the organist that the lay vicars should be allowed to sing glees and part-songs once a fortnight on Wednesday afternoons at Shoreham Gardens, for which they would receive £30 per annum plus expenses. This request, which would have involved a rearrangement of cathedral services, was refused, but a fortnight later the dean and chapter heard that a poster had been seen advertising that the lay vicars would sing at Swiss Gardens, Shoreham, on a Monday. The chapter warned the lay vicars that if they took part in this concert they would instantly cease to be members of the cathedral choir. The lay vicars replied that they knew nothing about the offending poster and regretted its publication. The chapter, as 'guardian of the character and status of the Cathedral body', reiterated that they must not sing at Shoreham and sent the chapter clerk there to see whether the views of the dean and chapter had been understood. He walked through part of the town, but failed to see any notice about the non-appearance of the lay vicars, except for a telegram posted outside the Gardens. He interviewed the promoter of the ill-fated concert who assured him that when he had received the telegram from the dean and chapter he had 'sent to all station masters up and down the line requesting them not to issue tickets to persons going for the purpose of the concert'.[328] When Oliver Milward, a lay clerk at Worcester for thirty-three years, died in 1898 he was remembered as 'one of the first to make a stand against the practice which he found prevailing among the lay clerks of repairing to public houses after service'.[329]

The chief fear of chapters about their lay clerks frequenting public houses was that they might become habitual drunkards and so bring disrepute upon the cathedral as well as disgrace, or worse, upon themselves. William Tootell, a lay vicar of Exeter, was admonished by the dean and chapter in 1834:

he had frequently been in a state unfit for his Cathedral duties in consequence of liquor and that he was in the general habit of frequenting pot houses contrary to the statutes of the Church, the rules of Ecclesiastical discipline and the laws of the land.[330]

Three years later he was suspended and later dismissed because of his habitual drunkenness.[331] Frederick Turner, a lay clerk at Bristol, was dismissed in 1850 for attending a service 'in a state of intoxication'.[332] William Simonds, a lay vicar of Winchester, was frequently absent as a result of his drinking, and another lay vicar there, by the name of Trenham, was involved in an affray with a man from Kingsgate Street as he left a public house after midnight one night in June 1857.[333] Five years later another Winchester lay vicar, George Richards, was fined a fortnight's stipend because of intoxication and improper conduct.[334] A particularly difficult case was that of J. D. Price, a lay clerk of Worcester Cathedral, who had already been in trouble with the chapter for an unauthorized absence and for hitting a chorister.[335] On 15 December 1876 Price came to the services in the cathedral 'in a state of intoxication' and was absent the following day. When he was suspended,[336] he pleaded financial worries:

> I was unable to take either food or sleep and a very little of anything would take that effect complain'd of; I have sacrificed my furniture for the benefit of any creditors. I am now living upon sufferance until I can pay for the goods I am now using and to resign my appointment would be to throw my wife and child into the streets or workhouse.

But the chapter found his excuses insufficient and he had to resign. He replied 'By the loss of my Cathedral appointment I was at once without incoming means of any kind. I am by all this reduced to much distress and I hardly know where to look.'[337] In 1898 a lay vicar at Chichester called Kelly was allowed to continue in office only if he avoided public houses and remained sober.[338]

Occasionally lay clerks were accused of more serious charges. In 1803 a lay vicar at Salisbury was accused of incest and suspended for a year.[339] At Winchester in 1814 a lay vicar by the name of Turner was accused of fraudulently altering 'the Choir Book for the purpose of procuring to himself greater pay than was justly his due'.[340] John Griffiths, a lay clerk of Worcester from 1791 to 1821, was a particularly troublesome character. Having been rebuked by the dean for not calling him 'Sir', he took advantage of a time when the dean was taking a service by adding 'Sir' to each phrase of the Lord's Prayer as he repeated it after the dean. On another occasion he made advances to the elderly sister of a prebendary on the banks of the Severn and was arrested and imprisoned for assault, although he only kissed her. He later infuriated the said prebendary by stealing up behind him and shouting 'Fire!' into his ear whenever he saw him in the street.[341] In 1816 Matthew Huby, a songman of York Minster, was dismissed by the chapter when they discovered that he was a bigamist and was about to marry a third woman.[342] In 1818 Edwin Ball, one of the lay vicars at Salisbury, was accused of adultery and of trying to procure an abortion, and was dismissed.[343] In 1852 Robert Bebby, a lay clerk at Gloucester, was charged with grossly neglecting his duty in the choir and behaving disgracefully in the palace of the Bishop of Hereford during the Three Choirs Festival.[344] Towards the end of the century a lay vicar at Winchester was dismissed after being imprisoned for contempt of court.[345]

Often choirs were hampered by ancient lay clerks whose voices were practically useless. Three of the eight lay clerks at Norwich were said in 1829 to be 'old and ineffective'.[346] As J. B. Dykes pointed out: 'There are at present no means of dispensing with the services of such members, either by pensioning them off, or supplying their place by paid substitutes.'[347] At Lichfield in 1854 the two oldest lay vicars were eighty-five and eighty,[348] and the lay vicars of Wells said in 1879 that five of their members were

> over 60 years of age, one of them considerably more than 70 and one of 85 years old. Each of these vicars has been here for more than 30 years and two for more than 40 years, engaged in the service of the Cathedral.

One Silas Fletcher had faithfully served Wells Cathedral as a lay vicar since 1811.[349] When Charles Lockey, a lay vicar choral of St Paul's, died in 1901, it was noted that owing to loss of voice he had been represented by a deputy since 1859.[350] At Salisbury, however, two lay vicars were retired in 1861 as a result of 'inefficiency from advanced age'.[351] The average age of cathedral lay clerks was much lower than these exceptional cases. In 1875 only Durham, Exeter, Lichfield, Norwich, St Paul's and Salisbury employed lay clerks over sixty, and in most cathedrals men in their twenties and thirties were common. But Bristol, Rochester and Wells declined to give any ages to this enquiry.[352] The dean and chapter of Hereford were certainly aware of imperfections among the voices of their lay clerks. In 1882 they reflected 'that the sad state of Mr Izod's health, and the imperfections at times of the voices of Mr Flint and Mr Andrews make the Bass parts not so strong and less satisfactory than could be desired'.[353] Of the nine lay vicars at Winchester in 1883, two or three 'manage to mar all the music of our services'.[354] John Hooker, a lay vicar at Exeter in the middle of the century, was found to be very incompetent in both the verse and chorus parts of anthems and services. He was erratic in his attendance and neglected the opportunities made for him to have private instruction. The organist, Alfred Angel, told the chapter that he even had to warn two choristers to supply the alto part if Hooker went wrong. Hooker appealed to Bishop Phillpotts, but he agreed that the dean and chapter were right to dismiss him.[355] In 1885 the dean and chapter of Gloucester decided that new lay clerks should be appointed for a ten-year period.[356] Dean Liddell of Christ Church once personally intervened to persuade a worn-out alto that he should sing bass,[357] but at Canterbury half the lay clerks were said to be passengers.[358] Edward Vine Hall, precentor of Worcester, repeatedly complained in his annual reports about the problem of useless voices among the men.[359] His successor, H. H. Woodward, reminded the chapter in his report in 1893 that Gloucester, Hereford and Chester Cathedrals had all made arrangements to dismiss unsatisfactory lay clerks. The real trouble, of course, was that the pensions offered to retiring lay clerks were derisory. F. J. O. Helmore, a Canterbury minor canon, told the cathedral commissioners in 1884 that the pensions of lay clerks were too often a 'miserable pittance'.[360]

From time to time, however, efforts were made to tackle this problem. When Samuel Dangerfield, a Worcester lay clerk, retired in 1828 he was allowed a pension equivalent to his former stipend, which had amounted to an average of £38 10s over the preceding seven years.[361] When two more Worcester lay clerks retired in 1836 they received the same pension in addition to lump sums of £50 and £35 respectively.[362] The senior lay clerk at Norwich was paid a pension of £40 per annum in 1841 and the same sum was paid as a pension at Peterborough in 1880.[363] In 1854 the dean and chapter of Canterbury told the Cathedral Commission that their lay clerks were entitled to a pension of £25 per annum. Additional gratuities meant that two former lay clerks were each in receipt of £40 per annum.[364] One of the lay vicars at Chichester whose voice had failed was given a pension of £25 per annum in 1869 and re-employed as a verger. In 1874 Joseph Barber, a lay vicar there for nearly forty years, was given a pension of £40 per annum.[365] In 1890 the dean and chapter of Chichester agreed to increase the stipends of the lay vicars when the amount paid in pensions to former lay vicars lapsed through their death. No new pensions had been allowed since 1888, but two of the lay vicars complained that they had previously been promised pensions.[366] The dean and chapter of Salisbury decided in 1899 that all new lay vicars must contribute to a pension fund.[367]

There were other ways in which chapters showed their concern for the well-being of their lay clerks. In 1801 the dean and chapter of Bristol generously gave 5 guineas to each of their lay clerks 'on account of the great dearness of provision'.[368] Thomas Cox at Chichester was allowed a loan of £120 by the chapter there 'to enable him to exercise and carry on his trade or business of a shoemaker within the City of Chichester'.[369] The dean and chapter of Worcester gave £10 in 1830 to James Bateman in consideration of his 'severe indisposition and distressed circumstances',[370] while at Winchester in 1862 a sick lay vicar was given £100 on his resignation through ill health.[371] Eight years later they gave £10 to Penual Cross, to enable him to purchase some false teeth.[372] There was a tragic event at Norwich in 1880, however, when a lay clerk committed suicide in the cathedral.[373] H. J. Dyke at Worcester was given 5 guineas in 1891 towards the cost of 'special medical attendance', but died soon afterwards.[374]

Increasingly during the nineteenth century, cathedral chapters began to employ supernumerary lay clerks. In 1818 John Barrett, a singing-man at Bristol, was allowed to provide a deputy to sing in his place when he was at St Augustine's Church, where he was the parish clerk.[375] Two supernumeraries were engaged at Winchester in 1841 to sing on all Sundays and major feasts, as well as at two weekday services each week.[376] Four supernumeraries were engaged at Gloucester in 1851 at 2s 6d for each Sunday and festival.[377] In the following year the choir at St Paul's was doubled by the engagement of six assistant choirmen.[378] George Townshend Smith, the organist of Hereford Cathedral, wanted in 1859 to recruit 'six of the most respectable members of the Choral Society, giving preference to old choristers' to augment his choir on Sundays.[379] At Chichester in 1868 it was decided that the lay vicars should in future be responsible for finding and paying their own substitutes.[380] Two supernumeraries were admitted there in 1869 to sing on Sundays, Wednesdays and Fridays during the following six months for £10 each.[381] The supernumeraries at Worcester were considered an advantage to the choir in 1872 – four seem to have been employed.[382] The reliance at St Paul's on supernumerary voices led to eight men being employed in 1873 to attend eight weekday services and to sing at all choral celebrations on condition that they attended a weekday rehearsal.[383] In 1875 there was one supernumerary lay clerk at Bristol, Durham, Hereford and Lichfield, two at Carlisle, three at Rochester and Winchester, four at Salisbury (including the assistant organist) and Worcester (Sundays only), five at Peterborough, eleven at Lincoln and twelve at York. At Ely there was one daily supernumerary and four Sunday men. At Exeter, in addition to the eight statutory lay vicars and six secondaries, there was one supernumerary lay clerk and also a substitute for the organist. Manchester had two supernumeraries on weekdays and an unspecified number on Sundays. Salisbury employed three Sunday men plus an assistant organist.[384] When a supernumerary lay vicar at Winchester retired in 1883 after thirty years' service, he was told that he could sing with the choir whenever he wished.[385] Eight supernumeraries were appointed at Winchester in 1895 to sing at the Sunday services for £5 per annum, provided they attended the newly established weekly practice on Saturdays.[386]

On the whole, life was not easy for Victorian lay clerks, but through their faithfulness they preserved the traditions of English cathedral music – a responsibility that they shared, of course, with the choristers. At the beginning of the nineteenth century the life of cathedral choristers was not only onerous but almost completely devoid of proper education. They found a valiant ally in Miss Maria Hackett, by whose zeal and courage cathedral chapters were eventually persuaded to improve conditions for their boys. In 1827 Miss Hackett printed statistics about the choristers in various cathedrals. Their statutory number varied between six (at Carlisle, Chichester, Peterborough and Wells) and fifteen (at Lincoln). In many cases the actual number of choristers fell short of what was intended by the statutes. There were only ten choristers at Lincoln and Exeter, where the statutory number was fifteen and fourteen respectively, and only eight at Lichfield and Salisbury, where there were supposed to be fourteen in each case. Many cathedrals had their proper complement of eight or ten choristers, and at Hereford and Winchester there were even one or two extra choristers.[387] R. L. Caley, the Precentor of Bristol Cathedral, urged the Cathedral Commission in 1854 to increase the number of choristers there.[388] At Bristol, Wells, Winchester and elsewhere, supernumerary choristers were being recruited in the middle years of the century,[389] and at Chester the number of choristers was increased from eight to twelve by Dean Anson.[390] But at Chichester as late as 1864 there were only six choristers, though this number was raised to ten and then to twelve shortly afterwards.[391] At Worcester in 1869, however, William Done, the organist, told the dean and chapter that it was difficult to obtain choristers.[392] When two choristerships were advertised at Worcester in 1875 no satisfactory applications were received.[393] The choir at Hereford was in such a poor state in 1881 that two extra boys were hired from Novellos to sing at the Christmas services.[394] By 1891 there were sixteen choristers at Winchester, six of whom were regarded as foundation boys. There were also between four and eight probationers, who occupied seats adjacent to the choristers and attended one service daily as well as all practices.[395] At Bristol the choristers were divided into three shifts, each shift attending in turn all the services for two successive weeks and then school only for the third week. All the choristers, however, were obliged to attend the weekly Friday practice.[396] Six probationers were added to the choir at Bristol in 1893.[397] The number of choristers at Norwich was increased from fourteen to sixteen in 1897 and then to twenty in 1899.[398]

Maria Hackett told Dean Pretyman of St Paul's in 1811 that the choral duties of the boys interfered with their education.[399] Two years later she found one boy at St Paul's who, after seven years in the choir, 'could neither play a bar of music nor read at sight'.[400] From 1812 the St Paul's boys were looked after by William Hawes, who was a vicar choral and held the post of almoner. Together with boys from the Chapel Royal, he boarded the four senior St Paul's choristers in a large house in Adelphi Terrace. He arranged engagements for the boys to sing in outside public concerts and oratorios, claiming that 'it contributed an important part towards their musical education'.[401] But they received scant education in the theory of music or playing the harpsichord. They 'have merely been called into the parlour occasionally in an evening to sing to their Master's company', while the four juniors met their master only 'accidentally'.[402] So ill prepared were they for the confirmation in 1824 that they 'did not seem to be aware of its occurrence'.[403] When Dean Coplestone arrived at St Paul's in 1827, he reorganized the choir school.

In 1802 the dean and chapter of Salisbury decided that their choristers should learn English and writing rather than Latin. They therefore ordered that they should be instructed only in their own school, their writing master being paid 5 guineas per annum, and should not be obliged to learn Latin.[404] In 1818 Dean Talbot told Maria Hackett that they were taught music by the organist, and learnt the three Rs, together with Latin and Greek, from Mr Greenly, one of the priest vicars. They were paid £8–12 per annum, plus an apprentice fee of £30 on superannuation.[405] At Bristol the dean and chapter drew up careful regulations for the education of the choristers in 1802.[406]

Choristers were generally paid a small amount each year, bound as apprentices and given a leaving bursary. At Winchester their pay was raised from £30 to £40 per annum in 1806.[407] Six years later the dean and chapter decided that they should be formally bound as apprentices to the organist and given 15 guineas on leaving the choir.[408] At Durham, however, those who left the choir under the age of thirteen were not to be given any apprentice fees. The others had a salary of £8–9 plus perquisites, with two suits of clothes annually.[409] The salaries at Worcester were increased by £1 per annum in 1824.[410] A sliding scale of allowances was introduced in 1825 at Chichester,[411] where the leaving bursaries were fixed at £12 each, and at Worcester in 1876.[412] The indentures for a chorister at Wells provided for him to continue until eighteen if his voice had not broken by then.[413] The apprentice fee at Winchester was increased to £30 in 1844.[414] At Salisbury a fund was formed 'for the purpose of defraying the expenses of placing ex-choristers as apprentices to respectable tradesmen'.[415] The ten choristers at Rochester received an average of £7 13s in 1849, according to Robert Whiston.[416] At Bristol choristers who left the choir were paid £6 for four years' service with an additional £4 for each extra year in the choir.[417] A typical indenture was that of Alfred Chiswell at Wells in 1856. He was eleven years old, and with his father's approval he agreed to serve for three years 'in case his voice shall so long continue useful'. He was given board, lodging, washing, mending and a proper education, but his father agreed to pay any medical charges and to clothe him. Unlike most boys (who presumably served longer), he was not entitled to a leaving present.[418] At Winchester the dean and chapter required each boy to pay 10s a quarter into a savings bank. The dean and chapter undertook to pay in the same sum so that a considerable sum (with interest) could be built up as a leaving present.[419] The apprenticing of choristers at Gloucester was discontinued in 1867.[420] Boarding fees at

Hereford were fixed at £30 per annum for boys over twelve (of which the dean and chapter paid £10 and the parents the rest) and at £25 for those who were twelve or under, of which the dean and chapter paid £5. The dean and chapter also paid for half the cost of the furniture in each bedroom.[421] A new scheme was introduced in the following year. The boys were to receive free education and books at the Cathedral School, apart from their French tuition. The boarder probationers were paid £2 per annum in their first year with annual increments, and when they became full choristers they were paid quarterly at the rate of £10 per annum. Half of this went to the parents and the other half was deposited in a bank 'to accumulate until the boy leaves the choir when it will be applied with such further sum as the Dean and Chapter may think fit...'[422] Indentures were still required at Exeter in 1876 'in order to prevent the removal of boys at their parents' will, thereby affecting the efficiency of the choir and the musical education of the boys'.[423] Dean Plumptre of Wells left £2,000 in 1891 for the benefit of the old choristers.[424]

In 1810 the dean and chapter of Gloucester ordered that the choristers should be taught English, writing and arithmetic in addition to Latin and Greek.[425] When the Worcester choristers were asked by the dean and chapter in 1812 about the education they received from William Kenge, the organist, they replied that they had had no lesson from him for weeks.[426] In 1812 the master who was responsible for the care and instruction of the choristers at Salisbury was reprimanded for neglect,[427] while at Winchester three years later the dean and chapter caused a register to be kept showing the attendance of the choristers at school.[428] Maria Hackett gave details of the education of the choristers at several cathedrals in a series of articles that she published in the *Gentleman's Magazine*, beginning in 1817.[429] At Bristol the choristers had a daily music lesson, as well as instruction in reading, writing and arithmetic. Miss Hackett approved of the arrangements made for their education, which also included optional teaching of classics.[430] At Canterbury, where the choristers were taught singing three times a week in the song-school, their general education was at various private schools at the expense of the dean and chapter.[431] The six choristers at Carlisle had occasional lessons in singing from the organist, but Miss Hackett was unable to find out any more about their education.[432] Greek and Latin, writing and arithmetic were all learnt by the choristers at Chester, who had preferential elections as King's Scholars, though this favour was not to be found in every new foundation cathedral.[433] At Chichester, however, the choristers' education was unsatisfactory: 'There is no choir in England, with the single exception of Carlisle, which promises so few advantages to the young persons educating under the auspices of the Chapter.'[434] At Durham too their education could have been better: 'Their antient [*sic*] and well-endowed school has greatly declined; and the singing boys receive a mere charity school education and wear a corresponding dress.'[435] The choristers at Ely received no education, except in music, while at Exeter

the choristers wear scholars' habits and by application to the Dean and Chapter they have the benefit of a classical education, with the addition of writing and arithmetic. They are instructed by the organist in singing from seven till nine every morning.

At Hereford she found that the choristers had a free education, except in writing and arithmetic, which they had to pay for.[436] At Lichfield a choir school had recently been established by the dean and chapter, and at Peterborough the choristers received a basic education at the King's School. The three Rs, Latin and music were taught at Salisbury, Wells, Worcester and York, while at Winchester, the schoolmaster made 'a weekly return of the conduct of the boys, which lies upon the Chapter House table for the inspection of the Dean and Resident Prebendaries'.[437] The eight choristers at Christ Church, Oxford, were given dinner daily in the College Hall, and their clothes and the expenses of short journeys were also paid for. They learnt Latin, Greek, writing and arithmetic and were at school from 11 a.m. till 1 p.m. and from 2 p.m. until 3.30 p.m. They were also permitted to belong to any other choir in Oxford provided that this did not interfere with their attendance at the cathedral.[438]

Ten years later Miss Hackett gave some more information about the contemporary care and education of cathedral choristers.[439] She commended the authorities at Hereford, where the older choristers studied Virgil, Horace, Euclid and Greek plays, and also had lessons on the organ and piano:

The daily performance of the choral service will bear comparison with that of any Cathedral in England....The boys enjoy good health and a death has not occurred among the children of the choir within memory.[440]

Elsewhere the situation was less favourable. At Carlisle the six choristers 'have for several years been greatly neglected, in consequence no doubt of the ill-health and increasing infirmities of the late Dean'.[441] But she had heard that at Chichester the choir school had 'greatly sunk in public estimation'.[442] As a result of pressure from Miss Hackett, the lot of the choristers at St Paul's improved considerably. Around 1836 we hear that they rose at 7.30 a.m. and had milk, bread and butter for breakfast, while dinner at 2 p.m. consisted of a good square meal, with meat every day, and vegetables, together with at least half a pint of beer. One morning a week the six senior boys learned Italian for an hour from a master supplied by Miss Hackett, while in the evening the choristers were taught reading, writing and arithmetic and the Church catechism. Supper, consisting of bread, butter and beer, was served at 8 p.m. and they were in bed by 9 p.m.

They changed their linen at least twice a week and their beds – they slept two in a bed – were clean and warm. A maid was kept to wash and comb the hair of the younger boys. She was supervised by Miss Hawes, who usually also carved the joint at dinner.[443] There are a few details of the boys' diet in other cathedrals: in 1818 the dean and chapter of Chichester gave 'an half quarter loaf of bread' to each chorister each week;[444] the dean and chapter of Salisbury were concerned about their choristers' diet in 1878 and agreed that they should have more milk and a small supper each evening.[445]

Later in the century chapters began to take better care of their choristers. At Wells the chapter asked the master of the grammar school and the deputy organist to present quarterly reports about them.[446] The dean and chapter of Chichester decided in 1850 to establish a new school for the choristers in a house near the east end of the cloisters, but three years later Mr Bucket, the master of the school, was admonished by the chapter after complaints had been received from some of the boys' parents.[447] In 1851 a separate master of the choristers was appointed at Worcester,[448] but in 1869 William Done, the organist, told the dean and chapter that if a higher standard of education could be offered to the choristers he would have less difficulty in recruiting suitable boys.[449] The dean and chapter of Exeter bought a cricket field for the use of their choristers in 1870.[450] At Winchester the choristers experienced frequent changes of schooling. They were under the care of a lay vicar called Garrett for forty years, but then had several moves before becoming day boys at a house in the close. From 1879 some boarders were accepted, but this led to friction between the two groups of boys.[451] A chorister of the time later recalled that:

> The House was in a very dilapidated condition, the interior being distinctively unattractive. A glass of milk and a bun was served out to each boy every morning. A Miss Jacob (daughter of Archdeacon Jacob) took a deep interest in the school, and her Bible Class was a regular feature. The education in comparison with present-day standards could be described as 'homely'; ... the choir during this period was strong vocally, solo boys of very good calibre being a marked feature, supported by day-boys from the city.[452]

In 1888 Bishop John Wordsworth suggested that one of the canons at Salisbury might concern himself with the religious instruction of the choristers, pointing out that when he had been a canon at Rochester, 'it was the custom for every Canon-in-Residence to give similar catechetical instruction on the Collect, Epistle and Gospel before morning service on Sundays'.[453]

Most cathedral choristers have to undergo two initiation ceremonies: one formal and during a service; the other no less formal but entirely organized by the other choristers. At Salisbury Cathedral in the last century this latter ceremony involved a new chorister being 'boxed and crowned'. A temporary imprisonment in a cupboard was followed by a new chorister having his head knocked against an episcopal tomb three times.[454] A more official form of admission of a chorister was drawn up by Dean Hook of Chichester in 1866. After the psalms, while a voluntary was played on the organ, the two senior choristers fetched the new boy from the vestry, placed him in his seat and said: 'By order of the Dean and Chapter, I, *AB*, do admit you, *CD*, a chorister of this Cathedral Church of Chichester in the room of *EF.*' The service then proceeded.[455]

The clothes normally worn by the Salisbury choristers consisted of 'trousers, waistcoat and tail-coat of claret-coloured broadcloth, ornamented with brass buttons; white socks, shoes, a black satin cravat, white linen frill and a tall black beaver hat'. A new suit was given to each boy every Whitsunday and a top-coat every other year at Christmas.[456] In 1853 a new uniform was authorized: 'they shall in future have a round jacket and tweed trowsers [*sic*]; each boy being allowed two pairs of trousers in each year.'[457] The eight Winchester choristers were allowed two suits of clothes a year, beginning in 1844.[458]

The conventional uniform of cassock and surplice was by no means common in the nineteenth century. The Norwich choristers wore surplices once a week only as late as 1854;[459] for the rest of the week they wore purple gowns and sat in the organ loft.[460] About the same time the boys at Worcester wore black gowns during Lent instead of their 'full and plenteous surplices'.[461] At Ely the dean and chapter gave a surplice to each chorister in 1817 and an additional one a few months later, 'that they may always appear clean and decent at divine service in the Cathedral'.[462] The choristers at Salisbury were provided with clean surplices once a fortnight.[463] At Hereford in 1856 each probationer chorister was required to provide his own surplice and a Bible.[464] Mackenzie Walcott noted in 1865 that the boys at Chester, Winchester, Gloucester, Wells and Canterbury wore square academic caps, while at Norwich, Ely and Peterborough the caps had red tassels. Both the lay clerks and the choristers at Durham wore gowns under their surplices.[465] Surplices were provided for the lay clerks at Hereford in 1869, with the dean and chapter also being responsible for washing them.[466] At Exeter in the same year the chapter took over from the choristers' parents the care of the boys' surplices.[467] The dean and chapter of York introduced cassocks and surplices for the choristers in 1871 and the songmen were similarly robed in the following year. Previously the boys had worn coats trimmed with fur, with black gowns during Lent and times of mourning.[468] A correspondent told the *Church Times* in 1874 about the slovenly condition of the choir's robes at Canterbury: 'a more untidy and ill-fitting set of surplices could not have been seen, many of them not even having the recommendation of cleanliness'.[469]

There was consternation at Manchester in the time of Dean Cowie when the choir wore purple cassocks for the first time and entered the church singing a processional hymn, with the wardens carrying their staves.[470] 'Sufficient and proper surplices' which were 'thrown on as a cloak over ordinary dress and fastened with a single button' were ordered for the Worcester choristers in 1876,[471] and a further supply of surplices and cassocks was obtained four years later.[472] Precentor Vine Hall of Worcester even suggested that all the male singers in the chorus at the Three Choirs Festival should wear surplices.[473] An invitation to three vicars choral at Wells to attend the opening of Truro Cathedral led to a discussion about cassocks. The chapter clerk of Wells was asked to make enquiries about the custom at other cathedrals, and found that there were eighteen where cassocks were worn and eleven where they were not worn.[474] In 1889 the dean and chapter ordered cassocks for the lay vicars to prevent their appearing in clothes of different colours.[475] Cassocks for the choristers and lay vicars were introduced at Exeter in 1887–8 and for the evening choir in 1892.[476] Cassocks for the lay vicars at Salisbury were introduced in about 1890, to the satisfaction of Bishop Wordsworth.[477] In 1895 scarlet cassocks for the choristers at Worcester were bought[478] and violet cassocks replaced black for use in Lent in 1897.[479] The choristers of St Paul's wore cassocks from 1872 and the vicars choral from 1873.[480]

Although through the efforts of Maria Hackett and others the care for cathedral choristers increased considerably during the century, proper concern for their welfare was by no means universal. S. S. Wesley told the cathedral commissioners in 1854 that in many places the choristers were

> for a great part of each day on their own hands; and in winter, from being about the streets, they take cold and so sing badly at church. They seem both to require and deserve a degree of care which it cannot be difficult to bestow, but which is not commonly bestowed at present.[481]

The commissioners found that the annual stipend of choristers varied between £29 per annum at Durham and £3 6s 8d 'in the least wealthy Cathedrals', plus the lump sum of up to £30 on leaving the choir. The Salisbury choristers were still 'under the special care of one of the Residentiary Canons'.[482]

There are several examples, however, of earlier attempts to place the care and nurture of choristers on a sound footing. In 1819 at Chichester, for example, the dean and chapter drew up some careful rules for them. They were to attend services regularly and to be attentive and well behaved. They were not allowed to be absent from the cathedral or the school without permission, and were barred from singing in any concert or private parties without leave. Further, 'they are not on any account to sing in a publick house or at any club or convivial meeting'.[483]

J. A. Harsthorne, who was later ordained, described in 1900 his life as a chorister at Christ Church, Oxford, in about 1850:

> The daily routine of a Chorister's life was as follows: 9–10 school; 10–11 Cathedral service; 11–1 school; 1–2 Practice about three times a week at Dr Corfe's house in Merton Street; at 2 o'clock dinner in the Chapter House. Joint of meat daily except on Wednesdays and Fridays, when there was nothing but pudding. No Beer. Water in a quart cup from which all drank. No superintendent. On Sundays, boys dined at their lodgings. At 5 o'clock on Fridays each boy could receive a jam tart from the buttery.
>
> Afternoon, 3–4 school; 4–5 Cathedral service. Evening, lessons to be prepared for the next day.
>
> In term time, Dr Corfe had a Madrigal Class at the music room, Holywell Street at 8 o'clock once a week which his boys attended. We received about 15s each for our attendance.
>
> A field was hired for us where we could play cricket and football. Everything for the games was provided and sometimes a tent and hamper of provisions...our holidays were six weeks in summer and four at Christmas. Every Saint's day was a whole holiday. Wednesday and Saturday were half-holidays.[484]

W. K. Hamilton drew up a careful list of forfeits for the choristers at Salisbury in 1851. Any boy who came to the cathedral with dirty hands or face forfeited 2d. The same fine was imposed on any boy who ran in the cathedral or wore his hat there, or who laughed, talked or made a noise. The sum of 3d was the fine for late arrival at the singing school or at the services, for leaving music in the stalls, for arriving at the cathedral overheated, for kicking another boy, for banging a door on entering the cathedral, or for throwing a stone. Double fines were imposed on Sundays.[485] Sir Frederick Ouseley, the non-resident precentor of Hereford, was very critical of the choristers there in 1857. Too many of them had difficulty in reading, let alone understanding the psalms. No one seemed to be responsible for their religious and moral training, and their behaviour in church was offensive and irreverent. Further, they were subject 'to very vulgarizing, if not demoralizing, influences when they are at home'. The dean and chapter should do as much as they could to prepare them for their subsequent life, and thus they ought to be educated at the grammar school.[486] George Townshend Smith, the organist, reiterated some of the problems at Hereford in a letter to the chapter two years later: 'Boy after boy has left long before the loss of voice; in the present year the two seniors thus quitting have made it very difficult to provide for the service.' He suggested that the dean and chapter should put aside an annual sum for each boy as an inducement to parents not to remove them from the choir.[487] In 1861 a start was made by boarding two senior choristers at the Cathedral School.[488]

A new choir school was opened at St Paul's in 1875 under a newly appointed clerical headmaster, Alfred Barff. This was an inspired appointment and Barff soon established a thriving school.[489] Liddon told William Bright in 1879 that when he first came to St Paul's

> all or nearly all our boys lived with their parents, or with friends – generally, too, in the suburbs of London. They came to the Cathedral in time for the 10 o'clock service, and spent the interval between it and the 4 o'clock service at 1 Amen Court (which was then occupied by Mr Coward), partly in school, partly at dinner, and partly at play. At 5 p.m. they went home.

> London, of course, affords exceptional opportunities for getting into mischief and evil of every description, and our poor boys made the most of them, on their way to and from the Cathedral...

> Nothing but a very strong feeling that the evils to which these boys were exposed were a direct consequence of their employment in the service of the Church would have led the Chapter to face the great expenses which were necessary to remedy it. The *site* and buildings of the new Choir House cost us a sum which still cripples us; and we could not have done what we have done had not the Ecclesiastical Commissioners behaved very generously.... Our new house is built to hold forty choristers, the number to which we hope to raise the choir in the course of a few years...

> As we did what we could to improve the education given in the school, and provided the boys, at our own expense, with a very comfortable home, the parents were glad enough to assent to our terms. We have found it necessary to make another change. The boys *were*, almost all of them, the sons of tradesmen – we have been driven to admit only the sons of gentlemen, chiefly of poor clergymen. Not merely the cockney pronunciation in church, but weightier reasons made this restriction necessary; although in *the abstract* I regretted the change, as partly cutting off the Cathedral from the sympathies of the people. But the event has justified our decision.[490]

Dean Duncombe reorganized the choir school at York. The choristers had been taught in a chapel in the Minster which was also used as the archbishop's court. There were frequent complaints by inspectors of schools. Duncombe persuaded the Ecclesiastical Commissioners in 1873 to make available a house in Minster Yard as a proper school for the choristers. Dean Purey-Cust transferred it to another house in 1880, but it closed in 1887, only to reopen in 1903.[491]

By way of contrast, the dean and chapter of Norwich took no responsibility for the boarding, clothing or lodging of their choristers. They received a 'scanty education' from one of the lay clerks, and were paid between £14 and £4 per annum, with a leaving present of not more than

£10.[492] At Hereford the dean and chapter presented a Bible and a prayer book to each new chorister,[493] and at Bristol a man was paid £10 per annum to escort the choristers to and from the cathedral.[494] One of the choristers at Exeter Cathedral in the 1890s was G. Barrington-Baker, who has left an account of his time there in the choir.[495] The morning classes at school began at 7.20 a.m. and ended only thirty-five minutes later when the boys lined up for breakfast. They were required at the cathedral for a rehearsal at 9.30 a.m., followed by matins at 10.30 a.m., but returned to school for an hour at 11.45 a.m. Afternoon school lasted from 2.00 p.m. until 2.45 p.m., followed by evensong at 3.00 p.m. They were then free until tea at 6.00 p.m. A further class began at 6.30 p.m., followed by their preparation from 7.15 p.m. until 8.15 p.m., when they were fed with bread and cheese. At 8.30 p.m. the headmaster conducted night prayers and the lights in the dormitory were extinguished at 9 p.m. They had a fortnight's holiday in January and a further three weeks in the late summer.[496] By the end of the century several choir schools were well regarded, including those at Winchester, Worcester, Bristol, Salisbury and Lincoln.[497] Choristers therefore led a busy and demanding life in the nineteenth century, but their proper care and nurture was only gradually achieved. Illness also took its toll – there was, for example, an outbreak of scarlet fever at Wells in 1899.[498]

Two particular problems that exercised chapters in the nineteenth century in their concern for their choristers were the soliciting of gifts and singing at Glee Clubs and private parties. Until about the middle of the century the choristers at Chichester roamed the city streets carol-singing and asking for money.[499] At Manchester also, it was the custom for the four foundation choristers to go round to members of the congregation and ask for a New Year's gift.[500] In 1823 at Hereford, however, the dean and chapter stated their disapproval of the choristers soliciting Christmas boxes and said that they would not allow it to happen again. Six years later they were obliged to repeat their prohibition and to warn the choristers that if any of them repeated the offence he would be expelled.[501] The custom was prohibited at Salisbury in 1852,[502] while Dean Plumptre proposed in Wells in 1886 that twice-yearly services should be held, with the offertory being devoted to the choristers, instead of allowing them to collect Christmas boxes.[503] The soliciting of Christmas gifts by the choristers from the congregation was forbidden at Bristol in 1900.[504] A similar, but less objectionable, practice was spur-money. At several cathedrals the choristers claimed the right to demand 6d from any man who entered the cathedral wearing spurs. This custom was certainly observed at Salisbury, Hereford, Bristol, St Paul's and Westminster Abbey,[505] and possibly at Peterborough, Southwell and Durham. The purpose was to prevent the jingling of spurs from interrupting the services.[506]

Maria Hackett was appalled to discover in 1811 that when the choristers at St Paul's went out at night to sing at concerts no one was appointed to look after them and they had to wander home alone at midnight.[507] A difficult situation arose at Exeter when S. S. Wesley discovered that two boys had sung privately at a Glee Club without his permission, although they claimed to have the dean's permission. Wesley complained to the Dean, but angered the dean and chapter by his brutal treatment of the two offending choristers:

> John Homeyard stated that on the previous Sunday before the Morning Service, Mr Chamberlain (Dr Wesley's apprentice), Robert Kitt and himself had been practising a glee without the organ, when Dr Wesley had come in late, and, having heard them, asked if they had been practising for the Glee Club concert with Mr Risdon and Mr Cole, the night before. They said that they had. Wesley then inquired who had given them orders to go. They replied that the men had asked the dean, who had given leave for them. Dr Wesley declared that the dean was not their master and that he was their master. And he went over to the window, turned round and ran over to the Choristers, and said that they should not have gone without his leave. He next struck Homeyard, several times, hard blows with his fist on the back. By that time, Homeyard was holding down his head in order to avoid the blows; and he then received another blow on the point of his chin by a kick from Dr Wesley, a hard blow, and subsequently there had been a mark on his chin for several days.
>
> Kitt, next, took up his side of the story by reporting how, as he quitted Homeyard, Dr Wesley had struck him, too, a blow on the side of his face and had knocked him down with another blow, and how, when he was on the floor, Dr Wesley had kicked him.[508]

Not long afterwards the dean and chapter at Exeter resolved that the choristers were not allowed to sing in houses of anyone except the dean and canons, nor to attend and take part in any musical performance without express leave of the chapter and only under the personal care of the organist.[509] A similar rule was made at Winchester in 1864, when the choristers were not allowed to go to any entertainment, public or private, out of the close.[510] The dean and chapter of Chichester prohibited their choristers from singing elsewhere in 1871,[511] and the permission of the canon-in-residence was required at Gloucester in 1875 if the choristers were invited to sing at any public entertainment.[512] At Worcester also a similar rule was made in 1879.[513]

At Norwich there was a 'respectable tavern' in the Ethelbert Gate of the close, where the cathedral Glee Club used to meet at monthly intervals. Some of the cathedral clergy and the élite of the city were members, and James Valentine Cox, a chorister, vividly remembered

the bountiful supply of delicious veal cutlets, boiled sausages, and mashed potatoes with which he and other Cathedral choirboys, who took part in the proceedings, were regaled after the concerts, this refreshment being supplemented, in the way of beverages, by lemonade and small glasses of hot punch 'to keep out the cold', the repast concluding with 'delicious stewed pears'.[514]

As well as attempting to control the behaviour of the choristers outside the cathedral, deans and chapters were naturally responsible for their discipline during services and on their way to and from them. In 1807 some of the choristers at Durham were accused of stealing lead.[515] The choristers' seats at Winchester were raised in 1812, so that they could be seen by the minor canons and lay vicars. In 1814 the dean and chapter of Winchester fined two boys 10s each for throwing stones and asked Dr Chard, the organist, to thrash them.[516] James Turle, who later became organist of Westminster Abbey, was a chorister at Wells at about this time. Not only did the choristers play and throw stones in the nave, they would also 'rush from their places during the reading of the lessons, in order to watch the action of the celebrated clock in the north transept'.[517]

The dean and chapter of Winchester required the choristers' schoolmaster to submit a weekly report on them, and mainly he submitted a favourable one. But in 1820 John Bishop and William Dyer were in trouble for cracking and eating nuts during the services.[518] Dyer was accused later the same month for obtaining leave under false pretences, and he continued to be often in trouble.[519] The choristers of Chichester were said to be disorderly during the 1820s[520] and one Alfred Angel was expelled in 1828 'for improper conduct in the Cathedral'.[521] Further examples of this sort of action were not uncommon at various cathedrals.[522] In June 1826 John Langridge, a chorister at Salisbury, had a quarrel with the head boy, John Arnold, and stabbed him with his pocket-knife. Langridge was a terror to the other boys and was dismissed by the dean and chapter.[523] When G. J. Elvey was a chorister at Canterbury Cathedral he once had the audacity to take a jackdaw into a service, hiding it under his surplice.[524] At Salisbury the boys once caught a jackdaw in the cathedral and brought it to the school.[525] In 1846 William Henshaw, the organist of Durham Cathedral, complained that the boys were 'neither punctual...nor obedient'.[526] At Peterborough, though, the choristers were given £1 each 'for exemplary conduct'.[527] Zechariah Buck would punish miscreant choristers at Norwich by shutting them in his summer-house on a diet of biscuits and water.[528] At Hereford the dean or hebdomadary had the power to fine choristers 5s for misconduct.[529] Fines of 6d per offence were allowed at Worcester in 1878, but the parents of two naughty boys questioned this right.[530]

In 1878 the dean and chapter of Wells were the defendants in an action brought in the County Court for the wrongful dismissal of a chorister.[531]

The boys at Wells were allowed to play on the open space in front of the cathedral so long as they did not play football or any other ball-game.[532] Four years later two of the choristers were accused of maiming a magpie and using 'foul and improper language'.[533] In 1899 the priest vicars at Wells were asked to superintend the boys' behaviour.[534] Following several complaints about the choristers' misbehaviour, strict instructions were issued to regulate their conduct.[535] But the chapter's difficulties had not ended. In the following year a priest vicar 'who had treated with imprudence and a lack of delicacy boarders in the school house' was given a grave reprimand, following a complaint by the father of a chorister.[536]

Unauthorized absences by choristers were also a problem from time to time, and could lead to suspension or expulsion.[537] At Hereford in 1831 the senior chorister was ordered to keep an account of any absences at each service in a special book which he had to show to the dean or hebdomadary on Saturday mornings.[538] Three years later Dean Merewether wrote to the parents of each chorister, asking them to inform him if illness caused their boy to be absent.[539] When W. S. Blandford, one of the choristers at Worcester, was absent on the Sunday following the Three Choirs Festival in 1881, he was fined 5s.[540] A fine of 6d per service was introduced at Hereford in 1888 and printed forms of application for leave, which had to be countersigned by the organist and succentor, were made available to choristers' parents.[541] At Salisbury one of the choristers was given the unique title and distinction of being the bishop's chorister. Formally admitted to this office by the bishop, it was his duty to ascertain before every service whether the bishop would be present and on such occasions to walk in procession immediately in front of the bishop's apparitor.[542]

In 1877 Dr (later Sir) Walter Parratt, who was then organist of Magdalen College, Oxford, was asked to examine the choristers at Worcester Cathedral and to report to the chapter. He found them 'very satisfactory' and said that

> their knowledge of scales, time and Musical Notation generally shows great care on the part of their instructor. Their voices are well selected and trained, and any little harshness that I noticed in one or two cases seemed to be chiefly owing to their Worcestershire dialect of which traces were sometimes apparent....If I might hint a weakness anywhere it is in the high notes of the boys' voices, which they are apt to get a little flat, and a few high scales every day would soon remedy this.[543]

Earlier in the year the bad behaviour of the choristers had been mentioned in chapter,[544] but the following year the precentor noted that it had 'improved in reverence: and it will still further improve when the desks are raised to a higher level, which will prevent their lounging upon them as they do at present'.[545] Precentor Vine Hall complained of listlessness among the boys in his report for 1879 and suggested that some small prizes each quarter might act as incentives. He gave weekly classes on the catechism and prayer book to the choristers.[546] Twice the dean and chapter forbade choristers to sing at public concerts without permission from the dean or precentor,[547] and doubtless to keep them away from such dangerous pursuits a guild was formed for them in 1882.[548] In that year, however, the choir school was revived through the initiative of Canon Butler – at first in a room in what is now known as the Old Palace, then used as the deanery, but it moved to a house in College Green on 3 November. The choristers' master was Minor Canon (later Precentor) H. H. Wood-ward, but the main teaching responsibility was in the hands of the assistant master, Mr Charles Shuttleworth. Butler allowed the boys to play beside his house, much to the delight of his successor, Mandell Creighton.[549] Part of the choristers' stipend was used to defray the cost of their education,[550] and the Creightons arranged Christmas parties for them.[551] In the 1873 edition of her *Brief Account*, Maria Hackett said that each of the canons at Chichester took the choristers on a day's holiday during his annual residence, while at Norwich four choristers dined alternately once a week on Sundays at the deanery.[552] Dean Goulburn was cross when he found the choristers playing in his garden without permission, but generously entertained them to supper, followed by a display of fireworks.[553] Twelve months later they played various games (such as bran-tub, bullet pudding and shooting the ball into the mouth) before supper. One boy, whom Dr Buck had forbidden to come because of his truancy, turned up and was sent away.[554] On New Year's Day 1869 Goulburn entertained the choristers to supper with Dr Buck and Precentor Symonds: 'We had magic lantern, with slides of Aladdin (whose story I told), Robinson Crusoe, the Abys-sinian War, etc....Dismissed them all with a sixpence each.'[555] At Ely, on Christmas Day 1816, the sum of £8 was divided among the choristers.[556] Canon Adam Sedgwick of Norwich was very generous to the choristers. In 1868 he hired some boats for the boys and took them on a river trip:

We then returned to my house where my housekeeper had prepared a capital tea in the drawing-room, of which indeed the tea and coffee formed the smallest part. And in my dining-room there was a pre-paration for more than 20 connected with our choir. A round of beef; a sirloin of beef; cold veal pies; gooseberry pies; cakes; loads of straw-berries, etc., etc., to help out the tea and coffee. And the lads did ample justice to Mrs Barnes' fare. That done...the choristers, men and boys all turned out into my little garden. The evening was lovely and they sang very beautifully. The chorus of Handel, 'See the conquering hero comes' was sung twice over very admirably. About ten more strawberries and cakes and a good dose of home-made champagne. Then 'God save the Queen'; ... goodnight and away.[557]

In 1863 the dean and chapter of Exeter gave £4 to entertain the choristers on the occasion of the wedding of the Prince of Wales.[558] In 1898 the American magazine *The Churchman*, in an article on 'Noted English Choirs',[559] described the twenty choristers and eight to ten probationers at Worcester as

> a truly admirable set... the training of the boys calls for high praise; they do not fail in a single point. The volume of tone is noteworthy and sounds satisfactory even far down the nave. The breathing is excellent, not a vestige of effort being apparent. The gradations of tone are also very good, the mezzo-piano being particularly beautiful.

Of course there were those who attacked the choristers' life. A correspondent wrote to the *Guardian* in 1898 that in view of the long hours of services they attended,

> the fatigue and strain involved in such hours cannot fail to be injurious to both body and mind with young boys, and it is equally harmful to their religion by making worship a weariness and routine.[560]

Dean Stephens of Winchester replied that not only were the boys at his cathedral healthy and happy, but were 'amongst the most proficient' in their school.[561] Precentor Woodward of Worcester, after pointing to the academic success of ex-choristers, said that he was 'constantly receiving letters from them and that they speak always in the most grateful way of their training at Worcester'.[562]

In the later nineteenth century it became more common for cathedral choirs to have short holidays from their duties. The choristers at Lincoln had few holidays earlier in the century, but enjoyed picking and eating fruit in the organist's garden.[563] At Norwich, too, holidays were practically unknown.[564] In July 1858 a visitor to Carlisle discovered the cathedral virtually shut for three weeks while the staff were on holiday.[565] In August and September 1873 half the choristers at St Paul's were given a month's holiday in turn, and they also had a week after Christmas and Easter. In the same year at Winchester the chapter looked at the question of whether the choir could be given a holiday.[566] From the summer of 1886 the *whole* school at St Paul's was away for a month in the summer each year, and seven to ten days' holidays after two festivals became normal after 1896.[567] The Worcester choristers had a three-week break together in the summer in 1888 and two weeks in the following January.[568] Before this the boys went away in 'batches', when the result was 'a weak and languid choir, which often draws forth remarks of surprise and disappointment from visitors'.[569] When the choristers were absent, the Worcester lay clerks continued to sing, supplemented by the boys of the voluntary choir. Meanwhile the choristers benefited from the change of air and the company of their parents.[570]

Voluntary choirs were quite common in the late nineteenth century, but those at St Paul's and Worcester were perhaps the most flourishing. The voluntary choir at St Paul's was formed when the Sunday evening services were started in 1858. It included 200 trebles and altos (including women), 150 tenors and the same number of basses.[571] They sat in a transept on a semi-circular platform and were conducted by one of the vicars choral from a special box. The congregation faced southwards into the transept. When Stainer succeeded Goss as organist, and the Sunday evening services became regular throughout the year, the choir was reconstructed and transferred to the quire. The women were asked to leave, the number of men was reduced, and only the cathedral choristers were kept as trebles.[572] Stainer held rehearsals for those who remained in the choir every Friday evening in the chapter-house and soon won their affection.[573] At first, however, he had to be very firm. The former members of the choir had resigned in a body, but Stainer had the support of the dean and chapter in reconstructing the choir and existing members were asked to contact him to learn the new conditions of membership. Within a short time, Stainer and the reconstructed choir were on the best of terms and the chairman of the choir said in 1877:

> I can remember the old Sunday Evening Choir; things are indeed changed. We were then located in a gallery over the south door: we had to buy our own music and surplices, and the admission for the public was by ticket....But now how different. We are seated in the proper place in the choir, all music and surplices found, and everything done to make us comfortable; the whole of the Cathedral free to the public, and a thoroughly congregational service....Dr Stainer and others have said we are not the same choir, musically speaking, we were a year ago; all thanks to Dr Stainer for that.[574]

The voluntary choir at Worcester was established by Canon Barry to sing at the Sunday evening services there. William Done, the organist, was enthusiastic and untiring in his endeavours to make it a success, with the ready co-operation of Minor Canon Cattley, who acted as secretary. The choir included doctors, lawyers, tradesmen from the porcelain works and clerks, and provided a valuable link between the cathedral and the city:

> The first service was an event not to be forgotten and the Cathedral was quite full ...we sang a processional hymn from the west end and I think the Custos carried the silver-headed staff before the procession. The service happily went very well and we were very relieved. This was the first attempt to make the Cathedral useful to the masses.[575]

John Randall went on to say:

> The silver-headed staff was commented on by some of the members of

the choir; they had never seen anything like it before; one of them said to me 'It's all very well, but if it comes to a *flag* I shan't walk behind it'.[576]

The choir was placed under the control of the precentor (or a minor canon appointed by him) in 1874,[577] and gratuities of £5 were given to each member of the choir in 1877.[578] The establishment of a voluntary choir at Worcester was welcomed by *The Choir*:

> Not only does it prevent an undue tax upon the regular choral body, who have already to sing at two services, but it also creates a lively interest in the cathedral among the amateur musicians of the town, and provides a strong body of choristers who can be united with the regular choir on festivals.[579]

Rules for the choir were drawn up in about 1885; there were weekly rehearsals that were voluntary and a compulsory monthly rehearsal. When Minor Canon Clifford took over the choir in November 1886 he recommended that the men should be disbanded, 'as the simplest and only effective method of getting rid of material which is worse than useless'. He also suggested that the number of boys be increased to fifty with three weekly practices and a Sunday afternoon class, with a guild for former voluntary choir choristers. He also wanted the choir to be equipped with cassocks and surplices, as 'the present state of robing is a great eyesore to many of the congregation'. He did not like the choir to be engaged in taking the collection and suggested that members of the congregation ought to do this.

The reconstruction of the choir advocated by Clifford seems to have been carried out, for in his report to the chapter for the years 1887–8 he said:

> The result has been, I consider, satisfactory: the standard of musical ability has been considerably raised, the fortnightly practices well attended, the services improved and there is a tone of increased reverence amongst the members.

There were twenty-one boys and twenty-seven members of the guild, whose object was the promotion of reverence with a rule of monthly reception of the eucharist. The guild gave a concert in 1888 in the Guildhall, but its devotional and social meetings had been curtailed since the house formerly used by the headmaster had been pulled down. The room they used there was also used for communicants' classes, and for a weekly Bible class for young men. But a room on the ground floor of Edgar Tower could be used instead, by kind permission of the chapter clerk, if £7 10s could be found to put it in order. Eleven of the boys were confirmed at Ascensiontide. Clifford was pleased that they all wore Eton collars and black ties, but criticized their surplices as being 'exceedingly untidy'. On

Sundays and special occasions they wore college caps with black tufts instead of tassels, to distinguish them from the choristers and King's School boys. The men of the voluntary choir also had college caps 'for use in the cloisters', but the dean and chapter disapproved of this.[580]

In November 1888 Clifford reported that the voluntary choir boys had sung in place of the cathedral choristers during August of that year and 'acquitted themselves with credit'. The new guild room was in use every weekday evening except Fridays.[581] In his report for 1889–90, Clifford said that twenty-nine cassocks and surplices had been bought for a total of £25. There were only ten ladies in the choir, compared with fifteen two years previously. The Sunday evening collections were now taken by junior members of the guild, who had recently been saddened by the death of one of their number, Edward Bladon, after only two days' illness. He had received the sacrament a few hours before he was taken ill and died 'with a prayer on his lips for the work of the guild he so much loved'. The choir wanted to buy a processional cross for use on great occasions in the cathedral, and another innovation was a band to accompany the choir four times a year. These services had attracted large congregations and Gloucester Cathedral had copied the idea. Twelve boys were confirmed that year and the guild had held a *conversazione* in the Guildhall attended by 150 guests. There had also been an excursion up the Severn to Red Rocks, near Stourport.[582] Clearly, the voluntary choir was going from strength to strength. In 1892 the dean and chapter were told, 'Practices for the boys of the choir and probationers are held every night in the week except Saturdays – on Wednesdays, in addition, there is a violin class conducted by an able teacher.' There were twenty-three members of the guild, with forty-six former choristers. There was a monthly communicants' class and monthly addresses and lectures by members of the chapter, various other classes and an intercessory prayer meeting each Saturday. The choir consisted of thirty-two men, six women, thirty-eight boys and fourteen probationers; the boys' annual outing had been to Scarborough.[583]

The 1893 report said that there were fifty adults and thirty-two boys in the choir; there were fortnightly practices for the whole choir, while the boys rehearsed three times a week. Once a fortnight some of the choir had visited the infirmary where they sang to the patients. In 1894 it was recorded that members of the choir were admitted formally by the dean or canon-in-residence. The boys had had an excursion to Bournemouth and the men had been to Dudley. Minor Canon Powell, in the report for 1899, said that during August the boys could have up to six services and practices a day. Ill-feeling, however, had been caused by collectors and servers at the Sunday evening service using the cassocks and surplices of the voluntary choir.[584]

In many ways, the voluntary choir at Worcester was an unqualified success. But it was the cause of friction between the dean and chapter and the incumbents of the city. Fourteen of them sent an address to the dean and chapter in 1894, and it was clear that there were certain misunderstandings that the chapter were anxious to clear up.[585] Careful regulations for the direction of the voluntary choir were laid down in 1897 and 1899, and the general impression that may be gained from all these comments is that the voluntary choir at Worcester was a most flourishing and useful institution. Its vigorous early life has no doubt contributed to its healthy state ever since.[586]

If the voluntary choirs at St Paul's and Worcester were the best known, they were not the only voluntary choirs to be found in cathedrals in the later nineteenth century. The voluntary choir at Manchester sang not only on Sunday evenings, but also at early choral celebrations and at confirmations.[587]

B. F. Westcott established a voluntary choir at Peterborough. He visited shops in the city and invited men to join. The practices were held in the hall of his house and there were soon fifty men in addition to the boys who joined.[588] A voluntary choir existed at Winchester for a time.[589] A suggestion from the organist and succentor in 1896 that some ladies should be introduced into the voluntary choir at Exeter on a regular instead of an occasional basis was refused by the dean and chapter.[590]

During the nineteenth century, then, cathedral choirs gradually became more professional and were better organized. Through the strenuous efforts of crusading reformers like Maria Hackett, S. S. Wesley and John Stainer, abuses were removed and chapters seem to have become increasingly concerned both for the welfare of choristers and lay clerks and for their contribution to the total life of a cathedral. Already the music of Stanford and Wood was finding a place in the cathedral repertoire and solid foundations were being laid for the great development of music and standards that has taken place in English cathedrals since the First World War.

9

CAPITULAR ESTATES
AND FINANCE

❄

The work of cathedrals in the nineteenth century was largely financed by the property owned by their deans and chapters. As corporate landowners, they can be compared with those who owned some of the great secular estates, but the administration of capitular estates underwent considerable changes during the course of the century as a result of the establishment of the Ecclesiastical Commissioners.

Most chapters owned three kinds of property – the houses in the close, which were mainly occupied by themselves and by other members of the cathedral foundation; various tenements in the cathedral city; and farms and woodland, often quite distant from the cathedral. Both the farms and the tenements were leased, and the income accruing from these fluctuated from year to year, since it included not only the annual rent, but also the fines paid by tenants in order to renew their leases. In addition, many members of chapters enjoyed the separate endowments of their own stalls.[1] Leases were sometimes for three lives, but increasingly capitular land was leased for terms of years or occasionally by rack-rents. This was an inefficient and deplorable system, since most of the income came from fines. These were garnered only every seven or twenty-one years.

The leases of some urban tenements were renewed only after forty years.[2] In 1839, the total number of leases for lives at fifteen capitular establishments was 792, but the total of leases for years was far greater at 2,862.[3] The dean and chapter of Exeter leased nineteen farms and seventy-five tenements in 1863, but there were problems associated with the use of urban property and at Bristol in 1844 a restriction was made on leases to prevent any capitular property being used as a brothel.[4]

To unravel the full extent and sources of capitular revenues in the early nineteenth century is an extremely complicated process, and within the limits of this chapter only a general picture can be attempted. In the 1830s the total revenues of English cathedral and collegiate churches was estimated at £208,289 net, with personal revenues of £66,465.[5] In 1854 it was estimated that over a seven-year period the average amount of capitular revenues per annum was £25,298 4s 6d, with the revenues for the year 1852 amounting to £313,005 2s6. The amounts received by fines varied considerably. Between 1801 and 1825 the amounts received by the dean and chapter of Gloucester from this source varied between £1,636 18s 6d in 1821 and £6,168 17s in 1825.[7] The individual fines demanded could amount to very substantial sums. In July 1832 the dean and chapter of Durham renewed the lease of a colliery to Lord Londonderry for £44,266,[8] and in 1838 another single fine secured £40,000 for the cathedral.[9] But Durham, with its rich coal-mines, was exceptional and other less fortunate cathedrals had to depend on lesser and more varied annual sums. At Worcester in 1829, £7,568 came in from fines, but two years later the income from this source was only £3,893.[10] It was not a very efficient system. The First Report of the Cathedrals Commission, published in 1854, said that

> the chapters in general derive the greater part of their revenues from the fines paid on the granting of renewal of leases...this system has hitherto been so beneficial to the lessees, that a considerable part of the annual value of the property is lost to the Church.[11]

W. K. Hamilton, however, argued strongly in favour of the right and competence of chapters to manage their own estates:

> There is no greater fallacy gone abroad than that Deans and Chapters cannot manage their own property....We have a chapter clerk, and one of the most admirable land surveyors. As far as the mere management of our property goes, it gives very little trouble indeed.[12]

Dean Pellew of Norwich agreed, and valued the contacts that existed between chapters and their tenants.[13] Sydney Smith believed in the value of capitular estates, even though he commended them in a typically extravagant way:

> Take, for instance, the Cathedral of Bristol, the whole estates of which are about equal to keeping a pack of fox-hounds. If this had been in the hands of a country gentleman, instead of Precentor, Succentor, Dean and Canons, and Sexton, you would have had huntsman, whipper-in, dog-feeder, and stoppers of earths; the old squire, full of foolish opinions, and fermented liquids, and a young gentleman of gloves, waistcoats and pantaloons.[14]

The key person in the management of capitular estates was the chapter clerk, generally a local solicitor, who acted as agent to the dean and chapter with the help of a number of subordinate stewards and bailiffs.[15] But chapters often took a direct interest in their estates. In 1802, for example, the Dean of Gloucester agreed to visit the capitular estates in Glamorgan on behalf of the chapter,[16] and in 1822 two of the prebendaries of Worcester were asked to visit one of the estates of that cathedral.[17] Bishop Monk of Gloucester and Bristol told the Cathedrals Commission in 1854 that chapters took a constant interest in the management of their

217

property.[18] The bailiffs employed by the dean and chapter of Worcester in 1800 were each paid according to the size of the estates in their care. Altogether £27 7s 6d was spent on bailiffs' salaries in that year.[19] The dean and chapter of Gloucester employed six bailiffs for their various estates in 1800, but none of them was paid more than 2 guineas. There were also two memorial stewards, who were paid £2 and 3 guineas respectively, while the surveyor of the estates received £50.[20] An agent was employed at Hereford in 1830 to inspect one of the capitular estates.[21]

Sometimes a bailiff could be a significant middleman between a dean and chapter and their tenants. The sensitive nature of his position may be glimpsed from incidents at Sandhurst in Gloucestershire in 1848 and at Churcham in the previous year. Thomas Frankis, the bailiff, told the dean and chapter of Gloucester that the trustees for the Sandhurst estate wished to fell six small oak trees. As they were young trees, he could not agree to their felling. He further recommended that landmarks should be erected on land belonging to the dean and chapter, especially as there were some places (such as Upleadon) where boundaries were disputed. This could be done 'by the assistance of some of the oldest men in the parish'. Twelve months earlier, Dr George Dangerfield, a tenant of the dean and chapter, who held a capitular estate at Churcham, complained that he had been 'ill-treated by your timber agent', who had subjected him to 'annoyance and unfair treatment'. Dangerfield told the dean and chapter that he had applied to George Whitcombe, the chapter clerk, for permission to cut down some trees to effect some repairs to the property. Frankis had eventually agreed to five unsatisfactory trees being felled. After a further delay he agreed to 'a little more timber of *very inferior quality*' being cut down. Dangerfield asked his carpenter to measure the tree that Frankis had chosen and he said that there would not be sufficient usable timber in it. Even a third visit from Frankis had not resulted in enough timber being made available. Unable to get any satisfaction from him, Dangerfield appealed directly to the dean and chapter.[22] At Wells the steward visited each manor belonging to the dean and chapter before the audit,[23] while at Chichester the chapter employed Messrs Appleby, Newman and Appleby as their surveyors on a commission calculated at the rate of 2½ per cent on the gross income. The commission was to cover travelling and all other expenses except stamps, dinners and audit expenses. The rents were to be collected every six months and were to be paid to the dean and chapter on 3 May and 1 November.[24]

Although the proceeds of the estates of chapters were mainly devoted to their own funds, they were certainly aware of their wider responsibilities. For example, in 1800 the dean and chapter of Hereford decided to send some of the grain normally delivered to the canons' bakehouse to the market, in order to be sold there to alleviate a general scarcity of grain.[25] Chapters were naturally responsible for holding manorial courts from time to time. The dean and chapter of Gloucester gave notice of them in the appropriate parish church on two successive Sundays.[26]

By the late 1830s the way in which chapters looked after their estates was being called into question and they were also under threat in other ways. In 1837, for example, the dean and chapter of Salisbury objected to five plans for railways to go through their lands.[27] Church land that was leased to tenants was often in a poor state, with neglected timber. It was even ignored by speculative builders.[28] A tenant of the dean and chapter of Canterbury published a pamphlet about the chapter's behaviour over the renewal of his lease on a house at South Lambeth, complaining that the deputy employed by their surveyor had never entered the house and that the amount claimed was sheer guess-work.[29] Under the terms of the 1840 Act, the Ecclesiastical Commissioners came to have an increasing share in capitular revenues as more and more canons' stalls were suspended and their income was transferred to the commissioners. In 1854 the cathedral commissioners said that the Ecclesiastical Commission had acquired property and revenue derived from five different sources: decanal and prebendal estates, of which 318 out of a possible 370 had come into their control since 1840; the income of fifty-nine out of a possible seventy-eight canonries; certain payments charged on deaneries and canonries; some surplus income 'to prevent any member of a chapter getting increased income'; and a portion of revenue derived from long leases.[30] In 1852 the contribution from capitular sources to 'the common fund for the benefit of the Church' amounted to £81,495. In the following year this figure had risen to £99,776 1s 5d.[31] 'Of the entire corporate revenues of the Chapters', the report estimated, 'about one sixth part is now paid to the Ecclesiastical Commissioners'. But the commissioners had no more than a nominal share in the management of these estates. There was an atmosphere of mutual distrust between the commissioners and the chapters, since the commissioners felt that they were being handicapped through the inefficient way in which the chapters managed their estates. The chapters were profoundly suspicious of the commissioners. There was open hostility in the dealings between the commissioners and the chapter clerk at Durham.[32] The whole subject of the Church's administration of its property was examined in 1849, when the Episcopal and Capitular Revenues Commission was appointed, 'for the purpose of inquiring into the present system of leasing and managing the real property of the church'.[33] In addition, the Commission was asked to find ways of replacing the fluctuating incomes of bishops, deans and chapters by fixed amounts. The Commission reported in the following year and recommended that the control of capitular estates should continue to be vested in the various chapters. So long as these estates produced sufficient income for the individual members of chapters and for the maintenance of the cathedral services, fabric and school, they felt that the existing arrangements should continue. Only if the estates produced more than was needed should the surplus be transferred to the Ecclesiastical Commission. Any surpluses in the fabric accounts of cathedrals should be accumulated to meet future demands.[34] A Bill based on the reports of this Commission was introduced in the House of Lords in 1851, but was opposed by many chapters. The dean and chapter of Winchester firmly opposed it and sent three of their members to attend a protest meeting in London.[35] It was substantially amended and became law.[36]

By this time the power and influence of the Ecclesiastical Commissioners was great and was steadily increasing. They wished to take over the capitular estates and run them more efficiently. In the 1850s and 1860s the majority of the chapters concluded agreements with the commissioners, which were ratified by the Ecclesiastical Commission Act of 1868.[37] The deans and chapters of York and Carlisle were the first to commute their estates in 1852.[38] The principle that was adopted was for the chapters to commute the whole of their estates to the commissioners in return for an annual payment until they could be re-endowed with a convenient estate which was supposed to produce the same annual income.[39] At Gloucester, for example, the capitular estates were commuted in 1855 for £8,460 per annum and the dean and chapter were re-endowed in 1866.[40]

The annual sum paid to each chapter took into consideration the annual income that they had received from their estates, the amounts required for the maintenance of the fabric and services of the cathedral, and the amount needed to ensure that the dean and each canon received the income to which they were entitled from the corporate revenues of the chapter.[41] By 1866 York, Peterborough and Carlisle had been re-endowed and Canterbury had nearly been re-endowed, while the calculations for Salisbury and some other cathedrals were pending.[42]

It was unfortunate that these negotiations were generally concluded in the years immediately preceding the Great Agricultural Depression. The chapters that had been re-endowed found themselves in considerable trouble. In 1884 the *Guardian* commented: 'The process has gone too far and it will be found a fatal error.'[43] Archbishop Benson said that it was not the fault of the chapters:

> They employ good agents and their estates are in good condition (as compared with estates in general) and their tenants satisfied. At the moment all agricultural interests are depressed. Many gentry suffer at least as much as the chapters.[44]

The appalling weather of the late 1870s and early 1890s and the flood of cheap imported grain, which more than halved the average price of a quarter of English wheat between 1867 and 1894, together with a depression in barley and wool, created very considerable difficulties for cathedral chapters as well as for the owners of secular estates.[45] Between

1879 and 1881, 6 million sheep died or were slaughtered, about a tenth of the number in the whole country.[46] The average price of wheat in 1870–4 was 55s a quarter. By 1895–9 this figure had fallen to 28s. The amount of grain imported from North America and Argentina more than doubled between 1870 and 1900. In the late 1860s the cost of bringing a quarter of wheat from Chicago to Liverpool was 15s 11d. By the early 1900s it was only 3s 11d. [47] The amount of wool imported from Australia quadrupled between 1864 and 1884.[48] The second phase of the Depression in the 1890s was caused more by low prices than by bad weather, though the cold summers of 1891 and 1892, followed by the drought of 1893 and a bad harvest in the following year, were sufficient to undo the limited recovery of the late 1880s. In 1894–5 the price of wheat was the lowest recorded for 150 years.[49] Between 1861 and 1901 over half a million people left the farms.[50]

No wonder cathedral chapters felt bitter. They had been led to believe that the process of commutation and re-endowment would leave them financially secure, but that proved to be wrong. A loose note inside the front cover of a volume of chapter acts at Salisbury ruefully records: 'Before the estates were handed over, the fee simple of the whole chapter property was valued at £549,903...now [1894] the *whole* net Chapter Revenue (Communar and Fabric) amounts to £4120.' This was less than the re-endowed sum of £4,700 per annum agreed in 1875.[51]

Most cathedrals experienced financial difficulties in the 1880s.[52] In 1884 the dean and chapter of Gloucester found that their accounts were showing a debit balance. The sum calculated to be the income from their re-endowed estates should have been £8,460 per annum. In 1883 it was only £6,030, which left a deficiency of £1,215 in the domus account. The chapter began to lobby the Ecclesiastical Commissioners and to introduce a strict method of cost control.[53] Dean Montagu Butler told Sir George Pringle of the Ecclesiastical Commissioners in October 1886:

> As to the chapter we go from bad to worse. The income which in 1879 was nearly £10,000 is now probably barely £5000, but the arrears are so serious and the reductions of rent so numerous and so repeated that it is impossible to say what our real income at any time is. For myself in 18 months I have received but £400. I can only live by borrowing on capital....The Cathedral does not any longer pay its own way. It is kept solvent, if solvent, by large sacrifices on the part of the Dean and Canons.[54]

In 1887 they sent a memorandum drawing attention to their plight to the Chancellor of the Exchequer, and reduced by 10 per cent all salaries, pensions and other payments to the minor canons and all other employees (except the schoolmaster and the beadswomen).[55] The overdraft on the general fund at Exeter had reached £973 by 1887. Payments to Sunday singers were discontinued, a stricter method of cost control was introduced, and the dean and chapter agreed that their gross personal incomes should be reduced until the debt was paid off. In the following year the dean and chapter blamed 'the present depressed state of agriculture' for not acceding to a request from the college of vicars choral for extra pay. By 1891 the overdraft had risen to £1,287 19s 10d. Further special payments to the choir were discontinued, but a year later the debt had increased to £1,590 19s 3d.[56] The same difficulties were being experienced at Winchester, where the excess of actual expenditure over the net annual income between 1879 and 1882 amounted to £5,586.[57] In 1884 the dean and chapter sent a long memorandum to the Ecclesiastical and Church Estates Commissioners asking for more money.[58] The plight of the chapters was certainly being taken seriously. A Treasury Minute of 11 June 1883 suggested, following a request for assistance with repairs from the Deans of Westminster and Peterborough, that cathedrals should hand over their estates to the Ecclesiastical Commissioners and be given instead a fixed annual grant, divided into two parts: for the maintenance of the fabric of cathedrals and their precincts, and for the expenses of their services and staffs. The Minute further suggested that each cathedral should be surveyed carefully 'in order that each Cathedral may be endowed with such an annual income as may be reported necessary for its maintenance in thorough repair'. These endowments would made inalienable and individual fabric funds would be vested in the Ecclesiastical Commissioners. If the revenues of individual cathedrals were inadequate, 'arrangements should, if possible, be made with the Ecclesiastical Commissioners for supplementing the revenues to the necessary extent'.[59]

Archbishop Benson tried hard to get additional funds for cathedrals, pointing out that Winchester was in a bad state, despite the immense sums that the commissioners received from its estates. Lincoln was impoverished, with inadequate amounts to maintain the services and the library. Much of the lump sum of £20,000 for fabric repairs agreed at the commutation had already been spent. At Peterborough the dean and chapter had borrowed £6,000 for fabric repairs, as it was wrongly supposed that no repairs would be needed for thirty years, and they were repaying this loan out of their own pockets. They needed to spend £60,000. Most canonical houses, such as those at Lincoln, were kept in repair by their occupants.[60] The Dean of Canterbury convened a meeting of 'landed chapters' in London in 1886. A committee was formed 'to draft and present a petition to Lord Salisbury to bring in a bill enabling the Ecclesiastical Commission to relieve the Chapters whose incomes fall short of the sums fixed at the time of their commutations', though a united front was spoilt by the Deans of Carlisle and Chester who said that their incomes had not fallen short. At Salisbury stipends and wages were reduced in 1888, after a London accountant had investigated the capitular accounts.[61] Ten years earlier the communar's accounts showed a profit of £625, but this had disappeared by 1885 and by 1888 each canon residentiary was receiving less than half of the £500 it was intended he receive when the estates were transferred.[62] The situation was no better at Chichester, where the dean and chapter sent a memorandum to the Ecclesiastical Commissioners in 1890 asking for a further grant, as the commutation of their estates had undermined their solvency.[63] At Bristol, too, the dean and chapter were in financial difficulties and had to seek an overdraft.[64] At the Exeter Church Congress of 1894 it was reported that Winchester, Salisbury and Peterborough were suffering from a greatly reduced income.[65] In 1893 the Dean of Canterbury convened a further meeting in London of deans and canons from various cathedrals to consider their straitened circumstances. The dean and chapter of Gloucester had already reduced their expenditure on such diverse outgoings as organ blowing, women cleaners and beadsmen's gowns, and informed the Ecclesiastical Commissioners of their plight. The estate income had fallen to £3,600. Dean Spence then began to negotiate a further exchange with the Ecclesiastical Commissioners in order to exchange all the capitular estates except Sandhurst for a tithe rent charge of £5,838 6s 2d each year.[66] Although the accounts showed a substantial improvement during the next few years, the value of the tithe rent charge also continued to fall. In the financial year 1900–1 the dean and chapter found that the overdraft on the domus account was rising again and it was not until 1906 that a credit balance was achieved.[67] The dean and chapter of Salisbury concluded a similar bargain in 1895 and contributed towards the expenses of a case being presented to the Privy Council on behalf of several distressed cathedrals.[68]

The estate records of Gloucester Cathedral in the 1880s illustrate, in a clear and moving way, the relations between the chapter and their tenants at this difficult time. The key men in the administration of the estates were George Whitcombe, the chapter clerk, and Canon Evans, the receiver, who was also Master of Pembroke College, Oxford. Whitcombe was assisted by an Oxford firm, Messrs Field and Castle of 18 Merton Street.

In May 1879 six of the chapter's tenants in east Gloucestershire wrote to Whitcombe for rent relief because of the decline in prices and because of 'adverse seasons [in which] our crops have more or less failed...at the same time our expenditure in rates and labour has been continuously increased and the result has been an unavoidable heavy loss'.[69] The following January, Whitcombe told Canon Tinling, another of the residentiary canons of Gloucester Cathedral, that several tenants were overdue in paying their rents.[70] Should the chapter seek different tenants when leases ran out? Messrs Field and Castle advised against it.[71] Nevertheless, some tenants drove a hard bargain with the chapter, such as Charles Barton of Coln Rogers, and a man named Cole from Ashbrook and South Cerney, who offered to renew their leases at reduced rents. Canon Evans even employed 'a capital bottle of port' during the negotiations, but the chapter eventually had to settle for a loss,[72] though Evans described part of the offered rent as 'simply preposterous'.[73] Barton was certainly in difficulties. He had paid nothing during the year preceding June 1880, despite the fact that he was known to be 'a well-to-do man, a good farmer with ample capital – in fact one of the best men all round in that part of the country'.[74] Evans described the list of arrears at that time as 'certainly formidable, very far in excess of our College arrears'. In July 1880 three of the chapter's tenants asked for time to pay, and by September matters were getting so urgent that Evans wrote to Whitcombe in the following terms:

> I have received letters from the Dean and Canon Harvey complaining of the non-payment of our rents in arrear, and suggesting that the tenants should be pressed for payment....And, perhaps, it would be well, if it is only to shew that we have the claim and have not written it off, to touch up those who are in arrear, *not* threatening 'proceedings' or coercive measures but stating that the members of the Chapter complain of the great inconvenience to which they have been put by the non-payment of so large an amount, and urging them to make an effort to pay it off. Poor devils! They are in a worse strait than we are, and it gives me a twinge to use anything like harshness towards them even in words; but, as a matter of business, it is our duty to the D. & C. [sic] to do what we can in the matter.[75]

In the following February Whitcombe received a letter from a man named Foreshew of Manor Barn, Withington, who had already revealed his difficulties the previous July:

> ...this year I have lost three-fourths of my sheep and this in addition to a very disappointing crop of grain; these two terrible disasters alone have been enough in themselves to bring me well nigh to ruin. I would also place before your notice the disastrous season of 1879 and tell you that the whole of the produce of grain grown on the farm in that year only realised me £125, and this amount represents every shilling that was made off 145 acres which simply means to me utter and total ruin unless you will assist me by making a substantial reduction in the rent of the farm. If you cannot meet me in this way, there will be no alternative left for me but to relinquish the holding and that as early as can be. This I should much regret to do after being here for thirty years.[76]

Whitcombe told Evans that Foreshew's lease was not due to expire till Michaelmas 1885, but Evans replied:

> With respect to Foreshew, we must keep him in play and we must reduce his rent; but as to the amount of the reduction we must be guided by Castle. You may tell him that his application is under consideration.[77]

A fortnight later Evans advised Whitcombe to go to Foreshew's farm with Castle, and in July 1881 his rent was reduced to £350 per annum.[78] Evans, Whitcombe and Castle were in almost daily correspondence over the estates, often making personal visits to the farms, seeking advice about possible new tenants, and making enquiries about their existing tenants. The degree of concern that they showed is impressive. Throughout those difficult years they had to maintain as high an income as possible for the benefit of the cathedral and chapter, and at the same time they knew that new tenants would be hard to find. It was therefore both sound financial prudence as well as an impressive compassion that governed their relations with their tenants.[79]

The rents from properties were paid to the dean and chapter at the twice-yearly audits, which were generally held at midsummer and in November. In order to encourage members of the chapter to attend the audits (which often lasted several days) at Gloucester Cathedral, an attendance allowance was paid in 1808.[80] J. W. Whitcombe, the chapter clerk, told Canon Townshend Selwyn in 1837:

> The order of Chapter respecting the attendance of members at the Audit requires that each member should be present at some time during the 26th November and should signify his presence by putting down his name in the Chapter Room and further that he should not absent himself from any of the meetings until the close of the audit on the 30th. The non-compliance with this order deprives the party of his right to share in the sumptus and seal fees.[81]

By 1815 it was decided that the November audit should always be considered adjourned to the following 1 January and the midsummer audit to the following 1 August to allow time for a proper report to be given on the moneys received. All money received by way of fines and rents was to be paid by the receiver into a bank account, which would then become the source of all payments by the dean and chapter, this account being kept separate from all other capitular accounts.[82] At Bristol, from 1862, a special chapter was held on the first Tuesday in each January and the first Tuesday in each July to audit the accounts.[83] The tenants of the dean and chapter of Gloucester were summoned by a circular sent out by the chapter clerk. In 1879 the tenants were told that the rents due on Lady Day should be paid to the chapter office between 10 a.m. and 3 p.m. on the first Thursday in June. Dinner would be served at the Bell Hotel at 3 p.m.[84] At Chichester the rents due at Michaelmas were to be paid on the first day of November.[85]

The internal financial arrangements of each cathedral varied considerably, and it is not easy to provide a comprehensive summary of them. At the new foundation cathedrals, two of the canons held the posts of receiver-general and treasurer. In broad terms the receiver-general was responsible for income and the treasurer for expenditure. In 1800, for example, the receiver-general at Worcester handled an income of £4,252 3s 4¾d and owed the chapter £1,459 17s 7¾d. He was also responsible for dividing among the dean and prebendaries the income received from the renewal of fines, together with other perquisites and heriots. In 1820 the receiver-general's total receipts amounted to £5,496 9s 0¼d and his outgoings came to £3,338 9s 9½d. The sum of £5,149 8s 0d was available to be divided among the members of the chapter. In 1850 the receipts had fallen to £2,988 2s 5¾d and the outgoings were £3,194 4s 9d, but £5,374 9s 5d was divided among the members of the chapter.[86] When we turn to the treasurer's accounts for 1800 we find that he was responsible for paying the statutory stipends of the dean, prebendaries, minor canons and other officers and servants of the cathedral. In addition he paid for the forty-six loaves that were given away each week to 'paupers' with an allowance for rent and coal. There were individual repairs to the cathedral that involved payments to tradesmen and other expenses, including washing the communion linen and sweeping the library. The ringers were paid £4 10s for ringing on special days, such as the anniversary of the King's accession, and the upkeep of the cathedral grounds cost over £13. Altogether the treasurer drew from the receiver-general £2,021 12s 5d during the year and spent £2,105 5s 2d, making a deficit of £76 4s 11d. Apart from 1802, the treasurer spent more than £2,000 in each of the first ten years of the nineteenth century. By 1870 he was spending nearly £3,800 in a year, but this figure had fallen to £3,060 by 1900.[87] The accounts of the treasurer of Gloucester were set out in a similar fashion, but with a careful distinction made between ordinary and extraordinary payments. In 1800 he spent £3,137 12s.[88] At Winchester also the treasurer was responsible for the payment of stipends and salaries and the making of charitable donations. The receiver collected rents and the vice-dean was responsible for the collection of fines. In 1799–1800 the treasurer's income was £7,775 16s 2½d, his expenses amounted to £2,772 10s 1¾d, and he paid £4,803 6s 0¾ to the dean and chapter in dividends.[89] By 1819–20 his turnover had risen to nearly £11,800 and by 1858–9 this figure had reached over £16,600, falling to £12,624 by 1868.[90]

At the old foundation cathedral of Salisbury the financial officer was known as the communar. He handled the income and payments to the individual members of the chapter, while the expenditure on the cathedral fabric was controlled by the master of the fabric, who kept his own accounts. In addition, the clerk of the works kept accounts and was responsible for the payments to workmen.[91] In 1813, at the general chapter meeting, it was agreed that a percentage amounting to 2½ per cent on all fines for the renewal of leases paid to individual members of the chapter should be paid to the master of the fabric or the communar, and this was embodied in a statute.[92] Archdeacon Webber, who was the communar at

Chichester in 1821, received £1,008 2s 10d mainly from rents and redeemed land tax. His payments totalled £684 9s 5d, leaving £323 to be divided among the dean and chapter.[93]

A new form of book-keeping was adopted at Chichester in 1815. The communar's accounts were to be submitted to the dean and chapter on the Tuesday in the week preceding Christmas Day each year and the communar for the following year would be appointed at that meeting.[94] At Hereford two of the canons (including the canon-in-residence) met to investigate the accounts of the chapter on the first Monday in October, to check that all bills were paid before the audit and to submit all necessary matters to the chapter.[95] There was no person in overall charge of the capitular finances at Hereford. The canons who held the posts of master of the library and master of the fabric were responsible for the accounts of their own departments, while the two other canons who held the posts of senior and junior claviger were similarly responsible for their own accounts. When Sydney Smith was a canon of St Paul's, the general and fabric funds were kept separately.[96]

Some cathedrals were finding it hard to pay their way in the early nineteenth century. In about 1812 the dean and chapter of Chester were £4,260 in debt and only strong advice from Bishop G. H. Law enabled them to recover their fortunes.[97] Even before the fire of 1829, the dean and chapter of York were in some financial difficulties and less than ten years later the enormous expense of restoration had forced them to live on capital.[98] At Salisbury the average annual capitular income during the three years up to 1835 was approximately £3,176 gross or £2,800 net, mainly from fines, rents and interest. On a seven years' average, the income was rather higher. The stalls of the dignitaries were well endowed, the dean's annual income being £2,679 and the treasurer's amounting to about £1,500. The chancellor and the (non-residentiary) precentor could expect £1,000 and £750 per annum respectively.[99] The statistics published by the Ecclesiastical Duties and Revenues Commission in 1835 enable us to form a comparative picture of the financial condition of cathedrals at this time.[100] Durham had the highest gross income, followed by Christ Church, Oxford, Canterbury and Winchester. The lowest was York, but this was because the bulk of the endowments were attached to particular stalls. Nevertheless, there was still a wide variation between the amount of surplus capitular revenue to be divided between the members of the chapter, varying in 1834 between £32,160 at Durham and £3,382 at Bristol.[101]

In 1854 the cathedral commissioners said that the average amount of the entire revenues of twenty-six cathedrals and two collegiate churches over the seven years from 1846 to 1852 amounted to £295,984 4s 6d, the revenue for the year 1852 being £313,005 2s. Of this total, £160,713 was available for distribution to members of chapters. About one-sixth of the corporate revenues was paid to the Ecclesiastical Commissioners, but they augmented the incomes of some poorer chapters, such as Chester and Ripon.[102] At Bristol the annual average income from the renewal of leases between 1846 and 1853 was £6,239.[103] Ten per cent of all fines renewed by the dean and chapter of Exeter were reserved for repairs to the fabric.[104] W. K. Hamilton pointed out the disadvantages to individual canons of relying on the division of surplus capitular income: 'Our annual incomes are very *unequal* in amount and very *uncertain*...I have experienced fluctuations in my professional income to the most inconvenient extent.'[105]

After the commutation of their estates, various deans and chapters began to reorganize their finances. A fixed income from the Ecclesiastical Commissioners meant that fixed payments could be paid as stipends, and various payments by way of corn rents, bread and sundry fees were discontinued. This was certainly the case at Chichester, where £400 was set aside each year as a fabric fund and £50 paid annually to the lay clerks' pension fund.[106] Approximately two-fifths of the income from the commissioners was spent on the cathedral and other capitular liabilities, and the remaining three-fifths formed part of the stipend of the dean and chapter.[107] The fabric fund at Salisbury was also reorganized in 1863.[108] In some notes drawn up by Harvey Goodwin in 1833 he said:

> My impression is that the needs of the fabric were always considered in commutation (certainly it was so at Ely and Carlisle), but the Ecclesiastical Commission did not insist upon or even always advise a *separate* fabric fund.

At Ely he insisted on 'a liberal allowance in the fabric, founded on experience; and at Carlisle there is a fabric fund applicable to the fabric only'.[109] At Winchester, the re-endowed chapter found itself overdrawn as early as 1871, but the situation had recovered by 1876.[110] The dean and chapter of Salisbury accepted in 1875 that they would have a fluctuating income when they were re-endowed.[111] Canon George Rawlinson complained to the Cathedrals Commission in 1880 that the disposable income of Canterbury Cathedral was insufficient to meet the chapter's responsibilities towards the fabric, services, staff and choir school. The income had fallen substantially since 1876 while demands continued to rise.[112] The situation was similar, if less acute, at Worcester. In 1876–7 the treasurer reported a surplus in both the domus and the fabric accounts. By 1877–8 this had been turned into a deficit in both accounts, though there were special circumstances that had helped to cause this situation. The domus account was still overdrawn in 1878–9 and the treasurer noted that the regular income was insufficient to meet the expected expenditure on this account, but there was a surplus on the fabric fund.[113] An indication of the increased cost of maintaining the services of cathedrals can be glimpsed at Bristol Cathedral. In 1850 the total stipends of six lay clerks and six choristers were £249 and £24 respectively, with the stipends of the organist, verger and schoolmaster amounting to £100, £20 and £60 respectively. By 1879 nine lay clerks were costing £540, and eighteen choristers were employed at a cost of £44, while the stipends of the organist and schoolmaster had doubled. The sum of £794 was spent in 1850 on the employment of twenty-four people. By 1879, thirty-nine people were employed at a cost of £1,838 per annum.[114]

The Agricultural Depression, as we have seen, caused considerable difficulties for several chapters.[115] Indeed, one could claim that many cathedrals have never wholly recovered from the effects of commutation and re-endowment, followed by the Depression. On the other hand, for those chapters that were able to realize that drastic reforms were necessary, the effects of the Depression forced them to overhaul their financial administration. One such cathedral was Winchester, where a financial committee, comprising the dean, treasurer and receiver, was established in 1893. Meetings of this committee were held before every chapter meeting, so that a monthly check could be kept on the cathedral's finances. The accounts of the receiver and treasurer were merged, so that all money due to the chapter was paid into this joint account. The agents on the capitular estates and the chapter clerk were obliged to submit quarterly statements and separate accounts were to be kept for the general fund, the charities accounts, the offertory account and for special funds of a temporary nature. The general fund income was derived from copyholds, dividends, rents, tithes, interest, boxes in the cathedral, rents of houses in the close and sundry other payments.[116] In 1898–9 the capitular estates at Winchester were exchanged for tithe-rent charge[117] and in 1900 Dean Stephens told Bishop Randall Davidson that 'the result so far has been satisfactory, even with tithe in its present depreciated condition'. The capitular income had fallen steadily since 1879, so that the members of the chapter had been receiving only half what they were due, but he now expected the income to rise again.[118] In his charge, Davidson realized that the reforms of the 1830s had impoverished chapters and complained that 'huge sums were taken from our cathedrals by those ruthless and ignorant men'.[119] Canterbury Cathedral also suffered from the effects of the Great Depression, though this was limited by the efficient administration of the seneschal, Colonel Dickenson, and Dean Farrar's soliciting of some £20,000 in special donations to the cathedral. From the early 1890s until 1912 the dean and canons of Canterbury gave up 'a considerable part' of their incomes in order to provide for the maintenance of the buildings and services.[120] Chichester Cathedral was still badly affected by the Agricultural Depression in 1899, the dean receiving only £560 instead of his official £1,000 and the canons receiving £280 instead of an official £500.[121] At St Paul's, however, where Robert Gregory became treasurer in 1871, the negotiations with the Ecclesiastical Commissioners about the commutation of the estates had been both protracted and careful in estimating the future needs of the cathedral. As a result, there were few financial problems at St Paul's in the late nineteenth century.[122]

Much was done during the century to try to put chapters on a sound financial footing. Unfortunately, by 1900, many cathedrals were in a precarious financial position, partly through the doctrinaire reforms of the 1830s, and partly through the effects of the Great Agricultural Depression, which rendered meaningless much of the basis upon which commutation and re-endowment agreements had been made. There were few outstanding figures in the field of cathedral finance – perhaps only Robert Gregory had any real ability – and few signs that chapters were really concerned to find expert lay help in this field. Excellent work was done by various experienced chapter clerks, but they were too firmly wedded to old procedures. The poverty of many cathedrals in the closing years of the century hampered their work and many of the problems that were revealed then have still not been adequately solved.

10

CATHEDRAL RESTORATION
IN THE NINETEENTH
CENTURY

In 1874 a leading article in the *Guardian* said that there was 'hardly a cathedral in England which had not been, or is not being restored'. The reason for this was 'simply because the whole idea of what a cathedral should be has been first restored'.[1]

Many English cathedral fabrics were in a deplorable condition in the early nineteenth century and the need to repair them from being completely ruinous was an important prerequisite to their later development and embellishment as useful religious centres. On Easter Monday 1786 the western tower of Hereford Cathedral collapsed, demolishing in its fall most of the Norman nave, and the memory of that calamitous event was revived in 1861 when the central tower and spire of Chichester Cathedral also collapsed. But Chichester was not the only cathedral to suffer very severe damage during the nineteenth century. York Minster was twice ravaged by fires that gutted the quire in 1829 and the nave in 1840.[2]

These, however, were exceptional catastrophes that simply highlighted the precarious state of so many cathedrals. A correspondent by the name of John Carter wrote to the *Gentleman's Magazine* in 1802 and described the state of the galilee at Durham which he had seen in 1795:

> The condition of this consecrated place was the most reprehensible, in regard to the roof being in many parts left without covering, the pavement strewed with heaps of coal and all kinds of building materials, the North aile [*sic*] partitioned off into offices...[3]

Winchester was similarly neglected. 'In several parts of the Nave,' wrote a visitor in 1806, 'the rain poured through in such torrents as to leave no doubt that the roof was in a deplorable state.'[4] Thomas Rickman warned the dean and chapter of Worcester of the risks involved in holding the Three Choirs Festival in the Cathedral in 1833: 'Though I do not say the roof will fall I do say that I think it dangerous to have the music meeting there with the Groining in the state it is, nor would I myself go to the Cathedral on the occasion.'[5]

Canterbury in 1845 was said to be similarly neglected, with broken windows, weed-covered sills, and walls streaked with green through lack of rainwater pipes. The chapter house was damp, disordered and littered, and the cloisters 'used as a dumping-place for ladders and stone'.[6]

In 1854 the Cathedrals Commission reported that two out of every three cathedrals were said to be in sound and good repair, but that many ornamental features were much decayed. Carlisle was in a poor way, but the Ecclesiastical Commissioners were expending £15,000 on it immediately. The commissioners noted that at several cathedrals considerable sums had been spent on restorations and repairs. In particular they mentioned the rebuilding of the north-west tower at Canterbury at a cost of £25,000 and a gradual restoration of the whole cathedral which had been continuing since 1823. The dean and chapter had spent nearly £100,000 on this work from capitular funds. The cost of repairing York after the two fires was said to be £106,560, £71,590 having been subscribed by the public, while further work (costing £5,000) to the chapter house and bells had been met through the proceeds of two bequests. Hereford was being rescued from the 'very dilapidated and unsafe condition' it was in in 1841. So far this had cost £27,398, of which £14,418 had been donated by the public. At Ely the commissioners mentioned the restoration of the south-west transept and the adjoining chapel, the opening of the interior of the west tower, and the reordering of the eastern arm. These and other works had cost £27,847, of which £15,800 had been donated. A handsome donation of £1,500 from Bishop Sparke was being used to repair the east window. The restoration of the quire at Wells had cost £13,000 over four years, of which £8,000 had been donated by the public. In the previous fourteen years, £370,000 had been spent in repairs at twenty-eight cathedrals and the collegiate churches of Westminster and Windsor. No less that £250,000 had been provided from capitular revenues, while £120,000 had been donated by the public.[7]

Some of the problems and achievements involved in the task of cathedral restoration may be best demonstrated by a closer examination of the work done in particular cathedrals. Ely, Hereford and Worcester are good examples of sustained restoration over several decades, while a study of Chichester highlights the problems caused by the worst structural calamity to befall a cathedral during the century. The new nave at Bristol is one of the most substantial Victorian additions to a cathedral, while the story of the redecoration of the interior of St Paul's shows how that vast building was increasingly cherished and valued.

When William Cobbett visited Ely in 1830 he found it 'in a state of disgraceful irrepair and disfigurement'. Many of the windows had been wholly or partially bricked up.[8] In 1848 John Hewett lamented the poor state of the Lady Chapel: 'its area filled with the most vile pewing, its carved work broken down, its windows – here robbed of their painted glass – there altogether blocked up, it presents an unusual picture of decay and desecration'.[9] The restoration of Ely Cathedral began in 1843 as the result of a gift of £200 from one of the canons, Edward Sparke, son of a former bishop of the diocese. He was keen to restore the south-west transept of the cathedral, which was disused and served as a workmen's store. A great partition was removed, the walls were strengthened, and the apsidal chapel rebuilt. In 1844 Jesus College, Cambridge, gave £100 towards the restoration of Bishop Alcock's Chapel, and under Dean Peacock's leadership plans were soon drawn up to make alterations at the east end, to place new windows in the lantern, and to re-order the quire.[10] In 1847 the *Guardian* reprinted a report from the *Cambridge Chronicle*, giving details of the restoration of over forty windows, and the work done in the south-west transept and the quire, as well as the plans that the dean and chapter had to spend some £8,000 on future improvements.[11] Gilbert Scott was appointed by the dean and chapter in 1847 to supervise the rearrangement of the quire.[12] The chapter agreed to a tender of £3,230 in 1848 for the construction of new stalls and a screen in accordance with his designs. He also designed a new organ case, font, and gates for the quire aisles.[13] In 1855 the west tower ceiling was painted by Henry Styleman le Strange, who went on to paint six bays of the nave ceiling before he died in 1862. Gambier Parry completed the work and later painted the lantern, and the roof of the south-west transept. There were some donations and bequests that helped pay for this work, but both le Strange and Parry gave their services.[14] The eastern lancets were filled with new glass in 1857 and in the following year Scott's elaborate reredos was finished, after five years' work.[15] Dean Peacock initiated the remodelling of the lantern by Scott, and the next two deans, Harvey Goodwin and Charles Merivale, continued the work of restoration as a memorial to him. Subscriptions amounted to around £10,000.[16] The nave floor was repaved in 1869–70 at a cost of £2,600 and the western tower was strengthened soon after.[17] The last pinnacle of the octagon was finished in 1879. The total cost has been put at £57,053 7s 9d. The dean and chapter had contributed nearly £23,000 out of their corporate funds, and nearly £15,000 as individuals. Some £3,600 was given by bishops of Ely and their families, £1,412 by officers and tradesmen of the chapter, £365 by inhabitants of Ely, and £13,840 by the general public.[18] In 1862 Murray's *Handbook* enthusiastically commended the work of restoration at Ely:

> When the nave roof has been completed there can be no doubt that Ely will be the most magnificently restored church in Europe, and will afford one of the most perfect examples of a great mediaeval cathedral in the height of its original splendour.[19]

Ely is a good example of a sustained restoration over a period of more than thirty years which was undertaken chiefly in order to beautify and enrich a splendid medieval building. The restoration of Hereford Cathedral, by contrast, owed its inception to an impending calamity and the vigour of one of the most remarkable of early Victorian deans, John Merewether.[20] Merewether had suggested improving the east end of the quire in 1835, but the chapter was divided on this matter; the serious disagreements that he had with the chapter during the next few years prevented any work being undertaken.[21] On 3 October 1840 Merewether was walking in the close with Philip Hardwick, the architect responsible for some alterations at the palace at Hereford. As they passed the east wall of the Lady Chapel, Hardwick remarked to Merewether, 'If you do not take care, you will surely have that beautiful building down.' This advice made a deep impression on Merewether, who was the only member of the chapter then at hand, and he took immediate measures to prop up the walls.[22] In the following spring the cathedral was examined by another architect, L. N. Cottingham, who found that the east wall of the Lady Chapel was very cracked, and indeed in a dangerous condition. The library, which then occupied the Lady Chapel, was removed, as was the Grecian screen and panelling in the quire. Scaffolding was erected under the tower, and the great ox-eye pillars on the north and south sides, together with the arches above them, were found to be in a dangerous condition. The state of the tower was found to be 'absolutely appalling', with wide and extensive cracks that continued down into the pillars supporting the tower. The core of the pillars had turned into dust. The foundations were examined and the screen, stalls and organ were removed. The main reason for removing the stalls under the tower was to prevent them from being damaged during its repair. Cottingham's anxiety about the extremely dangerous condition of the cathedral was confirmed by Professor Robert Willis of Cambridge and the building was closed. The contractor was John Carline, who submitted two estimates: the work on the tower was costed at £5,450 and the work on the Lady Chapel was expected to cost £2,730. Twenty-five per cent of the cost was not paid until three months after the completion of the contracts. This led to great difficulties for the builder, who had to borrow heavily from his brother and from his bank. Cottingham was elderly and unwell and visited Hereford only rarely. He agreed to few of John Carline's claims for additional work and materials and Carline had to bear the loss involved. Soon after Cottingham died in 1847, Carline stopped work at Hereford and moved to Lincoln.[23] The total cost of Cottingham's repairs was £27,000.[24] In 1854 Sir Gilbert Scott was called in. He advised the chapter to put in hand urgent repairs to the quire and eastern transepts. He also worked in the quire-aisles and the north porch, and replaced monuments that Cottingham had removed. He rearranged the old stalls east of the crossing and designed a metal screen which was executed by Skidmore.[25] Scott was clearly dubious about the new quire at Hereford:

Practically, for ordinary purposes, this was a gain; for great diocesan uses it was a loss. From an antiquarian view it was an error....The metal screen in its present form came about in this way: Mr Skidmore was anxious to have some great work in the exhibition of 1862, and offered to make the screen at a very low price. I designed it on a somewhat massive scale, thinking that it would thus harmonise better with the heavy architecture of the choir. Skidmore followed my design but somewhat aberrantly. It is a fine work, but too loud and self-asserting for an English church.[26]

Scott and Skidmore also produced the great *corona lucis* which was suspended from the centre of the tower:

The circlet of the crown sheds a soft and diffused light down upon the screen; and the standards surrounding the circle, which consists of groups of light enveloping a mass of crystals, produce a singular and gem-like appearance, suggestive of jewels on a crown, whilst serving the practical purpose of illuminating the upper part of the tower.... Beyond all question, the time when the entire building appears to the greatest advantage is Sunday evening, when the Corona and Standards are lighted, including in all more than 500 jets of gas, and producing a scene of more than Oriental magnificence.[27]

In 1884 the Cathedrals Commission noted that more than £45,000 had been spent on the restoration at Hereford, not including the cost of the reordering of the quire, the rebuilding of the organ, or the new heating and lighting.[28]

On the other side of the Malvern Hills, Worcester Cathedral was also undergoing a thorough restoration at the same time as Hereford.[29] This roughly coincided with the tenure of the deanery from 1845 to 1874 by John Peel, brother of Sir Robert Peel, the Prime Minister. The total cost between 1840 and 1875 was £114,295 11s 4d, more than that for any other cathedral during the same period.[30] It appears that during the period preceding the restoration a steady amount of repair work was done, since between 1818 and 1834 expenditure only fell below £500 twice and was often nearer £1,000.[31] A. E. Perkins, a local man, was the dean and chapter's architect; a pupil of Thomas Rickman, he began his work for the chapter by building some stables in College Green in 1845.[32] In the 1850s the amount spent in restoration increased considerably, partly through support given to the dean and chapter by the Ecclesiastical Commissioners. They commissioned their own architect, Ewan Christian, to provide them with reports, and it seems that Christian was more conservative than Perkins. The commissioners provided funds for the works from 1860 to 1866 and Christian was responsible for seeing that their money was well spent. It appears that Perkins took some trouble to point out various features to Christian and to make sure that he was quite satisfied.[33]

The turning point came in 1864 when dean and chapter, having spent £31,000 from their own resources, turned to the people of Worcestershire for help. The Lord Lieutenant, Lord Lyttelton, wrote to the magistrates and incumbents of the county and gave an account of what had so far been achieved:

> Externally, the whole Fabric east of the Tower has been restored: the East end and the two Eastern Transepts have been in great measure rebuilt. All the windows have been altered, and new Buttresses and Pinnacles erected. The two West Transepts have been thoroughly repaired and a large new window inserted in the north-west transept.
>
> Internally, the whitewash and plaster have been removed from the walls both of the Choir and the Nave, the whole of the Vaulting repaired, two large Piers rebuilt, two unsightly walls removed; the marble shafts and carved work restored, the Bosses re-gilt; and a part of the ancient painting renewed. Some ancient rooms have been converted into vestries and the Chapter Room restored within and without.[34]

But much still remained to be done, as Lyttelton went on to say:

> Externally the north-west and south sides of the Nave, including the North Porch, are to be restored: a new large west window inserted, and the Cloisters thoroughly repaired.
>
> Internally the Floor of the Nave is to be repaired at the charge of £1000; the Cathedral is to be lighted and furnished with a warming apparatus; the whole of the Choir re-modelled; a new Organ-screen and Reredos to be erected, the Organ to be reconstructed, the Floor repaired, and the stalls and fittings materially improved.

For all of this, nearly £22,000 was needed. A public meeting was held in the Guildhall on 7 April 1864 and a finance committee was elected to collect subscriptions. At the public meeting Lyttelton said that 'both the Bishop and the Dean felt it desirable that the laity should hold a prominent position in the work remaining to be done at the Cathedral', which was why he presided over it.[35] From this time onwards the work was superintended by a Joint Restoration Committee, consisting of prominent laymen as well as the dean and chapter. In addition to the planned work mentioned above, a decision was soon taken to restore the tower and improve the ring of bells.[36] The decision to restore the tower stemmed from an offer of £5,000 for this purpose from Lord Dudley and the pressure exerted by Minor Canon Richard Cattley, who wanted Worcester Cathedral to have the finest ring of bells in the country.[37] In 1866 three major contractors were at work on the cathedral: Hughes of Bristol, who were responsible for the north side of the nave and the tower; Collins and

A service in progress in the quire of Salisbury Cathedral, 1814

Top left   Sydney Smith, Canon of St Paul's Cathedral
Top right   Charles James Blomfield, Bishop of London
Bottom left   Sir Robert Peel, Prime Minister
Bottom right   John Merewether, Dean of Hereford

Top left   Richard William Church, Dean of St Paul's Cathedral
Top right   John William Burgon, Dean of Chichester
Bottom left   E. H. Plumptre, Dean of Wells
Bottom right   Robert Gregory, Canon and later Dean of St Paul's Cathedral

Top The Dean and Chapter of Worcester Cathedral, 1891
L. to R. W. Knox-Little, Dean John Gott, M. Creighton, D. Melville, T.L. Claughton
Bottom left Ralph Barnes, Chapter Clerk of Exeter Cathedral
Bottom right F. T. Havergal, Vicar Choral of Hereford Cathedral

Top   The vergers and beadsmen of Worcester Cathedral, 1891
Bottom   The choristers of Winchester Cathedral, 1877

Hereford Cathedral. 11th August 1851 (Canon in Residence)

Chants	Day of the Month	SERVICES.	ANTHEMS.	COMPOSERS.
	11	Mon. Clarke F. (Verse) Ev.	Sing praises — Bow thine Ear —	Croft Bird
	12	Tu. Porter D Ev.	Rejoice in the Lord — all People	Humphries Tallis
	13	Wed. Patrick G Ev.	(Litany) — Save Lord	Hayes
	14	Th. Aldrich A Ev.	Praise the Lord — In Jewry —	Hall Clarke
	15	Fri. Bryan G Ev.	(Litany) — Behold how good —	Nares
	16	Sat. Travers D Ev. Bishop D	God is gone up — Give the Lord —	Croft Kent
	17	Sun. Gibbons F Ev.	(Litany) — Why do the nations. —	Handel
	18	Mon. Russell A Ev.	O God thou art &c — I beheld &c —	Purcell Blow
	19	Tu. Hunt A Ev. E. Smith D	O give thanks — O Lord God of Hosts —	Tucker Crotch
	20	Wed. King D Ev.	(Litany) — I was in the Spirit —	Blow
	21	Th. Dare G Ev. Arnold B	O be joyful — Thou O God —	Bishop Greene
	22	Fri. Batten D Ev.	(Litany) — Behold now praise —	Rogers
	23	Sat. Boyce A. Full Ev. Aldrich G	My God — Lord for thy tender &c	Reynolds Farrant
	24	Sun. King F Ev.	(Litany) — O God who hast —	Corfe

Edward Howells.
Subchanter.

A music list from Hereford Cathedral, August 1851

Samuel Sebastian
Wesley, organist in
turn of Hereford,
Exeter, Winchester
and Gloucester
Cathedrals

Sir John Stainer,
organist of St Paul's
Cathedral

The ruinous state of the cloisters at Hereford Cathedral c. 1855

Chichester Cathedral following the fall of the spire in 1861

Truro Cathedral under construction, 1899

Top John Loughborough Pearson's perspective of Truro Cathedral
Bottom The bread dole at Worcester Cathedral. Although actually taken in 1909, this photograph perfectly captures the atmosphere of a regular event at many cathedrals in the late nineteenth century

The Three Choirs Festival, Hereford, 1897

The muniment room
at Salisbury
Cathedral, 1834

Walter Kerr Hamilton,
Bishop of Salisbury

Archibald Campbell
Tait, successively Dean
of Carlisle, Bishop of
London, and
Archbishop of
Canterbury

Harvey Goodwin,
successively Dean of Ely
and Bishop of Carlisle

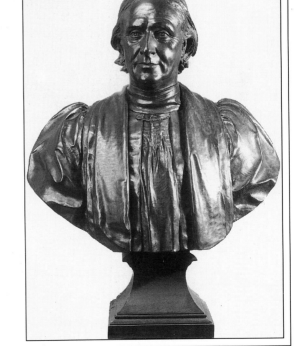

Edward White Benson,
successively Canon
Chancellor of Lincoln
Cathedral, Bishop of
Truro and Archbishop
of Canterbury

The enthronement of Randall Davidson as Bishop of Winchester in 1895

Cullis of Tewkesbury, who took over from Hughes and restored the cloisters; and Joseph Wood of Worcester, who restored the south side of the nave. Before 1864 the restoration work was in the hands of John Bennett of Birmingham. He employed thirty men in 1856 and increased the work-force to seventy in 1860 and to 100 in 1861.[38] In 1866 the work at Worcester was severely criticized by the *Saturday Review.*[39]

We have already seen how Scott was called in at both Ely and Hereford to continue a restoration that had begun under the direction of another architect. The same procedure occurred at Worcester, where he was responsible for the rearrangement of the quire, but also removed the old quire screen and canopies of the stalls. He also designed new paving for the nave and quire and designed the decoration of the quire vaulting. His proposals for the sites of the organs were overruled[40] and he later regretted the removal of the elegant sounding-board of the quire pulpit.[41] It should be stressed that Scott had little responsibility for the structural restoration of the cathedral and his designs for its refurnishing were very definitely controlled by the Joint Restoration Committee.[42] Indeed, the relationship between Scott and the Committee became yet more strained, since his report had been commissioned and accepted before the 1864 appeal, and the lay members of the Joint Restoration Committee had their own views about what should be done.[43] The work on the tower delayed the refurnishing of the quire until after a second public appeal in 1867. There was a third appeal in 1870. The dominant member of the Joint Restoration Committee was the Earl of Dudley. It was clear from the popular celebrations at the reopening of the cathedral in 1874 that he was regarded as the leading figure in all that had been achieved. Dudley became increasingly hostile to Scott, who suffered recurrent bouts of illness in the 1870s, and by 1873 he suggested that he himself should take over from Scott.[44] A major disagreement occurred over the furnishing of the nave. Dudley commissioned a new floor for the nave in 1872–3[45] and repeatedly pressed for a full set of liturgical furniture in the nave. He wanted the nave to be used for services so that it would not be available for the concerts of the Three Choirs Festival. Although Scott was in favour of a nave pulpit, he disapproved of the introduction of additional furniture into the nave.[46] But Dudley's views prevailed and Scott duly provided seats in the nave for the bishop, mayor, canons, choir and congregation. Although the dean and chapter resisted any definite undertaking in return for Lord Dudley's generosity, the 1875 Festival consisted entirely of church services and was known as the Mock Festival.[47]

In April 1874 there was an extensive festival to celebrate the reopening of Worcester Cathedral. Grand services were sung on three successive days, the cathedral choir being augmented by singers from St George's Windsor, Christ Church, Oxford, Eton College, and the cathedrals of Hereford and Gloucester. Other services were sung by the massed parochial choirs of the diocese, with a choral communion service on one day and early said celebrations on other days. After the opening sermon there was lunch in College Hall for over three hundred. Dean Peel, though very infirm, stood at the north door for half an hour to greet the notables of the city and county. At the Sunday evening service every spare inch of the cathedral was crammed with extra chairs.[48] The *Guardian* commented that 'there was a feeling towards the cathedral as really the mother church of the city and diocese'.[49]

Ely, Hereford and Worcester Cathedrals still bear considerable traces of their Victorian restorations, but the work done in each of them was essentially a re-dressing of an existing building. At Chichester and at Bristol a substantial amount of new work was necessary – in the former case resulting from the collapse of the spire in 1861, and in the latter case as a result of the desire to complete a building that had remained truncated since the sixteenth century. Dean Chandler of Chichester spent £3,000 from his own pocket on his cathedral between 1830 and 1859, and left a further £2,000 to be spent on making the building more suitable for public worship. This sum was increased by various public donations, and, as a memorial to Dean Chandler, it was proposed to remove the pulpitum known as the Arundel Screen, which stood between the western piers of the tower. Shortly before his arrival in Chichester in the summer of 1859, the new dean, W. F. Hook, wrote to the precentor, Canon C. A. Swainson, regretting that this plan had not been deferred until after his arrival, but the removal of the screen went ahead despite Hook's plea. By February 1861 it was clear that the tower had been seriously weakened as a result, and the spire collapsed on 21 February, while Dean Hook sat sobbing in his study. Nevertheless, he threw himself into the task of raising money for its rebuilding with the utmost vigour, establishing committees and addressing meetings. Queen Victoria gave £250 and the Prince Consort donated £100, while a meeting at Brighton only a month after the fall of the spire raised £14,300. Hook himself gave £1,000, his income for a whole year. Scott's estimate for rebuilding the tower and spire was £50,000.[50]

When Scott was called to advise about the reconstruction at Chichester, he did not displace the existing architect, a man named Slater, but shared the work with him, though the restoration committee acted as though Scott were in sole charge. The Duke of Richmond and Gordon was chairman of the committee, which Scott described as 'the finest committee I ever worked under; extremely numerous, and consisting of an admirable set of men'. Many old stones were re-used in the new tower and spire.[51] From 1861 to 1894, £78,000 was spent on the cathedral; the restoration of the spire cost £53,000. The cathedral was reopened in November 1867[52] with celebrations that included balloons, fireworks and a public dinner.[53] By 1878, however, it was apparent that much further restoration in the cathedral still remained to be done.[54] It was not until 1894 that fresh committees were appointed to carry forward the work of restoration.[55]

Bristol Cathedral had remained without a nave since the sixteenth century. In 1858–9 the interior suffered a disastrous reordering when the stalls were pushed to the extreme east end of the cathedral and the screen was destroyed.[56] The dean and chapter consulted Scott and J. S. Pope about the reordering, and Scott had recommended opening up the whole cathedral, shortening the quire, and making a 'nave' out of the three western bays. He disclaimed all responsibility, however, for the removal of the pulpitum.[57] In 1860 a new screen was erected under the eastern arch of the quire, but it was not connected to the stalls by side screens. The *Ecclesiologist* said that it was like 'a gate to a field with the hedges taken away'.[58] The new paving in the sanctuary was condemned by the same writer, who said that 'the pattern and materials are such as would disgrace a railway station', while the gas standards were of a 'hideous and ridiculous design'. Work began on a new nave in the 1860s. A local committee was formed in 1866, which pressed the dean and chapter to rebuild the nave. The sum of £11,000 had already been subscribed towards the work. Ten years later, however, a serious disagreement arose between the Nave Committee and the dean and chapter over the design of statues for the north porch.[59] The foundation stone of Street's new nave was laid in 1868 and it was complete apart from the west towers by October 1877. The central tower was underpinned by Scott in 1865, but its parapet and pinnacles were removed by Street ten years later. New pinnacles were added in 1893 when the tower was refaced. After Street's death in 1881, J. L. Pearson was appointed architect; he restored and enlarged the quire, bringing the stalls and altar back to their old positions, and finished off the west front.[60] In 1895 the *Guardian* said that Dean Elliott had transformed the truncated cathedral, which was formerly 'in a dilapidated and disgraceful condition' with broken windows. Under his leadership some £88,000 was spent on the building.[61] A further £24,000 was raised by Dean Pigou between 1891 and 1903.[62]

Although structurally sound, the position of St Paul's Cathedral in the middle of London meant that it was very dirty, and its internal decorations had never been completed. There were many openings through which the wind blew dust and soot. In 1842 'many loads of dirt' were taken away from the vaulting over the aisles, and the floors, walls, monuments and ceilings were covered in 'chronic filth'.[63] A great effort to clean and warm the cathedral was made by Archdeacon Hale. In 1841 he lime-washed the staircases and restored the Morning Chapel to a pristine condition. In 1842 he had the cathedral closed for over two months during the summer so that the quire and transepts, as well as the walls and monuments, could be dusted and painted. Two years later, despite a protest from *The Times*, the cathedral was again closed in order to clean the nave and the lower part of the dome.[64]

In Dean Milman's time, the frescoes under the dome were restored between 1853 and 1856, while in 1858 a committee was formed by the dean and chapter 'for assisting them in the special evening services and in the embellishment of the interior of the Cathedral'. Some windows were renewed, various parts of the cathedral were gilded, and two mosaics were inserted into the dome in 1864 and 1866. New stained glass was given for various windows, and by October 1868 the committee had spent £25,000 on the cathedral.[65] It also took away the quire-screen, moved the organ, and acquired a second-hand organ from the Panopticon of Science and Art in Leicester Square.[66] This committee was revived in 1870 and a public meeting was held at the Mansion House, with the Lord Mayor in the chair. An appeal was launched for £250,000, of which £25,000 was promised immediately. How the money should be spent was still to be decided.[67] As a result of the commutation of the capitular estates, which the dean and chapter agreed to in March of 1872, a capital sum of £30,000 became available for the repair, restoration and improvement of the cathedral and its ancillary buildings.[68] By March 1873 the Decoration Committee had collected nearly £56,000, with Queen Victoria heading the list of contributions with a personal gift of £1,000.[69]

The most pressing matter was the reconstruction of the organ and the question of whether it should be placed on a restored quire-screen or divided so that there was no screen between the dome and the quire. The chapter favoured the latter policy.[70] In July 1877 a Fine Arts Committee was appointed, consisting of six experts under the chairmanship of Dean Church. But the chapter had already entrusted the task of decoration to the architect, William Burges, whose dislike of the work of Sir Christopher Wren was well known. For two years the Fine Arts Committee and Burges contended with each other until eventually the Committee broke up, leaving Burges in sole charge. In the spring of 1874 Burges displayed his lavish plans at the Royal Academy; he estimated the cost at £400,000. Although for a while the dean and chapter supported Burges, both public and expert opinion condemned his plans and within a few months the chapter withdrew its support and suspended its plans for further decoration of the cathedral.[71]

When Canon Gregory became dean after Church's death in 1890, he was determined to revive the question of embellishing and decorating the cathedral. While Church was still alive, though increasingly unwell, Gregory had declined to act, but various improvements had been made, including a new chapel in the crypt in 1877, and a new floor in the quire. Walls and ceilings had been cleaned, masonry repaired, much of the roof re-leaded, steps in the geometrical staircase made safe, and wire guards, meant to exclude pigeons, fixed in the porticos.[72] A new and controversial reredos, designed by Bodley, had also been installed between August 1886 and January 1888, with accompanying work in the sanctuary. This all cost nearly £40,000. A new high altar was given in 1891 by Liddon's sister and a Jesus Chapel, in the apse behind the reredos, was dedicated at the end of that year.[73] Within a few weeks of Gregory's installation, the decoration of the cathedral was recommenced to a design by Sir William Richmond. The roof of the quire was filled with mosaics and gilding, and the work was completed by 1897. More work was done to the dome between 1892 and 1901 and the decoration of the aisles was finished by August 1907.[74] In December 1897 a great service was held to commemorate the bicentenary of the opening of the quire, and F. C. Penrose, the surveyor of the fabric, who had held office for forty-five years, retired.[75]

The story of the internal decoration of St Paul's is long and complicated, extending over several decades and including many schemes that eventually came to nothing. But it was brought to a triumphant conclusion at the end of the century and it illustrated, in a real and vivid way, the transformation that had been achieved at St Paul's in the last thirty years of the century, and which turned it from being a by-word for coldness and neglect into a shining example for the other English cathedrals.

Ely, Hereford, Worcester, Bristol, Chichester and St Paul's have been chosen as representative cathedrals that saw extensive restoration, extension or embellishment during the nineteenth century. However, virtually every cathedral in England was considerably restored at various times, and large sums of money were allocated for this. Only a summary account can be given of these restorations, but it is clear that a prodigious amount of work and care was expended by many deans and chapters and those whom they employed to repair and renovate the cathedrals for which they were responsible.

At Canterbury the cloisters were repaired,[76] and a new north-west tower was built.[77] After further repairs and renovations in the middle of the century,[78] Dean Farrar launched a successful appeal in 1895.[79] The restoration of Chester early in the century was clouded by a dispute with the architect, Thomas Harrison,[80] but later Scott did extensive work, energetically supported by Dean Howson.[81] Christ Church, Oxford, was internally reordered in 1856 and the effect was found pleasing.[82] In 1870–2 Scott rebuilt, repaired and refitted much of the cathedral and provided a striking east end.[83] At Durham, Dean Waddington, with the help of the architect Anthony Salvin, removed much of the seventeenth-century woodwork.[84] Dean Lake brought in Scott to do extensive repairs despite the opposition of Bishop Baring.[86] Exeter Cathedral was restored in the 1870s at a cost of over £50,000. There was 'immense opposition' to Scott's piercing of the pulpitum, and the new reredos caused a considerable controversy and was the subject of a legal case, *Phillpotts* v. *Boyd*.[87]

At Gloucester part of the white and yellow wash that disfigured the nave was removed in 1855,[88] while some years later Scott restored the stalls and canopies, and removed the side galleries, but did not interfere with the pulpitum.[89] In 1897 the Lady Chapel, which had been closed for over twenty-five years, was finally reopened. The cost of the restoration was said to be £9,892.[90] At Lichfield, after lamentable repairs early in the century,[91] Scott opened out and rearranged the quire.[92] The total cost of the repairs between 1856 and 1908, including further work by Scott's son, Oldrid Scott, was £98,000.[93] J. L. Pearson was appointed architect to Lincoln Cathedral in 1870. In his report to the dean and chapter in 1874 he noted that it was the only cathedral that had not been thoroughly restored. In the following year he proposed work to the west front that would cost £8,000–10,000 and general repairs to stonework estimated at over £50,000. The work was completed by 1880.[94]

Norwich Cathedral was extensively repaired in 1806 and a considerable number of alterations were made during the next forty years.[95] In the summer of 1829 the floor of the quire was covered in matting. This was very popular and led to increased congregations.[96] The restoration of the tower in 1842, including the use of a great deal of cement, caused considerable controversy.[97] Various work continued throughout the century and Scott estimated in 1867 that the cost of substantial repairs still needing to be done would be £12,000.[98] By the 1890s the interior of the quire was said to be in a deplorable condition.[99] Some of the windows were blocked; the inside of the tower piers could be seen, plaster was flaking off the walls, and the transepts were still behind screens.[100] Two years' work cost £3,357, of which the dean and chapter contributed over £2,000 out of their own pockets.[101] There was a remarkably prayerful atmosphere surrounding the restoration at Norwich, with Dean Lefroy leading the workmen in prayer every Monday morning. There were no accidents, and every time funds ran short there were redoubled prayers until the crisis was over.[102]

In 1860 Scott said that he had recently been asked to advise the dean and chapter of Peterborough. The north side of the cathedral was subsiding and needed to be shored up, and the central tower was in 'a very sad state'.[103] In 1882 J. L. Pearson found that its condition was dangerous, and thus it was carefully taken down, stone by stone. Pearson's proposals for its rebuilding led to a controversy that was eventually resolved by Archbishop Benson. By the time that the work on the tower and quire had been completed in 1890, it had cost nearly £32,000.[104] In 1884–5 the cathedral commissioners drew attention to the great expense of the repairs that the Peterborough chapter had had to meet.[105]

A new diocese was established at St Albans in 1877, and its ancient abbey became the cathedral of the new see. A restoration committee was formed, including Sir Edmund Beckett (later Lord Grimthorpe), whose name is indelibly linked with the restoration of St Albans. The first work to be put in hand was the raising of the nave roof. This was the subject of considerable debate among architects and antiquarians, but plans to restore the west front ran into even greater opposition.[106] By a faculty, Beckett was enabled to do what he liked with the building. An appeal was overruled and in May 1880 St Albans virtually became Beckett's property.[107] The restored nave was opened in October 1885.[108] Beckett then began to reconstruct the south transept.[109] There is no doubt that St Albans owed its preservation to Lord Grimthorpe, but the extensive alterations that he made, at a cost estimated between £120,000 and £140,000, have had few admirers and many critics.[110]

At Salisbury, after sporadic repairs in the early years of the century,[111] Scott began work in 1859, carefully replacing decayed stone throughout the building and examining all the foundations. With the support of Dean Hamilton he reordered the quire.[112] Scott's work at Salisbury was as extensive as his remodelling of the quire at Worcester.[113] He also introduced iron bars in the spire (which probably saved it from collapse) and restored the west front.

There was also a fair amount of restoration at Wells.[114] Until the early years of the century, the cathedral had been in a 'disfigured and discreditable condition', with unsightly galleries perched over the stalls and thick layers of white-wash and yellow ochre in the nave and transepts. In 1832 a new pavement was laid in the north and south quire aisles. The reforming zeal and generosity of Dean Goodenough and Archdeacon Brymer removed all the memorials inside the cathedral to the cloisters, thus enabling the Lady Chapel to be thoroughly restored. In 1844 the work of scraping was begun, but when funds ran out it had to be suspended. In the time of Dean Jenkyns the quire was restored with new stone walls designed by Salvin, and drastic repairs to the west front were begun in 1851. Through the zeal of some local citizens a new organ was built and brought into use in 1857.

The most notable work of restoration at Winchester in the late nineteenth century was to the reredos or great screen behind the high altar. Dean Bramston had wanted to replace the missing figures, but died before anything could be done. Work on the figures did not begin until 1888 and the screen was not finally restored until 1899. In the closing years of the century the nave roof was repaired and new windows were inserted in the Lady Chapel.[115]

York Minster was twice ravaged by fire within eleven years. The quire was gutted in 1829 and the nave in 1840.[116] Although the response to a public appeal following the first fire was generous, a lengthy dispute about the restoration of the pulpitum and the organ meant that there was much less public sympathy after the second calamity.[117] By 1854 the total cost of the two restorations amounted to £105,560. The second appeal had raised only £22,000, less than half the amount raised after the 1829 fire.[118]

At the end of the century J. C. Cox wrote an article entitled *The Treatment of Our Cathedral Churches in the Victorian Age*.[119] Although he admitted that the general condition of their fabrics was more sound than it had been sixty years earlier, he was nevertheless critical of many 'grievous faults' that had occurred in their restoration, giving several examples of work that he thought to be ill-advised or rash. He was particularly severe towards the destruction of screens and the desire to have 'unbroken vistas', and was ahead of his time in suggesting a national body to advise and warn chapters engaged in restoring and repairing their cathedrals.

Clearly the massive amount of restoration and repair work on so many cathedrals during the century must have cost a vast sum of money. It would be very hazardous to guess the total sum. Nevertheless, there are contemporary estimates for different times within the century that give some idea of the huge amounts involved. For instance, in 1835 the Ecclesiastical Revenues Commission said that more money had been spent on cathedral restorations in the years 1800–35 that in the whole of the preceding century.[120] In 1874 the *Quarterly Review* noted that nearly £400,000 had been given for repairs to various cathedrals.[121] It was reported to the Exeter Church Congress of 1894 that a total of £643,298 had been spent on cathedral restoration throughout England between 1874 and 1884.[122] In 1894 Dean Hole of Rochester calculated that over £10 million had been spent on church restoration in England and Wales between 1873 and 1892, of which a large proportion had been spent on cathedral repairs.[123]

Certainly by 1900, despite the sometimes over-zealous restoration work that Cox complained about, the cathedrals of England were in a much better structural condition than they had been a hundred years earlier. This notable achievement was made possible by several interlocking developments: the prodigious amount of money that was raised from the public, in addition to amounts given by the Ecclesiastical Commissioners, by individual members of chapters and from capitular funds; the skill and knowledge of great architects such as Scott and Pearson; the influence of the Cambridge Movement and the work of the Ecclesiological Society; the general progress of religion during the century and the industry and care shown by so many deans and chapters on behalf of the buildings in their care.

The restoration and repair of the cathedral itself was a major aspect of English cathedral life in the nineteenth century. Several English cathedrals were changed very considerably in appearance (both internally and externally) between 1800 and 1900, and without the vast amount of work that was carried out on them many would have crumbled into ruins.

11

THE MISSION OF
THE CATHEDRAL

❧

A lthough the cathedral commissioners said that 'the functions of the cathedral body have now more of an administrative than a missionary character,'[1] cathedrals inevitably have a relationship to the world outside the close. In this chapter we shall examine the ways in which that relationship was developed during the nineteenth century.

As the building that houses his *cathedra*, a cathedral has a special link with the diocesan bishop. E. W. Benson emphasized the essential idea of a chapter as that of a council to the bishop.[2] In the Middle Ages the main ways in which a bishop and his cathedral came into contact were through episcopal services in the cathedral, the appointment of canons, and visitations. The dean and chapter might indeed act as the bishop's council, and had certain legal rights, such as the election of a new bishop and the giving of their consent for certain episcopal acts.[3]

It was customary for the bishop's consistory court to be housed within the cathedral. The court was also used by the dean and others possessing peculiar jurisdiction before the abolition of peculiars in 1857. The place of the court in each cathedral varied considerably. The court at St Paul's was in the south-west corner of the nave, while at Winchester it was in the minstrels' gallery over the western bay of the north nave aisle. In many cathedrals a small room adjoining the cathedral, a disused chapel, or a corner in the nave or transept, or the chapter-house, was used for this purpose.[4]

Although consistory courts must have been held fairly frequently in the early years of the century, they often became used as storage places after 1857. The court at Wells was used as a vestry in 1881,[5] while at Carlisle it was used to store the instruments of the garrison band, and even jam-jars.[6]

The nineteenth century saw a revival of the enthronement of a new bishop in person, instead of by proxy. When Bishop Folliott Cornewall's proxy was enthroned at Hereford in 1803 he was met at the west door where he took the customary oaths. Then, preceded by the rest of the foundation, he was led by the two senior canons to the throne while the Te Deum was sung. There followed some prayers and the proxy exchanged the kiss of peace with all the foundation.[7] A similar ceremony was held at Wells in 1802 when the proxy of Bishop Beadon was enthroned.[8] At the

245

enthronement of Beadon's successor, Bishop Law, the Bishop of Lichfield and Coventry took part as commissary of the Archdeacon of Canterbury.[9] The enthronement of Archbishop Manners Sutton at Canterbury in 1805 was entirely in the hands of proxies. As the archiepiscopal chair was at the extreme east end of the cathedral, the procession to it caused a riot in the quire and many of the congregation, having rushed up into the sanctuary to get a better view, remained there for the rest of the service.[10] When John Fisher, Bishop of Exeter, was translated to Salisbury in 1807, he was met at Bishop's Down, two miles outside the city, 'by several clergy, gentry and citizens who attended his coach to the city'. He was there welcomed by the mayor and aldermen and conducted to the council chamber where a scholar of the Free School congratulated him with a Latin oration. He then went to the Sun and Lamb, where he robed and exhibited to the dean and chapter the Letters Mandatory and Commissional of the Archbishop of Canterbury. The chapter, preceded by the choir singing hymns, then led him through the north gate of the close and he received a second oration. The procession continued to the west door where he took the usual oaths, after which he was led to the high altar for prayers and was then enthroned by the dean and senior residentiary. The Te Deum was sung (begun by the dean), and after more prayers the new bishop was conducted to the chapter-house.[11] Proxy enthronements continued at Winchester until (and including) 1820,[12] and at Worcester Bishop Carr was enthroned by proxy in 1824.[13] When Bishop Maltby of Chichester and Bishop Phillpotts of Exeter were enthroned in 1831, however, they were installed in person.[14].

The enthronement of Archbishop Sumner at Canterbury in 1848 was a notable event. There was a vast congregation to see the first archbishop to be enthroned in person for 133 years.[15] The nomination of Renn Dickson Hampden as Bishop of Hereford and his subsequent election by the chapter was the ground of fresh controversy. When he was eventually enthroned in April 1848, the ceremony was performed by the hebdomadary, Dean Merewether having declined to attend.[16] E. W. Benson was one of Christopher Wordsworth's chaplains at his enthronement at Lincoln in 1869, and he wrote a fascinating account of the occasion.[17] When Lord Arthur Charles Hervey was enthroned at Wells early in 1870, the mayor and city council took an active part in the arrangements, offering the use of the town hall, joining the procession, and attending the service in state. The service was attended by many local dignitaries.[18]

Archbishop Tait's enthronement at Canterbury in 1869 developed the sense of a great occasion that had been glimpsed at that of Archbishop Sumner twenty years earlier. Seven bishops and 300 clergy escorted him in procession in the presence of a huge congregation. The minister of the local Huguenot congregation was also present.[19] Tait himself attended the enthronement of the first Bishop of St Albans in 1877,[20] while when E. W.

Benson was enthroned as the first Bishop of Truro in the same year the service was performed by the Bishop of Exeter.[21] When Bishop Maclagan was enthroned at Lichfield in 1878, he knocked on the west door for admittance, beginning an erroneous practice that has since spread to many other cathedrals during the last hundred years, and was enthroned by the precentor.[22] Lightfoot's enthronement at Durham in 1879 was said to be the first in person for a century and a quarter, and was accompanied by 'grand and impressive ceremonial such as had not been seen in Durham since the Reformation'.[23] The first Bishop of Southwell was enthroned by the Archdeacon of Nottingham,[24] and Dean Church enthroned Bishop Frederick Temple at St Paul's in 1885.[25] Edward King wore a cope of cloth of gold for his enthronement at Lincoln in 1885,[26] and the service included a celebration of holy communion. The first Bishop of Wakefield was enthroned by the Archbishop of York in 1888.[27] The enthronements of Carpenter at Ripon in 1884, Jayne at Chester in 1889, Westcott at Durham in 1890, Mandell Creighton at Peterborough in 1891, and Perowne at Worcester in 1891 were in each case performed by the dean of the cathedral concerned.[28] The traditional responsibility of the archdeacons of Canterbury undertaking enthronements in person in the southern province was revived by Edward Parry, who was also Bishop of Dover. He enthroned Bishop Browne of Winchester in 1873.[29]

The two chief occasions when the bishop conducted services at his cathedral were confirmations and ordinations. Confirmations could often be unseemly. On one occasion at Chester, 966 males and 1,131 females were confirmed by the bishop. They afterwards pelted each other with sods of earth in the graveyard and with cushions and prayer books inside the cathedral. Clanking tins were attached to the cloaks of the candidates as they walked up to kneel before the bishop, and some clergy had to use their fists to keep order.[30] At both Winchester and Worcester, however, the devotional nature of the occasion was enhanced by singing the litany at the beginning of the service,[31] though confirmations seem to have been held at Worcester only once every three years.[32] Confirmations at York were said to have become more dignified and reverent in the time of Dean Duncombe.[33] In March 1879 at Winchester two confirmation services were held on the same day. At 11.30 a.m. thirty-seven males and sixty-seven females were confirmed, while in the afternoon there were thirty-three males and seventy-six females.[34]

In the early nineteenth century public ordinations were practically unknown, but gradually the custom was introduced. In the early years of the century at Hereford the candidates were required to attend the daily services in the cathedral from the beginning of their examination until the day of the ordination.[35] Bishop Blomfield held his ordinations in St Paul's instead of in Fulham Palace Chapel,[36] but Bishop Pepys of Worcester conducted his services in a very peculiar manner, the candidates kneeling in a row at the altar rail while 'an official stood behind holding up a large card upon which was written the words to be used by the bishop'.[37] The ordination at Canterbury in 1868 was the first there for fifty years.[38] Dean Goulburn was quite ecstatic in describing an ordination at Lincoln in 1882 to Dean Lake of Durham: 'Christopher (Wordsworth) in a gorgeous cope, laying his hands on those youths....John Wordsworth holding with motionless rigidity a pastoral staff, the crook turned outwards, blazing with jewels.'[39] Harvey Goodwin emphasized the great value of a cathedral as a setting for an ordination in order to make a lasting impression on the candidates.[40]

At the Christmas ordinations at Rochester in the mid-nineteenth century there were sometimes as many as fifty or sixty candidates. When John Gott was Dean of Worcester, the candidates were lodged around the close during the ordination retreat and the chapel in the deanery (now known as the Old Palace) was used for their services. At the actual ordination, however, they were still ordained in their academic gowns.[41]

The right of bishops to conduct a visitation of their cathedral chapters was established by a decretal of Pope Innocent IV at the Council of Lyons in 1248.[42] In the eighteenth century, however, episcopal visitations of English cathedrals became quite rare. Bishop Carr's visitation of Chichester in 1825 was the first there since 1755, though it was closely followed by those of Bishop Maltby in 1832, Bishop Gilbert in 1844 and again in 1853, and Bishop Durnford in 1875.[43] Bishop Law of Bath and Wells conducted a visitation of Wells Cathedral in 1825, though he later revoked his articles of enquiry and disclaimed his right of visitation.[44] Bishop Grey conducted a visitation of Hereford Cathedral in 1835.[45] Archbishop Vernon Harcourt held a visitation of York Minster in 1841, but he was largely unsuccessful in controlling the notorious Dean Cockburn.[46] Bishop Hamilton told the Cathedrals Commission in 1854 that regular visitations should be encouraged.[47] Bishop Moberly's visitation at Salisbury in 1870 was soon followed by Bishop Christopher Wordsworth's at Lincoln in 1873.[48] Bishop E. H. Browne conducted two visitations of Winchester Cathedral, in 1878 and in 1884.[49] When A. C. Tait held a visitation of Canterbury Cathedral in 1880, all the members of the cathedral foundation, from the bell-ringers to the dean, were cited to appear before him in the south transept of the cathedral. In his charge, Tait said that new statutes should be provided with power for them to be amended in the light of circumstances, and applauded the work that was being done at St Paul's.[50] Bishop John Wordsworth held a notable visitation of Salisbury Cathedral in 1888. His articles of inquiry were largely based on those used by his father at Lincoln fifteen years earlier. The proceedings concluded with a solemn procession to the chapter-house after matins. Here the bishop held a short service and gave his charge. After the junior members of the foundation had been dismissed, the bishop and the dean and chapter conferred about the next steps to be taken, and gave careful directions about various aspects of the cathedral's life.[51] John Gott's visitation of Truro in 1896 followed a similar pattern, the proceedings opening with a sung Eucharist. In the chapter room, each section of the foundation was given an opportunity to raise any grievances.[52] At Bishop Randall Davidson's visitation of Winchester Cathedral, questionnaires were sent only to the clergy, with a more detailed list of questions being sent to the dean.[53] Visitations of minor cathedral corporations occurred from time to time, as at Wells in 1872, 1875 and 1888.[54]

Sometimes the bishop as visitor was required to settle points of difference within the cathedral foundation. In 1849 Dean John Lamb attempted to abolish the intoning of the responses at Bristol, but Bishop Monk ordered that choral services must be maintained in the accustomed manner.[55] When a minor canon of Worcester by the name of Rayson was admonished for being absent without leave and appealed to the bishop as visitor, the bishop upheld the admonition.[56] At Winchester, however, the bishop quashed the attempted dismissal of a lay vicar in 1876.[57]

The election of a new diocesan bishop by the cathedral chapter was usually a formality. When a new Bishop of Hereford was elected in 1803, the general chapter was cited to attend by means of a notice placed on the door at the west end of the quire and on the door of the chapter-house and in each of their stalls. Afterwards, the election was announced and a Te Deum was sung. A similar ceremony took place at Salisbury four years later, the election being announced there by two canons.[58] In some new foundations cathedrals (such as Peterborough and Ely) the bishop was elected only by the dean and the canons residentiary.[59] The elections of both R. D. Hampden at Hereford in 1847 and Frederick Temple at Exeter in 1869 were controversial. Despite a chorus of protest from all over the country objecting to Hampden, who had been censured by the University of Oxford in 1836 and barred from preaching before the University, Lord John Russell would not withdraw his nomination. Dean Merewether objected to Hampden, but most of the canons disagreed with him. When the general chapter met after matins on 28 December 1847 to elect a new bishop, Merewether was outvoted and Hampden was duly elected, consecrated and enthroned.[60] Temple's nomination over twenty years later was equally greeted by a storm of protest, in which Pusey and Deans Mansel and Burgon took a leading part. His successful election was very much in doubt, but in the end, of the nineteen prebendaries who cast their votes in the chapter-house at Exeter, thirteen voted for Temple and six voted against him. Four others were absent.[61]

As well as these formal occasions and links, there were many other ways in which Victorian bishops and their cathedrals related to one another. Bishop W. K. Hamilton of Salisbury constantly attended early morning prayers in the cathedral on weekdays and made a point of celebrating Holy Communion there on Sundays.[62] Bishop Pelham of Norwich was very regular in his attendance at the daily services,[63] as was Edward King at Lincoln when W. J. Butler was dean.[64] Dean Alford of Canterbury urged the 'absorption' of deans 'into the episcopal office' in 1869,[65] and E. W. Benson put this into practice when he became Bishop of Truro. Indeed the bishops of Truro continued to be deans of their cathedral until the 1950s. Benson would generally be present at his little cathedral once each Sunday.[66] His successor, G. H. Wilkinson, also became dean[67] and frequently attended services in the cathedral.[68] The first bishops of Southwell also acted as deans of their cathedral.[69] R. D. Hampden told the cathedral commissioners in 1854 that

> the diocesan ought to have more power over the cathedral than he now possesses in superintending and regulating the services performed in it...he should frequently attend the daily services and take part in them and preach from the cathedral pulpit.[70]

But Bishop Maltby of Durham saw no point in bishops attending cathedrals more frequently.[71] Bishop Henry Phillpotts's situation at Exeter was unique, as, like his predecessors, he was also treasurer and a canon residentiary of his own cathedral. As such he had regular opportunities to preach.[72] The Bishop of Salisbury also held a prebendal stall and Bishop Denison occasionally attended chapter meetings.[73] Elsewhere, however, there were bishops who had little to do with their cathedrals. John Jebb, later a canon of Hereford, wrote in 1843 that 'the bishop is no longer seen'.[74] Bishop Kaye of Lincoln was rarely present in his cathedral in the 1830s.[75] Archbishop Howley was seldom seen after being attacked by a mob during the disturbances over the Reform Bill in 1832.[76] The Bishop of Rochester lived in Essex after 1845 and visited his cathedral rarely.[77] Bishop Hampden of Hereford, despite his evidence to the Cathedrals Commission, was 'more or less a recluse' and had little to do with the city.[78] The *Hampshire Examiner* complained in 1860 that Bishop Sumner (who lived in Farnham) rarely visited Winchester and Bishop Pepys of Worcester seldom came to his cathedral except for ordinations and visitations.[79] E. H. Browne, when he became Bishop of Ely, asked the head verger where his predecessor, Dr Turton, had sat and what part he had taken in the cathedral services:

> The verger proved quite unable to supply the required information and said, in self-excuse, 'Well, you see, my Lord, his late Lordship wasn't at all a church-going gentleman', which being interpreted meant that on account of age and infirmity Bishop Turton had long confined his ministrations to his private chapel.[80]

Bishop Browne found this precedent a distinct disadvantage and complained that Dean Harvey Goodwin was reluctant to allow him more than a minor role in cathedral services.[81] Bishop Ellicott claimed the right to supersede the canon-in-residence as the preacher on Sunday mornings at Bristol and tried to insist on entering the cathedral separately from the dean and chapter. The dean and chapter were happy to allow him to preach.[82] At Chichester Dean Pigou took the initiative in asking the bishop to preach on Easter Day and to celebrate each Sunday.[83] Dean Close, however, felt that closer contact between bishops and deans and chapters would help to overcome the separation between them.[84]

In many cases, of course, the links between a bishop and his chapter depended on their personal relations with each other. Bishop Prince Lee of Manchester was never on intimate terms with his chapter,[85] while Samuel Wilberforce's relationship with the chapter at Christ Church, Oxford, was far from cordial, mainly because they treated him with 'scant courtesy'.[86] At York, too, there were difficulties between Archbishop Thomson and Deans Duncombe and Purey-Cust,[87] the archbishop even taking Dean Purey-Cust to law over details in the services in the Minster. Thomson's relations with successive deans were embittered by his high-handed manner towards them.[88] At Norwich, on the other hand, Bishop Stanley was very musical and every year arranged Christmas concerts in the palace. These were conducted by Zechariah Buck, the cathedral organist, and the cathedral choir took part.[89] Bishop John Wordsworth of Salisbury cultivated his relationship with the cathedral and attended matins regularly, joining in the responses with a voice that echoed down the nave, although during long choral services he would often turn to one of the many books he kept in his throne.[90] E. W. Benson took a critical interest in the affairs of Canterbury Cathedral after he became archbishop,[91] and Mandell Creighton's relations with the cathedral at Peterborough were no doubt aided by his experience as a canon of Worcester.[92]

When Dean Randall arrived at Chichester, Bishop Durnford told him that he had been on friendly terms with his two predecessors.[93] When E. R. Wilberforce became bishop, however, although he was kind and friendly, there were differences of opinion, chiefly over ceremonial, and it vexed Randall that Bishop Wilberforce should go out during the middle of choral celebrations, and that he did not attend weekday services or the special services in Advent and Lent.[94] One of the questions that the archbishops asked cathedral chapters in 1872 concerned the relationship of the bishop to the chapter. The dean and chapter of Salisbury referred to Bishop Denison's letter to the cathedral commissioners nineteen years previously and agreed that the bishop should have the right to preach and give directions about the cathedral just as in any other church in the diocese.[95] At St Paul's, Dean Gregory was on good terms with both Bishop Jackson and Bishop Temple, though on one occasion Temple arrived at the cathedral two minutes late and found the service had already started. Afterwards Gregory told him, 'When the clock strikes, we begin.' He was never late again.[96] When Temple became Archbishop of Canterbury in 1897, a special service was held in Exeter Cathedral attended by a large congregation.[97]

The traditional function of a cathedral chapter acting as the bishop's council was also continued occasionally in the nineteenth century. In 1844 the general chapter of Exeter Cathedral met to advise Bishop Phillpotts on the wearing of surplices.[98] In 1869 Bishop Selwyn of Lichfield summoned a meeting of the general chapter of his cathedral to consider the reports of the 1852–5 Cathedrals Commission and their local implications. Selwyn himself had unique powers to amend the statutes of his cathedral and a new code was ratified in 1875.[99] In 1872 Dean Goulburn replied to the Lambeth queries that Bishop Pelham of Norwich invited the whole cathedral body (honorary canons as well as residentiaries) to his palace annually 'for the purpose of discussing prominent church questions of the day'.[100] In 1878 Bishop Atlay of Hereford attended a meeting of his cathedral chapter which advised him to hold a diocesan conference.[101] E. W. Benson stressed the responsibility of the honorary canons at Truro to act as his council and consulted them over several diocesan matters.[102] After the Lambeth Conference of 1888, Bishop John Wordsworth, one of the pioneers of synodical government, also sought his chapter's advice about holding a synod of all diocesan clergy.[103] In 1892, Bishop Thorold of Winchester met his greater chapter and, after a celebration of holy communion, took counsel with them on the affairs of the diocese.[104]

The extent of the change in the relationship between bishops and their cathedrals during the nineteenth century is exemplified in little, but nevertheless significant, ways. When Sir Frederick Bridge was a chorister at Rochester Cathedral in the 1840s, the bishop, George Murray, still wore an episcopal wig.[105] In 1816 Bowyer Edward Sparke, Bishop of Ely and a noted pluralist and nepotist, attended a service of thanksgiving in his cathedral for the restoration of peace after a riot. He was preceded by his butler bearing his sword of state (he exercised civil jurisdiction over the Isle of Ely) and was attended by fifty of the leading citizens bearing white wands.[106] Seventy years later the model of a prince-bishop had given way to a more pastoral approach. In 1886 the dean and chapter of Chichester agreed to a request from the bishop that one of the sextons should carry his pastoral staff before him.[107]

As the bishop's church, a cathedral inevitably has a special relationship to the diocese. The importance of this was grasped only in the second half of the nineteenth century, when it was appreciated that some improvements in relations between dioceses and cathedrals were necessary. In 1871, during a debate in the House of Lords, Bishop Ellicott of Gloucester and Bristol said that 'cathedrals did not stand in sufficiently close relationship to the dioceses'. He wanted canons of cathedrals to be responsible for church building and diocesan societies, clerical charities, education and missionary agencies. Bishop Browne of Ely called for cathedrals to be 'much more intimately connected with the diocesan work than they had been'.[108] A leading article on cathedrals in the *Guardian* regretted the common division between cathedral and diocesan clergy.[109] Harvey Goodwin said in 1881 that cathedral clergy often seemed wrapped in 'a mysterious dignity' that kept them aloof from the diocese.[110] But how far were these criticisms true? Is it possible to detect any improvements during the last quarter of the nineteenth century?

One of the questions addressed by the Lambeth committee of deans and canons in 1872 asked each chapter about the relations between their cathedral and the diocese. Dean Goulburn told the committee that his chapter at Norwich was not indolent in this matter. Canon Robinson made it a point of his conscience to preach in a parochial pulpit every Sunday when he was in residence, and Canon Nisbet also did so frequently. Canon Heaviside and the dean preached in parishes when asked – 'and that we find to be very often' – and one of the canons was greatly occupied in attending all kinds of charitable board meetings.[111] At Salisbury one of the canons was an archdeacon, and another was secretary to the training school and examining chaplain to the bishop. The dean and canons were all on the board of education and attended its meetings, as well as those of many other diocesan institutions.[112] Two of the canons at Exeter were archdeacons, and three others had various diocesan duties, including ex-officio membership of the board of education and of the committee of the diocesan training college.[113]

Yet there were still grumbles. A. R. Grant, an honorary canon of Ely, admitted that 'cathedrals...are centres of spiritual life to the population about them', but concluded that 'they have no direct action on the diocese'.[114] A leading article also in the *Guardian* later in 1879 agreed that little progress had been made in reviving the diocesan functions of cathedrals.[115] It was no wonder that a canon of Lincoln told the editor that

the parochial clergy now, for the most part, regard the cathedral as an alien and separate institution, with which they have nothing to do, and which in their view often performs its work in an unsatisfactory manner; with services inferior to those in some parish churches, with indifferent sermons, and by no means perfect choirs.[116]

As a result of the establishment of the second Cathedrals Commission in 1879, several diocesan conferences appointed committees to consider the relation of the cathedral to the diocese and to offer such practical suggestions as might seem desirable.[117] The Dean of Exeter boldly said that there were *no* relations between the diocese and his cathedral and that it was a mistake to say that the cathedral was the life and centre of the diocese.[118] At Ely the daily services were claimed by the dean and chapter to be 'diocesan work of the highest and holiest character'.[119]

One notable way in which cathedral and diocese came together in the middle years of the century was through great choral festivals in which vast numbers from parochial choirs would flock to the cathedral and join together in a grand service. The *Ecclesiologist* said in 1857 that there was no better way of 'bringing home to the scattered portions of a necessarily large diocese the value – it might almost be said the existence – of its cathedral'.[120] Such occasions, however, did have various disadvantages. It was difficult to keep such a large body of singers together, and the practical arrangements were capable of improvement:

> Nothing could be more inconvenient than the want of arrangements for the surplices. Men and boys carrying their own in the town, boxes in one corner of the cathedral, bags in another, left to take care of themselves; between the services, surplices stuffed under or over the seats previously used.[121]

The first such festival seems to have been held at Lichfield in 1856, closely followed by others at Ely and Southwell (1858), Canterbury (1862 and 1864) and Salisbury (1863).[122] By 1869 the list included also York, Durham, Hereford, Llandaff, Norwich, Oxford, St Paul's, Peterborough and Rochester.[123] At Southwell in 1858 a surpliced choir of 200 was marshalled in the chapter-house and then went in procession to the west door to meet the bishop, preceding him up the nave for a service of matins, litany and holy communion.[124] The Canterbury festival in 1862 was spoilt by beginning half an hour late 'through the unpunctuality of the trains on the south-eastern line', and because most of the singers left after the Prayer for the Church Militant. Enough remained, however, to sing the Sanctus and Gloria in excelsis 'in a respectable style' and there were 300 communicants.[125] There were 1,400 singers at Salisbury in 1863.[126] Parish choirs in the neighbourhood of Chichester held a festival there in 1863. Some 300 singers rehearsed in the cathedral in the morning, and then marched, each choir behind its banner, to Priory Park where they had a cold lunch in a tent at 1s 9d a head. They then returned to the cathedral in surplices for the afternoon service, at which the congregation numbered 1,000.[127] In 1866 at Winchester no less than 956 singers from the United Choirs of the North and South Hampshire Association for the Improvement of Parish Psalmody came to two big services in the cathedral. There were 480 trebles, 110 altos, 144 tenors and 195 basses. Some 2,500 tickets were issued and 4,000 persons were estimated to be in the cathedral.[128] The mayor and city corporation attended the diocesan choral festival at Wells in 1883. The diocesan choirs robed in the cloisters, but were not allowed to use banners or processional crosses, though brass instruments were used in the band.[129]

In a less spectacular way the links between cathedral and diocese were strengthened through the appointment, under the terms of the 1840

Cathedrals Act, of honorary canons and prebendaries. Before 1840 a cathedral stall was nearly always held in plurality with several other positions, and generally regarded as merely a useful source of additional income. Gradually, however, as the new honorary incumbents of the stalls were appointed, the picture changed. At York in 1840 the thirty prebendaries held between them four other deaneries, three other canonries, two other prebendal stalls, one sinecure, eighteen parishes in Yorkshire and twelve parishes as far apart as Cumberland and the Isle of Wight. In 1857, of the twenty-three new prebendaries appointed since 1840, twenty-two were incumbents in Yorkshire.[130] Many of the rural deans of the diocese of Salisbury became non-residentiary canons of the cathedral.[131] The new and different composition of chapters through the introduction of a substantial diocesan element also led to a revival of meetings of the general or greater chapter.[132] Harvey Goodwin said in 1881 that he wanted his greater chapter at Carlisle to be 'a living thing, capable of action within defined limits'.[133] In 1885 Bishop Bickersteth of Exeter suggested to the dean and chapter that greater use should be made of the prebendaries. His suggestions included lectures to recently ordained clergy, special courses of sermons, monthly services for children (all of these could be either in the cathedral or in a church in the city) and missions, retreats and quiet days in various parts of the diocese. The dean and chapter, however, did not want the general chapter to be involved.[134] Non-residentiary prebendaries were also entitled to preaching turns in the cathedral, but these were often a source of great inconvenience and were frequently declined.[135]

The extensive restoration of cathedrals in the middle and late nineteenth century also enabled cathedral and diocese to come together in new ways. The joint restoration committee at Worcester in the 1860s included, alongside the dean and chapter, five local peers, Sir Edmund Lechmere and the Mayor of Worcester.[136] In 1885 a committee was formed at Winchester to include the bishop, the dean and chapter, one honorary canon and four laymen of the diocese; the purpose of this committee was to give advice to the chapter on all improvements, restoration and ornamentation in the cathedral.[137] The non-residentiary canons of Chichester agreed to spread public interest in the restoration of their cathedral in 1893, and in the following year a restoration committee, comprising the whole of the general chapter and some forty laymen, was established.[138]

Cathedrals were also used for diocesan synods and conferences, as at Worcester in 1892.[139] At Ely in 1866 Dean Harvey Goodwin curtained off a transept for a meeting of the diocesan conference.[140] A 'diocesan chapter' was held at Winchester in 1887, attended by the dean and chapter, the Archdeacon of the Isle of Wight, many honorary canons, all the minor canons and several rural deans.[141] In 1888 the Dean of Wells agreed to send regular news items about the cathedral for inclusion in the diocesan magazine.[142] Earlier in the century, the diocesan board of education used to meet in the chapter-house at Exeter Cathedral and the bishop also used it for legal proceedings and other formal occasions.[143]

Opinions varied as to the merit of combining cathedral and parochial work. When Robert Gregory went to St Paul's, two of the other canons held livings, but he refused to be Vicar of St Pancras and soon relinquished his vicarage in Lambeth, preferring to concentrate his energies on cathedral work.[144] When J. B. Dykes arrived at Durham, however, he immediately asked the Vicar of St Oswald's whether he could help him in the visiting of his parish.[145] Some parochial clergy badly needed help from cathedrals. In the early years of the century, the dean and chapter of Christ Church, Oxford, gave about £1,000 per annum to augment parochial stipends and towards the building of parsonages.[146] In 1854 the cathedral commissioners stated that the dean and chapter of Durham had made annual grants of £4,603 in augmenting parochial livings. From 1843 to 1854 they had spent some £36,000 in making parochial grants. The chapters at Exeter and Winchester pursued a similar policy, and there was an implied criticism of those at York and Carlisle who had already handed over their estates to the Ecclesiastical Commissioners, and so could not assist any poor incumbents.[147] But Benjamin Harrison told the cathedral commissioners in 1880 that the alienation of capitular revenues at Canterbury had left the cathedral 'powerless to help' poor parishes in the city.[148] An imaginative but unappreciated plan was introduced at Wells in 1879. Two furnished rooms near the cathedral were made available by the dean and chapter at a cost not exceeding £30 per annum for any diocesan clergy.[149] In 1888 a quiet day was held at Wells for readers and other laity in the diocese.[150]

For much of the nineteenth century capitular patronage was exercised more to the advantage of the individual members of the dean and chapter and their friends and relations than for the sake of the parish. Before the dean and chapter of Gloucester made any presentation to livings in their patronage, they sent their surveyor to inspect them.[151] Chapter livings at both Worcester and Chichester were offered to members in order of their seniority, either for their personal use or for the nomination of a suitable candidate.[152] A carefully drafted chapter act to the same effect was adopted at Wells in 1817.[153] When Dean Lamb of Bristol attempted to present himself to a living in the gift of the dean and chapter, three canons objected but eventually gave way.[154] The 1840 Cathedrals Act restricted capitular patronage to members of the cathedral foundation or clergy of the diocese.[155] It was alleged in 1848 that of the twenty-seven livings in the patronage of the dean and chapter of Lincoln, six were held by members of the chapter or their relatives, and four by minor canons. Chapter livings were notorious for their 'most forlorn wretched condition, with a starving parson, a falling Church and, for want of schools, a people degraded both morally and intellectually'.[156]

As late as 1881 Canon Gregory and Bishop Claughton wished to appoint relatives to livings in the gift of the dean and chapter of St Paul's, but Dean Church and Canon Liddon very properly expressed their disapproval. Ten years earlier Liddon had proposed that incumbents presented to livings in the patronage of the chapter must promise to reside within two miles of the parish church.[157] In 1888 the twelve livings in Cornwall in the patronage of the dean and chapter of Exeter were transferred to the chapter of Truro.[158] A speedier manner of choosing new incumbents was adopted at Exeter in 1895.[159] Some chapters exercised a peculiar jurisdiction over certain parishes in the early years of the century. This was certainly true at Salisbury, where the dean and chapter's peculiar consisted of six parishes, and at Wells and Lincoln.[160] At Salisbury the precentor and treasurer had their own peculiars, as they did at Wells, where the subdean also exercised peculiar jurisdiction in certain parishes. Even the prebendaries at Lincoln and Wells possessed certain rights within their jurisdictions. There were two parishes in the diocese of Hereford which formed the chancellor's peculiar.[161] In 1876 the dean and chapter of Chichester gave £24 to the churchwardens of the parish of St Peter the Great to help with service expenses, though they declined to respond to an appeal for the completion of the church.[162] In 1887 the dean and chapter of Winchester were seriously concerned that something should be done to relieve 'the suffering of the poorer clergy in their present distress'.[163]

On the other hand, there were some dioceses where the dignitaries of the cathedral showed little interest in diocesan affairs. H. W. Beadon wrote in 1880 that in over forty years he had not known a dean, of either Gloucester or Bristol, take any part in the management of any diocesan institutions or attend any meeting. The same could be said for all but two of the residentiary canons.[164] Sometimes dioceses took little interest in their cathedrals. Dean Pigou of Chichester complained that a dean could often be ostracized by the diocese and his pastoral experience neglected.[165] Where members of chapters did involve themselves in diocesan work, however, this was usually appreciated. During the time B. F. Westcott was a canon of Peterborough, he was anxious to play his part in quickening the intellectual and spiritual life of the diocese by holding devotional gatherings for clergy and churchwardens in the cathedral.[166] Dean Lefroy of Norwich established an 'Eggs and Bacon Society' and invited the junior clergy of the city and diocese to a monthly breakfast, followed by prayers and study of the Greek New Testament. He also planned to institute a 'Beefsteak Club' for older clergy, to include a midday meal after a morning's theological discussion.[167] Dean Gott of Worcester was a frequent visitor to country parishes and spiritual adviser to many clergy.[168] Edward King, in welcoming Dean Wickham to Lincoln, mentioned that Dean Butler had greatly improved the links 'between the cathedral and the city and diocese'.[169]

One of the ways in which cathedral and diocesan work could be linked was through the appointments of canons who were also archdeacons. E. B. Pusey pointed out in 1833 that two-fifths of the whole number of archdeacons held cathedral stalls.[170] The cathedral commissioners claimed in 1854 that many archdeacons were also canons, but M. E. C. Walcott estimated in 1865 that there were only eighteen archdeacons who also held canonries.[171] In 1832 Archdeacon King had to obtain a writ of *mandamus* to establish his claims to a prebend at Canterbury.[172] In 1840, under the terms of the Cathedrals Act, a fourth canonry was established at Lincoln to be held by an archdeacon.[173] But some archdeacons were little use to cathedrals and were to be seen there only during their months of residence, spending the rest of their time (like some canons) in their livings.[174] Archdeacon Hale, however, was full of zeal at St Paul's in the 1840s,[175] and the cathedrals of Chichester and Gloucester were used for archdeacon's visitations in 1864 and 1874 respectively.[176] Another archdeacon who was intensely interested in his cathedral was Arthur Bayly Crosse, who was a canon of Norwich between 1892 and 1909.[177]

Some bishops actively promoted the involvement of their cathedrals in the life of the diocese. E. W. Benson was anxious to associate mission work in the diocese of Truro 'definitely and closely with the Cathedral as the centre of the life and work of the diocese'.[178] Benson said that every diocese ought to have a large staff of missioners.[179] He quoted enthusiastically a suggestion that A. J. Mason had made at the first diocesan conference at Truro in 1877 when he had advocated that in addition there should be a band of missioners based on the cathedral. They should be organized by one of the canons, who would be known as the canon missioner.[180] Benson had been the first warden of a society of mission priests at Lincoln and had conducted a notable mission in the city of Lincoln, based on the church of St Peter-at-Arches, in 1876, preaching every night to a crowded congregation.[181] Towards the end of the century Canon Donaldson was able to report to the Church Congress at Norwich in 1895 that during the preceding year Truro Cathedral had helped various parishes in Cornwall on 130 occasions and that there was a diocesan society called the Cathedral Union which raised nearly £600 per annum for the cathedral, with secretaries in each deanery raising the subscriptions. Each parish had a 'Cathedral Sunday' and the offertories were devoted to the cathedral.[182]

When Dean Bramston was installed as Dean of Winchester, Bishop Samuel Wilberforce urged the vice-dean to invite as many of the diocesan clergy as possible to the service, and added, 'I think it a matter of such moment to knit together the Chapter and the Diocese. And what knitting together so strong as prayer?[183] Bishop John Wordsworth concluded his visitation of Salisbury Cathedral in 1888 by saying he expected the members of the chapter to concentrate on diocesan work 'and not to look on the title of Canon as a mere ornament'.[184] He advocated visits to the cathedral by parishes and more frequent invitations to city clergy to preach in the cathedral.[185] Canon Butler's preaching at Worcester was much in demand in the diocese in the 1880s: 'He preached right and left in the diocese with all the vigour and strength of a man carrying but half his years.'[186]

In 1900 Bishop Randall Davidson conducted a notable visitation of Winchester Cathedral. In particular he asked how links between the cathedral and diocese could be developed, and whether the dean and chapter or the greater chapter could usefully act as the bishop's council. The dean replied that the cathedral staff could be asked to undertake diocesan responsibilities and that he was always ready to hold special services in the cathedral for diocesan bodies, but warned of the difficulties involved in running the cathedral if too many members of staff were involved in diocesan work, and reminded the bishop that 'practical connexion with diocesan work' was not the principal function of cathedrals. Canon Erskine Clarke urged that the dean and residentiary canons should each go out to parishes on at least two Sundays a year. This would strengthen links between the cathedral and the diocese. Canon J. M. Lee pointed out that all the canons had diocesan responsibilities already and Canon Stenning said that Winchester Cathedral, which used to appear aloof from the diocese and to have little activity or interest outside its own walls, had gradually and increasingly come to play a large part in diocesan life.[187]

As well as having a relationship with the bishop and the diocese, every cathedral also had links with the city that surrounded it. But the influence that the dean and chapter might have in the city naturally varied. In 1841 the *British Critic* said that they had little influence.[188]

At Exeter, however, in the early nineteenth century, it seems that there was a great deal of goodwill between the ecclesiastical and civic authorities in the city.[189] One of the side-effects of Archbishop Vernon Harcourt's visitation of York Minster in 1841, and the uproar surrounding the charges against Dean Cockburn, was a wave of sympathy for the dean. A penny subscription for him was started in the city, and he was eventually presented with a handsome silver sugar bowl, engraved with a view of the Minster.[190] During his time as canon precentor of Salisbury, W. K. Hamilton became well known and liked, which stood him in good stead when he became bishop:

> He felt, so to speak, that he had his hand upon the pulse of his cathedral city; and this confidence was the result of his constant and intimate habits of intercourse with its inhabitants during his precentorship.[191]

Later in the century this aspect of a cathedral's life and work received particular emphasis. Something of this development can be seen if we look at four particular cathedrals – Canterbury, Worcester, Lincoln and Norwich – and mark the relationship between the deans and chapters and their cities. When Dean Alford instituted a sermon at Canterbury Cathedral on Sunday afternoons, 'the public responded with great congregations, and thus began that improved relationship between cathedral and city which since those days has, we believe, become cordial'.[192] The biography of Dean Alford stresses his great desire to break down the barriers between cathedral and city, 'and to promote the kindly intercourse of different classes of society'.[193] This policy was continued by Dean Farrar, who 'constantly strove to make others realise...the Cathedral as the living centre of social and spiritual life in the city'.[194] All this was a far cry from the time when Archbishop Howley arrived at Canterbury to make his primary visitation in 1832 and was greeted with gross insults and a call from the crowd that the cathedral should be converted into stables for cavalry horses.[195]

Lord Alwyne Compton was a popular Dean of Worcester. He and his wife were lavish in their entertainment, especially of the mayor and other city officials. When he was appointed Bishop of Ely, Compton received a presentation from the citizens and the mayor attended his enthronement.[196] This happy relationship continued during the time that Mandell Creighton was a canon of Worcester. The cathedral and the city were on the best of terms and the help of the chapter was often sought and freely given in many educational and philanthropic matters. The cathedral was regarded as a real centre of religious life in the city.[197]

When W. J. Butler, who had been a canon of Worcester, became Dean of Lincoln in 1885, the dean and mayor of Worcester jointly organized an appeal to commemorate his work in the city.[198] At Lincoln he was on good terms with the leading citizens and took an energetic role in the life of the city, with a particular interest in its educational institutions. A crowded congregation of all classes attended his funeral, witnessing to the success of his desire to break down barriers and bring people together more closely.[199] Edward King, writing to Gladstone in 1894, referred to the 'very friendly and valuable relation established between the Cathedral and the city'.[200]

Before Dean Lefroy's time, Norwich Cathedral was monopolized by wealth and social rank. Lefroy was a self-taught Dubliner, a former reporter on the *Irish Times* who had gained his preferment through much hard work in the diocese of Liverpool. At Norwich he organized mission services on Sunday, Wednesday and Friday evenings which attracted crowded congregations, including large numbers of dissenters. When he saw that the congregations at these services tended to be church people, he sent them into action as missionaries to the poor and the unchurched who frequented 'the alleys, the slums and the doors of public houses'. He abolished appropriated pews overnight and defeated the idea that the cathedral was only interested in the privileged classes. He was a familiar figure at every public occasion in the city.[201] He became chairman of the Norwich and Ely Training College, and instituted Bible classes for women on Wednesday afternoons and for men on Wednesday evenings.[202]

The links between cathedral and city were manifested in various ways. The most obvious of these was the relationship between a dean and chapter and the city council, but the involvement of various chapters in local education, health and welfare work also reveals their concern for the life of the cathedral city. In the early years of the century the dean and chapter of York were in dispute with the civic authorities over the lack of etiquette observed at the proclamation of peace in 1802 and a few years later they criticized the corporation's care of the city walls and gates and their proposals for rebuilding the Ouse Bridge.[203] George William Chard, the organist of Winchester Cathedral, was very involved in municipal affairs. In addition to being a freeman of the city and a justice of the peace, he was elected Mayor of Winchester in 1832.[204] Until 1835 the mayor and corporation of Norwich went in a carriage procession to the cathedral annually, preceded by swordsmen, musicians, standard-bearers and others. Sweet-scented rushes were strewn in the nave and the dean and chapter received them at the quire-screen.[205] The dean and chapter of Wells allowed the mayor and corporation to sit in the prebendal stalls on the north side of the quire between the pulpit and the subdean's stall.[206] Special stalls were designated for the use of the mayor, magistrates and corporation at Exeter in 1878 when they attended the cathedral in state.[207] In 1892 a special service was held at Worcester Cathedral for civic authorities throughout the diocese.[208] Cathedrals were often regarded with great affection by civic authorities, and the great programmes of restoration that took place in many cathedrals during the nineteenth century often enlisted their support and the enthusiasm of local citizens. After the 1829 fire at York Minster, the Lord Mayor presided at a large meeting in the Guildhall and started a public subscription towards the rebuilding with a personal donation of £50.[209] The chapter-house and library of Bristol Cathedral, however, were severely damaged when a mob that sacked the bishop's palace also broke into the cathedral.[210] In 1840 a second fire damaged York Minster, and the Lord Mayor and magistrates opened an inquiry the same afternoon. This time public criticism of the dean and chapter made the question of a subscription for the repairs more difficult.[211] When the dean and chapter of Hereford carried out improvements in the close in 1851, they received a resolution and vote of thanks from the Commissioners of Paving and Lighting in the city.[212] The plans to build a new nave at Bristol Cathedral were encouraged by a committee that included the mayor, the high sheriff and the Master of the Society of Merchant Venturers.[213] Although in 1868 the dean and chapter of Exeter had refused a request from the mayor, aldermen and overseers to make the north and south sides of the cathedral more visible to the public, in 1872 they invited the mayor, magistrates, town council, executive committee and their friends to view the restored cathedral. The town council passed a resolution expressing 'their high admiration of the energetic action of the Dean and Chapter', to which the chapter replied, thanking the mayor and council for their interest in the work of restoration.[214] Negotiations between the dean and chapter of St Paul's and the commissioners of sewers of the City of London, which lasted for forty years from 1834 onwards, eventually led to a great improvement to the western approach to the cathedral at the top of Ludgate Hill.[215] In the same year that this improvement at St Paul's was completed, the restoration work at Worcester Cathedral came to an end after nearly twenty-five years. The dean and chapter sent their effusive thanks to the mayor for his 'warm personal interest' in the festival that marked the reopening.[216] A similar cordiality prevailed at Bristol when the nave there was completed five years later.[217] A civic banquet and mayoral reception followed the consecration of Truro Cathedral in 1887.[218]

There were times, however, when a local council tried to interfere in the way in which the dean and chapter ran the cathedral.[219] At Worcester in 1874 the mayor, on behalf of the council, asked the dean and chapter to alter their arrangements for charging fees for entry to the eastern part of the cathedral and to introduce additional services, but the dean and chapter declined his request.[220] The dean and chapter of Chichester were attacked by the *Chichester Observer* in 1897 for reducing the amount of choral music, and this view was urged on the chapter by a petition signed by 400 citizens and a protest by the city council.[221]

The development of education during the nineteenth century afforded opportunities for members of cathedral chapters to take local initiatives in this field. In 1811 the dean and chapter of Salisbury gave £50 to the National Society for the Education of the Poor.[222] The dean and chapter of Lincoln elected two governors to the board of Lincoln Grammar School, [223] while at Carlisle Dean Close organized a Bible class for men at the deanery, a night school for adults, and occasional scientific lectures for the benefit of the general public.[224] At Worcester Dean Compton and Canon Butler took a leading part in the foundation of the Alice Ottley School,[225] and Dean Wickham was well known for continuing Butler's involvement with education at Lincoln.[226]

Many cathedral chapters also took an active interest in the public health of the cathedral city. The dean and chapter of Bristol gave £100 to the Bristol Infirmary in 1805,[227] while Deans Peacock and Goodwin were successively chairmen of the Ely board of health.[228] In 1866 a special service for Chichester Infirmary was held in the cathedral.[229] There were close links between the staff of Winchester Cathedral and the Royal Hampshire County Hospital. Both Dean Garnier and Dean Bramston took an active interest in it, several canons served as governors, and the chaplain was often one of the minor canons of the cathedral.[230] At Norwich, Canon Sedgwick combined his annual residence with two months' chaplaincy at the County Hospital. This involved prayers twice a week and prayers and a sermon on Sundays.[231] One of the minor canons at Chester was chaplain to the infirmary there.[232] Such corporate activity was also sometimes accompanied by individual acts of pastoral concern. In 1856 the Dean's wife and daughters were diligent in visiting the sick in infected parts of the city of Lincoln,[233] while Canon Burrows of Rochester used to pay weekly visits to the Infectious Hospital there.[234] The welfare of the poorer classes in cathedral cities also occupied the attention of many chapters. In 1800 the dean and chapter of Exeter gave £100 towards a plan for supplying herrings to the poor.[235] In 1801 the dean and chapter of Bristol gave 20 guineas towards the establishment of a soup kitchen in the city.[236] The golden jubilee of the coronation of George III was celebrated in Durham by a collection for poor families and the chapter gave a large sum to enable many of those imprisoned for small debts to be set free.[237] Fifty persons received the Winchester Dona in November 1800 and an additional donation was given to the county prison.[238] In 1820 and 1830 blankets and sheets were distributed to all who received the coal charity.[239] The manner in which the coal charity was organized was altered in 1873.[240] Prebendary Iremonger of Winchester was well known for his zeal for the relief of poverty and his early death in 1820 was greatly lamented.[241] Eighteen poor people were given a 2d loaf each week at Exeter, and this became a 5d loaf in 1828.[242] The distribution of pence at the cathedral doors on Maundy Thursday was discontinued in 1864,[243] but £40 was distributed as usual to the poor at Christmas in 1879 and over £33 in 1895.[244] Loaves were also distributed to the poor on Saturdays at Chichester. Recipients were required to produce certificates from their parish priests that they were members of the Church of England. Fifty poor people received bread in this way in 1850, but in 1872 no new recipients were admitted and donations were given instead to the Chichester Nurses' Association.[245] The dean and chapter of Bristol gave donations of £5 to the poor of various different parishes in turn.[246] The dean and chapter of Gloucester made several regular charitable donations, as well as some special ones.[247] At Exeter the dean and chapter gave £110 towards the cost of a public cemetery in 1835 and themselves served as improvement commissioners at the beginning of Queen Victoria's reign.[248] Following a heavy snowfall and a severe frost in January 1841, Dean Merewether attended a public meeting in Hereford at which the mayor presided. This meeting established 'a subscription for the relief of the poor in this inclement season'. The dean and chapter of Hereford gave £10 to the fund.[249] In 1848 the usual audit dinner at Wells was not held and £5 was spent on meat 'for such poor persons as were formerly in the habit of receiving the broken victuals after the dinner'. Six years later the dean and chapter of Wells gave £5 each to the poor of Wells, £5 to the poor of Bicknoller, and £7 to the poor of Winscombe to buy bread and coal.[250] At Salisbury W. K. Hamilton invited six or eight poor people to dinner on Sundays and heroically visited cholera victims in 1849.[251] Dean Bowers of Manchester gave a dinner to poor people on Christmas Day and his successors continued this tradition.[252] The dean and chapter of Manchester also maintained a 'Cathedral Country Home' in Derbyshire for women and children from the slums.[253] In 1874 the dean and chapter of Exeter gave a donation to enable the children from the workhouse to have an outing to the seaside.[254] At Worcester, Mandell Creighton was anxious to have a form of relief available in the 1880s, since beggars abounded in the city.[255]

Another way in which the presence of a cathedral affected the life of the city was in the provision of culture. In May 1838 the custos and vicars choral of Exeter announced their intention of rebuilding College Hall so that it could be used both as a clerical reading room and also as a general meeting-place.[256] Some cathedral libraries were open to subscribers,[257] and in 1882 Canon W. H. Lyttelton founded the Gloucester Cathedral Society 'with a view to promoting an intelligent interest in Gloucester Cathedral amongst all classes'. The society arranged a number of meetings in the chapter-house.[258] The inhabitants of cathedral cities also had many musical opportunities, often actively promoted by the cathedrals. Chief among these, of course, was the Three Choirs Festival, which was held annually in turn at Gloucester, Worcester and Hereford. The main burden of arranging and conducting this festival was undertaken by the cathedral organist.[259] F. E. Witts, a Gloucestershire clergyman, has left a vivid description of the scene at the 1823 Gloucester Festival:

> We obtained very good seats in the choir and the whole of the Cathedral was extremely crowded. The orchestra is erected in front of the organ, facing the altar; the area between the pulpit and the altar filled with benches; the space occupied by the altar is covered by raised sittings, one behind another in ranges, up to the top of the screen....On each side of the inner choir, the large arches above the stalls, opening into the transepts, were filled with temporary galleries, that on the right being appropriated to the friends of the lay stewards, that on the left to those of the clerical stewards. These galleries being almost wholly filled with ladies in elegant morning dresses present a most beautiful parterre to the eye....The Dettingen *Te Deum*, the Overture to *Esther*, Dr Boyce's Anthem (charity) and Knyvett's new Coronation anthem were the musical treats for the morning.[260]

In 1826 he again attended the Festival. He passed through the crowded, lively city and noted the 'large posse of constables' at the cathedral door, struggling to keep order:

By 11 o'clock the inner choir of the cathedral was fearfully crowded...an occasional scream or groan indicated distress or fainting; some were carried out, some struggled into the outer choir, the most persevering stood their ground...[261]

At Chester in 1842, however, the music festival had to be cancelled owing to the opposition of the bishop, and the dean and chapter, much to the chagrin of the citizens.[262] W. H. Longhurst, the organist of Canterbury Cathedral, was also conductor of the Canterbury Philharmonic Society, but its concerts did not take place in the cathedral.[263] At Gloucester, in about the year 1886, there were twelve free performances of sacred music in the cathedral during the winter which attracted large and varied congregations:

The thinly-clad women with children in their arms, the well-dressed county ladies, the town clergyman, the cab driver and the mechanic, and children with bare feet have been seen listening with eager attention to the solemn strains of Handel, Beethoven, Mozart and Mendelssohn.[264]

Dean Montagu Butler was especially anxious that the poor and needy should attend. In this he was loyally supported by C. Lee Williams, the conductor organist who 'visited the slums of the city, armed with bills and programmes'.[265] Butler's policy was remarkably successful, with 4,000 people attending the last concert during his term of office.[266] The *Musical Times* was glad to see that chapters were becoming more 'alive to the need that exists for strengthening the hold of the Church on the masses of the people'.[267] J. L. Naylor's cantatas were often performed in York Minster by the York Musical Society, of which he was the conductor. His successor, T. T. Noble, founded the York Symphony Orchestra.[268] In 1893 a great musical festival was held at Winchester Cathedral to commemorate the 800th anniversary of the Norman Cathedral. Dean Kitchin engaged the Stock Exchange orchestra, which was conducted by his nephew. Singers from choral societies in Portsmouth and Southampton, as well as Winchester, took part, and the precentor acted as secretary and conducted the psalms. Dr Arnold, the cathedral organist, refused to have anything to do with this festival which ended with a considerable deficit.[269]

In fact there was no end to the many and various ways in which the life of the cathedral and city impinged on each other. The dean and chapter of Bristol took an active interest in the Bristol Harbour Bill in 1803, even sending the chapter clerk with a petition to the House of Lords.[270] Fifteen years later they agreed to sell some land for the building of the new city gaol, and used the interest on the sum they received for its sale to establish a Sunday afternoon sermon.[271] In the same year the dean and chapter of Winchester asked the city magistrates not to relicense public houses near the cathedral, since they were 'notoriously disorderly houses'.[272] The dean and chapter of Salisbury were in the habit at this time of inviting the Assize judges to dine with them on Assize Sunday, the host being allowed 10½ guineas from the chapter's funds for this purpose.[273] At Wells the cathedral was regularly disfigured by notices from auctioneers and others being posted on the walls and doors, until the dean and chapter decided to prohibit this practice in 1831.[274] In 1834 the dean and chapter of Exeter gave a donation of £10 to the city commissioners for a nightly watch. Twenty-two years later they gave £30 to the city collection for celebrating peace following the end of the Crimean War.[275] In 1841 Dean Merewether took the chair at a general meeting of the Mechanics' Institution at Hereford. The members resolved to celebrate their anniversary with a procession to the cathedral, where the dean would preach a sermon.[276] A few days later, Merewether attended a public meeting, chaired by the mayor, to form a society 'for Aiding the Industrious'.[277] When another public meeting was held in November of the same year, to celebrate the birth of the Prince of Wales, he suggested that there should be a subscription for the relief of the poor and a dinner for them in the workhouse.[278] In 1867 the dean and chapter of Chichester protested to the mayor about the cattle market in West Street, and plans to move it to a different site were immediately put in hand.[279]

One area of particular sensitivity was the relationship between a cathedral and the parishes of the city. In some cases the parishes received valuable assistance from their proximity to the cathedral. In 1819 the parishioners of St Thomas's Church, Salisbury, were allowed to use the cathedral for their own services while their church was being repaired,[280] while the dean and chapter of Chichester provided bread and wine for the parish of St Peter the Great.[281] When the foundation stone of the new church of St Nicholas was laid at Hereford in 1841, there was a procession to and from the cathedral, and Dean Merewether entertained the company to luncheon after the ceremony.[282] Dean Johnson of Wells was also Vicar of St Cuthbert's,[283] and the cathedral commissioners stressed that one of the chief objects of cathedrals was 'the effective spiritual care of the cathedral cities'.[284] At St Paul's, two minor canons were appointed by the dean and chapter in 1876 to undertake pastoral work in the vicinity of the cathedral.[285] Some years earlier Dean Alford had described the parishes of cathedral cities as 'insignificant livings with poor little churches, serving to starve the incumbents and to keep down public church spirit'.[286] At Hereford the parishioners of St John the Baptist used the cathedral for their services. There were similar arrangements at Chester where the south transept was used as the parish church of St Oswald and at Chichester in the early years of the century where the congregation of St Peter the Great assembled in the cathedral until their own church was built immediately to the north of the cathedral.[287] At Norwich the parishioners of St Mary-in-the-Marsh were accustomed to having their own services at St Luke's Chapel in the cathedral. Bishop Pelham offered his own chapel for their use when the establishment of Sunday afternoon sermons in the cathedral effectively prevented them from continuing this arrangement.[288] The Lady Chapel of Ely was used as the parish church for the parish of Holy Trinity until 1938.[289]

Popular misconceptions about cathedrals on the part of those who lived near them were as common in the nineteenth century as today, and at least some chapters were aware of them. W. K. Hamilton told the Cathedrals Commission in 1854 that 'the general impression in Salisbury has been that every canon has £5,000 a year'.[290] The *Durham Chronicle* in 1821 criticized the dean and chapter for refusing to toll the cathedral bells to mark the death of Queen Caroline; the newspaper asserted that the canons 'had lost all semblance to ministers of religion'.[291] Forty years later it was the turn of the dean and chapter of Winchester to be pilloried by the *Hampshire Examiner* as 'a set of idle drones'.[292]

Dean Close of Carlisle told the archbishops in reply to the 1869 questionnaire that canons were seldom active as members of the committees of infirmaries, dispensaries, schools, or diocesan, educational or other charities. There was little contact between the families of canons and 'the social circle of the city', and as a result the cathedral became isolated from the city and unpopular.[293]

The life of a cathedral was therefore inevitably linked with that of the city that surrounded it. The power and privilege of a chapter was sometimes a cause of envy and hostility, but on the whole there are many more examples of any latent feelings of this kind being dispelled by the active way in which deans and canons took a lively interest in the life of the city. This was particularly true in the last thirty years or so of the century. In some cases a particular member of the chapter might be active in local civic affairs; in other instances, as in the entrusting of specific pastoral work to the minor canons of St Paul's in 1876, there was a definite commitment to local mission on the part of the dean and chapter. In either case, the criticism of the *British Critic* in 1841 that capitular bodies had little influence in cathedral cities was largely untrue by the closing years of the century.

To an increasing extent during the nineteenth century the mission of cathedrals involved not only links with the diocese and the city, but also with casual visitors. The hours during which the doors of cathedrals were open were extended and the development of railways encouraged tourism as never before. Early in the century it was quite common for cathedrals to remain closed except during services, as at Exeter in 1815.[294] The vergers there were prohibited from conducting guided tours around the building on Sundays.[295] In 1837 the dean and chapter of Norwich agreed to open the cathedral for one hour daily except on Sundays, in addition to the usual hours of service,[296] but Salisbury was not opened to the public until

1849.[297] In that year the nave was opened free of charge between 10.15 a.m. and 4 p.m. daily. From 1865 visitors were allowed to see the quire, chapter-house and cloisters for a charge of 6d.[298] In 1837 Lord John Russell tried to insist that the dean and chapter should keep St Paul's open to the public free of charge as a national monument. The chapter made a small charge of 2d (which formed part of the vergers' pay) and felt that this acted as a deterrent to unruly behaviour and helped to preserve a decent standard of conduct. An experimental free opening had had unfortunate results and the dean and chapter did not allow unrestricted free opening until 1851.[299] At Wells a new sacrist, John Barnard, was appointed in 1853. Part of his duties was to show the building to the public.[300] Bishop Hamilton of Salisbury told the Cathedrals Commission in 1854 that the doors of the cathedral should be left open all day and regretted that visitors were able to see only the nave.[301] The commissioners were certainly in favour of the public being given free access to cathedrals.[302] Gloucester Cathedral was opened on weekday afternoons in 1858. One of the sub-sacrists and the constable of the precincts were present to keep order and prevent any damage, but the tower, crypt and cloisters remained closed.[303] At Wells the dean and chapter ordered in 1862 that the cathedral should be closed for a week annually so that it could be cleaned.[304] Ten years later this was extended to two weeks in each year. A local incumbent complained that when he tried to go to a non-existent evensong during one of the weeks, he was shocked to discover the nave littered with orange peel and to detect a distinct smell of tobacco. Another visitor said that the air was so thick with dust during the preceding week that he had to wash his hands and brush his coat-tails after his visit.[305] One visitor to Worcester in 1881 was very indignant at finding the cathedral closed for cleaning, although Dean Compton pointed out that the services had been transferred to St Helen's Church. This was the first time the cathedral had been thoroughly cleaned since its reopening after restoration in 1874.[306] John Wordsworth managed to stop Rochester Cathedral being closed for cleaning in 1883,[307] but Bristol Cathedral was still closed for a fortnight in August for cleaning as late as 1889.[308] The hours when the cathedral at Salisbury was open were fixed in 1863. It was open from after the early morning service until five o'clock in the winter and until six o'clock in the summer.[309] Shortly after E. M. Goulburn went to Norwich in 1866, the chapter agreed to keep the doors of the cathedral open between services.[310] The nave of Lincoln Cathedral was open all day by 1869.[311] At Bristol in 1870 the cathedral was kept open each day after evensong until 5.15 p.m., so that those attending the service could look around the building. Fourteen years later new rules extended the hours of opening.[312] By 1872, according to Mackenzie Walcott, most cathedrals were left open each day free of charge.[313] Winchester was open from 9 a.m. until 5 p.m. in the winter and until 6.30 p.m. in the summer.[314] At Canterbury the nave was kept open, but visitors could view the quire only in an organized party. The guided tour was too rapid, though, and the cathedral was closed quite early in the afternoon.[315] At Hereford the cathedral was open each weekday from 9 a.m. to 6 p.m. There was no compulsory fee, but visitors were asked to contribute not less than 6d each. The vergers and sextons who were employed by the dean and chapter to show visitors around the cathedral were not allowed to accept gratuities.[316] In 1891 the dean and chapter decided that the cloisters at Chichester Cathedral should be locked on Bank Holidays and the chancel gates were also kept locked. In 1891 the dean and chapter decided that the cathedral should be closed each day between 1 p.m. and 2 p.m.[317] Worcester Cathedral was shut early in the afternoon of Accession Day 1897 after a special service to commemorate Queen Victoria's Diamond Jubilee.[318]

The development of the railway system led to a substantial increase in the number of visitors to cathedrals and their behaviour sometimes caused problems. In 1848 a train-load of mechanics from Derby visited Lincoln. For some hours, 'the cathedral was filled with an immense crowd of the lowest description of mechanics, many, nay most of them, wearing their hats, and all talking aloud, laughing and jesting in the most irreverent way'. The language was said to be disgusting and a blindfolded stranger in the Angel Choir 'would have thought that he was in the midst of the orgies of a low beershop'.[319] In the following year an outing of dissenters from Leeds visited Ripon and the cathedral was thrown open to them 'to do just what they liked in'. A priest from Bath was greatly shocked:

> Crowds of children were playing at hide-and-seek in all parts of it – throngs of men and women were rudely talking and laughing – the men for the most part with their hats on. A party of youths and girls had made their way to the font and were amusing themselves with splashing the water it contained on each other. Whilst in several of the pews social parties were busily engaged in sharing and eating the provisions they had brought for the day.[320]

A visitor to York in 1855 found a train-load of visitors, 'chiefly of the lower orders',

> behaving in a most unseemly and disgraceful manner. Refreshment-baskets were opened and their contents demolished; the men were laughing and talking loudly to each other; the men *with their hats on*, and, in more than one instance, *with cigars in their mouths*.[321]

F. T. Havergal, who was subtreasurer at Hereford, complained to the dean and chapter in 1870 that visitors were allowed access to the sanctuary where they frequently handled the books and cloth on the altar.[322] On Good Friday 1872 a party of 'rollicking sailors' invaded Wells Cathedral:

'Cries of "You're drunk" and the like were echoing along the aisles and transept, while a noisy scuffle was going on at the entrance to the choir.'[323] In 1899 the vergers at St Paul's were told 'to stop people eating, reading newspapers or secular books, and to watch "doubtful characters"'.[324] In view of these difficulties, some cathedrals promulgated series of rules for their visitors. No visitors were allowed into the quire at Exeter while the woodwork was being repaired.[325] At Chichester the dean and chapter published a notice to visitors in 1889 which requested them to abstain 'from any conduct unseemly and irreverent in the House of God',[326] and visitors were not allowed to enter the chancel unless accompanied by a verger.[327] The dean and chapter of Wells decided in 1868 that visitors who wished to climb the tower could do so only if they were accompanied, and smoking in the tower was forbidden.[328] Reliable statistics of the number of visitors to cathedrals during the nineteenth century are scarce, but Manchester was said to have 250 visitors a day in 1848, and 1,149 people visited Worcester Cathedral between May and December 1874 following its reopening in April.[329] St Paul's was obviously well placed to receive a much larger number of visitors: 48,000 people went there in 1840 and 71,000 in 1845.[330] Chester was much visited by Americans disembarking at Liverpool after crossing the Atlantic.[331] During 1877 Canon Gregory personally conducted 1,335 persons in nineteen parties around St Paul's.[332] H. E. Reynolds thought that visitors to cathedrals did not learn much, even from guided tours.[333] But at Bristol free guided tours were offered to working men on some summer Saturdays in 1893.[334] At Wells the needs of visitors were taken seriously: three seats were placed on the green and a 3d guide book was published.[335]

From time to time cathedrals welcomed distinguished visitors. When Lady Hamilton visited Canterbury early in the century, she could not resist singing aloud in the quire.[336] The Queen of Hawaii visited Wells in 1865, attending a special service at 11 a.m. and a public meeting in the chapter room in the afternoon.[337] In 1886 the Princess of Wales and three of her children visited Exeter as guests of Bishop Bickersteth; they were conducted around the cathedral by the dean and attended evensong.[338] Distinguished visitors to Norwich were guided around the cathedral by Dean Lefroy himself.[339]

There is therefore considerable evidence that cathedrals both stimulated and responded to a growing interest in them in the later decades of the century. Visitors sometimes caused problems and parts of the building had to be protected from them, but they did become a habitual source of income via the fees that were charged for admittance. Nevertheless, many deans and chapters recognized that they had a responsibility towards those members of the public who visited their cathedrals, and the awareness of this responsibility, added to the traditional links with the bishop, the diocese and the city, meant that cathedrals had a growing sense of mission during the nineteenth century. Canons such as Gregory, Benson, Liddon, Westcott, Butler, and Lightfoot were shining examples of men who cared deeply, not only for the cathedral and its services, but also for its impact on the life of the city and diocese and on the general public. They recognized that cathedrals had a great role in the life of the Church, and their zeal, vigour and enthusiasm were very influential in developing the mission of cathedrals.

12

CATHEDRALS AND
EDUCATION

❀

Education has traditionally been an important part of the work of
cathedrals. In France in the twelfth century many great cathedrals
maintained schools that were really embryonic universities. In England,
cathedrals such as Hereford and Lincoln were developing in the same
way, and the present Cathedral School at Hereford traces its ancestry back
to the medieval chancellor's grammar school. The secular cathedrals also
provided for the education of choristers, while the monastic cathedrals
often established almonry schools where boys could be educated. The new
foundation cathedrals established by Henry VIII usually included a
grammar school as an integral part of the foundation, as at Canterbury,
Rochester, Worcester, Gloucester, Peterborough, Chester, Bristol, Carlisle,
Durham and Ely. There was no need for such a school at Oxford, where
the chapel of Christ Church became the cathedral of the new diocese, since
Wolsey's Cardinal College, which the king refounded, amply demonstrated the educational work of the cathedral. The existence of Winchester
College immediately south of the cathedral removed the need for a
grammar school there. Only at Norwich was no provision made for a
grammar school, though here (as at other cathedrals where there was no
grammar school) a school for choristers was maintained.[1]

By the beginning of the nineteenth century many of these schools were
in a precarious position, though a local guide at Worcester said that in
1799 at the King's School, 'Besides a regular preparation for the University, Music, Drawing, the French, Spanish and Italian Languages, and
other fashionable accomplishments are taught by proper masters.'[2] Fifteen
years later it was said that this school was 'conducted on a liberal plan,
affording regular preparation for the University, as well as instruction in
music, drawing and in the modern languages, nor are the lighter fashionable accomplishments neglected.'[3] A. B. Evans, the headmaster of the
King's School at Gloucester, was 'a thoroughly good Greek scholar',
though his successor Dr Thomas Evans 'flogged boys mercilessly'.[4]
Religious instruction was not neglected at Hereford, where the boys
received regular instruction in the catechism.[5] The education of cathedral
choristers had been a particular concern of Maria Hackett. After her early
efforts to improve their lot at St Paul's, she published a more general

survey in 1827.[6] At Rochester the cathedral grammar school was decaying. In 1825 there were only sixteen boys and by 1838 there were no pupils at all. In 1842 Robert Whiston was appointed headmaster; he persuaded the dean and chapter to erect a new school-room, and brought with him the pupils of his own private school.[7] In 1848 Whiston began a spirited battle with the dean and chapter of Rochester to restore the value of the scholarships at the grammar school. In 1849 he published an inflammatory pamphlet entitled *Cathedral Trusts and Their Fulfilment*.[8] Whiston contended that at Rochester, as at Canterbury and other new foundation cathedrals, the cathedral grammar school was shabbily treated. Using documents prepared by or sent to the Ecclesiastical Commissioners, Whiston showed that the dean and canons were receiving very large sums of money as their share of the cathedral's revenues, while other officers (and especially the grammar school boys) were receiving even less than the sixteenth-century statutes had laid down. Whiston's criticism of the dean and chapter led to his dismissal, but after a legal wrangle that lasted nearly five years and that rocked the ecclesiastical world, he was re-instated in 1853 and remained headmaster until 1877.

Shortly before the middle of the century it is plain that all was not well with some cathedral schools. At Hereford the headmaster complained to the dean and chapter in 1841 that the schoolhouse was dilapidated and dangerous,[9] while the dean and chapter of Worcester were horrified to find that College Hall was also in a dilapidated state. This had been caused by wanton damage by the boys. They ordered Octavius Fox, the headmaster, to make sure that no boys were allowed to remain in College Hall after school hours and told him to supervise their behaviour more carefully.[10]

In 1854 the cathedral commissioners made enquiries about cathedral schools and printed a summary of their findings.[11] They also printed the replies that they received from the headmasters and others.[12] One of the fullest replies came from Charles Lowry, the headmaster of the King's School at Carlisle. He said that in 1843 there were no pupils, but when he was appointed in 1849 he found sixteen at the school. Since then the school had expanded considerably. New and excellent school-rooms had been built as a result of the generous donations by the dean, chapter and the public, and there were now over eighty pupils, half of them in the 'classical' school and half in the 'commercial' school. The latter was favoured by the middle class as the only way of obtaining a good education. He had appointed two other masters and paid their salaries, which left him with a little under £200 per annum. There were no boarders and the choristers received a free education. Because of their musical commitments they received 'a very scrambling education'.[13]

At Chester there was a grammar school, also known as the King's School, which included twenty-four King's Scholars and sixteen other boys. There was also a choristers' school, where the boys were taught by a

273

lay clerk.[14] The school at Chichester, known as St Faith's Choristers' School, was very small and catered for just eleven boys.[15] John Ingle, the headmaster of the grammar school at Ely, also found the inclusion of the choristers irksome, not least because of the wide age range, and suggested that they would benefit more from a commercial than from a classical education. Ingle had become headmaster less than two years previously, when he found the school

> in the lowest stage of decay. The pupils were the sons of servants, mechanics, and in one or two instances, of clerks or small trades-men....The boys had no notion of school work or school discipline to get even a short and simple English lesson learnt with accuracy.

The dean and chapter had assisted in improving the school-rooms and had appointed an assistant master. The tone and character of the school had improved and the curriculum had been widened. But Ingle wanted yet more progress and hoped that the cathedral might become the educational centre of the diocese.[16]

There was no school of any kind at Exeter, where the choristers were educated by a pupil of the diocesan training school.[17] Robert Hancock, the headmaster of the grammar school at Bristol, was troubled by the choristers: 'Their attendance on Divine Service twice every day the whole year without intermission is injurious to their health, education and morals.' He suggested doubling the size of the choir so that they could take it in turns to attend services.[18] The choristers at Hereford entered the school at a very young age when they could scarcely read or write.[19] There was no grammar school at Lichfield, Norwich or Christ Church, Oxford, but a small school in each case was maintained for the choristers.[20] Lincoln had a grammar school, with ninety-one pupils, and the choristers attended it.[21] At Rochester Robert Whiston complained that the twenty foundation boys were obliged to attend cathedral services on saints' days:

> They are required to leave a warm school-room, where they have been sitting for an hour and a quarter, to go through hail, rain or snow, in all weather, and to sit or stand for an hour and three-quarters or more in a bitterly cold, stone-walled and stone-floored cathedral, where anything like devotion, with a temperature at freezing point, is out of the question.[22]

John Richard, the headmaster of the school at Salisbury, complained that the schoolhouse was unsuitable both for his family and for the accom-modation of boarders: 'The dormitories of the choristers are very deficient in height (being in the slope of the roof), have no fire-places, and their proper warming and ventilation is almost impossible.' There were eight choristers and thirty-two other boys.[23] The cathedral commissioners concluded from their survey of cathedral schools that

...although laudable efforts have been made, in some instances, to reinvigorate them in recent years, yet for the most part, they are not in a flourishing state and do not occupy the place in the capitular institutions which their founders designed for them.

In particular, the masters and assistant masters were badly paid.[24]

There were 100 pupils at the school at Gloucester in the late 1860s, but by 1887 there were only twenty-four plus the choristers. By 1880 the numbers were rising again. On saints' days the boys attended the morning service in the cathedral and sat in the gallery above the stalls on the south side.[25] But the educational value of the school was limited. A. H. Brewer said that in the 1870s

the school buildings were very inadequate. Nearly all the forms were held in one room and the pandemonium caused by the masters competing with each other in their attempts to drive the rudiments of Latin, Greek and arithmetic into the heads of the boys, all at the same time, was indescribable.[26]

At Winchester the choristers were taught in various places by William Garrett for much of the first half of the century. Later a house in the close was used as a school for them. A young lay vicar, William Southcott, was appointed as their schoolmaster and for a while they were joined by the college quiristers. Southcott proved to be unsatisfactory and was asked to resign by the dean and chapter in 1887.[27]

For some twenty years, from the mid-1860s to the mid-1880s, many chapters did much to strengthen and improve their schools. Section 27 of the Endowed Schools Act of 1869 authorized the Ecclesiastical Commissioners to make grants to deans and chapters for this purpose.[28] Radical changes were made at St Paul's and a new choir school was opened in 1873 with Albert Barff as headmaster.[29] At Ely there were two schools – the ancient grammar school on one side of the cathedral and a new school for the choristers on the other side which Dean Harvey Goodwin had built in 1860.[30] Canon T. C. Durham, writing in 1872, praised the recent efforts of many chapters to improve their schools.[31] There were fifty-seven applicants for the headmastership of the choir school at Chichester in 1879, an appointment that was linked to the prebendal stall of Highleigh.[32] W. E. Bolland, the headmaster of the grammar school at Worcester, complained about the lack of classrooms and the poor state of his own house.[33] Earlier, however, this school had won much praise from James Bryce, who visited it in 1865 on behalf of the Endowed Schools Commissioners. 'Few schools in England,' he said, describing College Hall, 'have a school-room comparable to that at Worcester Cathedral. It is the refectory of the great Benedictine monastery....It is thus large enough to accommodate all the classes, the noise being moderated by the height of the room.' He went on to praise the knowledge and demeanour of the boys and concluded: 'The Worcester Cathedral School is in some respects a model of what a grammar school in a large provincial town ought to be.'[34] The title 'The King's School' was revived for the cathedral grammar school at Worcester in 1896.[35] On the other hand, J. M. W. Young, the organist of Lincoln Cathedral, said in 1880 that the school there had a very poor standard: 'The boys we get, with a rare exception, have not been taught to speak well before they come choristers; one half of the time of the singing lesson is taken up with the pronunciation alone.'[36] The cathedral school at Wells was practically extinct by 1870 and the choristers were transferred to a local private school. Dean Johnson revived it, though, and it reopened in 1881. In 1884 new premises were opened in the north liberty.[37] A new building was opened for the cathedral school at Hereford in the 1870s, the dean and chapter contributing over £3,000 towards the cost. In 1893 a major constitutional change occurred when the Charity Commissioners approved a scheme under the 1869 Endowed Schools Act which placed the school on a definite foundation. The Ecclesiastical Commission gave £7,000 towards the endowment of the school, but the dean and chapter remained the sole governors until after the end of the century.[38]

Many deans and individual canons took a great interest in their schools. Dean Lake greatly improved the buildings and grounds of the school at Durham,[39] and both Canon Burrows and Canon Wordsworth were supporters of King's School, Rochester. Wordsworth helped to acquire a cricket-ground for the school and also assisted in the design of the choir school;[40] and Burrows took a leading part in obtaining new buildings and other facilities.[41] Dean Farrar took a great interest in the boys of the King's School and the choir school at Canterbury. He would often invite them to breakfast on a Sunday morning or to tea in his garden during the summer.[42] Dean Law of Gloucester invited members of the sixth form at Gloucester to dine with him at the deanery each year.[43]

Progress in education was one of the most important achievements of Victorian England, and it is clear that cathedrals played their part in this. With the encouragement of the Endowed Schools Act of 1869, the ancient grammar schools were developed and expanded so that many of them were comparable with public schools, while the special needs of choristers were recognized and often catered for by the provision of separate choir schools. If cathedral schools were a clearly visible indication of the educational work of cathedrals, their character as places of learning also depended on their libraries. These were often hidden away in obscure parts of the building, and in some cases had been neglected for many years.

The library at Hereford Cathedral was housed in the Lady Chapel. One of the residentiary canons was master of the library and, under the terms of the cathedral's Laudian statutes, it was his duty to take care that the Library be kept in good repair, cleansed from all filth, that the books be fastened with chains, and the keys put away, and that if need be they be repaired, and a list of them be set up at the end of every shelf.

New books were bought with the proceeds of admission fees, for every new canon or prebendary had to pay 40s into the library fund. The master of the library rendered an annual account to the dean and chapter. There were three copies of the library catalogue and each year the dean and two of the canons were obliged to inspect the library.[44] The provisions for the library at Hereford were certainly fuller than those at some other cathedrals. At Winchester, for example, the only reference to the library was in the statute dealing with the work of the dean, who was to 'preserve with the utmost care the common Library and the books thereof, or with the consent of the Chapter shall cause it to be preserved by any other fit person'.[45]

The condition of cathedral libraries in the early nineteenth century varied considerably. At Ely George Millan, librarian and sacrist from 1813, constructed a new library on the east side of the south transept. New shelves were provided and the books were rearranged, catalogued and labelled. There was also careful provision made for the cleaning, super-vision, heating and opening hours of the new library.[46] Bristol Cathedral library was severely despoiled in the riots of 1831; over 5,000 books were destroyed by fire and many of the remaining ones were damaged.[47] The muniments of Salisbury Cathedral 'strewed the floor' in 1834, 'a feast for moths and spiders'.[48] Wells Cathedral library was 'in a state of disorder' in 1833, and as late as 1871 some muniments were being used by students of the theological college to light fires.[49] It was alleged in the House of Commons in 1848 that some cathedral libraries were so neglected that none of the canons knew who had the key, and that the lock was so rusty that the key would not turn or the door open.[50] The researches of Beriah Botfield in 1849 confirmed that this impression was not exaggerated. He reported that the library at Chester was neglected, with empty shelves.[51] The library at Exeter, like that of Hereford, had been housed in the Lady Chapel, 'exposed to the inroads of idle curiosity and subject to the chilling influence of damp and neglect'.[52] Many books at Salisbury were still buried in dust and covered in eighteenth century cobwebs.[53]

At several cathedrals, however, notable improvements had been carried out. Many of the books at Ripon were neglected and decayed, but they had been transferred to the deanery where they were 'preserved with commendable attention'.[54] Extensive repairs and rebinding had been carried out at Canterbury, where the books were 'generally in a very good condition'.[55] At Durham the books were well arranged and free from damp,[56] as they were at Gloucester.[57] The library at Lichfield was carefully housed above the chapter-house and the manuscripts were kept in locked cases.[58] The library at Norwich was in one of the houses in the close,[59] while the care and attention given to York Minster Library, which had been housed in the former chapel of the archbishop since 1810, was 'highly creditable'.[60] Through the initiative of Dean Markham, much had been done to improve this library in the early years of the century. He expanded the collection and initiated regular binding and lettering. In 1808 the dean and chapter began to give the library a regular income, which meant that nearly 100 books could be bought each year. In 1841 Archbishop Vernon Harcourt issued various injunctions about the library; they were designed to restrict unauthorized spending, to appoint a vicar choral as librarian and to encourage proper regulations to be drawn up about the use and management of the library. In the following year Edward John Raines was appointed librarian. His successor was Thomas Falkner, who held office from 1858 to 1872. The real development of the library was the work of James Raine, a local incumbent from 1856 until 1881 when he became a residentiary canon. He was chancellor from 1891 until his death five years later. Gifts of books and donations were solicited, the library was made warm and comfortable, and a new catalogue was compiled. Only Durham had a larger collection of books. Under Raine's guidance, the Minster library 'grew from good to outstanding', and he was described by Neil Ker as 'one of the great cathedral librarians'.[61] In 1854 the cathedral commissioners discovered in response to their enquiries that Durham, with 11,000 volumes, had the largest collection of books. York and St Paul's came next with 8,000, and most of the others contained between 2,000 and 5,000 volumes. Access to them was generally restricted, except at York and Durham. The income of most libraries was very small; Durham with £200 and York with £80 headed the list. The dean and chapter gave £30 at Canterbury, Ely and Norwich, and £20 at Exeter. At Carlisle only £5 was allowed for the purchase of books. The librarian at Durham was paid £40 in 1845, rising to £70 in 1864 and to £100 after 1865.[62]

The library at St Paul's remained in a neglected state until W. Sparrow Simpson became librarian in 1862. Many books were simply disintegrating.[63] Simpson rebound nearly one hundred volumes a year, some 3,428 books in total before his death in 1897. He also doubled the number of books in the library.[64] At Ely, by contrast, few additions to the library were made after 1869,[65] and the dean and chapter of Chichester lamented in 1881 that their library was 'in a state of utter decadence from want of funds'.[66] Dean Howson of Chester said in 1879 that the library of his cathedral was 'much impoverished in earlier years by grievous neglect', but was gradually improving.[67] At Worcester a suggestions book was placed in the chapter-house in 1838 for the canons to write down the names of books they thought should be added to the library, and a new librarian was appointed in 1865 at a salary of £20 per annum. The books were moved from Edgar Tower to the present library above the south aisle in 1866. In 1873 Maurice Day, the headmaster, was asked to produce a new catalogue and to improve the facilities for the use of the library by the clergy of the diocese.[68] The great library at Durham was extended between the years 1848 and 1854, with a new floor and additional book cases being added.[69] In 1880 H. E. Reynolds, the librarian of Exeter Cathedral, told the cathedral commissioners that the libraries at York, St Paul's, Salisbury, Canterbury, Durham, Oxford and Truro were in a tolerable condition, but those at Chichester, Exeter, Hereford, Lichfield, Lincoln, Wells, Carlisle, Ely, Norwich, Rochester, Winchester, Worcester, Bristol, Chester, Gloucester, Peterborough, Manchester and Ripon were poorly maintained. In some cases the libraries were 'awkward of access and insufficiently warmed', and others were 'very damp and not large enough and inconvenient'. At his own library at Exeter, some valuable books had been attacked by mildew, the binding of all the books was disintegrating, while recently 'a piece of marble, weighing many pounds, became detached from a capital and fell upon the bookcases'.[70] Reynolds sent some thirty questions in the late 1870s to various cathedral libraries to discover what changes had taken place during the previous twenty-five years. He found that the library was in the chapter-house at Chester, Exeter, Rochester and Chichester; and that at both Exeter and Canterbury the chapter-house was 'repeatedly used for meetings of the diocesan clergy'. At Carlisle and Lichfield a room above the chapter-house was used and at Bristol an adjoining room. At Ely and Chichester the books were contained in an aisle or chapel. The library at York was still in the archbishop's chapel, while at Wells, Winchester and Lincoln rooms over the cloisters were used. The library at Peterborough was in the chapel above the west door and that at Worcester above the south aisle of the nave. The library at Salisbury was specially built by Bishop Jewel, while at Ripon and Norwich it was in a house in the close. There were appropriate quarters at Durham (in the former dormitory) and at Gloucester in a room off the cloisters. The library at Chester was lit by gas and, like Lichfield, was warmed by a gurney stove. The temperature at Ely and Worcester was maintained at fifty degrees. York had a hot water system and Gloucester was warmed by hot air; elsewhere, only a fireplace was available – and in some places there was no heating at all.

Few deans or canons had recently given or bequeathed books to their libraries.[71] After two substantial private bequests of books at Exeter, the dean and chapter decided in 1886 to build a new library on the site of the former cloisters, demolishing a verger's house in order to do so.[72] When Mandell Creighton became Bishop of Peterborough he found the books in the chapter library 'in a rather dirty and neglected condition'. He therefore persuaded the canons' wives to set to work and dust them.[73]

Various rules governing the use of cathedral libraries in the nineteenth century have survived. At Worcester in 1818 no book was to be lent, except to the minor canons and the schoolmaster, without the consent of the chapter, and no book purchased without their approval. A fire was to be lit in the library each day and a subscription for the *Quarterly Review* was to be made.[74] At Hereford in 1821 no book was to be lent without permission from the dean or canon in residence, whose consent was also needed for the verger to admit visitors.[75] The rules drawn up at Exeter in the following year restricted the lending of books to the dean and canons, though the prebendaries and others were allowed to borrow with special permission.[76] Fifty-four years later it was made clear that borrowers were responsible for replacing any lost books; and only two volumes at a time could normally be borrowed for a maximum period of four weeks, with a fine of 1s a week for overdue books.[77]

In addition to William Sparrow Simpson and James Raine, two other notable librarians were F. T. Havergal at Hereford and J. F. Wickenden at Lincoln. The library at Hereford was removed from the Lady Chapel in 1841 and the books were stored in the college of vicars choral until about 1855, when they were transferred to the room above the north transept aisle. The bookcases were stored in the crypt until they were re-erected in 1857, but the work was badly done. Havergal, who was one of the vicars choral, obtained £10 in 1857 to renovate the shelves and the fittings. He was a meticulous and conscientious librarian who kept a careful note of the dates and prices paid for all repairs to the books. Sometimes he paid for repairs himself and he also kept a note-book in which he recorded details of any work done in the library. He compiled two important books on the history of Hereford Cathedral: *Fasti Herefordenses*, published in 1869, and *Monumental Inscriptions of Hereford Cathedral*, published in 1881. He has been described as 'the first modern librarian to take a keen interest in his work'.[78] In November 1854, while the books were still stored in the college of vicars choral, he said that he had carefully dusted and checked all the books, which were generally in a good condition, though some bindings needed attention.[79] He added that fires lit in damp weather would be an advantage and said that over 200 people had visited the library during the previous six months. He had also catalogued all the volumes of music. Seven years later he reported that over thirty volumes had been borrowed during the previous year and that all had been safely returned.[80]

When E. W. Benson became chancellor of Lincoln Cathedral he persuaded the dean and chapter to commission a report on the state of the muniments. Joseph Burtt, assistant keeper of the public records, told the dean and chapter in 1873 that a large mass of loose documents were 'in a very lamentable condition'. Many 'were crushed up together and packed as though they had been loose shavings or the sweepings of a workshop'.[81] Soon afterwards, J. F. Wickenden, a friend of Benson's, was invited to stay 'for weeks together' at the chancery to begin work on sorting out the muniments. A. C. Benson confirmed that he had taken on a daunting task:

> I shall never forget the sight of the place – deal boxes, shelves, pigeon holes, crammed with bundles of papers black with ages, shrivelled parchments, deeds with huge beeswax seals attached, the whole thing incredibly filthy and neglected.[82]

From 1874 until his death in 1883, Wickenden cleaned, examined and repaired some 5,000 documents, attaching descriptions to each. For some thirty years after Wickenden's work, numerous muniments from the cathedral's collection were published.[83]

The archives of Exeter Cathedral were the scene of much labour on the part of Dean Lyttelton and two chapter clerks, Nicholas Webber and Ralph Barnes. But it was Stuart Moore who provided a comprehensive calendar and rescued them from decay. He wrote in 1873:

> The archives have suffered a great deal from neglect and damp. Their place of deposit was unfortunately chosen, for being on the northern side of the Cathedral, the sun seldom or never shines upon it: the massive walls have drawn up the damp from below, and the documents deposited in wooden presses standing against the walls have suffered terribly. The jealous care of their late custodian for some 40 or 50 years has helped the ravages of the moisture, for the room had until I came into it neither ventilation nor warmth, and many previous documents have been lost to us in consequence. Now, however, that a free circulation of air has been provided and the walls thoroughly dried, there will be less danger.[84]

The work of men like Wickenden, Havergal, Sparrow Simpson and Raine is often neglected when developments in cathedrals during the nineteenth century are considered. But in their own quiet way they did much to improve their particular side of cathedral work. They would have endorsed Reynolds's desire that cathedral libraries should be efficient and active elements in cathedral life and work.[85]

The educational work of cathedrals was also promoted by lectures of various kinds. Some cathedrals had long recognized the value of this element in their life and mission. The seventeenth-century statutes at Hereford, for example, provided for 'a sacred Lecture, out of the books of the Bible' every Tuesday. During Lent, two lectures were delivered each week. The lectures were normally to be delivered by a dignitary known as the praelector, usually the holder of the bishop's prebend. Each of the canons and prebendaries and other ministers of the cathedral was obliged to attend his lectures.[86] Regular lectures were also customary at some new foundation cathedrals. A Sunday afternoon lecture was given at Winchester from at least 1673 until early in the present century, formerly by the deans and prebendaries in course, but by the minor canons from 1754 till 1873.[87] Theological lectures were, of course, an innovation of the Reformation; the earliest order for them appears to be in the royal injunctions for Salisbury issued in 1535–6.[88] Early morning lectures were given at Exeter on Tuesdays and Fridays, but these were discontinued in 1828.[89]

In addition to these statutory provisions, however, several deans and canons began to deliver lectures of various kinds in the second half of the nineteenth century. One of the first to do so was Charles Kingsley at Chester.[90] Harvey Goodwin tried to begin a working men's college at Ely in 1861. This was not a success, but he gradually established a scheme of lectures on literary and scientific subjects. These were delivered to working men on winter evenings with the help of friends from Cambridge.[91] Divinity lectures on a Lent weekday were an established feature at Lincoln in 1869,[92] though Chancellor Massingberd had encountered initial opposition when he tried to introduce them in 1864. They outgrew the morning chapel and were seriously disturbed by people walking about in the nave. They were therefore transferred to the nave itself, and became so popular that many had to stand.[93] When E. W. Benson succeeded Massingberd he started a Bible class for mechanics, gave lectures on church history in the chapter-house during Lent, and started night schools in the city. Some 400 men and boys came to the first of these and they proved very successful.[94]

Sir Frederick Ouseley was invited to give a lecture at Norwich Cathedral in 1869 on the different parts of the choral service. Dean Goulburn said it was 'excellent and well-attended'.[95] Canon Gregory was responsible for the initiation of lectures at St Paul's in 1871. Over 1,200 young men attended the first one, despite Gregory's insistence that women should be excluded. A St Paul's Lecture Society and the Amen Court Guild were established.[96] Canon Newbolt expanded the pastoral work of the cathedral and arranged courses on 'Catholic faith and practice' and weekend retreats. He also started a weekly Bible study class in his house for young warehousemen in 1898.[97] Canon Barry began to give some lectures at Worcester in 1878 on the theme of 'The Church of England before the Reformation'.[98] Mandell Creighton began an evening course of lectures on church history in the chapter-house in 1886 and continued to do so every summer until 1890. In 1889 he gave a series of addresses during Lent on 'Teachers of Holiness'. He also organized lectures for the diocesan clergy in the chapter-house given by distinguished Oxford scholars,[99] and a further course of theological lectures was introduced in 1890.[100] Dean Merivale of Ely also gave lectures on ecclesiastical history.[101] At Salisbury a course of lectures for young men was arranged in 1880. These took place on Thursday evenings and seats under the tower were reserved for the men. The lecturer wore a surplice and said certain collects. There were two hymns and the choristers were available to lead the congregational singing.[102] One of the prebendaries of Hereford suggested that daily catechizing and classes in the nave of the cathedral would be the best means of attracting working men, but the idea was not taken up.[103]

A further way in which cathedrals began to develop their educational role during the nineteenth century was in the field of theological education. Pusey drew attention in 1833 to the suitability of cathedrals for theological research and teaching.[104] The first theological college to be founded in a cathedral city was at Chichester in 1838, with Charles Marriott as its first principal. Wells followed two years later and other examples were Lichfield in 1857, Salisbury and Exeter in 1861, Gloucester in 1868, Lincoln in 1874, and Ely in 1876. The students at Chichester attended one of the cathedral services each day, wearing their hoods and gowns, while the college at Wells used vicars' hall for its library and the vicars' chapel as the college chapel.[105] The dean and chapter allowed the college to use a room over the west cloister as a lecture room and later they used the Lady Chapel for their services. The students, whose numbers rose from four in 1840 to over sixty in the 1890s, lived in lodgings in Vicars' Close or nearby and attended evensong daily in the cathedral. J. H. Pinder, the first principal of the college, was elected a residentiary canon in 1854. C. M. Church, who was principal between 1866 and 1880, was also a member of the chapter. Dean Plumptre said that he had been attracted to Wells in 1881 by the presence of the college, but no principal became a residentiary canon between 1880 and 1920.[106] When the theological college at Exeter was established in 1862, it was placed 'under the management of the Dean and Chapter', but it lasted only a few years.[107] When E. W. Benson was appointed chancellor of Lincoln in 1872, Bishop Christopher Wordsworth specifically asked him to undertake theological education.[108] Benson was determined to start the new college quietly,[109] but gradually lectures were established:

> The Bishop gives us (I hope) two lecture rooms, fires and a servant. I have got the Chapter to consent to a revival of the early Morning Prayers at quarter before eight in the Cathedral, so that I shall not send the men to over long Service in the morning when they ought to be reading. Monday next we all meet for the first time.[110]

An early student who later became an American dean wrote:

> How vividly one recalls the Chancellor. His quick, strong, nervous step as he enters the lecture-room, the prayer usually concluding with the Lord's Prayer in Greek, the students reciting it with him: and the strong, brilliant intellect glowing and lighting up a wondrously beautiful face, pouring forth stores of learning.[111]

The beginnings of the theological college at Ely in 1876 were similarly modest. Bishop Woodford appointed H. M. Lucock as a canon of the cathedral on the understanding that he would be principal of the new college. At first the students lived in Lucock's own house, but they were soon transferred to another house overlooking Palace Green. The foundation stone of the new college was laid in 1879 and the new buildings were opened in 1881. Woodford was keen to link the cathedral and the college and regarded the students as an important part of the cathedral congregation. They often came to evensong at the cathedral and said a shortened form of matins at 8.30 a.m. in St Catherine's Chapel. On Wednesdays and Fridays the litany was said, followed by a short address.[112] The presence of a theological college undoubtedly contributed to the devotional and worshipping life of those cathedrals that were able to develop the work of ordination training, and helped to raise standards of worship in both the cathedrals and the colleges.[113]

On the whole, the recovery of their educational role is one of the most impressive features of Victorian cathedrals. Their schools were revitalized and placed on a sound financial footing; their libraries were restored and catalogued; imaginative schemes of lectures and other forms of adult education were founded in the shadow of their walls. This aspect of their life, so strongly commended by Pusey in the face of much hostile criticism of cathedrals early in the 1800s, had become a living reality by the end of the century.

13

CATHEDRAL REFORM

❄

A s we saw in Chapter 2, the general clamour for the reform of the Church in the early 1830s included a desire that cathedrals should not be left unreformed. Many pamphlets were published, of which the most famous and influential was *A Plan of Church Reform* by Lord Henley. Seeing on the one hand 'an unchristianised land' in which 'the deepest ignorance and irreligion prevail' and, on the other, the substantial wealth of cathedrals, he desired 'to apply the superfluities on the one side of this melancholy account, to the deficiencies on the other'.[1] Henley was no lover of cathedrals. The work of canons was worthless in his opinion:

> They are connected with no poor, who look up to them as their protectors and guides; they have no sick and dying to pray with; no children to catechise; no flocks towards whom the sympathies and affections of a Pastor can be called forth.

Their work was simply 'a cold and pompous ceremonial'.[2] Henley's plan, which formed the basis of later legislation, was to transfer all the estates of bishops and chapters to a corporation that would have 'exclusive control' over them, and distribute them to poor parishes as needed. The liturgical needs of cathedrals could be adequately performed by a dean and two chaplains. Cathedral worship should be 'more parochial and therefore more devotional and spiritual in its nature'. He particularly detested cathedral music, including 'such reliques of Popery as chanting, and all anthems, solos, duets, voluntaries, etc.', and called instead for simple and easy psalmody which would be universal and congregational.[3]

Henley's proposals were so radical that they raised a storm of protest,[4] but by far the most weighty reaction came from Pusey.[5] Pusey strongly opposed the popular view that cathedrals were useless and should be abolished. He did not accept that cathedral services were cold and formal; it was, he said a question of feeling, and some people found them very devotional. Pusey saw the attraction of cathedrals, with their libraries and canonical houses, as being centres of theological training and education, though he did not see this as 'the only mode in which they might be serviceable'.[6] He was particularly concerned about the moral principles involved in seeking to redistribute cathedral property and endowments. Henley had taken the view that the public good should prevail over the intentions and wishes of long-dead private donors, but Pusey objected to this.[7] A wholesale redistribution of ecclesiastical endowments he condemned as 'national robbery'.[8]

Pusey's spirited defence of cathedrals did little to withstand the force of Henley's proposals, which were soon translated into action when his brother-in-law, Sir Robert Peel, became Prime Minister two years later. On the other hand, as we have seen, Pusey's plea for cathedrals as centres of theological education bore considerable fruit later in the century.

The proposals of the Ecclesiastical Commission in the late 1830s for the reform of cathedrals were, as we have already seen above, strenuously resisted by most chapters.[9] Their proposals were also criticized by several individuals such as Sydney Smith, William Selwyn, G. A. Selwyn, E. B. Pusey and Henry Manning.[10] But the threat to cathedrals was not without its value. As Pusey himself said:

> The body of cathedral clergy have been called to re-examine the nature of their institutions, their duties, and responsibilities, and the means of fulfilling them. While impressing upon others the importance of their office in the Church, they have probably deepened their own consciousness of it.[11]

John Merewether, Dean of Hereford, was a cathedral clergyman who was keenly aware of the faults in his own cathedral.[12] As he told Bishop Grey in 1837, 'It is impossible...not to deny the necessity for reform in this body.'[13] But there was little that even a passionate reformer like Merewether could do without the support of his chapter. From 1840 onwards cathedrals were in a state of transition as stalls were gradually suppressed when they became vacant. With smaller chapters, the work to be done had to be shared out less widely and so a growing understanding of the role and purpose of cathedrals began to evolve.

The first pressure for further external reform, however, came from a layman. A member of Parliament, Edward Horsman, told the House of Commons in 1848 that an inquiry into cathedrals should be established to see 'whether they may not be rendered more conducive to the services of the Church and the spiritual instruction of the people'.[14] Horsman was certainly critical of the present state of cathedrals at the time: 'They brought discredit upon the service of the Church, created disrespect for her ministers – they weakened her congregations and strengthened her enemies.' In the debate that followed, W. E. Gladstone stressed the important task of deans and chapters in maintaining cathedral fabrics and worship, but he felt, as did Pusey, that the promotion of learning was one of the highest functions of these institutions. Lord John Russell said in reply that the whole question required further attention on the part of the government and that further legislation about cathedrals would be introduced.[15]

A Royal Commission was eventually appointed on 10 November 1852 'to inquire into the State and Conditions of the Cathedrals and Collegiate Churches in England and Wales'.[16] The Commission recognized that cathedrals were in a transitional stage, fifty-nine canonries having been suspended between 1840 and 1854.[17] Their avowed intention was to make cathedrals 'once more, as they were originally, integral and effective parts of our Ecclesiastical organisation'.[18] The commissioners included both archbishops (J. B. Sumner and T. Musgrave), the Bishops of London (Blomfield) and Oxford (Wilberforce), Christopher Wordsworth (later Bishop of Lincoln), W. F. Hook (later Dean of Chichester), J. Jackson (later Bishop of Lincoln and of London), Canon W. Selwyn, H. Montagu Villiers (later Bishop of Carlisle and of Durham), the Marquess of Blandford, the Earl of Harrowby, Sir John Dodson, Sir John Patterson and Vice-Chancellor Page Wood.[19] Their first action was to ask each cathedral to send them a copy of their charters and statutes. They then addressed a list of questions to the cathedral chapters,

> intended to elicit detailed information on the original and the existing constitution of each Chapter, the present course of Divine Services, and the various institutions of education and charity connected with each establishment.

They also asked for suggestions from the chapters, and the opinions of the bishops, and financial statements from each chapter for a period of seven years up to the end of 1852, as well as comments from minor cathedral officers, the Ecclesiastical Commission and the universities.[20] Although Blomfield had been the dominant figure on the Ecclesiastical Commission nearly twenty years earlier, he was overshadowed this time by Canon William Selwyn.[21]

In their third report the commissioners included some definite recommendations. By a majority they were in favour of each dean and canon residing for nine months in each year. They also proposed that a permanent commission should be created for a period of ten years to draw up revised statutes for each cathedral. Believing that the daily choral services were being better performed and were becoming more widely appreciated, they recommended that cathedral choirs should be 'maintained in full strength' with additional singers on Sundays. They deprecated any permission for lay clerks to be absent from weekday services. But they also called for simpler music: a metrical psalm, in which the whole congregation could join in, was thought to be a useful component in cathedral worship. The commissioners also called for more frequent and more varied services on Sundays, with not less than two sermons each Sunday, one of which might be accompanied by short prayers and a hymn. Said services with sermons on weekdays were also recommended. Although some improvements had been made to cathedral schools, in general they were not in a flourishing state. They needed to be better endowed. The commissioners also encouraged the establishment of theological colleges at cathedrals and pressed chapters to make sure that all members of their foundations were paid a proper stipend. The fluctuating personal incomes of individual deans and canons were unfortunate, and the absence of special provisions for the maintenance of the fabric and capitular buildings was also regretted. Only men of the highest calibre should be appointed to positions in cathedrals and they ought to receive appropriate remuneration for their work, so that they might 'take the lead in works of charity in the city and diocese and to discharge the various duties of these posts with a dignified liberality'.[22] Much hard work was put into the Commission. Its reports, together with the evidence submitted to it, provide a most valuable insight into cathedrals in the mid-nineteenth century. Although it did not result in parliamentary legislation, the Commission helped to make the Church of England more aware of its cathedrals.[23]

While the Commission was sitting, there appeared two more important demands for the reform of cathedrals from men who were working in them. W. K. Hamilton was Precentor of Salisbury until he succeeded Denison as bishop of the see. In 1853 he addressed an open letter to his namesake, Dean H. P. Hamilton. He wished to make the cathedral a real centre of educational and musical life and to give the cathedral clergy, both canons and vicars choral, important pastoral duties in the city. He wanted to abolish the distinction between the two grades of clergy and allow vicars choral to hold prebendal stalls and have a place and voice in the chapter.[24] Two years later Hamilton (by this time bishop) published a pamphlet entitled *Cathedral Reform*. This included a reprint of his letter to Dean Hamilton and the dean and chapter's response to the enquiries of the cathedral commissioners, as well as two letters sent to the Commission by Bishop Denison. The new material took the form of an open letter from Bishop Hamilton to his diocese. He listed eleven principles that permeated his suggestions about cathedrals. These included: the furtherance of education; the worthy celebration of worship; the constant residence of deans and canons; the proper care of parishes in the patronage of the dean and chapter; the proper endowment of parochial cures in cathedral cities; the payment of proper stipends to cathedral employees and the abolition of fees; the restoration of the dignitaries and prebendaries to their proper functions; the association of the cathedral with areas of pastoral care; more frequent and more varied popular services; and a reformed relationship between the bishop as visitor and the cathedral body. Of these, Hamilton regarded residence and the revival of the proper functions of the dignitaries and prebendaries as being the most important.[25] Hamilton was determined to do what he could to reform cathedrals and make them 'a type and model of order, zeal, self-denial, faithfulness and charity'.[26]

The second important publication about cathedral reform at this time was written by A. C. Tait, who was then Dean of Carlisle. In an article in the *Edinburgh Review* in 1853 he pleaded against any further reduction in cathedrals and called for their revitalization as model centres of diocesan life in the fields of education, pastoral care, charity, preaching and scholarship.[27] 'The time seems to have come,' he said, 'for an effectual reform of the Cathedral Establishments of England.'[28] There was no time to be lost. Reform was inevitable and must be thorough.[29] Tait laid considerable stress on the advantages of a cathedral's responsibility for hospitality.[30] He also realized that it was important for individual members of chapters to have definite duties: one might have a cure of souls, one might be in charge of schools, another could run a theological college, while two more could combine their cathedral work with a city living and an archdeaconry. Every dean and canon should have 'a distinct sphere in which he is free to act'.[31] He also insisted on 'a marked distinction being established between the private income of the dean and canons and the money they are to spend on public purposes'. Tait felt that cathedral worship could be 'somewhat cold' and said that cathedrals should have a greater pastoral role:

> We should protest loudly against any scheme to make cathedrals mere parish churches; but we are firmly convinced that, without some parochial bond, uniting the cathedral congregation and those who minister in it, cathedrals never can be real places of devout, hearty worship.[32]

Tait even anticipated the recent Chichester Report on the Faculty Jurisdiction Measure by calling for

> some central control for the preservation of the monuments and other antiquities in cathedrals. The fabrics will probably never again be allowed to go to ruin: public opinion may secure this, but there is absolutely no guarantee for the preservation of the smaller historical or archaeological curiosities with which our cathedrals abound.[33]

By 1860 there were men like Hamilton and Tait who had had cathedral experience and who were holding high office in the Church. They recognized that there must be changes. If Parliament was unable to reform cathedrals, then the reform would have to come from within.[34]

The next discussion about the role and purpose of cathedrals began at the Church Congress at Norwich in 1865, when Harvey Goodwin gave an address on 'Cathedrals and Capitular Bodies and How to Increase Their Usefulness'. Goodwin said that cathedrals needed to have new statutes, and attacked the so-called reforms of the 1830s.[35] Four years later, Henry Alford published an article in the *Contemporary Review*.[36] Alford argued that cathedrals were in an exceptional position at the centre of diocesan life. It was right that they should not have parochial ties so that they could do their proper work fully, especially with respect to music and preaching. But they should not be independent of the bishop and be regarded as 'the private chapel of Deans and Chapters'. By nature, chapters were cautious and in many ways cathedrals were a hindrance to the work of the Church.[37] Alford did not want to alter the liturgical and musical character of cathedrals, but felt that substantial constitutional reforms were necessary. A dean and two archdeacons could easily run a cathedral, while the other clergy at his own cathedral – Canterbury – whether they were honorary canons, six preachers or minor canons, could be merged into one body and styled as canons. Alford agreed with Goodwin that cathedral statutes needed to be overhauled, and called for a new body to revise them.[38]

A few months earlier, in May 1869, the Archbishops of Canterbury and York (Tait and Thomson) had summoned a meeting of deans at Lambeth Palace 'to consider the best mode of introducing certain salutary changes in our cathedral system'. As a result of the meeting, a committee was formed to continue the discussion with the archbishops, who wrote to all deans on 29 May 1869 asking for 'a statement suggesting any change which you may consider as of great importance for the Cathedral over which you preside...'.[39] Alford's article was described as 'the substance of the writer's article to the enquiry', though in fact it was an expanded version of a letter he sent on 29 June 1869.[40] The chapter of Canterbury Cathedral informed the archbishops that they did not agree with the dean's views, but declined to express their own opinions.[41]

The archbishops' enquiry elicited from E. M. Goulburn a lengthy response which he published separately under the title *The Functions of Our Cathedrals*.[42] He believed strongly that cathedrals preserved that element in the life of the Church which emphasized that study, worship and prayer were just as important as active pastoral work. What should be reformed was not cathedrals, but the men appointed to cathedral chapters. They ought to be 'men specially qualified for the duties of *a cathedral*, gifted with the love of study, with the love of devotion...and with a contemplative turn of mind'.

Goulburn's specific suggestions for reform were more constant attendance by canons at cathedral services, an improvement in the income and status of minor canons, better payment and education for choristers, and the provision of pensions for minor canons and lay clerks. He also suggested that cathedrals should provide schools of sacred music for their dioceses. Theological colleges should be founded alongside cathedrals, and deans and canons should be obliged 'to make some contribution to theological literature once in five years'. If canons were better paid, then they should be made to reside for eight months in each year.

In the following year Goulburn published a collection of eight sermons under the title *The Principles of the Cathedral System*. He recognized the importance of cathedral music, but also stressed the value of 'sacred learning, study, devotion, retirement from the world, and the maintenance of the perpetual worship of God'.[43] Goulburn saw that the principal function of cathedrals was the regular worship of God, and that every other responsibility flowed from this central activity:

The Cathedral is a place rather where God is worshipped than where man is impressed...but do not, in a fit of indiscreet zeal, confuse or obliterate their leading idea; do not parochialize, or turn them into vast parish churches. The very core and centre of all their proceedings is not a sermon to the masses...but the daily office in the choir, solemn, effective, dignified, rendered as perfect as possible by the accessory of beautiful music, and ever striving and yearning to represent more perfectly upon earth the adoration which ceaselessly goes on in the courts of heaven.[44]

If regular worship was the principal function of cathedrals, then it followed that members of chapters should be diligent and enthusiastic in attending services.[45] For those clergy who could make use of them, cathedrals had many advantages:

The stalls in them offer a certain access to books, a certain amount of leisure for study, a certain amount of retirement from secular and parochial distractions, and above all, a life made happy, calm and solemn, by constant exercises of public devotion.[46]

Goulburn's third contribution to the debate about the reform of cathedrals was a pamphlet that he published in 1872.[47] He stressed that cathedrals were definitely improving:

The development of Cathedrals is progressing on the whole at a satisfactory rate of speed....Chester is not only exhibiting the comely proportions of its nave, but attracting vast congregations, and making itself quite a centre of spiritual activity to the city and neighbourhood.

And at Peterborough, York and Hereford there was much for which to be thankful.[48]

Some of the other replies to the archbishops' enquiry in 1869 are illuminating. Dean Close of Carlisle urged the abolition of pluralities and a stricter enforcing of residence for canons, which he called 'the two great fundamental vices of the system'. It was also important that cathedrals should be less isolated from the normal life of the Church and more closely identified with the bishop. He also called for the revision of cathedral statutes by a specially appointed commission.[49] Dean Howson of Chester said that the statutes of his cathedral emphasized its role as a place of diligent preaching, a school of sacred learning, a centre of religious education, and an opportunity for the exercise of charity. He agreed that all cathedral statutes should be revised and brought into harmony with the practice and demands of the time, and said that 'the main idea of a cathedral' was that it should be 'a diocesan institution'. Howson also urged that canonries should be severed from parochial appointments. The canons should have 'prescribed diocesan duties', with larger incomes. He wished to associate honorary canons more closely with the life of the cathedral, and desired pensions for elderly lay clerks and minor canons. Howson also added his voice to those who were already calling for a new commission.[50] Harvey Goodwin warned against treating cathedrals 'upon one uniform system', but agreed that some central authority was needed to supervise the revision of statutes. In his view, as in those of many other deans, the contant residence of canons was essential. He thought that the prebendaries of old foundation cathedrals and the honorary canons of new foundation cathedrals ought to be placed on an equal footing, particularly as regards preaching. His own preaching turns as Dean of Ely were too few, and he deemed a more flexible system to be necessary. Bishops should have a closer relationship with their cathedrals, and preach more often in them. Goodwin took a highly individual line about the revision of statutes:

> They should be rendered as simple and as open to modification as possible. The practical rules of a living active body cannot be stereotyped: and if the general principles were defined by statute, I would leave the details as much as possible to settle themselves, or rather to be settled by the chapter orders of the existing body.

He felt that cathedral schools should be separately endowed and would benefit from having lay as well as capitular governors. Any corporations of lay clerks should be dissolved and an adequate pension should be provided. Goodwin was firmly in favour of a theological college at Ely and favoured stronger links with the University of Cambridge. He did not think that cathedrals should be reduced in the way, for example, that Dean Alford had suggested.[51] Dean Boyd of Exeter made one interesting suggestion in his reply to the archbishops. He advocated the appointment of prebendaries by the chapter instead of by the bishop, as he felt that this would result in 'greater harmony of action and feeling'.[52] The Dean of Gloucester saw no reason why his chapter should not be reduced to one or two canons, provided they each resided for nine months. The capitular estates should be handed over to Queen Anne's Bounty or other commissioners, who would be responsible for paying the stipends of all members of the foundation. They should also pay the dean and chapter 'a sum sufficient to defray expense of lighting, warming, cleaning and etc., the cathedral, and keeping the precincts in order'. The patronage of the dean and chapter should be transferred to the bishop, as well as their 'rights and jurisdiction' over cathedral schools. Those to whom the capitular estates were transferred should pay the salaries of the school-masters and maintain the fabric of the cathedral and the capitular houses. The dean and chapter should be ready to undertake diocesan work at the bishop's request, and all their deeds, documents and minute books should be transferred to the diocesan registry.[53] Of all the replies to the arch-bishops, this was the one that sought to obliterate most fully the distinctive character of cathedrals.

Dean Bowers of Manchester pointed out that his cathedral was also the parish church of a very busy parish. He needed more than two minor canons to cope with the immense amount of pastoral work. As there were only four lay clerks, he clearly needed some extra singers.[54] Dean Goulburn's reply has already been mentioned, but he forwarded to the archbishops the views of three of his canons. Canon Heaviside suggested that the committee established by the archbishops should include some canons as well as deans. He felt that the stipends both of canons, minor canons and of lay clerks should be increased, and that a modernization of the statutes would be an advantage.[55] Canon Nisbet suggested smaller dioceses, and the combination of the office of dean and bishop. He also wanted an increase in the number of theological colleges attached to cathedrals. If the dean was not also bishop, he could be the head of such a college.[56] Canon Robinson, who was also master of a Cambridge college, was against any reduction in chapters, but did not make any positive suggestions. Dean Saunders of Peterborough said that cathedral statutes were scarcely known among church people in general, and this led to neglect and disobedience. They should be translated, published and sold 'boldly and publicly'. There were insufficient clergy to minister to 'the crowded congregations in which we now more and more rejoice'. The power to compel the retirement of aged, infirm and incompetent members of the foundation was also necessary.[57]

There was no corporate reply from Rochester Cathedral, but Canon Hawkins and Archdeacon Grant replied individually. Hawkins was not in favour of annexing all canonries to other positions of responsibility, and did not want to see any further theological colleges founded alongside cathedrals. Deans might become assistant bishops, which would increase their usefulness.[58] Archdeacon Grant agreed with Hawkins that deans might be given some episcopal functions, but felt more strongly than he did that canonries should be annexed to other responsibilities. He suggested that one canonry should be held by a theologian on a leasehold basis. He would teach in the theological college and 'publish in each year a treatise bearing on the theological questions of the day'. Deans and canons should be able to retire with a pension, and should be compelled to resign if found incompetent.[59]

Dean Mansel of St Paul's said that more care should be taken to find men suitable of holding cathedral appointments. The income of canons should be increased and longer periods of residence enforced, though he doubted whether the offices of canon and parish priest should be separated in all cases. Cathedral libraries should also be improved. Additional houses would be needed at those cathedrals where there was only one residentiary house. Mansel did not want chapters to be further reduced or any change made in the duties attached to them which would merge the work of a dean with that of a bishop, or a canon with that of a parish priest. The Church needed

> men competent to do service as students and divines, as well as those fitted for administrative and pastoral duties; and our cathedral preferments are the only means of making provision for clergymen of the former kind.

At St Paul's, though, three of the four canonries were held by clergymen who also held parishes in London, and it was difficult to see how this could be altered as the canonical houses were inconvenient – and one was even occupied by the cathedral choristers. Canon Gregory, he told the archbishops, disagreed with this and said that the residentiary canons of St Paul's should be given definite responsibilities in the cathedral and diocese, though this would restrict the choice of men well qualified to combine these responsibilities with their duties as residentiary canons.[60]

At York, Dean Duncombe said that there were several areas of the Minster's work where there were no adequate funds to maintain them. Neither minor canons nor lay clerks should hold their appointments indefinitely, and choristers should be apprenticed to trades and other professions. Some of the canons had made more novel suggestions, such as increasing the number of canons to twelve but demanding only one month's residence per year from each of them, or merging the office of the dean with either that of the precentor or of the archdeacon of the city churches. On the whole, however, Duncombe felt that any changes required 'calm and mature consideration' and more careful discussion.[61]

It will be seen from these replies that while some deans stressed the need for strengthening cathedrals in various ways, others wanted to make them fit more naturally into the life of the diocese. There were several deans who did not bother to reply, but these suggestions do represent a useful cross-section of opinion about the reform of cathedrals among men who were actually working in them.

Two other influential articles appeared at about this time; they were written by B. F. Westcott and E. W. Benson. In 1869 Westcott published an article on cathedrals in *Macmillan's Magazine*.[62] He blamed the current difficulties in cathedrals on the 1840 Act, which, 'based upon the popular conception of cathedral bodies at the time, first crippled their resources and then destroyed or obscured their special work'. He listed the statutes that governed the life of each cathedral and drew from them 'four great principles':

> Two contain the theory of cathedral life; two contain the theory of cathedral work. The life is framed on the basis of *systematic devotion* and *corporate action*: the work is regulated by the requirements of *theological study* and *religious education*.[63]

He argued that further information about the purpose of cathedrals could be gleaned from the injunctions issued at the beginning of the reign of Elizabeth I, which he examined in some detail.

Not long after Westcott's article appeared, E. W. Benson published an article in the *Quarterly Review*.[64] He gave a detailed account of Lincoln and its constitution, based on a study of medieval sources. He went on to stress the role that cathedrals should fulfil as colleges of sacred learning and as centres for theological education. He believed that the course of theological training should include some pastoral experience in groups attached to parishes. Benson revised and expanded this article when he published a fuller study of the role of cathedrals seven years later.[65]

Following the 1869 meeting of deans at Lambeth Palace, a further meeting was held in March 1872 between representatives of the bishops and the deans and representative canons of several cathedrals. Tait later said:

> The object of calling that meeting was to see whether it was or was not desirable that some immediate steps should be taken for improving the cathedral system throughout the country, and whether it was or was not desirable that the legislature should be invoked in order to assist in this good cause.[66]

The committee considered revising statutes to enable those who worked in cathedrals to do so more freely. Other subjects discussed included the widening of the chapters of cathedrals along the model of York, special preachers, and a Royal Commission on Cathedral Statutes; but in the end it was decided that more time should elapse during which each cathedral might consider carefully what improvements could be made in its own life and system.[67] Three resolutions were adopted: first, that Tait should contact the Prime Minister and discuss whether a parliamentary Bill should be introduced to give chapters greater freedom in fulfilling their duties; secondly, that the dean and chapter of each cathedral should be asked to give answers within two weeks to various questions sent to them by the archbishop. These answers would be considered by the archbishops and bishops. Thirdly, it was agreed that a committee should frame the questions to be asked.[68]

The first question was about cathedral statutes. Was there any way of revising them, or should a Bill be introduced in Parliament to deal with this problem? This could either be by a general Bill, 'covering all the cathedrals and stating in detail the improvements thought desirable', or by a Bill that enabled a special commission to deal with each cathedral separately. The second question was about the relationship of the bishop to the chapter; how should it be defined? Thirdly, the archbishop enquired about the diocesan duties of members of chapters. Should these be increased and, if so, how? If there were a theological college, how would it be financed and staffed? Another question related to sermons and services in cathedrals and asked who organized them. The remaining questions included the following queries: should the number of canons in a cathedral be increased or diminished? Should they keep a longer period of residence and was it desirable to restrict the kind of post that could be combined with a canonry? How should canons be appointed? Was it desirable to establish or recognize the greater chapter? Should members of the greater chapter have a say in such matters as statutes, services, expenditure and patronage? If there were a college of minor canons, vicars choral or lay clerks, should this be modified in any way? Finally, the chapters were asked if there were any special hindrances to their work.[69]

Further research might elicit why these enquiries, conducted with some urgency, did not result in any action. The answer probably lies in the political situation at the time. Gladstone was anxious to discourage contentious items of ecclesiastical business being discussed in Parliament. There was a great deal of ecclesiastical legislation before Parliament in 1872 (including the Deans and Canons Resignation Act) and further moves requiring parliamentary consent were best left in abeyance.[70]

The other outstanding event of 1872 was the publication of a book entitled *Essays on Cathedrals by various writers*, edited by J. S. Howson, Dean of Chester. The contributors included Harvey Goodwin, B. F. Westcott, E. A. Freeman, A. J. B. Beresford Hope, E. W. Benson and Sir Frederick Gore Ouseley. There were also contributions by Canon J. P. Norris of Bristol, from Dean MacDonnell of Cashel on Irish cathedrals, by Canon Massingberd of Lincoln, by Canon J. J. S. Perowne on Welsh cathedrals, by Canon T. C. Durham on cathedral schools and by Canon E. Venables on cathedral architecture. Howson, in his introduction, stressed 'the immense opportunities possessed by the Cathedral system' and the urgent need 'to bring new life out of old forms'.[71] He was well aware of the calls for a public inquiry into cathedrals, and believed that his collection of essays would provide some useful and well-considered background information. Cathedrals were 'rapidly becoming the most popular parts of the system of the Church of England' and this volume of essays is clear evidence of the widespread interest being taken in them at the time.[72]

Harvey Goodwin's essay looked back over his time as Dean of Ely and stressed the importance of daily worship as the principal work of cathedrals. They were the natural setting for large diocesan services such as ordinations and choral festivals, or even for such occasions as diocesan conferences. Many cathedrals had also begun to have successful and popular Sunday evening services. Although cathedrals were places of quiet contemplation and theological study, the members of chapters should be occupied in diocesan work. Cathedral statutes needed to be reviewed and reformed. Much had been achieved in the previous twenty years, but there were boundless opportunities for further work.[73]

J. P. Norris reviewed the work of cathedral canons and stressed the need for them to involve themselves in the task of training ordination candidates. Canons had a fivefold ministry: the daily worship of God; diligent preaching, studying and lecturing; ministering to the poor and giving advice to the bishop as the members of his council. But it was in training ordination candidates that cathedrals would most easily prove their usefulness.[74] Beresford Hope's essay on 'Cathedrals in their Missionary Aspect' contains some valuable suggestions from a well-known layman. He was in favour of more cathedrals and pointed to the growing number of new cathedrals in Australia and the United States. He did not believe that cathedrals should be further mutilated, but wanted 'a more mixed and elastic constitution' for them.[75] He was critical of some of the contemporary suggestions for their reform:

> The chapter cut down to two members besides the Dean in order to concentrate residence, is evidently undermanned. The rotary chapter of four or six members, is weak on the side of co-operation. The chapter of learned theologians, or distinguished veterans, does not help the diocesan work, while the chapter of active officials may be destitute of the erudition, stability and devotion which such a body ought to foster.[76]

Recognizing that each cathedral had different needs, he suggested that additional canons or prebendaries might be appointed. These additional canonries should be of two classes, one permanent and held in conjunction with specified offices, and the other personal and unlimited in numbers. The offices might be diocesan posts, and the headship of educational institutions, or the incumbencies of important parishes in the diocese which had a quasi-cathedral role in their own areas. Itinerant missionaries, supplementing the work of the parochial clergy in large towns and scattered rural areas, might also be attached to the cathedral. It ought to be as easy to create additional canonries as it was to create new parishes. In old foundation cathedrals they could be grafted on to existing prebends, and in Chichester Cathedral there was an example of this, since the prebends of Highleigh and Wittering were still endowed and attached to the mastership of the prebendal school and to the divinity lectureship.[77] All canons, whether residentiary, non-residentiary or supernumerary, should be allowed to come into residence at will. The endowment of supernumerary canonries might well be made by private munificence. Beresford Hope was in favour of closer contacts between cathedrals and dioceses. Diocesan synods, informal conferences of clergy and laity, confirmations, ordinations, choir festivals, and special services for harvest and other times, would all find a natural setting in a cathedral. Large voluntary choirs might become a feature of them. If such a policy were adopted, cathedrals would become the centres of missionary work.[78]

B. F. Westcott contributed a thoughtful essay on 'Cathedral Foundations in Relation to Religious Thought'.[79] Basing his remarks on his earlier article in *Macmillan's Magazine*, Westcott said that because cathedral clergy were relieved of much direct pastoral work, they should give more time to theological study and the training of candidates for ordination. The diocesan clergy should also be involved and the cathedral might be a useful means of encouraging them in their studies. There should be gatherings of clergy for study and for devotion and opportunities for personal spiritual training. Westcott also believed that cathedral clergy should set an example in 'a simpler and more frugal mode of living'. When they entertained clergy from the diocese there should be no 'display or lavish expense', but the social advantages of such meetings would be considerable. In conclusion, Westcott added a note about the staffing, courses and cost of such a scheme, which would repay careful investigation by many cathedrals even today.

E. A. Freeman's contribution was an essay on 'The Cathedral Churches of the Old Foundation'.[80] This was largely an historical study, but Freeman believed that some reforms were necessary and wished that all cathedrals might follow the York pattern where the non-residentiary canons were considerably involved in the affairs of the cathedral. Indeed, he said that this was 'an essential feature of all cathedral reform'. He also believed that periods of residence should be increased from three to nine months or more: 'Residentiaries must really reside at the Cathedral; it must be their home, and they must hold no office which involves residence elsewhere.' The dignitaries should be merged with the residentiary canons and also do work as diocesan officers, though he believed that archdeacons should not also be residentiary canons and that there should be some residentiary canons who were not also dignitaries. Freeman believed that colleges of vicars choral should be turned into theological colleges, the lay vicars forming the choir during their years of training.

Canon Massingberd's essay was on the subject of 'Cathedral Reform – Past, Present, Future'.[81] Massingberd regretted much that had been swept away through over-hasty legislation, but admitted that much progress had been made in several cathedrals during the preceding forty years. He wanted residentiary canons to be chosen from the prebendaries of the same cathedral – which might well lead to a higher calibre of prebendaries

– and for them to be given definite duties. Massingberd also wanted a closer relationship between bishops and cathedrals and more definite arrangements made for the pastoral care of lesser members of cathedral foundations. He did not want any further legislation concerning cathedrals; such changes as were necessary could be introduced by the making of a canon. He was not wholly in favour of abolishing pluralities, since he believed that canons who were also parish priests could still do useful work in both these offices, provided that their parish was within the diocese. The peculiar jurisdiction of deans in cathedral cities should be revived. On the whole, Massingberd's essay was unimaginative and shallow, and contributed little to the continuing debate about the role and function of cathedrals.

Sir Frederick Ouseley had founded St Michael's College, Tenbury, in 1856 as a specialist choir school, and was therefore well qualified to write about 'The Education of Choristers in Cathedrals'.[82] Too often, he said,

> the Choristers have been chosen from the very lowest rank of society, badly schooled, badly cared for in morals and in religion, snubbed, despised, slighted, and eventually sent forth into the world with no adequate provision for their maintenance.[83]

Their education was an important responsibility for the dean and chapter and he believed that the choristers' school should effectively become the nucleus of a general school.[84] Ouseley believed that choristers' education should include musical, physical, intellectual, moral and religious training. They should learn to play an instrument, and the choristers' school should be, musically speaking, 'a model and a rallying point for the whole Diocese'. Their physical well-being should be carefully superintended with the help of an experienced matron, and they should be given a good classical, mathematical and liberal education. They should not be exposed to moral danger, either from the careless talk of young lay clerks or from the unwholesome atmosphere of public dinners where they sometimes sang. Their religious instruction should not be left to chance and they should be taught to value highly their part in the services of the cathedral and not to behave with irreverence, as was too often the case with lay clerks. Ouseley deprecated the rehearsal of music in choir-stalls rather than in a practice-room: 'It is a very fruitful source of irreverence, and engenders a cold and perfunctory habit of performance most injurious to all who are brought within its scope.'[85]

Day-boy choristers were liable to particular dangers. If they were the children of poor parents, they might regard their place in the choir from a too mercenary angle. In going to and from home through the streets and lanes of the city a chorister might encounter 'vicious and immoral sights and sounds most defiling to a boy's mind'. Even his home life might undermine the influence of the cathedral.[86] It would be much better if he could board with a good and responsible master. A solemn ceremony of admission to the choir was valuable, and vestry prayers before and after services were also beneficial in creating a quiet and devout atmosphere. Fuss and disturbance during the actual services should be avoided, and permission to be absent from services given only rarely. The demands made upon a chorister by the cathedral should not be allowed to interfere with his school lessons, but with care and a little flexibility on both sides it should be possible for a boy to combine school-work and choir-work. Ouseley concluded his essay by sketching an ideal picture of a musical boy who becomes a chorister at his local cathedral, where he is well looked after and educated. The atmosphere of the cathedral makes a profound impression on him, and he begins to think about ordination. He obtains his degree at university, studies theology, and eventually is ordained to a minor canonry in his old cathedral. Ouseley realized that education was much in the public mind at the time (the Endowed Schools Act of 1869 and Forster's Education Act of 1870 are still regarded as important landmarks) and said that the work of Maria Hackett needed to be consolidated.

E. W. Benson contributed a scholarly and substantial essay on 'The Relation of the Chapter to the Bishop'.[87] He traced the development of chapters and their distinctive life from the time of Chrodegang in the eighth century, and concluded that the essential feature of a chapter was 'the right of aiding the bishop's work'. A bishop should consult his chapter and visit it. Several actions of the bishop in theory required the consent of his chapter and they inherited many of his responsibilities during a vacancy in the see. There were specific occasions when the bishop and his chapter exercised a *vis simultanea*. A good example of this was in the appointment of prebendaries – the bishop had the power of nomination and the chapter that of installation. In recent years the chapter and the bishop had drifted apart, but it would not be too difficult for them to resume their former relationship. Convocations, synods and conferences of clergy had been revived and chapters should also recover their ancient conciliar role.

Canon T. C. Durham's essay on 'Cathedral Schools' argued that education had been part of the work of cathedrals from the earliest times. In England the cathedrals of the old and new foundations had different kinds of schools. A fresh opportunity to revive moribund cathedral grammar schools was now available under the provisions of the 1869 Endowed Schools Act, but in order to compete with the great public schools (especially in preparing boys for Oxford and Cambridge) the value of their scholarships needed to be increased. But there were good grounds for optimism.[88]

The final essay, by Canon E. Venables, was on 'The Architecture of Cathedral Churches of England considered historically'. He gave a detailed account of several medieval cathedrals and showed how in recent years they had been used for a multitude of services and occasions of all kinds. He ended on a very positive note by prophesying that 'A new and glorious future is now opening before our Cathedrals'.[89] Howson's volume of essays was timely, as it provided a substantial collection of informed and authoritative views on a subject that was in the forefront of attention and debate.

At the Church Congress in 1872 Dean Lake of Durham read a paper on 'Suggested Improvements in Cathedrals'. He stressed that he was not calling for any 'violent' changes, but called for increased residence, a closer obedience to the statutes, more theological colleges at cathedrals, and improved relations between the cathedral and the diocese. He believed that in old foundation cathedrals the precentor and chancellor should be always resident. The third canon should be an archdeacon and the fourth might be a canon missioner. As far as theological colleges were concerned, he thought that these were of value to cathedrals as they ensured 'the constant presence of men devoted to learning'. He was not in favour of giving too much power to the general or greater chapter either as a bishop's council, or in relation to the day-to-day affairs of the cathedral. The careful and reverent conduct of cathedral worship and the opportunity that cathedrals gave for effective preaching were very important, while their statutes, if conscientiously followed, would enable the ideal of cathedral life and work to be achieved. Lake earnestly desired that each of those who worked in cathedrals 'may feel that he has a real work to do in his Cathedral', and looked forward to seeing these principles put into practice.[90]

Soon after Benson became Bishop of Truro in 1877, he made a further contribution to the study of cathedrals and their reform in a book that he published in 1878.[91] Much of this was a recapitulation of his earlier publications, but he added further material because he felt that 'cathedral life and cathedral work were never more needed or more yearned after'.[92] Benson believed that they had an important role in the field of ordination training and that 'the foremost place in the functions of the Cathedral must be assigned to it as a home and hearth of theological learning'.[93] Cathedrals could also have a useful role in promoting the mission of the Church.[94]

Another way in which cathedrals could be of use was in arranging lectures for and ministering to the young men who worked in the offices, shops and warehouses of cathedral cities.[95] The training of readers and deaconesses could also be centred on cathedrals; the libraries and music of cathedrals were of great value; and the inspection of diocesan schools and training in hospital work could be based in them.[96] Benson was quite clear that canons should be obliged to keep proper terms of residence; they should be given distinct responsibilities in the cathedral and should resign their parishes. Suspended canonries should be restored and the cathedrals would be the homes for 'colleges of families'.[97] The concluding section of this book is his own address to the first diocesan conference at Truro about 'the Cathedral Body'.[98]

In the early 1870s, then, there was a clear desire among many deans and canons for a thorough overhaul of what they called 'the cathedral system', and it was felt that the best means of achieving this would be by means of a new Commission. In 1876 Tait asked Disraeli to appoint one, but he declined to do so until 1879. Tait described this in his diary as

> an important event. It is now 25 years since I wrote my article on Cathedral Reform, and perhaps I shall live to see my plans carried out. This Cathedral movement has excited a desire in me for some further work before I die.[99]

Harvey Goodwin, by now Bishop of Carlisle, introduced a Bill to reform cathedral statutes in the House of Lords in 1879. This gave Tait the opportunity to repeat his suggestion of a Commission.[100] Besides Tait and Goodwin, the commissioners appointed included Lord Cranbrook and Lord Coleridge, Sir Henry Mather Jackson, Mr C. Dalrymple and Mr A. J. B. Beresford Hope. Later on, Lord Blachford and Sir Walter Charles James were added.[101] Beresford Hope told the Leicester Church Congress in 1880 that the purpose of the Commission was to improve and develop cathedrals:

> We wish to take up and develop the Cathedrals of the Old Foundation, borrowing the best features of the new; and to improve the new Cathedrals, borrowing the best features of the old. We wish to preserve the best features both of the Old and of the New Foundations and yet leave them their distinctive characteristics as Old and New foundations.[102]

In 1882 Lord Cranbrook told the House of Lords that the first decision of the commissioners was to send out questionnaires to bishops, deans and chapters and everyone connected with cathedrals, asking what changes they thought should be made to their statutes. Then the dean and one canon from each cathedral attended a meeting of the Commission to amplify the points made in the written answers. The Commission's recommendations for each cathedral were sent to the bishop and the dean and chapter concerned. The Commission proposed presenting their report on each cathedral to the House of Lords and to the Privy Council, and the new statutes would be laid on the table of the House of Lords.[103] Altogether the Commission held 128 meetings in six years,[104] and published three reports, which included all the replies they had received from the various cathedrals. The commissioners' final report was largely the work of Harvey Goodwin. He tried many times to introduce in the House of Lords legislation based on the work of the Commission, but without success.[105]

While this Commission was meeting, the Convocation of Canterbury established a committee to consider the question of cathedral reform under the chairmanship of Canon Gregory. The committee recommended that the cathedral chapters would be more useful if individual members could be influential throughout the diocese, and form a kind of diocesan chapter. The cathedral should be a model to the churches of the diocese. Its services should present the worship of the Church of England 'in its most winning aspect', and should be characterized by reverence and devotion. If the canons of cathedrals were really expert in the fields of divine worship, sacred learning and church finance, they might do much good work for the diocese as a whole. For example:

> The Precentor should be, not merely to the Cathedral staff, but to the whole Diocese, a director and counsellor in all matters connected with choral worship – organizing a system of choir-training and seeing to the circulation of good Church music...few, if any, could be found more eligible for preferment to the Precentor's stall than one who had for some years ably fulfilled the duties of succentor.

In the same way, one of the canons should give lectures to theological students, and the cathedral treasurer might also act as the diocesan secretary. The director of education should also be linked to the cathedral as a non-residentiary canon. The committee did not want all cathedrals to be identical, and stressed that at least one canon in each cathedral should be exempt from diocesan work.[106]

It is unfortunate that the last picture of cathedral reform in the nineteenth century should be of the unsuccessful efforts of Harvey Goodwin to initiate legislation based upon the proposals of the 1879–85 Cathedrals Commission, for few men of his time had done more to encourage the contribution that cathedrals could make to the life of the Church. The constitutional reforms that this Commission advocated had to wait some fifty years before they were achieved in the 1930s, and the story was taken a stage further by the Cathedrals Measure of 1963. Yet constitutional reforms, however desirable, were not absolutely essential. As St Paul's demonstrated between 1870 and 1890 and Worcester in the 1880s, it was certainly possible for cathedrals to become very active and very successful without far-reaching reforms. As the work increased and new standards of excellence were set, so men's expectations of cathedrals rose. The enforcement of residence and the abolition of pluralities ceased to be pressing problems simply because the volume of cathedral work increased. Many cathedrals had been reformed from within, and so by the end of the century there was little demand for further action. This improvement was certainly apparent to those who were involved in it. When William Done, the organist of Worcester Cathedral, received the robes of his Lambeth Doctorate in Music in 1894, he contrasted the 'miserably cold and dirty' cathedral of the 1830s with the atmosphere sixty years later, where the worship was among the best in England.[107] By 1900 cathedral reform was a less pressing matter because so much had been achieved in this respect during the century.[108]

14

THEN AND NOW

❀

By the closing years of the nineteenth century, English cathedral life was both more varied and more purposeful than ever before. It had acquired a distinctive social flavour, based on the shared experience of several households serving a building that was increasingly well used and well ordered. The petty fascination of the social scene of a cathedral close in the early nineteenth century, as described by Sydney Smith in 1838,[1] had been replaced by a society that, at Winchester for example, could include such notable religious personalities as Mary Sumner, the founder of the Mothers' Union, and Josephine Butler, well known for her work among prostitutes.[2]

When men looked back on what had been achieved during the century, they found much to praise. A leading article in the *Guardian* in 1891 spoke of the 'wonderfully increased strength' of cathedrals and their 'really noble work for the Church of the nation'.[3] Worcester Cathedral, as late as 1855, was said to be vast and cold in appearance, with a broken and uneven nave floor.[4] By 1886 it had improved out of all recognition. The worship was said to be 'most reverent and thoroughly earnest', the preaching 'powerful', and the fabric 'in such excellent order that it stands as a model to all Cathedral churches'.[5] The *Guardian* in 1874 said that cathedrals were displaying 'vitality and power', while Dean Plumptre, in a sermon at Wells Cathedral on Christmas Day 1881, spoke of 'The Ideal of Cathedral Life', based on a loyal and friendly staff and frequent services. Dean Gott's first sermon at Worcester displayed similar high ideals of what a cathedral meant to the life of the Church.[6]

Were these claims justified? Was it true that the cathedrals of England had demonstrated by 1900 that they were a vital and essential element in the life of the Church? Can one identify distinctive opportunities and problems in the life and work of nineteenth-century cathedrals that have a bearing on contemporary issues a hundred years later? To what extent were nineteenth-century deans and chapters able to keep a proper balance between their various responsibilities?

Some cathedrals in the later nineteenth century certainly showed signs of increasing vitality. St Paul's and Worcester are the obvious examples,[7] but others, such as Norwich under Dean Lefroy,[8] were also making a considerable local impression. Most cathedrals were in a much better structural state than they had been earlier in the century,[9] and their worship was offered with greater care and dignity. More frequent communion services, including full choral eucharists, were provided.[10] Their choirs had often been transformed and there was a new respect for outstanding organists of the calibre of Stainer and Sinclair.[11] Brilliant preachers, such as H. P. Liddon at St Paul's or Creighton and Knox-Little at Worcester, had drawn thousands to cathedrals.[12] Enterprising experiments in mission and education had been undertaken[13] and popular Sunday evening services in some cathedrals helped forge new links with many who rarely attended cathedral services.[14]

The cathedrals of the south and west of England shared in this general progress, but to differing degrees. At Bristol a new nave had been completed,[15] but the music, which was in the hands of George Riseley, was unsatisfactory.[16] On the other hand, Canon Percival and Dean Pigou had shown that there was a ready need for popular Sunday evening services.[17] Chichester Cathedral had recovered from the collapse of its spire,[18] but Dean Burgon's unhappy reign[19] was followed by further difficult times under Deans Pigou and Randall.[20] At Exeter, after the controversy about the reredos, efforts were made by Bishop Bickersteth to make the cathedral less of a backwater, but these were only partially successful.[21] Gloucester Cathedral was hampered by poverty as a result of the Agricultural Depression,[22] but new links with the city had been developed through the enterprising free concerts that attracted many of the poorer classes.[23] The great restoration of Hereford Cathedral was followed by an era of liturgical progress as a result of pressure from Ouseley and Jebb,[24] but the choir continued to be in a weak state until George Sinclair's appointment as organist in 1889.[25] Salisbury Cathedral also emerged from its mid-century restoration to enjoy a period of prestige. Bishops Moberly and Wordsworth, Dean Boyle and various other learned clergy were highly regarded, but here too the Agricultural Depression impoverished the cathedral.[26] Wells enjoyed a golden era under Dean Plumptre,[27] while at Winchester the restoration of the Great Screen[28] and the far-sighted appointment of a committee to advise the dean and chapter about alterations to the cathedral were substantial achievements, which were not diminished by the indifferent state of the choir under Dr Arnold.[29] None of these cathedrals, however, could point to such substantial achievements as Worcester, where the great restoration of the cathedral in the middle years of the century had been followed by an era of rapid improvement in all departments of the cathedral's life.[30]

When we look at the way in which English cathedral life changed and developed during the nineteenth century, we can see several features that are relevant to cathedrals today. The most recent general survey of the contemporary life and work of cathedrals was conducted in 1989 by Canon Owen Conway.[31] Other recent contributions include an essay by Alan Webster and the late Jack Churchill and a university sermon preached at Oxford in May 1991 by the Dean of Winchester, Trevor Beeson.[32] Most of the issues facing cathedrals in the late twentieth century are identified in these studies. Many of them are recurring problems that were either familiar in the nineteenth century, or may be better understood in the light of developments at that time.

The relationship between cathedrals and their bishops and dioceses was emphasized by Conway, who called for more changes in this area than either Churchill, Webster or Beeson.[33] Yet many of these matters were recognized and emphasized during the nineteenth century. Episcopal visitations became more frequent and several, such as those of Bishop Browne or Bishop Davidson at Winchester, or Bishop Wordsworth at Salisbury, proved to be notable events in the development of the life and work of the cathedral.[34] W. K. Hamilton was right to call for regular visitations.[35] If properly conducted, such occasions can make a real and important contribution to the solving of problems and the clarifying of ideas. Some nineteenth-century bishops recognized the value of sharing in the daily life of their cathedrals,[36] but Bishop Hampden's desire for more power at Hereford is a warning that the delicate relationship between a bishop and his chapter can easily be misunderstood.[37] Large-scale confirmations, and indeed ordinations, were not uncommon in Victorian cathedrals, and successful experiments were made in holding diocesan synods and other meetings at them.[38] Perhaps the most obvious way in which cathedrals promoted parish life in the nineteenth century was the widespread popularity of festivals of parish choirs.[39] Many Victorian cathedral clergy actively helped parishes by preaching, lecturing and missionary work, including such notable men as Westcott, Lefroy, Gott, Butler, Creighton and Benson.[40] Benson was keen to involve cathedral clergy in diocesan work,[41] but divided loyalties inevitably cause tensions, and the autonomy of a dean and chapter, linked to, but not controlled by, the synodical system, is a freedom that needs to be carefully guarded. There is a continuing debate about this question. Bishop David Say, in his visitation of Rochester Cathedral in 1984, looked forward to 'a synod that is concerned with the ministry, mission and money of the Cathedral as well as of the parishes',[42] but the dean and chapter, in their formal response, argued for a variety of church life and warned that the relationship of cathedrals to the synodical structure should be one of partnership rather than integration.[43] The revival of more frequent meetings of the greater or general chapter in the nineteenth century was an important achievement, but much greater use could be made of them today.[44]

All four of those who have recently studied the contemporary problems of cathedrals have drawn attention to a range of issues relating to the staffing and administration of cathedrals. These include the establishment of a highly skilled administrative structure in which committed lay people play a full part, thus enabling cathedral clergy (who may not necessarily have much business experience) to have more time for theological study. Great care is needed in making appointments to cathedral posts, at all levels, and in working out the relationship between individual and corporate responsibilities. Many of these matters have financial implications and require great skill in public relations.[45]

The lack of time for proper study was felt to be a problem by many cathedral clergy in the nineteenth century, including Harvey Goodwin, A. C. Tait and E. M. Goulburn.[46] On the other hand, the degree to which an individual canon should have autonomy in his own department, and whether chapters had the necessary financial and business skills for their work, was rarely seen as a difficulty in the nineteenth century. An unwarranted appropriation of power by individuals no doubt lies behind some of the complaints against Dean Duncombe and Canon Swainson.[47] But a united chapter, as at St Paul's in the 1870s and 1880s, was a great strength, and here Gregory's financial and administrative ability was crucial.[48] Earlier W. K. Hamilton had defended the competence of chapters in financial matters.[49] Good lay advice from the chapter clerk and others was vital, but despite the support of Archbishop Benson the possibility remains that the financial difficulties experienced by so many cathedrals in the closing decades of the last century were partly caused by the ineptness of their chapters and the Ecclesiastical Commissioners.[50] This point cannot be emphasized too strongly. Many cathedrals today have had to make substantial appeals for funds to carry out vital and often urgent repairs, to strengthen their endowments, and to extend their mission. The root cause of this financial problem lies in the bad bargains made by so many chapters in the mid-nineteenth century over the commutation of their estates, a situation made much worse by the Agricultural Depression. Attempts to alleviate the problem since then – notably the extra funds provided by the Church Commissioners under the terms of the Cathedrals Measure 1963 and the very recent promise of help by the Department of the Environment – have not tackled its root cause. Too much money was taken away from cathedrals in the last century, and that is why they have too little money today.

There is a growing demand for canonries to be held on a leasehold basis. In the nineteenth century there were some canons whose longevity was a real impediment to the development of their cathedrals. At Worcester the deafness of Canon Benson and the feeble condition of Canon Seymour could not have provided a greater contrast to their more energetic successors.[51] There is, however, a great danger that a solution to one problem may well cause other greater problems in another direction. Conway's call for more 'interchange' between cathedral and parochial posts may be a disguised version of the 'diocesanization' of cathedrals that others have criticized.[52] The highly specialized and often intricate responsibilities of cathedrals need *more* relevant experience in their administration, not less. One solution might be to encourage greater mobility between chapters, so that experience gained as a canon of one cathedral could be used profitably elsewhere. It should also be possible to regard a vocation to collegiate life as equally valid as a vocation to monastic life or the parochial ministry. This was certainly the view of E. W. Benson[53] and should be seriously considered at the present time. It is sad, as Conway points out, that there are so few full-time minor canonries in cathedrals today. When one considers the distinguished contribution to the life of their cathedrals that men like Sparrow Simpson of St Paul's,[54] or J. B. Dykes at Durham,[55] or F. T. Havergal at Hereford[56] made in the last century, one cannot but regret that such useful opportunities for cathedral work are now so limited.

The rigid hierarchical and social distinctions observed by Canon Wray at Manchester[57] should have no place in a modern cathedral, where a partnership between the dean and chapter and other clergy and laity is vital. The opportunities opening out for cathedrals today are leading to substantial lay involvement (both paid and unpaid) in their work. The financial resources for this are often inadequate and the administrative pressures are considerable. During the nineteenth century there were several chapter clerks, such as Ralph Barnes of Exeter, Sir George Raper at Chichester, George Whitcombe of Gloucester and J. H. Knight at Hereford, who made an outstanding contribution to the administration of the cathedrals they served.[58] Victorian chapters certainly recognized the value of competent administration, and the work of the joint restoration committee at Worcester in the 1860s and the advisory committee at Winchester in the 1880s are early examples of partnerships being developed between chapters and laity.[59]

Conway makes several suggestions relating to the ecumenical and missionary work of cathedrals today.[60] In the nineteenth century religious differences were so marked that there was little incentive or opportunity for cathedrals to engage in ecumenical work, though Dean Peel of Worcester was on friendly terms with the local Roman Catholic priest. The great growth in the number of visitors to cathedrals in the last thirty years has led to many new initiatives and developments.[61] Although Victorian cathedrals were engaged in this work to a much lesser extent, it is clear that chapters were certainly aware of some of the problems and opportunities that it involved.[62] They were also involved in developing links with many kinds of society in the city and beyond, though the recent educational work of cathedrals with groups of children is largely new.[63]

Cathedral worship has changed very considerably in the last 150 years. It is certainly more eucharistic. Conway's plea for more eucharists each day and the retention of choral matins on Sundays needs to be understood in the light of the development of cathedral worship in the nineteenth century.[64] The interior reordering of cathedrals to adapt them to new fashions in liturgy was as controversial in the nineteenth century as it may be today, as one can see from the records of the refurnishing of Worcester Cathedral.[65] Visiting choirs are a new phenomenon in cathedral life, but the voluntary choirs established at several nineteenth-century cathedrals show how their chapters were sensitive to changing liturgical, musical and pastoral opportunities.[66] Regular cathedral congregations are generally larger and often more vigorous now than they were a hundred years ago.[67] The influence of parish church cathedrals – as well as Ripon, St Albans and Truro, which have substantial parochial responsibilities, not to mention the implications of synodical government – is causing many chapters to consider the role of their congregations in their daily life. Both pastoral and constitutional questions are involved.[68] Although there is a great need, here as elsewhere, to guard against cathedrals being over-parochialized, since one of their great strengths is the way they differ from the priorities and character of parish churches, the value of 'colleges of families' in cathedral life was stressed by E. W. Benson and the implications of his insight need to be developed.[69]

The perceptive reader may well identify other contemporary issues that could be illuminated by a consideration of some of the material contained in preceding chapters of this book. The pressures facing deans and chapters and the cathedral councils of parish church cathedrals today inevitably raise questions of priority. This is a perpetual problem and one of the great dangers is that chapters will try to tackle too many problems at the same time. If we look again at the six cathedrals whose nineteenth-century restorations were discussed above[70] (Ely, Hereford, Worcester, Chichester, Bristol and St Paul's), we can see that their physical restoration was linked to their revival as religious centres. In some cases – notably Hereford and Worcester – the restoration of the fabric preceded the burgeoning of their work in other directions. At Ely, however, there was an overlap between the two, while the rebuilding of the spire at Chichester and the completion of the nave at Bristol can best be seen as expressions of confidence in the opportunities that were developing for cathedrals. At St Paul's, the desire to embellish the interior of the cathedral went hand in hand with the cathedral's famous revival in the closing decades of the century. The nineteenth century has been described as an age of improvement, and all aspects of cathedral life were involved in this process. Certainly the *Guardian* could point in 1891 to a wide range of cathedral activities where progress could be discerned:

Vast and on the whole satisfactory restorations have been effected; knowledge of our great historic minsters has been put, through the energy of Deans and Canons, within reach of a multitude of visitors; the life of the Close and the Chapter has helped to quicken as well as been quickened by the life of the diocese, and the cathedral has become a *rendezvous* and centre for the various diocesan societies and agencies. Notwithstanding the increased calls of active clerical life, an atmosphere of study and literary culture has lingered round the capitular bodies, while series of lectures on the history of the cathedrals and of the diocese have been well promoted or assisted by Deans and Canons in many cathedral cities, and the intellectual life of the cathedral *entourage* has been raised and stimulated.[71]

The revitalization of English cathedrals was one of the most impressive achievements of the Victorian Church, as romantic in its way as the Gothic Revival or the Oxford Movement, and as heroic as the great efforts that were made to advance the mission of the Church in the industrial slums of so many growing cities. To reform an institution with a long history is often harder than to make important new initiatives. That such notable progress was made in so many cathedrals in the closing decades of the nineteenth century is a remarkable tribute both to the untiring energy of their chapters and staff, and also to their willingness to learn from one another. Such progress was founded on a growing perception of the distinctive role that cathedrals might have in the life of the Church; and the sustained enthusiasm that, for example, surrounded the building of Truro Cathedral shows that this perception was widely appreciated.

As the twentieth century draws to a close, we can look back on the life of Victorian cathedrals with a new understanding of their achievements. To evaluate the problems and opportunities of cathedrals today needs a further examination of their continuing development during this century, but the nineteenth century gives us crucial evidence with which to begin. We can take our leave of Barchester with affection and admiration.

NOTES

❈

INTRODUCTION

1 *CCR* 1872, p. 225.
2 The best account of these is by K. Edwards, *The English Secular Cathedrals in the Middle Ages* (2nd edn, Manchester 1967).
3 cf. H. Bradshaw and C. Wordsworth, *Statutes of Lincoln Cathedral* (London 1892), vol. I, p. 38.
4 cf. W. H. Frere, *Visitation Articles and Injunctions of the Period of the Reformation* (London 1910), vol. I, *passim*.
5 cf. Bradshaw and Wordsworth, vol. I, p. 38.
6 cf. H. E. Reynolds, *Wells Cathedral: Its Foundation, Constitutional History and Statutes* (Leeds 1881), and J. Jebb and H. W. Phillott, *The Statutes of the Cathedral Church of Hereford* (Hereford 1882).
7 For a good account of one of them, cf. R. B. Dobson, *Durham Priory, 1400–1450* (Cambridge 1973). Two further medieval cathedral monasteries that did not survive the Reformation were Bath and Coventry. Their position was unusual as there was already a secular cathedral, at Wells and Lichfield respectively, in each diocese. For a recent survey, cf. R. B. Dobson, 'English Monastic Cathedrals in the Fifteenth Century', *Transactions of the Royal Historical Society*, sixth series, vol. I (1991), pp. 151–172.
8 31 Henry VIII, c.9.
9 1 Mar., sess 3, c.9.
10 cf. 1 and 2 Phil. and Mar., c.8.s.18.
11 6 Anne, c.75.
12 R. Phillimore, *The Ecclesiastical Law of the Church of England* (2nd edn., ed. by W. G. F. Phillimore, London 1895), vol. I, pp. 146–50. The fullest account of new foundation cathedrals is in J. M. Falkner and A. H. Thompson, *The Statutes of the Cathedral Church of Durham* (Surtees Society, vol. cxliii, 1929), pp. xxvi–lxvi; cf. D. M. Owen, 'The Early Years of Cathedrals of the New Foundation', *Friends of Peterborough Cathedral Annual Report*, 1983, pp. 2–4, and the same author's article, 'From Monastic House to Cathedral Chapter: the experiences at Ely, Norwich and Peterborough', in D. Marcombe and C. S. Knighton, eds, *Close Encounters: English Cathedrals and Society since 1540* (Nottingham 1991), pp. 4–15; cf. also S. E. Lehmberg, *The Reformation of Cathedrals* (Princeton 1988).
13 G. L. Prestige, *St Paul's in its Glory, 1831–1911* (London 1955), pp. 9–10.
14 As well as more general works such as Edwards, op.cit., studies of individual corporations of vicars choral include the following: A. R. Maddison, *A Short Account of the Vicars Choral, Poor Clerks, Organists and Choristers of Lincoln Cathedral* (London 1878); J. F. Chanter, *The Custos and College of the Vicars Choral of the Choir of the Cathedral Church of St.Peter, Exeter* (Exeter 1933); N. Orme, *The Minor Clergy of Exeter Cathedral, 1300–1548* (Exeter 1980); F. Harrison, *Life in a Mediaeval College* (London 1952); P. L. S. Barrett, *The College of Vicars Choral at Hereford Cathedral* (Hereford 1980).

15 For cathedrals in the reign of the later Tudors, cf. Lehmberg, pp. 101–306; cf. also D. Marcombe, 'Cathedrals and Protestantism: the search for a new identity, 1540–1660' in Marcombe and Knighton, pp. 43–61.

16 cf. C. Cross, '"Dens of Loitering Lubbers": Protestant Protest against Cathedral Foundations, 1540–1660', in D. Baker, ed., 'Schism, Heresy and Religious Protest', *Studies in Church History*, vol. ix (Cambridge 1972).

17 cf. P. le Huray, *Music and the Reformation in England 1549–1660* (London 1967).

18 For Laud's work at Gloucester, cf. S. Eward, *No Fine but a Glass of Wine: Cathedral Life at Gloucester in Stuart Times* (Wilton 1985). For Laud's visitation, cf. *The Works of William Laud* (Oxford 1853), vol. v, and F. Bussby, *Winchester Cathedral* (Southampton 1980), p. 123. Details of Laud's visitation of Salisbury are given in D. H. Robertson, *Sarum Close* (London 1938), pp. 185–94 and K. Edwards, 'The Cathedral of Salisbury, 1075–1950', *VCH Wiltshire*, vol. iii, 1956, p. 190; for his visitation of St Paul's, cf. W. R. Matthews and W. M. Atkins, *A History of St Paul's Cathedral* (London 1957), pp. 164–6; cf. also C. Cross, 'Conflict and Confrontation: The York Dean and Chapter and the Corporation in the 1630s', in Marcombe and Knighton, pp. 62–71.

19 F. R. Goodman, *The Diary of John Young* (London 1928).

20 L. G. Wickham Legg, ed. 'A relation of a short survey of the western counties, made by a lieutenant of the military company in Norwich in 1635', *Camden Miscellany*, vol. xvi (London 1936).

21 cf. Bussby, pp. 134, 137; D. I. Hill, *Christ's Glorious Church* (London 1976), pp. 60–2; L. S. Colchester, ed., *Wells Cathedral: A History* (Shepton Mallet 1982), p. 159.

22 G. Cobb, *English Cathedrals: The Forgotten Centuries* (London 1980), p. 10.

23 cf. I. M. Green, *The Re-establishment of the Church of England, 1660–1663* (Oxford 1978), pp. 61–79, 99–116.

24 There are useful articles by P. E. Morgan, 'Hereford Cathedral in the 1680s', *Three Choirs Festival Programme 1985*, pp. 23–7, and p. Mussett, 'Norwich Cathedral under Dean Prideaux, 1702–24', in Marcombe and Knighton, pp. 88–114.

25 cf. Bussby, pp. 153–4; J. H. Srawley, *Michael Honywood, Dean of Lincoln (1660–81)* (Lincoln 1950); N. Linnell, 'Michael Honywood and Lincoln Cathedral Library', in Marcombe and Knighton, pp. 72–87.

26 cf. L. P. Curtis, *Chichester Towers* (New Haven and London 1966).

27 cf. Chapter 13.

28 cf. Chapter 7, pp. 129–30, 144.

29 T. S. Gowland, 'Ripon Minster and its Precincts', *Yorkshire Archaeological Journal*, no.35, 1943, pp. 270f.; cf. Walcott, *Traditions*, p. 96.

30 PP 1854, xxv, p. 943; PP 1884, xxii, pp. 293, 304.

31 PP 1884–5, xxi, p. 303; J. M. Elvy, *Recollections of the Cathedral and Parish Church of Manchester* (Manchester 1913), pp. 26–9, 43; A. Boutflower, *Personal Reminiscences of Manchester Cathedral 1854–1912* (Leighton Buzzard 1913), p. 22 (cf.Chapter 4, p. 36); J. C. Cox, 'The Treatment of our Cathedral Churches in the Victorian Age', *Archaeological Journal*, vol. liv, 1897, p. 269; *Guardian*, 1884, p. 603; 1885, p. 518; 1895, p. 593.

32 cf. Chapter 10, pp. 242–3.

33 *Guardian*, 1879, p. 1117.

34 P. Ferriday, *Lord Grimthorpe, 1816–1905* (London 1957), pp. 81, 130; P. V. Coghlan, 'Cathedral Worship in the Church of England 1815–1914' (Leicester University M. Phil. thesis 1984), p. 151; *Guardian*, 1900, p. 1065. No residentiary canons were appointed until 1936 (Coghlan, p. 169); cf. also W. O. Chadwick, 'The Victorian Diocese of St. Albans', in R. A. K. Runcie, ed., *Cathedral and City: St Albans Ancient and Modern* (London 1977).

35 H. M. Brown, *A Century for Cornwall – The Diocese of Truro 1877–1977* (Truro 1976)

p. 1; A. B. Donaldson, *The Bishopric of Truro* (London 1902), p. 53; cf. 39 & 40 Vict., c.54 and 41 & 42 Vict., c.44.

36 Brown, pp. 26, 30; Donaldson, p. 112.

37 A. Quiney, *John Loughborough Pearson* (London 1979), pp. 133–4, 143.

38 ibid., p. 143; Brown, p. 31; *Guardian*, 1880, pp. 684–6; *The Times*, 21 May 1880. For Benson's own account, cf. A. C. Benson, *The Life of Edward White Benson, sometime Archbishop of Canterbury* (London 1899), vol. I, pp. 453f.

39 Brown, p. 32.

40 T. F. Barham, *The Creation of a Cathedral* (Falmouth 1976), p. 20. For an impression of this building, cf. *Trefoil*, p. 266.

41 50 & 51 Vict., c.12.

42 Donaldson, pp. 47, 104–8, 110; cf.Bradshaw and Wordsworth, vol. II, pp. 748f., and G. W. Prothero, *A Memoir of Henry Bradshaw* (London 1888), pp. 282, 345. For the statutes, cf. PP 1883, xxi, pp. 47–78. For the earlier regulations that Benson issued in 1878, cf. PP 1883, xxi, pp. 82–5.

43 Donaldson, pp. 104, 111, 273; cf. Phillimore, vol. I, p. 189. The honorary canons met three times a year and acted as the bishop's council (Donaldson, pp. 237–8).

44 Donaldson, pp. 272–85.

45 ibid., pp. 238f., 245f.; Barham, pp. 30–1; Quiney, p. 145.

46 Donaldson, pp. 344, 349. For Bishop Wilkinson's efforts on behalf of Truro Cathedral, cf. A. J. Mason, *Memoir of George Howard Wilkinson* (London 1909), vol. II, pp. 119–38.

47 Donaldson, pp. 126–7; Barham, p. 56.

48 Barham, p. 62; Donaldson, p. 222. For liturgical details of the new cathedral, cf. Chapter 7, pp. 138, 141.

49 Donaldson, pp. 60, 235–6.

50 Quiney, p. 148. For a recent brief survey of Truro, cf. H. M. Brown, *The Story of Truro Cathedral* (Penryn 1991).

51 W. B. Forwood, *The Liverpool Cathedral: The Story of Its Foundation, 1885–1914* (Liverpool 1925), p. 21; J. Riley, *Tomorrow's Cathedral* (London 1978), pp. 20–1; V. E. Cotton, *Liverpool Cathedral: The Official Handbook of the Cathedral Committee* (11th edn, Liverpool 1951), pp. 10–11; Phillimore, vol. I, p. 189.

52 L. Creighton, *Life and Letters of Mandell Creighton* (London 1904), vol. I, p. 240.

53 47 & 48 Vict., c.33; Phillimore, vol. I, p. 189; *Guardian*, 1900, p. 1065.

54 R. M. Beaumont, *The Chapter of Southwell Minster* (Nottingham 1956), p. 33; cf. *Cathedral Church of the Blessed Virgin Mary of Southwell: Regulations* (Nottingham 1887).

55 cf. W. O. Chadwick, *The Victorian Church* (London 1970), vol. II, p. 389, quoting *CCR* 1885, p. 250; cf. also L. Ridding, *George Ridding, Schoolmaster and Bishop* (London 1908), pp. 161–7.

56 *Guardian*, 1888, p. 941.

57 ibid., 1898, p. 81.

CHAPTER 1: *English Cathedral Life in the Early Nineteenth Century*

1 W. Cobbett , *Rural Rides* (Penguin edn, ed. G. Woodcock, London 1967), p. 253; cf. F. Bussby, *Winchester Cathedral 1079–1979* (Southampton 1979), pp. 214–5. Bussby has checked this description with the attendance register and finds that the dean was present at the service, together with three prebendaries and four lay vicars. It is not known how many choristers were there, but there were only six in the choir at the time.

2 Cobbett, p. 323. For a similar anonymous account of a visit to Chichester in 1816, cf. T. J. McCann, *Restricted Grandeur: Impressions of Chichester 1586–1948* (Chichester 1974), p. 35: 'While our Breakfast at Chichester was preparing we walked over the

Cathedral. Service had just commenced and as we walked thro' the Cloisters the solemn sound of the Organ had an awful effect and increased the monastic impression upon the mind – save these Cloisters we observed little to admire of the interior no monuments adorned the Walls which looked damp and unwholesome. To walk from Church at the commencement of Prayers is not a very decorous Step but Hunger and pleasure pleaded...'

3 Report dated 24 November 1834, *Winchester Cathedral Chronicle*, 1800–1865, pp. 2–21; cf. P. L. S. Barrett, 'Winchester Cathedral in the Nineteenth Century', in D. Marcombe and C. S. Knighton, eds, *Close Encounters: English Cathedrals and Society since 1540* (Nottingham 1991), p. 115.

4 F. E. Gretton, *Memory's Hark-back through Half a Century, 1808–1858* (London 1889), pp. 4–5. For a description of Wells in the early nineteenth century, cf. L. S. Colchester, 'The Victorian Restoration of Wells Cathedral (Barnard Ms.)', *TAMS*, n.s., vol. iv, 1956, pp. 79–80.

5 CCF 3189, quoted in P. L. S. Barrett, 'Hereford Cathedral in the Nineteenth Century', *FHCAR*, 1986, p. 13.

6 cf. G. Cobb, *English Cathedrals: The Forgotten Centuries* (London 1980), pp. 144–7, for an account of Wyatt's work at Lichfield.

7 ibid., pp. 111–13. For Wyatt's work at Durham, cf. R. A. Cordingley, 'Cathedral Innovations: James Wyatt, Architect at Durham Cathedral 1795–1797', *TAMS*, n.s., vol. iii, 1955, pp. 31–55.

8 Cobb, pp. 76–7.

9 The origin for this early said service may be found in the Royal Injunctions for Cathedrals, 1547 (W. H. Frere and W. Kennedy, *Visitation Articles and Injunctions of the Period of the Reformation* (London 1910), vol. II. p. 138). Further details are given in the Royal Injunctions for Salisbury Cathedral, 1559 (Frere, vol. III, p. 33; cf. the injunctions for Wells, and for Exeter in ibid., pp. 36, 41); for evidence of similar services at Rochester in 1565, cf. vol. III pp. 148, 152; for St Paul's in 1598, cf. W. P. M. Kennedy, *Elizabethan Episcopal Administration* (London 1924), vol. III, p. 305.

10 e.g. Worc. C. Mss., Sacrist's Accounts, 24 August 1800, pp. 324–6.

11 ibid., 1827, pp. 428–30.

12 *Gentleman's Magazine*, vol. lxxii, pt 1, 1802, p. 33, quoted in P. C. Moore, 'The Organisation and Development of Cathedral Worship in England, with special reference to choral services, from the Reformation to the nineteenth century' (Oxford D. Phil. thesis 1954), p. 122, fn.4.

13 cf. Bussby, pp. 198–9, and G. H. Blore, *Thomas Rennell, Dean of Winchester 1805–1840* (Winchester 1952).

14 Quoted in A. Bell, *Sydney Smith* (Oxford 1980), pp. 145–6.

15 ibid., p. 162, quoting L. Strachey and R. Fulford, eds, *The Greville Memoirs* (Cambridge 1938), vol. iii, p. 113.

16 ibid., pp. 162–3, quoting G. S. Hillard, *Life, Letters and Journals of George Ticknor* (1876), vol. I, p. 414.

17 Bussby, p. 206.

18 W. J. Rees, *A Memoir of the Life and Character of the late John Napleton*, pp. 43–4 (Ms. in HCL).

19 ABVC Hereford, 26 November 1816.

20 Quoted in Moore, p. 271. The dean and chapter of Winchester gave £50 to the Waterloo sufferers (ABDC Winchester, 23 June 1815).

21 ABDC Worcester, 21 November 1801; cf. ibid., 23 November 1811, 6 January 1812.

22 ABDC Worcester, 4 May 1801.

23 ABDC Worcester, 19 August 1803, 20 November 1816.

24 ABDC Winchester, 19 January 1809.

25 ABDC Salisbury, 20 February 1810.

26 ABDC Winchester, 8 February 1833.

27 E. B. Pusey, *Remarks on the Prospective and Past Benefits of Cathedral Institutions in the promotion of Sound Religious Knowledge occasioned by Lord Henley's Plan for their Abolition* (London 1833).

28 ibid., p. 91.

29 Bussby, pp. 197–8.

30 ibid., pp. 200, 204. Another attractive Winchester prebendary at this time was Philip Williams: cf. P. L. S. Barrett 'Philip Williams – The Acceptable Face of Pluralism', *Winchester Cathedral Record*, no.57, 1988, pp. 13–26; and Marcombe and Knighton, pp. 116–17.

31 W. O. Chadwick, *The Victorian Church* (London 1966), vol.I, pp. 39, 560–1; cf. C. J. Stranks, *This Sumptuous Church* (London 1973), p. 89, and J. Greig, ed., *The Farington Diary* (London 1922–8), vol. VII, 119.

32 C. E. Woodruff and W. Danks, *Memorials of the Cathedral and Priory of Christ in Canterbury* (London 1912), p. 354.

33 M. Hackett, *Correspondence, Legal Proceedings and Evidences respecting the Ancient Collegiate School attached to St Paul's Cathedral* (3rd edn, London 1832), p. 42.

34 ABDC Worcester, 15 February 1806, 4 April 1808.

35 M. E. C. Walcott, 'Cathedral Reform', in O. Shipley, ed., *The Church and the World* (London 1866) p. 78. In fact the Durham chapter was well endowed with bishops: the deanery was occupied by the Bishop of St David's, while the Bishops of Chester, Exeter and Bristol held three of the twelve stalls (PP 1835, xxii, pp. 68–9). Bishop Phillpotts of Exeter was a canon of Durham from 1831 until his death nearly forty years later (G. C. B. Davies, *Henry Phillpotts* (London 1954), p. 96). The chapter of Lincoln Cathedral included the deans of Peterborough and Rochester (PP 1835, xxii, pp. 80–1) while that of St Paul's Cathedral included Dean Gaisford of Christ Church, Oxford, and Dean Rennell of Winchester, and the Bishop of Carlisle. The deanery was held by the Bishop of Llandaff (ibid., pp. 86–8).

36 E. B. Pusey, 'The Royal and Parliamentary Ecclesiastical Commissions', *British Critic*, vol. 23, April 1838, p. 493.

37 W. K. L. Clarke, *Chichester Cathedral in the Nineteenth Century* (Chichester Papers no.14, Chichester 1959), pp. 6–7; ABDC Chichester, 2 May 1806, 2 May 1821, 2 May 1822.

38 ABDC Worcester, 13 April 1828, 23 June 1829; cf. G. Van Loo, *A Victorian Parson* (Upton-on-Severn 1989).

39 Chadwick, *York*, pp. 282, 288–9; A. S. Leak, 'Conflict and reform at York Minster in the Nineteenth Century' (Oxford B. D. thesis 1988), p. 200.

40 R. J. Fletcher, *A History of Bristol Cathedral* (London 1932), p. 56.

41 M. H. Fitzgerald, *The Story of Bristol Cathedral* (London 1936), pp. 57–8.

42 D. King, 'Winchester Cathedral under Deans Rennell and Garnier', *Winchester Cathedral Chronicle*, 1972; cf. also Pretyman to James Lampard, 3 November 1832 (Win.CA, Ecclesiastical Commissioners' Box).

43 Woodruff and Danks, p. 354.

44 Greenhalgh, *Wells*, p. 181.

45 R. B. Beckett, *John Constable and the Fishers* (London 1952), pp. 20, 42. He was later made an archdeacon.

46 cf. C. K. F. Brown, *A History of the English Clergy 1800–1900* (London 1953), p. 24, fn.41.

47 King, 'Winchester Cathedral under Deans Rennell and Garnier', 1972; cf. also W. Gibson, 'Continuity and Change: The Cathedral Chapter at Winchester in the Nineteenth Century', *Proceedings of the Hampshire Field Club and Archaeological Society*, vol. 45, November 1989, pp. 167–72.

48 Greenhalgh, *Wells*, p. 181.

49 J. W. F. Hill, *Victorian Lincoln* (London 1974), pp. 256–7.

50 Moore, p. 355, quoting a letter of Maria Hackett, 22 November 1853. At Lincoln a footman stood behind the chair of each of his dinner guests (A. C. Benson, *The Life of Edward White Benson, Sometime Archbishop of Canterbury* (London 1899), vol.I, p. 365).

51 J. W. F. Hill, *Georgian Lincoln* (Cambridge 1966), p. 301, fn.4, quoting B. Ferrey, *Recollections of A. N. Welby Pugin and his father, Augustus Pugin* (London 1861), p. 88; cf. Benson, vol.I, p. 365. Another canon known for the speed with which he departed from services in the cathedral was Moses Toghill, Precentor of Chichester in the early years of the century. He was so addicted to fox-hunting that when choir and clergy turned east to recite the creed he would slip away for the meet (W. D. Peckham, 'The Vicars Choral of Chichester Cathedral', *Sussex Archaeological Collections*, vol. 78, no.xxxvii, 1937, p. 154.)

52 Woodruff and Danks, p. 355.

53 R. T. Holtby, 'Carlisle Cathedral Library and Records' (*Transactions of the Cumberland and Westmorland Antiquarian and Archaeological Society*, vol. 66, 1966, p. 206).

54 Beckett, p. 109; cf. also p. 42.

55 J. T. Fowler, *Life and Letters of John Bacchus Dykes* (London 1897), pp. 45–6, 48.

56 M. R. Craze, *King's School, Worcester (1541–1971)* (Worcester 1972), pp. 183–4, quoting the issue of 3 October 1833.

57 Gretton, p. 3.

58 ABDC Worcester, 11 January, 28 May, 23 June, 12 September, 19–25 November 1800.

59 B. Trueman, 'The Administration of Hereford Cathedral 1776–1786', *FHCAR*, 1976, p. 36.

60 ABDC Hereford, 11 November 1830.

61 cf. Chapter 9, p. 217.

62 e.g. ABDC Worcester, 23 June and 3 February 1801.

63 Worcester Cathedral Treasurer's Accounts, 1808, 1820. The audit expenses at Worcester in 1800 were £106 2s 11d (ibid., 1800). In 1808 the dean and chapter of Winchester resolved to allow the receiver an extra £10 'on account of the increased expenses of the entertainments at the audit' (ABDC Winchester, 25 November 1808). The dinners given at the midsummer chapter at Gloucester in 1800 cost £9 2s 0d (Gloucester Cathedral Treasurer's Accounts, 1786–1910, pp. 383f. (Gloucester CRO, D 936 A/1/9). In 1808 the dean and chapter of Gloucester, 'for the purpose of encouraging due attendance at the Audits', set aside the sum of £56 for the midsummer audit and £80 for the one in November, to be divided among the canons who attended (ABDC Gloucester, 30 November 1808).

64 *Winchester Cathedral Chronicle*, 1800–65, pp. 62f. Dean Luxmoore of Gloucester used to send potted lampreys from Gloucester to Canterbury (where he had been a prebendary) for the audit dinner (Woodruff and Danks, p. 356). This custom of three separate feasts with three different menus on special occasions such as the wedding of a landowner was a well-known contemporary feature in landed society (cf. F. M. L. Thompson, *English Landed Society in the Nineteenth Century* (London 1963), p. 77). Some form of entertainment was customary; Lord Verulam had glee singers performing at his audit dinner in 1824 (ibid., p. 906). For a secular audit dinner later in the century, cf. G. L. Mingay, *Rural Life in Victorian England* (London 1977), pp. 142–3.

65 ABDC Winchester, 2 February 1815, 25 November 1818; P. M. J. Crook, 'Fifty Years of Choral Misrule: George Chard and the Choristers of Winchester Cathedral', *Winchester Cathedral Record*, no.56, 1987, p. 34.

66 cf. B. Matthews, *The Music of Winchester Cathedral* (London 1974), p. 21; cf. also

ibid., p. 19, and P. M. J. Crook, 'Half-a-century of Choral Indiscipline: George Chard and his choir, 1802–1849', *Southern Cathedrals Festival Programme*, 1981, pp. 11–13, for more information on Chard.

67 G. L. Prestige, *St Paul's in its Glory, 1831–1911* (London 1955), p. 4; D. Scott, *The Music of St Paul's Cathedral* (London 1972), p. 25; Moore, pp. 317–20 (quoted in P. L. S. Barrett, 'English Cathedral Choirs in the Nineteenth Century', *JEH*, vol.xxv, no.1, January 1974, p. 19). Recent articles on Maria Hackett include B. M. Taylor, 'Angel Voices ever Singing', *The Lady*, vol.clxxxx, no.4911, 26 July 1979, pp. 132, 150; D. Gedge, 'Maria Hackett – The Choristers' Friend', *The World of Church Music*, 1983, pp. 41–9; D. Gedge, 'The Redoubtable Miss Hackett', *Musical Opinion*, vol. 108, no.1297, December 1985, pp. 441–6 and vol. 109, no.1298, January 1986, pp. 11–14; cf. D. H. Robertson, *Sarum Close* (London 1938), pp. 278–80, and P. L. Smith, ed., 'The Recollections of John Harding of his time as a chorister at Salisbury Cathedral, 1826–1832', *The Hatcher Review*, no.10, Summer 1980, pp. 3–22. For Attwood, cf. W. J. Gatens, *Victorian Cathedral Music in Theory and Practice* (Cambridge 1986), pp. 84–102.

68 Moore, p. 276, quoting Hackett, p. 37.

69 J. E. West, *Cathedral Organists Past and Present* (London 1899), p. 73.

70 Hill, *Georgian Lincoln*, p. 301.

CHAPTER 2 *Church Reform and Cathedrals*

1 cf. R. A. Soloway, *Prelates and People* (London 1969), pp. 3–4; G. F. A. Best, *Temporal Pillars* (Cambridge 1964), pp. 147–51, 199–200.

2 43 George III, c.84; 53 George III, c.149; 58 George III, c.45; cf. M. H. Port, *Six Hundred New Churches* (London 1961).

3 For the political background, cf. Lord Mahon and E. Cardwell, eds, *Memoirs of Sir Robert Peel* (London 1856–7), vol.I, *passim*; C. S. Parker, ed., *Sir Robert Peel* (London 1899), vol.II, pp. 92–3, 104–6, 166–70; M. Brock, *The Great Reform Act* (London 1973), pp. 51–5, 86–130.

4 cf. M. H. Fitzgerald, *The Story of Bristol Cathedral* (London 1936), p. 61. Sydney Smith commented on the rampant anti-clericalism at this time: 'It was not safe for a clergyman to appear in the streets. I bought a blue coat and did not despair in time of looking like a layman' (quoted in Best, p. 272). Bishop Marsh of Peterborough said in his charge of July 1831: 'If we except the period which preceded the Church's overthrow in the time of Charles I, there never was a time when the clergy were assailed with so much calumny and so much violence as they are at present' (quoted in W. L. Mathieson, *English Church Reform, 1815–1840* (London 1923), p. 45).

5 For the political developments leading up to the passing of the 1832 Reform Act, cf. W. O. Chadwick, *The Victorian Church* (London 1966), vol.I, pp. 24–32; Parker, vol.II, pp. 173f.; G. M. Trevelyan, *British History in the Nineteenth Century and After (1782–1919)* (London 1937), pp. 214–39; Brock, pp. 131–313; and D. C. Moore, *The Politics of Deference* (Hassocks 1976), pp. 137–242.

6 *The Times*, 17 November 1832, quoted in Chadwick, vol.I, p. 35.

7 ibid., p. 47.

8 The dean and chapter of Durham saw the storm coming and used some of their vast wealth to found a new university at Durham. 'It appears to be morally certain,' wrote a prebendary of Durham in 1831, 'that as soon as the Reform Bill is disposed of, an attack will be made on deans and chapters and as certain that Durham will be the first object. It has occurred to us that it will be prudent, if possible, to ward off the blow and that no plan is so likely to take as making the public partakers of our income by annexing an establishment of enlarged education to our college.... We regard this as a premium to be paid to ensure the remainder' (E. Hughes, 'The

Bishops and Reform, 1831–3: Some Fresh Correspondence', *EHR*, vol.lvi, 1941, p. 461).

9 Best, p. 277.

10 O. J. Brose, *Church and Parliament* (Stanford, USA 1959), pp. 123–4; cf. also Best, pp. 283–8; Mathieson, pp. 68–9.

11 Peel, *Memoirs*, vol.II, pp. 33–5; cf. Parker, vol.II, pp. 263–5.

12 Quoted in Chadwick, vol.I, p. 102; longer quotation in Best, pp. 296–7; full text in Peel, *Memoirs*, vol.II, p. 58f.

13 Best, p. 296; cf. also pp. 334f.; cf. Peel, *Memoirs*, vol.II, pp. 69–72.

14 Parker, p. 276.

15 A. Blomfield, *A Memoir of Charles James Blomfield* (London 1863), vol.II, pp. 154–5, quoted in Brose, p. 125 and Mathieson, p. 171.

16 Brose, pp. 125–6:'Strictly speaking, the Ecclesiastical Duties and Revenues Commissioners and the Ecclesiastical Commissioners were different things. But since their membership was identical, and the latter form adopted simply to give effect to the recommendations made in the former, the Ecclesiastical Commissioners are most sensibly to be thought of as dating (in fact if not in form) from 1835 and Peel's first ministry than from 1836 and Melbourne's second' (Best, p. 298; cf. also Mathieson, pp. 129f.).

17 Peel's own views are set out in his letter to Lord Harrowby on 12 January 1835; cf. Peel, *Memoirs*, vol.II, pp. 72–5.

18 Chadwick, vol.I, p. 106. For a more caustic comment, cf. Best, p. 298. For a recent discussion of the foundation of the Ecclesiastical Commissioners, cf. W. O. Chadwick, *Church and Historical Endowment in the Victorian Age* (London 1986).

19 Best, p. 300; Blomfield, p. 167.

20 Brose, p. 217. There is a useful summary of all five reports in Best, pp. 302–5.

21 Brose, p. 130.

22 Best, p. 304.

23 ibid., p. 331.

24 ibid.

25 PP 1836, xxxvi, p. 20.

26 6 & 7 William IV, c.77. For details, cf. Best, pp. 306–7.

27 1 & 2 Vict., c.106.

28 3 & 4 Vict., c.113.

29 *Communications addressed to His Majesty's Commissioners appointed to consider the state of the Established Church in England and Wales.... Communications made to the same Commissioners from Cathedrals and Collegiate Churches in England and Wales, and from their several Chapters, Dignitaries, Members and Officers* (PP 1837, xli, p. 37, summarised by C. K. F. Brown, *A History of the English Clergy, 1800–1900* (London 1953), pp. 55–60).

30 ibid., p. 44.

31 ibid., p. 44. This view was shared by the dean and chapter of Carlisle, who said they were 'well aware that with that limited number it is very difficult, and often impracticable, to secure the constant attendance of one of the body at daily prayer, more especially when sickness or old age may happen to prevent individuals from fulfilling their own wishes in that respect' (ibid., p. 47). The same point was made by the dean and chapter of Ely (ibid., p. 54).

32 ibid., p. 45.

33 ibid., pp. 44–5; cf. ABDC Bristol, 23 June 1837.

34 ibid., pp. 48–9.

35 ibid., p. 49.

36 Quoted in ibid., p. 57.

37 PP 1837, xli, pp. 54–5.

38 ibid., pp. 56–7.
39 ibid., p. 58, quoted in Brown, pp. 57–8.
40 ibid., p. 57, quoted in Brown, p. 57; cf. also G. Pellew, *A Letter to Sir Robert Peel on the Means of Rendering Cathedral Churches Most Conducive to the Efficiency of the Established Church* (London 1837), p. 21.
41 PP 1837 xli, p. 62; cf. Brown, p. 58, and P. L. S. Barrett, in D. Marcombe and C. S. Knighton, eds, *Close Encounters: English Cathedrals and Society since 1540* (Nottingham 1991), p. 20.
42 PP 1837 xli, p. 82; cf. Brown, p. 59.
43 Quoted in Brown, p. 59. There was concern about the patronage proposals at Salisbury. The dean and chapter deplored 'any such attempt to deprive them of chartered rights which they have enjoyed in their corporate capacity since the time of the conquest to be unjust as it is uncalled for' (ABDC Salisbury, 6 April 1836).
44 CCF 3189.
45 cf. Mathieson, p. 140; E. B. Pusey, *Form of Petition against the Disposition of Cathedral Properties in the Fourth Report* (Oxford 1836); H. P. Liddon, *Life of Edward Bouverie Pusey* (London 1893), vol.I, pp. 396–8.
46 ABDC Salisbury, 6 July 1836, 4 April 1838. Bristol also sent two canons (ABDC Bristol, 14 July 1836).
47 ibid., 7 January 1837.
48 J. H. Spry, *Some Observations on the Tendency of a Measure for the Future Regulation of Cathedral and Collegiate Bodies* (London 1838), pp. 37–8.
49 ABDC Hereford, 22 February 1838. Mr Knight Bruce and Mr Hope appeared before the House of Lords on behalf of the chapters on 23 and 24 July 1840 (*British Critic*, vol. 29, January 1841, pp. 114f.; cf. ibid., April 1838, pp. 508–9). The dean and chapter of Winchester contributed £38 to Dr Spry's Cathedral account as their proportion of the expenses incurred by 'the committee for watching over the interests of the chapters during the progress of the late bills relating to Ecclesiastical Duties and Revenues' (ABDC Winchester, 25 November 1840). There are several letters from Spry in Norfolk CRO (Dean Pellew's letters, nos.116f.).
50 S. Smith, *First Letter to Archdeacon Singleton* (London 1837), p. 8.
51 Quoted in P. J. Welch, 'Contemporary Views on the Proposals for the Alienation of Capitular Property in England (1832–40)', *JEH*, vol. V, 1954, p. 186.
52 ibid.
53 ibid., p. 187.
54 cf. Best, p. 315.
55 W. Selwyn, *An Attempt to Investigate the True Principles of Cathedral Reform* (London 1839).
56 G. A. Selwyn, *Are Cathedral Institutions Useless?* (London and Eton 1838), p. 2. Another who wrote to Gladstone in a similar vein was J. W. Blakesley, Dean of Lincoln (cf. Welch, p. 187).
57 G. A. Selwyn, p. 15.
58 ibid., p. 84.
59 ibid., p. 103.
60 'The Royal and Parliamentary Ecclesiastical Commissions', *British Critic*, vol. 46, April 1838. The author was Pusey, according to Liddon.
61 ibid., p. 472.
62 ibid., p. 476: 'No one member of a cathedral was examined, heard or listened to.'
63 ibid., p. 476.
64 ibid., p. 477.
65 ibid., p. 478.
66 A. J. B. Beresford Hope, 'Cathedral Reform', *Christian Remembrancer*, vol. xxix, no.55, 1855, p. 341. Bishop Denison of Salisbury made a similar comment in his

Charge of 1848: 'The changes then made were not measures of reform, properly so called. They were directed merely to the abstraction from those bodies of a portion of their revenues to be employed on other purposes which were deemed to be of greater utility: but they called forth in them no new powers of usefulness, or effected any adaptation of their resources to the altered state of the Church' (cf. L. W. Cowie, 'The Church of England since 1837', *VCH Wiltshire*, vol.III, 1956, p. 65).

67 H. E. Manning, *The Principle of the Ecclesiastical Commission Examined* (London 1838), and his *The Preservation of Unendowed Canonries, a Letter* (London 1840).

68 Manning, *The Principle of the Ecclesiastical Commission Examined*, p. 7.

69 ibid., p. 9.

70 ibid., p. 31; cf. D. Newsome, *The Parting of Friends* (London 1966), pp. 214–15, and Brose, pp. 143–5. Others strongly opposed to the Ecclesiastical Commissioners and their plans included C. R. Sumner, Bishop of Winchester, and Henry Phillpotts, Bishop of Exeter. For Sumner's views, cf. Best, pp. 315–16; for Phillpotts' opinions, cf. ibid., pp. 313–14 and G. C. B. Davies, *Henry Phillpotts, Bishop of Exeter, 1778–1869* (London 1954), pp. 155–6. Richard Bagot, Bishop of Oxford, did not hide his feelings in his Charge of 1838: 'In the appointment of the Board of Ecclesiastical Commissioners we have witnessed the creation of a power as irresponsible as it is gigantic – an *imperium in imperio* which, before long, must supersede all other authority in the Church, and whose decrees are issued in such a manner as to render expostulation and remonstrance unavailing.... I take this solemn occasion of recording my protest against both the Commission and its proceedings. I disapprove the Commission as utterly unconstitutional in its *permanency*, in the *extent* of its *powers*, and in the obstacles which it throws in the way of fair and open discussion.' As to the commissioners' plans for cathedrals, he said: 'my settled conviction [is] that while those edifices themselves, many of them the beauty and the glory of the country, must eventually fall to ruin and decay through the inadequacy of the funds now left to support the necessary expenditure of repairs, the Established Church generally will receive no proportionate benefits from the alienation of Cathedral property' (R. Bagot, *A Charge Delivered to the Clergy of the Diocese of Oxford* (Oxford 1838), pp. 7–9).

71 J. Kaye, *A Letter to His Grace the Archbishop of Canterbury on the Recommendations of the Ecclesiastical Commission* (London 1838), quoted in Brose, pp. 149–50; cf. also Welch, pp. 190–1.

72 J. H. Monk, *A Charge to the Clergy of the Diocese of Gloucester and Bristol* (London 1838), pp. 17–18, quoted in Best, pp. 336–7. Peel himself had said much the same thing in a letter to Phillpotts in 1835 as he was setting up the Ecclesiastical Commission: 'After providing for the maintenance of the fabric and the proper performance of all Cathedral services, in what mode can the superfluous wealth of Cathedrals be made available for the spiritual instruction of the people, with the greatest effect and the least violation of principle? It is in vain to disguise from ourselves that either by friendly or unfriendly hands, ecclesiastical sinecures must share the fate to which all other sinecures have been doomed. I think it is impossible to maintain the principle that an office of the Church, without corresponding duties, shall have large endowments attached to it, while the cure of souls in some populous districts is wholly unprovided for' (Peel, *Memoirs*, vol.II, p. 76; see also his letter to Van Mildert, Bishop of Durham, ibid., pp. 80–4. For his views in 1839, cf. Parker, vol.II, pp. 411–12).

73 For Howley's contribution, cf. Best, pp. 345–7.

74 cf. Welch, pp. 191–2.

75 Quoted in Best, pp. 343–5; cf. *Mirror of Parliament*, 30 July 1840.

76 R. Burrows, *Halsbury's Statutes of England*, vol.vii, pp. 1024–50 (London 1949). By 1845 the commissioners reported that thirty-eight canonries had been suspended

and that they were in receipt of the endowments of the separate estates of seven deaneries and canonries and 156 prebends (L. T. Dibdin and S. E. Downing, *The Ecclesiastical Commission* (London 1919), p. 37; cf. also Mathieson, pp. 152–4). The last estate to fall into the hands of the commissioners was the prebend of Wiveliscombe in Wells Cathedral in 1891 (Best, p. 501; Chadwick, *Church and Historical Endowment in the Victorian Age*, p. 15).

77 The *British Critic* commented prophetically in 1841: 'We can hardly remember any subject on which the rise, growth and mastery of a right principle has been so marked as that of the Ecclesiastical Commission.... From the steady opening of a clear insight into the nature of Cathedrals, and the vast growth of moral power to the Church, arising from the discussions on Cathedral revenues, we bode a great work hereafter' (*British Critic*, vol. 29, 1841, p. 150; quoted in Brose, p. 155).

CHAPTER 3 *The Environment of the Cathedral: The Close*

1 For some work in this area, cf. M. E. C. Walcott, 'The Arrangement of Secular Cathedral Closes', *Associated Architectural Societies Reports and Papers*, vol. xv, 1879, pt 1, pp. 70–8; E. Lega-Weekes, *Some Studies in the Topography of the Cathedral Close at Exeter* (Exeter 1915); I. C. Hannah, 'Houses in the Close at Chichester', *Sussex Archaeological Collections*, vol. 68, 1927, pp. 133–58; A. H. Thompson, *The Cathedral Churches of England* (London 1928), pp. 153–94; P. E. Morgan, 'The Cathedral Close', *FHCAR*, 1976, pp. 15–19; M. Binney, 'Hereford Cathedral Close', *Country Life*, vol. clxviii, no.4336, 25 September 1980, pp. 1026–9. Some of the buildings in the close at Winchester have been studied by P. M. J. Crook: cf. *A History of the Pilgrims' School and earlier Winchester Choir Schools* (Chichester 1981), pp. 101–33, and 'The "Gumble" Affair and the House of Thomas Ken', *Winchester Cathedral Record*, 1983, no.52, pp. 5–16; cf. also the popular booklets about the closes at Winchester, Gloucester and elsewhere by Aylwin Sampson. Southwell Minster became a cathedral only in 1884, but the buildings of this collegiate church (including the prebendal houses) have been studied by N. Summers, *A Prospect of Southwell* (Chichester 1974). There is information about the topography of Wells in D. S. Bailey, 'The Liberty, Wells', in N. Coldstream and P. Draper, eds, *Mediaeval Art and Architecture at Wells and Glastonbury* (British Archaeological Association Conference Transactions 1978) (London 1981), pp. 54–61; and W. Rodwell, 'The Buildings of Vicars' Close', in L. S. Colchester, ed., *Wells Cathedral: A History* (Shepton Mallett 1982), pp. 212–26. For a detailed study of the houses in the liberty at Wells, cf. D. S. Bailey, *The Canonical Houses of Wells* (Gloucester 1982). For Lincoln, cf. K. Major, *Minster Yard* (Lincoln 1974); S. Jones, K. Major and J. Varley, *The Survey of Ancient Houses in Lincoln I: Priorygate to Pottergate* (Lincoln 1984).

2 Thompson, pp. 157–8.

3 cf. Morgan, p. 15. As late as 1475 one of the reasons given by the vicars choral of Hereford in asking for a new college closer to the cathedral was the fear of assault on their way to matins (A. T. Bannister, ed., *The Register of John Stanbury, Bishop of Hereford 1453–1474* (Hereford 1918), pp. v–vi).

4 ABDC Hereford, 13 November 1800.

5 ABDC Bristol, 25 June 1802. In the same year Mr Mann, the close porter at Winchester, was rewarded by the chapter for catching a thief red-handed in the close (ABDC Winchester, 25 November 1802).

6 ABDC Salisbury, 22 January 1807; cf. A. S. Leak, 'Conflict and Reform at York Minster in the Nineteenth Century' (Oxford B. D. thesis 1988), pp. 9–10, 96–9, 105–6 for a similar arrangement at York.

7 ABDC Exeter, 3 May 1800, 16 October 1819. There was a brewery opposite the North Porch at Wells (cf. Bailey, p. 127).

8 ABDC Exeter, 30 March 1822. Bonfires and fireworks were still a problem at Exeter

in 1853 – cf. ABDC Exeter, 22 October 1853, cf. ABDC Gloucester, 23 June 1826, for the close constable's duties there. The office of the close porter at Exeter had been discontinued in 1815 (ABDC Exeter, 19–20 December 1815).

9 ABDC Hereford, 28 November 1826. For the arrangements made at York in 1825 to patrol the Minster Yard and Bedern, which was full of thieves and prostitutes, cf. Leak, pp. 121–2.

10 ABDC Exeter, 14 February 1829, 9–10 December 1830.

11 ABDC Hereford, 27 September 1831.

12 ABDC Chichester, 2 May 1845. When a new porter was appointed at Winchester in 1874 he was required to trim the trees in the close and keep the paths clear of snow (ABDC Winchester, 13 May 1874).

13 Wells CM, 15 May 1858.

14 P. A. Welsby, *Rochester Cathedral in the time of Charles Dickens* (Rochester 1976), p. 9.

15 ABDC Hereford, 25 March 1861.

16 ABDC Chichester, 13 February 1875, 30 May 1876. In 1865 the dean and chapter had employed Charles Goddard to take oversight of the cloisters and precincts each day from 12 noon till 2 o'clock and from 4 p.m. to 5 p.m. (except Sundays) at a rate of 5s per week, as both windows and the cloisters had been damaged by the throwing of stones (ABDC Chichester, 20 January 1865).

17 ABDC Salisbury, 23 August 1881.

18 P. V. Coghlan, 'Cathedral Worship in the Church of England 1815–1914' (Leicester University M. Phil. thesis 1984), p. 94, quoting ABDC Norwich, 28 March 1883.

19 ABDC Winchester, 3 February 1885.

20 ABDC Worcester, 1 January 1892. In 1847 the dean and chapter had ordered that the gates leading through the Dark Alley should be closed for the whole of one day each year (ABDC Worcester, 25 November 1847). In 1824 there were three porters at Worcester, supervising the North Gate, the East Gate and the Water Gate (ABDC Worcester, 24 November 1824). There were porters at Canterbury, Durham, Carlisle, Peterborough and Winchester in 1865 (M. E. C. Walcott, *Cathedralia* (London 1865), p. 153). For details of those who could use the ferry at the Water Gate at Worcester free of charge, cf. ABDC Worcester, 31 March 1884. In 1867 a porter was appointed to be responsible for the area to the west of the cathedral and college yard 'which he is to keep in perfect order, having the grass regularly mown and preventing all nuisance and trespass' (ABDC Worcester, 10 May 1867). He was reminded of his responsibilities in 1888 and the porter at Edgar Tower was told to keep a book in which the names of all who entered and left after the gates were closed were to be entered (ibid., 19 November 1888).

21 ABDC Worcester, 1 May 1896.

22 Hebdomadary's Book (HCA), p. 454. For the similar duties given to the close porter at Salisbury, cf. ABDC Salisbury, 9 September 1869. For Winchester, cf. ABDC Winchester, 25 November 1870. An anonymous letter was sent to Dean Pellew of Norwich in 1835 complaining about prostitutes occupying prominent seats *inside* the cathedral: 'I am sure no mother will dare to take her daughter to the Cathedral' (Dean Pellew's letters, no.219, Norfolk CRO).

23 F. G. Bennett, R. H. Codrington and C. Deedes, *Statutes and Constitutions of the Cathedral Church of Chichester* (Chichester 1904), p. 50.

24 Chapter Archives, Chichester: Visitation Book 1/7/1, p. 137.

25 ibid., draft acts 1874–88 (Cap.I/3A/1). At Salisbury in 1898 the constable was directed to remove from the close children who congregated at the corner by the theological college (ABDC Salisbury, 2 May 1898).

26 ABDC Chichester, 20 January 1857.

27 ibid., 11 October 1858.

28 ibid., 6 August 1885. Games in the close were an old problem at Hereford. In

November 1796 it was ordered that 'no Boys except Mr Squire's (the Cathedral School) be suffered to play in the Church Yard and that they be restrained from playing at all in the Walks or within the Rails at Cricket, Bandy or any other Diversion that may endanger the Passengers or the Windows of the Cathedral' (Morgan, p. 17; cf. ABDC Hereford, 13 November 1800, and Leak, p. 104 for a similar problem at York in 1836).

29 ABDC Worcester, 6 April 1843.
30 Wells CM, 30 September 1861.
31 ABDC Winchester, 11 December 1883; in the same year a public urinal in the close at Winchester was found to be offensive and was removed (ABDC Winchester, 7 August and 1 September 1883). Forty years earlier, privies had been removed from the gardens of some of the houses at Worcester (ABDC Worcester, 6 April 1843).
32 ABDC Chichester, 6 August 1885.
33 ABDC Winchester, 23 June 1809.
34 ABDC Salisbury, 8 October 1852.
35 ABDC Winchester, 12 April 1806.
36 ABDC Exeter, 19 September 1818.
37 M. R. Craze, *King's School, Worcester (1541–1971)* (Worcester 1972), p. 182.
38 ABDC Gloucester, 30 November 1836.
39 ABDC Exeter, 11 February 1837. A sewer was introduced into the college of vicars choral in 1831. (ABDC Exeter, 19 November 1831).
40 ABDC Hereford, 16 February 1846.
41 ibid., 25 June 1870.
42 Morgan, p. 18; ABDC Hereford, 8 December 1851. For the Hereford improvement commissioners, cf. D. J. Mitchell, 'Hereford in the Age of Reform 1832–1856', *TWNFC*, vol.xliv, 1982, pp. 105f.
43 Wells CM, 30 November and 30 December 1884, 2 January 1889.
44 ABDC Exeter, 12 June 1830.
45 ibid., 23 October 1830.
46 ibid., 26 November 1831.
47 ibid., 26 November 1831, 18 February 1832, cf. 3 March 1832, 22–23 March 1832, 9 June 1832. In 1882 they supported the dean and chapter of Norwich in their objections to having a railway in their close (ABDC Exeter, 11 March 1882).
48 ibid., 6 August 1835.
49 Chadwick, *York*, p. 288, fn.37, pp. 311–2. Carts left by the deanery wall on market days were a nuisance at Wells in 1860 (Wells CM, 17 August 1860, 10 September and 20 October 1861).
50 ABDC Salisbury, 18 June 1856.
51 F. Kilvert, *Kilvert's Diary 1870–1879* (one volume edition, ed. W. Plomer, London 1944, reprinted 1967), p. 91 (1 December 1870).
52 cf. Chapter 1, p. 5.
53 G. L. Prestige, *St Paul's in its Glory, 1831–1911* (London 1955), pp. 8–9.
54 H. W. Beadon, *The Cathedrals and the Diocese* (Gloucester 1880), p. 3.
55 ibid., p. 7.
56 ABDC Gloucester, 30 November 1813.
57 ABDC Worcester, 25 November 1842. For a detailed account of alterations to the deanery at Norwich, cf. Dean Pellew's note-book, 1829–32, DCN 120/2, Norfolk CRO.
58 ABDC Worcester, 17 February 1846. Some of the old prebendal houses in the precincts at Canterbury were also demolished (cf. D. I. Hill, *Christ's Glorious Church* (London 1976), p. 75). The houses in the Bedern at York were demolished in 1883 (cf. G. Benson, *An Account of the City and County of the City of York from the Reformation to the year 1925, being a continuation of 'Later Mediaeval York' by G. Benson* (York 1925), vol. III, facing p. 113).

59 ABDC Exeter, 1–2 June 1843.

60 4 & 5 Vict., c.39, s.18.

61 ABDC Winchester, 25 November 1863; cf. 25 June 1864.

62 ibid., 25 October 1873.

63 ABDC Bristol, 6 January 1885.

64 Wells CM, 1 July 1899.

65 ibid., 2 October 1899; Bailey, p. 26.

66 W. O. Chadwick, *The Victorian Church* (London 1970), vol. II, pp. 368, 371; Anon., 'Cathedral Life and Cathedral Reform', *Contemporary Review* (n.d.), p. 498; W. K. L. Clarke, *Chichester Cathedral in the Nineteenth Century* (Chichester Papers no.14, Chichester 1959), p. 11; J. Jebb, *The Choral Service of the United Church of England and Ireland* (London 1843), p. 72; L. Smith, *The Story of Ripon Minster* (Leeds 1914), pp. 256–7.

67 Chadwick, vol.II, p. 371 (cf. PP 1884–5, xxi, pp. 303, 367). In 1874 two of the canons who did not have a house at Chichester were given £25 per annum by the dean and chapter towards their lodging expenses. The tenant of the Chantry was given notice to quit so that the house could be used as a canonical residence (ABDC Chichester, 1 August 1874).

68 Quoted in S. E. R. Chitty, *The Beast and the Monk* (London 1974), p. 258.

69 C. A. E. Moberly, *Dulce Domum* (London 1911), p. 209.

70 Clarke, p. 11. At Peterborough the population of the precincts in 1831 was 198 – 68 males and 130 females lived in 37 inhabited houses. These figures included 10 male and 35 female servants (R. S. Wingfield Digby, *Friends of Peterborough Cathedral Annual Report* 1966, pp. 3–4).

71 I. C. Hannah, 'The Vicars' Close and Adjacent Buildings, Chichester', *Sussex Archaeological Collections*, vol. 56, 1914, pp. 92, 108.

72 R. V. H. Burne, *Chester Cathedral* (London 1958), pp. 253–4.

73 see Chapter 5, p. 69.

CHAPTER 4 *The Office and Work of a Dean*

1 If one excepts the bishop's palace. For relations between bishops and cathedrals, see Chapter 11, pp. 245–52.

2 F. E. Gretton, *Memory's Hark-back Through Half a Century, 1808–1858* (London 1889), p. 4.

3 F. Bussby, 'Winchester Cathedral 1789–1840', *Winchester Cathedral Record*, no.44, 1975, p. 27.

4 Chadwick, *York*, p. 292.

5 A. H. Brewer, *Memories of Choirs and Cloisters* (London 1931), p. 43; W. H. B. Proby, *Annals of the Low Church Party in England* (London 1888), vol.II, pp. 456–7. Dean Stevens was Dean of Rochester for fifty years until his death in 1870, at the age of ninety-three. 'A mild mannered, timid, generous person' with 'an exceptionally beautiful speaking voice', he was said to be 'easily led, essentially honest but rather simple-minded'. The *Church Times* claimed that he had been incapable of performing any clerical duties for some years before his death, though he had attended a chapter meeting as recently as six weeks before he died (P. A. Welsby, *Rochester Cathedral in the Time of Charles Dickens* (Rochester 1976), p. 11; cf. also J. F. Bridge, *A Westminster Pilgrim* (London 1919), p. 23).

6 ABDC Salisbury, 8 August 1811. For the personal responsibility of the porter to the dean at Salisbury, cf. Chapter 6, p. 111.

7 J. Jebb, *A Plea for What is Left of the Cathedrals* (London 1852), p. 16. Dean Farrar of Canterbury was well known for his constant attendance at daily services towards the end of the century (R. Farrar, *The Life of Frederic William Farrar, sometime Dean of Canterbury* (London 1904), p. 328).

8 cf. for an example the election of Dean Talbot of Salisbury (ABDC Salisbury, 13 and 21 March 1809). The matter is explained in R. Phillimore, *The Ecclesiastical Law of the Church of England* (London 1895), vol. I, p. 127. The bishop's right to institute a dean in an old foundation cathedral was stoutly urged by Bishop John Wordsworth at Salisbury (E. W. Watson, *Life of Bishop John Wordsworth* (London 1915), pp. 239–40). Dean Goulburn claimed that the Dean of Norwich was unique among new foundation deans in not needing to take the oath of canonical obedience (B. Compton, *Edward Meyrick Goulburn, Dean of Norwich* (London 1899), p. 73).

9 ABDC Exeter, 10, 24 and 26 January and 25 February 1839.

10 ABDC Exeter, 9, 23 and 30 March, 4, 6 and 9 April and 1 May 1839.

11 ABDC Exeter, 14 and 27 June, and 1 August 1839.

12 cf. R. Barnes, *Report of the Case of the Queen v. The President and Chapter of the Cathedral Church of St Peter in Exeter* (London 1841).

13 cf. G. C. B. Davies, *Henry Phillpotts, Bishop of Exeter, 1778–1869* (London 1954), pp. 159–62; R. J. E. Boggis, *A History of the Diocese of Exeter* (Exeter 1922), pp. 509–10.

14 3 & 4 Vict., c.113, s.24.

15 4 & 5 Vict., c.39, s.5.

16 ABDC Exeter, 6 July 1861.

17 Hansard, P. D., vol. cl, 4 June 1858, pp. 1522f.;cf. also p. 47 above.

18 *Guardian*, 1884, p. 96. When he left Manchester he was presented with a silver tea service, a silver inkstand and a book of photographs (ibid., 1884, p. 47); cf. also M. Hennell, *The Deans and Canons of Manchester Cathedral, 1840–1948* (Manchester 1990), pp. 13–19.

19 H. W. Massingham, 'The Nationalisation of Cathedrals', *Contemporary Review*, vol. 60, no.309, September 1891, pp. 364–5.

20 E. M. Goulburn, *John William Burgon, Dean of Chichester* (London 1892), vol.II, p. 152.

21 H. D. Rawnsley, *Harvey Goodwin, Bishop of Carlisle* (London 1896), p. 85; cf. F. Pigou, *Odds and Ends* (London 1903), p. 205: 'It was a too long prevalent notion that a Dean lived for the rest of his days on a sofa or sat in easy armchair *en luxe*, chewing the cud of past experience, enjoying to the full the *otium cum dignitate*, not regarding the Cathedral as a great trust and great centre of varied activity.'

22 P. V. Coghlan, 'Cathedral Worship in the Church of England 1815–1914' (Leicester University M. Phil. thesis 1984), p. 93.

23 F. Arnold, *Our Bishops and Deans* (London 1875), vol.I, p. 299; cf. *The Cathedral Bodies and what they cost* (Facts for Churchmen no.6, PHPR 9486, p. 2); and Hansard, P. D., vol.clxi, 1861, p. 1948.

24 PP 1871, lv, p. 198, quoted in W. O. Chadwick, *The Victorian Church* (London 1970), vol. II, p. 372.

25 Pigou, p. 219. Dean Gott of Worcester wrote to congratulate him on his appointment, saying 'Rest at last', but Harvey Goodwin told Pigou that 'there is a career of usefulness open to those who are called to that "very reverend" office' (F. Pigou, *Phases of My Life* (London 1898), pp. 354–5.

26 Hansard, P. D., vol.cxii, 1850, pp. 1410f.; cf. also A. Tait, 'Cathedral Reform', *Edinburgh Review*, vol.xcvii, January 1853, pp. 152, 156, 160–1.

27 PP 1854, xxv, p. 797.

28 ibid., p. 832.

29 K. Lake, ed., *Memorials of William Charles Lake* (London 1901), p. 216. In the early years of the century (until 1840), some deans (such as those of Chichester, Hereford and Salisbury) exercised absolute jurisdiction in their 'peculiar'. At Chichester this consisted of most of the city with the exception of the parish of All Saints, Pallant. Within the peculiar, the dean possessed supreme ecclesiastical authority, admitting churchwardens, granting marriage licences, proving wills, issuing faculties and hearing cases of 'defamation and slander' (W. K. L. Clarke, *Chichester Cathedral in the*

Nineteenth Century (Chichester Papers no.14, Chichester 1959), p. 8; cf. ABDC Salisbury, 29 December 1809, 24 July 1819). The Dean of Salisbury had a very substantial peculiar jurisdiction, including forty parishes in Wiltshire, Berkshire and Dorset, where he was the undisputed authority, and another thirty-eight where he had quasi-episcopal authority (P. Stewart, *Diocese of Salisbury: Guide to the Records of the Bishop, the Archdeacons of Salisbury and Wiltshire and other Archidiaconal and Peculiar Jurisdictions and to the Records from the Bishop of Bristol's sub-registry for Dorset* (Wiltshire 1973), p. 71. There were thirty-two parishes and chapelries in the dean's peculiar at Hereford. (I am grateful to the late Miss P. E. Morgan for this information.)

30 E. Stuart, *Do Away with Deans: Cathedral Reform* (London 1869).

31 F. Alford, *Life, Journals and Letters of Henry Alford, Dean of Canterbury* (London 1873), p. 434; cf. H. Alford, 'Cathedral Reform', *Contemporary Review*, vol.xii, September 1869, p. 43. In a further article in the November 1869 issue of the same magazine, he wrote: 'The objection that the Bishops are already overworked simply does not apply. They are not likely to have much more work added by becoming deans. Among the possible changes of name and modifications of duty which may befall the Deans it is quite likely that their absorption into the episcopal office may be the best solution for the interests of the Church' (ibid., November 1869, p. 365).

32 Hansard, P. D., 3rd series, vol.clxiv, 1861, p. 179.

33 J. S. Howson, ed., *Essays on Cathedrals by Various Writers* (London 1872).

34 John Gott described his work as Dean of Worcester as that of 'a man who did odd jobs about the diocese' (A. J. Worlledge, *Letters of Bishop Gott* (London 1918), p. 26).

35 Howson, p. 15. Alford's average attendance at the daily service at Canterbury was over 200 services per annum (H. Alford, p. 44).

36 He was installed on 5 January 1850.

37 R. T. Davidson and W. Benham, *Life of Archibald Campbell Tait, Archbishop of Canterbury* (London 1891) vol.I, pp. 150–1.

38 Goulburn, vol.II, p. 123.

39 LPL, Tait Papers, vol. 27. For E. M. Goulburn's early days at Norwich, cf. his diary in Norwich Cathedral Library: entries for 27 and 28 February 1867.

40 ibid., vol. 27, 10 May 1850.

41 ibid., vol. 27, 7 August 1850.

42 ibid., vol. 24, 17 October 1851; cf. vol. 32, 5 December 1852.

43 ibid., vol. 24, 22 October 1851.

44 ibid., vol. 33, 21 May 1854; cf. vol. 32, 5 December 1852, 2 April 1853.

45 ibid., vol. 33, 4 June 1854.

46 ibid., 30 July and 17 December 1854, 14 January 1855.

47 Davidson and Benham, vol.I, pp. 185–6.

48 Tait Papers, vol. 39 (LPL), contains a full account of their illnesses and deaths.

49 ibid., vol. 42.

50 Compton, p. 71. For an appreciation of Goulburn's work at Norwich, cf. R. Hale, in C. Barringer, ed., *Norwich in the Nineteenth Century* (Norwich 1984), pp. 171–2.

51 J. W. Burgon, *Chichester Cathedral – Suggestions submitted to the Cathedral Commissioners* (Chichester 1879), p. 11. Earlier in the century Edward Copleston was a diligent Dean of St Paul's, despite also being Bishop of Llandaff. Between 1832 and his death in 1849, he missed only eight or nine chapter meetings out of a possible ninety-eight, four of them during the last two years of his life (G. L. Prestige, *St Paul's in its Glory, 1831–1911* (London 1955), p. 14).

52 A. J. Butler, *Life and Letters of William John Butler* (London 1897), pp. 347–8. For various appreciations of Butler's work at Lincoln, cf. L. Ragg, *A Memoir of Edward Charles Wickham, Dean of Lincoln* (London 1911), pp. 120, 124 (quoting a letter of

Edward King to Gladstone, 15 January 1894); W. O. Chadwick, *Edward King, Bishop of Lincoln 1885–1910* (Lincoln 1968), p. 23; J. W. F. Hill, *Victorian Lincoln* (London 1974), pp. 270–1.

53 cf. P. L. S. Barrett, 'John Merewether, Dean of Hereford 1832–50', *FHCAR*, 1977, pp. 23–39.

54 ABDC Hereford, 14 June and 10 July 1832.

55 ABDC Hereford, 31 March 1837.

56 ABDC Hereford, 9 July 1835, ABVC, 9 July 1835 – summarized in Barrett, pp. 28–9. In 1836 Merewether told Lord John Russell: 'Your Lordship may probably be aware that I have not been wanting in endeavours to render the different departments of this establishment efficient and to induce all members personally and punctually to perform the duties for which they were designed and responsible' (CCF 3208).

57 cf. above. This was hardly tactful to Grey, who had been the previous dean! The following quotation may be found in ABDC Hereford, 31 March 1837.

58 See Chapter 10, pp. 233–5.

59 cf. J. Merewether, *Diary of a Dean* (London 1851).

60 Chadwick, *The Victorian Church*, vol.I, pp. 241–2.

61 The fullest account is Chadwick, *York*, pp. 272f; cf. A. S. Leak, 'Conflict and Reform at York Minster in the Nineteenth century' (Oxford B. D.thesis 1988), pp. 140–95.

62 cf. J. S. Kerr, *Improvers and Preservers* (York 1973).

63 Chadwick, *York*, p. 282.

64 ibid., pp. 284–5.

65 Cockburn to C. A. Thiselton, October 1840; quoted in ibid., p. 284; Leak, pp. 156–7.

66 Chadwick, *York*, p. 286; Leak, p. 172.

67 J. Raine, *A Memorial of the Honourable and Very Reverend Augustus Duncombe, DD* (London and York 1880), p.viii.

68 He was appointed on the initiative of Queen Victoria herself (cf. A. C. Benson and Viscount Esher, eds, *The Letters of Queen Victoria* (London 1907), vol.II, pp. 47–8).

69 C. E. Woodruff and W. Danks, *Memorials of the Cathedral and Priory of Christ in Canterbury* (London 1912), p. 355.

70 Worc. C. Add.Mss., 128, p. 14.

71 ibid., 141, p. 3.

72 ibid., 128, p. 14; 137, p. 2.

73 ibid., 137, p. 1; 141, p. 3.

74 ibid., 137, pp. 1–2.

75 ibid., 141, pp. 2–3.

76 ibid., 128, p. 14; cf. 137, p. 2; 141, p. 3.

77 ibid., 128, pp. 16–17; 141, p. 3.

78 ibid., 128, p. 15.

79 There is a condensed summary of lay clerk John Randall's reminiscences of Dean Peel in R. B. Lockett, 'George Gilbert Scott, the Joint Restoration Committee and the Re-furnishing of Worcester Cathedral, 1863–74' *TWAS*, 3rd series, vol. 6, 1978, p. 26, fn.19.

80 Hansard, P. D., vol. cl. 1522 (4 June 1858); cf. also Chadwick, *York*, pp. 294–5, quoting Archbishop Musgrave to Lord Derby, 4 May 1858 and *The Times*, 7 June 1858. See also above, p. 36.

81 PP 1884–5, xxi, pp. 442–3, quoted in Chadwick, *York*, p. 296. The precentorship was held by the Dean at Salisbury for some years. See Chapter 5, p. 65.

82 *Yorkshireman*, 29 May 1858, quoted in Chadwick, *York*, p. 297.

83 ibid., 3 July 1858.

84 *CCR* 1866, p. 196.

85 cf. H. Kirk-Smith, *William Thomson, Archbishop of York 1819–1890* (London 1958), p. 85; Leak, pp. 303–4.

86 Raine, p.vii.
87 The fullest account of Duncombe's work is in Chadwick, *York*, pp. 294–306. For the work of his successor, A. P. Purey-Cust, cf. ibid., pp. 307f; L. W. Cowie, 'Worship in the Minster', *VCH* (City of York) (London 1961), p. 355; Kirk-Smith, p. 92, for the hostile view of one of his canons.
88 C. J. Stranks, *This Sumptuous Church* (London 1973), p. 98.
89 ibid., p. 107, fn.46, quoting A. Hare, *The Story of My Life*, (London 1900), vol.V, p. 424.
91 Lake, p. 140. For a delightful account of Lake's dignified predecessor, George Waddington, and his predilection for boxing, church restoration and the delights of the dinner table, cf. Stranks, pp. 90–2.
92 Lake, p. 135. For his right to control the service at Durham, cf. PP 1884–5, xxi, p. 90. In 1880 he wrote to Tait: 'to compel us to bring our arrangements for services before our Chapters is either to doom Cathedrals to immobility or to doom deans to a life of worry which is intolerable' (Lake, p. 242; cf. p. 258; cf. also J. T. Fowler, *Durham University, Earlier Foundations and Present Colleges* (London 1904), p. 118).
93 Lake to Tait, 10 November 1872, quoted in Lake, p. 222.
94 Lake, p. 238; see Chapter 11, p. 247.
95 Goulburn, vol.II, pp. 123–6.
96 J. W. Burgon, *Dr Swainson and the Dean of Chichester* (Chichester 1878), pp. 4–9.
97 Burgon, *Chichester Cathedral*, *passim*
98 ibid., p. 11; cf. p. 41 above.
99 ibid., pp. 11–12; PP 1884–5, xxi, p. 368. Burgon was not the only dean to complain of his poverty. In the early nineteenth century decanal incomes had varied considerably. That of the Dean of Durham had risen from £2,000 per annum in 1788 to £9,000 in 1840 (Stranks, p. 85), while that of the Dean of Gloucester rose from £1,172 9s 4d in 1802 to £1, 580 1s 10d in 1809, before falling to £857 9s 9d in 1820 (Gloucestershire CRO, D 936/A20, 41). Early nineteenth century deans of Chichester received a very small income from the deanery (probably about £300) (Clarke, p. 5). The deaneries of Ripon and Chester were also very poorly endowed (W. L. Mathieson, *English Church Reform 1815–1840* (London 1923), p. 153), but George Gordon, Dean of Lincoln from 1809 to 1845, managed to accrue an income of £20,000 from his various preferments (Hill, p. 256). By 1836 he was 'old and inactive' (ibid., p. 301). In the 1830s the Dean of Salisbury was not only the richest member of the chapter with an average annual income of £2,679, he was only exceeded by the Deans of St Paul's and Lincoln among old foundation cathedrals (K. Edwards, 'The Cathedral of Salisbury 1075–1950', *VCH Wiltshire* (London 1956), vol.III, p. 201). For full details of decanal incomes in the 1830s, cf. PP 1835, xxii, pp. 36f; cf. also Anon., *The Case of the Deans of the Old Cathedrals Stated and Examined* (London n.d.) (copy in Sarum Capitular Archives, Press II, Box 7). In the 1850s, however, the dean's income was much reduced, falling to as low as £40 in 1857–8 (Sarum DRO, Press V, Box 5, bundle of miscellaneous papers). Although some deans were rich and generous to their cathedrals, such as Duncome of York or Hook of Chichester, others made no secret of their lack of means. After 1840, when decanal incomes were in general limited to £1,000 per annum, this became a considerable problem. Dean Johnson of Wells was unable to keep up his large house, 'the most expensive decanal residence in England', which needed five or six servants and a gardener, despite some assistance from his chapter and heavy borrowing of money (Chadwick, *The Victorian Church*, vol.II, p. 368; Greenhalgh, *Wells*, p. 191; Wells CM, 23 September 1878, 1 July 1880; Johnson to Ecclesiastical Commissioners, Sarum DRO, Press II, Box 7, (c.1845?), bundle re income of old foundation deans; cf. G. F. A. Best, *Temporal Pillars* (Cambridge 1964), pp. 437–40; for details of Johnson, cf. Greenhalgh, *Wells*, p. 187). E. H. Plumptre left the cathedral commissioners in no doubt of the difficulties he would encounter in succeeding

Johnson (PP 1883, xxi, p. 256). Another dean saddled with a large and expensive house was J. J. S. Perowne of Peterborough – cf.PP 1884–5, xxi, pp. 280–1. In 1893 the Dean of Peterborough considered letting the deanery, 'on account of the great agricultural depression and the consequent reduction in the income of the dean' (Peterborough Audit Book 3, 13 February 1893, quoted in Coghlan, p. 97). The situation had not improved by the 1890s. H. W. Massingham printed a table of decanal income, with Durham at £3,000 at the top and Winchester at £500 at the bottom (Massingham, pp. 309, 366; cf. Chadwick *The Victorian Church*, vol.II, p. 367). When Francis Pigou went to Chichester in 1888, he found that the value of the deanery had fallen to £500 per annum (Pigou, *Phases of My Life*, p. 350), and F. W. Farrar's acceptance of the deanery of Canterbury in 1895 involved a considerable drop in income (Farrar, p. 313). Dean Pellew of Norwich, however, was criticized in 1861 for the amount of income he received from his deanery and a living in Kent (Anon., *Cathedral Wealth and Cathedral Work* (London 1861), p. 18).

100 Burgon, *Chichester Cathedral*, p. 28. Burgon read a solemn protest at the chapter meeting on 20 August 1878 (cf. ABDC Chichester, 20 August 1878). He had earlier quarrelled with the lay vicars, who appealed to the chapter that they did not like being kept back after services to hear the dean's frequent complaints about their singing and that of the choristers, which he described as a 'disgusting noise' (Chichester Cathedral Draft Acts 1874–88, Cap.I/3A/1, July 1878).

101 Burgon, *Chichester Cathedral*, p. 28.

102 ibid., p. 30.

103 ibid., p. 31.

104 ibid., p. 32. In 1881 the dean and chapter adopted the practice of putting a mourning frontlet on the stalls of all deceased dignitaries (ABDC Chichester, 21 January 1881).

105 Burgon, *Chichester Cathedral*, p. 33.

106 ibid., p. 35; cf. J. W. Burgon, *Remarks on Dr Swainson's Two Letters addressed to the Canons, Dignitaries and Prebendaries of Chichester Cathedral* (Chichester 1879), p. 6: 'No one can fail to perceive that *jealousy of the Dean's office* is the root of bitterness out of which all his remarks spring: and that those remarks are in reality aimed *at me.*'

107 Goulburn, vol.II, pp. 239–40, 273; Pigou, *Phases of My Life*, p. 361.

108 Goulburn, p. 309. There is a similar account of J. W. Blakesley, Dean of Lincoln, on his way to a service there in *Trefoil*, pp. 114–17: 'He must have been a man of a little over 60 when he went to Lincoln...they lived a rather remote and shadowy life so far as the Close was concerned. My own idea of the Dean was a kindly but formidable man, with a quiet and impressive manner, entirely removed from all contact with life, turning over the pages of lexicons, I supposed, in a gloomy study...

A private flagged pathway led from the Deanery to the door of the North Transept and the Dean's dignity was such that it was impossible for him to enter the Cathedral without the escort and assistance of a verger with a silver wand. I seem to myself to be standing outside the choir-screen on a Sunday afternoon in the fading light. Very faint and far away in the western towers the bells are ringing for the service, slowly and demurely, with an almost honeyed sweetness. The Dean's verger is standing at the transept door. He (presumably) hears footsteps, for he opens the door and stands to attention. The Dean comes in, stands for a moment in silence; the verger closes the door, comes round into position, cocks the silver wand and then advances, slowly and rhythmically, with a curious rocking motion, the Dean following. They pass close in front of us. The Dean is a very solemn and dignified figure, walking in rather a constrained way, moving only from the hips, his body held rigidly and slightly stooping. He is sombrely apparelled; a velvet skull-cap low down on his forehead, black scarf, black BD hood, full surplice, but no cassock in the old academical fashion. It is an austere-looking face with a grave and scholarly abstraction, large dark eyes, an aquiline nose, firm lips and chin, and grizzled hair. He passes by, looking neither to left nor right, apparently entirely unaware of his surroundings.' For his predecessor, Dean Jeremie, cf. A. C. Benson, *The Life of Edward White Benson, sometime Archbishop of Canterbury* (London 1899), vol.I, p. 274. Benson preached at Lincoln Cathedral (where he was a prebendary, but not yet chancellor and canon residentiary) on New Year's Day 1871 (a Sunday) and lunched at 2 p.m. with Dean Jeremie the next day. He described him as 'most amusing – acute – witty – his quotations from French – his plain but perfect table – make me always think of a French ecclesiastic before the Revolution. The very last of the type....The merry, pleasant anecdotage of the conversation is all that one can carry away; and certainly if deans and minor canons live this life of elevated gossip always, it is very different from the earnest life of the Bishop's House.' For Sir Charles Anderson's views on Jeremie, cf. Hill, p. 260.

109 There are two studies of Church: M. C. Church, *Life and Letters of Dean Church* (London 1895) and B. A. Smith, *Dean Church* (London 1958); cf. also W. O. Chadwick, 'The Oxford Movement and Its Historian', in R. Holloway, ed., *The Anglican Tradition* (Oxford 1984).

110 Church, pp. 160–1.

111 Prestige, p. 119.

112 Church, pp. 202–3.

113 ibid., p. 203.

114 ibid., p. 200. That the canons of St Paul's expected something of their new dean is shown by a comment of Liddon's: 'Our new Dean...will not be a fossil-dignitary – say a Plesiosaurus, such as more than one Dean I know of' (H. P. Liddon to Mrs Lear, 28 August 1871 in Pusey House Mss., quoted in C. E. Beswick, 'Liddon of St Paul's' (Exeter University MA thesis 1974), p. 6.

115 E. F. Braley, ed., *More Letters of Herbert Hensley Henson* (London 1954), no.94.

116 ABDC Hereford, 30 August 1814; cf. above pp. 42–3 and ABDC Hereford, 25 January 1837. The Dean of Salisbury was also a residentiary canon of his cathedral until 1840 and continued to hold the prebendal stall of Heytesbury after that; cf. M. E. C. Walcott, *Cathedralia* (London 1865), pp. 41, 45, 49.

117 Wells CM, 21 October 1839. An earlier Dean of Wells, G. W. Lukin, who was dean from 1799 to 1812, tried to overrule his chapter, became involved in a dispute about bull-baiting, and laid down so much wine that Dean Plumptre was quite shocked when he found a memorandum of the amount pinned to the cellar door of the deanery (Greenhalgh, *Wells*, p. 179); cf. Chapter 5, p. 78.

118 Rawnsley, p. 94.

119 ibid. For Goodwin's 'high ideal of worship', cf. pp. 103, 112; cf. also his contribution in Howson, pp. 3–34.

120 Compton, pp. 63–4. Bates says he was 'almost a recluse, known to few outside the Cathedral precincts towards the end of his life' (F. Bates, *Reminiscences and Autobiography of a Musician in Retirement* (Norwich 1930), p. 49).

121 PP 1884, xxii, p. 88. For an estimate of Goulburn's work at Norwich, cf. H. Leeds, *Norwich Cathedral Past and Present* (Norwich 1910), pp. 59–60.

122 B. Rainbow, *The Choral Revival in the Anglican Church, 1839–1872* (London 1970), p. 204.

123 H. L. Thompson, *Henry George Liddell* (London 1899), p. 152. He was also responsible for the internal reordering of the cathedral (ibid., pp. 151–2, 154).

124 W. E. Dickson, *Fifty Years of Church Music* (Ely 1894), pp. 62, 67.

125 ibid., p. 74, quoted in P. C. Moore, 'The Organisation and Development of Cathedral

Worship in England, with special reference to choral services, from the Reformation to the Nineteenth Century' (Oxford D. Phil. thesis 1954), p. 369, fn.2.

126 C. E. Woodruff, 'Reminiscences of the Cathedral and its Personnel Seventy-five Years Ago', *Canterbury Cathedral Chronicle*, no.39, September 1943, p. 15; cf. Chapter 7, p. 147.

127 Worc. C. Add. Mss., 104, p. 6–7; cf. H. W. Shaw, *The Three Choirs Festival* (Worcester 1954) pp. 54f.

128 Worc. C. Add. Mss., 137 p. 11; 141, p. 44.

129 Clarke, p. 16; cf. Chapter 11, p. 262. For an account of Randall's unhappy time at Chichester, cf. J. F. Briscoe and H. F. B. Mackay, *A Tractarian at Work* (London 1932), pp. 181–9.

130 A. Trollope, *Clergymen of the Church of England* (1866, new edn Leicester 1974), pp. 36–7. Tait said in 1853 that among his contemporaries as deans were 'the first Greek scholar in Britain, if not in Europe; the only two really able ecclesiastical historians in our church (one also a poet); the greatest mathematician of Cambridge; two of the most eminent geologists of this or any other country' (Tait, p. 153).

131 F. Close, *Memorials of Dean Close by 'One Who Knew Him'* (London 1885), p. 35.

132 J. M. Elvy, *Recollections of the Cathedral and Parish Church of Manchester* (Manchester 1913), p. 59. For an impression of Dean Bowers, cf. ibid., p. 26 and Hennell, pp. 6–9.

133 H. B. J. Armstrong, ed., *Armstrong's Norfolk Diary* (London 1963), p. 184; cf. Bates, p. 46.

134 H. Leeds, *Life of Dean Lefroy* (Norwich 1909); cf. also the same author's *Norwich Cathedral Past and Present* (Norwich 1910), p. 61.

135 Farrar, p. 328. For an earlier Dean of Canterbury, W. R. Lyall (1845–57) and his circle, cf. C. Dewey, *The Passing of Barchester* (London 1991).

136 PP 1854, xxv, p. 1017. Traditionally the Dean of Christ Church was the bridge between the canons and the students, the chapter and the college (cf. E. G. W. Bill and J. F. A. Mason, *Christ Church and Reform 1850–1867* (Oxford 1970), p. 6).

137 Wells CM, 12 January 1891; cf 13 October 1883, 18 May 1891 and Greenhalgh, *Wells*, pp. 193, 195f. Dean Dawes of Hereford was well known for his interest in education. For the kindness of F. W. Farrar of Canterbury towards the choristers and boys from the King's School, and the hospitable actions of Dean Law of Gloucester, see Chapter 12, p. 276.

138 cf. B. Massingham, *Turn on the Fountains: A Life of Dean Hole* (London 1974); cf. also S. R. Hole, *The Memories of Dean Hole* (London 1893), and Hole's *More Memories* (London 1894); and G. A. B. Dewar, *The Letters of Samuel Reynolds Hole* (London 1907).

139 D. King, in *Winchester Cathedral Chronicle*, 1972; cf. A. E. Garnier, *The Chronicles of the Garniers of Hampshire* (Norwich 1900), and B. Carpenter Turner, *Winchester* (Southampton 1980), pp. 172–3.

140 For Liddell, cf. p. 54. For Scott, cf. E. Wordsworth, *Memorials of Henry William Burrows* (London 1894), p. viii.

141 cf. above, n.108.

142 cf. Woodruff and Danks, p. 367; F. Alford, *passim*.

143 cf. F. Bussby, *Winchester Cathedral 1079–1979* (Southampton 1979, 2nd edn 1987), p. 237.

144 Butler, pp. 320–1.

CHAPTER 5 *Canons and Capitular Government*

1 At Canterbury, Durham and Winchester there were twelve prebendaries; at Worcester there were ten; at Ely, eight; at Rochester, Chester, Gloucester, Bristol, Oxford and Peterborough, six; and at Carlisle, four (J. M. Falkner and

A. H. Thompson, *The Statutes of the Cathedral Church of Durham* (Surtees Society, vol. cxliii, Durham 1929), p. xxxiii).

2 It is important to emphasize that the terms 'canon' and 'prebendary' are really interchangeable: cf. E. A. Freeman: 'What I want you to bear in mind is that, when a non-residentiary canon becomes a residentiary, he is not changed from a prebendary into a canon. He was a canon before, and he remains a prebendary afterwards' (quoted in F. W. Harper, *What are the York Residentiary Canonries?* (Selby 1880), p. 52); cf. also W. H. Jones, *Canon or Prebendary* (Bath 1877).

3 F. G. Bennett, R. H. Codrington and C. Deedes, *Statutes and Constitutions of the Cathedral Church of Chichester* (Chichester 1904), pp. 54f.

4 J. Jebb and H. W. Phillott, *The Statutes of the Cathedral Church of Hereford* (Hereford 1882), pp. 2–3: 'vacante autem Canonicatu, aut Dignitate aliqua, ad Dominum Episcopum spectat collatio'. ('The collation of every Canonry and Dignity when void belongs to the Lord Bishop'.)

5 ABDC Salisbury, 20 August 1803; cf. ABDC Exeter, 18 and 31 December 1802. For the election of T. H. Lowe at Exeter in 1832, cf. ABDC Exeter, 15 September and 27–8 December 1832.

6 3 & 4 Vict., c.113, s.25; cf. R. Phillimore, *The Ecclesiastical Law of the Church of England* (2nd edn, London 1895), vol.I, p. 179; W. D. Peckham, 'Two Dukes and the Chichester Chapter', *Sussex Notes and Queries*, vol.xvii, no.5, May 1970, pp. 146f.; cf. Bennett, Codrington and Deedes, p. 51; cf. also above, p. 78.

7 cf. Canon Swainson's *Miscellanea* (Chichester Cathedral Archives), p. 91; W. K. L. Clarke, *Chichester Cathedral in the Nineteenth Century* (Chichester Papers no.14, Chichester 1959), p. 5.

8 Phillimore, pp. 179–80; M. E. C. Walcott, *Cathedralia* (London 1865), p. 42; A. S. Leak 'Conflict and Reform at York Minster in the Nineteenth Century' (Oxford B. D. thesis 1988), p. 305.

9 Chadwick, *York*, p. 288.

10 F. Harrison, *York Minster* (London 1927), p. 154; cf.Chadwick, *York*, p. 286.

11 A. R. M. Finlayson, *The Life of Canon Fleming* (London 1909). For Prebendary George Trevor's savage attack upon this appointment, cf. PP 1884–5, xxi, p. 444; Hansard, P.D. 1879, vol.ccxlvi, pp. 1887ff. For a fuller account of this episode and its background, cf. Chadwick, *York*, pp. 303–6; cf. also H. Kirk-Smith, *William Thomson, Archbishop of York 1819–1890* (London 1958), p. 87; and Leak, pp. 307–20.

12 A. Judd, 'The Office of Subdean', *Church Quarterly Review*, vol. 166, 1965, p. 39. This was also the case at St Paul's.

13 Jebb and Phillott, pp. 6–11; cf. ABDC Hereford, 27 February 1800 and 12 January 1801. In 1870 there was a dispute between Archdeacon Waring and Canon Jebb as to which should become a residentiary. This was settled in the Queen's Bench, though a death on the chapter enabled both of them to become residentiaries. The dean and chapter waived their admission fees of £40 (ABDC Hereford, 22 March and 4 April 1870). At Chichester, until 1870, a new residentiary was obliged to give the dean a pottle (half a gallon) of wine, a pottle of claret and 2 pounds of sugar; to each residentiary a quart of sack, a quart of claret and one pound of sugar, prandio (*ad fabricam*), £3; and the sum of £33 6s 8d to the fabric fund, with fees to the subtreasurer, vicars, clerks, ringers and other minor officials, making a total of £40 14s 8d (M. E. C. Walcott, *The Early Statutes of the Cathedral Church of the Holy Trinity, Chichester* (London 1877), p. 75; Clarke, p. 18. For the original purpose of entrance fees of this nature, cf. K. Edwards, *The English Secular Cathedrals in the Middle Ages* (2nd edition, Manchester 1967), pp. 63–7.

14 Jebb and Phillott, pp. 2–5; for the oath, cf. ibid., pp. 144–9. New prebendaries at Wells in the early nineteenth century had to swear true allegiance to the sovereign, to abjure the authority of the Pope, to observe the customs of the cathedral, and to

pay canonical obedience to the dean and chapter (ABDC Wells, 1817–32, p. 1). At Chichester, a new canon or prebendary was given a baton in addition to a Bible and a loaf: the baton (*regula*) being a mistranslation for statutes (Clarke, p. 17).

15 ABDC Salisbury, 3 June 1802.

16 H. W. Pullen, *Mediaeval Mummery in 1870* (Salisbury 1870), pp. 3–4. For the installation of Canons Gregory and Liddon at St Paul's, cf. Chapter 7, p. 129.

17 C. Wordsworth and D. Macleane, *Statutes and Customs of the Cathedral Church of the Blessed Virgin Mary at Salisbury* (London 1915), p. 459 fn., quoting F. Lear, 'Reminiscences of Eighty Years', *SDG*, vol. 23, July 1910.

18 PP 1835, xxii, pp. 36f.

19 ibid., pp. 38–9. At St Paul's the value of the prebends varied between £10 and £1,500 (G. L. Prestige, *St Paul's in its Glory, 1831–1911* (London 1955), p. 9).

20 PP 1835, xxii, pp. 40–1, 68–9. At Winchester, a prebendary had to be present during the November audit chapter to receive his share of the dona (ABDC Worcester, 25 November 1808).

21 W. K. Hamilton, *Cathedral Reform* (London, Oxford and Salisbury, 1855), p. 18; cf. Chapter 9, p. 228.

22 A. Boutflower, *Personal Reminiscences of Manchester Cathedral 1854–1912* (Leighton Buzzard 1913), p. 52.

23 PP 1854, xxv, p. 56.

24 PP 1854, xxv, p. 58.

25 Chadwick, *York*, p. 309; cf.Fleming to Thomson, 17 July 1885, quoted in Kirk-Smith, p. 92.

26 K. Edwards, 'The Cathedral of Salisbury, 1075–1950', *The Victoria History of the Counties of England* (London 1956), vol.III, p. 205. For canonical incomes in 1890, cf. H. W. Massingham, 'The Nationalisation of Cathedrals', *Contemporary Review*, vol. 60, no. 309, September 1891, pp. 365–6.

27 ABDC Hereford, 25 June 1800.

28 ABDC Wells, 1 October 1800. In 1801 the dean and chapter of Bristol arranged the residences for the ensuing twelve months. Eight residences of six weeks each were allotted to the dean and six canons. Altogether the dean was resident for three months (ABDC Bristol, 23 June 1801).

29 ABDC Worcester, 24 November 1800; cf. Chapter 1, p. 5.

30 ABDC Worcester, 4 February 1808; cf. also 24 November 1810, 6 January 1812, 1 August 1827. At Winchester in 1825 three of the prebendaries obtained a royal dispensation from residence (ABDC Winchester, 23 June 1825). For later examples, cf. 23 June 1853, 21 February and 5 May 1854, 31 March 1855, 11 June and 17 July 1856, 14 May and 21 October 1857. In 1859 Canon Jeune of Gloucester obtained a licence enabling him to be non-resident during his term of office as vice-chancellor of Oxford University (Gloucester Cathedral Archives no.129).

31 Jebb and Phillott, pp. 10–11; ABDC Hereford, 12 January 1801.

32 ABDC Gloucester, 30 November 1802.

33 ABDC Bristol, 15 September 1807.

34 ABDC Winchester, 25 November 1807.

35 ABDC Winchester, 25 November 1811.

36 ABDC Worcester, 25 November 1819; cf. also 24 November 1825.

37 Prestige, p. 11 (quoting *The Times*, 1 and 15 January 1829); cf. Chapter 1, p. 5.

38 ABDC Hereford, 19 July 1834.

39 ABDC Bristol, 24 June 1834; these fines were paid to the fabric fund (ABDC Bristol, 30 November 1843). The sum of 5s was the fine at Salisbury in 1854 for any canon who missed a service of his residence. If any canon neglected to keep the whole of his term of residence and did not provide a deputy, the fine was £100 (ABDC Salisbury, 1 July 1854).

40 ABDC Bristol, 23 June 1837. This custom ceased in 1839, but it was not until 1853 that the four residentiary canons each kept the three months' annual residence required by the 1840 Act (R. J. Fletcher, *A History of Bristol Cathedral* (London 1932), p. 58).

41 PP 1837, xli, p. 54.

42 ibid., p. 68; cf. *British Critic*, vol. 23, April 1838, pp. 455f.

43 P. C. Moore, 'The Organisation and Development of Cathedral Worship in England, with special reference to choral services, from the Reformation to the nineteenth century' (Oxford D. Phil. thesis 1954), p. 329.

44 Walcott, *Cathedralia*, p. 45.

45 PP 1854–5, xv, p. 89. Earlier in the century William Welfitt, who was a prebendary of Canterbury for forty-seven years, had been an exception among the members of the chapter. He resided for at least nine months in each year and attended the services twice daily. There was one year, shortly before his death, in which he missed only one service in the entire year (C. E. Woodruff and W. Danks, *Memorials of the Cathedral and Priory of Christ in Canterbury* (London 1912), p. 355; D. I. Hill, *Christ's Glorious Church* (London 1976), p. 77).

46 ABDC Wells, 13 September 1852.

47 PP 1854–5, xv, p. 45.

48 W. K. Hamilton's evidence to the Cathedral Commission, Salisbury Chapter Muniments, Press I, Box 39; cf. also F. Lear, 'Reminiscences of Eighty Years', *SDG*, vol. 23, July 1910, pp. 121–2.

49 *Guardian*, 1864, p. 1129; cf. Hamilton, pp. 6, 20, and A. C. Tait, 'Cathedral Reform', *Edinburgh Review*, vol. xcvii, January 1853, p. 153.

50 E. M. Goulburn, *Reasons for not signing 'Report of Her Majesty's Commissioners for Inquiring into the condition of Cathedral Churches in England and Wales upon the Cathedral Church of Norwich'*, PHPR 4978, p. 12.

51 *Chronicle of Convocation of Canterbury*, 1881, Lower House, 19 May, p. 316.

52 ABDC Exeter, 8–9 March 1872.

53 PP 1884, xxii, p. 268.

54 *Chronicle of Convocation of Canterbury*, 1881, Lower House, 19 May, p. 310.

55 G. Trevor, *Cathedral Reform* (Hull 1880), p. 14.

56 Bennett, Codrington and Deedes, p. 51.

57 ABDC Worcester, 25 November 1830.

58 ABDC Worcester, 22 January 1841.

59 *London Gazette*, 8 June 1841, 14 June 1842.

60 ABDC Bristol, 16 January 1852. Several cathedrals applied to the Ecclesiastical Commissioners for financial aid for the payment of substitute canons (PP 1850, xlii, p. 109) and various grants were made.

61 ABDC Winchester, 23 June 1863.

62 Wells CM, 5 May 1870.

63 ibid., 27 January 1874.

64 ABDC Winchester, 23 June 1877.

65 ABDC Bristol, 6 January 1891.

66 ABDC Gloucester, 13 December 1899.

67 *London Gazette*, 28 May 1844. For the form of installation at Winchester, cf. ABDC Winchester, 8 May 1844; cf. also ABDC Gloucester, 23 June 1853.

68 CCR 1865, p. 83. At Norwich the honorary canons were invited to preach at morning services, being entertained as weekend guests by the bishop (ibid., p. 97). For Peterborough, cf. ABDC Peterborough, 11 June 1857, cited in P. V. Coghlan, 'Cathedral Worship in the Church of England 1815–1914' (Leicester University M. Phil. thesis 1984), p. 105.

69 ABDC Worcester, 20 November 1873.

70 L. Creighton, *Life and Letters of Mandell Creighton* (London 1904), vol.I, p. 240.

71 PP 1883, xxi, p. 270.

72 PP 1884, xxii, p. 195. In 1894 the dean and chapter of Worcester claimed that their relations with the honorary canons, apart from one exception, were of 'the most cordial and fraternal character' (ABDC Worcester, May 1894).

73 PP 1884, xxii, p. 155. Only one member of the chapter, Dr Jelf, was present at the installation of the first honorary canon of Christ Church on 23 July 1866 (E. G. W. Bill and J. F. A. Mason, *Christ Church and Reform 1850–1867* (Oxford 1970), p. 117, fn.2).

74 A. C. Tait, *Some Thoughts on the Duties of the Established Church of England as a National Church* (London 1876), p. 6.

75 A. B. Donaldson, *The Bishopric of Truro* (London 1902), pp. 237–8.

76 J. H. Srawley, *The Origin and Growth of Cathedral Foundations as illustrated by the Cathedral Church of Lincoln* (Lincoln 1951), p. 9.

77 36 & 37 Vict., c.39; cf. Phillimore, vol.I, p. 178.

78 Prestige, p. 129.

79 ABDC Gloucester, 26 February and 26 September 1890.

80 C. Jenkins, ed., *The Statutes of the Cathedral and Metropolitical Church of Christ, Canterbury* (Canterbury 1925).

81 Donaldson, p. 104.

82 P. Ferriday, *Lord Grimthorpe, 1816–1905* (London 1957), p. 130.

83 R. M. Beaumont, *The Chapter of Southwell Minster* (Nottingham 1956), p. 33.

84 E. B. Pusey, *Remarks on the Prospective and Past Benefits of Cathedral Institutions in the Promotion of Sound Religious Knowledge occasioned by Lord Henley's Plan for their Abolition* (London 1833), p. 112. A. C. Benson said that when his father, E. W. Benson, went to Lincoln as chancellor, all he was legally required to do was 'to reside for three months, preaching once each Sunday, and by tradition to deliver a few lectures in the Chapter-house' (*Trefoil*, p. 72). Dean Alford of Canterbury said in 1869: 'There is no position so much looked up to and courted as that of a Cathedral dignitary. And this, not because it is a post of usefulness, but because it is a post of ease. The general idea of such preferment is that there is "plenty of money and nothing to do". And though the reality may in many instances fall short of this ideal elysium, there cannot be much doubt that in the main and in character the estimate is right' (H. Alford, 'Cathedral Reform', *Contemporary Review*, vol.xii, September 1869, p. 41). Tait had made a similar point in 1853: 'At present, every right-minded clergyman, residing at his cathedral without any very definite practical duties assigned to his office, considers it a point of conscience to seek such duties for himself; and a good deal of time and energy is usually lost in the search' (Tait, 'Cathedral Reform', p. 157). Contrast Dean Close's views in PP 1884, xxii, p. 132.

85 H. P. Liddon, *Walter Kerr Hamilton, Bishop of Salisbury* (London 1869), pp. 31–2.

86 F. W. Joyce, *The Life of Rev. Sir F. A. G. Ouseley, Bart.* (London 1896), pp. 87, 220. For a study of Ouseley's music, cf. W. J. Gatens, *Victorian Cathedral Music in Theory and Practice* (Cambridge 1986), pp. 147–69. H. W. Shaw has recently produced *Sir Frederick Ouseley and St Michael's, Tenbury* (Birmingham 1988).

87 Prestige, pp. 9–10; cf. Introduction, p. xv.

88 Liddon, pp. 22–59; A. E. Bridge, 'Walter Kerr Hamilton; The Making of a Tractarian Bishop, 1808–1854' (Oxford M. Litt.thesis 1988), pp. 108–31 and the same author's 'The Nineteenth Century Revivification of Salisbury Cathedral: Walter Kerr Hamilton, 1841–1854', in D. Marcombe and C. S. Knighton, eds, *Close Encounters: English Cathedrals and Society since 1540* (Nottingham 1991), 137–60. For the formal instructions sent by Dean Merewether at Hereford to his precentor, cf. ABDC Hereford, 18 August 1835. For the duties of the precentor at Lichfield, Wells, Hereford, Salisbury and Exeter in 1892, cf. Bristol, DC/A/13/5.

89 *Trefoil*, pp. 118–20.
90 Chadwick, *York*, p. 296; Walcott, *Cathedralia*, p. 49; ABDC Salisbury, 15 July 1881; ABDC Exeter, 27 May 1889.
91 *Chronicle of Convocation of Canterbury*, 1881, Lower House, 19 May, p. 315.
92 PP 1854, xxv, pp. 38–9. The first two suffragan bishops in the southern province were also canons of their cathedrals, as was Bishop Parry of Dover, who somehow managed to combine being a suffragan bishop, an archdeacon and a residentiary canon of Canterbury (W. O. Chadwick, *The Victorian Church* (London 1970), vol.II, p. 379; Hill, p. 79). In 1895 Canon Browne of St Paul's became Bishop of Stepney, but continued to hold his canonry (Prestige, p. 122).
93 Walcott, *Cathedralia*, p. 143. At Winchester each canon in turn held the post of vice-dean during his period of residence (ABDC Winchester, 11 December 1883).
94 Prestige, p. 119. When Gregory arrived in 1868, two of the other canons held parishes (W. H. Hutton, ed., *The Autobiography of Robert Gregory* (London 1912), p. 166). Other cathedrals with widely based chapters included Carlisle, where (in 1869) only one canon lived locally, the others living in Northumberland, Hertfordshire and Devon. At Norwich, Canon Adam Sedgwick was Professor of Geology at Cambridge, while the other canons included the Master of St Catharine's College, Cambridge, the Rector of St Giles-in-the-Fields, London, and a former Professor of the East India College (Chadwick, vol.II, p. 371; cf. PP 1871, lv, pp. 201, 227). For Sedgwick's life at Norwich, cf. above pp. 67–8. When W. H. Fremantle was a canon of Canterbury, he only resided there for two months in each year, spending the rest of his time at Oxford, where he was Chaplain of Balliol College (W. H. Fremantle, *Recollections of Dean Fremantle* (London 1921), pp. 98–100).
95 PP 1883, xxi, p. 253.
96 PP 1884–5, xxi, p. 443.
97 R. J. E. Boggis, *A History of the Diocese of Exeter* (Exeter 1922), p. 532. For Dean Close's negative views on the value of definite duties being given to canons, cf. PP 1884, xxii, p. 132.
98 Coghlan, p. 105, quoting ABDC Peterborough, 19 December 1882.
99 *CCR* 1865, p. 83; cf. ABDC Wells, 30 September 1852.
100 M. E. C. Walcott in O. Shipley, ed., *The Church and the World* (London 1866), p. 78. For their status at Salisbury, cf. ABDC Salisbury, 2 April 1867. For the rights of the prebendaries and others at St Paul's to take part, cf. Prestige, pp. 63–4.
101 Clarke, p. 9.
102 J. W. F. Hill, *Georgian Lincoln* (Cambridge 1966), p. 301, fn.1. For other early nineteenth-century canons, cf. Chapter 1, pp. 5–7.
103 A. Bell, *Sydney Smith* (Oxford 1980), p. 145. The chapter at Bristol in the years immediately preceding Sydney Smith's appointment certainly contained some curious characters. Canon Randolph was known as 'Belshazzar Randolph' after he compared George IV with that king in a sermon. Three other canons were related to Lord Chancellor Eldon, including Lord William Somerset, a younger brother of the Duke of Beaufort. He had been a cavalry officer and declared that he would 'rather lead his men to the cannon's mouth than go into the pulpit'. During his twenty-nine years as a canon he was not known to preach more than twice and he almost certainly never wrote a sermon. After weekday services he would climb on to the box of his 'four-in-hand' which was waiting for him outside the north porch and drive off, 'the greatest of whips and the least of theologians' (M. H. Fitzgerald, *The Story of Bristol Cathedral* (London 1938), p. 59).
104 ibid., p. 168.
105 ibid., pp. 168–71; cf. Prestige, pp. 19–20, 26–7 and Chapter 1, p. 3.
106 J. W. Clark and T. McK. Hughes, *The Life and Letters of The Reverend Adam Sedgwick* (Cambridge 1890).

107 ibid., vol.I, pp. 501–2.
108 ibid., vol.II, p. 571; for further details of his life at Norwich, cf. also ibid., vol.II, pp. 564f., 572.
109 ibid., vol.I, p. 502; vol.II, pp. 65–6.
110 A. C. Benson, *The Life of Edward White Benson, sometime Archbishop of Canterbury* (London 1899), vol.I, pp. 365–9, 380; cf. Chapter 12, p. 283.
111 D. King, in *Winchester Cathedral Chronicle*, 1972; cf. also W. Gibson, 'Continuity and Change: The Cathedral Chapter at Winchester in the Nineteenth Century', *Proceedings of the Hampshire Field Club and Archaeological Society*, vol. 45, November 1989, pp. 167–72.
112 Worc. C. Add. Mss., 128, p. 19; 141, pp. 5–6; cf. 137, p. 3.
113 ibid., Add. Mss., 128, p. 19; 137, p. 2; 141, p. 1.
114 ibid., 128, p. 21; 141, p. 7.
115 ibid., 128, p. 22; 137, p. 3; 141, p. 9.
116 ibid., 137, p. 19; 141, pp. 10–11.
117 ibid., 137, p. 21.
118 ibid., 104, p. 2; 137, p. 15.
119 A. J. Butler, *Life and Letters of William John Butler* (London 1897), pp. 302f.; Worc. C. Add. Mss., 104, pp. 8–9, 12.
120 e.g. ABDC Worcester, 19 November 1880.
121 Creighton, vol.I, p. 315.
122 ibid., vol.I, pp. 311–12.
123 ibid., vol.I, pp. 312, 381, 389, 397. For Knox-Little, see Chapter 7, pp. 136–7. T. W. Surette, an American visitor to the Three Choirs Festival at Worcester in 1899, wrote: 'Many people living near the Cathedral kept open house during the Festival, lunch being often laid in a lovely garden, where one could walk about and chat with the other guests. The conductor's door was open to composers, artists and newspaper men, and around his hospitable board one met many of the celebrities' (*MT*, 1 March 1900, p. 169). This hospitable tradition is still maintained at the Festival each year.
124 Prestige, pp. 119–20. Scott Holland himself says of the St Paul's chapter in the 1870s (before his own appointment): 'It was not, as is so usual in Cathedral bodies, an odd assortment of stray goods, a collection of contradictory specimens, each of which had been specially selected in order to neutralize the others. It was a corporate body that was animated by a single purpose, and possessed of sufficient coherence to prosecute this purpose with some consistency and continuity of will. It was ready and able to act together in its integrity, so that it might create a regularity in the life and the worship associated with the Cathedral' (quoted in M. C. Church, *Life and Letters of Dean Church* (London 1895), p. 218, and J. O. Johnston, *Life and Letters of Henry Parry Liddon* (London 1904), p. 154).
125 Hutton, pp. 226–7.
126 cf. Chapter 2, p. 136.
127 Johnston, pp. 301–2.
128 ibid., p. 219.
129 C. E. Beswick, 'Liddon of St Paul's' (Exeter University MA thesis 1974), pp. 7–8.
130 Prestige, p. 196.
131 ibid.
132 S. Paget, *Henry Scott Holland* (London 1921), pp. 152–3.
133 Prestige, p. 119.
134 W. J. Rees, pp. 51–2, quoted in P. L. S. Barrett, 'Hereford Cathedral in the Nineteenth Century', *FHCAR*, 1986, p. 14.
135 D. I. Hill, p. 77; cf. n.45 above.
136 Greenhalgh, *Wells*, p. 184; cf. p. 79 above.
137 P. A. Welsby, *Rochester Cathedral in the Time of Charles Dickens* (Rochester 1976), p. 11,

quoting J. W. Burgon, *Lives of Twelve Good Men* (London 1888), vol.I, p. 411; cf. J. F. Bridge, *A Westminster Pilgrim* (London 1919), p. 23.

138 E. Wordsworth, *Memorials of Henry William Burrows* (London 1894), pp. 189, 192, 193, 212.

139 E. W. Watson, *Life of Bishop John Wordsworth* (London 1915), pp. 132–4.

140 A. Westcott, *Life and Letters of Brooke Foss Westcott* (London 1903), vol.I, p. 364; Henry Scott Holland (cf. ibid., pp. 310–11) described one of his lectures: 'He was giving lectures on St John in a side chapel; and all through the first lecture we could hardly believe our eyes. This tiny form, with the thin, small voice, delivering itself with passionate intensity, of the deepest teaching on the mystery of the Incarnation, to two timid ladies of the Close, under the haughty contempt of the solitary verger, who had been forced to lend the authority of his 'poker' to those undignified and new-fangled efforts – was this really Dr Westcott?'

141 ibid., p. 312; cf. Benson, vol.I, p. 358.

142 Greenhalgh, *Wells*, pp. 192–3.

143 Chadwick, *York*, p. 282.

144 W. J. Humfrys, *Memories of Old Hereford* (Hereford n.d.), pp. 11–12.

145 ibid., pp. 13–14. Archdeacon Hony at Salisbury spent the time of sermons 'in a snug nook between the bays, where he ate his sandwiches out of a newspaper parcel and drank his half-bottle of port' (D. H. Robertson, *Sarum Close* (London 1938), p. 303).

146 *Trefoil*, pp. 126–7; cf. also pp. 128–9.

147 Chadwick, vol.II, pp. 391–2; J. M. Elvy, *Recollections of the Cathedral and Parish Church of Manchester* (Manchester 1913), p. 30; cf. also Boutflower, pp. 54, 58; M. Hennell, *The Deans and Canons of Manchester Cathedral, 1840–1948* (Manchester 1990), pp. 2–3.

148 R. E. Prothero and G. G. Bradley, *The Life and Correspondence of Arthur Penrhyn Stanley* (London 1893), vol.I, pp. 429–30, 469.

149 R. B. Beckett, *John Constable and the Fishers* (London 1952), p. 123.

150 R. Newton, *Victorian Exeter 1837–1914* (Leicester 1968), p. 21.

151 J. W. F. Hill, *Victorian Lincoln* (London 1974), p. 263. The *Ecclesiologist* complained about the scraping of the exterior of Lincoln Cathedral in 1861 and said that of the five members of the chapter 'two from infirmity are utterly incapable of taking a part in the duties belonging to their position, and two others ingenuously confess that they have no knowledge whatever of architecture' (*Ecclesiologist*, vol.xxii, 1861, pp. 222–4; cf. pp. 245–7).

152 Prothero and Bradley, vol.I, p. 468.

153 Chadwick, *York*, pp. 298–9.

154 F. W. Gretton, *Memory's Hark-back through half a century, 1808–1858* (London 1889), pp. 5–6.

155 Fitzgerald, p. 59. At Wells the canons defended their rights to act independently of the dean (ABDC Wells, 4 December 1801, 3 April 1802).

156 Chadwick, *York*, p. 287.

157 F. Pigou, *Phases of My Life* (London 1898), p. 363; F. Pigou, *Odds and Ends* (London 1903), p. 219.

158 *Chronicle of Convocation of Canterbury*, 1881, 19 May, p. 324.

159 H. Leeds, *Life of Dean Lefroy* (Norwich 1909), p. 28.

160 Wells CM, 1 January 1900.

161 Bell, pp. 171–2.

162 Quoted in Walcott, *Traditions*, pp. 62–3.

163 J. A. Merivale, ed., *Autobiography of Dean Merivale* (London 1899), p. 302.

164 Certainly in new foundation cathedrals this distinction did not really exist before the 1840 Act; cf. pp. 74–5.

165 ABDC Salisbury, 11 June 1813.

166 Watson, pp. 161, 233; Walcott, *Cathedralia*, p. 83. An attempt to revive the meetings

in 1879 failed: twenty-nine canons signed a petition asking for their revival, but Dean Hamilton refused to consider it (K. Edwards, 'The Cathedral of Salisbury, 1075–1950', p. 204). Archdeacon Carpenter recalled the meetings that Bishop Wordsworth summoned: 'The questions discussed were mostly brought forward by the Bishop himself; generally schemes of diocesan action which he was anxious to launch. His own personality and exhaustive treatment of the subjects he introduced left little to be said by anybody else, and I don't think, as a rule, the Chapter discussions helped him much, but with characteristic simplicity he generally wound up with grateful thanks for support, so that he could proceed "after consultation with the Chapter", to take this or that step. One used to smile rather, but it was quite real to him, and I am sure he was right to call the Greater Chapter together in this way' (Watson, p. 233).

167 Clarke, p. 6.
168 ABDC Worcester, 6 March 1824.
169 A. J. B. Beresford Hope, 'Cathedral Reform', *Christian Remembrancer*, vol. xxix, no. 88, 1855, p. 341.
170 ABDC Bristol, 30 November 1836.
171 ABDC Gloucester, 30 November 1855, 2 January 1856.
172 Win.CA, Bishop Davidson's visitation papers, Canon Erskine Clarke's reply. According to the *Guardian*, this was the decision-making body (*Guardian*, 1880, p. 979).
173 ABDC Hereford, 13 November 1873.
174 Chichester general chapter minute book, 2–3 November 1876, 9 December 1879, 5 December 1893, 11 January 1895; cf. ABDC Chichester, 23 January 1893. In 1875 the general chapter of Chichester met twice within a month to advise the bishop about the establishment of a diocesan conference (W. R. W. Stephens, *Cathedral Chapters Considered as Episcopal Councils: A Letter to the Right Reverend The Lord Bishop of Chichester* (London 1877), p. 5); cf. W. R. W. Stephens, *A Memoir of Richard Durnford* (London 1899), pp. 158–60, 360.
175 ABDC Worcester, 11 December 1889.
176 ABDC Salisbury, 25 May 1899.
177 Winchester Greater Chapter minutes, 1892–1907.
178 ABDC Worcester, 24 November 1826; ABDC Winchester, 29 September and 3 November 1874.
179 ABDC Exeter, 1 March 1800.
180 ABDC Winchester, 16 January 1800.
181 ABDC Hereford, August 1841.
182 Prestige, pp. 47, 94–5, 122; Hutton, p. 169.
183 Wells CM, 1 July 1874; Salisbury CM, 4 January and 27 September 1878, 20 October 1882; ABDC Worcester, 20 November 1882.
184 ABDC Wells (1841–55), quoting 3 & 4 William IV, c.31.
185 ABDC Gloucester, 1 April 1891.
186 Clarke, p. 17; cf. ABDC Chichester, 20 January, 19 February, 2 May, 1 August 1800.
187 ABDC Chichester, 1 August 1865.
188 cf. for example, ABDC Gloucester, 11 January 1866.
189 LPL, Tait Papers, vol. 33, 27 November 1853; cf. 25 November 1854.
190 ABDC Gloucester, 30 November 1867.
191 ABDC Bristol, 6 July 1869; cf. also 2 December 1862. There were six special chapter meetings at Norwich in 1822 (Coghlan, p. 130).
192 ABDC Hereford, 6 May 1800.
193 ABDC Gloucester, 29 October 1824.
194 ABDC Bristol, 29 November 1831.
195 Wells CM, 22 May 1843; but cf. 14 January 1832 for a meeting at the deanery.
196 ABDC Worcester, 9 February 1872.

197 ABDC Chichester, 2 February 1886, 2 May 1898.
198 Clark and Hughes, vol.II, pp. 471–2.
199 ABDC Worcester, 11 January, 28 May, 23 June, 12 September, 19–25 November 1800; cf. Chapter 1, p. 8. On 1 January 1800 the dean and five canons of Salisbury agreed to a notice of a meeting of the trustees of the college of matrons, summoned the porter to appear at the next chapter for neglect of duty, and sealed three leases (ABDC Salisbury, 1 January 1800). On 10 October 1801 they elected the following officers – keeper of the muniments, two masters of the fabric, a master of the choristers (one of the canons), a communar and a sub-communar (ibid., 8 October 1801).
200 ibid., 4 February, 13 March, 23 June, 4 August, 2 September, 19–25 November 1830.
201 Prothero and Bradley, vol.I, pp. 428–9.
202 NCL, Goulburn's diary, 22 April and 4 June 1867.
203 ABDC Worcester, 1 January, 6 January, 1 March, 14 May, 3 June, 23 June, 1 August, 7 August, 1 September, 1 October, 19–22 November, 1 December, 22 December 1890. D. I. Hill has noticed a similar change in the business transacted at Canterbury (cf. D. I. Hill, p. 76).
204 Win.CA, Davidson visitation papers 1900, Canon Warburton's reply. Canon Valpy suggested additional meetings to discuss services (with the minor canons included) and gifts to the cathedral.
205 ABDC Wells, 7 December 1805.
206 ABDC Winchester, 24 June 1811, 23 June 1812.
207 ABDC Salisbury, 8 October 1811; one canon was also thought insufficient for a quorum at Wells in 1873 (Wells CM, 9 September 1873). A chapter at Norwich was cancelled in 1828 during a vacancy in the deanery (ABDC Norwich, 2 December 1828, quoted in Coghlan, p. 96).
208 ABDC Gloucester, 30 November 1815.
209 ABDC Gloucester, 1 April 1818, 4 January 1819.
210 ABDC Salisbury, 8 October 1827.
211 ABDC Worcester, 25 November 1835.
212 ABDC Chichester, 20 January 1864.
213 Gloucester chapter minute book, 12 January 1865.
214 ABDC Worcester, 23 November 1872.
215 ibid., 31 July 1874.
216 Chichester Draft Acts 1874–88, January 1877.
217 Gloucester chapter minute book, 31 March 1881.
218 Worc. C. Mss., Compton to Hooper, 1 September 1882. Ten days was agreed as the minimum notice for chapter meetings later that year (ABDC Worcester, 20 November 1882; cf. 13 July 1892).
219 ABDC Chichester, 29 October 1889.
220 ibid.
221 Greenhalgh, Wells, pp. 182, 184–5.
222 cf.F. M. L. Thompson, English Landed Society in the Nineteenth Century (London 1963), pp. 162–3. At Wells, however, the chapter clerk and the chapter agent, scribe and registrar were two separate functionaries (ABDC Wells, 1826).
223 ibid., pp. 160–2, 178. In 1865 the chapter clerks of Lichfield, York, Salisbury and Ripon received respectively £230, £200, £31 and £190 per annum. For examples of local solicitors being employed as agents, cf. P. L. R. Horn, The Changing Countryside in Victorian and Edwardian England and Wales (London 1984), p. 19.
224 G. E. Mingay, Rural Life in Victorian England (London 1977), p. 129.
225 ibid., pp. 129–30, 139, 142–3, 145. At Bristol in 1825 the chapter clerk was empowered to conduct the annual progress in the absence of any member of the chapter (ABDC Bristol, 23 June 1825).

226 For details of the work, cf. E. Richards, in G. E. Mingay, ed., *The Victorian Countryside* (London 1981), vol.II, pp. 439–56.

227 Massingham, pp. 366–7.

228 ABDC Exeter, 1 September 1810; cf. p. 81.

229 ABDC Bristol, 25 January 1808, 5 July 1803. At Peterborough in 1839 the chapter clerk was instructed to keep a careful watch on the affairs of Parliament and to scrutinize any Bills introduced there which might affect the rights and interests of the dean and chapter (Coghlan, quoting ABDC Peterborough, 9 January 1839).

230 R. V. H. Burne, *Chester Cathedral* (London 1958), pp. 236–7.

231 ABDC Winchester, 23 June and 29 July 1814.

232 Chadwick, *York*, p. 290 (cf. Ecclesiastical Commissioners' file 8083/2024/51). Another cause for complaint as a result of government interference was the repeated series of enquiries and questionnaires sent to cathedrals. The completion of these was usually given to the chapter clerk. The chapter clerk at Hereford was 'over-wearied' by 'your interminable queries' and told the Ecclesiastical Commissioners: 'I may as well shut my office door against all professional business for the next two or three months' (quoted in O. Brose, *Church and Parliament* (Stanford, USA, 1959), p. 166).

233 ABDC Bristol, 17 March 1841.

234 ABDC Bristol, 19 March 1856.

235 Walcott, *Cathedralia*, p. 141.

236 ABDC Gloucester, 11 January 1866.

237 Chichester Draft Acts, 20 September 1875. For his involvement in the Shoreham Gardens saga, cf. Chapter 8, p. 192.

238 ABDC Bristol, 1 April 1879. Two joint chapter clerks were appointed at Salisbury in 1888 (cf. ABDC Salisbury, 13 November 1888 for their duties). The salary of the chapter clerk at Peterborough in 1898 was £60 per annum (ABDC Peterborough, 25 October 1898, cited in Coghlan, p. 129).

239 ABDC Winchester, 6 March, 3 October, 11 December 1883, 8 January 1884. Cluttons proved unsatisfactory and in 1886 the dean and chapter engaged Messrs Field and Castle of 18 Merton Street, Oxford. They also acted for the dean and chapter of Gloucester in association with George Whitcombe, the chapter clerk; cf. also Win.CA, Bishop Davidson's visitation papers, dean's reply.

240 Salisbury DRO, Press V, Box 5.

241 ABDC Bristol, 12 September 1838.

242 Wells CM, 20 August 1863.

243 ABDC Exeter, 6 March 1869.

244 ABDC Chichester, 2 August, 15 November 1887.

245 ABDC Salisbury, 25 June 1888.

246 ABDC Hereford, 17 April 1890.

CHAPTER 6 *The Cathedral Staff*

1 See above, Introduction, p. xv, and n.14 on p. 313 for various studies of individual corporations of vicars choral.

2 cf. P. L. S. Barrett, *The College of Vicars Choral at Hereford Cathedral* (Hereford 1980), *passim*, and ABVC Hereford, 2 July 1853. The distinct nature of the college was emphasized in the 1637 statutes at Hereford: 'Quia Collegium Vicariorum Choralium Herefordense commune quoddam est, et Corpus per se distinctum' ('Forasmuch as the College of Vicars Choral of Hereford is a sort of community and body distinct by itself') (cf. J. Jebb and H. W. Phillott, *The Statutes of the Cathedral Church of Hereford* (Hereford 1882), pp. 108–9).

3 ABVC Hereford, 15 December 1802, 15 December 1803.

4 ABDC Hereford, 25 June 1836. For an example of an advertisement at Wells (presumably for a lay vicar), cf. Wells CM, 11 May 1868.

5 ABDC Hereford, 5 September 1849.

6 Wells CM, 2 January 1858.

7 ABVC Wells, 2 March 1855.

8 ABDC Hereford, 10 September and 14 November 1867.

9 F. G. Bennett, R. H. Codrington and C. Deedes, *Statutes and Constitutions of the Cathedral Church of Chichester* (Chichester 1904), p. 186. In addition, no vicar was allowed to go into the city wearing a sword or carrying a hawk! For restriction on dogs at Hereford, cf. ABVC Hereford, 30 April 1807 and 15 March 1817. When F. T. Havergal's fowls and poultry began to cause damage in the college garden at Hereford in 1858, the vicars decided that in future no poultry should be allowed within the college (ABVC Hereford, 17 April 1858).

10 ABVC Wells, 21 September 1800.

11 ABVC Hereford , 26 September 1800.

12 Walcott, *Traditions*, p. 63; M. E. C. Walcott, *Cathedralia* (London 1865), p. 143. For the fire, cf. p. 85.

13 ABVC Hereford, 6 August 1803; cf. P. L. S. Barrett, 'Hereford Cathedral in the Nineteenth Century', *FHCAR*, 1986, p. 15.

14 ABVC Hereford, 4 February 1809.

15 ABVC Hereford, 23 October 1810.

16 ABVC Hereford, 27 October and 22 November 1810, 26 March and 6 June 1811.

17 ABVC Hereford, 24 April and 30 April 1813.

18 ABVC Hereford, 20 September 1810, 26 November 1816.

19 ABVC Hereford, 24 March 1820, 9 August 1828; Barrett, 'Hereford Cathedral in the Nineteenth Century', pp. 16–17.

20 ABVC Hereford, 1 May 1833.

21 ABDC Hereford, 12 November 1874.

22 ABVC Hereford, 6 March and 23 June 1875.

23 ABVC Hereford, 9 June 1866, 8 November 1886; MBVC Wells, 22 September 1890.

24 J. Jebb, *The Choral Service of the United Church of England and Ireland* (London 1843), p. 112; cf. also pp. 97, 101. There were eleven vicars choral at Wells in 1825 (ABDC Wells, 13 December 1825) and fourteen in 1875 (MBVC Wells, 28 October 1875). For the appointment of lay vicars at Wells, cf. MBVC Wells, 29 August and 1 September 1853, and Wells CM, 3 December 1860.

25 HCA 5071.

26 cf. the rules for the choir at Wells, ABDC Wells, 8 December 1831.

27 Jebb commented in 1843: 'it is a modern abuse to devolve the principal part of this sacred duty chiefly upon laymen' (Jebb, p. 102).

28 CCF 3208.

29 ABDC Exeter, 20 May and 18 November 1815.

30 ABDC Exeter, 26–7 March 1827. Four years later the dean and chapter declined to interfere in an arrangement by which the two senior priest vicars paid two juniors £20 each for relieving them of their of their Sunday duties so that they might take curacies in the city or district (ABDC Exeter, 2 April 1831). Two priest vicars were also expected to attend services at Wells on Sundays, especially the communion service (Wells CM, 26 August 1853). The rule of two vicars at Sunday services was also observed at Hereford (ABVC Hereford, 31 January 1867 – cf. CCF 37357, letter of 21 May 1867).

31 ABDC Exeter, 18 December 1817.

32 W. D. Peckham, 'The Vicars Choral of Chichester Cathedral', *Sussex Archaeological Collections*, vol. 78, no. xxxvii, 1937, p. 146. Later the dean and chapter stipulated that the duty priest vicar must attend early celebrations and any special services

during the week, though A. H. Glennie, the principal, pleaded for an additional income for the extra work involved (ABDC Chichester, 2 August 1888, 21 January and 19 March 1889; cf. Dean Pigou to Principal Glennie, 19 July 1889; Glennie's reply 19 October 1889, Chichester Capitular Archives, III/5/4, pp. 59, 63).

33 See Chapter 7, p. 120.

34 ABDC Hereford, 20 December 1890.

35 *Guardian*, 1896, p. 2081; cf. *Hereford Journal*, 19 June 1897.

36 ABDC Exeter, 9 January, 10 April, 15 April, 21 April 1869. At Chichester in 1877 the dean and chapter decided to collect fees on behalf of the priest vicars from prebendaries of endowed stalls who failed to keep their preaching turns (ABDC Chichester, 2 May 1877). This followed an occasion when the Vicar of Boxgrove had declined to pay as he had been superseded by an ordination, calling the vicars' request 'a piece of impertinency on your part'. The priest vicars sent the whole correspondence to the dean and chapter and asked them to protect them from such discourteous treatment (Chichester Capitular Archives, III/5/4, p. 25).

37 *Guardian*, 1898, p. 511.

38 Greenhalgh, *Wells*, p. 189.

39 F. E. Gretton, *Memory's Hark-back Through Half a Century, 1808–1858* (London 1889), p. 7; Barrett, *The College of Vicars Choral at Hereford Cathedral*, p. 24; W. Cooke, *Memorials of the Vicars Choral*, no.65.

40 Gretton, pp. 7–8. For more details of Kidley, cf. Barrett, 'Hereford Cathedral in the Nineteenth Century', p. 14.

41 ABDC Hereford, 12 November, 28 November, 1 December 1807, 25 February and 2 April 1808; ABVC Hereford, 17 August 1805, 18 August 1807.

42 ABVC Hereford, 30 April 1831.

43 ABDC Hereford, 26 June 1848. Although in his early days in the college Pearce had been something of a recluse, he was later the life and soul of the college, thoroughly enjoying the comforts of the common room: 'None could fail to be captivated by the liveliness of his repartee.' Towards the end of his life, he spent many hours poring over his Hebrew Bible, and his voice became as tremulous as his whole body had always been, the effect of an accident with a gun at Ross-on-Wye while he was a boy (Barrett, *The College of Vicars Choral at Hereford Cathedral*, p. 24, quoting Cooke, no.61).

44 Dawes to Ecclesiastical Commissioners, 18 March 1851, CCF 3208, quoted in Barrett, 'Hereford Cathedral in the Nineteenth Century', p. 30.

45 ABVC Hereford, 11 October 1813.

46 ABVC Hereford, 1 February 1836.

47 Barrett, *The College of Vicars Choral at Hereford Cathedral*, pp. 24–5; Cooke, no.76; ABVC Hereford, 27 November 1819.

48 J. F. Chanter, *The Custos and College of the Vicars Choral of the Choir of the Cathedral Church of St Peter, Exeter* (Exeter 1933), pp. 38–9.

49 PP 1837, xli, p. 67; cf. A. S. Leak, 'Conflict and Reform at York Minster in the Nineteenth Century' (Oxford B. D. thesis 1988), pp. 256–302. In 1869 Subchanter William Bulmer died. He had been a vicar choral at York for sixty-eight years (Leak, p. 272).

50 ABDC Hereford, November 1834.

51 PP 1854, xxv, p. 909.

52 ABVC Hereford, 2 February 1867.

53 ABDC Hereford, 9 April and 26 April 1875.

54 ibid., 26 April 1875. The *Guardian* alleged in 1858 that the dean and chapter of Wells had appointed two priest vicars 'without any trial of their musical qualifications' (*Guardian*, 1858, p. 107, and Chapter 7, p. 146).

55 ABDC Hereford, 9 April 1888.

56 ABDC Hereford, 24 March and 9 April 1870, 24 March 1871, 13 November, 12 December and 19 December, 4 June 1873; ABVC Hereford, 16 June 1873; cf. Leak, pp. 276–7 for a similar dispute at York.

57 H. W. Pullen, *Mediaeval Mummery in 1870* (Salisbury 1870), p. 5.

58 ABDC Salisbury, 2 March 1869, Dean to Pullen, 4 March 1869.

59 ABDC Hereford, 13 November 1800.

60 See pp. 86–7 above.

61 ABDC Hereford, 11 November 1819; cf. ABVC Hereford, 27 November 1819.

62 ABDC Hereford, 3 March 1829.

63 ABDC Hereford, 14 February 1832.

64 ABDC Hereford, 19 July 1834; Merewether to vicars, 28 July 1834; cf. ABVC Hereford, 23 August 1834.

65 ABDC Hereford, 17 November 1834.

66 ABVC Hereford, 7 October 1837; cf. ibid., 25 September 1840.

67 CCF 3208.

68 ibid.

69 L. W. Cowie, 'Worship in the Minster', *The Victoria History of the Counties of England: A History of Yorkshire: The City of York* (London 1961), p. 353.

70 F. Harrison, *Life in a Mediaeval College* (London 1952), pp. 279–80.

71 ABVC Hereford, 7 November 1857.

72 ABDC Hereford, 31 January and 25 March 1867.

73 Wells CM, 25 January 1870; cf. 7 January 1874, MBVC Wells, 23 July 1874.

74 Wells CM, 13 September and 30 September 1876; cf. 12 November 1880.

75 PP 1883, xxi, pp. 254–5.

76 Wells CM, 1 April 1887.

77 Wells CM, 3 October 1888.

78 Wells CM, 1 April 1899.

79 ABDC Hereford, 24 March, 4 April, 20 April 1870; cf. 24 October 1872.

80 ABDC Hereford, 9 November 1876.

81 ABDC Hereford, 9 December 1878.

82 ABDC Hereford, 25 March 1894, 12 October 1895, 24 March 1899; cf. Barrett, 'Hereford Cathedral in the Nineteenth Century', p. 35.

83 ABDC Hereford, 9 April, 25 June, 12–14 November 1846; cf. ABVC Hereford, 2 April 1846.

84 Wells CM, 30 September 1868.

85 ABDC Hereford, 4 December and 7 December 1872.

86 ABDC Hereford, 24 March 1873; in return the dean and chapter objected to the presence of a married vicar choral living with his children in the college (ABDC Hereford, 12 November 1874).

87 Wells CM, 18 December 1874, 31 March, 10 April, 31 May, 15 June 1875; cf. ABDC Wells, 10 April, 7 and 16 June 1875.

88 Wells CM, 30 April 1879, 17 January 1880.

89 PP 1883, xxi, pp. 268–9.

90 Chanter, p. 37.

91 *Guardian*, 1888, p. 526.

92 ABVC Hereford, 23 January 1800.

93 ABVC Hereford, 2 November 1807.

94 The list of fines and the vicars' account book are in Salisbury Chapter Muniments, Press III, Box 'Vicars Choral' / 29, p. 3. In the first few years the fines received by the Salisbury vicars averaged £37 and their annual revenues were approximately £437 gross or £243 net. In other words, each of the four vicars received some £40 in addition to what they were paid by the dean and chapter; cf. K. Edwards, 'The Cathedral of Salisbury, 1075–1950', *VCH Wiltshire*, 1956, vol.iii, p. 201.

95 MBVC Wells, 8 February 1802.

96 ABVC Hereford, 4 February 1809.

97 ABVC Hereford, 27 September 1822.

98 ABDC Exeter, 22–3 March and 23 June 1832, 25–28 March 1846, 14–15 March 1849.

99 ABDC Hereford, 14 November 1850.

100 ABVC Hereford, 2 July 1853. Dean Dawes told the Ecclesiastical Commission in 1851 that the property of the college of vicars choral ought to be vested in the dean and chapter: 'the property is ill-managed and might be improved – the greater part of the College buildings entirely useless' (CCF 3208). Nearly fifty years later Dean Leigh said: 'I only wish that it were possible for the Ecclesiastical Commissioners to take over the *whole* of the property of the Custos and Vicars, including the College buildings which are only inhabited by *two* of the vicars choral, whereas they were intended for twelve and which from not being occupied are getting into a very bad condition....I believe we could rent the Vicars' College from the Ecclesiastical Commissioners for the use of the Cathedral School or other purposes. There is a nice Hall, good library and small chapel *unused* or put to *wrong purposes* and as it is we have no power to make any use of them. Can nothing be done?' (Dean Leigh to A. de Brock Porter, 18 April 1898, CCF 37357).

101 Chanter, p. 32.

102 ABDC Chichester, 1 August 1865, ABVC Chichester, 10 July 1875. In 1880 the Chichester vicars choral told the cathedral commissioners that before the commutation of their estates they were worth £869 per annum, plus an average of £200 per annum from fines on the renewal of leases. The Ecclesiastical Commissioners had allowed them £300 per annum after the commutation and they had an additional income of £183 from various other sources (ABVC Chichester, 6 July 1880).

103 Harrison, pp. 36, 273. For some examples of York leases, cf. ibid., pp. 268f.

104 MBVC Wells, 31 July 1852, 15 March, 9 July, 21 September 1866.

105 Orders in Council, 4 November 1867, 14 May 1868. For the Exeter settlement, cf. Chanter, p. 36.

106 *Guardian*, 1887, p. 430.

107 ABDC Hereford, 10 October 1893.

108 MBVC Wells, 5 March 1864. They were also not to come to the Hall (as the formal meeting was termed) 'in slippers or in a dirty or indecent dress' or they were liable to a fine of 3s 4d (MBVC Wells, 21 September 1809).

109 ABVC Hereford, 4 January 1868.

110 ibid., 3 October 1870, 12 August 1871, cf. Barrett, *The College of Vicars Choral at Hereford Cathedral*, p. 28.

111 ABVC Hereford, 6 March 1875.

112 ABVC Chichester, 10 July 1875.

113 MBVC Salisbury, 26 July 1864.

114 ABVC Hereford, 1865, 4 March 1866.

115 MBVC Wells, 8 November 1872, 7 October 1875, 18 October 1888.

116 ibid., 8 November 1894.

117 cf. Chapter 8, n. 47. Dean Merewether told Archbishop Howley in 1836: 'I am convinced from experience obtained as Dean and Ordinary of the Peculiar of the Deanery of Hereford, in which many of the vicars choral have livings and curacies, that the two offices are not compatible with each other, at least so as to afford due attention to both...' (CCF 3208). Bishop Hervey of Bath and Wells expressed the same opinion in 1880 (PP 1883, xxi, p. 251).

118 J. W. F. Hill, *Victorian Lincoln* (London 1974), p. 177.

119 Peckham, p. 132. The dean and chapter of Chichester seem to have encouraged their vicars choral to be active pastorally outside the cathedral. In 1884, in a printed

note about the emoluments of the vicars choral (or minor canons – the terms seem to have been used interchangeably), it was stated: 'A minor canon who is not beneficed can materially increase his income by helping his beneficed brethren with their Sunday duty in their parishes. The last minor canon who was not beneficed received betwen £60 and £70 per annum in this way' (Chichester Draft Acts, 10 October 1884).

120 Index to leases, Salisbury Chapter Muniments, Press III, Vicars Choral/10.

121 G. L. Prestige, *St Paul's in its Glory, 1831–1911* (London 1955), pp. 20–1.

122 ABDC Chichester, 10 October 1868; cf. also 16 October and 8 December 1899.

123 ibid., 2 May 1876.

124 Prestige, pp. 153–4; W. J. S. Simpson, *Memoir of The Reverend W. Sparrow Simpson* (London 1899), pp. 62–77; cf. Chapter 12, p. 278.

125 ABDC Chichester, 2 February 1886, 10 October 1890.

126 ABDC Exeter, 27 December 1890, 23 February 1895; for further details of the duties of the succentor at Lichfield, where he was known as the subchanter, Hereford and Salisbury in 1892, cf. Bristol DC/A/13/5.

127 cf. Jebb and Phillott, p. 129. The term also seems to have been in use for the vicars choral at Salisbury (cf. Salisbury CM, 24 May, 28 May, 20 June, 30 July, 3 August, 29 November 1864).

128 Prestige, p. 6.

129 ibid., p. 7.

130 ibid., p. 8.

131 Jebb, p. 111.

132 E. Taylor, *The English Cathedral Service: its Glory, its Decline and its Designed Extinction* (London 1845); see also Chapter 7, p. 163 (*Guardian*, 1854, p. 918).

133 Prestige, pp. 64–5.

134 38 & 39 Vict., c.74.

135 Prestige, pp. 126–7; cf. W. H. Hutton, ed., *The Autobiography of Robert Gregory* (London 1912), p. 202.

136 Prestige, p. 169.

137 ibid., pp. 169–73; *Guardian*, 1883, p. 1807. The need for such work had become apparent in 1870, when the dean and chapter received a petition from local workers who wanted a place set aside in St Paul's for private prayer (St Paul's CM, 29 June 1870, cited in P. V. Coghlan, 'Cathedral Worship in the Church of England 1815–1914' (Leicester University M. Phil. thesis 1984), p. 147).

138 ABDC Bristol, 1 December 1824.

139 ABDC Bristol, 23 June 1837.

140 cf. 3 & 4 Vict., c. 113, s.45. For the reduction at Winchester, cf. A. W. Goodman and W. H. Hutton, *The Statutes governing the Cathedral Church of Winchester* (Oxford 1925), p. 5, fn.2. By 1854 there were only three minor canons at Norwich (B. Rainbow, *The Choral Revival in the Anglican Church, 1839–1872* (London 1970), p. 245). The number of cathedral chaplains was reduced to six by 1860 (E. G. W. Bill and J. F. A. Mason, *Christ Church and Reform 1850–1867* (Oxford 1970), p. 195, fn.1).

141 Jebb, pp. 121–2.

142 PP 1884–5, xxi, p. 92.

143 ABDC Winchester, 25 November 1807.

144 ABDC Winchester, 25 November 1812.

145 ABDC Worcester, 23 and 25 November 1833.

146 ABDC Worcester, 24 November 1824; cf. 24 November 1825. Meanwhile, at Winchester the minor canons were awarded an extra £15 in 1825 (ABDC Winchester, 25 November 1825).

147 PP 1835, xxii, pp. 36–7.

148 PP 1836, xxxvi, p. 25. The 1835 figures were made the basis of a pamphlet pleading

for higher salaries for minor canons which appeared in 1839: *The Case of the Minor Canons and inferior officers of the Cathedrals of the New Foundation particularly with reference to Canterbury Cathedral* (Canterbury 1839). At Bristol, four dean and chapter livings were retained for the minor canons, though they complained when the members of the chapter opted to keep the richer livings for themselves or appointed outsiders (ABDC Bristol, 24 April 1806, 30 November 1829; PP 1837, xli, pp. 46–7). Difficulties were caused at Gloucester in 1819 when a minor canon tried to retain his living after resigning his minor canonry (ABDC Gloucester, 13 April 1819). At Winchester one of the minor canons was also chaplain of Winchester College (ABDC Winchester, 29 September 1852). So common was the practice of combining minor canonries with city livings that the *Guardian* said in 1852: 'There are few inhabitants of Cathedral cities who have not painful recollections of the overworked minor canon, pausing in his sermon, and listening anxiously for the Cathedral bell' (*Guardian*, 1852, p. 821).

149 P. C. Moore, 'The Organisation and Development of Cathedral Worship in England, with special reference to choral services, from the Reformation to the nineteenth century' (Oxford D. Phil. thesis 1954), p. 329, quoting C. J. Blomfield in *Mirror of Parliament*, vol.vi, 30 July 1840, p. 5079, and *The Ecclesiastic*, 1846, vol.I, p. 365.

150 ABDC Gloucester, 30 November 1840; cf. ABDC Winchester, 25 November 1840.

151 ABDC Worcester, 25 November 1854. The dean and chapter of Bristol had agreed to pay their minor canons £150 each in the previous year (ABDC Bristol, 7 December 1853).

152 Worc. C. Mss., Bundle marked 'Corn rents'.

153 ABDC Worcester, 28 November 1868, 30 July 1870, 19 November 1874.

154 Coghlan, p. 110, citing ABDC Norwich, 25 January and 3 April 1865.

155 H. Alford, 'Cathedral Reform', *Contemporary Review*, vol. xii, September 1869, p. 46; cf. C. Jenkins, ed., *The Statutes of the Cathedral and Metropolitical Church of Christ, Canterbury* (Canterbury 1925), pp. 133–4.

156 ABDC Gloucester, 21–2 December 1887, 12 July 1888. At Winchester, where Dean Kitchin said that the dean and chapter's annual average income had fallen to £9,126 instead of an intended £12,904, the problem was overcome by reducing the four minor canons to three and paying them £218 per annum (Win.CA, *Cathedralia Winton – Minor Canons 1860–1918*, 15 July 1890).

157 PP 1884, xxii, p. 95.

158 Winchester Cathedral Mss., *Cathedralia Winton: Minor Canons 1860–1918*; cf. ABDC Gloucester, 30 November 1813.

159 See Chapter 3, p. 31.

160 H. A. Hudson in introduction to J. M. Elvy, *Recollections of the Cathedral and Parish Church of Manchester* (Manchester 1913), pp. 9–10.

161 Rainbow, pp. 244–5, quoting J. S. Bumpus, *A History of English Cathedral Music, 1549–1889* (London 1908), vol.II, p. 356.

162 Moore, p. 267.

163 R. J. Fletcher, *A History of Bristol Cathedral* (London 1932), pp. 51–2; cf. ABDC Bristol, 15 September 1807, 5 December 1848.

164 ABDC Gloucester, 30 November 1808; cf. 30 November 1841, 30 November 1842. At Ely two minor canons were needed at each service. One intoned the collects and the other read the lesson and performed the remaining parts of the service. The rota was drawn up carefully to avoid the parochial commitments of the minor canons (ABDC Ely, 1 October 1852, quoted in Coghlan, p. 143).

165 Fletcher, p. 61; cf. ABDC Bristol, 1 March and 7 December 1853.

166 PP 1852–3, lxxviii, p. 11.

167 ABDC Winchester, 23 June 1858.

168 PP 1865, xli, p. 434; cf. LPL, Tait Papers, vol. 27, 5 February 1850.

169 ABDC Worcester, 3 and 22 November 1870, 22 November 1871, 11 January, 9 February, 29 June 1872, 31 July and 19 November 1874, 25 September 1875.

170 ABDC Worcester, 13 January 1876; T. L. Wheeler to Dean, 4 February 1876, Worc. C. Mss., bundle marked 'Memorials from the minor canons'.

171 ABDC Worcester, 6 April, 7 June, 27 December 1881. In 1900 the dean and chapter said that two minor canons were required on Sunday afternoons (ABDC Worcester, 20 November 1900).

172 ABDC Winchester, 22 June, 3 August, 26 November 1878, 7 January 1879.

173 ABDC Gloucester, 30 November 1882. The Gloucester minor canons were responsible for reading both lessons at the early morning service each day (ABDC Gloucester, 25 September 1873). At Canterbury they read the lessons from their stalls on weekdays (C. E. Woodruff and W. Danks, *Memorials of the Cathedral and Priory of Christ in Canterbury* (London 1912), p. 19).

174 Coghlan, p. 107, quoting ABDC Peterborough, 30 November 1883.

175 ibid., pp. 107–8, quoting ABDC Peterborough, 31 May 1872, 29 April 1881.

176 ABDC Bristol, 3 April 1888 (letter of 11 February 1888).

177 ABDC Worcester, 15 July, 1 August, 2 September 1889.

178 Winchester Cathedral Mss., *Cathedralia Winton: Minor Canons 1860–1918*, 15 July 1890.

179 Woodward to Hooper, 20 November 1896, Worc. C. Mss., Precentor's Reports.

180 Fletcher, pp. 51–2; ABDC Bristol, 2 December 1824, 5 December 1848.

181 Coghlan, p. 130, citing St Paul's CM, 9 May 1853.

182 ABDC Winchester, 23 June 1873.

183 ABDC Worcester, 19 November 1877, 19 November 1880.

184 PP 1884, xxii, p. 274.

185 Worc. C. Mss., Woodward to Dean, 3 March 1896, Sacrists' Reports.

186 Winchester Cathedral Mss., *De Precentore*, 1900.

187 ibid., Davidson visitation papers, 1900.

188 Moore, p. 210. There was a similar practical audition at Exeter in 1808 (ibid., p. 268, quoting ABDC Exeter, 23 January 1808).

189 ABDC Gloucester, 30 November 1835.

190 *Parish Choir*, vol. 1 p. 135. For a comment on the unfortunate effect of having unmusical minor canons, cf. Moore, p. 325.

191 Winchester Cathedral Mss., *Cathedralia Winton: Minor Canons 1860–1918*, 2 July 1862.

192 ABDC Worcester, 6 February 1875.

193 Winchester Cathedral Mss., *Cathedralia Winton: Minor Canons 1860–1918*, 1 October 1878, 13 October 1878. For E. Vine Hall's application for the precentorship of Worcester Cathedral in 1877, cf. Worc. C. Mss., Choir Bundle.

194 ABDC Gloucester, 2 June 1882, 30 April 1895.

195 Elvy, p. 35; A. Boutflower, *Personal Reminiscences of Manchester Cathedral 1854–1912* (Leighton Buzzard 1913), p. 47.

196 Woodruff and Danks, p. 19. Nicholas Westcombe was elected a minor canon of Winchester in 1769 and held the post until he was murdered in 1813. His son Thomas succeeded to the minor canonry which he held until 1848 (C. E. Moxley, 'Minores Canonici – Part I: Nicholas Westcombe', *Winchester Cathedral Record* no.58, 1989, pp. 24–33; 'Minores Canonici – Part II: Thomas Westcombe', in ibid., no.59, 1990, pp. 23–34.

197 *Trefoil*, p. 132.

198 J. T. Fowler, *Life and Letters of John Bacchus Dykes* (London 1897), pp. 152–4. Other notable librarians among junior cathedral clergy were J. F. Wickenden at Lincoln and F. T. Havergal at Hereford; cf. Chapter 12, pp. 280–1.

199 Worc. C. Add. Mss., 141, p. 10; cf. Add. Mss., 104, pp. 159–60.

200 Bristol Capitular Archives DC/A/7/6/2.

201 *Guardian*, 1881, p. 791. When Joseph Jameson resigned as a minor canon of Ripon in 1875, he had served there for over fifty years (L. Smith, *The Story of Ripon Minster* (Leeds 1914), p. 270).

202 Goodman and Hutton, pp. 49–50.

203 ABDC Winchester, 2 February 1815.

204 ABDC Bristol, 26 June 1832, 24 June 1834; cf. 10 May 1849, 7 December 1853, 12 January 1869. He was asked to give the attendance book to the canon-in-residence on the first Monday in each month, but was not allowed to buy music without the approval of the dean and chapter (ABDC Bristol, 13 December 1888, 8 January 1889).

205 ABDC Gloucester, 30 November 1853. For examples of his reports, cf. 1 December 1854 and 8 January 1857.

206 ABDC Winchester, 26 November 1860.

207 ABDC Worcester, 4 July 1862.

208 ABDC Worcester, 3 August 1876.

209 Worc. C. Mss., Precentor's Reports; cf. ABDC Worcester, 3 December 1879. According to Walcott, the stipends of the precentors of Norwich and Peterborough in 1865 were £244 and £175 respectively (Walcott, p. 176). It appears, however, that the Precentor of Norwich was paid more generously, for he had an income of £255 as a minor canon, with £20 as precentor and £11 as librarian (ABDC Norwich, 25 January 1865, cited in Coghlan, p. 111). When T. L. Wheeler retired as Precentor of Worcester in 1877 and was given a pension of £60 per annum, he was also allowed the use of a stall in the quire (ABDC Worcester, 23 June 1877, 19 November 1877). Precentor Vine Hall told the dean and chapter in 1899 that he had been giving religious instruction once a month to the beadsmen in one of the chapels of the cathedral: 'I have reason to think that they value these little gatherings. Certainly they listen to what I have to say to them with the utmost attention and seem grateful for the help then given' (Worc. C. Mss., Sacrists' Reports, 1889).

210 ABDC Worcester, 19 November 1883.

211 PP, 1884–5, xxi, p. 284; cf. also ABDC Peterborough, 6 March 1869, 31 May 1870, cited in Coghlan, p. 111.

212 ABDC Bristol, 30 June 1899.

213 Bristol DC/A/13/5.

214 ibid. When a new precentor of Winchester was appointed in 1890, he was formally introduced to the organist and choir by the dean at the Monday evening choir practice. He made a speech to the lay clerks and choristers, encouraging them to try to achieve a higher standard of singing and asking for their 'hearty co-operation' (Winchester Cathedral Mss., *De Precentore*, 22 September 1890). At Ely, where the precentor was also sacrist, he rehearsed the choir and taught the choristers religious knowledge, with an additional stipend of £70 per annum (ABDC Ely, 1 October 1895, cited in Coghlan, p. 111).

215 Fowler, pp. 49–50.

216 W. G. Roe and A. Hutchings, *J. B. Dykes, Priest and Musician* (Durham 1976), p. 2.

217 F. G. Kitton, *Zechariah Buck* (London 1899), p. 37.

218 S. S. Wesley to H. E. Ford, 19 September 1858 (Royal School of Church Music Library), quoted in Moore, pp. 357f.

219 M. P. Chappell, *Dr S. S. Wesley: Portrait of a Victorian Musician* (Great Wakering 1977), pp. 98–9, quoting *Musical Times*, June 1899, pp. 377–8. For an impression of T. T. Griffith, Precentor of Rochester, cf. Bridge, pp. 16–17.

220 Worc. C. Add. Mss., 141, pp. 32–3.

221 Worc. C. Add. Mss., 137, p. 4

222 Worc. C. Add. Mss., 104, pp. 2–3.

223 Worc. C. Add. Mss., 137, p. 16.
224 ibid.; cf. Worc. C. Add. Mss., 141, p. 37.
225 Taylor, pp. 32–3.
226 Bristol DC/A/7/4/3.
227 Winchester Cathedral Mss., *De Precentore*, 1879, p. 71.
228 ibid., November 1880.
229 ABDC Worcester, 1 December 1887.
230 E. Vine Hall to dean and chapter, 9 December 1887, Worc. C. Mss., Choir Bundle.
231 Goodman and Hutton, pp. 50–1. For the similar duties of the sacrist at Chester, cf. PP 1883, xxi, p. 157. The sacrist of Canterbury was pastorally responsible for the precincts and also a non-parochial area formerly part of the archbishop's palace, but currently occupied by the King's School (PP 1884, xxii, p. 226).
232 Worc. C. Add. Mss., 19, p. 24. For a weekly donation of 10s to a verger whose wife had a broken thigh, cf. ABDC Worcester, 1 March 1827. A verger at Peterborough who was disabled through blindness caused by an accident at work was given only a charitable allowance of £4 per annum from Michaelmas 1829 (ABDC Peterborough, 30 November 1829, cited in Coghlan, p. 128).
233 ABDC Bristol, 7 December 1853, 12 January 1869.
234 Worc. C. Mss., Precentor's Reports; cf. ABDC Worcester, 11 December 1869.
235 H. Clifford to chapter clerk, 18 November 1891, Sacrist's Report, 1892, Worc. C. Mss.
236 ibid., 1894.
237 Walcott, p. 182.
238 ABDC Chichester, 20 January 1804.
239 F. C. and P. E. Morgan, *Hereford Cathedral Libraries and Muniments* (Hereford 1970), p. 10.
240 ABDC Bristol, 30 November 1827.
241 ABDC Exeter, 14 February 1829.
242 Wells CM, 4 June 1832.
243 ABDC Gloucester, 18 January 1858. A further reorganization of the duties was implemented in 1876 (ABDC Gloucester, 24 June and 28 September 1876).
244 ABDC Salisbury, 7 December 1866. For the duties of the verger at Hereford, cf. ABDC Hereford, 9 May 1874.
245 ABDC Winchester, 6 June 1882. For an earlier account of their duties, when they were known as clerks, cf. ABDC Winchester, 3 February and 29 September 1874. (For the duties of the vergers at Norwich in 1883, cf. ABDC Norwich, 6 March 1883, cited in Coghlan, p. 124.)
246 ABDC Worcester, 3 August 1876.
247 ibid., 10 January 1874. At Ely the verger's salary was only £85 (ABDC Ely, 21 April 1885, cited in Coghlan, p. 127); cf. pp. 107–8, and n.252.
248 ABDC Worcester, 5 February, 21 March, 13 July 1892.
249 ibid., 27 June and 19 November 1895 (for details of Custos Simpson, cf. Worc. C. Add. Mss., 104, pp. 10–12).
250 Bristol DC/A/7/3/4.
251 Bristol DC/A/7/4/3. A. Poole to I. Trott, 17 April 1865, A. Poole to canon-in-residence, 26 June 1866; cf. Chapter 7, p. 159.
252 Chichester Draft Acts 1889, pp. 21–2. In 1891 the bishop appointed his butler to be his verger, and the dean and chapter acquiesced in this appointment (Chichester chapter minute book, August 1891). The stipends of vergers remained low at most cathedrals throughout the century. At Winchester in 1817 they were entitled to £25 per annum plus perquisites (ABDC Winchester, 23 June 1817. A new verger at Bristol in 1827 was paid only £20 per annum (ABDC Bristol, 30 November 1827). The four vergers at St Paul's were mainly dependent on the 2d visitors' fees. From

NOTES

1837 to 1843 these enabled each verger to have an average income of over £100. This rose to over £130 during the next four years, but fell back back to £112 from 1848 to 1850 (Prestige, p. 29). Visitors' fees were abolished at St Paul's in 1851 when the Ecclesiastical Commissioners offered £400 to augment the stipends of the four vergers (ibid., p. 68). Some £30 per annum was the income of the sexton and dean's verger at Chichester in 1860 and they were not allowed to receive any pew rents or visitor's fees (ABDC Chichester, 20 January 1860). The basic income of many vergers in different cathedrals in the 1860s was still very low (cf. Walcott, p. 182). At Hereford in 1868 the verger received £65 per annum and the two sextons £50 each.They were allowed 10 per cent of visitors' fees, plus installation fees, but were not allowed to have any gratuities (CCF 32508). The rates of £130 and £50 fixed at Salisbury in 1866 would have been regarded as generous (ABDC Salisbury, 7 December 1866, 29 January 1867). The dean and chapter of Exeter established the salaries of their two senior vergers at £200 in 1873 (ABDC Exeter, 15 March 1873) and even the junior verger was paid £100 (ibid., 9 February 1884). The sum of £130 per annum and no fees or gratuities was the salary offered to a new senior verger at Exeter in 1898 (ABDC Exeter, 18 June 1898).

253 Salisbury CM, 18 July and 1 August 1899.
254 ABDC Chichester, 10 October 1900.
255 Prestige, p. 25.
256 ibid., pp. 164–5; cf. St Paul's CM, 4 February 1890, cited in Coghlan, p. 126.
257 H. D. Rawnsley, *Harvey Goodwin, Bishop of Carlisle* (London 1896), pp. 115–16. The verger at Christ Church, Oxford, kept his beer in a cupboard on the north side of the quire. (H. L. Thompson, *Henry George Liddell* (London 1899), pp. 149–50).
258 Coghlan, p. 126, citing ABDC Ely, 21 April 1885.
259 Wells CM, 1 April 1873. For a similar notice at Salisbury, cf. ABDC Salisbury, 7 December 1866; cf. also *Guardian*, 1888, p. 1096. The paying of 6d to see the east end of York Minster was said to be an old custom in 1888 (*Guardian*, 1888, p. 1937).
260 ABDC Winchester, 3 February 1874.
261 *Guardian*, 1888, p. 1736; cf. ibid., p. 1773. An entrance fee paid to the vergers was necessary at Lincoln in 1866 (*Guardian*, 1866, p. 867). Fees of 6d were also demanded at St Albans in 1888, except from inhabitants of the city and diocesan clergy (ibid., 1888, pp. 1656, 1814). There was an income of £200 per annum from visitors' fees at Exeter (*Guardian*, 1888, p. 443); cf. Chapter 11, pp. 268–9.
262 *Guardian*, 1888, p. 1774. Precentor Venables defended the system at Lincoln, claiming that it would be impractical to open the whole cathedral to the huge crowds that came on excursions trains. The income from the fees had been used to buy new furnishings (*Guardian*, 1888, p. 1936).
263 ABDC Winchester, 25 November 1889; cf. ABDC Exeter, 15 March 1873. Dean Duncombe gave the vergers at York Minster fixed salaries in 1858 and forbade them to receive any fees (see above, Chapter 4, p. 47). Before this the vergers were paid only £11 per annum, plus tips (Chadwick, *York*, p. 293). A visitor to Winchester Cathedral in 1806 complained about 'a kind of griping, avaricious propensity with the officers deputed to show the nave to strangers' (D.N. King, in *Winchester Cathedral Chronicle*, 1972, p. 1).
264 J. S. Howson, ed., *Essays on Cathedrals by Various Writers* (London 1872), p. 24.
265 A. C. Coxe, *Impressions of England* (New York, 2nd edn 1856), p. 13.
266 J. E. West, *Cathedral Organists Past and Present* (London 1899), p. 10.
267 Thompson, pp. 149–50.
268 ABDC Bristol, 1 December 1801.
269 Wells CM, 1 October 1832.
270 ABDC Worcester, 31 July 1874.
271 Prestige, p. 106; cf. Coghlan, pp. 126–7.

272 ABDC Chichester, 12 May 1890.

273 Coghlan, pp. 126–7.

274 ABDC Exeter, 15 March 1809.

275 ibid., 21–22 December 1826.

276 Coghlan, p. 124, quoting ABDC Norwich, 13 November 1830, 13 and 24 March 1831.

277 ABDC Winchester, 1 August 1844.

278 ABDC Winchester, 23 June 1862.

279 Wells CM, 6 June 1873.

280 Prestige, p. 182. John Allgate, a verger at Worcester, was reinstated in 1879 on condition that he ceased to occupy or manage the public house where he lived (ABDC Worcester, 4 December 1879; cf. 28 February 1880).

281 ibid., pp. 174–81.

282 F. Pigou, *Odds and Ends* (London 1903), pp. 255–6.

283 *MT*, 1 February 1905, p. 87; cf. ABDC Chichester, 1 August 1861.

284 P. A. Welsby, *Rochester Cathedral in the time of Charles Dickens* (Rochester 1976), p. 12.

285 *Trefoil*, pp. 147–8.

286 R. A. Godfrey, 'Cathedral Virgers through the Centuries', *Winchester Cathedral Record*, no.47, 1978, p. 24, quoting *Winchester Cathedral Chronicle*, 1854–1916, p. 131.

287 ABDC Hereford, 13 November 1800.

288 ibid., 11 November 1809. In 1874 they were told to wear gowns in the cathedral (ABDC Hereford, 25 June 1874).

289 ABDC Worcester, 22 November 1822, 16 January 1835. Two were in office in 1867. For their salaries and duties (generally to assist the custos), cf. ABDC Worcester, 10 May 1867.

290 ibid., 10 October 1868. Another of the sextons at Chichester was authorized to carry the bishop's staff before him (ABDC Chichester, 2 August 1886).

291 ABDC Hereford, 6 April 1882.

292 Prestige, p. 81.

293 Goodman and Hutton, pp. 56–7, 62–3. One of the beadsmen at Rochester was a veteran of Waterloo (Bridge, p. 21). At Christ Church, Oxford, however, where there were twenty-four almsmen, they were not required to attend services or wear distinctive dress (PP 1854, xxv, pp. 1008–9). For their duties at Winchester in 1874, and Bristol in 1884, cf. ABDC Winchester, 25 November 1874, and Bristol DC/A/ 7/3/4; cf. also ABDC Bristol, 7 January 1887.

294 ABDC Worcester, 24 November 1824. There were further increases in 1869 and 1874; cf. ABDC Worcester, 19 November 1869, 20 May, 23 June, 31 July 1874.

295 Coghlan, p. 128, citing ABDC Norwich, 1 December 1818, 28 November 1887.

296 PP 1854, xxv, p. 43. Walcott gives details of their numbers and pay at various cathedrals (*Cathedralia*, pp. 139–40).

297 ABDC Worcester, 26 April 1887.

298 ABDC Worcester, 17 November 1888; Worc. C. Mss., Sacrist's Report, 1889.

299 Winchester Cathedral Mss., Davidson's visitation 1900. There were six beadsmen or almsmen at St Paul's in 1853, an unusual instance in an old foundation cathedral (St Paul's CM, 9 May 1853, cited in Coghlan, p. 129).

300 Worc. C. Add. Mss., 141, p. 11; ABDC Worcester, 17 November 1888.

301 Coghlan, p. 128, citing ABDC Norwich, 6 March 1883.

302 ABDC Bristol, 23 June 1818, 25 June 1823; ABDC Worcester, 21 January 1861, 13 April 1874, 7 August 1877, 2 February 1882, 11 July 1885, 20 September 1886, 24 August 1891, 3 January 1896, 29 May 1896.

303 PP 1884–5, xxi, p. 281. At Gloucester there were two beadswomen in 1800 (ABDC Gloucester, 20 January 1800).

304 Coghlan, p. 92.

305 For some examples, cf. Chapter 3, pp. 26–9.

306 ABDC Worcester, 24 November 1826, 20 November 1846.
307 ABDC Winchester, 23 June 1839; ABDC Worcester, 25 November 1841.
308 Salisbury Cathedral Mss., Vicars Choral Account Book.
309 Salisbury DRO, Press V, Box 2, W. Boucher to Archdeacon Macdonald, 5 January 1833.
310 ABDC Exeter, 24 May 1800, 15 June and 31 August 1811, 22–3 December 1824, 1 March 1828; Thompson, pp. 149–50.
311 Gretton, pp. 8–9, quoted in Barrett, 'Hereford Cathedral in the Nineteenth Century', p. 20.
312 ABDC Gloucester, 2 April and 30 November 1827. Ringing was allowed only at official practices in 1882 (ABDC Gloucester, 28 September 1882). By 1890 the bells were unringable and the ringers no longer paid (ABDC Gloucester, 26 February 1890).
313 Walcott, p. 140.
314 Wells CM, 4 May 1866. The Grandison bell was tolled at Exeter in 1817 for the death of Princess Charlotte (ABDC Exeter, 1817).
315 Wells CM, 25 January 1870. The sum of £5 was the rate for enthronements at Worcester. The ringers received £4 for ringing at the installation of a dean and £2 for the installation of a canon (ABDC Worcester, 21 November 1871).
316 ABDC Hereford, 8 November 1866.
317 ABDC Hereford, 24 March 1877.
318 ABDC Worcester, 23 June 1900.
319 ABDC Chichester, 2 May and 25 July 1878.
320 ABDC Chichester, 20 January 1879.
321 ABDC Chichester, 22 May 1879. A nightwatchman was appointed at York following the fire in 1829 (Chadwick, York, p. 277).
322 ibid., 5 August 1889, 4 December 1889.
323 ibid., 4 December 1889. Lowther Clarke says that a morrow bell was rung at 6 a.m. and the curfew bell at 9 p.m., the number of days in the month and the number of the month being rung (W. K. L. Clarke, Chichester Cathedral in the Nineteenth Century (Chichester Papers no.14, Chichester 1959), p. 17).
324 ibid, 10 October 1890.
325 Worc. C. Mss., Precentor's Report, 1884. The bells at Exeter were chimed for five minutes only before services (ABDC Exeter, 20 January 1891).
326 Worc. C. Mss., Report of W.G. Melville (Sacrist) on the ringers, 1895.
327 ABDC Winchester, 6 April 1899.
328 ABDC Exeter, 4 April and 24 October 1807.
329 ABDC Winchester, 25 November 1835.
330 ABDC Winchester, 29 September 1856.
331 Wells CM, 2 January 1872.
332 Wells CM, 1 July 1886.
333 Wells CM, 24 March and 8 August 1888.
334 Hill, p. 271.
335 Prestige, pp. 146–7.
336 ABDC Wells, 13 October 1883.
337 ABDC Worcester, 10 January 1874, 24 November 1875; cf. also 22 November 1869. The chimes were rung six times a day (ABDC Worcester, 1 February 1873). New arrangements for winding the clock (formerly a duty of the vergers) were made at Exeter in 1817 (ABDC Exeter, 18 December 1817).
338 ABDC Worcester, 24 November 1870, 28 June 1886.
339 ABDC Exeter, 16 October 1830.
340 Wells CM, 1 April 1833.
341 ABDC Salisbury, 5 September 1849; Prestige, p. 99.

342 ABDC Exeter, 17 October 1874.

343 ABDC Gloucester, 28 September 1876.

344 Salisbury CM, 12 August 1879.

345 PP 1883, xxi, p. 157.

346 Wells CM, 1 October 1880, 2 January 1882; cf. 2 October 1882.

347 ABDC Chichester, 12 May 1890.

348 ABDC Chichester, 2 May 1898. For other examples of annual cleaning of cathedrals, cf. Chapter 11, p. 268.

349 ABDC Worcester, 24 June and 20 November 1876.

350 Salisbury CM, 12 and 18 August and 6 October 1879; cf. 16 March 1880.

351 Worc. C. Mss., Sacrist's Report, 1899.

352 Boutflower, p. 29.

CHAPTER 7 *Cathedral Worship in the Nineteenth Century*

1 J. S. Howson, ed., *Essays on Cathedrals by Various Writers* (London 1872), p. 12.

2 Quoted in ibid., p. 14.

3 ABDC Worcester, 22 November 1825. A divided Sunday morning service was the rule at Hereford in the early nineteenth century, where matins was sung by the full choir at 8 a.m., but only the choristers were available for the 11 a.m. service of litany, holy communion and sermon, since the vicars choral, who supplied the lower parts in the choir, were busy taking services in their parish churches (J. S. Bumpus, *A History of English Cathedral Music, 1549–1889* (London 1908), vol.II, pp. 374–5).

4 ABDC Worcester, 24 November 1826.

5 PP 1854, xxv, p. 28 (these figures include the Welsh cathedrals and the royal peculiars of Westminster and Windsor); F. E. Gretton, *Memory's Hark-back Through Half a Century, 1808–1858* (London 1889), p. 4; D. King in *Winchester Cathedral Chronicle*, 1972. It appears that by 1872 at Ely matins was sung at 9 a.m. on Sundays, with the litany and holy communion at 11 a.m. (Walcott, *Traditions*, p. 97).

6 *Guardian*, 1849, p. 654.

7 ABDC Hereford, 14 November 1850.

8 ibid., 13 November 1851; ABDC Exeter, 21–22 December 1858. By 1896 the Sunday morning service at Hereford had been fixed at 11 a.m., with evensong at 6.30 p.m. (*Guardian*, 1896, p. 2081).

9 NCL, Goulburn's diary, 21 April and 9 June 1867.

10 C. E. Beswick, 'Liddon of St Paul's' (Exeter University MA thesis 1974), pp. 11–12 (quoting St Paul's CM of 14 October 1872 and 14 June 1873); cf. W. H. Hutton, ed., *The Autobiography of Robert Gregory* (London 1912), p. 169. The times of weekday and Sunday services at St Paul's in 1880 are given in PP 1883, xxi, pp. 122–3. For other cathedrals at this time, cf. ibid., p. 162 (Chester), p. 211 (Bristol), p. 251 (Wells), p. 330 (Rochester); PP 1884, xxii, p. 47 (Ely), p. 91 (Norwich), p. 130 (Carlisle), p. 153 (Christ Church, Oxford), p. 191 (Worcester), p. 228 (Hereford), p. 265 (Canterbury), p. 299 (Ripon); PP 1884–5, xxi, p. 46 (Winchester), p. 135 (Salisbury), p. 182 (Lichfield), p. 240 (Gloucester), p. 278 (Peterborough), p. 301 (Manchester), p. 334 (Exeter), p. 365 (Chichester), p. 407 (Lincoln), p. 442 (York).

11 G. L. Prestige, *St Paul's in its Glory, 1831–1911* (London 1955), p. 162. The service at Chichester also lasted from 10.30 a.m. until 1 p.m. Dean Pigou described it as 'the most sleep-inducing I have ever had to attend' (F. Pigou, *Phases of My Life* (London 1898), p. 358).

12 ABDC Salisbury, 25 May and 26 November 1886. Bishop John Wordsworth criticized these arrangements (cf. C. Wordsworth and D. Macleane, *Statutes and Customs of the Cathedral Church of the Blessed Virgin Mary at Salisbury* (London 1915), p. 481.

13 ABDC Worcester, 28 February 1887. The Sunday afternoon pattern at Worcester included a children's catechizing at 3 p.m. (replaced by a service for men on the last

Sunday of the month) and an anthem and litany at 4 p.m. (ABDC Worcester, 20 November 1886). Five years later the pattern was as follows: 8 a.m. holy communion; 11 a.m. morning prayer (to end of third collect), followed by an anthem, the litany, a sermon and holy communion; 3 p.m. children's service; 4 p.m. evening prayer; 6.30 p.m. short evening prayer (ABDC Worcester, 19 November 1891). There was a similar pattern at Chichester, except that there was a short anthem at matins (ABDC Chichester, 29 October 1889). For Wells, cf. Wells CM, 2 July and 1 October 1894.

14 ABDC Exeter, 23 February 1811; cf. 5 January 1818, 13 November 1819, 5 January and 1 March 1828.

15 ibid., 29 January 1814; cf. 22 January 1820, 12 January 1828, 4 January 1829, 16 January 1830, 1 January 1831, 22–23 December 1835, 6 February 1836.

16 ABDC Exeter, 28 October 1865.

17 ibid., 24 January 1891.

18 ABDC Gloucester, 30 November 1843.

19 J. Jebb, *The Choral Service of the United Church of England and Ireland* (London 1843), p. 189.

20 ABDC Gloucester, 12 January 1865; cf. 11 January 1866.

21 ABDC Gloucester, 30 November 1870.

22 ABDC Hereford, 14 November 1811, 10 April 1821.

23 ABVC Hereford, p. 57 (reverse pagination).

24 ibid., p. 59, p. 61; cf. Jebb, p. 226.

25 Walcott, *Traditions*, p. 99.

26 H. P. Liddon, *Walter Kerr Hamilton, Bishop of Salisbury* (London 1869), p. 24. Hamilton's evidence to the Cathedrals Commission, Salisbury Chapter Muniments, Press I, Box 39; cf. Walcott, *Traditions*, p. 101; cf. A. E. Bridge, in D. Marcombe and C. S. Knighton, eds, *Close Encounters: English Cathedrals and Society since 1540* (Nottingham 1991), pp. 141–2.

27 ABDC Salisbury, 19 July 1875.

28 Walcott, *Traditions*, p. 100. The early service at York was discontinued during the winter of 1826–7 (L. W. Cowie, 'Worship in the Minster', *The Victoria History of the Counties of England: A History of Yorkshire: The City of York* (London 1961), p. 353).

29 Walcott, *Traditions*, p. 101; Jebb, pp. 124, 226. For Worcester, cf. Worc. C. Mss., Attendance Book 1836–42, 28 December 1838. The service survived at St Paul's until 1901, despite an attempt to suppress it in 1836 by Sydney Smith. The minor canons were technically responsible for it, but often hired deputies to perform the duty for them (Prestige, pp. 10–11, 164–5). For Durham in 1822, cf. C. J. Stranks, *This Sumptuous Church* (London 1973), p. 92. For further details at various cathedrals, cf. Walcott, *Traditions*, p. 102.

30 cf. Chapter 1, p. 3.

31 Jebb, p. 504.

32 *Parish Choir*, vol.I, p. 135; cf. Jebb, p. 511. The custom of the choir going into the sanctuary was stopped in 1850; cf. ABDC Durham, 20 July 1850, quoted in P. C. Moore, 'The Organisation and Development of Cathedral Worship in England, with special reference to choral services, from the Reformation to the Nineteenth Century' (Oxford D. Phil. thesis 1954), p. 122, fn. 3.

33 Jebb, p. 461.

34 Walcott, *Traditions*, pp. 117–18. W. L. Hillsman, citing *The Christian's Miscellany*, 1861, pp. 29–30, says that Exeter may have had a monthly sung Eucharist in 1841 (W. L. Hillsman, 'Trends and Aims in Anglican Music 1870–1906, in relation to developments in churchmanship' (Oxford D. Phil. thesis 1985), p. 316).

35 T. F. Bumpus, *The Cathedrals of England and Wales* (London 1905), vol.II, p. 250.

36 Winchester Cathedral Mss, *De Precentore*, 29 March 1864.

37 Cowie, pp. 354–5; cf. Chadwick, *York*, p. 300; PP 1867, xx, p. 777.

38 Worc. C. Add. Mss.137, pp. 23–4. Another lay clerk at Worcester, John Randall, said that before 1857, after the singing of an anthem and the litany at 11 a.m., the choir sang the Sanctus 'while the celebrant and his assistants proceeded to the altar with much ceremony'. The creed was sung, but the choir and most of the congregation left after the sermon, except on great festivals when the choir remained until the end of the service and sang the Sanctus (presumably a second time) and the Gloria in excelsis. Randall adds that on these occasions all the communion plate was placed on the altar, which he believed to be a survival of pre-Reformation ritual (Worc. C. Add. Mss., 128, p. 7). For the introduction of more frequent services, cf. ABDC Worcester, 19 November 1888, Worc. C. Mss., Precentor's Report, 1889, ABDC Worcester, 19 November 1891, 13 July 1892.

39 Worc. C. Mss., Precentor's Report, 1891.

40 ibid., 1892; cf. ABDC Worcester, 19 November 1892, when it was also agreed that the altar candles should be lit.

41 Worc. C. Mss., Precentor's Report, 1896. A further difficulty arose in 1900 when the start of the Eucharist was delayed on several Sunday mornings by the slowness of the congregation in leaving the cathedral after matins, and the first part of the Eucharist being interrupted by a band playing outside the cathedral (Worc. C. Mss., Precentor's Report, 1900).

42 ABDC Worcester, 19 November 1896.

43 J. S. Bumpus, vol.I, p. 415; St Paul's CM, 1 March and 14 June 1873, cited in P. V. Coghlan, 'Cathedral Worship in the Church of England 1815–1914' (Leicester University M. Phil. thesis 1984), p. 148; Gloucester chapter Minute Book, 29 November 1873. At Wells, however, the dean and chapter ordered that the Nicene Creed and the Athanasian Creed should be read, not sung (Wells CM, 16 May 1856). At Norwich in 1812 the Nicene Creed was chaunted, not sung, and began with 'a terrific blast' from the organ (Walcott, *Traditions*, pp. 116–17). Jebb said that the Creed was often performed carelessly (Jebb, p. 353; B. Rainbow, *The Choral Revival in the Anglican Church, 1839–1872* (London 1970) p. 254). The Sanctus was rarely sung as an introit after 1880, Wells and Liverpool in approximately 1890 being the last examples (Hillsman, p. 317). Introits at York after 1866 were mainly by George Macfarren (N. Temperley, *The Athlone History of Music in Britain: Volume 5: The Romantic Age, 1800–1914* (London 1981) p. 181).

44 W. A. Frost, *Early Recollections of St Paul's Cathedral* (London 1926) p. 21.

45 Prestige, p. 106; Frost, p. 46. The first one was on Whitsunday 1872. The St Paul's service was described by Gregory as 'one of the most attractive and beautiful services in the Church of England' (Hutton p. 199).

46 Salisbury CM, 8 December 1886.

47 Wells CM, 22 May 1886.

48 *Guardian*, 1889, p. 770.

49 ABDC Chichester, 12 May 1890. Settings of the offertory sentences were also sung at St Paul's (Hillsman, p. 317). For further details, including a psalm during the ablutions at St Paul's, cf. Hillsman, pp. 317–18.

50 ABDC Chichester, 2 May 1892. At Exeter the offertory sentence was sung by the choir and the confession and Lord's Prayer were accompanied on the organ (ABDC Exeter, 12 May 1888).

51 PP 1854, xxv, p. 28.

52 cf. above, p. 115.

53 C. K. F. Brown, *A History of the English Clergy, 1800–1900* (London 1953), p. 57.

54 *Guardian*, 1853, p. 763.

55 Prestige, p. 80; cf. A. Milman, *Henry Hart Milman* (London 1900), p. 241. Dean Milman wrote of these services in 1865: 'The congregations at the special services

NOTES

at St Paul's are very far the largest that have ever met Sunday after Sunday within the walls of any church in England....I cannot describe the effect of a solemn and impressive lesson from the Old or New Testament on the vast congregation: the breathless, reverential attention was most striking' (ibid., pp. 237–8; cf. also D. Scott, *The Music of St Paul's Cathedral* (London 1972), p. 26; W. M. Sinclair, *Memorials of St Paul's Cathedral* (London 1909) p. 297). The St Paul's services were inspired by Dean Stanley's success with similar services at Westminster Abbey (Hillsman, p. 301, citing M. S. Stancliffe in E. Carpenter, ed., *A House of Kings* (London 1966), pp. 295–6, 298).

56 Prestige, p. 85.

57 W. O. Chadwick, *The Victorian Church* (London 1970), vol.II, p. 381.

58 Bristol DC/A7/3/4, 13 January 1863.

59 L. E. Elliott-Binns, *Religion in the Victorian Era* (London 1936), p. 433; W. Temple, *Life of Bishop Percival* (London 1921), p. 80.

60 R. J. Fletcher, *A History of Bristol Cathedral* (London 1932), p. 66.

61 F. Pigou, *Odds and Ends* (London 1903), p. 265; Pigou, *Phases of My Life*, p. 379; cf. *Guardian*, 1895, p. 689.

62 L. Smith, *The Story of Ripon Minster* (Leeds 1914), p. 263; cf. also *The Choir*, 2 October 1875, p. 622.

63 P. A. Welsby, *Rochester Cathedral in the Time of Charles Dickens* (Rochester 1976), p. 9.

64 E. W. Watson, *Life of Bishop John Wordsworth* (London 1915), p. 134.

65 W. J. Humfrys, *Memories of Old Hereford* (Hereford n.d.), pp. 10–11; cf. *Guardian*, 1867, p. 78.

66 R. Cant in A. Stacpoole, ed., *The Noble City of York* (York 1972), p. 57; Cowie, pp. 354–5; PP 1867, xx, p. 777; Chadwick, *The Victorian Church*, vol.I, p. 330, quoting PP 1884–5, xxi, pp. 444–5. Duncombe said in 1867 that he thought that the large numbers attending the Sunday evening services in York Minster made 'very little difference to the congregations in the parish churches'. They were almost exclusively composed of working men, most of whom never attended any other place of worship (PP 1867, xx, p. 777). From Advent Sunday 1888 the Sunday pattern of services at Exeter was altered so that the afternoon service consisted of a hymn, the litany, an anthem, the bidding prayer and a sermon. Evensong was sung at 7 p.m., with three hymns, but with chants for the canticles. Six choristers were present at the evening service, but only one priest vicar was required on a Sunday afternoon (ABDC Exeter, 24 November 1888).

67 *Guardian*, 1878, p. 1482. Charles Kingsley's Sunday evening sermons at Chester were so popular that people would queue outside the cathedral for them (S. E. R. Chitty, *The Beast and the Monk* (London 1974), p. 274; cf. also *CT*, 8 July 1870).

68 C. E. Woodruff and W. Danks, *Memorials of the Cathedral and Priory of Christ in Canterbury* (London 1912), pp. 366, 368; C. E. Woodruff, 'Reminiscences of the Cathedral and its Personnel Seventy-five Years Ago', *Canterbury Cathedral Chronicle*, no.39, September 1943, p. 15; D. I. Hill, *Christ's Glorious Church* (London 1976), p. 80. The establishment of Sunday evening services at Canterbury was opposed by the clergy of the city parishes who had large and regular congregations and feared a 'counter-attraction' (LPL, Benson Papers, XII, p. 191).

69 Pigou, *Phases of My Life*, p. 358.

70 Chichester Capitular Archives, III/5/4, pp. 8–9; Swainson to Principal, 20 December 1867; Principal to Swainson, 23 December 1867.

71 ABDC Chichester, 19 November and 24 December 1881, 10 October 1882.

72 ABDC Chichester, 1 August 1890.

73 K. Lake, ed., *Memorials of William Charles Lake* (London 1901), p. 135.

74 ABDC Gloucester, 30 November 1869, 31 March 1870.

75 ABDC Gloucester, 26 September 1878, 24 June 1879.

76 ABDC Gloucester, 23 June 1883, 24 June 1884.
77 cf. Howson, pp. 28–9; cf. also PP 1871, lv, p. 212.
78 *Guardian*, 1878, p. 1482. Sunday evening services, attended by the full choir, became a regular feature at Ely in 1888 (ABDC Ely, 26 November 1888, cited in Coghlan, p. 148).
79 A. J. Butler, *Life and Letters of William John Butler* (London 1897), p. 323; J. W. F. Hill, *Victorian Lincoln* (London 1974), p. 265. Sunday evening services began at Exeter in 1881 (ABDC Exeter, 2 November 1881).
80 J. M. Elvy, *Recollections of the Cathedral and Parish Church of Manchester* (Manchester 1913), pp. 33–4; *Guardian*, 1884, p. 45; cf. also *The Choir*, 7 August 1875, and M. Hennell, *The Deans and Canons of Manchester Cathedral, 1840–1948* (Manchester 1990), pp. 57–8.
81 H. Leeds, *Life of Dean Lefroy* (Norwich 1909), pp. 25, 70; cf. CCR 1894, p. 57.
82 Chadwick, *The Victorian Church*, vol. II, p. 381, quoting PP 1884–5, xxi, p. 54.
83 A. Westcott, *Life and Letters of Brooke Foss Westcott* (London 1903), vol.I, pp. 313–4, 358, 364.
84 Greenhalgh, *Wells*, p. 195.
85 Wells CM, 1 July and 1 October 1886.
86 Worc. C. Add. Mss., 141, pp. 32, 35; cf. also *The Choir*, 22 August 1874, p. 114.
87 Worc. C. Add. Mss., Voluntary Choir Bundle, E. V. Hall to Dean Compton, 13 April 1882; R. Cattley to Compton, 12 April 1882. Disputes between these two minor canons were no new thing: cf. ABDC Worcester, 16 April 1878. Dean Goulburn introduced a collection between the prayer of St John Chrysostom and the grace at Sunday afternoon evensong at Norwich in 1867, 'but most of the people in the Presbytery ran away from the collection' (NCL, Goulburn's diary, 23 June 1867).
88 Worc. C. Mss., *Record of Some of the Principal Events relating to the Cathedral of Worcester, the Dean and Chapter and their property*, p. 5.
89 Hillsman, pp. 320–1, quoting CT, 12 February 1892, p. 145.
90 ABDC Exeter, 29–30 December 1857; Walcott, *Traditions*, p. 110. At York, until at least 1818, the four dignitaries of the chapter each had a seven-branched candlestick placed before them in their stalls on the vigils of certain holy days (Walcott, *Traditions*, p. 106).
91 W. E. Dickson, *Fifty Years of Church Music* (Ely 1894), p. 67. Regular simple services during Advent and Lent were introduced at Peterborough in 1860, but the choir and the minor canons were not expected to attend (ABDC Peterborough, 31 October 1860, quoted in Coghlan, p. 148). Special services on Good Friday were introduced at Wells in 1872 (Wells CM, 1 April 1872). Walcott noted that the organ was not used during Holy Week at Chichester until the evening service on Easter Even (Walcott, *Traditions*, p. 111).
92 *Guardian*, 1873, pp. 20–1.
93 Prestige, p. 100; W. R. Matthews and W. M. Atkins, *A History of St Paul's Cathedral and the Men Associated with it* (London 1957), p. 268.
94 *Guardian*, 1878, p. 1482; for the Christmas Eve service at Canterbury, cf. *Guardian*, 1873, pp. 20–1. The *St Matthew Passion* was sung at St Paul's every Tuesday in Holy Week from 1873 (Prestige, p. 103 ; P. Charlton, *John Stainer and the Musical Life of Victorian Britain* (Newton Abbot 1984), pp. 64–5, 72f). There were services on Wednesday evenings in Advent and Lent at Rochester by 1880 (PP 1884, xxii, p. 330).
95 Worc. C. Add. Mss., 104, p. 5. There was instrumental music at the Sunday evening services at Worcester four times a year in 1890 (ABDC Worcester, 3 June 1890). At Norwich in 1886, on the four Wednesdays in Advent, there were performances of Spohr's *Last Judgement* and Mozart's *Requiem*, with short prayers and an address. Tickets were only issued after written application, and it was feared that the poorer classes would be deterred by this and the fact that there was a collection (*MT* 1

December 1886, p. 713). F. Bates, the organist of Norwich, engaged a cavalry band to play during the Jubilee services in 1887 (F. Bates, *Reminiscences and Autobiography of a Musician in Retirement* (Norwich 1930), pp. 37–8).

96 *Guardian*, 1880, p. 427.

97 Worc. C. Add. Mss., 137, p. 23. A Three Hours' Service was introduced at Winchester in 1895 (*Winchester Cathedral Chronicle*, 1895–1932, p. 4).

98 Wells CM, 25 February 1884.

99 *Guardian*, 1884, p. 572; 1885, p. 517.

100 ABDC Worcester, 20 November 1884; cf. Worc. C. Add. Mss., 104, p. 9; special services on Monday evenings during Lent were introduced at Wells in 1882 (Wells CM, 2 January 1882).

101 ABDC Worcester, 19 November 1887.

102 ABDC Worcester, 19 November 1888. B. F. Westcott wrote from Peterborough and told his wife in December 1880: 'Yesterday evening the rendering of the selections from the *Last Judgement* was admirable; better than anything I have heard here before. There was a large congregation and the manner of the choir was most reverent, and Dr. Keeton's accompaniment perfect. I saw Mr Phillips and Dr. Keeton after, and I must see the choir today. Mr P. says that they have taken most kindly to the extra work, and shown the greatest interest in it' (Westcott, vol.I, pp. 313–14).

103 HCA 5818.

104 Prestige, p. 164.

105 ABDC Chichester, 17 February 1890; cf. also ABDC Exeter, 11 December 1886.

106 Winchester Cathedral Mss., *De Precentore*, 1890–1, 1893–4. At Norwich a special weekday evening service, including carols, was held at Christmas 1890 in the nave of the cathedral (ABDC Norwich, 4 November 1890, cited in Coghlan, p. 148). Benson's Service of the Nine Lessons with carols was first used in the temporary cathedral at Truro in 1880 (Temperley, p. 174).

107 Worc. C. Mss., Precentor's Report, 1894. There was an 8 p.m. service on Easter Eve at Salisbury in 1882 (Salisbury CM, 21 March 1882).

108 Hillsman, p. 321, citing *CT*, 9 April 1880, p. 235; *Church Musician*, 15 January 1895, p. 11; *CT* 10 April 1896, pp. 420–1; YML scrapbook, p. 416; Salisbury CM, 5 October 1898.

109 D. Verey, ed., *The Diary of a Cotswold Parson (F. E. Witts) 1783–1854* (Gloucester 1978), pp. 57, 69.

110 Wells CM, 17 September 1849.

111 Prestige, p. 97.

112 Charlton, pp. 65–9; for a list of special services in St Paul's between Michaelmas 1879 and August 1880, cf. PP 1883, xxi, p. 123; cf. also W. S. Simpson, *A Year's Music at St Paul's Cathedral* (2nd report, London 1879), pp. 6–7, 28–9.

113 Prestige, pp. 74–5. In 1872 a great service of public thanksgiving for the recovery of the Prince of Wales was held in St Paul's, attended by Queen Victoria and most of the royal family. Liddon was in the cathedral for over two hours before the service 'making people take off their hats and in otherwise trying to find them seats and to keep order' (Prestige, p. 143; cf. also B. A. Smith, *Dean Church* (London 1958), p. 161). Gregory thought it was the publicity that the cathedral received through this service that really made the revival of cathedral work at St Paul's nationally known (Hutton, p. 183). For Queen Victoria's Diamond Jubilee in 1897, St Paul's was filled with a glittering congregation including the Prince and Princess of Wales, most of the uncrowned royalty and half that of Europe. The Russian Orthodox Archbishop of Finland, the diplomatic corps and a great number of members of the legal profession were present. The Queen was too infirm to leave her carriage and the service was held on the west steps. The dean and chapter wore copes for the first

time with skullcaps of cardinal red velvet (Prestige, p. 229; Sinclair, pp. 359–60).

114 H. B. J. Armstrong, ed., *Armstrong's Norfolk Diary* (London 1963), p. 49.

115 ibid., p. 132. Stringent conditions were imposed for the use of St Paul's for such services (Prestige, p. 167).

116 *Guardian*, 1855, pp. 632, 771.

117 *CCR* 1865, p. 93; for the reopening of Lichfield, cf. *Saturday Review*, 1861, vol.II, p. 432: 'It was solely and simply a church-going gala on a weekday, and yet that was sufficient to put half a county – comprising the Potteries and the Black Country – into a state of pleasurable excitement.'

118 W. J. S. Simpson, *Memoir of the Reverend W. Sparrow Simpson* (London 1899), p. 49; Prestige, p. 105. For the annual performances of Mendelssohn's oratorio *St Paul*, the cathedral choir was joined by singers from other London churches. The *Daily Chronicle* said in 1885 that 'from first to last a more imposing and reverential musical service has probably never been given within the walls of a Cathedral than that of yesterday afternoon' (Charlton, p. 70). One service that had been an annual event at St Paul's was discontinued after 1877. This was the charity schools' service which was held in June and necessitated the closure of the cathedral throughout the preceding month in order to enable huge stands to be erected under the Dome. By the 1850s the increased emphasis being placed on the importance of the daily services at St Paul's meant that such a severe disturbance of the normal routine could no longer be tolerated (Prestige, p. 103; B. Rainbow, 'Singing for their Supper', *MT*, vol.cxxv, no.1694, April 1984, pp. 227–9). Berlioz was present at the 1851 service and, disguised as a clergyman in a black coat and surplice, sang with the choir in the organ loft. He was 'deeply stirred' by the singing of the 6,500 children (Scott, p. 26).

119 *Winchester Cathedral Chronicle*, 1873–91, p. 72.

120 R. Cant in Stacpoole, p. 57. Regular and territorial soldiers from all parts of Yorkshire attended this service and special trains were later provided for the congregation; by 1909 it is said that there were 2,000 soldiers and a congregation of 10,000 civilians in the cathedral (Chadwick, *York*, pp. 309–10).

121 ABDC Exeter, 15 April 1886.

122 ABDC Winchester, 25 April 1893.

123 Wells CM, 25 January 1900; *Winchester Cathedral Chronicle*, 1895–1932, p. 66.

124 *Guardian*, 1872, p. 550.

125 Winchester Cathedral Mss, *De Precentore*, 1873.

126 ABDC Worcester, 1 February 1873, 10 January, 21 February, 13 April 1874; Worc. C. Add. Mss., 128, p. 17; cf. *Guardian*, 1874, pp. 454–7; R. B. Lockett, 'George Gilbert Scott, the Joint Restoration Committee and the Refurnishing of Worcester Cathedral, 1863–1874' *TWAS*, 3rd series, vol. 6, 1978, p. 26 (cf. Chapter 10, pp. 237–8). For Bishop Wilberforce's comments on the services marking the reopening of Hereford Cathedral in 1863, cf. A. R. Ashwell and R. G. Wilberforce, *Life of The Right Reverend Samuel Wilberforce* (London 1883), vol.III, p. 90.

127 Lake, p. 143.

128 ABDC Exeter, 29 May 1876, *Guardian*, 1878, p. 1545, ABDC Chichester, 1 August 1890. In 1894 Norwich Cathedral was reopened, and Archbishop Benson preached at the great service to mark this event. The band of the King's Dragoon Guards took part, together with many local mayors (Bates, p. 50). In 1899 the nave of Norwich Cathedral was reopened after restoration. Tickets were issued to those who had subscribed to the restoration, but the general public was admitted only to the triforium. The procession included not only clergy and civic dignitaries, but also freemen, oddfellows and foresters (ABDC Norwich, 27 May 1899, cited in Coghlan, p. 167).

129 ABDC Gloucester, 1 April 1880; *Winchester Cathedral Chronicle*, 1886–94, p. 41.

130 Stacpoole, p. 1165; Cowie, p. 355. Harvest Festivals were introduced at Worcester in 1884, at Wells in 1885, and at Salisbury in 1886; 1,500 were present at the 1886 Wells Harvest Festival (ABDC Worcester, 20 November 1884; Wells CM, 1 July 1885, 21 August and 1 October 1886; Salisbury CM, 14 September 1886).
131 ABDC Exeter, 27 November 1894.
132 Lake, p. 288.
133 D. I. Hill, p. 76. For the opening service at Canterbury in 1888, cf. A. C. Benson, *The Life of Edward White Benson, sometime Archbishop of Canterbury* (London 1899), vol.II, p. 213, quoted in A. M. G. Stephenson, *Anglicanism and the Lambeth Conferences* (London 1978), p. 77. For choral festivals, cf. Chapter 11, p. 254.
134 J. T. Fowler, *Durham University, earlier foundations and present colleges* (London 1904), pp. 31–2, 67–8 (cf. also pp. 42, 45).
135 J. W. F. Hill, p. 263, fn.5.
136 H. W. Shaw, *The Three Choirs Festival* (Worcester 1954), p. 58. In 1984, however, the traditional opening service was replaced by a short opening ceremony before one of the concerts at Worcester. The normal practice was restored at Hereford in 1985, but seems to have been dropped at Worcester.
137 J. W. Clark and T. McK. Hughes, *The Life and Letters of the Reverend Adam Sedgwick* (Cambridge 1890), vol.I, p. 434.
138 Prestige, pp. 93–4.
139 ibid., p. 100. For Benson's account of his own installation at Lincoln, cf. Benson, vol.I, pp. 355–6. For the forms for installing a canon that he drew up at Truro, cf. PP 1883, xxi, pp. 70–4.
140 ABDC Hereford, 25 February 1809.
141 ibid., 6 April 1809. For Alford's installation at Canterbury in 1857, cf. F. Alford, *Life, Journals and Letters of Henry Alford, Dean of Canterbury* (London 1873) p. 270; for Bramston's installation at Winchester in 1872, cf. *Winchester Cathedral Chronicle*, 1873–91, pp. 71, 74–5.
142 H. Leeds, *Life of Dean Lefroy* (Norwich 1909), pp. 22–3. For the form for the installation of a dean that Benson compiled at Truro, cf. PP 1883, xxi, pp. 68–70.
143 Prestige, p. 166.
144 Elvy, pp. 21–3; A. Boutflower, *Personal Reminiscences of Manchester Cathedral 1854–1912* (Leighton Buzzard 1913), p. 28. Dean Bowers said in 1869 that there were over 3,300 baptisms every year (PP 1871, lv, p. 219).
145 Cowie, p. 356.
146 Elvy, pp. 18, 38; Boutflower, p. 28; J. F. Bridge, *A Westminster Pilgrim* (London 1919), p. 57. In 1869 Dean Bowers said that there were 2, 500 marriages per annum at Manchester (PP 1871, lv, p. 219).
147 ABDC Wells, 14 March 1861; Wells CM, 12–14 March 1861; ABDC Chichester, 21 March 1863.
148 J. W. F. Hill, p. 260, fn.4.
149 ABDC Bristol, 31 January 1805.
150 ABDC Exeter, 30 July 1808.
151 *HT*, 16 November 1842, quoted in P. L. S. Barrett, 'Hereford Cathedral in the Nineteenth Century', *FHCAR*, 1986, pp. 29–30; J. E. West, *Cathedral Organists Past and Present* (London 1899), p. 43.
152 R. E. Prothero and G. G. Bradley, *The Life and Correspondence of Arthur Penrhyn Stanley* (London 1893), vol.I, p. 41. For the funeral of the Duke of Wellington at St Paul's, cf. Sinclair, pp. 304–5.
153 *Guardian*, 1884, p. 528.
154 *Hereford Journal*, 23 March 1867. I am indebted to the Revd S. C. Parsons for this reference. For details of the funeral of Dean Hook of Chichester, cf. W. R. W. Stephens, *The Life and Letters of Walter Farquhar Hook* (London 1885), pp. 567–8. When Dean

Payne-Smith of Canterbury died in 1895, the coffin was laid on a purple bier in the midst of the nave, flanked by the choir and canons. The archbishop's beadsmen had black ribbons tied on their white staves (D. I. Hill, p. 84).

155 ABDC Chichester, 21 January 1881. The stalls of deceased canons at St Albans were draped in black in 1891 (Coghlan, p. 106).

156 ABDC Chichester, 10 October 1891; for rules re clergy funerals at Exeter, cf. ABDC Exeter, 3 December 1881.

157 F. Kilvert, *Kilvert's Diary 1870-9* (one volume edn, ed. W. Plomer, London 1944, reprinted 1967), pp. 93–5.

158 Boutflower, p. 26.

159 J. Jebb and H. W. Phillott, *The Statutes of the Cathedral Church of Hereford* (Hereford 1882), pp. 45–57.

160 C. Jenkins, ed., *The Statutes of the Cathedral and Metropolitical Church of Christ, Canterbury* (Canterbury 1925), p. 31.

161 A. W. Goodman and W. H. Hutton, *The Statutes governing the Cathedral Church of Winchester* (Oxford 1925), pp. 31–3, 98.

162 ABDC Chichester, 1 August 1800.

163 ABDC Hereford, 13 November 1800.

164 ABDC Exeter, 18 December 1817. At St Paul's one of the minor canons was appointed to the post of Divinity Lecturer. His principal task was 'to be ready and in attendance to preach' on all holy days in case the dignitary or prebendary whose turn it was failed to appear (Prestige, pp. 11–12; for details of the customary preachers later in the century, cf. PP 1883, xxi, p. 114).

165 ABDC Worcester, 24–25 November 1825, 25 November 1826. The rate was the same for a substitute sermon at Winchester (ABDC Winchester, 25 November 1808). Two guineas (or 3 guineas if in place of the dean) was still the rate at Worcester in 1874 (ABDC Worcester, 20 May 1874).

166 ABDC Hereford, 29 July 1834.

167 ABDC Hereford, 16 July 1834.

168 W. K. L. Clarke, *Chichester Cathedral in the Nineteenth Century* (Chichester Papers no.14, Chichester 1959), p. 12.

169 ABDC Chichester, 11 October 1841.

170 E. Denison, *A Charge Delivered to the Clergy of the Diocese of Salisbury* (London 1842), p. 28.

171 ABDC Winchester, 25 November 1846; cf. Goodman and Hutton, p. 98.

172 Jebb, p. 493; cf. Prestige, pp. 11–12; and PP 1883, xxi, p. 113.

173 M. E. C. Walcott, *Cathedralia* (London 1865), p. 32.

174 Wells CM, 2 January 1858; cf. also 6 December 1859. In 1883 Lord Arthur Hervey, Bishop of Bath and Wells, publicly rebuked a priest vicar for his preaching during a substitute sermon, which he said was 'a perversion of scripture' (Greenhalgh, *Wells*, p. 195). The priest vicar, D. G. Manning, complained to the dean and chapter, but they declined to comment or take any action (Wells CM, 2 April 1883).

175 Wells CM, 5 July 1858. B. F. Westcott said in 1872 that only about half of the honorary canons of Peterborough fulfilled their preaching turns (Howson, p. 123).

176 PP 1883, xxi, p. 268.

177 PP 1883, xxi, p. 253; cf. Greenhalgh, *Wells*, p. 190.

178 ABDC Winchester, 23 June 1873.

179 ABDC Worcester, 19 November 1877, 19 November 1880.

180 Salisbury Chapter Muniments, Press V, Box 5; cf. Wordsworth and Macleane, pp. 502–15. At a discussion about preaching turns at the general chapter at Salisbury in 1889, Archdeacon Lear said that honorary canons in new foundation cathedrals had no right to preach in the cathedral and were anxious to establish one. But some of the canons did not find regular preaching turns an easy

responsibility. Canon Whitefoord said that he had 'great difficulty' in preaching on Trinity Sunday, while Canon Sir J. Philipps mentioned that the late Subdean Eyre had complained that he had exhausted the subject of the conversion of St Paul (ABDC Salisbury, 13 June 1889). At Lichfield the stipends of two prebends had been allotted to the repair funds of the cathedral in 1803. The preaching turns of these lapsed stalls were undertaken by the canon-in-residence (H. Baylis, 'The Prebends in the Cathedral Church of Saints Mary and Chad in Lichfield', *South Staffordshire Archaeological and Historical Society* 1960–1, vol.II, pp. 33–52).

181 ABDC Salisbury, 13 March 1872; a list of preachers at Chester Cathedral from Advent 1878 to Ascension Day 1879 and from Advent 1879 to Whitsunday 1880 may be found in PP 1883, xxi, pp. 159f.; an earlier list from Trinity Sunday until Advent Sunday 1869 is in PP 1871, lv, pp. 205–7. For preaching turns at Truro, cf. PP 1883, xxi, pp. 61–2.

182 ABDC Chichester, 20 January 1877.

183 ABDC Gloucester, 26 September 1900.

184 Pigou, *Phases of My Life*, p. 358; Pigou, *Odds and Ends*, p. 216.

185 W. H. Fremantle, *Recollections of Dean Fremantle* (London 1921), p. 128. The sermon preceded evening prayer until 1848 (Walcott, *Traditions*, p. 86).

186 F. Alford, pp. 271, 516; Woodruff, p. 15; D. I. Hill, p. 78; cf. p. 120.

187 Pigou, *Phases of My Life*, p. 358; Stephens, pp. 522–3. In 1889 the dean and chapter ordered that Sunday afternoon sermons should begin with the trinitarian invocation (ABDC Chichester, 2 May 1889).

188 Jebb, p. 412; cf. Walcott, *Traditions*, p. 86, who says that the sermons were preached in the nave at Exeter from 1859.

189 ABDC Bristol, 30 November 1818; cf. Fletcher, p. 51. There were Sunday afternoon sermons at Norwich from 1831 to 1842 (Dean Pellew's note-book, DCN 120/2, Norfolk CRO). They were restarted in 1858 (ABDC Norwich, February 1858, cited in Coghlan, p. 99).

190 ABDC Bristol, 10 May 1849.

191 LPL, Tait Papers, vol. 27, 4 May 1850.

192 ibid., vol. 32, 5 December 1852.

193 Gloucester chapter minute book 1865–91, 11 January 1866.

194 *Guardian*, 1869, p. 182. When Benson preached on Sunday afternoons, 'the nave of the Cathedral was crowded with intelligent listeners' (Benson, vol.I, p. 380).

195 F. Lear, 'Reminiscences of Eighty Years', *SDG*, vol. 23, July 1910, pp. 121–2.

196 ABDC Chichester, 20 May 1884, 30 January 1889.

197 CCF no.3189.

198 ABDC Chichester, 11 January 1866.

199 Wells CM, 22 January 1868.

200 ABDC Worcester, 19 November 1872; cf. 2 December 1879 when the dean and chapter ordered sermons to be preached on Friday evenings in Lent and Advent. At Hereford there was a weekly evening sermon in Lent and a daily sermon in Holy Week (ABDC Hereford, 23 January 1868).

201 Wells CM, 8 February 1876.

202 ABDC Chichester, 28 January 1878; cf. 5 August 1889 when the eve of festivals was preferred; cf. also 23 January 1893.

203 ABDC Worcester, 4 January 1893.

204 ABDC Worcester, 30 October 1900.

205 Butler, p. 325. Towards the end of the century it became increasingly common for chapels to be used for short services (cf. ABDC Chichester, 21 January 1889, 12 July 1897). The Bishop of Salisbury used the Morning Chapel there to catechize the boys of the Bishop's School (Salisbury CM, 18 January 1890) and the theological college at Wells was allowed to use the Lady Chapel in the cathedral for its daily services

(Wells CM, 27 May 1895). In 1873 the dean and chapter of St Paul's received a request from fifty-eight young men in the city asking for a short evening service in one of the chapels, based on compline. A similar lunchtime service, based on sext, was compiled by Liddon and brought into use in 1881 (Prestige, p. 184).

206 ABDC Exeter, 20 October 1881, 22 February 1884 (cf.15 November 1884, 14 February 1885, 21 November 1885).

207 B. Compton, *Edward Meyrick Goulburn, Dean of Norwich* (London 1899), p. 78.

208 G. Cobb, *English Cathedrals: The Forgotten Centuries* (London 1980), p. 78, quoting H. Goodwin's *Ely Gossip*. Dickson says that this custom changed in 1843, not 1852, and adds that 'the space west of the organ screen was known as the "sermon-place" and was encumbered by benches of various patterns, some of them cushioned and baize-covered and jealously claimed as pews by leading citizens and their families. The lay clerks and boys ascended into the organ-loft and sang a hymn, standing on its western side' (Dickson, p. 58). Earlier in the century, great confusion prevailed at Ely where the congregation would leave their places in the quire during the singing of the Nicene Creed in order to move into the nave to hear the sermon (Jebb, pp. 493–4).

209 ABDC Chichester, 12 November 1885, 30 January 1889.

210 ABDC Worcester, 24 November 1885.

211 ibid., 31 July 1874.

212 ABDC Exeter, 12 February 1881. For a similar plan at Wells, cf. Wells CM, 20 December 1873. For Worcester, cf. ABDC Worcester, 19 November 1874. Visiting preachers at Chichester were paid expenses (ABDC Chichester, 12 May 1890). At Hereford, however, a plan to invite the Revd Luke Rivington, Superior of the Holy Ghost, to preach in the Lady Chapel caused 'great scandal in the city' (ABDC Hereford, 25 June 1870).

213 *Guardian*, 1883, p. 1807 (reprint of an article which originally appeared in the *Pall Mall Gazette*). In 1872 it was decided that the bishop should choose the preachers from January to March, the dean choose those between April and June and the canons choose those for the rest of the year (St Paul's CM, 14 October 1872, cited in Coghlan, p. 100).

214 ABDC Worcester, 7 March 1884. In 1888 the dean and chapter of Worcester ordered that the list of anthems and services be sent each week to the offices of the *Worcester Journal* and the *Herald* (ABDC Worcester, 1 August 1888).

215 A. C. Tait, 'Cathedral Reform', *Edinburgh Review*, vol. xcvii, January 1853, p. 176.

216 *CCR* 1872, p. 224. The development of preaching in cathedrals had been strongly recommended by the Cathedrals Commission (cf. PP 1854–5, xv, p. 52).

217 His shortest sermon lasted forty-five minutes and the longest was eighty minutes (Beswick, p. 20).

218 Prestige, p. 101; cf. J. O. Johnston, *Life and Letters of Henry Parry Liddon* (London 1904), p. 140. Beswick says that the first seats were occupied over an hour before the afternoon service when Liddon preached (Beswick, p. 13).

219 Benson, vol.I, p. 403, quoted in Johnston, p. 303.

220 Johnston, p. 304.

221 ibid., pp. 389–90. There is a fuller account of Liddon's preaching in ibid., pp. 305–6 (quoting *Guardian*, 24 July 1889), and another by Darwell Stone in 'Dr Liddon as a Preacher', *Henry Parry Liddon, 1829–1929: A Centenary Memoir* (London 1929), pp. 17–23.

222 M. C. Church, *Life and Letters of Dean Church* (London 1895), p. 217.

223 L. Creighton, *Life and Letters of Mandell Creighton* (London 1904), vol.I, pp. 312–3.

224 Worc. C. Add. Mss., 104, p. 13.

225 ibid., letter of 30 January 1913.

226 Worc. C. Add. Mss., 137, p. 20; cf. Add. Mss., 141, p. 39.

227 Prothero and Bradley, vol.I, p. 430.

228 cf. Lake pp. 136–7.

229 Westcott, vol.I, p. 314.

230 Benson, vol.I, p. 380.

231 Elvy, p. 13.

232 Humfrys, pp. 12–13; cf. Chapter 5, p. 72.

233 *Guardian*, 1891, p. 1548.

234 T. G. Willis, *Records of Chichester* (Chichester 1928), pp. 217–8.

235 cf. Chapter 1, p. 3.

236 Bishop Maltby's visitation, Visitation Book, f.159.

237 Wells CM, 13 December 1825.

238 Walcott, *Traditions*, p. 101; cf. PP 1854, xxv, p. 281 and p. 115 above.

239 H. L. Thompson, *Henry George Liddell* (London 1899), p. 153.

240 Armstrong, p. 110.

241 CCR 1865, p. 97. Worc. C. Mss., Sacrist's accounts, 24 August 1800, f.324–6, 1827, f.428–30. Canon Sedgwick was 'shocked' at the very idea of a weekly communion at Norwich (Clark and Hughes, vol. II, p. 588).

242 Chadwick, *York*, p. 286; cf. R. Cant in Stacpoole, p. 57 and Cowie, p. 353.

243 Jebb, pp. 504, 511.

244 *Guardian*, 1849, p. 726. This was not true of Worcester, where a weekly celebration was not achieved until 1851. (cf. Worc. C. Add. Mss., 24).

245 Thompson, p. 159.

246 ABDC Hereford, 8 November 1866. A proposal to have a weekly communion at Wells was considered by the dean and chapter in 1872 (Wells CM, 27 August 1872; cf. also Greenhalgh, *Wells*, p. 188). Lincoln had a weekly celebration by 1869 (J. W. F. Hill, pp. 264–5) and Ripon in 1875, though Canon Charles Dodgson, father of Lewis Carroll, had earlier pressed for one (cf. Smith, p. 261).

247 Bristol Capitular Mss., DC/A/7/4/3. Canon J. P. Norris told the cathedral commissioners in 1880 that for eight years all four canons had pressed for a weekly communion, but that celebrations on saints' days and choral eucharists were still forbidden (PP 1883, xxi, p. 210). More frequent celebrations began at Salisbury in 1881 (Salisbury CM, 28 February 1881).

248 R. Hale in C. Barringer, ed., *Norwich in the Nineteenth Century* (Norwich 1984), p. 165.

249 ABDC Hereford, 12 November 1868. B. Rainbow's article, 'John Jebb (1805–1886) and the Choral Service' in L. Dakers, ed., *The World of Church Music 1986* (Croydon 1986), attempts to assess Jebb's place in the development of nineteenth century cathedral worship.

250 ABDC Hereford, 25 June 1869, 25 June 1870.

251 ABDC Peterborough, 30 December 1869, cited in Coghlan, p. 148.

252 Prestige, p. 106.

253 ABDC Worcester, 3 December 1879. The service was at 8.15 a.m. in the summer and noon in the winter. In 1895 the dean and chapter decided that the celebration on all red letter days, with the exception of Lady Day and the Nativity of St John the Baptist, when it was held in the Lady Chapel and St John's Chapel, should be held at the High Altar (ABDC Worcester, 27 June 1895). The Jesus Chapel was used in 1896 when the Lady Chapel was out of action owing to the construction of the new organ (ibid., 29 May 1896).

254 Salisbury CM, 3 February 1880.

255 Wells CM, 2 January 1882, 1 July 1882. Red letter days were observed with an early celebration and an additional one after morning prayer at Exeter from 1884 (ABDC Exeter, 22 February 1884).

256 NCL, Goulburn's diary, 11 June 1887; ABDC Norwich, 2 December 1873, quoted in Coghlan, p. 148.

257 ABDC Chichester, 29 October 1889.

258 ABDC Winchester, 25 November 1895.

259 Prestige, pp. 106, 184.

260 *Guardian*, 1883, p. 1807.

261 H. M. Brown, *A Century for Cornwall – The Diocese of Truro 1877–1977* (Truro 1976), p. 43.

262 *CCR* 1894, p. 38.

263 J. F. Briscoe and H. F. B. Mackay, *A Tractarian at Work* (London 1932), p. 182; cf. ABDC Chichester 21 January 1894, 8 November 1895, 23 October 1896, 2 May 1898.

264 *Guardian*, 1897, p. 6.

265 K. Edwards, 'The Cathedral of Salisbury, 1075–1950', *VCH Wiltshire*, vol. iii, 1956, pp. 203–4. Bristol did not have a daily celebration until 1935 (M. H. Fitzgerald, *The Story of Bristol Cathedral* (London 1936), p. 68)

266 ABDC Salisbury, 5 September 1849; cf. Walcott, *Traditions*, p. 102. This was as a result of pressure from W. K. Hamilton (cf. L. W. Cowie, 'The Church of England since 1837', *VCH Wiltshire*, vol. iii, 1956, p. 65; Liddon, p. 24; *Guardian*, 1849, p. 654). In 1878 the dean and chapter of Salisbury agreed with the request of a petition 'signed by many communicants resident in the Close' and determined to have a second celebration of the eucharist every Sunday (Salisbury CM, 16 December 1878).

267 Chadwick, *York*, p. 1295.

268 Fitzgerald, p. 68; Fletcher, p. 65; ABDC Bristol, 10 January 1873. They were the custom at Lincoln in the same year (*Guardian*, 1869, p. 182).

269 Walcott, *Traditions*, pp. 117–18; for Chichester, cf. ABDC Chichester, 20 January 1873, 20 January 1877, and A. S. Duncan-Jones, *The Story of Chichester Cathedral* (London 1933), p. 127. For Durham, cf. Lake, p. 135; for Peterborough (where early celebrations were introduced by Westcott), cf. Benson, vol.I, p. 310. At the early celebration on New Year's Day at Norwich in 1869, the bishop celebrated and the choristers sang 'O God our help in ages past' and the Gloria at the Gospel, before being dismissed after the Creed (NCL, Goulburn's diary, 1 January 1869).

270 Prestige, p. 107.

271 *Guardian*, 1873, pp. 20–1. Before the 8 a.m. celebration was begun, the number of communicants on the greater festivals at the single long morning service was sometimes so numerous that the service did not end until long after one o'clock (Woodruff, p. 21).

272 D. King, 'Winchester Cathedral under Deans Rennell and Garnier' *Winchester Cathedral Chronicle* 1972; ABDC Norwich, 2 December 1874, cited in Coghlan, p. 148.

273 ABDC Worcester 21 November 1874. An early service once a month was started at Exeter in 1881(ABDC Exeter 12 November 1881).

274 ABDC Worcester, 25 November 1875, 19 November 1880, 21 January, 26 February, 21 November 1881, 20 March and 29 April 1882, 7 March 1884 (cf.ABDC Chichester, 2 May 1891); 17 September and 20 November 1884, 16 April and 31 August 1885, 26 April 1887, 1 May and 3 June 1893.

275 Butler, pp. 319, 327–8. An early service on each Sunday and saints' day was begun at Gloucester in 1881 (ABDC Gloucester, 31 March 1881).

276 Wells CM, 1 April 1887. There was an early celebration at Wells on Easter Day 1881, since 'a considerable number of worshippers at the Cathedral desired the additional service' (Wells CM, 13 April 1881; cf. also 1 July and 2 July 1883).

277 ABDC Salisbury, 18 May 1887; cf. Salisbury CM, 7 January 1887.

278 ABDC Chichester, 2 May 1889; cf. 1 August 1894.

279 ABVC Chichester, 18 October 1889.

280 ABDC Peterborough, 13 February 1893; St Albans I, vol.ii, 30 June 1894, both cited in Coghlan, p. 148.

281 Prestige, p. 12.
282 Hutton, p. 160.
283 Johnston, p. 219.
284 Jebb, p. 479.
285 Wells CM, 30 January 1861.
286 Armstrong, p. 110.
287 Lake, p. 135.
288 *Guardian*, 1869, p. 182; cf. J. W. F. Hill, pp. 264–5. At Exeter the dean and chapter ordered that the celebrant should himself place the alms and elements and remains of the elements on the altar (ABDC Exeter, 29 May 1876). At Worcester, the chalice was mixed in the chapter-house before the service. For midday celebrations, the vessels were placed beforehand in Prince Arthur's chantry and taken from there to the altar by the celebrant or by a minor canon (ABDC Worcester, 3 June 1893). At Wells the dean and chapter rather grudgingly agreed to a request by the bishop 'that the long established custom observed in the Cathedral of placing the bread and wine upon the table before the commencement of morning service should be abandoned and that they be placed there immediately before the Prayer for the Church Militant' (Wells CM, 5 May 1870). Dean Close told the Royal Commission on Ritual in 1867 that at Carlisle the bread and wine were placed on the altar by a minor canon before the service began and that two lay clerks collected alms from the congregation (PP 1867, xx, pp. 773–4).
289 Chichester chapter minute book, 2 May 1892.
290 ibid., 12 May 1893.
291 Chichester Draft Acts, f.73 (Cap. 1/3A/2).
292 ABDC Worcester, 19 November 1895, 3 March 1896.
293 Worc. C. Mss., Sacrists' Reports. The dean and chapter clarified the issue in an Act of 3 March 1896; cf. Chapter 6, p. 100.
294 ABDC Worcester, 2 December 1896.
295 ABDC Winchester, 1 October 1850. A pair of new chairs was presented at Norwich in 1845 'expressly for the purpose of placing either side of the altar' (ABDC Norwich, 8 December 1845, quoted in Coghlan, p. 145).
296 Armstrong, p. 170. Dean Duncombe told the Royal Commission on Ritual in 1867 that he took the first part of the communion service from the north end of the altar, adopting the eastward position at the beginning of the Prayer of Consecration (PP 1867, xx, p. 777).
297 Johnston, p. 145; Prestige, pp. 107–8. For Dean Church's defence of the eastward position, cf. B. A. Smith, p. 181; cf. also Matthews and Atkins, pp. 269–70. The dean and chapter of St Paul's had petitioned Parliament in 1874, asking that cathedrals should be exempted from the Public Worship Regulation Act, and Dean Church led the opposition to it (St Paul's CM, 23 May 1874, quoted in Coghlan, p. 156).
298 Pigou, *Phases of My Life*, p. 363; cf. ABDC Chichester, 2 May 1889.
299 J. W. F. Hill, p. 246.
300 Elvy, p. 27.
301 ABDC Gloucester, 30 November 1808; ABDC Bristol, 23 June 1828. New velvet coverings for the altar were bought at York in 1806 (D. M. Owen, in G. E. Aylmer and R. Cant, eds, *A History of York Minster* (Oxford 1977), p. 258).
302 Worc. C. Add. Mss., 128, pp. 4–5.
303 PP 1867, xx, p. 778.
304 ABDC Exeter, 4 December 1872.
305 Worc. C. Mss., Sacrists' Reports, 1891, 1896–1900.
306 Coghlan, p. 162, citing ABDC Peterborough, 16 October 1891.
307 Moore, p. 122.
308 ABDC Exeter, 16 May 1885. Candles were used at the early services at Exeter early

in the century, though it is not clear whether they were used liturgically or merely to provide light on dark mornings. The sub-treasurer was responsible for giving candle stubs to the vergers as perquisites (ABDC Exeter, 15 March 1809). There were candlesticks on the altar at York in 1867, but they did not contain any candles (PP 1867, xx, p. 777). The dean and chapter of Chichester accepted a gift of a pair of candlesticks in 1868 (ABDC Chichester, 10 October 1868), as did the dean and chapter of Hereford in 1871, where Canon Jebb presented them with a specific request that they 'should be allowed to remain upon the Holy Table and be used when the Cathedral is otherwise lighted' (ABDC Hereford, 9 November 1871). Salisbury Cathedral was given some candlesticks in 1887 (ABDC Salisbury, 18 October 1887), while at Worcester it was ordered in 1888 that the practice of the candles above the altar at evensong should be continued throughout the year (ABDC Worcester, 17 November 1888). Gloucester Cathedral received a gift of candlesticks and other altar furnishings in 1889 (ABDC Gloucester, 28–9 March 1889). The dean and chapter of Worcester ordered that the altar candlesticks should be lit at the monthly choral celebration at midday (ABDC Worcester, 19 November 1892). In 1893 it was found that it would be more convenient to light them before matins if a choral celebration followed (ABDC Worcester, 3 June 1893). At Salisbury the dean and chapter decided in 1900 that the altar candles should be lit during the winter and on any dark days (Salisbury CM, 5 June 1900). At Manchester there was an old custom of lighting two candelabra with tall wax candles during the Christmas and Epiphany seasons, while two large candlesticks with tall candles had 'always' stood on the altar (Boutflower, pp. 27–8; cf. H. A. Hudson, 'The Christmas Lights at Manchester Cathedral', *TLCAS*, vol.xxix, 1912).

309 A. B. Donaldson, *The Bishopric of Truro* (London 1902), pp. 285–6; H. M. Brown, p. 47. The gradual movement towards High Church ceremonial may also be observed at Worcester (cf. Worc. C. Add. Mss., 137, pp. 22–3) and Chichester (Willis, p. 216). Wells is another example of the same trend. In 1893 the services were described as 'careful and reverent' though there was a danger that 'the spirit of devotion may be smothered under ceremony and form' (Greenhalgh, *Wells*, pp. 193–4; cf. also Wells CM, 5 and 13 October 1898).

310 *Gentleman's Magazine*, 1802, vol.lxxii, pt 1, pp. 32–3.

311 ibid., vol. lxxiv, pt 1, p. 232, quoted in Walcott, *Traditions*, p. 121.

312 Walcott, *Traditions*, p. 122.

313 L. Smith, pp. 268–9.

314 Prestige, p. 108; W. J. S. Simpson, p. 49.

315 ABDC Winchester, 4 January 1872.

316 Lake, p. 262; see Chapter 11, p. 248.

317 *Trefoil*, p. 112.

318 *Guardian*, 1892, p. 876 and 1894, p. 746.

319 Prestige, p. 187; Coghlan, p. 162.

320 Worc. C. Add. Mss., 128, p. 9.

321 Boutflower, p. 47.

322 E. M. Goulburn, *The Functions of our Cathedrals* (Oxford 1869), pp. 11, 15, cited in Coghlan, p. 157.

323 ABDC Chichester, 21 January 1822. For other examples, cf. ABDC Peterborough, July 1823, cited in Coghlan, p. 133; cf. ABDC Hereford, 1 December 1860. The times of daily services at Hereford in 1835 were 11 a.m. and 3 p.m. (CCF 3189); ABDC Chichester, 31 December 1864; ABDC Bristol, 2 July 1867; Hutton, p. 169. The times of services at St Paul's before 1869 were 9.45 a.m. and 3.15 p.m. (R. D. Fenwick, 'An Early Victorian Organist at Work: II – The Latter Years of John Goss at St Paul's Cathedral, 1860–1872', *The Organ*, vol. 64, no.254, October 1985, p. 159); NCL, Goulburn's diary, 4 June 1867; PP 1867, xx, pp. 773–9.

324 ABDC Exeter, 19 April 1871.

325 ABDC Worcester, 21 February and 20 May 1874, 26 April 1876. This decision was reversed in 1878 to avoid interfering with the choristers' education (ibid., 22 November 1878). For the same reason evensong was rearranged at 5 p.m. in 1883 (ABDC Worcester, 28 April 1883); cf. also Salisbury CM, 16 December 1878, 1 November 1879; ABDC Winchester, 19 May 1891; *Guardian*, 1896, p. 2081.

326 *Guardian*, 1848, p. 355; Walcott, p. 197.

327 Church, pp. 210–12.

328 Rainbow, *The Choral Revival in the Anglican Church, 1839–1872*, p. 246; J. C. Cox, 'The Treatment of Our Cathedral Churches in the Victorian Age', *Archaeological Journal*, vol.liv, 1897, p. 240.

329 PP 1854, xv, p. 52. At Manchester in about 1855 the services on Sundays were more congregational than the daily services (cf.Boutflower, p. 22). At Norwich there was a hybrid evensong, 'partly choral, partly parochial' for three months of the year at 2.30 p.m. (Walcott, *Traditions*, p. 102). Dean Close told the Royal Commission on Ritual in 1867 that he believed that the daily choral service was having a harmful effect at Carlisle: 'I can speak decidedly though sorrowfully, that it certainly keeps away the working classes. They have given me as a reason, that they cannot follow the choral service. Mechanics and respectable people of that class have often stated that as an objection' (PP 1867, xx, p. 773; cf. ibid., p. 774).

330 Winchester Cathedral Mss., Davidson's visitation 1900, Canon Warburton's reply.

331 Winchester Cathedral Mss., *De Precentore*, November 1890.

332 Salisbury CM, 3 January 1899. Dean Close was in favour of the congregation singing during the settings and the anthem (F. Close, *Thoughts on the Daily Choral Services in Carlisle Cathedral* (Carlisle 1865), p. 8).

333 ABDC Exeter, 1 August 1818, 16 October 1819.

334 ibid., 5 August 1865, 10 March 1866.

335 Coghlan, p. 141, citing ABDC Peterborough, 9 March 1830.

336 ABDC Hereford, 14 August 1841, 15 January 1844; West, p. 43; CCF 3208.

337 Worc. C. Add. Mss., 137, pp. 8–9.

338 Prestige, p. 84.

339 ABDC Chichester, 1 August 1861; Clarke, p. 13.

340 ABDC Salisbury, 9 March 1866.

341 Wells CM, 5 August 1874. At Hereford in 1869 the services were suspended for a week during the cleaning of the cathedral (ABDC Hereford, 21 April 1869), but at Worcester in 1881 the services were transferred to St Helen's Church while the cathedral was cleaned (*Guardian*, 1881, p. 1404).

342 *Parish Choir*, vol.II, p. 185; vol.III, p. 9.

343 Walcott, *Traditions*, p. 102. This was a matter for comment in the *Guardian* (1869, p. 1168). Daily sung evensong was started in 1875 (L. Smith, pp. 261, 270). The weekday services at St Albans were sung by boys' voices only (*Guardian*, 1900, p. 1065), with a full service only on Saturday afternoons (T. F. Bumpus, vol.III, p. 223). The services on Wednesdays and Fridays were plain at Carlisle in 1867 (PP 1867, xx, p. 774).

344 Woodruff, p. 15.

345 Salisbury CM, 17 July 1883.

346 ABDC Chichester, 30 January 1889.

347 P. Aston, *The Music of York Minster* (London 1972), p. 12. Before this, the service was sung by the songmen only.

348 Coghlan, p. 99, citing ABDC Ely, 14 June 1888.

349 ABDC Worcester, 1 August 1887.

350 Worc. C. Mss., Precentor's Report, 1890.

351 Hillsman, p. 326, fn.57, citing ABDC Lichfield, 24 June 1887, and ABDC Ely, 14 June 1888.

352 Hillsman, p. 305, fn.58, citing ABDC Salisbury, 29 August 1877, and ABDC Ely, 25 November 1887.

353 Wells CM, 2 January 1899; cf. ibid., 1 October 1900. For further details of choir holidays, cf. Chapter 8, pp. 211.

354 Hillsman, p. 315, citing YML Add.Mss, 157/2, p. 292, and Frost, p. 72; cf. NCL, Goulburn's diary, 23 March 1867.

355 For psalm-singing, cf. pp. 149–50. One service a week was sung by men's voices only at St Paul's in the later nineteenth century (cf. Prestige, pp. 157, 159; Frost, pp. 48–9). Unaccompanied services were rare but not unknown. Jebb recorded that in many cathedrals the organ was not used in Passiontide or on Wednesdays and Fridays during Lent. Canterbury and Winchester had had successful unaccompanied services during repairs to the cathedral (Jebb, p. 313; cf. Walcott, *Traditions*, p. 111). T. L. Wheeler, the Precentor of Worcester, complained in 1866 that the choral services there were often marred by an inadequate organ (Wheeler to Peel, Worc. C. Mss., Restoration Box, 1 January 1866).

356 Walcott, *Traditions*, p. 114; cf. Jebb, p. 382. The anthem was also omitted on litany days at St Paul's (Jebb, p. 371).

357 e.g. ABDC Worcester, 24 November 1826, 19 November 1883; Wells CM, 1 October 1831.

358 West, p. 73; cf. Jebb, p. 122.

359 ABDC Worcester, 2 February 1807.

360 ABDC Gloucester, 30 November 1808; cf. D. C. St.V. Welander, *The History, Art and Architecture of Gloucester Cathedral* (Stroud 1991), p. 435.

361 ABDC Worcester, 25 November 1825.

362 Worc. C. Mss., Attendance Book 1836–42, 28 December 1838. A similar custom was in force at Christ Church, Oxford, in the late 1840s. The *Parish Choir* complained that 'the Litany is *not sung* by the priest at all, but only *read* with the absurd anomaly of the choir singing the responsion. There is a crying necessity for reform in the services of the cathedral, where the prayers are always *read* with gross inconsistency of *choral* responses' (*Parish Choir*, vol.III, p. 33).

363 Coghlan, p. 141, citing ABDC Peterborough, 9 March 1830.

364 W. Howitt, *Visits to Remarkable Places* (London 1840–2), vol.II, p. 64.

365 D. Robertson, *The King's School, Gloucester* (Chichester 1974), p. 105.

366 Jebb, p. 122.

367 ibid., p. 103, quoted in Rainbow, *The Choral Revival in the Anglican Church, 1839–1872*, p. 254.

368 J. Jebb, *Three Lectures on the Cathedral Service of the Church of England* (Leeds, 1845), pp. 5, 8.

369 Jebb, *The Choral Service of the United Church of England and Ireland*, pp. 249–50, 263.

370 ibid., p. 239.

371 ABDC Bristol, 5 December 1848, 13 and 23 February, 10 May, 26 June, 5 and 6 December 1849; DC/A/7/8/1; Fletcher, pp. 60–1; *Guardian*, 1848, pp. 768–9, 781–2; 1849, pp. 7, 16, 65, 81, 129, 153. There is a full account of this controversy by D. Gedge, 'In quires and places (ii)', *Musical Opinion*, vol. 104, no.1244, June 1981, pp. 323–8, 354.

372 *Guardian*, 1849, p. 156.

373 Rainbow, *The Choral Revival in the Anglican Church, 1839–1872*, p. 256.

374 ibid., p. 256.

375 *Guardian*, 1858, p. 107.

376 Wells CM, 23 September 1858.

377 *Guardian*, 1859, p. 819.

378 Walcott, *Traditions*, p. 114; T. F. Bumpus, vol.III, p. 161.
379 ABDC Bristol, 19 October 1869. Ripon eventually began to have intoned offices(Hillsman, p. 313, citing *The Choir*, 20 February 1875, p. 114).
380 F. Alford, pp. 282, 516; cf. Chapter 4, p. 54.
381 NCL, Goulburn's diary, 30 March and 21 April 1867.
382 Coghlan, p. 143, citing ABDC Ely, 2 July 1853, ABDC Peterborough, 27 November 1856.
383 Win.CA, *Cathedralia Winton: Minor Canons 1860–1918*, 12 March 1897. A similar custom at Exeter lasted until 1878 (ABDC Exeter, 8 June 1878).
384 ABDC Chichester, 2 May 1891. Jebb commended organ accompaniments for sung amens (Jebb, *The Choral Service of the United Church of England and Ireland*, p. 478).
385 Chichester Draft Acts, f.29–30, Mee to Dean, 11 October 1889 (Cap.I/3A/2).
386 Worc. C. Mss., Attendance Book 1836–42, 28 December 1838.
387 Jebb, *The Choral Service of the United Church of England and Ireland*, p. 436; Walcott, p. 150; T. F. Bumpus, vol.I, p. 58, has a slightly different list.
388 ibid., p. 439.
389 ibid., pp. 194, 435; cf. also, for various litany places, Walcott, *Traditions*, p. 114.
390 Jebb, *The Choral Service of the United Church of England and Ireland*, p. 446. The choristers at York were notorious for 'gabbling the responses with truly wonderful rapidity' during the litany (*Parish Choir*, vol.II, p. 173).
391 *Trefoil*, pp. 143–4; cf. *Guardian*, 1858, pp. 604, 546; *Parish Choir*, vol.III, pp. 56–7.
392 Worc. C. Add. Mss., 137, p. 4.
393 NCL, Goulburn's diary, 5 May 1867.
394 ibid., 23 December 1868.
395 Hillsman, p. 315, citing J. S. Bumpus, *The Organists and Composers of St Paul's Cathedral* (London 1891), p. 192, and Frost, p. 68.
396 Salisbury CM, 3 February and 16 March 1880.
397 ABDC Hereford, 6 April 1882. A short afternoon service, including the litany, was established at Ely in 1888 (ABDC Ely, 26 November 1888, cited in Coghlan, p. 148) and at Worcester in 1890 (Hillsman, p. 316). The *Church Times* deprecated replacing capitular evensong by the litany and claimed that a popular Sunday evening evensong was no substitute (Hillsman, p. 316, citing *CT*, 12 February 1892, p. 145).
398 ABVC Chichester, 13 June 1889.
399 ABDC Bristol, 28 December 1871; ABDC Chichester, 10 October 1871; ABDC Worcester, 21 November 1871; ABDC Hereford, 10 November 1871; ABDC Exeter, 16 December 1871; Wells CM, 19 December 1871.
400 Jebb, *The Choral Service of the United Church of England and Ireland*, p. 330. Adam Sedgwick, however, was noted for his dramatic reading of the lessons at Norwich (Clark and Hughes, vol.II, pp. 583–4).
401 Jebb, *The Choral Service of the United Church of England and Ireland*, p. 327. At Norwich in 1827 a chorister read the lesson (Walcott, *Traditions*, p. 114), though perhaps this was an isolated incident as Dean Pellew records that a lay clerk read the first lesson at the daily offices until he secured agreement for the duty minor canon to do so (Dean Pellew's note-book, 1829–31, p.lv, DCN 120/2, Norfolk CRO).
402 Jebb, *The Choral Service of the United Church of England and Ireland*, p. 347.
403 ibid., p. 331.
404 ABDC Gloucester, 30 November 1866.
405 ABDC Gloucester, 25 September 1873.
406 ABDC Wells, 5 May 1870.
407 ABDC Hereford, 8 September 1873.
408 *Guardian*, 1898, p. 170.
409 ABDC Exeter, 16 January 1830.
410 N. Temperley, *The Music of the English Parish Church* (Cambridge 1979), vol.I, p. 290.

411 cf. ibid., pp. 220f. and Rainbow, *The Choral Revival of the Anglican Church, 1839–1872*, pp. 83f., 297. But Temperley himself has pointed out that Janes' psalter was preceded by such collections as John Beckwith's collection in 1808 and J. E. Dibb's *Key to Chanting* in 1831. (N. Temperley, *Jonathan Gray and Church Music in York, 1770–1840* (York 1977), pp. 19, 21). Dibb gives examples of the varied pointing to be found at Lincoln, Norwich, York, Canterbury, St Paul's, Bangor and Chester (ibid., pp. 22–3).

412 *Parish Choir*, vol.I, p. 135.

413 W. E. Dickson, *Fifty Years of Church Music* (Ely 1894), p. 51, quoted in Temperley, *The Music of the English Parish Church*, vol.I, p. 51. At Winchester a metrical psalm was sung before the sermon (D. King). Psalms were also sung before the sermon at Bristol (ABDC Bristol, 23 June 1836).

414 H. D. Rawnsley, *Harvey Goodwin, Bishop of Carlisle* (London 1896), p. 245. A proposal at St Paul's in 1886 to have plainsong psalms for men's voices services was unpopular with the choir (Frost, p. 78; Scott, p. 28). Gregorian tones were used at York on Wednesday afternoons from 1883 to 1891 (Hillsman, p. 313, citing Aston, p. 12).

415 H. W. Pullen, *The Real Work of a Cathedral and why it is not done* (London 1869), p. 11.

416 Worc. C. Mss., Precentor's Report, 1882; cf. ABDC Worcester, 27 December 1881.

417 Hillsman, p. 306; Temperley, *The Music of the English Parish Church*, vol.I, pp. 330–1; *Guardian*, 24 October 1860, p. 924.

418 J. Sutton, *A Short Account of Organs* (London 1847), p. 3, quoted in Moore, p. 382.

419 Worc. C. Mss. (music library), A/1/6(5).

420 Bristol DC/A/11/3/2.

421 Frost, p. 18; cf. R. D. Fenwick, 'An Early Victorian Organist at Work: I – John Goss in Quire at St Paul's Cathedral, 1838–1860', *The Organ*, vol. 62, no 245, July 1983, pp. 100–1.

422 Moore, p. 189, n.l. Corrections in the books at Wells were ordered in 1831 after several mistakes were found (ABDC Wells, 8 December 1831). For other examples, cf. Bristol DC/A/11/31.

423 ABDC Worcester, 4 November 1816. No books could be borrowed at Winchester without written permission (ABDC Winchester, 2 February 1815). At Hereford, however, the vicars choral were allowed to borrow music (ABDC Hereford, 13 November 1800). When several volumes were found to be missing at Exeter in 1808, a careful search for them was ordered; if they could not be found a reward would be offered for their safe return (ABDC Exeter, 14–15 December 1808). Later, stricter regulations were introduced at Hereford (ABDC Hereford, 2 March 1830) and at Exeter (ABDC Exeter, 24 April 1841). A catalogue of the music books was made at Hereford in 1834 (ABDC Hereford, 9 December 1834), at Exeter in 1878 (ABDC Exeter, 7 September 1878) and at Bristol in 1900 (ABDC Bristol, 10 March 1900).

424 ABDC Worcester, 2 February 1861. The Precentor of Winchester was asked to investigate the condition of the books there in 1825 (ABDC Winchester, 1825).

425 ABDC Worcester, 23 November 1865.

426 ABDC Worcester, 23 November 1865.

427 ABDC Worcester, 1 August 1889.

428 ABDC Exeter, 28 July 1821.

429 ibid., 29 April 1848.

420 Bridge, p. 16.

431 ABDC Chichester, 20 January 1858.

432 ABDC Exeter, 23 May 1877.

433 ABDC Worcester, 1876; cf. also 25 November 1875.

434 Wells CM, 1 April and 1 July 1899.

435 Bristol DC/A/11/3/2.

436 Dickson, p. 63. At Exeter in about 1834 the choristers were required to arrive fifteen minutes before each service, not only to rehearse but 'to look out the hymns and

anthems, in order to prevent as far as possible the interchange of messages during prayer time'(*Mirror*, vol.xxiv, no.682, 20 September 1834, p. 195; vol.xxiv no.685, 11 October 1834, p. 243). At Hereford in 1863 the choristers had to arrive ten minutes before each service in order to arrange their books according to rules drawn up by the succentor (CCF 32508).

437 ABDC Chichester, 2 May 1876.

438 Quoted in D. H. Robertson, *Sarum Close* (London 1938; new edn 1970), pp. 279–80. At Hereford the choristers distributed the anthem books during the services (ABDC Hereford 13 November 1800; Barrett, p. 18).

439 cf. Chapter 1, p. 10. In 1824 the dean and chapter of Exeter ordered that the music must not be changed after a service had commenced (ABDC Exeter, 2 October 1824).

440 Worc. C. Mss., Attendance Book 1836–42, 27 September 1839.

441 ABDC Worcester, 2 February 1861. A similar order was made at Hereford in 1800 (ABDC Hereford, 13 November 1800).

442 Worc. C. Add. Mss., 137, p. 5 – the anthem being, of course, 'The Lord hear thee in the day of trouble', by John Blow.

443 Rainbow, *The Choral Revival in the Anglican Church, 1839–1872*, p. 256, quoting the *Parish Choir*, vol.I, p. 135.

444 W. H. Havergal to Maria Hackett, 23 September 1846, quoted in Moore, pp. 297–8. Dean Merewether of Hereford, however, ordered in 1834 that the Te Deum and Jubilate must be sung to proper settings on litany days, instead of being simply chanted. The same applied to the canticles at evensong and the anthem was never to be omitted (ABDC Hereford, 30 July 1834). Twenty years later, George Townshend Smith, the organist at Hereford, was able to tell the cathedral commissioners that the aim there was 'to make no difference as regards the performance or selection of the music between the Sunday and other days, striving to make the daily service as excellent as possible, whether it is attended by few or many' (PP 1854, xxv, p. 938).

445 *Guardian*, 1852, p. 617.

446 PP 1854, xxv, p. 925.

447 ibid., p. 923.

448 cf. Moore, supplement (HCA 5915). For the repertoire in use at Chester in 1824, cf. J. C. Bridge, 'The Organists of Chester Cathedral, part 2', *Journal of the Architectural, Archaeological and Historical Society for the County and City of Chester and North Wales*, n.s., vol. xix, pt 2 (Chester 1913), pp. 118–9. Several music lists of the time were printed in the *Quarterly Musical Magazine and Review* in 1824 (pp. 26–7, 310–17). At the reopening of Hereford Cathedral in 1863, anthems by Goss and Ouseley and Townshend Smith were sung, while *Ouseley in C* (double choir) was used for the eucharist as well as matins and evensong (Bumpus, *The Organists and Composers of St Paul's Cathedral*, p. 165); cf. also E. H. Fellowes, *English Cathedral Music from Edward VI to Edward VII* (London 1941, new edns 1970, 1973), p. 257, for a Bristol list of 1827. For the Durham list, cf. B. Crosby, 'A service sheet from June 1680', *MT*, vol.cxxi, no.1648, June 1980, pp. 399–401. For a discussion of Victorian cathedral music, cf. W. J. Gatens, *Victorian Cathedral Music in Theory and Practice* (Cambridge 1986), *passim*.

449 Rainbow, *The Choral Revival in the Anglican Church 1839–1872*, pp. 329f. The following cathedrals are represented: York, Chester, Lichfield, Salisbury, St Asaph, Bristol, Carlisle, Hereford, Ripon, Gloucester, Lincoln, Peterborough, Manchester and St Paul's, in addition to various other foundations. For a comment on the Lincoln repertoire in 1857, cf. A. L. Kirwan, *The Music of Lincoln Cathedral* (London 1973), p. 12. In 1870 the *Musical Standard* published tables of music sung at St Paul's, Lichfield, Wells, Ely, Worcester, Salisbury, Peterborough, Durham and York (Hillsman, p. 352).

450 cf. Maria Hackett's notes quoted in Moore, pp. 317–20.

451 For the old method of copying these lists and the introduction of printed lists, cf. H. Woodward (precentor) to J. Hooper (chapter clerk), 20 November 1896 (Worc. C. Mss., Precentor's reports).

452 Aston, p. 13.

453 *Letters to the Editor of the Musical World*, pp. 47–8. Printed schemes have survived at York from 1881, Christ Church, Oxford, from 1886, Chichester from 1888 and Hereford from 1892 (cf. Aston, p. 12; Christ Church Misc. Papers, Bodleian Library, Oxford; West Sussex CRO, Cap.VI/4/1; HCA 5818). Schemes at Salisbury and Lincoln for 1895 have been published (cf. M. Foster, *The Music of Salisbury Cathedral*, (London 1974), p. 22; Kirwan, p. 12).

454 Dickson, p. 72.

455 Worc. C. Mss., Precentor's Reports.

456 Worc. C. Mss., Precentor's Report, 1890. In 1882 the dean and chapter made an attempt to curb the expanding repertoire of anthems at Exeter (ABDC Exeter, 11 February 1882). Eight years earlier they had taken the unusual step of prohibiting the repetition of an anthem which they found objectionable (ABDC Exeter, 23 May 1874). At Lichfield the dean and chapter spent £75 on new music in 1882 (Hillsman, p. 310, citing ABDC Lichfield, 22 September 1882).

457 Scott, p. 28.

458 Charlton, p. 75. For details of music sung at St Paul's in 1878–9, cf. W. S. Simpson, especially pp. 15–16, 19–27. The service settings were chosen in a fourteen-week cycle (ibid., pp. 10–11). Hillsman's table on p. 311 of his thesis seems to indicate that most cathedrals had a preponderance of nineteenth century music in their repertoire between 1857 and 1906 (Hillsman, p. 311).

459 S. S. Wesley to H. E. Ford, 19 September 1858, quoted in Moore, p. 357. Some years later Precentor Wray of Winchester had an unpleasant dispute with Archdeacon Jacob about the choice of music for services. Jacob had asked another minor canon to substitute on the list music by Wesley for a setting by Aldrich and wrote to Wray as follows: 'I confess when I saw the bill I expected Mr Beckwith would have yielded the service as he had done the anthem. For I had asked the substitution of Wesley for Aldrich, not only on the grounds of my dislike of Aldrich generally, but that for persons coming from the country as I expected the congregation to be, Wesley was more intelligible and appropriate. Mr Beckwith remarked that this of *Aldrich in E* was peculiarly suited to country people; it was the very class of music which one would submit as a sample of cathedral music. I expressed my dissent. Now I quite believe that Mr Beckwith's word, that had he understood my wish to be persevered in for Wesley's service, he would have changed the service as he did the Anthem. But conceiving that he adhered to Aldrich on a principle, I resolved to act on a principle also, or to quote my own saying, to "try the right" – and I substituted Wesley for Aldrich. I claim to do again what I did last week.' Wray protested to the dean and chapter, adding that if individual canons could exclude composers at whim, 'the result would be that Anglican Church Music would sink to the popular taste instead of those tastes which require formation being raised to the best style' (Winchester Cathedral Mss., *De Precentore*, 1–2 June 1864; but cf. ABDC Winchester, 25 November 1828). Precentor Symonds of Norwich remarked that he generally chose excerpts from oratorios and anthems 'with a good tune' on Sundays, with more traditional music on weekdays, since those who came to the cathedral on Sundays were less used to cathedral music (F. G. Kitton, *Zechariah Buck* (London 1899), p. 28). In 1878 the dean and chapter of Winchester made the organist responsible for the first choice of music to be sung. He was to submit this to the precentor, and then to the dean or canon-in-residence. In the event of a disagreement between the precentor

and the organist, the dean or canon-in-residence had the final decision. No subsequent alteration could be made without the approval of the organist, precentor and dean or canon-in-residence (ABDC Winchester, 26 November 1878, 7 January 1879). There was a further dispute about the choice of music in 1889 (*De Precentore*, 21–22 May 1889).

460 Prestige, p. 153. He had the reputation of a careful choice of music from every period from Redford to Sullivan (W. J. S. Simpson, p. 68).

461 H. Woodward to J. Hooper, 20 November 1896 (Worc. C. Mss., Precentor's Reports). For W. K. Hamilton's principles in choosing music at Salisbury, cf. Rainbow, *The Choral Revival in the Anglican Church 1839–1872*, p. 261. Dean Randall of Chichester thought that the canticles and anthems should be sung to short and simple music and would leave his stall on Sunday afternoons if he thought the anthem was too long (Briscoe and Mackay, p. 186; cf. ABDC Chichester, 25 January 1897). A shorter setting of the morning canticles was also desired by the dean and chapter of Hereford in 1878 (ABDC Hereford, 12 June 1878). H. P. Liddon asked for shorter anthems on Sunday afternoons at St Paul's during his months of residence (Beswick, pp. 15–16). A more liberal policy was adopted at Gloucester where the boarders at King's School were allowed to choose the anthem on the last Sunday of each half year (D. Robertson, p. 121).

462 ABDC Chichester, 10 October 1893.

463 cf. F. Close, *Memorials of Dean Close by 'One who Knew Him'* (London 1885), pp. 39–42. For an earlier dispute at York, cf. A. S. Leak, 'Conflict and Reform at York Minster in the Nineteenth Century' (Oxford B. D. thesis 1988), pp. 261–6.

464 Pigou, *Odds and Ends*, p. 230.

465 ABDC Worcester, 19 November 1869; cf. ibid., 21 January 1870; *Parish Choir*, vol.II, p. 152.

466 Prestige, p. 106; W. J. S. Simpson, p. 49; Welsby, p. 10; ABDC Bristol, 29 May 1866; Greenhalgh, *Wells*, p. 188; ABDC Hereford, 11 March 1869; ABDC Exeter, 24 December 1870; ABDC Chichester, 10 October 1877. Hymns from the Christian Knowledge Society's Collection were still occasionally chosen at Wells (Wells CM, 24 October 1868).

467 Worc. C. Mss., Precentor's Report, 1882; cf. also the 1883 report.

468 *Guardian*, 1884, p. 1960. Sometimes hymns replaced anthems several times a week (Hillsman, p. 309, citing *CT*, 25 September 1896).

469 ABDC Chichester, 25 January 1897.

470 Beswick, pp. 15–16.

471 ABDC Chichester, 20 January 1806. For examples of printed schemes, cf. n.463.

472 ABDC Exeter, 11 January 1812.

473 ABDC Winchester, 2 February 1815.

474 ABDC Wells, 8 December 1831; cf. Wells CM, 1 October 1885.

475 ABDC Hereford, 29 July 1834.

476 ABDC Gloucester, 26 September 1900.

477 F. Hannam-Clark, *Memories of the College School, Gloucester* (Gloucester 1890), pp. 80–1.

478 For a description of the custom at Salisbury in about 1830, cf. D. H. Robertson, pp. 278–9.

479 B. Rainbow, *The Choral Revival in the Anglican Church 1839–1872* (London 1970), p. 254. For details at Canterbury, cf. Woodruff and Danks, p. 359.

480 Rainbow, p. 254; cf. Jebb, *The Choral Service of the United Church of England and Ireland*, p. 229.

481 Dean Pellew's note-book, 1829–32, p. 2, DCN 120/2, Norfolk CRO, quoted in Coghlan, p. 136.

482 Jebb, *The Choral Service of the United Church of England and Ireland*, p. 231.

483 ABDC Worcester, 6 April 1843. For the custom at Worcester later in the century, cf. Worc. C. Add. Mss., 137, p. 7.

484 Moore, p. 256, quoting ABDC Lichfield, 25 September 1842.

485 Wells CM, 4 May 1847. Voluntaries before the services on greater festivals were ordered at Winchester Cathedral in 1864 (ABDC Winchester, 30 March 1864). The rule of *seniores priores* for the procession at the end of the service was introduced at Winchester in 1873 (ABDC Winchester, 25 November 1873).

486 *Parish Choir*, vol.I, p. 143, quoting S. H. Tyng, *Recollections of England* (London 1847), p. 266. A similar custom was observed at Christ Church (T. F. Bumpus, vol.III, p. 161). Bowing to the altar survived until after 1800 at Exeter (Walcott, *Traditions*, p. 103). When a proposal was made at Chichester in 1889 that the dean and chapter should bow to the altar on entering and leaving the quire, it was decided to leave this to the liberty of each member of the chapter (ABDC Chichester, 2 May 1889). At Manchester Cathedral the choir turned east for the Gloria Patri (Walcott, *Traditions*, p. 103; T. F. Bumpus, vol.III, p. 267). One of the minor canons at Carlisle in 1867 was accustomed to bow to the altar (PP 1867, xx, p. 774).

487 Lake, p. 135; cf. Chapter 4, p. 49. The chapter-house was used as a vestry at Chichester (ABDC Chichester, 1 August 1833). A vestry was brought into use at Norwich on Advent Sunday 1829. Before this, 'the Dean and Chapter and other members were obliged to go at once from their houses into the choir, and consequently were very liable to drop in after the service commenced' (Dean Pellew's note-book, 1829–32, p. 2, DCN 120/2, Norfolk CRO).

488 ABDC Winchester, 25 November 1856.

489 *Guardian*, 1861, p. 996.

490 ABDC Winchester, 30 March 1864.

491 Prestige, pp. 96–8; cf. Frost, p. 17. At Norwich until 1867 the choir sat together in the organ gallery for Sunday services (H. Leeds, *Norwich Cathedral Past and Present* (Norwich 1910), p. 85; cf. Kitton, p. 93). The choir at Christ Church, Oxford, sang in lofts on 'surplice prayer-days' before 1885 (Thompson, pp. 149–50).

492 *Guardian*, 1869, p. 144.

493 ibid., 1874, pp. 454–5; cf. Hillsman, p. 318, citing *CT*, 5 January 1900, for an example of psalms chanted in procession at St Paul's. A Gregorian Te Deum was chanted in procession at Lichfield in 1872 and a Benedicite at Southwell in 1888 (ibid., citing *CT*, 5 July 1872, p. 311, and 10 February 1888, p. 110).

494 ABDC Chichester, 28 January 1878. This was also the custom at Worcester (ABDC Worcester, 4 January 1893). Several variations in the normal order of procession are given in Walcott, *Traditions*, p. 76. After some bitter disputes at Norwich, where two archdeacons were members of the chapter, the bishop ruled that the vice-dean took precedence over the rest of the canons (ABDC Norwich, 10 January 1900, quoted in Coghlan, p. 102).

495 ABDC Chichester, 2 May 1829. This matter was still in dispute at Salisbury in 1896 (Salisbury CM, 8 December 1896).

496 ABDC Hereford, 24 March 1859.

497 ABVC Hereford, 6 March 1875.

498 Wells CM, 10 April 1882.

499 ABVC Chichester, 29 October 1889; cf. ABDC Chichester, same date. The dean and chapter agreed to provide a verger to precede the vicars.

500 ABDC Salisbury, 13 June 1889.

501 ABDC Chichester, 5 August 1889. Two vergers walked together before the clergy at Worcester until 1894 when the custom was abolished (ABDC Worcester, May 1894; cf. 19 November 1895). This was also the custom at Winchester (Goodman and Hutton, p. 52).

502 ABDC Chichester, 29 October 1889. In 1890 the dean and chapter stressed that the

same order of procession should be observed at eucharists as at the offices (ABDC Chichester, 10 October 1890). In 1898 the dean and chapter ordered that the prebendaries had precedence in the order of their installation as prebendaries (ABDC Chichester, 20 January 1898).

503 ABDC Worcester, 4 January 1893.

504 ABDC Worcester, 2 May 1899. For earlier rules, cf. ABDC Worcester, 19 November 1892, 19 November 1895, 23 December 1895.

505 ABDC Worcester, 5 February and 13 July 1892.

506 ABDC Worcester, 1 April 1892.

507 ABDC Worcester, 12 July and 19 November 1897.

508 Worc. C. Add. Mss., 137, pp. 9–10. Ely had weekly processional hymns on a Sunday evening (Hillsman, p. 318, citing ABDC Ely, 25 November 1888).

509 Prestige, pp. 166–7; cf. ABDC Chichester, 2 May 1891; Wells CM, 15 March 1900.

510 Hillsman, pp. 318–9; CT, 6 August 1897, p. 136; CT, 27 October 1899, p. 479.

511 Walcott, *Traditions*, p. 76; cf. Howson, p. 227, and ABDC Hereford, 14 November 1889. This custom was also introduced at Chester in about 1869 and at Lincoln in about 1871 (Chadwick, vol.II, p. 376).

512 Coghlan, p. 154, quoting St Paul's CM, 30 March 1872, and ABDC Norwich, 2 December 1873; cf. Prestige, p. 96.

513 ABDC Chichester, 2 May 1876.

514 ABDC Gloucester, 29 September and 30 November 1881.

515 Chichester chapter minute book, October 1891; cf. ABDC Chichester, 2 May 1896.

516 ABDC Chichester, 2 May 1892.

517 D. M. Owen in Aylmer and Cant, p. 271.

518 Prestige, pp. 3–4. Two years later the average number at weekday evensong was between fifteen and twenty (Matthews and Atkins, p. 254). But on Easter Day 1800 there were only six communicants at the morning celebration at St Paul's, (Temperley, *The Athlone History of Music in Britain: Volume 5: The Romantic Age, 1800–1914*, p. 171).

519 Worc. C. Add. Mss., 24, pp. 31–3. Dean Duncombe said that there were forty communicants at York at the Sunday Eucharist in the winter, with seventy on the first Sunday of the month when there was a choral communion, and 200 on Easter Day (PP 1867, xx, p. 778).

520 Chadwick, *York*, p. 279, quoting PP 1884, xxi, p. 444. There were sixty-four communicants on Easter Day, 1849 (Leak, p. 272, citing ABDC York, 4 May 1849).

521 *Parish Choir*, vol. I, p. 143.

522 Hansard, 3rd series, 1848, vol. xcviii (16 May); *Guardian*, 1848, p. 322.

523 Hansard, vol. cxii, 1850, p. 1410 (15 July).

524 J. Jebb, *A Plea for What is Left of the Cathedrals* (London 1852), p. 18.

525 LPL, Tait Papers, vol. 27.

526 ibid., vol. 31, pp. 113, 116.

527 PP 1867, xx, p. 773.

528 PP 1854, xxv, p. 283.

529 Bishop Hamilton's evidence to Cathedrals Commission, 12 July 1854 (Salisbury Chapter Muniments, Press I, Box 39, pp. 3, 5).

530 PP 1854, xxv, p. 919.

531 Chadwick, vol.II, p. 366, quoting PP 1871, lv, p. 218. The daily attendance at weekday services was between thirty and forty.

532 *Ecclesiologist*, vol. 2, nos.14–24, November 1842, pp. 34–5; for extra seats in the quire at Exeter, cf. ABDC Exeter, 6 June 1818.

533 W. Russell, *St Paul's in the Early Nineteenth Century* (London 1920), p. 18; *The Times*, 9 July 1824, both quoted in Fenwick, p. 100.

534 Fenwick, p. 100.

535 ABDC Bristol, 10 July 1805, 24 June 1831.

536 Bristol DC/A/7/3/4; cf. also Chapter 6, p. 107. In 1891 the dean and chapter ordered that only men could sit in the actual stalls, the seats in front of the stalls being reserved for female relatives and families of the cathedral staff (ABDC Bristol, 10 November 1891).

537 ABDC Exeter, 31 December 1828, 1 January 1829, 26 January 1877, 24 February 1877, 14 March 1877; 600 rush-seated chairs were bought for the nave at Worcester in 1874 (ABDC Worcester, 23 June 1874). Some 108 chairs for the nave were bought at Chichester in 1864 for 24s a dozen (ABDC Chichester, 10 October 1867).

538 ABDC Worcester, 13 April 1874. For seating in the quire at Worcester before 1874, cf. Worc. C. Add. Mss., 128, p. 7; cf. also ABDC Worcester, 1 June 1894, 2 December 1896.

539 ibid., 23 April 1874; cf. 21 November 1892. For clergy seating, cf. 19 November 1896.

540 ibid., 23 November 1882, 2 September 1889.

541 ABDC Hereford, 13 November 1800, 13 November 1871.

542 ABDC Chichester, 10 October 1879.

543 Wells CM, 1 October 1862.

544 ibid., 15 June 1868.

545 ibid., 26 August and 16 October 1890.

546 Bristol DCA/13/4.

547 ABDC Gloucester, April 1816.

548 ABDC Winchester, 25 November 1818; for Walcott's comments on galleries or pews at Winchester, Worcester, Peterborough and Durham, cf. Walcott, *Traditions*, p. 53.

549 Coghlan, p. 28.

550 J. W. F. Hill, p. 262, quoting Hansard, P. D., 1848, 3rd series, vol.xcviii, pp. 1076–7.

551 Close, *Thoughts on the Daily Choral Services in Carlisle Cathedral*, pp. 3, 6–7; cf. also Worc. C. Add. Mss., 141, p. 7. Very soon after he arrived in Carlisle in 1850, Tait noted in his diary: 'The Bedesmen must be made to come into the choir during service and some plan must be devised for keeping the people in the nave quiet during the service. The number who come for the anthem in the afternoon and stay out is very great' (LPL, Tait Papers, vol. 27, 27 January 1850). Indeed, Tait found the cathedral congregation at Carlisle rather unsatisfactory: 'So long as a cathedral congregation consists mainly of stray officers from the neighbouring garrison, and strangers who are passing a vacant Sunday at the principal inn, and the few musical amateurs of the town, whom probably none of the Cathedral body except the organist know even to speak to, and a few old ladies, whose families have once had some official connection with the Close, added to a body of unruly school-children who are brought to the Cathedral only because it is difficult to find room for them in any other church – and so long as all these fortuitously assembled worshippers have no personal religious intercourse with any of the clergy who participate, we cannot have in our cathedrals such real hearty worship as we find in a parish church' (Tait, p. 168).

552 J. W. F. Hill, p. 263; cf. Lake, pp. 117, 135, for a similar problem at Durham; cf. also Hansard, 1848, vol.xcviii, 16 May.

553 ABDC Exeter, 21–22 December 1826; cf. ABDC Exeter, 17 September 1831; entry via the west door of the quire was also prohibited at Winchester in 1860 (ABDC Winchester, 23 June 1860). The situation at Exeter was still as bad in 1851 (Benson, vol.I, pp. 106–7). Guided tours at Gloucester during services were a nuisance in 1830 (ABDC Gloucester, 5 April 1830).

554 F. G. Bennett, R. H. Codrington and C. Deedes, *Statutes and Constitutions of the Cathedral Church of Chichester* (Chichester 1904), p. 50; Visitation Book, f.142. The verger, sextons and beadle at Hereford were required in 1800 to prevent people walking and talking during services (ABDC Hereford, 13 November 1800; Barrett, p. 18).

555 Wells CM, 1 July 1862; cf. Greenhalgh, *Wells*, pp. 190–1. This order was rescinded in

the following year. There was a similar habit at Worcester (cf. Worc. C. Add. Mss., 141, p. 7). For a notice intended to quell this problem at Winchester in about 1872, cf. *Winchester Cathedral Chronicle*, 1873–91, p. 75, and 1866–94, p. 42 (17 June 1892).

556 Salisbury CM, 5 June and 1 July 1899.

557 *Guardian*, 1849, p. 654; cf. also Salisbury CM, 25 July 1877.

558 Quoted in E. Royle, *The Victorian Church in York* (York 1983), p. 21; cf. Leak, p. 100.

559 *Contemporary Review*, vol.II, May–August 1866, p. 506; cf. F. Alford, p. 516.

560 *CCR* 1866, p. 196.

561 Westcott, vol.I, p. 302. The Dean of Peterborough spoke of 'the crowded congregations in which we now more and more rejoice' in a letter to the bishops, 8 June 1869 (PHPR 1419).

562 *Guardian*, 1869, p. 1227.

563 ibid., p. 1168. Another visitor to Rochester spoke of the character of the service there and noted only eight persons in the congregation (ibid., p. 1110). At Salisbury at least one canon and one vicar choral were always present at the services (Hamilton, *Cathedral Reform: A Letter to the Members of his Diocese* (London, Oxford and Salisbury 1855), p. 25) At Bristol, however, there was once a Christmas Day on which the whole service and the sermon were in the hands of a minor canon, the only clergyman present (Fitzgerald, pp. 58–9). At Exeter in 1800 there were several occasions when no canon was present (ABDC Exeter, 29 March and 1 August 1800, 18 July 1801). Dean Alford boasted in 1869 that he was present on over 200 days, and that one of the archdeacons had been present for over 300 services (H. Alford, 'Cathedral Reform', *Contemporary Review*, vol.xii, September 1869, p. 44). For correspondence between Dean Herbert of Hereford and J. R. G. Taylor, the custos of the vicars choral, cf. ABDC Hereford, 9 December 1878. At Durham the attendance of members of the chapter was not all it might have been. Canon Evans, the absent-minded Professor of Greek, often forgot what was happening during services and wandered away from his stall. Once, while being led to the pulpit, he walked straight on and went home. Canon Farrar frequently strolled in late for services, and on Advent Sunday 1882 he did not appear until the end of the service, which was conducted entirely by the precentor. Canon Tristram occasionally 'blustered in in the middle of the psalms' and another frequent absentee was Canon Body. Even Dean Lake was often absent or late (Stranks, *This Sumptuous Church*, pp. 97–8; for further reference to Evans, cf. Fowler, p. 139). At Canterbury, however, Dean Farrar was a constant attender at the daily services (R. Farrar, *The Life of Frederic William Farrar, sometime Dean of Canterbury* (London 1904), p. 318). The unexpected appearance of the whole body of the minor canons of St Paul's at services during 1851 occasioned much surprise until it was revealed that they were entitled to a share in the admission fees to the Whispering Gallery and that the increase of visitors during the Great Exhibition made it worthwhile for them to attend (*Guardian*, 1854, p. 918). Exact figures of the attendance of Dean Church and the canons of St Paul's at the daily services from 1873 to 1878 are given in PP 1883, xxi, p. 114.

564 *Guardian*, 1869, p. 895; cf. PP 1871, lv, p. 214.

565 Bristol DC/A/7/6/2; cf. PP 1871, lv, p. 225. There were thirty communicants at Norwich on Sunday, 3 March 1867, less than fifty on Easter Day, and about forty on 5 May (NCL, Goulburn's diary, 3 March, 21 April, 5 May 1867).

566 Sedgwick to Duke of Argyll, 20 October 1857; Clark and Hughes, vol.II, pp. 334–5.

567 *Guardian*, 1872, pp. 323, 388.

568 ibid., 1874; cf. p. 128 above.

569 PP 1884, xxii, p. 195.

570 Hansard, vol. cclxxi, 1882, 22 June.

571 *Guardian*, 1884, p. 572. Nearly 2, 000 attended the Three Hours' Service at St Paul's in 1885 (*Guardian*, 1885, p. 517).

572 Coghlan, p. 151.
573 G. Barrington-Baker, *Quam Dilecta! A Chorister's Recollections* (Oxford 1948), p. 7.
574 Quoted in E. Routley, *The Musical Wesleys* (London 1968), pp. 254–5.
575 T. F. Bumpus, vol.I, p. 97.
576 Temperley, *The Athlone History of Music in Britain: Volume 5: The Romantic Age, 1800–1914*, pp. 172–3, quoting *Musical World*, vol.iv (1837), p. 37.
577 Jebb, *The Choral Service of the United Church of England and Ireland*, p. 439.
578 ibid., p. 102–3.
579 *Ecclesiologist*, vol. 7 (new series vol. 4) nos. 55–60 (new series nos. 19–24), January–June 1847, pp. 47–59, quoted in Rainbow, *The Choral Revival in the Anglican Church, 1839–1872*, p. 211; cf. also Thompson, pp. 149–50.
580 *Guardian*, 1849, p. 15.
581 *Guardian*, 1848, p. 547. Similar experiences at Lincoln were noted by visitors in 1816 and 1836 (ibid., p. 602).
582 *Guardian*, 1849, p. 552; cf. ibid., pp. 653, 668.
583 *Parish Choir*, vol.I, p. 143; cf. Tyng, pp. 260–1: 'I saw enough of these singing, formal services in the Cathedrals and Chapels of England to disgust me with the system completely. With but few exceptions this whole plan of worship is irreverent and light, the deportment of the choristers almost uniformly very unexceptionable and the influence of the system very unedifying' (ibid., p. 193).
584 *Ecclesiologist*, vol. 13 (new series vol. 10), nos. 88–93 (new series nos. 52–57), February–December 1852, pp. 77–8.
585 *Guardian*, 1858, p. 564; Creighton, vol.I, p. 25.
586 *Parish Choir*, vol.I, pp. 47–8; cf. Rainbow, *The Choral Revival in the Anglican Church, 1839–1872*, p. 225.
587 *Guardian*, 1854, p. 918.
588 *Ecclesiologist*, vol. 15 (new series vol. 12), nos. 100–105 (new series nos. 64–69), February–December 1854, p. 249.
589 Armstrong, p. 79; cf. ibid., p. 130. The *Norwich Spectator* condemned the worship at Norwich in 1862 as 'irreverent, careless and undevotional': 'A more cold and miserable service I have seldom heard. Not a dignitary was present. The prayers were read with a most depressing effect, and as if to show how little was cared about the Christian Year – nay, seemingly to run counter to it – the anthem was 'Unto us a boy is born' – thoroughly out of place at Ascensiontide' (R. Hale, 'The Church of England in Nineteenth Century Norwich', in Barringer, pp. 164–5).
590 *Guardian*, 1859, p. 872.
591 *MT*, 1 November 1869, pp. 263–4.
592 *Guardian*, 1869, p. 1168.
593 ibid., p. 1110.
594 Welsby, p. 9; for a similar comment by A. J. B. Beresford Hope, cf. *Christian Remembrancer*, vol.xxix, no.88, 1855, p. 354.
595 Hillsman, p. 305.
596 *Guardian*, 1876, pp. 1116–17.
597 Prestige, pp. 21–2, 94, 148; cf. Gregory's description of St Paul's at this time in Hutton, pp. 164–5, Prestige, pp. 97–8, and Fenwick, pp. 151, 157, for extracts from his note-books describing disorderly services at St Paul's.
598 NCL, Goulburn's diary, 12 July 1868.
599 *Guardian*, 1880, p. 283.
600 Winchester Cathedral Mss., *De Precentore*, 22 September 1890.
601 Worc. C. Mss., Precentor's Report 1900; cf. Chapter 8, pp. 183–4.
602 T. F. Bumpus, vol.I, p. 161, quoting *Gentleman's Magazine*, 30 July 1830.
603 Quoted in Bumpus, *The Organists and Composers of St Paul's Cathedral*, pp. 125–6. S. Butler said in 1833: 'I cannot conceive how it is possible to attend the solemnities

of Cathedral worship without having the affections purified, and a warmer glow of devotion excited in the mind' (S. Butler, *Thoughts on Church Dignities* (London 1833), pp. 8–9.

604 T. F. Bumpus, vol.I, pp. 96–7. The *Ecclesiologist* described the services at Ely as 'the most real and hearty and thoroughly devotional which it has ever been my lot to witness' (*Ecclesiologist*, vol.xv, 1854, p. 249).

605 Jebb, *The Choral Service of the United Church of England and Ireland*, pp. 240, 311.

606 *Guardian*, 1848, p. 664.

607 ibid., 1851, p. 283. The service is described in careful detail: cf. ibid., 1854, p. 897.

608 A. C. Coxe, *Impressions of England* (2nd edn, New York 1856), p. 77. The reform of the early 1870s had begun to take effect by 1877. Dean Church said that the consecration of E. W. Benson as Bishop of Truro in April of that year was carried out 'with all the order and beauty of a perfected musical service' (Church, p. 257), while Dean Hole of Rochester, preaching at St Paul's in the 1880s, said: 'I was thoroughly delighted with St Paul's. Such a dignified service, and such sublime music' (B. Massingham, *Turn on the Fountains: A Life of Dean Hole* (London 1974), p. 159). John Bumpus, in an article in *The Musical Standard* in 1881, said: 'for beauty of music, dignified and impressive yet simple ritual, and facilities for accommodating an immense congregation, the service now at St Paul's will challenge comparison with any other English Cathedral' (quoted in Charlton, p. 61).

609 *Trefoil*, pp. 140f., where there is a long description of the services at Lincoln.

610 T. F. Bumpus, vol.I, p. 167.

611 Worc. C. Mss., Precentor's Report, 1885.

612 Worc. C. Add. Mss., 141, p. 28.

613 *Guardian*, 1898, p. 614.

614 *Winchester Cathedral Chronicle*, 1895–1932, p. 74.

615 For contemporary appreciations of the value of cathedral worship, cf. A. J. B. Beresford Hope, *The English Cathedral of the Nineteenth Century* (London 1861), p. 117, quoted in Coghlan, p. 133; and Creighton, vol.I, p. 315.

CHAPTER 8 *Cathedral Choirs in the Nineteenth Century*

1 PP 1854, xxv, p. 3.

2 ibid., p. 931.

3 ibid., cf. p. 933.

4 ibid., p. 944. Twelve years previously three lay vicars was the maximum number to be found at Salisbury, which Hamilton described as 'a caricature' (Salisbury Chapter Muniments, Press I, Box 39, pp. 8–10; Hamilton's evidence to the cathedral commissioners 1854). PP 1854, xxv, p. 97, gives the number of lay clerks as seven, but each of them had one day off every week.

5 ibid., p. 936.

6 ibid., pp. 934–5. In 1842 the choir at Ely was described as having 'quiet dignity and gravity' (W. E. Dickson, *Fifty Years of Church Music* (Ely 1894), p. 53). PP 1854, xxv, p. 80, says there were twelve choristers. There were sixteen choristers and fourteen men on Sundays in about 1860 (Dickson, p. 59).

7 PP 1854, xxv, p. 937.

8 ibid., pp. 920–2.

9 B. Rainbow, *The Choral Revival in the Anglican Church 1839–1872* (London 1970), p. 209.

10 PP 1854, xxv, p. 933. W. E. Dickson says that 'under his management, the Chester services were orderly and careful; the choir, though numerically weak, was of good quality; the prayers, however, were read, not chanted' (Dickson, p. 49). Mendelssohn said that Gunton played 'like velvet' (J. E. West, *Cathedral Organists Past and Present* (London 1899), p. 15).

11 PP 1854, xxv, p. 27. In their analysis of the answers from deans and chapters in reply to the first series of questions, the commissioners included the following details of other cathedral choirs:

Canterbury	12 lay clerks	10 choristers
York	14 lay clerks	10 choristers
	(6 daily; 8 on special occasions)	
St Paul's	6 lay clerks	12 choristers
Durham	10 lay clerks	10 choristers
Winchester	16 lay clerks	8 choristers
	(at least 4 on weekdays)	(plus two supernumeraries)
Wells	7 lay clerks	8 choristers
	(half on weekdays)	
Chichester	7 lay clerks	10 choristers
	(one attends only 4 days per week)	
Gloucester	6 lay clerks	8 choristers
Bristol	6 lay clerks	6 choristers and
	(plus 5 supernumeraries)	2 probationers
Hereford	6 minor canons and	8 choristers and
	6 lay vicars	2 probationers
Lichfield	5 minor canons and	8 choristers and
	6 vicars choral	4 or 6 probationers
Lincoln	8 lay clerks	10 choristers
	(plus 3 supernumeraries)	
Manchester	4 lay clerks	4 choristers plus 6 extras
	(plus 6 Sunday men)	
Norwich	8 lay clerks	10 choristers and
	(plus 2 supernumeraries)	2 probationers
Peterborough	6 lay clerks	10 choristers
Ripon	6 lay clerks	10 choristers
Rochester	6 lay clerks	8 choristers
Worcester	8 lay clerks	10 choristers

12 *Parish Choir*, vol.III, pp. 56–7; cf. *Guardian*, 1848, p. 602.
13 W. K. L. Clarke, *Chichester Cathedral in the Nineteenth Century* (Chichester Papers no. 14, Chichester 1959), p. 13.
14 M. Foster, *The Music of Salisbury Cathedral* (London 1974), pp. 15, 17.
15 W. K. Hamilton's evidence, Salisbury Chapter Muniments, Press I, Box 39, pp. 14–16.
16 Greenhalgh, *Wells*, p. 189.
17 Bishop Browne's visitation 1884, *Winchester Cathedral Chronicle*, 1873–91, pp. 86f.
18 ABDC Chichester, 10 October 1871; cf. ABDC Chester, 25 November 1867, quoted in P. C. Moore, 239
19 W. O. Chadwick, *The Victorian Church* (London 1970), vol.II, p. 374.
20 A. Boutflower, *Personal Reminiscences of Manchester Cathedral 1854–1912* (Leighton Buzzard 1913), p. 22; cf. PP 1854, xxv, p. 941.
21 Rainbow, p. 287.
22 W. A. Frost, *Early Recollections of St Paul's Cathedral* (London 1926), p. 16.
23 *Guardian* 1880, p. 283; cf. PP 1884–5, xxi, p. 243, and Chadwick, vol. II, p. 374. The organists also called for choristers to be boarded and for increased salaries and houses for themselves, so that they could be set free from augmenting their cathedral salaries by teaching.
24 Chadwick, vol.II, p. 374; cf. PP 1884–5, xxi, p. 200.
25 PP 1884–5, xxi, p. 340. The number of lay clerks in each cathedral in 1875 was as follows:

Bristol	10	Manchester	4
Canterbury	12	Norwich	8
Carlisle	4	Christ Church,	
Chester	6	Oxford	9
Chichester	6	Peterborough	8
Durham	10	Ripon	0
Ely	8	Rochester	6
Exeter	8	St Paul's	6
(+ 6 secondaries)		Salisbury	7†
Gloucester	6	Wells	8
Hereford	7*	Winchester	9
Lichfield	9	Worcester	8
Lincoln	4	York	13‡

* This is the number of assistant vicars choral, who included two priest vicars and five lay vicars.

† This figure includes the organist.

‡ This is the total number of songmen employed during the year ending 25 March 1865. Eight were still employed at that date (PP 1876, lviii, pp. 539–49).

26 *Guardian*, 1883, p. 1807. For various recent statutes governing the vicars choral, assistant vicars choral, and choristers at St Paul's, cf. PP 1883, xxi, pp. 104–8, 114–5, 117–18.

27 PP 1884–5, xxi, p. 306. For the difficulties involved in running the choir at Manchester, cf. J. F. Bridge, *A Westminster Pilgrim* (London 1919), p. 55. The rehearsals were the responsibility of the precentor who left them in the hands of 'a very able double-bass player'.

28 PP 1883, xxi, pp. 157, 172–3.

29 ibid., p. 212; cf. p. 213.

30 ibid., p. 45.

31 ibid., p. 86. By 1899 the number of choristers at Norwich had risen to eighteen, with two probationers (ABDC Norwich, 6 June 1899; cf. ibid., 4 November 1897, and H. Leeds, *Norwich Cathedral Past and Present* (Norwich 1910), pp. 83–4, all cited in P. V. Coghlan, 'Cathedral Worship in the Church of England 1815–1914' (Leicester University M. Phil. thesis 1984), p. 138).

32 PP 1883, xxi, pp. 223–4.

33 PP 1884–5, xxi, p. 177.

34 ibid., p. 330.

35 Winchester Cathedral Mss. Davidson visitation papers.

36 PP 1854, xxv, p. 919; cf. Chadwick, vol.II, p. 374.

37 Chadwick, *York*, p. 293.

38 ibid., p. 301; cf. P. Aston, *The Music of York Minster* (London 1972), p. 13, and Chapter 4, p. 48.

39 ABDC Salisbury, 16 June 1806, 16 July 1806; cf. 27 February 1808.

40 ibid., 9 September 1809; cf. ABDC Salisbury, 5 December 1815. A similar rule was made at Worcester in 1828. The lay clerks had often been absent from matins (ABDC Winchester, 23 June 1828). After several occasions when only one or two lay clerks were present, Worcester introduced a similar provision in 1838 (Worc. C. Mss., Attendance Book 1836–42, rule 1838).

41 ABDC Salisbury, 8 August 1820, 2 December 1820; cf. ABDC Hereford, 24 March 1868.

42 ABDC Exeter, 22–23 December 1807, 2 April 1814.

43 Bristol Cathedral Mss., DC/A/11/1/2.

44 ABDC Worcester, 4 November 1816.

45 ABDC Worcester, 25 November 1816, 25 November 1820, 5 February 1821.

46 Worc. C. Mss., Attendance Book 1836–42, 4 September 1837, 29 November 1837, 2 December 1837, 3 December 1837, etc.

47 Moore, p. 184, n.1. In A. T. Bannister, *The Cathedral Church of Hereford* (London 1924), p. 106, it is said that since 1800 those of the Hereford vicars who also held livings were allowed to be absent from the cathedral on Sunday mornings to attend to their parochial duties; cf. ABDC Hereford, 25 June 1792, 25 June 1795 (quoting ABDC Hereford, 13 December 1680, 9 November 1739), 13 November 1800. The absence of the vicars choral from services was certainly causing concern to the chapter in the 1830s and Dean Merewether fought a spirited battle with the vicars choral over this matter: cf. ABDC Hereford, 14 February 1832, 9 August and 18 October 1834, 17 November and 1 December 1834; dean to succentor, 15 July 1834, dean to each of the vicars, 19 July and 28 July 1834; succentor to dean, 29 July 1834, custos and vicars to dean, 6 August 1834; dean to succentor, 6 August and 16 October 1834; cf. J. Merewether to Archbishop Howley, 11 August 1836 (CCF 3208) and M. P. Chappell, *Dr S. S. Wesley: Portrait of a Victorian Musician* (Great Wakering 1977), pp. 25–6. G. T. Smith pointed out the difficulties caused by absence among the lay clerks in 1854 (PP 1854, xxv, p. 938).

48 W. M. Sinclair, *Memorials of St Paul's Cathedral* (London 1909), p. 309. For details of choir attendance at services in St Paul's in 1834, cf. Moore, pp. 317–20; for the situation in 1870, cf. G. L. Prestige, *St Paul's in its Glory, 1831–1911* (London 1955), p. 148. The small numbers of vicars choral in the choir at St Paul's may have been caused by chapter orders such as one of 8 August 1847 that merely stipulated that one tenor and one counter-tenor (or their deputies) should attend the daily services, though Maria Hackett had noted very sparse attendances in 1832 (St Paul's CM, 8 April 1847, cited in Coghlan, p. 137; *Harmonicon*, 1832, p. 271). Goss told the cathedral commissioners in 1854 that he needed a bigger choir with professional lay vicars (PP 1854, xxv, p. 920).

49 S. S. Wesley, *A Few Words on Cathedral Music* (London 1849), p. 9. See n. 168 on p. 390.

50 D. H. Robertson, *Sarum Close* (London 1938; new edn 1970), p. 284.

51 K. Edwards, 'The Cathedral of Salisbury, 1075–1950', *VCH Wiltshire*, vol iii, 1956, p. 201; cf. ibid., p. 204.

52 ABDC Salisbury, 10 January 1852. In 1853 the dean and chapter of Salisbury told the lay vicars that they were all expected to attend on Sundays, Tuesday afternoons and some seventeen other days during the year, and daily during Holy Week. They must also attend the service for the anniversary of the infirmary, public days and services for meetings of church and diocesan societies (ABDC Salisbury, 7 October 1853).

53 B. Crosby, *Durham Cathedral Choristers and Their Masters* (Durham 1980), p. 29.

54 ABDC Hereford, 13 November 1823. For rules made by the dean and chapter of Hereford for the regulation of the cathedral choir in 1863, cf. CCF 32508.

55 ABDC Exeter, 29 May 1841. However, absences were still causing problems in 1856 (ABDC Exeter, 28 June 1856).

56 ABDC Winchester, 25 November 1856.

57 ibid., 25 November 1859.

58 ABDC Winchester, 2 August 1887.

59 ABDC Winchester, 29 December 1891, 1 January 1892, 1 June 1897.

60 *Guardian*, 1867, p. 102. The dean and chapter of Gloucester had a long tradition of careful rules for their lay clerks. In 1831 they approved the usual attendance of three lay clerks at each weekday service, but more were required on Tuesday and Thursday mornings when more elaborate music was sung (ABDC Gloucester, 30 November 1831).

61 W. H. Hutton, ed., *The Autobiography of Robert Gregory* (London 1912), p. 168.

62 Mansel to Gregory, 4 November 1869; Hutton p. 172.
63 Frost, pp. 36–7. The lay vicars choral were required to produce a certificate, signed by an official of the railways, if they were delayed in travelling to St Paul's for services. One of them got into considerable trouble with the dean and chapter for tearing down a notice in the vestry about lapses in duty (cf. Prestige, pp. 160–1). For further references at St Paul's and Lichfield, cf. W. L. Hillsman, 'Trends and Aims in Anglican Music 1870–1906, in relation to developments in churchmanship' (Oxford D. Phil. thesis 1985), p. 326, fn.56.
64 ABDC Chichester, 3 February 1876
65 PP 1854, xxv, pp. 921–2.
66 ABDC Hereford, 26 June 1805.
67 See Chapter 1, pp. 9–10; for earlier efforts to enable Chard to have proper rehearsals, cf. ABDC Winchester, 25 November 1800.
68 Moore, p. 237; ABDC Gloucester, 23 June 1828, 30 November 1828.
69 ABDC Exeter, 9–10 December 1830.
70 M. Hackett, *A Brief Account of Cathedral and Collegiate Schools* (London 1827 edn), p. 31.
71 ABDC Wells, 8 December 1831.
72 Wells CM, 4 December 1832.
73 Wells CM, 8 August 1858.
74 Chichester Cathedral Mss., Visitation Book, p. 155.
75 Rainbow, p. 245; F. G. Kitton, *Zechariah Buck* (London 1899), pp. 23–4. For fuller details of Buck's methods, cf. Kitton, pp. 4–5, 8, 10, 62f., 90–1.
76 Prestige, p. 23.
77 ABDC Winchester, 29 September 1840.
78 ABDC Winchester, 25 November 1840.
79 ABDC Winchester, 29 September 1841.
80 ABDC Winchester, 23 June 1843; cf. P. M. J. Crook, *A History of the Pilgrims' School and earlier Winchester Choir Schools* (Chichester 1981), p. 16.
81 ABDC Worcester, 24 November 1842.
82 Exeter Cathedral Mss., Bundle 7062, quoted in Moore, pp. 353–4; cf. p. 207 above. When Alfred Angel, his successor, was appointed, the dean and chapter of Exeter stipulated that it was his duty 'to teach the choristers in all things necessary for the due performance of divine service and to practice [*sic*] them daily for such time and at such hours as the Chapter shall appoint, not only in what they have to learn but likewise in what they know already'. Rehearsals of both old and new music was essential, 'it being very desirable even for the oldest members of the choir to join with the younger in such practice occasionally in order that they may all sing well together, for without a common understanding with each other and with the organist, it is impossible that the proper effect of a musical service can be produced. Convenient hours will, of course, be fixed for this purpose, so as to interfere as little as possible with the studies of the boys or the employments of the men elsewhere' (ABDC Exeter, 2 April 1842). At Salisbury the lay vicars and supernumeraries were instructed to practise with the choristers in the singing school once a week (ABDC Salisbury, 7 October 1853).
83 B. Matthews, *Samuel Sebastian Wesley 1810–1876* (Bournemouth 1976), p. 5.
84 ABDC Winchester, 5 May 1854, 25 November 1858.
85 *Guardian*, 1860, p. 899. At Ely, at about the same time, the choristers had a daily practice with the precentor at 9 a.m. for an hour. The organist, Robert Janes, had long ceased to do this and had left the task to his articled pupils (Dickson, p. 59).
86 Moore, p. 237, quoting ABDC Norwich, 25 June 1868.
87 Kitton, p. 9, quoted in Moore, p. 295.
88 T. L. Wheeler to dean and chapter, 17 November 1869 (Worc. C. Mss., Precentor's Reports).

89 W. Done to Dean and Chapter, 17 November 1869 (Worc. C. Mss., Precentor's Reports); cf. Worc. C. Add. Mss., 137, p. 8.
90 Moore, p. 306, n.2.
91 Rainbow, p. 289; Prestige, p. 153. Frost says that regular rehearsals were not established for some years, unless there was a special anthem (Frost, p. 47). There were twice-weekly rehearsals by 1878–9 (W. S. Simpson, *A Year's Music at St Paul's Cathedral* (2nd report, London 1879), p. 8).
92 ABDC Bristol, 9 April 1872, 9 January 1877; cf. DC/A/7/4/3.
93 ABDC Bristol, 1 April 1873, 9 January 1877.
94 ABDC Bristol, 11 February 1886. For Riseley, cf. pp. 180–1 above.
95 PP 1876, lviii, p. 547.
96 A. H. Brewer, *Memories of Choirs and Cloisters* (London 1931), pp. 3–4.
97 ABDC Salisbury, 29 August 1877; cf. Salisbury CM, 21 December 1877.
98 ABDC Exeter, 24 May, 15 November, 22 November 1879; cf. 16 December 1876.
99 See above, p. 174–5. The boys had a daily practice, except on Mondays and Fridays when there was a full practice (ABDC Hereford, 8 November 1877; cf. 4 July 1874). There was a single weekly full practice in 1863. This was held in the quire or the chapter room each Saturday between 5 p.m. and 6 p.m. (CCF 32508).
100 Worc. C. Mss., Precentor's Reports, 1882.
101 ibid., Precentor's Reports, 1891 and 1892.
102 Worc. C. Add. Mss., 137, p. 18; cf. printed rules of office for the precentor (c.1877), no.4 (Worc. C. Mss., bundle of Precentor's Reports); cf. also Chapter 6, pp. 103–4.
103 *Guardian*, 1884, p. 508; cf. also P. L. S. Barrett, 'English Cathedral Choirs in the Nineteenth Century', *JEH*, vol. xxv, no. 1, January 1974, pp. 24–5. For another account of a choristers' practice at St Paul's, cf. *MT*, 1 March 1900, pp. 303–6.
104 Bridge, p. 10.
105 G. Barrington-Baker, *Quam Dilecta! A Chorister's Recollections* (Oxford 1948), p. 2.
106 Winchester Cathedral Mss., Bishop Davidson's visitation papers.
107 L. W. Cowie, 'Worship in the Minster', *The Victoria History of the Counties of England: A History of Yorkshire: The City of York* (London 1961), p. 353.
108 A. L. Kirwan, *The Music of Lincoln Cathedral* (London 1973), p. 11; J. W. F. Hill, *Georgian Lincoln* (Cambridge 1966), p. 271, fn.1.
109 ABDC Winchester, 2 February 1815.
110 ibid., 25 November 1818.
111 ABDC Exeter, 3 January 1818.
112 *Mirror*, no.685, 11 October 1834, p. 243.
113 ABDC Hereford, 10 April 1821.
114 Prestige, p. 20.
115 A. Bell, 'The Letters of Sydney Smith', *Bulletin of the John Rylands Library*, vol. 59, no.1, 1976–7, p. 37; cf. A. Bell, *Sydney Smith* (Oxford 1980), p. 168.
116 J. Jebb, *The Choral Service of the United Church of England and Ireland* (London 1843), p. 246, quoted in Rainbow, p. 255.
117 ABDC Gloucester, 17 April 1844, 6 May 1844.
118 ABDC Hereford, 25 June 1846; cf. also 12–14 November 1846.
119 ABDC Hereford, 26 June 1848; CCF 3208; cf. also P. L. S. Barrett, 'Hereford Cathedral in the Nineteenth Century', *The Friends of Hereford Cathedral Annual Report*, 1986, pp. 29–30.
120 ABDC Winchester, 29 September 1857.
121 Chadwick, *York*, p. 279, quoting Ecclesiastical Commissioners' Papers 11778.
122 ABVC Hereford, 22 August 1857.
123 *Guardian*, 1860, p. 924.
124 ibid., p. 8.

125 Hillsman, p. 305, citing J. Hullah to dean and chapter of Lichfield, 17 May 1864, in Lichfield Joint Record Office.

126 ABDC Hereford, 7 November 1865.

127 *MT*, 1 November 1869, p. 264.

128 *Guardian*, 1869, pp. 126, 182.

129 ABDC Exeter, 8 October 1870.

130 J. O. Johnston, *Life and Letters of Henry Parry Liddon* (London 1904), pp. 137, 141; cf. C. E. Beswick, 'Liddon of St Paul's' (Exeter University MA thesis 1974), pp. 16–17.

131 Chichester Cathedral Mss., Draft Acts, July 1878.

132 ABVC Hereford, 4 December 1880. These remarks are misattributed and wrongly dated in Moore, pp. 199–200, and Barrett, 'English Cathedral Choirs in the Nineteenth Century', p. 26.

133 Chichester Cathedral Mss., Draft Acts, pp. 29–30, 11 October 1889; cf. Clarke, p. 14.

134 ABDC Bristol, 7 January 1896; for Riseley, cf. pp. 180–1 above.

135 ABDC Bristol, 28 May 1896.

136 M. Elvey, *Life and Reminiscences of George J. Elvey* (London 1894), p. 13.

137 Chappell, p. 42.

138 *Parish Choir*, vol.I, p. 135. For details of the choir at Durham, cf. C. J. Stranks, *This Sumptuous Church* (London 1973), p. 94.

139 Kitton, p. 17.

140 Kirwan, p. 11. He was a skilled accompanist and was 'unrivalled' as a trainer of boys' voices (T. F. Bumpus, *The Cathedrals of England and Wales* (London 1905), vol.I, pp. 131–2).

141 Chadwick, vol.II, p. 370. W. E. Dickson, the Precentor of Ely, wrote in 1867 that those cathedral choirs that practised secular music could learn from it 'niceties of light and shade' (Hillsman, p. 306, citing *Contemporary Review*, December 1867, p. 462).

142 *Guardian*, 1876, p. 145. For a comment on the choir at Norwich in 1835, cf. Chappell, p. 33. For a full account of the choir at Norwich, cf. Kitton, *passim*. Dean Goulburn noted in 1867 that 'the singing at the early service was beautiful, specially that of Heber's Trinity Hymn' (NCL, Goulburn's diary, 16 June 1867).

143 Chadwick, vol.II, p. 376.

144 Hillsman, p. 306, citing *CT*, 8 September 1876, p. 453, and YML Add.Mss., 157/2, p. 341.

145 Worc. C. Mss., Precentor's Report, 1873.

146 ibid., 1878.

147 ibid., 1883.

148 ibid., 1889.

149 W. S. Simpson, p. 5.

150 A. B. Donaldson, *The Bishopric of Truro* (London 1902), p. 284.

151 West, p. 15.

152 For an interesting exchange of correspondence on this subject at Winchester in 1879, cf. Winchester Cathedral Mss., *De Precentore*, 4 and 6 December 1879. This was also a problem at Bristol: cf. ABDC Bristol, 5 January 1892.

153 West, p. 91.

154 ibid., p. 10.

155 Brewer, p. 15. When pedal stops were added to the organ at Lichfield in 1860, Samuel Spofforth, the organist, protested, 'You may put them there but I shall never use them' (W. L. Sumner, *The Organ*, 4th edn, (London 1973), p. 183). J. M. W. Young, who was appointed to Lincoln in 1850, was the first organist there to use pedals (ibid., p. 185).

156 ABDC Hereford, 25 June and 26 November 1805.

157 F. E. Gretton, *Memory's Hark-back Through Half a Century, 1808–1858* (London 1889), p. 8. Dare was also admonished in 1813–14 for neglecting his duties (cf. ABDC

Hereford, 16 November 1813, 30 August 1814, 10 November 1814).

158 M. R. Craze, *King's School, Worcester (1541–1971)* (Worcester 1972), p. 178; West, pp. 28, 91. At some cathedrals the organ loft was almost a family business. Joseph Corfe, organist at Salisbury Cathedral from 1792 to 1804, was succeeded by his son A. T. Corfe, who was in office until 1863. J. L. Hopkins (1841–56) was succeeded at Rochester by his brother, John Hopkins, who remained organist there until 1900. The Camidge family provided three generations of organists at York: John Camidge (1756–1799) being succeeded by his son Matthew Camidge (1799–1842), who was succeeded by his son John Camidge (1842–59) (cf. West, pp. 79, 73, 94).

159 See above, Chapter 1, pp. 9–10, and this chapter, p. 170; cf. P. M. J. Crook, *A History of the Pilgrims' School and earlier Winchester Choir Schools*, pp. 13–14; P. M. J. Crook, 'Half-a-century of Choral Indiscipline: George Chard and his Choir, 1802–1849', *Southern Cathedrals Festival Programme*, 1981, pp. 11–13; P. M. J. Crook, 'Fifty Years of Choral Misrule: George Chard and the Choristers of Winchester Cathedral', *Winchester Cathedral Record*, no.56, 1987, pp. 30–6.

160 L. S. Colchester, R. Bowers and A. Crossland, *The Organs and Organists of Wells Cathedral* (Wells 1974), pp. 22–3; cf. p. 170 above.

161 West, p. 37.

162 Dickson, p. 54, quoted in West, p. 31. The organist was generally allowed to use the cathedral organ for teaching his organ pupils (cf. ABDC Exeter, 26 November 1808).

163 cf. Chappell, p. 21.

164 For his appointment at Hereford, cf. ABDC Hereford, 10 July 1832. He was poorly paid both at Hereford (ABDC Hereford, 11 January 1836) and at first at Exeter (Chappell, p. 34). For his appointment and duties at Exeter, cf. ABDC Exeter, 8 August, 15 August, 24 October 1835. For his resignation, cf. ABDC Exeter, 7 June and 20 November 1841, 2 April 1842. For his duties at Winchester, cf. ABDC Winchester, 21 August 1849, and Chappell, p. 74; for the conditions of his employment at Gloucester, cf. Chappell, p. 105, and ABDC Gloucester, 18 February 1865. When C. H. Lloyd took over the choir at Gloucester following Wesley's death in 1876, it was 'in a state of insubordination' (*MT*, 1 June 1899, p. 373).

165 For recent studies of Wesley's music, cf. K. Long, *The Music of the English Church* (London 1971), pp. 340–51; W. J. Gatens, *Victorian Cathedral Music in Theory and Practice* (Cambridge 1986), pp. 128–46; and D. Hunt, *Samuel Sebastian Wesley* (Bridgend 1990), pp. 63–90.

166 Summarized in Chappell, p. 55.

167 *Morning Post*, 26 February 1845, quoted in ibid., p. 55.

168 New edition with introduction by W. F. Westbrook and historical note by G. W. Spink published in 1965. For a study of Wesley's writings, cf. Hunt, pp. 91–108.

169 Wesley, p. 44.

170 ibid., pp. 74–5.

171 *Reply to the Inquiries of the Cathedral Commissioners relative to the Improvement in the Music of Divine Worship in Cathedrals* (London 1854).

172 PP 1854, xxv, p. 923.

173 ibid., p. 925.

174 For a summary, cf. Chappell, pp. 86–8.

175 ABDC Winchester, 25 November 1859.

176 For Merewether, cf. Chapter 4, pp. 41–4. There is some attempt to understand Wesley's complex psychology in H. W. Shaw, 'Samuel Sebastian Wesley', *English Church Music*, 1976, pp. 22–30; see also H. W. Shaw, 'The Achievement of S. S. Wesley', *MT*, April 1976, pp. 303–4.

177 West, p. 63. Buck began his career at Norwich in 1807 when he was barely seven years old. He stayed a chorister for seven years and his solo singing was so

exceptional that one of the canons, Dr Pretyman, secretly provided for him (Leeds, p. 73). Another organist who gave a lifetime of service to the same cathedral was W. H. Longhurst. He became a chorister at Canterbury in 1827 and was later assistant organist and a lay clerk there, succeeding T. E. Jones as organist in 1873. When he retired in 1898 on a pension equivalent to his full yearly salary, he had completed seventy years' service to the cathedral (West, p. 10; *Guardian*, 1898, p. 1992). For his complaints about his inconvenient house, cf. PP 1884, xxii, p. 277.

178 Kitton, pp. 5–6; Philip Armes, later organist of Durham Cathedral, was a chorister at Norwich under Buck and described him as 'a wonderful judge of tone: the tone that he obtained from us boys was of the purest kind and it was most successful' (*MT*, 1 February 1900, p. 81).

179 Kitton, pp. 6, 10, 64–5.

180 ibid., pp. 10, 24; cf. Leeds, p. 75.

181 Kitton, pp. 71–2.

182 *Guardian*, 1900, p. 586.

183 D. Gedge, 'John Goss (1800–1880) of St Paul's', *English Church Music*, 1980, pp. 25–35; and Gedge's 'The Gentle Mr Goss', *Musical Opinion*, vol. 108, no.1290, pp. 139–45, 202–7; cf. also R. D. Fenwick, 'An Early Victorian Organist at Work: I – John Goss in Quire at St Paul's Cathedral, 1838–1860', *The Organ*, vol. 62, no.245, July 1983, pp. 98–111, and Fenwick's 'II – The Latter Years of John Goss at St Paul's Cathedral, 1860–1872', *The Organ*, vol. 64, no.254, October 1985, pp. 146–65. Goss's music has recently been studied by Long, pp. 352–5 and Gatens, pp. 115–27.

184 Fenwick, II, p. 156.

185 *Musical World*, 7 January 1888, quoted in P. Charlton, *John Stainer and the Musical Life of Victorian Britain* (Newton Abbot 1984) p. 82; cf. ibid., p. 83 and Prestige, p. 148. For studies of Stainer's music, cf. Gatens, pp. 170–91, and Long, pp. 325, 364–5.

186 ABDC Bristol, 18 August 1884.

187 ibid., 3 July, 1 October, 6 October 1885, 11 November 1885. For Brewer's account of the saga, cf. Brewer, pp. 38, 43.

188 ibid., 4 February 1886; cf. *Quarterly Musical Review*, vol. 2, London 1886, pp. 43f.

189 ABDC Bristol, 11 February 1886.

190 ibid., 7 July 1886.

191 ABDC Bristol, 1 October 1886.

192 ABDC Bristol, 2 October 1894.

193 ABDC Bristol, 4 January 1895.

194 ibid., 4 June 1895.

195 ibid., 2 July and 1 October 1895.

196 ibid., 7 January 1896.

197 ibid., 1 April 1896.

198 ibid., 1, 9, 18 July 1898.

199 ABDC Bristol, 4 October and 18 October 1898, 4 January 1899.

200 ABDC Worcester, 25 June 1844. A similar obligation to remain in the organ loft during services was imposed on Chard and his assistant at Winchester in 1838 (ABDC Winchester, 25 November 1838). The deputy organist, Benjamin Long, was allowed a further £10 per annum in compensation for this (ibid., 23 June 1869). In 1890 the dean and chapter of Chichester restricted those allowed to be in the organ loft at Chichester during services (ABDC Chichester, 1 August 1890). As an example of the problems caused when the organist left the organ loft before the end of the service, cf. Winchester Cathedral Mss., *De Precentore*, 20 March 1866: 'I do not know whether your assistant also told you that I again complained about the noise in the organ loft, which was most annoying this afternoon. As soon as the anthem is concluded and you have gone away, the boys begin to talk and make a disturbance. I saw today both men and boys on the *decani* side looking up to see

what was the matter, and to myself who am just underneath it is most disturbing....I have spoken to your pupils twice; Mr Beckwith once; and you also, at my request have done the same; yet the evil still continues.'

201 Worc. C. Add.Mss., 141, p. 25.
202 Worc. C. Add.Mss., 137, p. 5.
203 Worc. C. Mss., Wheeler to dean and chapter, 17 November 1869. E. H. Thorne was officially appointed choirmaster at Chichester in 1865 (ABDC Chichester, 20 January 1865).
204 Worc. C. Mss., Done to dean and chapter, 17 November 1869.
205 Worc. C. Mss., Done to dean and chapter, 22 June 1874. The low pay of cathedral organists was a constant problem and source of irritation throughout the century. G. W. Chard's salary at Winchester was increased to £100 per annum in 1803 (ABDC Winchester, 25 November 1803). Edmund Larkin, the organist of Peterborough Cathedral, was paid £63 per annum in 1822. By 1853 he was receiving £150 with an additional bonus of £20 for regular attendance (ABDC Peterborough, 12 August 1822, 5 July 1853, October 1853, all cited in Coghlan, p. 115). The post was worth £80 per annum at Bristol in 1825 (ABDC Bristol, 23 June 1825), but was raised to £100 per annum in the following year (R. J. Fletcher, *A History of Bristol Cathedral* (London 1932), p. 52). At Exeter the organist was paid £200 per annum in 1849 (ABDC Exeter, 3 December 1849), but the figure at Chichester in the following year was only £120 per annum (ABDC Chichester, 1 August 1850). Henry Bennett of Chichester complained to the cathedral commissioners of 'the very inadequate salaries of the cathedral organists' which varied, he said, between £90 and £130 per annum. Out of this they had to pay an assistant about £50 per annum (PP 1854, xxv, p. 933). The commissioners found that the organists of Durham (£209) and Exeter (£200) were the highest paid (PP 1854, xxv, p. 41). The commissioners were not informed of John Camidge's salary at York, which was £210 per annum (Aston, p. 12). The figures had not changed by 1865 (M. E. C. Walcott, *Cathedralia* (London 1865), p. 153). In response to enquiries made by the Ecclesiastical Commissioners to cathedral organists in 1867, George Townshend Smith of Hereford said that his income during the years 1864–6 had been £160 per annum. He occupied a prebendal house rent free by favour of the bishop, but he had to insure it and found that it was expensive to repair (CCF 32508). The organist's salary at Ely in 1870 was £200 per annum (ABDC Ely, 14 June 1870, cited in Coghlan, p. 115). Done's salary was increased by £25 per annum at Worcester in 1874 (ABDC Worcester, 31 July 1874). At some cathedrals, such as Lichfield, the organist was also a lay vicar and derived most of his income from the latter post. Thomas Bedsmore, organist of Lichfield from 1864 to 1881, complained in 1880 that a third of his salary was spent on renting a house near the cathedral: 'If a residence was found (free), it would enable myself and all future organists to devote more time to the cathedral duties, without having to undergo the drudgery of giving lessons to make out a living' (PP 1884–5, xxi, p. 184). C. W. Lavington, who was organist of Wells from 1859 to 1895, was the first organist there not to have also been a vicar choral (Colchester, Bowers and Crossland, pp. 15, 22–3). Done was also obliged to live in his own house and felt that he was one of the worst paid organists in the country (PP 1854, xxvi, p. 198). Precentor Vine Hall said that organists, in common with minor canons, lay clerks and choristers, were 'miserably paid' (PP 1884, xxii, p. 196). Riseley was paid £200 per annum at Bristol (Fletcher, pp. 65–6), while at Wells, Percy Buck's salary was raised to £250 per annum in 1899 (Wells CM, 9 January 1899). John Naylor was appointed organist at York in 1883 at a salary of £300 per annum, rising to £400 on the death of his predecessor, E. G. Monk (Aston, p. 12). Sir George Grove described Naylor as 'an excellent cathedral organist, a musician of catholic tastes, and a composer of no mean merit' (Chadwick, *York*, p. 422).

206 ABDC Worcester, 19 November 1877.
207 ABDC Worcester, 23 June 1877.
208 ABDC Worcester, 14 January 1889; West, p. 91; Worc. C. Mss., Precentor's Reports, 1891–2.
209 Worc. C. Mss., Precentor's Report, 1895.
210 ABDC Hereford, 17 October 1889. For an account of Sinclair, cf. *MT*, 1 October 1900, pp. 661–2; H. W. Shaw, *The Organists and Organs of Hereford Cathedral* (Hereford 1976), p. 24; P. M. Young, 'George Robertson Sinclair, 1863–1917', *Three Choirs Festival Programme*, 1985, pp. 28–32. For details of his work at Truro, cf. Donaldson, pp. 284–5; cf. also E. W. Atkins, 'George Robertson Sinclair – A Festival Centenary and His Influence on the Three Choirs 1891–1912', *Three Choirs Festival Programme*, 1991, pp. 27–31.
211 *MT*, 1 January 1900, p. 26. F. Bates, the organist of Norwich Cathedral, was a well-known conductor in Norfolk. He directed the Gate House Choir which combined with Norwich Philharmonic Society to form Norwich Choral Society (F. Bates, *Reminiscences and Autobiography of a Musician in Retirement* (Norwich 1930), pp. 103–4).
212 ABDC Worcester, 2 December 1896, 23 July 1897.
213 Worc. C. Mss., Woodward to Dean Forrest, 25 November 1896; cf. Blair to chapter clerk, 18 June 1897, and chapter clerk to Blair, 23 July 1897.
214 Worc. C. Mss., Precentor's Report, 1897.
215 Worc. C. Mss., Precentor's Report, 1900.
216 Worc. C. Mss., Atkins to dean and chapter, 22 November 1900.
217 ABDC Worcester, 3 December 1900; Worc. C. Mss., Woodward to Forrest, 2 December 1900; Forrest to Atkins, 3 December 1900.
218 cf. E. W. Atkins, *The Elgar–Atkins Friendship* (Newton Abbot 1984).
219 Robertson, p. 262.
220 H. D. Rawnsley, *Harvey Goodwin, Bishop of Carlisle* (London 1896), p. 105.
221 Wells CM, 22 May 1886.
222 ABDC Worcester, 19 November 1896.
223 ABDC Hereford, 13 November 1800.
224 Winchester Cathedral Mss., *De Precentore*, 22 February 1865.
225 ABDC Winchester, 30 March 1864.
226 ABDC Hereford, 25 June 1870. In the same year, a voluntary was substituted for a hymn at Sunday afternoon evensong at St Paul's (Fenwick, II, p. 159).
227 Walcott, *Traditions*, p. 118.
228 ABDC Hereford, 8 November 1877. They were the standard practice at St Paul's from Advent Sunday 1869 (Fenwick, II, p. 159).
229 E. H. Fellowes, *English Cathedral Music from Edward VI to Edward VII* (London 1941, new edns 1970, 1973), p. 35; cf. B. Matthews, *The Music of Winchester Cathedral* (London 1974), p. 24, quoting W. A. Fearon, *The Passing of Old Winchester* (Winchester 1924).
230 Jebb, p. 317.
231 ABDC Winchester, 25 November 1805. Sir Frederick Bridge pointed out that seven ex-choristers of Rochester had become cathedral organists, and three had become professors of music (Bridge, p. 6).
232 ABDC Exeter, 28 December 1822.
233 ABDC Exeter, 9–10 December 1830.
234 ABDC Hereford, 1 October and 12 November 1835. For Hunt's conditions of service, cf. ABDC Hereford, 22 September 1835. There seems to have been no deputy before then. During the interregnum a local organist by the name of Mills was engaged at one guinea per week (ABDC Hereford, 22 September 1835). There was, however, a 'temporary' organist in 1820, just before Aaron Hayter was

dismissed, by the name of Robert Woodward. One James Prosser was cited in the Dean's Court for brawling and assaulting him in the organ loft during a service on 6 May 1820 (HCA 5349).

235 Wells CM, 1 December 1846.
236 ABDC Exeter, 25 November 1865.
237 Prestige, pp. 99, 149–51.
238 ABDC Gloucester, 21 March 1872.
239 ABDC Exeter, 12 February 1875.
240 CCF 32508.
241 PP 1884–5, xxi, p. 97; for Armes, cf. *MT*, 1 February 1900, pp. 81–6.
242 Worc. C. Mss., Precentor's Report, 1887; cf. 1886 report. For Blair's appointment at £50 per annum, cf. ABDC Worcester, 28 June 1886.
243 ABDC Worcester, 22 December 1888.
244 See above, p. 182.
245 Worc. C. Mss., Precentor's Reports, 1891–2.
246 Worc. C. Mss., Precentor's Reports, 1890–1, 1893. One of them, Henry Holloway, was rather unreliable (cf. ABDC Worcester, 1 December 1890).
247 ABDC Worcester, 4 August 1897.
248 Moore, p. 244, quoting ABDC Durham, 20 November 1820.
249 *MT*, 1 February 1900, p. 84.
250 ibid., pp. 84–5 (cf. 1 March 1900, p. 169). When the dean and chapter of Wells were searching for a successor to Percy Buck in 1899, two candidates were each asked to come and take a service at Wells (Wells CM, 9 January 1899).
251 Coghlan, p. 114, citing ABDC Peterborough, 12 March 1870.
252 ABDC Chichester, 7 August and 31 August 1876. For Precentor Wray's suggestion to the dean and chapter of Winchester in 1865, when they were considering a successor to S. S. Wesley, cf. Winchester Cathedral Mss., *De Precentore*, 22 February 1865.
253 Worc. C. Mss., bundle of the duties of organists.
254 *Guardian*, 1897, p. 1993. The vacant post of organist at Norwich in 1885 attracted 168 applicants. F. Bates, who was eventually appointed, was one of three shortlisted candidates. He was required to take a choristers' rehearsal and later played for evensong (Bates, pp. 29–30).
255 ABDC Salisbury, 9 January 1884; for the duties at Bristol in 1899, cf. ABDC Bristol, 4 January 1899.
256 cf. J. Jebb, *Three Lectures on the Cathedral Service of the Church of England* (Leeds 1845), p. 18; Moore, p. 168; PP 1854, xxv, p. 938; ABDC Hereford, 9 April 1846; ABVC Hereford, 18 April 1846. For the introduction of additional lay clerks at Hereford, cf. ABDC Hereford, 14 November 1850, 22 February 1851, G. T. Smith to Dean Merewether, 11 November 1850. The names and length of service of all the nineteenth century lay clerks at Hereford are recorded in HCA 5909. Dean Herbert unsuccessfully tried to introduce ordinands as lay clerks at Hereford later in the century (W. J. Humfrys, *Memories of Old Hereford* (Hereford n.d.), p. 19). Lay singers were not unknown at Hereford in the early part of the century. In 1836 Dean Merewether told Archbishop Howley: 'There are indeed four deacons, who were originally chosen with regard to their musical qualifications, but they have only £4 p.a. each of right and only attend on Sundays (when the vicars choral are absent at the 11 o'clock service at their parochial cures) and are not capable of performing the service in general, although I have thought it right to press upon them the necessity of studying music and endeavouring to supply as far as possible the want of the regular ministers of the choir at a time when they seem to be especially missed' (CCF 3208).
257 cf. Chapter 6, p. 98.

258 PP 1883, xxi, p. 269.

259 cf. 'Rules for the Junior Vicars and Supernumerary Singing Men' at Lincoln, PP 1884–5, xxi, p. 417. For numbers in various cathedrals, cf. n. 25 above.

260 For 1854, cf. n.11 above. A document in Hereford Cathedral Archives (HCA 5071) gives the following figures for 1893:

Canterbury	12	York	11	Chester	6
Norwich	8	Durham	10	Bristol	9
Worcester	8	Salisbury	7	Gloucester	6
Ely	8	Carlisle	6	Lincoln	9
Exeter	8	Lichfield	10	Hereford	7
Wells	11	Rochester	6		

261 PP 1854, xxv, p. 923.

262 Worc. C. Mss., Treasurer's Accounts 1800.

263 ABDC Winchester, 25 November 1801, 25 November 1802. For choir regulations and salaries at Winchester, cf. ABDC Winchester, 23 June 1809, 26 November and 29 November 1810.

264 ABDC Exeter, 22 December 1803.

265 ABDC Bristol, 30 November 1818.

266 Coghlan, p. 118, citing ABDC Peterborough, 12 August 1822 and 10 July 1826.

267 ABDC Worcester, 24 November 1824; cf. also 24 November 1831.

268 ABDC Chichester, 2 May 1826.

269 ABDC Winchester, 25 November 1826. At Norwich in 1829 the eight lay clerks received an average of £52 12s per annum (Dean Pellew's note-book, 1829–32, DCN 120/2, Norfolk CRO).

270 ABDC Winchester, 23 June 1840.

271 C. Sandys, *The Memorial and Case of the Clerici-Laici or Lay-clerks of Canterbury Cathedral* (London 1848), p. 9.

272 ibid., p. 31.

273 ABDC Winchester, 25 November 1853; cf. 26 November 1855.

274 PP 1854, xxv, p. 41.

275 ABDC Chichester, 1 August 1854.

276 Worc. C. Mss., Bundle marked 'Corn rents, Lay Clerks'. When Philip Armes's father became a lay clerk at Rochester in 1848, his salary was £50 per annum. He also worked in the chapter clerk's office and brought up seven children on £150 per annum (*MT*, 1 February 1900, p. 82).

277 For details, cf. ABDC Worcester, 22 November 1859; Worc. C. Add. Mss., 71; ABDC Salisbury, 2 April 1862; ABDC Gloucester, 7 April 1864; *Guardian*, 1867, p. 102; Hereford lay clerks to Ecclesiastical Commissioners, 17 August 1861 in CCF 3208 (cf. 32508); NCL, Goulburn's diary, 11 December 1868; Dean Pellew's letters, no. 428, 3 February 1865, Norfolk CRO; Coghlan, p. 118, citing ABDC Norwich, 22 July 1875, ABDC Ely, 26 November 1888, ABDC Peterborough, 11 March 1881; PP 1876, lviii, pp. 542, 546.

278 *MT*, 1 November 1869, p. 264. In 1862 all cathedral lay clerks sent a petition to Parliament asking for an income of £100 per annum, together with a residence allowance (Coghlan, pp. 118–19).

279 ABDC Salisbury, 8 December 1869.

280 ABDC Winchester, 4 October 1873.

281 PP 1876, lviii, pp. 539–49.

282 Coghlan, p. 119; the income from the lay clerks' estates at Ely fell from £336 in 1880 to £60 in 1895 (ibid.).

283 PP 1884, xxii, p. 139

284 PP 1884–5, xxi, p. 445.

285 PP 1884–5, xxi, p. 378.

286 HCA 5071.

287 MBVC Wells, 2 November 1891; ABDC Worcester, 1 October 1892; Precentor's Report, 1892.

288 H. Goodwin, 'Recollections of a Dean' in J. S. Howson, ed., *Essays on Cathedrals by Various Writers* (London 1872), p. 16; cf. Rawnsley, pp. 108, 309–10. Perhaps it was Dean Goodwin's policy that led to the 'good working relationship' which the Ely lay clerks claimed to have with the dean and chapter (Coghlan, p. 92). They certainly seemed quite satisfied: 'We in Ely are fortunate in many respects (although we seldom have a professional engagement). We live in one of the healthiest and cleanest towns in the kingdom, where the necessaries of life are very reasonable...' (quoted in Coghlan, p. 119; cf. H. P. Liddon's lecture to the choir at St Paul's on 25 August 1873: 'I went at length into the intentions of the Chapter in insisting on having communicants; we wanted *religious* men first; then, if we could get them, accomplished musicians' (Johnston, p. 141); cf. Precentor to lay clerk Pimlott on his appointment to Winchester in 1864: 'The Chapter moreover will expect you to be a regular communicant and it would be well for you to act on some settled resolve to avoid laxity on this point. I hope you will agree with me that once a month and on the great festivals is the least a Christian man should do in this respect. We have seen such falling off in this by others that I feel sure the Chapter will not retain a man whether sworn in or not who does not fulfil his duty in this respect. Make up your mind to do what is right without caring for the opinions of others, and you will be happy and contented, and possess the respect and esteem of all with whom you are brought into contact – even of those who are careless as to their own religious duties' (Winchester Cathedral Mss., *De Precentore*, February 1864, p. 12). The dean and chapter of Winchester were also insistent that no new lay vicar who was in debt could be admitted (ABDC Winchester, 25 November 1874). In 1879 Precentor Crowdy wrote to lay clerk Gardiner on his appointment that, as there had been 'so much falling-off' in regular communicating among the members of the choir, 'we feel constrained to impress on you very strongly our confident hope that you will take a high view of your Christian duty in this respect, paying no heed to the opinion or habits of others' (*De Precentore*, 25 November 1879).

289 ABDC Exeter, 7 January 1804.

290 ABDC Bristol, 23 February 1803; ABDC Winchester, 25 November 1831.

291 Winchester Cathedral Mss., *De Precentore*, February 1881, p. 75.

292 Dean Pellew's letters, no. 344, Norfolk CRO.

293 PP 1854, xxv, p. 944.

294 PP 1884–5, xxi, p. 416. The Lincoln lay clerks of the 1870s were described by A. C. Benson in *The Trefoil*: 'The outstanding personalities of the choir were Barraclough, a busy-looking, whiskered man, very hearty and friendly, who kept a stationers' shop by the Exchequer Gate. He was the senior vicar choral and his voice, though forcible, was harsh and over-emphatic. The other tenor was appointed in our time, Dunkerton, a very handsome young man, with a beautiful voice and with a devotional beauty, both of mien and utterance, as though the whole service was to him an act of worship and devout intention, which was a contrast to the unconcerned air of some of the older lay clerks. Two altos I remember: Plant, a striking-looking clean-shaven man, with the air of an early Victorian artist, and Mason, a tall, grey-bearded figure like a minor prophet in a stained-glass window; but I confess that an alto duet, such as sometimes occurred in a leisurely old anthem, was generally more a humorous performance than an act of worship' (*Trefoil*, pp. 144–5).

295 *MT*, 1 September 1904, p. 572.

296 Worc. C. Mss., Precentor T. L. Wheeler to dean, 4 February 1876, bundle of memorials from minor canons.

297 Winchester Cathedral Mss., *De Precentore*, February 1879. At Manchester it was difficult to get good candidates for voice trials (cf. Bridge, pp. 58–9).

298 Worc. C. Mss., Precentor's Report, 1884.

299 Worc. C. Mss., Precentor's Report, 1899.

300 ABDC Chichester, 17 February 1890.

301 NCL, Goulburn's diary, 6 July 1867.

302 Coghlan, pp. 126–7.

303 cf. Howson, p. 222. Bishop Carr was shocked to find in 1825 that the lay vicars at Chichester did not attend holy communion (F. G. Bennett, R. H. Codrington and C. Deedes, *Statutes and Constitutions of the Cathedral Church of Chichester* (Chichester 1904), p. 50; cf. Visitation Book, f. 135). In 1890 Bishop Harvey Goodwin found that the lay clerks at Carlisle did not communicate for months on end (Rawnsley, pp. 309–10). Bishop Hamilton said in 1854, however, that most of the lay vicars at Salisbury were communicants (Salisbury Chapter Muniments, Press I, Box 39, p. 14). Later in the century Dean Pigou complained that such habits had not disappeared: 'Lay clerks have tricks, not to speak of whispering and unnecessary communication with each other: there are sadly listless attitudes, singing with folded arms, not kneeling when they ought to kneel; not bowing the head when they should bow it; not reciting the Creed; looking over music during the reading of the lessons, studying the anthem when presumably joining in prayer and divers sundry and other "tricks"' (F. Pigou, *Odds and Ends* (London 1903), p. 246).

304 ABDC Bristol, 25 August 1801.

305 ABDC Gloucester, 5 April 1830, 23 June 1831; cf. 31 December 1824.

306 Dean Pellew's letters, no. 104, Norfolk CRO.

307 ABDC Bristol, 23 June 1858.

308 ABDC Winchester, 1 October 1860.

309 ABDC Hereford, 1 October 1864.

310 P. A. Welsby, *Rochester Cathedral in the time of Charles Dickens* (Rochester 1976), p. 9. A bankrupt lay vicar at Wells, who was continually absent, was expelled in 1891 (MBVC Wells, 2 November 1891).

311 ABDC Worcester, 1 September 1870.

312 Worc. C. Mss., Choir Bundle, E. Vine Hall to dean, 4 July 1879. The dean and chapter of Worcester ordered in 1872 that it was the duty of the minor canon present, if he noticed any 'irregularity of conduct' among the choir, to remonstrate with the offender and report him to the dean or canon-in-residence (ABDC Worcester, 29 June 1872).

313 PP 1883, xxi, p. 269. In 1873 a lay vicar at Wells had been dismissed for bad behaviour and 'his uselessness as a singer' (Wells CM, 1 October 1873). It is clear that there were considerable difficulties at Wells at this time. The dean and chapter complained in 1875 that their attendance was irregular, some of them were unable to sing, and their authority had been flouted by 'a spirit of insubordination' (PP 1876, lviii, p. 540). Two of them had been suspended for misconduct and they had omissions of duty varying from 204 to 702 services.

314 ABDC Ely, 24 May 1887, cited in Coghlan, p. 117.

315 Winchester Cathedral Mss., *De Precentore*, June 1889.

316 ABDC Chichester, 12 May 1890.

317 Winchester Cathedral Mss., *De Precentore*, 24 December 1894. Sir Frederick Bridge recalled that in his early years at Rochester the alto soloist in Elvey's anthem 'Unto thee have I cried' refused to sing in the middle of the performance, and there were some heated altercations after the service (Bridge, p. 34).

318 ABDC Winchester, 28 September and 28 December 1896, 25 February 1898.

319 Salisbury CM, 5 June 1896.
320 Winchester Cathedral Mss., Davidson's visitation 1900, Canon Warburton's reply. In 1888 it was arranged at Worcester that the dean or canon-in-residence should hold a monthly meeting for the lay clerks and beadsmen in order to give them spiritual instruction (ABDC Worcester, 17 November 1888).
321 Hillsman, p. 304.
322 ABDC Winchester, 25 November 1864; *De Precentore*, 13 May 1865.
323 Winchester Cathedral Mss., *De Precentore*, 25 November 1879.
324 Salisbury CM, 22 December 1883, 7 January 1884. In 1893 the dean and chapter of Salisbury issued new regulations reminding the lay vicars that they were not allowed to frequent public houses, to sing at 'a house licensed for the sale of intoxicating liquors' or at a place of public entertainment without permission from the dean or canon-in-residence. The lay vicars were expected to have regular jobs in addition to their cathedral duties (ABDC Salisbury, 7 March 1893).
325 ABDC Winchester, 5 April 1887.
326 Worc. C. Mss., Precentor's Report, 1896. At Hereford in 1885 the dean and chapter registered their disapproval of the five lay vicars taking part in 'smoking concerts' at the Green Dragon Hotel. They were not to do this again 'or at any establishment where intoxicating liquors are sold' (ABDC Hereford, 7 December 1885).
327 ABDC Worcester, 19 November 1896.
328 ABDC Chichester, 4 May, 22 May, 24 May 1875; P. L. S. Barrett, 'Chichester Cathedral Choir in the Nineteenth Century', *Southern Cathedrals Festival Programme*, 1980, p. 30.
329 Worc. C. Mss., Precentor's Report, 1898.
330 ABDC Exeter, 24 May 1834.
331 ABDC Exeter, 22–23 December 1835, 9 January and 19 March 1836.
332 ABDC Bristol, 4 December 1850.
333 ABDC Winchester, 23 June 1855, 23 June 1856, 23 June 1857.
334 ABDC Winchester, 25 November 1862. Other examples are given by Crook, *A History of the Pilgrims' School*, p. 14; Crook, 'Fifty Years of Choral Misrule', p. 33. For examples at Salisbury, cf. ABDC Salisbury, 8 December, 15 December, 31 December 1863, 9 April 1864.
335 ABDC Worcester, 26 November 1868; for the chorister incident, see above, p. 191.
336 ABDC Worcester, 23 December 1875, 13 January 1876.
337 Worc. C. Mss., Choir Bundle, J. D. Price to precentor, 20 December 1875; J. D. Price to dean and chapter, 14 February 1876.
338 ABDC Chichester, 15 November 1898.
339 ABDC Salisbury, 10 November 1803, 6 January 1804.
340 ABDC Winchester, 23 June 1814. There was a similar case at Salisbury two years later (ABDC Salisbury, 10 February 1818).
341 J. Noake, *The Monastery and Cathedral of Worcester* (London 1866), pp. 491–4.
342 D. M. Owen in G. E. Aylmer and R. Cant, eds, *A History of York Minster* (Oxford 1977), p. 245.
343 ABDC Salisbury, 17 February 1818; cf. 24 February 1818, 2 December 1820.
344 ABDC Hereford, 30 November 1852; cf. 1 December 1852.
345 ABDC Winchester, 30 July 1890, 25 March 1891; Winchester Cathedral Mss., *De Precentore*, 30 January 1891. There were forty-five applicants for the vacant post.
346 Dean Pellew's note-book, 1829–32, DCN 120/2, Norfolk CRO.
347 PP 1854, xxv, p. 922; cf. Dean Close's comment in PP 1884, xxii, p. 132; cf. ibid., p. 138.
348 PP 1854, xxv, p. 939.
349 PP 1883, xxi, p. 270.
350 W. R. Matthews and W. M. Atkins, *A History of St Paul's Cathedral and the Men Associated with it* (London 1957), p. 274. Canon Gregory said in 1889 that the dean and chapter of St Paul's had found it impossible to dismiss a lay vicar choral who

had been appointed in 1812 but was still in office in 1875, even though he could not sing at all. Apparently, at his election, the only alternative was a notorious drunkard, 'and the Chapter had decided upon the appointment of the man who could not sing in preference to that of the drunkard' (*Guardian*, 1889, p. 361).

351 ABDC Salisbury, 20 November 1861.

352 PP 1876, lviii, pp. 539–49.

353 ABDC Hereford, 3 April 1882.

354 Chadwick, vol.II, p. 376.

355 ABDC Exeter, 6, 12, 19, 20, 29 October 1849, 3 December 1849, 3 October 1850.

356 Gloucester chapter minute book, 25 March 1885. The insecurity felt by lay clerks in temporary appointments is reflected in a letter of the Salisbury lay vicars to the dean and chapter, 5 July 1853 (ABDC Salisbury, 6 July 1853).

357 H. L. Thompson, *Henry George Liddell* (London 1899), p. 152.

358 Woodruff, p. 21.

359 Worc. C. Mss., Precentor's Reports, 1880, 1883, 1885, 1887 and 1889.

360 PP 1884, xxi, p. 276. The vicars choral of Wells had told the Ecclesiastical Commissioners in 1867 that the pensions given to the lay vicars were inadequate (MBVC Wells, 31 March 1867).

361 ABDC Worcester, 24 November 1828.

362 ABDC Worcester, 25 November 1836; cf. also 22 November 1859, 29 June 1872.

363 Coghlan, p. 119, citing ABDC Norwich, June 1881, and ABDC Peterborough, 25 May 1888.

364 PP 1854–5, xv, p. 87.

365 ABDC Chichester, 11 October 1869, 20 January 1870, 2 May 1874.

366 ABDC Chichester, 18 February and 12 May 1890.

367 Salisbury CM, 5 June 1899. A Choir Benevolent Fund was set up in 1851 to assist former cathedral lay clerks and organists. The dean and chapter of Salisbury sent £20 to it in 1865 (ABDC Salisbury, 20 March 1865). In 1889 the lay clerks of Worcester Cathedral toured Devon to raise funds for it (ABDC Worcester, 1 August 1889; cf. also Bridge, p. 10). The dean and chapter of St Paul's made arrangements for their assistant lay vicars choral to have pensions (Hutton, p. 202).

368 ABDC Bristol, 23 June 1801; cf. 24 June 1802.

369 ABDC Chichester, 20 January 1809.

370 ABDC Worcester, 22 November 1830.

371 ABDC Winchester, 25 August 1862.

372 ABDC Winchester, 23 June 1870. S. S. Wesley wrote some of the famous bass solos in his anthems for Cross, who had a splendid voice. He was appointed in 1847 and retired in 1890. (Fellowes, p. 226). Another famous bass was Stock of Manchester, who for a while sang on Saturday nights at the Theatre Royal and at the cathedral the next day (Bridge, p. 57; Boutflower, pp. 22–3). The dean and chapter of Durham had been similarly generous to one of their lay clerks in 1847, giving him £20 'to defray the expense of a set of teeth and of his journey to London for that purpose' (ABDC Durham, 2 January 1847, quoted in Chappell, p. 65).

373 Leeds, p. 93.

374 ABDC Worcester, 18 February 1891. For Dean Forrest's appreciation of the Worcester lay clerks, cf. Chapter 4, p. 54.

375 ABDC Bristol, 23 June 1818.

376 ABDC Winchester, 25 November 1841.

377 ABDC Gloucester, 27 November 1851; cf. 1 December 1852; PP 1854, xxv, p. 919. C. Z. Crawley, the precentor of Gloucester, commented: 'I do not think the plan has succeeded so well as was expected partly from the want of inducement to attend as volunteers... and partly from the deficiency of the previous education' (PP 1854, xxv, p. 937).

378 Prestige, p. 68. Even so, it was 'clearly impracticable to secure full and regular attendance on the daily services' (PP 1854, xxv, p. 283). For the unsuccessful attempt of the dean and chapter of St Paul's to introduce new regulations for the (lay) vicars choral in 1843–7, cf. Prestige, pp. 43, 44–7. More stringent rules for them were introduced following Bishop Blomfield's visitation of the cathedral in 1848 (cf. W. S. Simpson, *Registrum Statutorum et Consuetudinum Ecclesiae Cathedralis Sancti Pauli Londinensis* (London 1873), p. 317).

379 ABDC Hereford, 10 November 1859; cf. also 24 March 1865. The vicars choral felt in 1868 that the introduction of lay clerks had not been satisfactory and wished to replace them by assistant vicars choral in holy orders (CCF 32508).

380 ABDC Chichester, 10 October 1868.

381 ibid., 20 January 1869.

382 ABDC Worcester, 6 April 1872, 19 November 1873.

383 Frost, p. 36; cf. Prestige, pp. 152–3. For details of their auditions, cf. Frost, p. 38. Their numbers were increased to twelve in 1878, though fourteen was given as the number in 1875. They had been appointed because the dean and chapter were 'dissatisfied with the inefficient condition of the choir' (PP 1883, xxi, pp. 104–8, 117–18; PP 1876, lviii, p. 545).

384 PP 1876, lviii, pp. 539–49. For St Paul's, cf. n. 374 above.

385 ABDC Winchester, 6 February 1883.

386 Winchester Cathedral Mss., *De Precentore*, 1895, p. 116.

387 Hackett (1873 edn), p.vii. For a short account of Maria Hackett's crusade on behalf of the choristers at St Paul's, cf. B. M. Taylor, 'Angel Voices ever singing', *The Lady*, vol. clxxxx, no. 4911, 26 July 1979, pp. 132, 150; and D. Gedge, 'Maria Hackett – the Choristers' Friend', *The World of Church Music*, 1983, pp. 41–9; and D. Gedge, 'The Redoubtable Miss Hackett', *Musical Opinion*, vol. 108, no. 1297, December 1985, pp. 441–6; vol. 109, no. 1298, January 1986, pp. 11–14; vol. 109, no. 1299, February 1986, pp. 49–53.

388 PP 1854, xxv, p. 937.

389 ibid., Wells CM, 1 October 1857; ABDC Winchester, 4 July 1862, 16 August 1863. Sir Frederick Bridge recalled that when he joined the choir at Rochester Cathedral at the age of six, he was one of six probationers (Bridge, pp. 4–5).

390 PP 1854, xxv, p. 931.

391 W. D. Peckham, 'The Vicars Choral of Chichester Cathedral', *Sussex Archaeological Collections*, vol. 78, no. xxxvii, 1937, p. 144; ABDC Chichester, 1 August 1866. M. E. C. Walcott gave details of the number of choristers and their pay at various cathedrals in 1865 (Walcott, pp. 142–3).

392 Worc. C. Mss., Done to dean and chapter, 17 November 1869, Bundle of Precentor's Reports, 1869–1918.

393 ABDC Worcester, 6 February 1875. Five years later the dean and chapter wanted to increase their number to twenty (ABDC Worcester, 28 February 1880). The choristers' payments were reorganized at Wells in 1885 and Dean Plumptre believed that 'this scheme would attract boys of a better class and with more musical proficiency to start with'. Vacancies were advertised in the *Wells Journal* and the *Guardian* (Wells CM, 21 August 1885). Tait noted in 1850 that many of the eight choristers at Carlisle were the sons of such tradesmen as a shoemaker, a dyer, a joiner and a weaver (Tait Papers, vol. 27, 5 May 1850), cf. n. 486 below. At Norwich in about 1865 a system of 'trial boys' had led to 'a constant succession of good singers' (Dean Pellew's letters, no. 429, Norfolk CRO).

394 ABDC Hereford, 10 November 1881.

395 ABDC Winchester, 6 January 1891.

396 ABDC Bristol, 6 March 1891.

397 ABDC Bristol, 10 October 1893.

398 Leeds, pp. 83–4.

399 cf. Moore, p. 278.

400 ibid., p. 276.

401 Prestige, pp. 4–5, quoting J. S. Bumpus, *The Organists and Composers of St Paul's Cathedral* (London 1891), pp. 137f.; cf.also Prestige, pp. 23–4, 47–8.

402 Maria Hackett in a letter of 4 April 1814, quoted in Moore, p. 284.

403 ibid., p. 286.

404 ABDC Salisbury, 20 March 1802. The writing master at Exeter was paid £5 18s 6d (ABDC Exeter, 3 July 1802).

405 Robertson, p. 260.

406 ABDC Bristol, 8 January 1802; see n.430 below.

407 ABDC Winchester, 11 December 1806.

408 ibid., 23 June 1812.

409 Crosby, pp. 30–1.

410 ABDC Worcester, 24 November 1824.

411 ABDC Chichester, 20 January 1825.

412 ABDC Worcester, 26 April 1876; for the sliding scale introduced by E. H. Fellowes at Bristol in 1897, cf. ABDC Bristol, 1 July 1897.

413 ABDC Wells, 1 October 1829.

414 ABDC Winchester, 25 November 1844.

415 J. E. Millard, *Historical Notices of the Office of Choristers* (London 1848), p. 11.

416 R. Whiston, *Cathedral Trusts and Their Fulfilment* (London 1849), p. 40.

417 ABDC Bristol, 1 March 1853.

418 Greenhalgh, *Wells*, p. 189.

419 ABDC Winchester, 23 June 1865.

420 ABDC Gloucester, 30 November 1867.

421 ABDC Hereford, 6 January and 23 January 1868.

422 ABDC Hereford, 2 June 1869. For details of educational and other payments at Winchester, cf. ABDC Winchester, 8 January 1891.

423 ABDC Exeter, 8 February 1876.

424 ABDC Wells, 18 May 1891.

425 ABDC Gloucester, 23 June 1810.

426 ABDC Worcester, 6 January 1812.

427 ABDC Salisbury, 21 February 1812.

428 ABDC Winchester, 2 February 1815.

429 The following details are taken from *Gentleman's Magazine*, vol. 87, 1817, pt 1, pp. 327f., and vol. 88, 1818, pt 1, pp. 104f., and pt 2, pp. 6f. These articles formed the basis of her publication *A Brief Account of Cathedral and Collegiate Schools* which first appeared in 1825. For a summary of this, cf. Gedge, 'The Redoubtable Miss Hackett', pp. 11–14.

430 ibid., vol. 87, 1817, pt 1, pp. 327–8. The boys' parents paid for their books, slates and pens (Fletcher, p. 51).

431 ibid., vol. 87, 1817, pt 1, p. 419.

432 ibid., vol. 87, 1817, pt 2, p. 104.

433 ibid., vol. 88, 1818, pt 1, p. 104.

434 ibid., vol. 88, 1818, pt 1, p. 392. For a summary of the choristers' education at Chichester at various times during the nineteenth century, cf. Clarke, p. 13.

435 ibid., vol. 88, 1818, pt 1, p. 487.

436 ibid., vol. 88, 1818, pt 1, p. 487. An independent account of the choristers' education at Exeter says: 'there seems to be a prevalent opinion that their education, with the exception of music, has lately been much neglected' (*Mirror*, 11 October 1834, no.685, p. 243).

437 ibid., vol. 88, 1818, pt 2, pp. 6f. Of Worcester, Maria Hackett said: 'There are few

Cathedrals in the United Kingdom which can boast a greater number of distinguished names among those who received the rudiments of their musical education under the superintending care of the Dean and Chapter' (quoted in Craze, p. 178).

438 ibid., vol. 81, 1819, pt 1, p. 102.

439 Hackett (1827 edition), p.ix. The ordinary schooling of the choristers at Norwich in Dr Buck's time was 'terribly neglected'. They were supposed to have two hours a day in school, but Buck often required some of this time for the training of his solo boys: 'It will readily be imagined how imperfect their general education must necessarily have been and when their voices broke (thus rendering them useless as choristers) how ill-equipped were the boys for fighting their way in the world' (Kitton, pp. 6–7).

440 Hackett, p. 6.

441 ibid., p. 13.

442 ibid., p. 17.

443 Prestige, pp. 23–4.

444 ABDC Chichester, 20 January 1818.

445 Salisbury CM, 11 January 1878.

446 Wells CM, 2 October 1848.

447 ABDC Chichester, 1 August 1850, 2 May 1853. The parents of choristers at Worcester complained about the education given to their sons in 1878 (ABDC Worcester, 10 July 1878).

448 ABDC Worcester, 20 November 1851.

449 Worc. C. Mss., Done to dean and chapter, 17 November 1869, Precentor's Reports, 1869–1918.

450 ABDC Exeter, 5 November 1870.

451 Winchester Cathedral Mss., Choristers' Box File (memorandum about the choristers and their school, 25 September 1883). An earlier attempt was made to attract boarders in 1856 (cf. Crook, *A History of the Pilgrims' School*, p. 17). In 1860 the dean and chapter felt that the choristers' school was in an unsatisfactory state and urged S. S. Wesley to give it his personal attention (ABDC Winchester, 26 November 1860). In 1868 the chapter reduced the number of choristers to twelve, but undertook to provide them with free board, lodgings and education. Their parents paid £4 per annum to the dean and chapter, who invested it to provide a lump sum when the boys left the choir. The parents were also required to provide two suits of clothing, including caps and boots, and also any necessary books (ABDC Winchester, 25 November 1868).

452 Quoted in Crook, *A History of the Pilgrims' School*, p. 20. In 1884 the chapter told the Ecclesiastical Commissioners: 'The choir is not what it might be and the school arrangements are very defective and unsatisfactory' (Winchester Cathedral Mss., Ecclesiastical Commissioners Box; Dean Kitchin to commissioners, 5 February 1884): 'Our present schoolmaster is a most conscientious and diligent person, and an efficient teacher; but he is single-handed and can undertake only part of the education we desire to give. The result is that the standard of the school is very little higher than that of a good elementary school, except indeed in the subject of Music....Our position is painful; with every wish to have a fitting school for our boys we find ourselves unable to advance a step for lack of funds. We cannot organise a good day school and a boarding school is utterly out of the question. Apart from the important question of the efficiency of the choir in church, there is so strong feeling abroad that a choir school ought, from its historic position and in its religious aspect, to be a pattern-school, that we feel confident that we shall not appeal in vain to the Commissioners to enable us to reorganise and maintain in due efficiency the school entrusted to our care.' They therefore asked the commis-

sioners for assistance under the 1866 Act (29 and 30 Vict., c.iii, s.18).

453 C. Wordsworth and D. Macleane, *Statutes and Customs of the Cathedral Church of the Blessed Virgin Mary at Salisbury* (London 1915), p. 487.

454 Robertson, pp. 269–70.

455 ABDC Chichester, 10 October 1866. Similar forms were used at Norwich (ABDC Norwich, 2 June 1868, quoted in Moore, pp. 253–4) and St Paul's (Prestige, p. 157). The Norwich form was directly borrowed from Chichester (cf. NCL, Goulburn's diary, 19 March and 12 July 1867; ABDC Norwich, 2 December 1873, quoted in Coghlan, p. 154). For the form for the admission of the Bishop's Chorister at Salisbury, cf. E. E. Dorling, *Register of Old Choristers of Salisbury Cathedral 1810–97* (London 1898), p. 38. For the Truro form, cf. PP 1883, xxi, pp. 75–6.

456 Robertson, p. 270.

457 ABDC Salisbury, 26 January 1853.

458 ABDC Winchester, 25 November 1844.

459 Rainbow, p. 245; Kitton, p. 76.

460 Kitton, p. 76; Walcott, *Traditions*, p. 109; Millard, p. 61; Hackett (1827 edn), p. 41; *Guardian*, 1860, p. 899; they were given new surplices in 1867 (NCL, Goulburn's diary, 18 July 1867).

461 Worc. C. Add. Mss., 128, p. 8 and 137, p. 10.

462 Coghlan, p. 139, quoting ABDC Ely, 14 June and 25 November 1817.

463 ABDC Salisbury, 7 January 1853.

464 ABDC Hereford, 13 November 1856.

465 Walcott, *Traditions*, p. 65. Adam Sedgwick was shocked by the red tassels (J. W. Clark and T. McK. Hughes, *The Life and Letters of the Reverend Adam Sedgwick* (Cambridge 1890), vol.II, p. 588).

466 ABDC Hereford, 11 November 1869. The vicars choral refused to help wash them (ibid., 24 March 1873). Until at least 1865 the lay vicars of Chichester wore surplices embroidered with the letters 'RS' (Walcott, *Traditions*, p. 66; Clarke, p. 58). At Peterborough the dean and chapter ordered in 1822 'that the lay clerks shall attend divine service regularly in clean surplices and appear neat and decent in their own person and that they shall be ready in their seats before the hour at which prayers are to begin: also that they stand upright in their places and all take their due share in the service' (Coghlan, p. 139, quoting ABDC Peterborough, 11 July 1822).

467 ABDC Exeter, 11 December 1869.

468 Cowie, p. 354.

469 Quoted in D. I. Hill, *Christ's Glorious Church* (London 1976), pp. 78–9.

470 Boutflower, p. 23.

471 ABDC Worcester, 3 August 1876.

472 ibid., 28 February 1880. The lay vicars of Chichester asked for new surplices in 1880 (Chichester Draft Acts, 3 August 1880).

473 Worc. C. Mss., Precentor's Report, 1881.

474 Wells CM, 1 October, 25 October, 10 November 1887.

475 Wells CM, 1 July 1889.

476 ABDC Exeter, 17 December 1887, 28 April 1888, 23 April 1892.

477 ABDC Salisbury, 30 May 1890.

478 ABDC Worcester, 27 June 1895. The Gloucester choristers were put into cassocks in the same year (ABDC Gloucester, 6 March 1895).

479 ABDC Worcester, 19 November 1897; cf. also Worc. C. Add. Mss., 137, and Precentor's Report, 1897.

480 Prestige, p. 154; cf. Frost, p. 17. The clergy at St Paul's began to wear cassocks in 1870 (Prestige, p. 95).

481 PP 1854, xxv, p. 927.

482 PP 1854, xxv, p. 42; cf. Rainbow, p. 261.

483 ABDC Chichester, 20 January 1819.

484 J. H. Swistead, ed., *Christ Church Cathedral School; Register of Choristers, Probationers, Masters, Precentors, Organists from 1837–1900* (Salisbury 1900), p. 7. For details of the choristers' timetable at Norwich, cf. Kitton, p. 78.

485 Dorling, pp. 32–3. At Winchester the choristers were not allowed to leave the singing school between their practice and morning service, nor to play in the close before and after any service (ABDC Winchester, 26 November 1860). For further rules at Winchester, cf. *De Precentore*, February 1864.

486 F. A. G. Ouseley to dean and chapter, 21 July 1857 (ABVC Hereford, 22 August 1857); cf. p. 173 above. In 1877 the headmaster of the Cathedral School at Hereford complained of the choristers being selected 'from so low a class' (ABDC Hereford, 8 November 1877; cf. ABDC Hereford, 7 November 1865). The Gloucester choristers who were (and still are) all day-boys were mainly from the 'inferior classes' (F. Hannam-Clark, *Memories of the College School, Gloucester* (Gloucester 1890), p. 79). Dean Alford said of the Canterbury choristers in 1869 that they were 'at present the least satisfactory part of our establishment, owing to the mingled influences under which their boyhood is passed' (H. Alford, 'Cathedral Reform', *Contemporary Review*, vol.xii, September 1869, p. 46); cf. n. 393 above. Hillsman believes that around the middle of the century Salisbury and Lincoln may have been the only cathedrals to board even some of their choristers (Hillsman, p. 303).

487 ABDC Hereford, 10 November 1859.

488 ibid., 23 September 1861. In 1868 the dean and chapter of Hereford told the Ecclesiastical Commissioners: 'We are now arranging with one of the assistant vicars to take some of the choristers to board and lodge in his house, the parents paying £20 p.a. toward the expence thereof and we paying £10 p.a. for boys over 12 and £5 for boys under 12' (CCF 32508). At Peterborough the choristers boarded until 1879, when the organist, Haydn Keeton, wanted to have only day-boys in the choir. Eventually only two of the choristers continued to board (ABDC Peterborough, 9 January 1879, cited in Coghlan, pp. 122–3).

489 Prestige, pp. 156–7. The foundation-stone of the new school was laid in January 1874 during a snow-storm. The choir sang at this and their wet surplices were dried before evensong over the vestry fire by Green, the head verger (Frost, p. 54).

490 Johnston, p. 142. For the arrangements for the choristers at St Paul's in the 1840s, cf. Prestige, pp. 47–50.

491 Chadwick, *York*, p. 301.

492 PP 1884, xxii, p. 95. Leaving presents of £20 were paid to the choristers at Ely, but at Peterborough they had to make do with a 5s book. The leaving scholarships at St Paul's totalled £250 in 1888 (ABDC Ely, 19 February 1864; ABDC Peterborough, 29 March 1905; St Paul's CM, 8 November 1888, all cited in Coghlan, p. 123).

493 ABDC Hereford, 3 April 1884.

494 ABDC Bristol, 13 December 1888.

495 Barrington-Baker, *passim*.

496 Swistead, pp. 10, 12. Dean Goulburn attempted to found a guild for ex-choristers at Norwich. This was revived in 1893 (ABDC Norwich, 3 December 1901, cited in Coghlan, p. 123).

497 Hillsman, p. 303.

498 Wells CM, 1 July 1899.

499 Walcott, *Traditions*, p. 64.

500 Boutflower, p. 23.

501 ABDC Hereford, 13 November 1823, 23 March 1829.

502 ABDC Salisbury, 7 January 1852.

503 Wells CM, 1 October 1886.

504 ABDC Bristol, 4 January 1900.

505 Robertson, pp. 280–1.

506 Walcott, *Traditions*, p. 88 (quoting *Notes and Queries*, 2nd series, vol.xii, pp. 229, 259); cf. *Chamber's Journal*, 8 January 1887, p. 28.

507 M. Hackett, *Correspondence, Legal Proceedings and Evidences Respecting the Ancient Collegiate School Attached to St Paul's Cathedral* (3rd edn, London 1832), p. 2.

508 Exeter Cathedral Mss., 7061, 7062; cf. also Chappell, pp. 40–1.

509 ABDC Exeter, 3 April 1842.

510 ABDC Winchester, 25 November 1864.

511 ABDC Chichester, 20 January 1871; cf. also 31 August 1876, 1 August 1890.

512 Gloucester chapter minute book, 31 March 1875.

513 ABDC Worcester, 26 January 1879; cf. also 21 November 1881. For a good description of the atmosphere of these Glee Clubs in about 1870, cf. J. N. Moore, *Edward Elgar: A Creative Life* (Oxford 1984), pp. 44–5.

514 Kitton, pp. 18–19.

515 Crosby, p. 32.

516 ABDC Winchester, 23 June 1812, 23 June 1814; cf. Crook, *A History of the Pilgrims' School*, p. 14; Crook, 'Fifty Years of Choral Misrule', p. 34.

517 Quoted in T. F. Bumpus, vol.II, p. 286.

518 Winchester Cathedral Mss., Reports on Choristers, 1819–22, 2 September 1820.

519 F. Bussby, *Winchester Cathedral 1079–1979* (Southampton 1979, second edn 1987), p. 209, and Crook, *A History of the Pilgrims' School*, p. 15; Crook, 'Fifty Years of Choral Misrule', pp. 34–5. Bussby calls him 'the villain of the choir'.

520 Bp.Carr's Injunctions (F. G. Bennett, R. H. Codrington and C. Deedes, p. 50).

521 ABDC Chichester, 20 January 1828; cf. ABDC Exeter, 12 January 1828.

522 cf. ABDC Worcester, 23 September 1842; ABDC Exeter, 3 July 1847; Crosby, p. 30.

523 Robertson, p. 269.

524 Elvey, p. 4.

525 Robertson, p. 275.

526 Crosby, p. 32.

527 ABDC Peterborough, 26 January 1849, cited in Coghlan, p. 139.

528 Kitton, p. 9. But corporal punishment was not unknown at Norwich. Dean Goulburn wrote in 1868: 'After Church the Precentor and I examined into Livock's conduct, and finding that the charges of drunkenness and lying were substantiated, had him caned by Alden. Fearnside was also caned; and Butler and Livock were excluded from the Firework supper on Thursday next' (NCL, Goulburn's diary, 25 June 1868, cf. 8 September 1868). In December 1868 Goulburn complained of the boys fidgeting in the organ gallery (ibid., 31 December 1868).

529 ABDC Hereford, 14 January 1869; cf. 25 July 1882.

530 ABDC Worcester, 19 January and 10 July 1878; cf. 31 March 1877 and Precentor's Report, 1878.

531 Wells CM, 1 February 1878.

532 ibid., 30 December 1884.

533 ibid., 17 October 1888.

534 ibid., 9 January 1899.

535 Wells CM, 25 May 1899.

536 ibid., 28 May 1900. There was an apparently similar difficult incident at Norwich in 1867, involving a chorister named Kendall and a Mr Chamberlain. But Kendall's father had been caught stealing pears and Dean Goulburn threw him out of the deanery (cf. NCL, Goulburn's diary, 7–10 June and 13–16 June 1868).

537 cf. ABDC Worcester, 7 September 1818, 6 August 1829.

538 ABDC Hereford, 27 September 1831.

539 ibid., 27 October 1834.

540 ABDC Worcester, 22 November 1881.
541 ABDC Hereford, 24 March and 9 April 1888.
542 T. F. Bumpus, vol.I, pp. 162–3; cf. F. G. Edwards, 'The Musical Associations of Salisbury Cathedral', *MT*, February 1903.
543 Report of Parratt to dean and chapter, 23 July 1877 (Worc. C. Mss., Precentor's Reports); cf. ABDC Worcester, 7 August 1877, and Barrett, 'English Cathedral Choirs in the Nineteenth Century', pp. 34–5. For some general details of the choristers at Norwich at this time, cf. PP 1884, xxii, p. 95. Ouseley and W. D. V. Duncombe examined the probationers at Hereford in 1870, but regarded their musical progress as unsatisfactory: 'more especially as to reading music from note – of this we cannot say that one seemed to have an idea: they all seemed to know what they do *entirely by ear* which we cannot consider an altogether satisfactory or safe system' (ABDC Hereford, 25 June 1870).
544 ABDC Worcester, 31 March 1877.
545 Worc. C. Mss., Precentor's Report, 1878.
546 ibid., Precentor's Report, 1879; ABDC Worcester, 3 December 1879.
547 ABDC Worcester, 26 January 1879, 21 November 1881.
548 ibid., 20 March 1882.
549 cf. Craze, pp. 223–4, 246–7, 258; ABDC Worcester, 22 November 1881, 19 June 1882; L. Creighton, *Life and Letters of Mandell Creighton* (London 1904), vol.I, p. 311; Worc. C. Mss., Precentor's Reports, 1892–3.
550 ABDC Worcester, 22 January 1884.
551 Creighton, vol.I, p. 397; cf. F. Alford, pp. 284, 472, for a similar custom at Canterbury.
552 Hackett, *Brief Account* (1873 edition), pp. 5, 8–9.
553 NCL, Goulburn's diary, 10 July 1867.
554 ibid., 14 July 1868; cf. 4 July 1868.
555 ibid., 1 January 1869; a week earlier, on Christmas Day, they were given shillings and mince pies (ibid., 25 December 1868).
556 Coghlan, citing ABDC Ely, 25 November 1816.
557 Kitton, p. 18. Dean Goulburn spoke warmly of Canon Sedgwick in his reply to the questionnaire issued by a Lambeth committee of eight deans and canons in March 1872. He described him as 'the great pride and boast of our chapter, one who at the age of 86 is in brightness of mind, tenderness of heart, singleness of purpose, and general force of character, worth all the rest of us put together' (Bristol DC/1/A/7/6/2); cf. Clark and Hughes, especially vol.II, pp. 578–9.
558 ABDC Exeter, 21 February 1863. For some of the entertainments and leisure pursuits of the choristers at Salisbury, cf. Robertson, pp. 317–21, 327–30.
559 'Noted English Choirs', *The Churchman*, vol.lxxvii, no. 2765, 15 January 1898.
560 *Guardian*, 1898, p. 564.
561 ibid., p. 1143.
562 *Guardian*, 1898, pp. 1142–3.
563 J. W. F. Hill, p. 301, fn. 1.
564 Kitton, p. 86.
565 *Guardian*, 1858, p. 564.
566 ABDC Worcester, 26 April 1873.
567 Prestige, pp. 156, 158. Half-holidays for each chorister once a fortnight were introduced at Wells in 1885 (Wells CM, 1 July 1885) and they were allowed thirteen days in the summer – but only two boys could be absent each Sunday (ibid., 16 June 1887).
568 ABDC Worcester, 12 January, 27 February, 17 November 1888.
569 Worc. C. Mss., H. Woodward to Canon Melville, 8 January 1888, Precentor's Reports. In 1879 the dean and chapter of Exeter decided to discontinue sending all the choristers away at once and reverted to the older custom of sending two of

them on holiday at a time (ABDC Exeter, 30 April 1879).

570 Worc. C. Mss., Precentor's Report, 1890. At Bristol the lay clerks were obliged to take their holidays in August, but were also obliged to ensure that six lay clerks were always present except on the Sunday during the annual cleaning of the cathedral, which was sung by trebles only (ABDC Bristol, 7 January 1887). At Peterborough the lay clerks had two weeks' holiday each year with a rota of half-day absences on Mondays (ABDC Peterborough, 23 May 1868, quoted in Coghlan, p. 119).

571 D. Scott, *The Music of St Paul's Cathedral* (London 1972), p. 26.

572 Prestige, p. 85.

573 ibid., p. 154.

574 *CT*, 2 February 1877, quoted in Charlton, pp. 57–8.

575 Worc. C. Add. Mss., 104, p. 4–5; 141, pp. 32, 35.

576 Worc. C. Add. Mss., 128, p. 8.

577 ABDC Worcester, 19 November 1874.

578 ibid., 31 March 1877.

579 Hillsman, p. 320, quoting *The Choir*, 22 August 1874, p. 114.

580 Worc. C. Mss., Bundle marked 'Voluntary Choir'. In February 1888 the dean and chapter consented to the use of the lower hall in Edgar Tower for voluntary choir practices, and allowed the boys to wear college caps and the arms of the cathedral (ABDC Worcester, 27 February 1888).

581 ibid., Voluntary Choir Report 1888.

582 ibid., Voluntary Choir Report 1889–90. The dean and chapter required a certificate of character from the incumbent for every new member of the choir (ABDC Worcester, 19 November 1891).

583 ibid., Voluntary Choir Report, 1892.

584 ibid., Voluntary Choir Reports, 1893–4, 1899.

585 ABDC Worcester, 26 February 1894.

586 ABDC Worcester, 19 November 1897, 6 January 1899.

587 J. M. Elvy, *Recollections of the Cathedral and Parish Church of Manchester* (Manchester 1913), p. 35; cf. Hillsman, p. 320.

588 A. Westcott, *Life and Letters of Brooke Foss Westcott* (London 1903), vol. I, pp. 313, 358, 364. There was opposition to the voluntary choir at Peterborough from Haydn Keeton, the cathedral organist. He refused to work with it in 1891 and wanted it to be disbanded (ABDC Peterborough, 29 December 1891, cited in Coghlan, p. 144).

589 Winchester Cathedral Mss., *Winchester Cathedral Chronicle, 1873–91*, p. 39; the voluntary choir at Gloucester had 100 singers in 1886 (Hillsman, p. 320, citing *MT*, 1 November 1886, p. 641).

590 ABDC Exeter, 6 June 1896.

CHAPTER 9 *Capitular Estates and Finance*

1 At Chichester in 1825 Bishop Carr instructed the dignitaries and prebendaries to send the counterparts of their leases to be entered in a special book kept by the dean and chapter (F. G. Bennett, R. H. Codrington and C. Deedes, *Statutes and Constitutions of the Cathedral Church of Chichester* (Chichester 1904), pp. 49f.).

2 G. F. A. Best, *Temporal Pillars* (Cambridge 1964), p. 370. For contemporary secular practice, cf. F. M. L. Thompson, *English Landed Society in the Nineteenth Century* (London 1963), p. 229. For the procedure at Worcester, cf. ABDC Worcester, 24 June 1811.

3 PP 1839, viii, p. 245.

4 ABDC Exeter, 29 July 1853; ABDC Bristol, 25 June 1844. In 1809–10 the chapter clerk at Bristol was responsible for collecting rents from 218 properties belonging to the dean and chapter (Bristol Cathedral Archives, DC E/4/3). In 1831 the dean

and chapter of Wells were involved in a difficult situation when they tried to prevent floodwater flowing from a neighbouring garden into houses leased by them in the market place, and they encountered opposition from the Misses Parfitt who currently occupied the garden (Wells CM, 6 December 1831).

5 C. K. F. Brown, *A History of the English Clergy, 1800–1900* (London 1953), p. 50.

6 PP 1854, xxv, p. 55.

7 Gloucestershire CRO, D 936 A 20. In 1838 Messrs Whitcombe and Helps, who acted for the dean and chapter, told Mr C. Canning that 'the custom of the Chapter is to have their houses and property valued previous to a renewal of the leases; and upon that valuation they calculate the fine' (Gloucestershire CRO, D 936 C1/1. 96, 16 June 1838).

8 Brown, p. 45; PP 1835, xxii, pp. 36f.

9 Anon, *Cathedral Wealth and Cathedral Work* (London 1861), p. 12 fn.

10 Worc. C. Mss., Bundle marked 'Ecclesiastical Commissioners'. The amounts received from fines in 1810, 1820 and 1830 respectively at Worcester were £3,830 10s 9d, £941 5s 6d and £5,460 14s 4d (Worc. C. Mss., Receiver-General's Accounts, ad.loc.). For a list of fines totalling £85, 224 11s 6d received between 1838 and 1859, cf. Salisbury DRO, Press V, Box 5 (bundle of miscellaneous papers).

11 PP 1854, xxv, p. 58.

12 Salisbury Chapter Muniments, Press I, Box 39, p. 91, Minutes of Oral Evidence.

13 PP 1854, xxv, pp. 876–8, quoted in Best, p. 459.

14 S. Smith, *Second Letter to Archdeacon Singleton* (London 1838), p. 8.

15 cf. Chapter 5, pp. 79–81. Christopher Hodgson served as registrar, chapter clerk and bailiff of the manors and bailiwicks at St Paul's from 1802 to 1869 and William Sellon served there as receiver and steward of the manors from 1835 to 1869 (G. L. Prestige, *St Paul's in its Glory, 1831–1911* (London 1855), p. 91.

16 ABDC Gloucester, 30 November 1802.

17 ABDC Worcester, 23 November 1822. The chapter clerk of Bristol was asked to attend the yearly progress in 1825 if the dean was unable to do so (ABDC Bristol, 23 June 1825).

18 PP 1854, xxv, pp. 854–5.

19 Worc. C. Mss., Receiver-General's Accounts 1800.

20 Gloucester Cathedral Mss., Treasurer's Accounts 1786–1840, p. 400. For full details of the tenant holdings, buildings and fields of each estate owned by the dean and chapter of Gloucester in the early nineteenth century, together with the amounts of arable, meadow, and pasture land, the tenants, terms of leases and rents, cf. Gloucestershire CRO, D 1740/E2; D 936/E/3/1–2, p. 6. The dean and chapter of Ely employed a gamekeeper (P. V. Coghlan, 'Cathedral Worship in the Church of England 1815–1914' (Leicester University M. Phil. thesis 1984), p. 97.

21 ABDC Hereford, 11 November 1830.

22 Gloucestershire CRO, D 936/E/254, General Estate Correspondence 1842–9. For general regulations about the timber on the estates of the dean and chapter of Gloucester, drawn up in 1847, cf. Gloucestershire CRO, D 936/CI/4, p. 371.

23 Wells CM, 7 December 1858.

24 ABDC Chichester, 20 January 1866.

25 ABDC Hereford, 18 September 1800.

26 ABDC Gloucester, 30 November 1815.

27 ABDC Salisbury, 4 January 1837.

28 Best, p. 372. For some severe criticisms of the chapters at Lincoln and Gloucester at this time, cf. Anon, *Cathedral Wealth and Cathedral Work* (London 1861).

29 W. Heseltine, *A Tenant's Statement of the Conduct Recently Pursued towards Him by the Dean and Chapter of Canterbury at the Occasion of His Renewing His Lease* (2nd edn, London 1839).

30 PP 1854, xxv, p. 56. Some of these estates were very valuable. The prebend of Finsbury at St Paul's was worth £7,000 in 1859 and was bringing in nearly ten times this amount by 1872 (Prestige, p. 68). Some individual estates were commuted, especially at York, and this led to the commutation of corporate estates. Dean Cockburn of York had particularly prolonged negotiations with the Ecclesiastical Commissioners over his estates (Chadwick, *York*, p. 291); for the York estates, cf. A. S. Leak, 'Conflict and Reform at York Minster in the Nineteenth Century' (Oxford B. D. thesis 1988), pp. 196–255.

31 PP 1854, xxv, p. 57.

32 Best, pp. 455–6.

33 O. J. Brose, *Church and Parliament* (Stanford USA 1959), p. 165; cf. Best, pp. 378f.

34 PP 1850, xx, pp. 35f. For an example of a capitular reply to the Commission's enquiries, cf. ABDC Hereford, 12 February 1849.

35 ABDC Winchester, 30 May 1851. Two years later a meeting was held in the Jerusalem Chamber at Westminster Abbey between the cathedral commissioners and representatives of chapters about the management of capitular estates (ABDC Exeter, 29 September 1853).

36 For further details of this Bill and the recommendations of Ralph Barnes, the chapter clerk at Exeter, cf. Brose, p. 167. Lord Blandford wished to transfer the whole management of episcopal and capitular property to the Ecclesiastical Commissioners, but he was thwarted year after year by those who feared that this would effectively imply a change of ownership (ibid., p. 173).

37 31 & 32 Vict., c. 114; cf. Prestige, p. 72; R. Phillimore, *The Ecclesiastical Law of the Church of England* (London 1895), vol. I, p. 188, and vol. II, p. 1669. Eighteen chapters acted in this way between 1852 and 1867 and eventually only Hereford, Manchester and Christ Church, Oxford, remained independent (cf. L. T. Dibdin and S. E. Downing, *The Ecclesiastical Commission* (London 1919), pp. 39f. for a useful summary of these matters).

38 J. E. Prescott, *The Statutes of the Cathedral Church of Carlisle* (Carlisle 1879), p. 16; Chadwick, *York*, p. 292. The value of the commutation payment at Chester was £5,680 per annum (PP 1864, xliv, p. 31).

39 For a good example of the negotiations involved, cf. Salisbury DRO, Press V, Box 5 (bundle of miscellaneous papers) and ABDC Salisbury, 5, 7 and 27 August 1861, and 23 July 1874. In 1875 the dean and chapter of Salisbury were re-endowed with property worth £4,700 per annum (K. Edwards, 'The Cathedral of Salisbury, 1075–1950', *VCH Wiltshire*, vol. iii, 1956, pp. 203–4). The total value of the capitular estates in the hands of the Ecclesiastical Commission in 1871 was estimated to be £8,123,000 (PP 1871, lv, pp. 246–7) with a further £4,530,000 worth of other estates which had not been fully valued.

40 ABDC Gloucester, 3 May and 6 July 1855, 16 April 1866, and Gloucester Cathedral Archives no. 69; cf. also I. M. Kirby, *Diocese of Gloucester: A Catalogue of the Records of the Dean and Chapter including the former St Peter's Abbey* (Gloucester 1967), p. xiv. For details of the commutation of the capitular estates at Chichester, cf. ABDC Chichester, 10 October and 26 November 1859, 2 March 1860; and W. K. L. Clarke, *Chichester Cathedral in the Nineteenth Century* (Chichester Papers no. 14, Chichester 1959), p. 10; for the commutation and re-endowment of the Worcester estates, cf. ABDC Worcester, 29 and 30 November 1859, 22 November 1869, an Order in Council of 29 November 1859 published in the *London Gazette* on 16 December 1859 and 'Record of some of the Principal Events relating to the Cathedral of Worcester, the Dean and Chapter and their property', pp. 13–16. R. B. Lockett says that they were commuted in return for £15,300 per annum (R. B. Lockett, 'The Victorian Restoration of Worcester Cathedral', *Mediaeval Art and Architecture at Worcester Cathedral* (British Archaeological Association Conference Transactions for the Year

1975), p. 167). For the details at Winchester, cf. ABDC Winchester, 1 February, 4 May, 23 June, 1 October 1860, 25 March and 25 April 1861, and 29 September 1864; for the commutation of the Bristol estates, cf. R. J. Fletcher, *A History of Bristol Cathedral* (London 1932), pp. 62–3, and ABDC Bristol, 6 November 1860, 5 March 1861, 21 January and 17 April 1862; for St Paul's, cf. Prestige, pp. 72, 114 and 123–4; W. H. Hutton, ed., *The Autobiography of Robert Gregory* (London 1912), pp. 189–90 and PP 1883, xxi, p. 115. The capitular estates at Exeter were commuted in 1862 for £11,500 per annum (ABDC Exeter, 9 August 1862). The dean and chapter of Lincoln were criticized for their slowness in commuting their estates (cf. J. W. F. Hill, *Victorian Lincoln* (London 1974), p. 129) and eventually made a bad bargain in 1870 (ibid., p. 267). Many estate documents were also transferred to the commissioners (cf. D. M. Williamson, *Lincoln Muniments* (Lincoln 1956), pp. 12–13). The estates of Canterbury Cathedral were commuted for £17,500 per annum (C. E. Woodruff and W. Danks, *Memorials of the Cathedral and Priory of Christ in Canterbury* (London 1912), pp. 364–5; cf. also C. Jenkins, ed., *The Statutes of the Cathedral and Metropolitical Church of Christ, Canterbury* (Canterbury 1925), pp. 130f. The dean and chapter of Hereford opened negotiations about the commutation of their estates in 1866 and agreed to the proposed terms five years later, but the scheme was left in abeyance (ABDC Hereford, 25 June 1866, 11 December 1871). For Wells, cf. ABDC Wells, 9 July 1866, Wells CM, 1 February 1856, 10 March 1866, 1 October 1877. For Gloucester, cf. ABDC Gloucester, 3 May 1855.

41 Dibdin and Downing, p. 43.

42 *Contemporary Review*, vol. II, May–August 1866, p. 244.

43 *Guardian*, 1884, p. 45.

44 LPL, Benson Papers, I, p. 412.

45 Thompson, pp. 308–10; P. J. Perry, ed., *British Agriculture 1875–1914* (London 1973), pp. xviii–xx; F. M. L. Thompson in G. E. Mingay, ed., *The Victorian Countryside* (London 1981), vol. I, pp. 108–9. For the impact of the Agricultural Depression on the University of Oxford and its colleges, cf. A. J. Engel, *From Clergyman to Don* (Oxford 1983), pp. 202–56.

46 E. L. Jones, *Seasons and Prices* (London 1964), pp. 87, 175; Perry, p. xviii; P. J. Perry, *British Farming in the Great Depression 1870–1914* (Newton Abbot 1974), p. 57.

47 Perry, *British Agriculture 1875–1914*, p. xiv.

48 R. S. Sayers, *A History of Economic Change in England, 1880–1939* (London 1967), p. 108.

49 Perry, *British Agriculture 1875–1914*, pp. xxi, 7, 10; Jones, pp. 176–7; Sayers, p. 109; J. H. Clapham, *An Economic History of Modern Britain* (Cambridge 1952), vol. III, pp. 75, 78; F. M. L. Thompson in Mingay, vol. I, p. 109.

50 Perry, *British Agriculture 1875–1914*, p. vii; F. M. L. Thompson in Mingay, vol. I, p. 111.

51 ABDC Salisbury, 1878–89; cf. n. 39 above. For York, cf. Leak, pp. 218–20.

52 W. O. Chadwick, *The Victorian Church* (London 1970), vol. II, p. 367.

53 ABDC Gloucester, 8 January, 25 March, 24 June 1884, 28 January 1885, 27–28 September and 20 December 1886.

54 Gloucester CRO, D 936 C/5.

55 ABDC Gloucester, 1–2 July and 29–30 September 1887. Stipends were also reduced at Norwich about this time (F. Bates, *Reminiscences and Autobiography of a Musician in Retirement* (Norwich 1930), p. 52). It is said that at Gloucester, when Dean Spence-Jones greeted the organist, C. Lee-Williams, on the first Christmas Day after this reduction, he said, 'A happy Christmas, Mr Organist'; to which Lee-Williams replied, 'The same to you, Mr Dean, less ten per cent' (H. W. Sumsion, 'Random Reminiscences', in B. Still, ed., *250 Years of the Three Choirs Festival* (Hereford 1977), p. 52.

56 ABDC Exeter, 21 May 1887, 24 April 1888, 9 May 1891, 29 April 1892.

57 *Guardian*, 1885, p. 645. In 1884 the dean and chapter told the Ecclesiastical Commissioners that the £6,450 per annum that they received from them under the terms of the commutation agreement in 1860 was insufficient and pleaded for extra grants under the Act of 1866 (29 & 30 Vict., c. 111) to cover the stipends they paid to the organist, lay vicars, officers and other servants of the cathedral and to improve the choir school (Win. CA, Ecclesiastical Commissioners Box).

58 Win. CA, Ecclesiastical Commissioners Box, 5 February 1884. The dean and chapter had suspended their charitable donations the year before (ABDC Winchester, 3 March 1883).

59 LPL, Benson Papers, I, pp. 399f.

60 ibid., pp. 410–11; cf. Treasury Minute, 17 August 1883.

61 NCL, Goulburn's diary, 30 November 1886; ABDC Salisbury, 25 June 1888; Salisbury CM, 1 November 1887.

62 Edwards, p. 205.

63 ABDC Chichester, 17 February 1890.

64 ABDC Bristol, 8 July 1890.

65 *CCR* 1894, pp. 32–3; cf. also C. Wordsworth and D. Macleane, *Statutes and Customs of the Cathedral Church of the Blessed Virgin Mary at Salisbury* (London 1915), p. 486.

66 ABDC Gloucester, 28 April and 26 May 1893, 25 January, 1 March, 23 May and 7 September 1894; Kirby, p. xiv. Under the Tithe Act of 1891, unpaid tithe could be recovered through the County Courts (cf. G. E. Mingay, *Rural Life in Victorian England* (London 1977), p. 151).

67 *CCR* 1894, pp. 32–3; Gloucestershire CRO, D 936 A/3 (printed summaries of treasurer's and receiver's accounts).

68 ABDC Salisbury, 5 March, 3 August, 4 November 1895, 10 April 1896. For the agreement reached with the dean and chapter of Winchester, cf. ABDC Winchester, 28 July 1898, 31 January and 28 February 1899. The national average rent per acre fell from 29s 4d in 1875–7 to 20s in 1899–1900. For a comparison between the average rent of agricultural land in England and Wales in 1900, 1872, 1877 and 1846, cf. R. J. Thompson, 'An Inquiry into the Rent of Agricultural Land in England and Wales during the Nineteenth Century', in W. E. Minchinton, ed., *Essays in Agrarian History* (Newton Abbot 1968), vol. II, pp. 65, 66, 72.

69 Gloucestershire CRO, D 936/C2, file 599, bundle no. 1, letter of 5 May 1879.

70 ibid., Whitcombe to Tinling, 27 January 1880.

71 ibid., Field and Castle to Whitcombe, 17 February 1880.

72 ibid., Evans to Whitcombe, 15 April 1880; Whitcombe to Evans, 27 March 1880.

73 ibid., Evans to Whitcombe, 28 March 1880.

74 ibid., Evans to Whitcombe, 20 June 1880.

75 ibid., Evans to Whitcombe, 29 September 1880. The agent of Christ Church, Oxford, admitted in 1883 that it was impossible to let land at its proper value: 'It is notorious that the number of farms vacant far exceeds the number of tenants with sufficient capital who are able and willing to take them, and the rental, if the landlord is determined to let, will be fixed by what a tenant can be found to give, rather than by what ought to be obtained.' Four years later a rent rebate of 15 per cent from the dean and chapter of Christ Church was made conditional on the tenant remaining on the farm (P. L. R. Horn, *The Changing Countryside in Victorian and Edwardian England and Wales* (London 1984), pp. 34–5, quoting Christ Church estate records). One tenant of Christ Church in 1878 was so much in arrears with his rent that the dean and chapter seized his belongings and retained him only as a farm manager. He lost everything in this disaster, even his furniture (ibid., pp. 71–2).

76 Gloucestershire CRO, D 936/C2, file 599, bundle no. 1, Foreshew to Whitcombe, 21 February 1881.

77 ibid., Evans to Whitcombe, 17 March 1881.

78 ibid., Whitcombe to Foreshew, 4 July 1881.

79 Rent reductions were common on comparable secular estates, including that of the Duke of Bedford (cf. Perry, *British Agriculture 1875–1914*, pp. xxv–vi, quoting Duke of Bedford, *A Great Agricultural Estate* (London 1897), pp. 116–22. The Marquess of Ailesbury's Savernake estate was heavily in debt by 1895, and Lord Stradbrooke's Suffolk estate had a rental income in 1895 which was only a third of that received in 1877. The Duke of Richmond and Gordon at Goodwood was also suffering from a diminished income (Horn, p. 32).

80 ABDC Gloucester, 30 November 1808; cf. above, Chapter 1, n. 63.

81 Gloucestershire CRO, D 936 C1/1, p. 96, Whitcombe to Selwyn, 25 November 1837; cf. also Whitcombe to Dean, 18 November 1840.

82 ibid., 30 November 1815.

83 Bristol DC/A/7/3/4.

84 Gloucestershire CRO, D 936/C2, file 599. For details of audit dinners at Winchester in the early nineteenth century, cf. Chapter 1, p. 9; for an example of a secular audit dinner in the late nineteenth century, cf. Mingay, *Rural Life in Victorian England*, pp. 130, 142–3.

85 ABDC Chichester, 1 August 1865.

86 Worc. C. Mss., Receiver-General's Accounts 1800–50.

87 Worc. C. Mss., Treasurer's Accounts 1800–1900.

88 Gloucestershire CRO, D 936 A/1/9 (Treasurer's Accounts 1786–1810). The total capitular income at Bristol in 1810 was £1,767 11s 4d, with expenditure amounting to £1,712 15s. In the second half of the nineteenth century these figures had risen to an average of £9,000 (Bristol Capitular Archives, DC E/4/3). For the income and expenditure of the dean and chapter of Winchester in 1873, cf. ABDC Winchester, 19 November 1873.

89 Win. CA, Treasurer's Book, 1794–1804.

90 ibid., 1805–22, 1838–45, 1845–68.

91 Salisbury Cathedral Archives, Communar's Accounts 1770–1833, Master of the Fabric Account Book 1794–1810, 1828–32, Clerk of the Works Weekly Accounts 1791–1802; cf. also ABDC Salisbury, 27 January 1849, for a general account of the financial administration of the dean and chapter of Salisbury, and ibid., 4 May 1853, for new provisions.

92 Wordsworth and Macleane, pp. 456f.

93 West Sussex CRO, Cap. 1/23/6, Communar's Accounts 1821–65.

94 ABDC Chichester, 2 May 1815.

95 ABDC Hereford, 13 October 1829.

96 Prestige, p. 24.

97 R. V. H. Burne, *Chester Cathedral* (London 1958), pp. 237–9.

98 Chadwick, *York*, p. 279.

99 Edwards, p. 201.

100 PP 1835, xxii, pp. 36f.

	Average gross yearly income	Average yearly payments	Average net yearly income
Bristol	4,280	1,191	3,629
Canterbury†	21,551	5,569	15,982
Carlisle	6,443	1,125	5,318
Chester	2,135	1,501	634
Chichester	5,361	1,416	3,721
Durham	35,071	27,933	7,138

Ely	8,651	2,246	6,405
Exeter	10,438	2,782	7,052
Gloucester	5,407	1,510	3,897
Hereford	4,426	822	3,544
Lichfield	1,638	327	1,311
Lincoln	7,692	706	6,986
Norwich	7,811	2,566	5,245
Christ Church, Oxon*	25,899	12,663	12,203
St Paul's, London	11,140	1,710	9,049
Peterborough	6,357	1,239	5,118
Rochester	7,178	2,072	5,106
Salisbury	3,176	377	2,799
Wells	8,378	1,799	6,579
Winchester	15,573	2,790	12,783
Worcester	12,088	3,609	8,479
York	1,788	138	1,352

† cf. Woodruff and Danks, pp. 364–5.
* Cathedral and College.
For details of receipts and expenditure at most cathedrals in England in 1860–3, cf. PP 1865, xli, pp. 441–50, 454–5, 457–74, 477–93. Unfortunately these details are presented in such a diverse way that it is impossible to make an accurate comparison between different cathedrals at the time.

101 Chadwick, *York*, pp. 287–8; R. Whiston, *Cathedral Trusts and Their Fulfilment* (London 1849), p. 24. Tait referred in 1853 to the widespread impression that capitular property was administered 'so as to promote the private interests of the members of the several chapters than to make it produce the greatest amount of good to the Church and the nation' (*Cathedral Wealth and Cathedral Work*, (London 1861), title page).
102 PP 1854, xxv, pp. 55–7.
103 Bristol Capitular Archives, DC/E/4/54.
104 ABDC Exeter, 3 February 1849.
105 W. K. Hamilton, *Cathedral Reform: A Letter to the Members of His Diocese* (London, Oxford and Salisbury 1855), p. 18; cf. Chapter 5, p. 61.
106 ABDC Chichester, 20 January and 2 May 1860. For further details of the finances of Chichester Cathedral in the early nineteenth century, cf. Clarke, pp. 9–10; cf. ABDC Gloucester, 22 June 1855; Wells CM, 31 August 1866.
107 ABDC Chichester, 1 August 1865; for Canterbury, cf. *Contemporary Review*, vol. II, May–August 1866, p. 499.
108 ABDC Salisbury, 13 November 1863.
109 H. Goodwin, notes written on 4 July 1883, in LPL, Benson Papers, I, p. 407.
110 ABDC Winchester, 24 March 1871, 9 December 1876.
111 ABDC Salisbury, 2 March 1875.
112 PP 1884, xxii, p. 271.
113 ABDC Worcester, 19 November 1877, 19 November 1878, 2 December 1879. H. W. Massingham gives the impression that only at five cathedrals (Chester, St Paul's, Norwich, Carlisle and Durham) was a special fabric fund established, and only at Chester, where £2,400 was set aside, were the funds for repairs adequate. Other cathedrals besides these five had fabric funds (H. W. Massingham, 'The Nationalisation of Cathedrals', *Contemporary Review*, vol. 60, no. 309, September 1891, pp. 366–7).
114 Chadwick, vol. II, p. 369. For the balance sheet at Wells in 1878, cf. PP 1883, xxi,

p. 255. In 1882 the dean and chapter of Wells asked for an increased grant from the Ecclesiastical Commissioners to improve the 'scanty and inadequate' stipends of the priest vicars (Wells CM, 2 January 1882). For details of capitular expenditure at St Paul's in 1877–9, cf. PP 1883, xxi, p. 115.
115 Cf. above, pp. 220–3.
116 ABDC Winchester, 31 October 1893.
117 cf. above, n. 57.
118 Win. CA, Davidson's visitation Mss.
119 ibid.
120 Woodruff and Danks, pp. 369–70.
121 Clarke, p. 10; ABDC Chichester, 20 January 1899.
122 Hutton, pp. 180–1, 189–91.

CHAPTER 10 *Cathedral Restoration in the Nineteenth Century*
1 *Guardian*, 1874, p. 1476.
2 Chadwick, *York*, pp. 274–5, 280.
3 *Gentleman's Magazine*, vol. lxxii, January 1802, pt 1, p. 31.
4 Quoted in D. King, 'Winchester Cathedral under Deans Rennell and Garnier', *Winchester Cathedral Chronicle*, 1972; cf. above, Chapter 1, p. 2.
5 R. B. Lockett, 'The Victorian Restoration of Worcester Cathedral', *Mediaeval Art and Architecture at Worcester Cathedral* (British Archaeological Association Conference Transactions for the year 1975), p. 162.
6 *Ecclesiologist*, vol. 4 (new series vol. 1), nos. 1–6, January–November 1845, pp. 43–4, quoted in D. I. Hill, *Christ's Glorious Church* (London 1976), p. 77.
7 PP 1854, xxv, pp. 52–3.
8 Quoted in G. Cobb, *English Cathedrals: The Forgotten Centuries* (London 1980), p. 79; for a full account, cf. pp. 80–3.
9 Cobb, p. 82, quoting J. W. Hewett, *A Brief History and Description of the Conventual and Cathedral Church of the Holy Trinity, Ely* (1848), p. 22. For minor restorations at Ely in the nineteenth century, cf. P. V. Coghlan, 'Cathedral Worship in the Church of England 1815–1914' (Leicester University M. Phil. thesis 1984), pp. 32–4; for major restoration work, cf. ibid., pp. 51–7.
10 P. C. Moore, *Three Restorations of Ely Cathedral* (Ely 1973), pp. 10–12; B. E. Dorman, *The Story of Ely and its Cathedral* (new edn, Ely 1980), pp. 66–7. An American visitor noted that during the restoration of the quire, services were held in the chapel at the west end (T. F. Bumpus, *The Cathedrals of England and Wales* (London 1905), vol. I, p. 129).
11 *Guardian*, 1847, p. 366.
12 G. G. Scott, *Personal and Professional Recollections* (London 1879), pp. 280f.
13 Moore, p. 12.
14 ibid., pp. 13–14; Dorman, p. 68. For Scott's own account of his work at Ely, cf. Scott, pp. 280–3; cf. also D. Cole, *The Work of Sir Gilbert Scott* (London 1980), pp. 48–50.
15 Cobb, p. 81.
16 ibid.
17 Moore, pp. 12–14; Dorman, p. 68. For Harvey Goodwin's personal interest in restorations and the work done at Ely in his time, cf. H. D. Rawnsley, *Harvey Goodwin, Bishop of Carlisle* (London 1896), pp. 99–101.
18 Dorman, p. 68; Moore gives the total cost down to October 1873 as £70,000 (Moore, p. 14). Over £70,000 was said to have been spent between 1873 and 1898 (Cobb, p. 82).
19 Cobb, p. 81.
20 cf. P. L. S. Barrett, 'John Merewether, Dean of Hereford 1832–50', *FHCAR*, 1977, pp. 23f.
21 ABDC Hereford, 9 December 1835; Barrett, pp. 29–34.

22 J. Merewether, *A Statement of the Condition and Circumstances of the Cathedral Church of Hereford* (Hereford 1842), pp. 6–7.

23 HCA 6170; Barrett, pp. 35–6; Barrett, 'Hereford Cathedral in the Nineteenth Century', *FHCAR*, 1986, pp. 27–9; Merewether, *passim*. For contemporary accounts of the developing work of restoration, cf. *HT*, 1 May, 8 May, 15 May, 22 May, 5 June, 24 July 1841. For Merewether's own account, cf. also ibid., 8 January 1842 and CCF 3208. The cathedral services were held in All Saints' Church from 1842 to 1850 (Bumpus, vol. I, p. 214; J. E. West, *Cathedral Organists Past and Present* (London 1899), p. 43).

24 A. T. Bannister, *The Cathedral Church of Hereford* (London 1924), p. 108.

25 Scott, p. 288; cf. also Cole, pp. 65–6.

26 Scott, pp. 290–1.

27 Anon, *Hereford Cathedral, City and Neighbourhood* (Hereford 1867), pp. 26–7.

28 PP 1884, xxii, p. 203.

29 For a full account, cf. Lockett, pp. 161f., and Lockett's 'George Gilbert Scott, The Joint Restoration Committee and the Refurnishing of Worcester Cathedral 1864–1874', *TWAS*, 3rd series, vol. 6, 1978, pp. 7f.

30 cf. Lockett, 'The Victorian Restoration of Worcester Cathedral', pp. 161–2, quoting *Worcester Cathedral Restoration: Account of Receipts and Expenditure* (1875) and *The Builder*, 5 February 1876.

31 ibid., p. 162.

32 cf. Lockett, 'The Victorian Restoration of Worcester Cathedral', pp. 161, 177.

33 ibid., pp. 164–7.

34 Worc. C. Mss., Restoration Committee Box, Lord Lyttelton to magistrates, 1864.

35 ibid. Scott estimated that the cost of rearranging the quire alone would be £13,000. Lord Dudley said he would only support the appeal if the laymen were involved in superintending the restoration. He eventually gave over £20,000 (Lockett, 'George Gilbert Scott', pp. 8, 26).

36 Lockett, 'The Victorian Restoration of Worcester Cathedral', pp. 171–2.

37 For details of the tower restoration, cf. ibid., pp. 172–3.

38 ibid., p. 175.

39 Quoted in ibid., p. 163.

40 cf. Lockett, 'George Gilbert Scott', pp. 15–19, 21–2.

41 Scott, pp. 343–5.

42 Lockett, 'George Gilbert Scott', pp. 7–8; cf. Cole, pp. 99–110.

43 Lockett, 'George Gilbert Scott', p. 8.

44 ibid., pp. 11–12.

45 ibid., p. 15.

46 ibid., p. 23.

47 ibid., pp. 23–5.

48 *Guardian*, 1874, pp. 454–7; Lockett, 'George Gilbert Scott', p. 26.

49 *Guardian*, 1874, p. 444; cf. Chapter 14, p. 305.

50 W. R. W. Stephens, *The Life and Letters of Walter Farquhar Hook* (London 1885), pp. 521–2, 525, 531–3; cf. W. K. L. Clarke, *Chichester Cathedral in the Nineteenth Century* (Chichester Papers no. 14, Chichester 1959), p. 3.

51 Scott, pp. 309–11; cf. Cole, pp. 93–4.

52 Clarke, p. 4.

53 *Guardian*, 1866, p. 688.

54 J. W. Burgon, *Dr Swainson and the Dean of Chichester: An Address, a Protest and a Correspondence* (Chichester 1878), p. 9; cf. Burgon's *Chichester Cathedral: Suggestions Submitted to the Cathedral Commissioners* (Chichester 1879), pp. 3–4, and PP 1884–5, xxi, p. 367; cf. Chapter 4, p. 49.

55 Chichester general chapter minute book, 13 August 1894.

56 R. J. Fletcher, *A History of Bristol Cathedral* (London 1932), p. 62.
57 Cobb, p. 40.
58 ibid., p. 40, quoting *Ecclesiologist*, vol. 22 (new series vol. 19) nos. 142–147 (new series nos. 106–111), February–December 1861, p. 217.
59 ABDC Bristol, 9 November 1866, 9 May 1876, 17 August 1866; cf. Chapter 11, p. 261.
60 Cobb, p. 41. The *Quarterly Review* said in 1874 that the cost of the nave and west towers was estimated at £55, 000 (*Quarterly Review*, vol. 137, July/October 1874, p. 246). The dean sent an effusive note of thanks to the mayor for his support in the completion of the cathedral in July 1879 (newscutting in ABDC Bristol, 1879–1900).
61 *Guardian*, 1895, p. 689.
62 F. Pigou, *Odds and Ends* (London 1903), p. 265.
63 G. L. Prestige, *St Paul's in its Glory, 1831–1911* (London 1955), p. 3. As late as 1868, St Paul's was still notorious for its dirty condition: 'Dirt and neglect are, I find, the most prominent characteristics of the handsomest edifice of the wealthiest city in the world. The most prominent fact connected with any inspection of the monuments is their filth. Dust which is black in its thickness rests undisturbed upon the handiwork of Chantrey and Flaxman, converting classic groups into piebald monstrosities, turning white black....Black angels are conveying Ethiopian heroes to their long rest. Smutty-faced Britannias vie with much besoiled Glories and Fames in doing honour to English worthies to whom soap and a scrubbing-brush are a first necessity' (quoted in W. M. Sinclair, *Memorials of St Paul's Cathedral* (London 1909), p. 308).
64 Prestige, pp. 42–3. For minor nineteenth-century restoration work at St Paul's, cf. Coghlan, p. 40. For major works, cf. ibid., pp. 72–9; cf. also *Victorian Church Art*, catalogue of an exhibition at the Victoria and Albert Museum, London, 1971–2 (London 1971), pp. 86–9.
65 Prestige, p. 82.
66 ibid., pp. 83f.
67 ibid., p. 112.
68 ibid., p. 124.
69 ibid., p. 132.
70 ibid., p. 141.
71 ibid., pp. 144–6.
72 ibid., pp. 207–8.
73 ibid., pp. 211–13. Liddon was very interested in the design of the new reredos; cf. C. E. Beswick, 'Liddon of St Paul's' (Exeter University MA thesis 1974), p. 15.
74 ibid., pp. 214–15; cf. Sinclair, pp. 378f.
75 ibid., pp. 217–18.
76 C. E. Woodruff and W. Danks, *Memorials of the Cathedral and Priory of Christ in Canterbury* (London 1912), p. 355.
77 ibid., p. 361.
78 ibid., pp. 362, 368. For details of Dean Alford's restorations at Canterbury, cf. F. Alford, *Life, Journals and Letters of Henry Alford, Dean of Canterbury* (London 1873), pp. 536f.
79 R. Farrar, *The Life of Frederic William Farrar, Sometime Dean of Canterbury* (London 1904), pp. 316–17. For an account of this restoration, cf. *Guardian*, 1897, pp. 238–9, 604.
80 R. V. H. Burne, *Chester Cathedral* (London 1958), pp. 234, 243, 245–6.
81 Scott, pp. 330–5; cf. Cole, pp. 89–91, and PP 1883, xxi, p. 158.
82 H. L. Thompson, *Henry George Liddell* (London 1899), pp. 149–52.
83 Cole, p. 140.
84 C. J. Stranks, *This Sumptuous Church* (London 1973), pp. 90f.
86 K. Lake, ed., *Memorials of William Charles Lake* (London 1901), pp. 142–3; cf. J.

Fawcett, ed., *The Future of the Past* (London 1976), p. 93, for a modern account of restoration at Durham.

87 R. J. E. Boggis, *A History of the Diocese of Exeter* (Exeter 1922), p. 529; cf. Scott, pp. 345–7, and Cole, pp. 169–70.
88 *Guardian*, 1855, p. 859.
89 Scott, p. 337; for further details about Gloucester, cf. Cole, pp. 100–2 and D. C. St.V. Welander, *The History, Art and Architecture of Gloucester Cathedral* (Stroud 1991), pp. 428–31, 439–91.
90 *Guardian*, 1897, p. 1555; 1898; p. 118.
91 Cobb, p. 148.
92 Scott, pp. 291–3, 296–7. According to Canon Lonsdale's recollections, the nave was empty of all furniture in 1856 and used only as a promenade by nursery maids with their babies while the services were being sung in the quire (Cobb, p. 148); cf. Cole, pp. 66–7, 193–4.
93 Cobb, p. 149. Cole says that the work between 1877 and 1881 alone cost £165,000 (Cole, p. 194).
94 A. Quiney, *John Loughborough Pearson* (London 1979), pp. 129, 132.
95 J. A. Repton, *Norwich Cathedral at the end of the Eighteenth Century* (ed. S. R. Pierce) (Farnborough 1965), pp. 5–6, quoting *Archaeologia*, vol. xxii, 1847, pp. 405–6.
96 Dean Pellew's note-book, 1829–32, DCN 120/2, Norfolk CRO; Coghlan, p. 38; for minor nineteenth-century restorations, cf. ibid., pp. 36–40; for major restoration work, cf. ibid., pp. 57–63.
97 H. Leeds, *Norwich Cathedral Past and Present* (Norwich 1910), p. 93.
98 NCL, Goulburn's diary, 21 April 1867.
99 H. Leeds, *Life of Dean Lefroy* (Norwich 1909), p. 32. The cloisters were said to be 'falling to pieces' (*Guardian*, 1898, p. 399).
100 R. Hale in C. Barringer, ed., *Norwich in the Nineteenth Century* (Norwich 1984), p. 173.
101 Leeds, *Norwich Cathedral Past and Present*, p. 94.
102 W. C. Lefroy, *Echoes from the Choir of Norwich Cathedral* (London 1894), pp. 14–15. Bates says that Dean Lefroy had a remarkable gift for raising money (F. Bates, *Reminiscences and Autobiography of a Musician in Retirement* (Norwich 1930), p. 49.
103 Fawcett, p. 79; cf. Scott, pp. 298–9: 'For a very long time the Chapter, with one brilliant exception, did all in their power to shut their own eyes and those of the public to the truth. They called in another architect who preached "Peace, peace". They then sent for a third...' Harvey Goodwin said in 1883 that Peterborough was 'suffering from having had a Dean who was fast asleep *qua fabric* for some quarter of a century' (notes by Harvey Goodwin, 4 July 1883, Benson Papers, I, p. 407, LPL). For minor nineteenth-century restorations at Peterborough, cf. Coghlan, pp. 34–6. For major restorations, cf. ibid., pp. 63–72; cf. Cole, p. 67.
104 Fawcett, p. 97; Quiney, pp. 187–8. The Prince of Wales was invited to lay the foundation stone of the new tower, but he sent a substitute (P. Ferriday, *Lord Grimthorpe, 1816–1905* (London 1957), pp. 148).
105 PP 1884–5, xxi, p. 251; for these and later works at Peterborough, cf. Cobb, pp. 98–9, and Quiney, pp. 194–8. For the work of Dean Monk and Edmund Blore at Peterborough earlier in the century, cf. Cobb, p. 97; cf. also J. Fawcett, 'Nineteenth Century Restoration of Peterborough Cathedral', *Friends of Peterborough Cathedral Annual Report*, 1978, pp. 15–22; R. S. W. Digby, 'The Central Tower Saga', in ibid., 1981, pp. 7–17, and D. F. Mackreth, 'The Irvine Papers', in ibid., 1976, pp. 15–19.
106 Ferriday, pp. 89–90, 95–8, 99–100, 106. For a description of St Albans earlier in the century, cf. ibid. p. 93. Scott repaired the building early in the 1870s, but before it became a cathedral (cf. Cole, pp. 171–2). For minor nineteenth-century restorations at St Albans, cf. Coghlan, pp. 40–2. For major restoration work, cf. ibid., pp. 80–9.

107 Ferriday, p. 116; cf. p. 205 for the words of the faculty.
108 ibid., p. 149.
109 ibid., p. 152.
110 ibid., pp. 190–1. The total amount spent by Grimthorpe on the building since 1877 was said in 1898 to be £250,000 (*Guardian*, 1898, p. 1285).
111 ABDC Salisbury, 11 September 1822.
112 Scott, pp. 300–7.
113 Cobb, p. 113; cf. Cole, pp. 88–9.
114 L. S. Colchester, 'The Victorian Restoration of Wells Cathedral Church (Barnard Ms.', *TAMS*, n.s. vol. iv, 1956, pp. 79f.; D. M. Greenhalgh in L. S. Colchester, ed., *Wells Cathedral: A History* (Shepton Mallett 1982), pp. 179–203.
115 F. Bussby, 'The Great Screen – part II', *Winchester Cathedral Record*, no. 48, 1979, pp. 12–15; cf. F. Bussby, *Winchester Cathedral 1079–1979* (Southampton 1979; 2nd edn 1987), pp. 245–50.
116 For an account, cf. Chadwick, *York*, pp. 274–80.
117 ibid., pp. 278–9; cf. J. S. Kerr, *Improvers and Preservers: A dissertation on Some Aspects of Cathedral Restoration 1770–1830 and in Particular on the Great Screen Squabble of York Minster from 1829 to 1831* (York 1973).
118 Chadwick, *York*, p. 281.
119 *Archaeological Journal*, vol. 54, 1897, pp. 239–74.
120 PP 1835, xxii, p. 15.
121 *Quarterly Review*, vol. 137, July/October 1874, pp. 246f.
122 CCR 1894, pp. 32–3.
123 S. R. Hole, *More Memories, Being Thoughts about England Spoken in America* (London 1894), p. 63.

CHAPTER 11 *The Mission of the Cathedral*

1 PP 1854, xxv, p. vi.
2 E. W. Benson, *The Cathedral: Its Necessary Place in the Life and Work of the Church* (London 1878), pp. 44–74.
3 K. Edwards, *The English Secular Cathedrals in the Middle Ages* (2nd edn, Manchester 1967), p. 100.
4 For details, cf. R. S. Ferguson, 'Consistory Courts and Consistory Places', *Archaeological Journal*, vol. lvi, June 1899, pp. 85–119; ABDC Gloucester, 2 July 1863; Worc. C. Add. Mss., 128, p. 5; ABDC Worcester, 8 October 1889, 7 August 1890; ABDC Peterborough, 1899, cited in P. V. Coghlan, 'Cathedral Worship in the Church of England 1815–1914' (Leicester University M. Phil. thesis 1984), p. 100; Bristol DC/A/611.
5 Wells CM, 1 April 1881.
6 Ferguson, p. 92.
7 ABDC Hereford, 5 February 1803.
8 ABDC Wells, 7 June 1802.
9 ABDC Wells, 21 June 1824.
10 C. E. Woodruff and W. Danks, *Memorials of the Cathedral and Priory of Christ in Canterbury* (London 1912), p. 364.
11 ABDC Salisbury, 29 July 1807; for Bishop Hamilton's enthronement in 1854, cf. *Guardian*, 1854, p. 453; for Bishop Moberly's in 1869, cf. ABDC Salisbury, 13 November 1869.
12 *Winchester Cathedral Record*, no. 1, June 1932, p. 13.
13 M. R. Craze, *King's School, Worcester (1541–1971)* (Worcester 1972), p. 182. Chancellor Burton of Carlisle, who was enthroned and installed as the proxy of more than one bishop of the diocese, claimed the right to sit, and always sat, in the bishop's stall in the quire, the Bishop of Carlisle having both a stall and a throne (Ferguson, p. 119).

14 ABDC Chichester, October 1831; ABDC Exeter, 14 January 1831. Bishop Kaye was enthroned in person at Bristol in 1820 (ABDC Bristol, 7 August 1820). For the enthronement of Bishop Stanley at Norwich in 1837, attended by the mayor and corporation, cf. Dean Pellew's letters, nos. 238, 259, Norfolk CRO.

15 For details, cf. D. I. Hill, *Christ's Glorious Church* (London 1976), p. 76, and Woodruff and Danks, p. 363; *Guardian*, 1848, p. 285.

16 ABDC Hereford, 27 April 1848; HCA 4370.

17 cf. A. C. Benson, *The Life of Edward White Benson, Sometime Archbishop of Canterbury*, (London 1899), vol. I, pp. 262f.

18 ABDC Wells, 20 December 1869; for details of Samuel Wilberforce's enthronement at Winchester Cathedral in the same year, cf. Win. CA, Enthronement box. Precentor Wray established with difficulty his right to take part in the service, complaining that the canons always wanted to intone 'when they thought there was an opportunity of shewing off' (*De Precentore*, 1869).

19 *Guardian*, 1869, pp. 144, 156–7.

20 ibid., 1877, pp. 806–7.

21 A. B. Donaldson, *The Bishopric of Truro* (London 1902), p. 53; cf. H. M. Brown, *A Century for Cornwall: The Diocese of Truro 1877–1977* (Truro 1976), p. 1. The form of service that Benson drew up for succeeding enthronements at Truro may be found in PP 1883, xxi, pp. 66–8. When Benson was enthroned at Canterbury in 1883, the dean and chapter received 2,077 applications for nearly 7,000 seats (LPL, Benson Papers, III, p. 228,).

22 *Lichfield Cathedral: Order of Ceremonial and Services at the enthronement of the Bishop and the Diocesan Foreign Missions Festival, 11 July 1878* (Lichfield); cf. *Guardian*, 1878, p. 992.

23 K. Lake, ed., *Memorials of William Charles Lake* (London 1901), pp. 237–8.

24 *Guardian*, 1884, pp. 834–6.

25 ibid., 1885, p. 518.

26 G. W. E. Russell, *Edward King* (London 1912), p. 109; *Guardian*, 1885, p. 797.

27 *Guardian*, 1888, p. 941.

28 *Guardian*, 1890, p. 892; 1891, pp. 530, 794; 1884, p. 1340; 1889, p. 346.

29 *Guardian*, 1891, p. 1754; *Winchester Cathedral Chronicle* (1873–1891), p. 79.

30 T. F. Bumpus, *The Cathedrals of England and Wales* (London 1905), vol. I, pp. 260–1.

31 J. Jebb, *The Choral Service of the United Church of England and Ireland* (London 1843), p. 433.

32 Worc. C. Add. Mss., 141, p. 8.

33 L. W. Cowie, 'Worship in the Minster', *The Victoria History of the Counties of England: A History of Yorkshire: The City of York* (London 1961), pp. 354–5.

34 *Winchester Cathedral Chronicle*, 1873–91.

35 W. J. Rees, p. 49.

36 G. L. Prestige, *St Paul's in its Glory, 1831–1911* (London 1955), p. 33.

37 Worc. C. Add. Mss. 128, p. 12.

38 F. Alford, *Life, Journals and Letters of Henry Alford, Dean of Canterbury* (London 1873), p. 411.

39 Lake, p. 262. In December 1868 Goulburn noted that an ordination at Norwich had lasted 2½ hours: 'Another time, the people must be retained in Church by giving out a short hymn, without any pause, immediately after the sermon, during which we go to the altar' (NCL, Goulburn's diary, 20 December 1868).

40 H. Goodwin in J. S. Howson, ed., *Essays on Cathedrals by Various Writers* (London 1872), pp. 25–6.

41 A. J. Worlledge, *Letters of Bishop Gott* (London 1918), p. 28.

42 W. H. Frere, *Visitation Articles and Injunctions of the Period of the Reformation* (London 1910), vol. I, p. 90; cf. ibid., p. 75.

43 W. K. L. Clarke, *Chichester Cathedral in the Nineteenth Century* (Chichester Papers no. 14, Chichester 1959), pp. 6–7, 17; cf. Chichester Capitular Archives (WSCRO), 1/7/1; Cathedral Visitation Book, pp. 131f., 142; cf. F. G. Bennett, R. H. Codrington and C. Deedes, *Statutes and Constitutions of the Cathedral Church of Chichester* (Chichester 1904), pp. 49f.

44 ABDC Wells, 13 December 1825, 9 January 1828; cf. H. E. Reynolds, *Wells Cathedral: Its Foundation, Constitutional History and Statutes* (Leeds 1881), p. iii.

45 ABDC Hereford, 9 July 1835, and ABVC Hereford, pp. 52ff. (reverse pagination). For a summary, cf. P. L. S. Barrett, 'John Merewether, Dean of Hereford 1832–50', *FHCAR*, 1977, p. 28, and Barrett, 'Hereford Cathedral in the Nineteenth Century', in ibid., 1986, pp. 22–3.

46 Chadwick, *York*, pp. 282, 284–6; A. S. Leak, 'Conflict and Reform at York Minster in the Nineteenth Century' (Oxford B. D. thesis, 1988), pp. 140–95.

47 Bishop Hamilton's evidence to Cathedrals Commission 1854, Salisbury Chapter Muniments, Press I, Box 39, p. 113.

48 C. Wordsworth, 'On English Cathedrals', in *Miscellanies Literary and Religious* (London 1879), vol. III, p. 323; J. W. F. Hill, *Victorian Lincoln* (London 1974), p. 242; J. H. Overton and E. Wordsworth, *Christopher Wordsworth* (London 1888), p. 214.

49 *Cathedralia Winton: Minor Canons 1860–1918*, 1 October 1878; cf. *Winchester Cathedral Chronicle*, 1873–91, pp. 82–3, 86f.

50 *The Standard*, 27 September 1880.

51 Wordsworth and D. Macleane, *Statutes and Customs of the Cathedral Church of the Blessed Virgin Mary at Salisbury* (London 1915), pp. 467–92; ABDC Salisbury, 30 May 1890.

52 Donaldson, pp. 321–5.

53 The papers of this visitation are in the capitular archives at Winchester. For a summary, cf. F. Bussby, *Winchester Cathedral 1079–1979* (Southampton 1979, second edn 1987), p. 251; see also above, p. 259.

54 MBVC Wells, 8 November 1872, 7 October 1875, 18 October 1888.

55 cf. Chapter 7, p. 146.

56 ABDC Worcester, 3 November and 22 November 1870. At Wells in 1875 the dean and chapter asked the bishop to intervene in the election of a lay vicar (ABDC Wells, 10 August 1875). Twelve years later a row between two vicars choral at Wells was referred to the bishop (Wells CM, 1 April 1887).

57 ABDC Winchester, 4 April 1876. The permission of the Bishop of London was needed at St Paul's in 1880 before the litany could be said in the North Chapel (St Paul's CM, 13 November 1880, cited in Coghlan, p. 100).

58 ABDC Hereford, 18 January 1803; ABDC Salisbury, 11 June 1807.

59 Donaldson, p. 308.

60 cf. Barrett, 'John Merewether', pp. 37–8; ABDC Hereford, 16 December 1847.

61 E. G. Sandford, ed., *Memoirs of Archbishop Temple by Seven Friends* (London 1906), vol. I, pp. 281–91. Bishop Gott's election at Truro in 1891 was the first to be held in one of the newly founded cathedrals and great care was taken to ensure that every detail in the proceedings was correct (Donaldson, p. 310).

62 H. P. Liddon, *Walter Kerr Hamilton, Bishop of Salisbury* (London 1869), p. 24.

63 B. Compton, *Edward Meyrick Goulburn, Dean of Norwich* (London 1899), p. 73.

64 W. O. Chadwick, *Edward King, Bishop of Lincoln 1885–1910* (Lincoln 1968), p. 24.

65 H. Alford, 'Cathedral Reform – a Supplement', *Contemporary Review*, vol. xii, September 1869, p. 365.

66 Donaldson, p. 59.

67 ibid., p. 382.

68 ibid., p. 225.

69 R. M. Beaumont, *The Chapter of Southwell Minster* (Nottingham 1956), p. 33.

70 PP 1854, xxv, p. 814.

71 PP 1854, xxv, p. 797.

72 ABDC Exeter, 15 and 29 January, 12 February 1831; cf. also 13 March, 3 and 20 August 1803, 29 November and 13 December 1820, and 17 July 1830. At Chester the bishop regularly preached on the morning of the first Sunday of the month (PP 1883, xxi, p. 157).

73 ABDC Salisbury, 17 July and 11 December 1841.

74 Jebb, p. 32.

75 J. W. F. Hill, *Georgian Lincoln* (Cambridge 1966), p. 301, fn. 1.

76 D. I. Hill, p. 74.

77 P. A. Welsby, *Rochester Cathedral in the Time of Charles Dickens* (Rochester 1976), p. 10.

78 W. J. Humfrys, *Memories of Old Hereford* (Hereford n.d.), p. 2.

79 Quoted in D. King, *Winchester Cathedral Chronicle*, 1972, p. 3; Worc. C. Add. Mss., 128, p. 12.

80 Bumpus, vol. I, pp. 95–6. Harvey Goodwin said that he and Bishop Turton were never together in the cathedral for any service or other occasion (H. Goodwin, *Ely Gossip*, p. 97, quoted in Coghlan, pp. 165–6).

81 E. H. Browne, *Bishops and Cathedrals* (London 1872), p. 10.

82 R. J. Fletcher, *A History of Bristol Cathedral* (London 1932), pp. 64–5; ABDC Bristol, 24 October 1866; for the bishop's powers at Bristol, cf. G. F. Browne, *The Recollections of a Bishop* (London 1915), p. 400.

83 F. Pigou, *Odds and Ends* (London 1903), p. 216.

84 PP 1884, xxii, p. 132.

85 A. Boutflower, *Personal Reminiscences of Manchester Cathedral 1854–1912* (Leighton Buzzard 1913), p. 37.

86 H. L. Thompson, *Henry George Liddell* (London 1899), p. 156; cf. also S. Meacham, *Lord Bishop* (Harvard 1970), pp. 127–8; E. G. W. Bill and J. F. A. Mason, *Christ Church and Reform 1850–1867* (Oxford 1970), p. 117, fn. 2.

87 H. Kirk-Smith, *William Thomson, Archbishop of York 1819–1890* (London 1958), pp. 85–91; Leak, pp. 320–7.

88 Kirk-Smith, p. 95; cf. also Chadwick, *York*, pp. 303–9. Archbishop Thomson complained in 1882 that he had not been properly consulted by the Cathedrals Commission. He claimed that the fact that the bishops did not belong to the chapters of their cathedrals was 'the cause of much of the uselessness of cathedrals' (Thomson to Ellicott, 27 February 1882, Benson Papers, I, p. 383).

89 F. G. Kitton, *Zechariah Buck* (London 1899), p. 42; cf. *MT*, 1 February 1900, p. 82. Buck's successor, F. Bates, arranged a Rheinberger opera for the choristers to perform at his house at Christmas 1889 before an invited audience. The cathedral choir also gave madrigal concerts at St Andrew's Hall (F. Bates, *Reminiscences and Autobiography of a Musician in Retirement* (Norwich 1930), pp. 39–40).

90 E. W. Watson, *Life of Bishop John Wordsworth* (London 1915), pp. 175, 178, 183; cf. L. W. Cowie, 'The Church of England since 1837' *VCH Wiltshire*, vol. iii, 1956, p. 75. Bishop Ellicott of Gloucester was also bored by long anthems and amused himself by translating them into Hebrew and Greek and the longest into Arabic as well (A. H. Brewer, *Memories of Choirs and Cloisters* (London 1931), p. 86). Harvey Goodwin, however, asked to have a copy of the music when he attended his cathedral at Carlisle for evensong on Wednesdays (H. D. Rawnsley, *Harvey Goodwin, Bishop of Carlisle* (London 1896), pp. 140–1).

91 D. I. Hill, p. 84.

92 L. Creighton, *Life and Letters of Mandell Creighton* (London 1904), vol. II, p. 9.

93 J. F. Briscoe and H. F. B. Mackay, *A Tractarian at Work* (London 1932), p. 179.

94 ibid., p. 187.

95 ABDC Salisbury, 13 March 1872.

96 Prestige, p. 221.
97 ABDC Exeter, 30 January 1897.
98 R. Newton, *Victorian Exeter, 1837–1914* (Leicester 1968), p. 56; Exeter Cathedral Library no. 7170/41, Phillpotts to Barnes; G. C. B. Davies, *Henry Phillpotts, Bishop of Exeter, 1778–1869* (London 1954), pp. 181–4. But Benson said: 'There is not in any single answer from all the deans and chapters of England in 1854 any indication that they regarded themselves as in origin, foundation, design, attributes, rights, or powers, having even a theoretical connection with episcopal government or ecclesiastical counsel' (E. W. Benson, p. 101).
99 H. W. Tucker, *Memoir of the Life and Episcopate of George Augustus Selwyn* (London 1879), vol. II, pp. 273–4.
100 Bristol Capitular Archives, DC/A/7/6/2.
101 ABDC Hereford, 25 March 1878; cf. ABDC Chichester, 21 August 1876; and ABDC Wells, 30 August 1870.
102 PP 1883, xxi, p. 81.
103 ABDC Salisbury, 14 October 1888.
104 *Winchester Cathedral Chronicle*; 1866–94, p. 46.
105 J. F. Bridge, *A Westminster Pilgrim* (London 1919), p. 23.
106 B. E. Dorman, *The Story of Ely and its Cathedral* (Norwich 1945, new edn Ely 1980), p. 52.
107 ABDC Chichester, 2 August 1886.
108 Hansard, 1871, 3rd series, vol. ccvi, cols 461–2. In a pamphlet published in the same year, Ellicott said that cathedrals should be 'the Parish Churches of the dioceses to which they belong; to be the centres of spiritual energy and life; the examples of noble and reverent worship, of stirring services, and of faithful preaching...' (C. J. Ellicott, *Our Cathedral Institutions – Will They Stand?* (Gloucester 1871), p. 12). For Browne's views, cf. G. W. Kitchin, *Edward Harold Browne* (London 1895), p. 357.
109 *Guardian*, 1872, p. 377.
110 H. Goodwin, *Charge Delivered to the Clergy and Churchwardens of the Diocese of Carlisle* (Carlisle 1881), p. 5.
111 Bristol Capitular Archives, DC/A/7/6/2.
112 ABDC Salisbury, 13 March 1872. For Archbishop Tait's letter to the dean, setting out the procedures leading up to these questions, cf. ibid., 11 March 1872; cf. also Chapter 13, pp. 295–6.
113 ABDC Exeter, 8–9 March 1872. For a similar arrangement at Winchester, cf. Kitchin, p. 356.
114 *Guardian*, 1879, p. 353.
115 ibid., p. 1069.
116 ibid., p. 1121.
117 cf. W. E. Dickson, *The Relation of the Cathedral of Ely to the Diocese* (Ely 1879), p. 2.
118 R. J. E. Boggis, *A History of the Diocese of Exeter* (Exeter 1922), p. 531. Later Bishop Bickersteth appointed four new residentiary canons and assigned to them definite diocesan duties relating to education, missions, overseas missions and pastoral theology (ibid., p. 532); cf. also H. W. Beadon, *The Cathedrals and the Diocese* (Gloucester 1880), p. 4.
119 W. E. Dickson, *Fifty Years of Church Music* (Ely 1894), p. 11.
120 *Ecclesiologist*, vol. xviii, 1857, p. 360; for Harvey Goodwin's views, cf. Howson, p. 26; cf. *Ecclesiologist*, vol. xxiv, 1863, p. 171, and Bussby, p. 237.
121 *Ecclesiologist*, vol. xviii, 1857, p. 363.
122 cf. B. Rainbow, *The Choral Revival in the Anglican Church, 1839–1872*, (London 1970), p. 273; Bumpus, p. 52; Walcott, *Traditions*, p. 109; D. L. Adelmann, 'The Contribution of Cambridge and the Ecclesiological (late Cambridge Camden) Society to the Revival of Anglican Choral Worship, 1839–62' (Cambridge Ph.D. thesis 1991), pp. 223–32.

123 *Guardian*, 1869, p. 787.

124 *Ecclesiologist*, 1858, vol. xix, p. 175.

125 ibid., vol. xxiii, 1862, p. 211.

126 ibid., vol. xxiv, 1863, p. 174. By 1885 this figure had fallen to 250 (Salisbury CM, 12 January 1885).

127 Clarke, p. 14.

128 Win. CA, *De Precentore*, 5 June 1866; Bussby, p. 237.

129 Wells CM, 2 April 1883. F. Bates, the organist of Norwich Cathedral, did much to encourage the Diocesan Choral Association in his diocese in the closing years of the century (Bates, pp. 88–98).

130 cf. Chadwick, *York*, pp. 288–9.

131 PP 1854, xxv, p. 40. Bishop Denison promised in 1842 that new prebendaries would always be clergy of his diocese, since they would value their appointment 'as a means of connection with the Cathedral' (E. Denison, *A Charge Delivered to the Clergy of the Diocese of Salisbury* (London 1842), p. 27).

132 cf. chapter 5, pp. 74–5.

133 Goodwin, p. 7.

134 ABDC Exeter, 7 November 1885.

135 See Chapter 7, p. 133–4.

136 R. B. Lockett, 'The Victorian Restoration of Worcester Cathedral', *Mediaeval Art and Architecture at Worcester Cathedral* (British Archaeological Association Conference Transactions for the Year 1975), pp. 171, 182, fn. 109; see above, Chapter 10, pp. 236–7.

137 ABDC Winchester, 8 January 1885.

138 ABDC Chichester, 12 April 1893; Chichester Cathedral Archives, General chapter minute book 1876–1935, 5 December 1893 and 13 August 1894.

139 ABDC Worcester, 1 November 1892.

140 W. O. Chadwick, *The Victorian Church* (London 1970), vol. II, p. 385; Howson, p. 27; for the Salisbury diocesan synod, cf. Chapter 7, p. 127.

141 Win. CA, *Cathedralia Winton: Minor Canons 1860–1918*.

142 Wells CM, 22 October 1888.

143 ABDC Exeter, 5 November 1842, 1 April 1843, 10 November 1849, 16 November 1850.

144 W. H. Hutton, ed., *The Autobiography of Robert Gregory* (London 1912), pp. 166–7.

145 W. G. Roe and A. Hutchings, *J. B. Dykes, Priest and Musician* (Durham 1976), p. 2; cf. Chapter 6, p. 104. For a general discussion of the subject, cf. Chapter 5, pp. 62–3. For examples of vicars choral and minor canons combining cathedral and parochial duties, cf. Chapter 6, pp. 93–4, 97 and n. 148. In 1854 the cathedral commissioners encouraged cathedral clergy to help in city parishes as they thought this would increase their influence 'and the strengthening of the bonds of unity in the Diocese' (PP 1854, xxv, p. 29).

146 E. B. Pusey, 'The Royal and Parliamentary Ecclesiastical Commissions', *British Critic*, vol. 23, no. 46, April 1838, p. 536.

147 PP 1854, xxv, pp. 30–1.

148 PP 1884, xxii, p. 269.

149 Wells CM, 1 April 1879; cf. 30 April, 1 October, 22 December 1879; cf. W. H. Jones, *Canon or Prebendary: A Plea for the Non-residentiary Members of Cathedral Chapters* (Bath 1877), p. 3.

150 Wells CM, 3 July 1888.

151 ABDC Gloucester, 23 June 1800.

152 ABDC Worcester, 25 November 1814; ABDC Chichester, 18 October 1802.

153 ABDC Wells, 1 April 1817, revised 30 September 1858; cf. ABDC Bristol, 1 December 1840, revised 4 December 1855 (DC/A/7/3/4); ABDC Chichester, 10 October 1843.

154 ABDC Bristol, 4 February and 16 April 1845.

155 PP 1854, xxv, p. 40.

156 Hansard, P. D., 16 May 1848.

157 C. E. Beswick, 'Liddon of St Paul's' (Exeter University MA thesis 1974), p. 14.

158 ABDC Exeter, 22 November 1888.

159 ibid., 16 November 1895.

160 P. Stewart, *Diocese of Salisbury: Guide to the Records of the Bishop, Archdeacons of Salisbury and Wiltshire and other Archidiaconal Jurisdictions and to the Records from the Bishop of Bristol's Sub-registry for Dorset* (Wiltshire 1973), p. 108; Ferguson, pp. 100, 107; for decanal peculiars, cf. Chapter 4, n. 29; for peculiar jurisdictions at York, cf. Leak, p. 70.

161 Stewart, p. 89; HCA, A.5613, D.417.

162 ABDC Chichester, 2 May 1876.

163 ABDC Winchester, 1 March 1887.

164 Beadon, p. 5.

165 Pigou, p. 210.

166 A. Westcott, *Life and Letters of Brooke Foss Westcott* (London 1903), vol. I, p. 311.

167 CCR 1894, p. 56.

168 Worlledge, p. 27.

169 L. Ragg, *A Memoir of Edward Charles Wickham, Dean of Lincoln* (London 1911), p. 125.

170 E. B. Pusey, *Remarks on the Prospective and Past Benefits of Cathedral Institutions in the Promotion of Sound Religious Knowledge occasioned by Lord Henley's Plan for their Abolition* (London 1833), p. 102.

171 PP 1854, xxv, pp. 38–9; M. E. C. Walcott, *Cathedralia* (London 1865), p. 18.

172 R. Whiston, *Cathedral Trusts and Their Fulfilment* (3rd edn, London 1849), p. 50.

173 J. H. Srawley, *The Origin and Growth of Cathedral Foundations as illustrated by the Cathedral Church of Lincoln* (Lincoln 1951; third edn 1965), p. 9.

174 C. E. Woodruff, 'Reminiscences of the Cathedral and its Personnel Seventy-five Years Ago', *Canterbury Cathedral Chronicle*, no. 39, September 1943), p. 17; Win. CA, Davidson visitation papers, 1900, Dean's reply: 'The severance of the stall from the archdeaconry would be a gain in every way to the Cathedral'; Hill, *Victorian Lincoln*, pp. 271–2.

175 Prestige, pp. 40f.

176 ABDC Chichester, 2 May 1864; ABDC Gloucester, 17 February 1874.

177 Coghlan, p. 104.

178 Donaldson, p. 77.

179 E. W. Benson, p. 133.

180 ibid.; cf. M. Portal, *Our Cathedral* (Winchester 1886), pp. 9–10.

181 A. C. Benson, vol. I, pp. 378–9.

182 CCR 1895, pp. 600–1.

183 Win. CA, *Winchester Cathedral Chronicle*, 1873–91, p. 71. Harvey Goodwin urged in 1881 that cathedrals should be brought into closer involvement with the life of the whole diocese: 'as a general rule it seems right that the diocese should look to the Cathedral for assistance in theological teaching, for aid in preaching on special occasions, for encouragement in mission and such like extraordinary efforts – that the Cathedral should be, as it were, a reserve of spiritual power to be applied to the doing of God's work in the diocese' (Goodwin, pp. 6–7).

184 Wordsworth and Macleane, p. 481.

185 ibid., pp. 487–8.

186 CT, March 1886, preserved in Worc. C. Add. Mss., press cuttings, vol. I.

187 Win. CA, Davidson visitation papers; cf. Bussby, pp. 250–2. M. Portal had stressed the diocesan aspect of cathedrals in 1886. He said that Winchester Cathedral should be 'the centre of all teaching, the centre of all preaching, the centre of all

missionary work, aye, of all church work in the diocese' (Portal, p. 8; cf. p. 14).

188 *British Critic*, vol. 29, January 1841, p. 146.

189 cf. M. E. Curtis, *Some Disputes between the City and the Cathedral Authorities of Exeter* (Manchester 1932), p. 9. The dean and chapter were very pleased to receive this resolution and assured the chamber 'that the mutual good feeling which has so long subsided between the bodies has been a source of great satisfaction to themselves' (ABDC Exeter, 2 January 1836).

190 Chadwick, *York*, p. 287.

191 Liddon, p. 42.

192 Woodruff and Danks, p. 366; cf. Chapter 7, p. 120.

193 F. Alford, p. 517.

194 R. Farrar, *The Life of Frederic William Farrar, sometime Dean of Canterbury* (London 1904), p. 318; cf. p. 320.

195 Worlledge, p. 3.

196 Worc. C. Add. Mss., 104, p. 12.

197 Creighton, vol. I, pp. 311, 315.

198 A. J. Butler, *Life and Letters of William John Butler* (London 1897), p. 313.

199 ibid., pp. 320, 330. For Benson's mission to the city of Lincoln, cf. p. 258 above.

200 Ragg, pp. 124–5.

201 H. Leeds, *Life of Dean Lefroy* (Norwich 1909), pp. 23, 25–6, 35, 70; R. Hale in C. Barringer, ed., *Norwich in the Nineteenth Century* (Norwich 1984), pp. 171–2; cf. Coghlan, pp. 150–1, and Chapter 7 above, p. 122.

202 Leeds, p. 36; Coghlan, p. 94, citing ABDC Norwich, 9 September 1890.

203 Chadwick, *York*, pp. 269–70.

204 P. M. J. Crook, 'Half-a-century of Choral Indiscipline: George Chard and his Choir, 1802–1849', *Southern Cathedrals Festival Programme*, 1981, p. 11; Crook, 'Fifty Years of Choral Misrule: George Chard and the Choristers of Winchester Cathedral', *Winchester Cathedral Record*, no. 56, 1987, p. 31.

205 Walcott, *Traditions*, p. 88. Dean Goulburn records that the mayor and corporation came in state to Norwich Cathedral in 1867, but they left before the celebration of holy communion (NCL, Goulburn's diary, 5 May 1867).

206 Wells CM, 1 October 1862; for the city council's involvement in the enthronement of Bishop Hervey in 1870, cf. above, p. 246.

207 ABDC Exeter, 6 and 13 July 1878.

208 ABDC Worcester, 30 April 1892.

209 Chadwick, *York*, p. 277.

210 M. H. Fitzgerald, *The Story of Bristol Cathedral* (London 1936), p. 61; for consequent repairs, cf. ABDC Bristol, 29 November 1831.

211 Chadwick, *York*, pp. 280–1.

212 ABDC Hereford, 8 December 1851; cf. Chapter 3, pp. 29–30. In 1870 the town council at Hereford was asked by the dean and chapter to water the walks in the close (ABDC Hereford, 25 June 1870). Wells town council was thanked by the dean and chapter for sweeping the crossing outside the deanery in 1895 (Wells CM, 1 January 1895).

213 ABDC Bristol, 9 November 1866, 9 May 1876; cf. Chapter 10, p. 239.

214 ABDC Exeter, 28 December 1868, 19 October 1872.

215 Prestige, pp. 110–11.

216 ABDC Worcester, 13 April 1874.

217 Newscutting dated 2 July 1879 in ABDC Bristol, 1879–1900.

218 T. R. Barham, *The Creation of a Cathedral* (Falmouth 1976), pp. 30–1.

219 cf. Chapter 7, p. 115–16, for a civic petition at Hereford.

220 ABDC Worcester, 20 May and 23 June 1874. .

221 T. G Willis, *Records of Chichester* (Chichester 1928), p. 217.

222 ABDC Salisbury, 31 December 1811; cf. Chapter 1, p. 4.

223 Hill, *Victorian Lincoln*, pp. 56–7.

224 *Memorials of Dean Close*, 'by one who knew him', p. 35.

225 Worc. C. Add. Mss., 141, p. 36.

226 Ragg, pp. 135f. A cookery school was established in the close at Winchester in 1884 (ABDC Winchester, 23 June 1884).

227 ABDC Bristol, 10 July 1805.

228 Rawnsley, p. 115. Harvey Goodwin was very anxious to be a Guardian of the Poor and made it a personal objective to build a chapel at the workhouse (Coghlan, quoting H. Goodwin, *Ely Gossip*, pp. 167–8.

229 ABDC Chichester, 10 October 1866.

230 C. E. Moxley, *Cathedral, College and Hospital* (Winchester 1986), p. 71.

231 J. W. Clark and T. McK. Hughes, *The Life and Letters of The Reverend Adam Sedgwick* (Cambridge 1890), vol. II, p. 129.

232 PP 1883, xxi, p. 157.

233 Hill, *Victorian Lincoln*, p. 263.

234 E. Wordsworth, *Memorials of Henry William Burrows* (London 1894), p. 212.

235 ABDC Exeter, 23 December 1800.

236 ABDC Bristol, 5 March 1801.

237 C. J. Stranks, *This Sumptuous Church* (London 1973), p. 82. When George IV was crowned, the dean and chapter of Exeter gave £10 to a city subscription 'for regaling the poor' (ABDC Exeter, 21 July 1821).

238 ABDC Winchester, 25 November 1800.

239 ibid., 25 November 1820, 25 November 1830.

240 *Winchester Cathedral Chronicle*, 1873–91, pp. 38–9, which also contains details of various other charitable donations by the dean and chapter in the 1870s.

241 cf. Chapter 1, p. 41, for the *Hampshire Chronicle*'s comment on Iremonger and other examples of poor relief by chapters in the early nineteenth century.

242 ABDC Exeter, 18 January 1800, 22 March 1828.

243 ibid., 19 March 1864.

244 ibid., 20 December 1879, 14 February 1895.

245 Clarke, p. 18; ABDC Chichester, 2 May 1840.

246 ABDC Bristol, 30 November 1801, 30 November 1805, 1 December 1806, 30 November 1821, 30 November 1826, 30 November 1827.

247 ABDC Gloucester, 30 November 1800, 23 January 1812; Treasurer's Accounts 1786–1810, p. 400.

248 ABDC Exeter, 18 April 1835.

249 *HT*, 16 January 1841.

250 Wells CM, 31 October 1848, 17 January 1854, 2 February 1854.

251 Liddon, p. 42.

252 J. M. Elvy, *Recollections of the Cathedral and Parish Church of Manchester* (Manchester 1913), p. 59.

253 ibid., p. 47.

254 ABDC Exeter, 25 July 1874.

255 Creighton, vol. I, p. 382. At Winchester, however, the charity monies were transferred to the Charity Commissioners in 1861 and in 1883 the dean and chapter warned that the state of their finances compelled them to suspend their normal donations (ABDC Winchester, 25 November 1861, 3 March 1883).

256 J. F. Chanter, *The Custos and College of the Vicars Choral of the Choir of the Cathedral Church of St Peter, Exeter* (Exeter 1933), pp. 35–6.

257 cf. Chapter 12, n. 68.

258 W. Bazeley, *Records of Gloucester Cathedral* (Gloucester 1882–97), vol. I, p. 1.

259 cf. H. W. Shaw, *The Three Choirs Festival* (Worcester 1954), pp. 30–83, and B. Still, ed.,

250 Years of the Three Choirs Festival (Hereford 1977).

260 D. Verey, ed., *The Diary of a Cotswold Parson 1783–1854* (Gloucester 1978), p. 31.

261 ibid., p. 65; for a description of the 1900 Hereford Festival, cf. *MT*, 1 October 1900, pp. 657f.

262 *MT*, 1 September 1900, p. 592.

263 Woodruff, p. 21.

264 *Sacred Music for the People*, November 1886 (Gloucester City Library, Gloucester Collection, 25–10956). This initiative was copied at Norwich and attracted immense crowds for several winters (Bates, p. 38; NCL, Goulburn's diary, 3 March 1887; *MT*, 1 December 1886, p. 713; *MT*, 1 April 1887, p. 212).

265 *MT*, 1 November 1886, pp. 641–2; cf. also *CT*, 19 November 1886, p. 890, and *MT*, 1 January 1887, p. 45.

266 W. L. Hillsman, 'Trends and Aims in Anglican Music 1870–1906, in relation to developments in churchmanship' (Oxford D. Phil. thesis 1985), p. 322.

267 ibid., p. 322, quoting *MT*, 1 December 1886, p. 713; cf. also ibid., 1 February 1899, p. 92, 1 March 1900, p. 314, 1 June 1900, p. 411.

268 P. Aston, 'Music since the Reformation', in G. E. Aylmer and R. Cant, eds, *A History of York Minster* (Oxford 1977), p. 422.

269 Win. CA, *De Precentore*, 1893.

270 ABDC Bristol, 14 May and 5 July 1803.

271 ibid., 30 November 1818.

272 ABDC Winchester, 23 June 1818.

273 ABDC Salisbury, 29 September 1819.

274 Wells CM, 1 October 1831.

275 ABDC Exeter, 18–19 March 1834, 17 May 1856.

276 *HT*, 6 February 1841; cf. 1 May 1841.

277 ibid., 13 February 1841.

278 ibid., 27 November 1841.

279 ABDC Chichester, 10 October 1867.

280 ABDC Salisbury, 29 September 1819.

281 ABDC Chichester, 2 May 1821.

282 *HT*, 17 April 1841.

283 ABDC Wells, 10 September 1855.

284 PP 1854, xxv, pp. 29–30; cf. n. 145 above.

285 cf. Chapter 6, pp. 95–6.

286 H. Alford, 'Cathedral Reform', *Contemporary Review*, vol. xii, September 1869, p. 47. For friction between the cathedral and city parishes over Sunday evening services at Canterbury and Chichester, cf. Chapter 7, p. 120. For the views of local incumbents about the voluntary choir at Worcester, cf. Chapter 8, pp. 214–15.

287 ABDC Hereford, 17 November 1877; E. M. Jancey, 'Hereford Cathedral and the Parish of St John the Baptist', *FHCAR*, 1984, pp. 21–7; D. Cole, *The Work of Sir Gilbert Scott* (London 1980), p. 91; Clarke, p. 3.

288 Coghlan, p. 99, citing ABDC Norwich, February 1858.

289 Coghlan, p. 177; cf. G. Cobb, *English Cathedrals: The Forgotten Centuries* (London 1980), pp. 82–3.

290 Salisbury Chapter Muniments, Press I, Box 39, p. 37.

291 Stranks, pp. 82–3; Davies, pp. 38–40.

292 D. King, in *Winchester Cathedral Chronicle*, 1972, p. 3.

293 PP 1871, lv, p. 201.

294 ABDC Exeter, 16 March 1815.

295 ABDC Exeter, 11 October 1823. For the responsibility of vergers as guides at various cathedrals, cf. Chapter 6, pp. 108–9.

296 ABDC Norwich, 6 June 1837, quoted in P. C. Moore, 'The Organisation and

Development of Cathedral Worship in England, with special reference to choral services, from the Reformation to the nineteenth century' (Oxford D. Phil. thesis 1954), p. 167.

297 D. M. Robertson, *Sarum Close* (London 1938, new edn 1970), p. 293.

298 K. Edwards, 'The Cathedral of Salisbury, 1075–1950', *VCH Wiltshire*, vol. iii, 1956, p. 202; ABDC Salisbury, 5 September 1849. For further rules, cf. 7 December 1866; cf. Robertson, p. 302.

299 A. Bell, *Sydney Smith* (Oxford 1980), p. 173; cf. Prestige, pp. 30–1, and A. Milman, *Henry Hart Milman* (London 1900), p. 232. H. B. Barry said in 1852: 'It would not be easy to calculate the damage done to the Church in the opinion of the masses by the long-delayed and incomplete opening of St Paul's, and by the frequent rudeness of vergers generally. These may appear small things, but they are important, as they give the Church itself a repulsive instead of an inviting aspect' (H. B. Barry, *Thoughts on the Renovation of Cathedral Institutions* (London 1852), quoted in A. C. Tait, 'Cathedral Reform', *Edinburgh Review*, vol. xcvii, January 1853, p. 180). It was the Great Exhibition that finally threw open the doors of St Paul's. Tourists from all over England flocked to London with cheap railway excursion tickets and visited St Paul's at the rate of 6,000 an hour (R. D. Fenwick, 'An Early Victorian Organist at Work: I – John Goss in Quire at St Paul's Cathedral, 1838–1860', *The Organ*, vol. 62, no. 245, July 1983, p. 106).

300 ABDC Wells, 5 August 1853.

301 Salisbury Chapter Muniments, Press I, Box 39; cf. A. E. Bridge in D. Marcombe and C. S. Knighton, eds, *Close Encounters: English Cathedrals and Society since 1540* (Nottingham 1991), p. 141.

302 PP 1854, xxv, pp. 53–4.

303 ABDC Gloucester, 15 September 1858. The nave of Worcester Cathedral was opened freely in the same year (*Record of some of the Principal Events relating to the Cathedral of Worcester, the Dean and Chapter, and their property*, p. 8).

304 Wells CM, 29 September 1862; cf. ABDC Hereford, 21 April 1869.

305 *Guardian*, 1872, pp. 388, 455, 550.

306 *Guardian*, 1881, pp. 791, 1404.

307 Watson, p. 134.

308 ABDC Bristol, 9 July 1889.

309 ABDC Salisbury, 8 October 1863.

310 Compton, pp. 63–4.

311 *Guardian*, 1869, p. 182. Earlier the cathedral had been kept locked (Hill, *Victorian Lincoln*, p. 262.

312 ABDC Bristol, 5 July 1870, 1 May 1884; cf. Pigou, p. 265.

313 Walcott, *Traditions*, p. 81.

314 ABDC Winchester, 29 September 1874.

315 *Guardian*, 1875, p. 1057. For a complaint to Archbishop Benson about the early closing of Canterbury, and the reply of the Archbishop's Chaplain, cf. LPL, Benson Papers, XII, pp. 185, 191. A 6d fee was levied at Exeter to see all parts of the building except the nave (ABDC Exeter, 15 March 1873).

316 ABDC Hereford, 4 July 1876. Two years later visitors were *required* to pay 6d each (ibid., 14 November 1878). A fee of 6d was requested at Winchester in 1874 (ABDC Winchester, 3 February 1874) and at Chichester in 1886 (ABDC Chichester, 7 May 1886). A similar fee was demanded at Gloucester in 1876, though the nave was still freely open (Gloucester chapter minute book, 24 June and 28 September 1876). A fee of 6d was required in 1892 at Bristol to inspect certain parts of the building (ABDC Bristol, 5 January 1892); cf. Wells CM, 1 April 1873, and 27–28 June 1890. The income from visitors' fees at Exeter was said to amount to over £200 per annum in 1888. (*Guardian*, 1888, p. 526); cf. Chapter 6, p. 108.

317 ABDC Chichester, 2 May and 1 August 1891. The decision about the cloisters was rescinded in 1897 (ibid., 3 August 1897).
318 ABDC Worcester, 2 March 1897; cf. 10 May 1897.
319 *Guardian*, 1848, p. 578; cf. also *Guardian*, 1888, p. 1936. In 1841 a party of nearly 800 members of the Birmingham Mechanics' Institute went by rail to visit Gloucester Cathedral (*HT*, 31 July 1841).
320 *Guardian*, 1849, pp. 505, 567, 600.
321 *Guardian*, 1855, p. 676; cf. *Ecclesiologist*, vol. 2, nos. 14–24, November 1842, p. 34.
322 ABDC Hereford, 24 March 1870.
323 *Guardian*, 1872, p. 455.
324 Coghlan, p. 168, quoting St Paul's CM, 8 December 1899.
325 ABDC Exeter, 3 January 1873.
326 ABDC Chichester, 19 March 1889.
327 ABDC Chichester, 29 October 1889.
328 Wells CM, 24 October 1868, 1 October 1872; cf. ABDC Winchester, 3 February 1874. The fee for ascending the tower at Winchester was 1s; cf. also ABDC Worcester, 25 September 1875.
329 *Guardian*, 1848, p. 558; Worc. C. Add. Mss. 45.
330 Prestige, p. 29.
331 S. E. R. Chitty, *The Beast and the Monk* (London 1974), p. 274.
332 Prestige, p. 97. Gregory, Liddon and Lightfoot often took large parties of working men round St Paul's on Saturday afternoons (ibid., p. 106). Westcott was also keen to give guided tours at Peterborough (Westcott, vol. I, p. 318).
333 Reynolds, p. 747.
334 ABDC Bristol, 7 April 1893, 4 June 1895.
335 Wells CM, 1 July 1884, 9 January 1899.
336 Woodruff and Danks, p. 356.
337 Wells CM, 13 October 1865.
338 ABDC Exeter, 3 April 1886.
339 H. Leeds, *Norwich Cathedral Past and Present* (Norwich 1910), p. 70.

CHAPTER 12 *Cathedrals and Education*

1 For the medieval background, cf. K. Edwards, *The English Secular Cathedrals in the Middle Ages* (2nd edn, Manchester 1967), pp. 166–8, 176–7, 185–97, 204–5, 307–9, 311; M. D. Knowles, *The Monastic Order in England* (2nd edn, Cambridge 1966), pp. 487–92; N. Orme, *English Schools in the Middle Ages* (London 1973); for sixteenth-century developments, cf. J. M. Falkner and A. H. Thompson, *The Statutes of the Cathedral Church of Durham* (Surtees Society, vol. cxliii, Durham 1829), p. xlix; G. Butler, *Statutes of Peterborough Cathedral* (Peterborough 1853), pp. 23–5; D. Robertson, *The King's School, Gloucester* (Chichester 1974), pp. 31–7; M. R. Craze, *King's School, Worcester (1541–1971)* (Worcester 1972), pp. 14–17; S. E. Lehmberg, *The Reformation of Cathedrals* (Princeton 1988), pp. 297–301; and C. S. Knighton, 'The Provision of Education in the new Cathedral foundations of Henry VIII', in D. Marcombe and C. S. Knighton, eds, *Close Encounters: English Cathedrals and Society since 1540* (Nottingham 1991), pp. 18–42.
2 Quoted in Craze, p. 174.
3 ibid.
4 Robertson, pp. 102, 104–5.
5 ABDC Hereford, 8 November 1804.
6 M. Hackett, *Correspondence, Legal Proceedings and Evidences Respecting the Ancient Collegiate School Attached to St Paul's Cathedral* (3rd edn London 1832), and Hackett's *A Brief Account of Cathedral and Collegiate Schools* (London 1825, 1827, 1860 and 1873). For the education of choristers, cf. Chapter 8, pp. 197–201.

7 R. Arnold, *The Whiston Matter* (London 1961), pp. 10–13. The summary in this chapter is based on the full account to be found in Arnold's book.

8 cf. P. C. Moore, 'The Organisation and Development of Cathedral Worship in England, with special reference to choral services, from the Reformation to the nineteenth century' (Oxford D. Phil. thesis 1954), p. 352.

9 ABDC Hereford, 7 January 1845. St Peter's School at York was at a low ebb at this time under an unsatisfactory headmaster, William Hewson. For an account of the varying fortunes of this school during the nineteenth century, cf. A. S. Leak, 'Conflict and Reform at York Minster in the Nineteenth Century' (Oxford B. D. thesis 1988), pp. 8–9, 29–54.

10 ABDC Worcester, 23 June 1848.

11 PP 1854–5, xv, pp. 74–8.

12 PP 1854, xxv, pp. 969f.

13 ibid., pp. 971–5. Very soon after his arrival at Carlisle, Tait asked Canon Harcourt 'to superintend the religious instruction of the choristers' until he could make proper and permanent arrangements for them (LPL, Tait Papers, vol. 27, 28 January 1850).

14 PP 1854, xxv, p. 976.

15 ibid., p. 976.

16 ibid., pp. 977–9.

17 ibid., p. 980.

18 ibid., p. 981.

19 ibid., p. 981.

20 ibid., pp. 982–4. Dean Goulburn visited the choristers' school at Norwich very soon after his arrival in 1867. He described it as 'a poor mean cottage on the way to the ferry' (NCL, Goulburn's diary, 28 February 1867).

21 ibid., p. 983.

22 ibid., pp. 984–6.

23 ibid., pp. 986–8.

24 PP 1854–5, xv, p. 56.

25 PP 1884–5, xxi, p. 242. Robertson, pp. 120–1. Around 1850 the King's Scholars of Canterbury attended matins in the cathedral on saints' days and Fridays, and both matins and evensong on Sundays (C. E. Woodruff and H. J. Cape, *Schola Regia Cantuariensis*, London 1908). The grammar scholars at Salisbury Cathedral also attended matins on saints' days (ABDC Salisbury, 7 January 1852). At Hereford the Lady Chapel was used for the school's daily assembly, though the dean and chapter prohibited its use on saints' days and on the day of the chapter audit. On Sunday mornings the boys were instructed to leave the cathedral through the north porch 'to avoid the noise sometimes made in leaving the Cathedral' (ABDC Hereford, 8 November 1888). Children from the Episcopal or Bishop Blackall's School attended early prayers at Exeter in about 1828 (ABDC Exeter, 1 March 1828).

26 A. H. Brewer, *Memories of Choirs and Cloisters* (London 1931), pp. 4–5.

27 Winchester Cathedral Mss., *De Precentore*, 1 March 1887; P. M. J. Crook, *A History of the Pilgrims' School and earlier Winchester Choir Schools* (Chichester 1981), pp. 14–20; cf. also Chapter 8, p. 201.

28 cf. T. C. Durham, 'Cathedral Schools', in J. S. Howson, ed., *Essays on Cathedrals by Various Writers* (London 1872), pp. 298f.

29 G. L. Prestige, *St Paul's in its Glory, 1831–1911* (London 1955), pp. 156–7; cf. Chapter 8, p. 205.

30 Durham, in Howson, pp. 289–90; cf. H. D. Rawnsley, *Harvey Goodwin, Bishop of Carlisle* (London 1896), p. 108.

31 Durham, in Howson, pp. 294–5. On the other hand, it was widely felt that the education of cathedral choristers in the 1870s was 'still generally deplorable',

especially at Ely and Chester (W. L. Hillsman, 'Trends and Aims in Anglican Music 1870–1906, in relation to developments in churchmanship' (Oxford D. Phil. thesis 1985), p. 302, citing *Musical Standard*, 7 April 1877, p. 208; ibid., 2 October 1875, p. 223; and Moore, p. 371).

32 ABDC Chichester, 31 March 1879. The school received new statutes in the following year (ibid., 3 May 1880). For entry qualifications to the school in 1860, cf. ABDC Chichester, 10 October 1860; cf. also W. K. L. Clarke, *Chichester Cathedral in the Nineteenth Century* (Chichester Papers no. 14, Chichester 1959), pp. 14–15, and N. Ollerenshaw, *A History of the Prebendal School* (Chichester 1984), pp. 14–21, 77–82.

33 PP 1884, xxii, p. 197; Craze, pp. 217–8.

34 PP 1884, xxii, pp. 197–8.

35 Worc. C. Add. Mss., 55; Craze, p. 250.

36 PP 1884–5, xxi, p. 416.

37 Greenhalgh, *Wells*, p. 190; cf. PP 1883, xxi, p. 250.

38 HCA 1538; Charity Commissioners' Scheme no. 733, approved by an Order in Council, 26 June 1893; CCF 32508, letter of 28 June 1890.

39 K. Lake, ed., *Memorials of William Charles Lake* (London 1901), p. 133.

40 E. W. Watson, *Life of Bishop John Wordsworth* (London 1915), p. 134.

41 E. Wordsworth, *Memorials of Henry William Burrows* (London 1894), p. x.

42 R. Farrar, *The Life of Frederic William Farrar, sometime Dean of Canterbury* (London 1904), p. 322.

43 R. Hannam-Clark, *Memories of the College School, Gloucester* (Gloucester 1890), p. 58.

44 J. Jebb and H. W. Phillott, *The Statutes of the Cathedral Church of Hereford* (Hereford 1882), pp. 26–31.

45 A. W. Goodman and W. H. Hutton, *The Statutes governing the Cathedral Church of Winchester* (Oxford 1925), p. 12.

46 D. M. Owen, *The Library and Muniments of Ely Cathedral* (Ely 1973), p. 7.

47 B. Botfield, *Notes on the Cathedral Libraries of England* (London 1849), p. 4; cf. ABDC Bristol, 29 November 1831, 26 June 1832; Walcott, *Traditions*, p. 47.

48 Walcott, *Traditions*, p. 52.

49 Anon., *Wells Cathedral Library* (Wells 1974), pp. 10, fn. 29, 12. The dean became librarian in 1833 and Mr Aldrit, the master of the cathedral school, became sub-librarian at a salary of £10 per annum (Wells CM, 1 July 1833).

50 Hansard, P. D., 16 May 1848 (speech of Mr Horsman).

51 Botfield, p. 72.

52 ibid., p. 132.

53 ibid., p. 416.

54 ibid., pp. 384–5.

55 ibid., pp. 5f. Early in the century C. R. Bunce was responsible for sorting out the 5,000 or so mss. of the dean and chapter. It took him two years to complete the task and he wrote a careful index of their contents in a huge folio (M. Beazeley, 'History of the Chapter Library of Canterbury Cathedral', *Transactions of the Bibliographical Society*, vol viii, 1907, pp. 113f.; cf. ABDC Canterbury, 25 November 1804, 25 November 1806). The library was opened to the public for the first time in 1840 (Beazeley, p. 178).

56 Botfield, p. 89.

57 ibid., p. 171.

58 ibid., p. 259.

59 ibid., p. 330.

60 ibid., p. 508; cf. C. B. L. Barr, 'The Minster Library', in G. E. Aylmer and R. Cant, eds, *A History of York Minster* (Oxford 1977), p. 512.

61 N. R. Ker, 'Cathedral Libraries', in *Library History*, vol. 1, no. 2, Autumn 1967, p. 43; for fuller details about York Minster library, cf. Barr, in Aylmer and Cant,

pp. 512–23; cf. also O. S. Tomlinson, 'Libraries in York', in A. Stacpoole, ed., *The Noble City of York* (York 1972), p. 973.

62 Ker, pp. 42–3.

63 W. J. S. Simpson, *Memoir of the Reverend W. Sparrow Simpson* (London 1899), p. 39; cf. Prestige, p. 87.

64 Simpson, pp. 39–40.

65 Owen, p. 8. Ely library contained 4,000 books in 1852.

66 ABDC Chichester, 24 December 1881.

67 PP 1883, xxi, p. 157.

68 ABDC Worcester, 21 November 1838, 27 February, 22 November 1865, 1 April 1866, 20 November 1873. Visitors to the cathedral at Exeter in 1810 were not to be shown the library by the vergers without permission (ABDC Exeter, 20 December 1810). The clergy of the diocese of York were allowed access to the Minster library on any weekday (Barr, in Aylmer and Cant, p. 517) and the libraries at Wells and Exeter could also be used by diocesan clergy (Wells CM, 16 October 1850; ABDC Exeter, 30 December 1876). H. E. Reynolds complained that only seventeen persons used the Exeter library in 1877, compared with ninety at Canterbury, but they borrowed 124 books between them. Ker has shown that between 1877 and 1898 about 3,500 books were borrowed at an average rate of 160 a year (Ker, p. 44). The great library at Durham, however, was used most by dissenting ministers (P. Kaufman, 'Reading Vogues at English Cathedral Libraries of the Eighteenth Century', *Bulletin of the New York Public Library*, vol. 67, 1963, p. 651, quoting H. E. Reynolds, 'Our Cathedral Libraries', *Transactions and Proceedings of the first annual meeting of the Library Association, 1878*, p. 32f. Bishop Browne discovered at his visitation of Winchester Cathedral in 1884 that the books in Bishop Morley's library were hardly ever used, and other books were used only under stringent conditions (*Winchester Cathedral Chronicle*, 1873–91, pp. 86f.). In 1880 the *Guardian* made a plea for an increased use of cathedral libraries by clergy (*Guardian*, 1880, p. 153). In 1899 the library at Canterbury was open to the public on Tuesdays and Fridays each week (ibid., 1899, p. 34).

69 H. D. Hughes, *A History of Durham Cathedral Library* (Durham 1925), pp. xiv, 10.

70 PP 1884–5, xxi, p. 338. In 1878 several cathedral librarians and others met at Oxford and founded the Library Association of the United Kingdom. The dean and chapter of Exeter gave £5 to Reynolds to enable him to attend (ABDC Exeter, 28 September 1878). A very detailed table giving much information about the contemporary state of cathedral libraries from information supplied by Reynolds was published in PP 1884–5, xxi, p. 341.

71 Reynolds, p. 41.

72 L. J. Lloyd, *The Library of Exeter Cathedral* (Exeter 1967), p. 16; ABDC Exeter, 27 November 1886, 22 January 1887.

73 L. Creighton, *Life and Letters of Mandell Creighton* (London 1904), vol. II, p. 9.

74 ABDC Worcester, 23 November 1818; cf. also 22 November 1834.

75 ABDC Hereford, 10 November 1821.

76 ABDC Exeter, 14–15 March 1822.

77 ibid., 30 December 1876.

78 F. C. and P. E. Morgan, *Hereford Cathedral Libraries and Muniments* (Hereford 1970), pp. 10–12.

79 ABDC Hereford, 9 November 1854.

80 ibid., 14 November 1861.

81 D. M. Williamson, *Lincoln Muniments* (Lincoln 1956), p. 13. A correspondent in the *Guardian* wrote in 1869: 'The library, much augmented by gifts from the present dean, has been warmed by hot water and the manuscripts enclosed in cases, all the clergy of the diocese being at liberty to take out books' (*Guardian*, 1869, p. 182).

82 *Trefoil*, pp. 88–9.

83 Williamson, pp. 13–16; cf. HMC Report XII, appendix part ix, 1891, p. 553; for the work of Archdeacon Chapman at Ely, cf. ibid., p. 389.

84 S. Moore, *Calendar of Archives – Dean and Chapter of Exeter*, 1873 (manuscript in Exeter Cathedral library).

85 Reynolds, p. 39. W. K. Hamilton did much good work in the library and archives at Salisbury (cf. A. E. Bridge, in Marcombe and Knighton, p. 142).

86 Jebb and Phillott, pp. 56–65. At Chichester the responsibility of lecturing was exercised by the Prebendary of Highleigh (Walcott, *Traditions*, p. 85).

87 Goodman and Hutton, p. 31, fn. 1. Dean Bramston introduced other preachers besides the minor canons at these lectures: 'It may be added that the lecture is given *before* evensong and that a bell was formerly tolled, to give notice to the people, at its conclusion, that evensong was about to commence; thus showing the two, lecture and service, were totally unconnected' (Winchester Cathedral Mss., *Cathedralia Winton – Minor Canons 1860–1918*).

88 W. H. Frere, *Visitation Articles and Injunctions of the Period of the Reformation* (London 1910), vol, I, p. 126.

89 ABDC Exeter, 9 February and 1 March 1828.

90 S. E. R. Chitty, *The Beast and the Monk* (London 1974), p. 274.

91 Rawnsley, p. 114.

92 *Guardian*, 1869, p. 182.

93 J. W. F. Hill, *Victorian Lincoln* (London 1974), pp. 263–4.

94 A. C. Benson, *The Life of Edward White Benson, sometime Archbishop of Canterbury* (London 1899), vol. I, pp. 369–71, 380–1). For John Wordsworth's classes at Rochester for the dockyard workers from Chatham, cf. Chapter 5, p. 71; for Westcott's lectures at Peterborough, cf. Chapter 5, p. 71.

95 NCL, Goulburn's diary, 28 January 1869. For Burgon's lectures and classes at Chichester, cf. Chapter 4, p. 51.

96 W. H. Hutton, ed., *The Autobiography of Robert Gregory* (London 1912), pp. 197–8; Prestige, p. 107; *Guardian*, 1883, p. 1807; cf. Chapter 6, pp. 95–6.

97 Prestige, pp. 224–5.

98 *Guardian*, 1878, p. 1197; cf. Worc. C. Add. Mss., 141, p. 32.

99 Creighton, vol. I, pp. 318–9, 381–3, 389.

100 ABDC Worcester, 19 November 1890.

101 *Guardian*, 1878, p. 1581.

102 Salisbury CM, 4 October and 29 November 1880.

103 ABDC Hereford, 25 June 1884. Bishop Browne suggested at Winchester in 1884 that there should be lectures on theology, ecclesiastical history and law (*Winchester Cathedral Chronicle*, 1873–91, p. 86, qu.46); cf. Chapter 11, p. 264, for the lectures arranged by Gloucester Cathedral Society.

104 E. B. Pusey, *Remarks on the Prospective and Past Benefits of Cathedral Institutions in the Promotion of Sound Religious Knowledge occasioned by Lord Henley's Plan for their Abolition* (London 1833), pp. 15, 142, fn. 3. There have been two recent studies of this pamphlet: D. Galilee, 'Pusey: A Forgotten Text?', *Theology*, vol. lxxviii, no. 658, April 1975, pp. 196–202; and R. Jupp, '"Nurseries of a learned clergy": Pusey and the Defence of Cathedrals', in P. Butler, ed., *Pusey Rediscovered* (London 1983), pp. 139–61. Another early advocate of cathedrals as suitable centres for theological education was H. E. Manning, who also called in 1840 for cathedrals to found new intermediate schools between parochial schools and universities and to help train teachers for secondary schools (H. E. Manning, *The Preservation of Unendowed Canonries, a Letter* (London 1840); cf. D. Newsome, *The Parting of Friends* (London 1966), p. 220).

105 F. W. B. Bullock, *A History of Training for the Ministry of the Church of England in England and Wales from 1800 to 1874* (St Leonard's-on-Sea 1955), p. 58; MBVC Wells,

21 July 1860, 23 October 1872. For a general account of theological colleges in cathedral cities, cf. W. O. Chadwick, *The Victorian Church* (London 1970), vol. II, pp. 382–3.

106 Greenhalgh, *Wells*, pp. 192–3; cf. Chapter 5, pp. 71–2; cf. also W. M. Jacob, 'The Diffusion of Tractarianism: Wells Theological College 1840–1849', *Southern History*, vol. V, 1983, pp. 189–209.

107 ABDC Exeter, 18 January 1862; PP 1883, xxi, p. 81.

108 Wordsworth to Benson, 9 December 1872, quoted in Benson, vol. I, p. 344; cf. Benson's own account of the foundation of the college in J. H. Overton and E. Wordsworth, *Christopher Wordsworth* (London 1988), pp. 285–90. Benson stresses that the college 'became part of the Cathedral organisation in the truest sense' (ibid., p. 286).

109 Benson, vol. I, p. 372.

110 Benson to Cubitt, 16 January 1874, quoted in Benson, vol. I, pp. 373–4.

111 ibid., pp. 376–7. Benson was quick to initiate a 'cathedral school of divinity' at Truro. By 1879 there were twenty-five students, who attended morning prayer in the cathedral daily and were present at evensong at least three times a week (PP 1883, xxi, pp. 83, 85).

112 H. Stapleton, ed., *Tribute to Ely: Ely Theological College 1876–1964* (privately published 1980), pp. 16–17.

113 P. V. Coghlan, 'Cathedral Worship in the Church of England 1815–1914' (Leicester University M. Phil. thesis 1984), p. 91. Another way in which cathedrals supported theological education may be found at Exeter, where the dean and chapter resolved in 1877 to offer exhibitions of £50 per annum to ordinands to allow them to remain an extra year at university before ordination (ABDC Exeter, 21 July 1877). This plan was heavily criticized and E. W. Benson tried to divert the funds for his new theological college at Truro (PP 1883, xxi, pp. 82, 90–1). For W. K. Hamilton's connection with the Salisbury diocesan training school, the diocesan board of education, and the foundation of Marlborough College, cf. A. E. Bridge, in Marcombe and Knighton, pp. 149–50.

CHAPTER 13 *Cathedral Reform*

1 Lord Henley, *A Plan of Church Reform* (London 1832, 4th edn), p. vii. For a summary of his proposals, cf. R. Jupp, in P. Butler, ed., *Pusey Rediscovered* (London 1983), pp. 146–9.

2 Henley, p. 25; G. F. A Best, *Temporal Pillars* (Cambridge 1964), p. 287.

3 Henley, pp. 31, 34–5.

4 For examples of some comments and reactions, cf. Best, pp. 286–7.

5 cf. Chapter 1, p. 4, and Chapter 12, p. 283 and n. 104. Thomas Arnold's *Principles of Church Reform* (London 1833) was also a response to Henley's pamphlet, but his proposals went far beyond finding a new role for cathedrals.

6 E. B. Pusey, *Remarks on the Prospective and Past Benefits of Cathedral Institutions in the Promotion of Sound Religious Knowledge occasioned by Lord Henley's Plan for their Abolition* (London 1833), pp. 4–5, 61–2, 65, 76. For a summary of Pusey's work, cf. H. P. Liddon, *Life of Edward Bouverie Pusey* (London 1893), vol. I, pp. 227f., and Jupp, in Butler, pp. 149–55. The educational role of cathedrals was also stressed by Gladstone and Acland in 1840 (Hansard, P. D., 3rd series, vol. lv, pp. 200f., 207f., 29 June 1840).

7 Pusey, pp. 146f.

8 ibid., pp. 151f.

9 cf. Chapter 2, pp. 17–20.

10 cf. Chapter 2, pp. 20–2.

11 E. B. Pusey, 'The Royal and Parliamentary Ecclesiastical Commissions', *British Critic*, vol. 23, no. 46, April 1838, p. 558.

12 cf. Chapter 4, pp. 41–4.

13 ABDC Hereford, 31 March 1837.

14 Hansard, P. D., 3rd series, vol. xcviii, 16 May 1848. For Horsman, cf. W. O. Chadwick, *Church and Historical Endowment in the Victorian Age* (London 1986), pp. 11–13.

15 Hansard.

16 PP 1854, xxv, pp. 1–3; Hansard, P. D., 3rd series, vol. xcviii, 16 May 1848.

17 ibid., p. 9.

18 ibid., p. 60. Tait welcomed the establishment of the Commission and hoped it would result in legislation about cathedral duties as well as revenues (Tait, 'Cathedral Reform', *Edinburgh Review*, vol. xcvii, January 1853, p. 181).

19 ibid., cf. A. J. B. Beresford Hope, *The English Cathedral of the Nineteenth Century* (London 1861), pp. 22–3.

20 PP 1854, xxv, pp. 10–11.

21 C. Wordsworth, 'On English Cathedrals', *Miscellanies Literary and Religious*, III (London 1879), p. 315; G. F. A. Best, p. 433.

22 PP 1854–5, xv, pp. 45, 47, 52, 56–8, 60; cf. Chapter 7, p. 143.

23 For a more dismissive opinion, cf. Best, pp. 433–4.

24 D. H. Robertson, *Sarum Close* (London 1938, new edn 1970), pp. 286–7.

25 W. K. Hamilton, *Cathedral Reform: A Letter to the Members of his Diocese* (London, Oxford and Salisbury 1855), p. 4.

26 ibid., pp. 6, 14. For an appreciation and details of Hamilton's work, cf. H. P. Liddon, *Walter Kerr Hamilton, Bishop of Salisbury* (London 1869), pp. 22–4; B. Rainbow, *The Choral Revival in the Anglican Church, 1839–1872* (London 1970), p. 261; W. H. Hutton, ed., *The Autobiography of Robert Gregory* (London 1912), pp. 161–2; and A. E. Bridge, 'Walter Kerr Hamilton: The Making of a Tractarian Bishop, 1808–1854' (Oxford M. Litt. thesis 1988), pp. 108–31. Part of Bridge's thesis has been published – 'The Nineteenth Century Revivification of Salisbury Cathedral: Walter Kerr Hamilton, 1841–1854' in D. Marcombe and C. S. Knighton, eds, *Close Encounters: English Cathedrals and Society since 1540* (Nottingham 1991), pp. 137–60 – and includes an account of Hamilton's views on cathedral reform.

27 A. C. Tait, 'Cathedral Reform', *Edinburgh Review*, vol. xcvii, January 1853, pp. 152–81; cf. also P. T. Marsh, *The Victorian Church in Decline* (London 1969), p. 208.

28 Tait, p. 152.

29 ibid., p. 158.

30 ibid., p. 162.

31 ibid., pp. 166–7, 175.

32 ibid., pp. 167–8.

33 ibid., p. 179 fn.; cf. *The Continuing Care of Churches and Cathedrals: Report of the Faculty Jurisdiction Commission* (London 1984), pp. 123–38. The Care of Cathedrals Measure 1990 has enacted many of the proposals of this report.

34 For the views of Benjamin Jowett on cathedral reform, cf. E. Abbott and L. Campbell, eds, *Letters of Benjamin Jowett* (London 1899), pp. 8–13.

35 CCR 1865, pp. 75, 80. William Selwyn had made various suggestions in 1863 (PP 1863, vi, pp. 234–7).

36 H. Alford, 'Cathedral Reform', *Contemporary Review*, vol. xii, September 1869, pp. 38f.

37 Alford had said much the same a year earlier: 'The cathedral *esprit de corps* is ordinarily one of isolation from the diocese, and from common clerical work; the scrupulous maintenance of certain rights and privileges, as against the invasion of the wants and necessities of the age....The whole body is a phenomenon, in the estimation of the people, quite extraneous to anything which comes home to them in the work or influence of the Church.' He said that it was impossible for the

capitular system to survive. It was 'an evil in itself and must be reformed' (H. Alford, 'The Church of the Future', *Contemporary Review,* vol. ix, 1868, pp. 176–7).

38 H. Alford, 'Cathedral Reform', pp. 38, 41, 43–7.

39 H. Alford, 'Cathedral Reform', pp. 48–9; PP 1871, lv, p. 197.

40 H. Alford, 'Cathedral Reform', p. 49. For the shorter letter, cf. PP 1871, lv, pp. 197–9.

41 PP 1871, lv, p. 200.

42 PP 1871, lv, pp. 219–25; E. M. Goulburn, *The Functions of our Cathedrals* (Oxford and London 1869).

43 E. M. Goulburn, *The Principles of the Cathedral System Vindicated* (London 1870), p. xxxiv. When Goulburn advocated these advantages of cathedrals in his earlier pamphlet, he was sharply criticized by Dean Close: 'While thousands and tens of thousands of our people need better churches, more pastors, and, as we are assured, more bishops, we cannot afford some ten or twelve thousand per annum to each of our cathedrals to sustain a corps of ecclesiastical thinkers, writers, or masters of sacred song' (PP 1871, lv, p. 204). Dean Mansel supported Goulburn (ibid., p. 238).

44 Goulburn, *The Principles of the Cathedral System Vindicated,* pp. 14–15.

45 ibid., pp. 41, 45.

46 ibid., pp. 134–5.

47 E. M. Goulburn, *Suggestions to Facilitate Business at the Second Lambeth Conference on the Subject of Cathedral Reform* (Oxford 1872).

48 ibid., pp. 15–16.

49 PP 1871, lv, pp. 201–4.

50 ibid., pp. 204–10.

51 ibid., pp. 210–13.

52 ibid., p. 215.

53 ibid., p. 215.

54 ibid., p. 219.

55 ibid., pp. 225–6.

56 ibid., p. 226.

57 ibid., pp. 227–8.

58 ibid., pp. 229–30. Tait had suggested in 1853 that certain episcopal functions might be vested in deans (Tait, pp. 172–3).

59 ibid., pp. 231–2.

60 ibid., pp. 236–41.

61 ibid., p. 242.

62 B. F. Westcott, 'On Cathedral Work', *Macmillan's Magazine,* vol. xxi, 1869–70, p. 246; cf. also pp. 308f.

63 ibid., pp. 246–7.

64 E. W. Benson, 'Cathedral Life and Cathedral Work', *Quarterly Review,* vol. cxxx, no. 259, January 1871, pp. 225–55.

65 See above, pp. 301–2.

66 A. C. Tait, *Some Thoughts on the Duties of the Established Church of England as a National Church* (London 1876), pp. 8–9. Tait had clearly been considering a further move for some time. Towards the end of 1871 he discussed the matter with Dean Lake of Durham, who tried to dissuade him (cf. K. Lake, ed., *Memorials of William Charles Lake* (London 1901), pp. 219–20, 222). The *Saturday Review* welcomed this meeting: 'That some capitular reform is needful no one who knows anything about the subject can doubt' (*Saturday Review,* 1872, vol. I, p. 365).

67 Tait, *Some Thoughts on the Duties of the Established Church,* pp. 10–12.

68 ABDC Salisbury, 11 March 1872: Archbishop Tait to Dean, 4 March 1872. The eight men chosen for this committee were the Deans of Chester, Bristol, Durham and Rochester, and Canons Gregory, Harrington, Moore and Wood.

69 For replies of the dean and chapter of Salisbury, cf. ABDC Salisbury, 11 March

1872; for Exeter, cf. ABDC Exeter, 8–9 March 1872. Dean Herbert of Hereford said that there were no special hindrances. The cathedral 'has already been rendered fairly efficient and useful without any help from Parliament and if left alone will no doubt increase in usefulness and in popularity still more' (HCA 5685).

70 cf. P. T. Marsh, *The Victorian Church in Decline* (London 1869), pp. 98, 109–10.

71 J. S. Howson, ed., *Essays on Cathedrals by Various Writers* (London 1872), p. v. For a review of this book, cf. *Saturday Review,* 1872, vol. I, pp. 607–9.

72 Howson, pp. vi–xi.

73 ibid., pp. 3–34.

74 ibid., pp. 37–55.

75 ibid., pp. 77–94.

76 ibid., p. 95.

77 ibid., pp. 96–8.

78 ibid., pp. 99–105.

79 ibid., pp. 109–33.

80 ibid., pp. 139–65.

81 ibid., pp. 167–84.

82 ibid., pp. 211–34.

83 ibid., p. 215; cf. *The Choir,* 17 February 1872, p. 95, quoted in W. L. Hillsman, 'Trends and Aims in Anglican Music 1870–1906, in relation to developments in churchmanship' (Oxford D. Phil. thesis 1985), p. 302.

84 Howson, p. 217.

85 ibid., p. 223.

86 ibid., p. 225.

87 ibid., pp. 237–83.

88 ibid., pp. 287–306; cf. Chapter 12, pp. 275–6.

89 ibid., pp. 362–3.

90 CCR 1872, pp. 217–25.

91 E. W. Benson, *The Cathedral: Its Necessary Place in the Life and Work of the Church* (London 1878). Another example of cathedral reform put into practice was at Lichfield, where Bishop Selwyn was able to amend the statutes (H. W. Tucker, *Memoir of the Life and Episcopate of George Augustus Selwyn* (London 1879), vol. I, p. 30; J. H. Evans, *Churchman Militant* (London 1964), p. 172.

92 Benson, *The Cathedral,* p. 105.

93 ibid., p. 120.

94 ibid., p. 133; cf. Chapter 11, p. 258; cf. also J. Tiller, *A Strategy for the Church's Ministry* (London 1983), pp. 101–2, for a modern echo of this plan.

95 Benson, *The Cathedral,* pp. 134–5.

96 ibid., pp. 136–40.

97 ibid., pp. 142–9.

98 ibid., pp. 153–65.

99 Marsh, pp. 208–9; R. T. Davidson and W. Benham, *Life of Archibald Campbell Tait, Archbishop of Canterbury* (London 1891), vol. II, pp. 518–19. Tait was very interested in the new commission and worked hard on its behalf (ibid., pp. 521, 526).

100 Davidson and Benham, pp. 518–19; J. A. Merivale, ed., *Autobiography of Dean Merivale* (London 1899), p. 326; H. D. Rawnsley, *Harvey Goodwin, Bishop of Carlisle* (London 1896), p. 220; Hansard, P. D., vol. ccxlvi, 15 May 1879, pp. 381f.

101 PP 1883, xxi.

102 CCR, 1880, p. 387.

103 Hansard, vol. cclxxi, 22 June 1882, col. 9; cf. Elliott to Thomson, 2 August 1882, LPL, Benson Papers, I, pp. 384–5.

104 PP 1884–5, xxi, p. 455; for a detailed account of the way in which the commission worked, cf. G. E. Marindin, ed., *Letters of Frederic, Lord Blachford* (London 1896),

pp. 409–10. Cranbrook later described the work of the commission as 'a wasted employment to us all' (N. E. Johnson, ed., *The Diary of Gathorne Hardy, later Lord Cranbrook, 1866–1892: Political Selections* (Oxford 1981), p. 813 (27 November 1891). There are several references to the work of the commission in this diary.

105 cf. Marsh, p. 280, quoting PP 1882, xx, p. 20; Hansard, 3rd series, vol. cclxxi, 1882, pp. 4–11, and vol. cclxxiii, 1882, pp. 1918–21; Rawnsley, pp. 222, 245; cf. also Hansard, 3rd series, vol. cccxli, 1890, pp. 1131f., 1488, 1764; vol. cccxlii, 1890, p. 668; vol. cccxlvii, 1890, p. 1844; vol. cccxlix, 1890, pp. 108–9; vol. ccclv, 1891, p. 1272.

106 *Chronicle of the Convocation of Canterbury,* Lower House, 26 April 1881, pp. 6–10; cf. ibid., 19 May 1881, pp. 280–1, 310–24.

107 Worc. C. Mss., volume of press-cuttings (pre-1900).

108 Moore, pp. 375–6.

CHAPTER 14 *Then and Now*

1 S. Smith, *Second Letter to Archdeacon Singleton* (London 1838), p. 5.

2 F. Bussby, *Winchester Cathedral 1079–1979* (Southampton 1979; second edn 1987), p. 242; P. L. S. Barrett, 'Winchester Cathedral in the Nineteenth Century', in D. Marcombe and C. S. Knighton, eds, *Close Encounters: English Cathedrals and Society since 1540* (Nottingham 1991), pp. 129–30.

3 *Guardian,* 1891, p. 1548; for similar comments by Dean Payne-Smith, Archbishop Tait and Bishop Temple, cf. PP 1884, xxii, p. 267; Hansard, vol. cclxxi, 22 June 1882, col. 4f.; *Guardian,* 1882, p. 891, 1879, p. 715.

4 Worc. C. Add. Mss., 128, pp. 1–3f; 137, pp. 1–7.

5 *CT,* March 1886 (press-cutting in Worcester Cathedral library).

6 *Guardian,* 1874, p. 444; E. H. Plumptre, *The Ideal of Cathedral Life* (London 1882), pp. 13f.; A. J. Worlledge, *Letters of Bishop Gott* (London 1918), p. 25; cf. *Guardian,* 1878, p. 1482, 1879, p. 433.

7 For St Paul's, cf. Chapter 4, pp. 52–3; Chapter 5, pp. 69–71; Chapter 6, pp. 94–6; Chapter 8, pp. 179–80, 212; Chapter 10, pp. 239–41. For Worcester, cf. Chapter 4, pp. 45–7; Chapter 5, pp. 68–9; Chapter 6, pp. 104–5; Chapter 8, pp. 212–15, Chapter 10, pp. 235–8.

8 cf. Chapter 4, p. 55; Chapter 7, p. 122; Chapter 10, p. 242; Chapter 11, pp. 257, 260–1.

9 cf. Chapter 10, *passim.*

10 cf. Chapter 7, pp. 117–9, 137–9.

11 cf. Chapter 8, pp. 179–80, 182–3.

12 cf. Chapter 7, pp. 136–7.

13 cf. Chapters 11 and 12, *passim.*

14 cf. Chapter 7, pp. 119–23.

15 cf. Chapter 10, pp. 239.

16 cf. Chapter 8, pp. 180–1.

17 cf. Chapter 7, p. 119.

18 cf. Chapter 10, pp. 238–9.

19 cf. Chapter 4, pp. 37, 41, 49–51, 54.

20 F. Pigou, *Phases of My Life* (London 1898), p. 370; J. F. Briscoe and H. F. B. Mackay, *A Tractarian at Work* (London 1932), pp. 181–9.

21 cf. Chapter 10, p. 241; Chapter 11, pp. 253, 255.

22 cf. Chapter 9, pp. 221, 223–5.

23 cf. Chapter 11, p. 265.

24 cf. Chapter 10, pp. 233–5; P. L. S. Barrett, 'Hereford Cathedral in the Nineteenth Century', *FHCAR,* 1986, p. 33.

25 Barrett, p. 36.

26 K. Edwards, 'The Cathedral of Salisbury, 1075–1950', *VCH Wiltshire,* vol. iii, 1956, pp. 204–5.

27 cf. Chapter 4, p. 55.

28 cf. Chapter 10, p. 243.

29 cf. Chapter 11, p. 255; Chapter 7, p. 164; contrast Bishop Davidson's estimate in Chapter 7, p. 165.

30 cf. references given in n. 7 above.

31 O. C. Conway, *A Cathedral Pilgrimage* (privately published 1990).

32 J. H. Churchill and A. B. Webster, 'From Close to Open: A Future for the Past', in Marcombe and Knighton, pp. 161–84; T. R. Beeson, *Mission and Management in the Cathedral* (privately published 1991).

33 Conway, pp. 3–12.

34 cf. Chapter 11, pp. 248–9.

35 cf. Chapter 11, p. 248.

36 cf. Chapter 11, pp. 249–52.

37 cf. Chapter 11, p. 250.

38 cf. Chapter 11, pp. 247–8; Chapter 7, p. 127; Chapter 11, p. 255.

39 cf. Chapter 11, p. 254.

40 cf. Chapter 11, pp. 257–9.

41 cf. Chapter 13, pp. 300, 301–2. This view is strongly criticized by H. H. Henson, *Retrospect of an Unimportant Life* (London 1942), vol. I, pp. 151–2, and by A. S. Leak, 'What are Cathedral Chapters for?', *Theology*, vol. lxxxvi, no. 710, March 1983, pp. 106–13.

42 R. D. Say, *Visitation Charge delivered in the Cathedral (of Rochester) on 26 November 1984* (Rochester 1984), p. 14.

43 J. Arnold, *Rochester Cathedral – Visitation 1984: Response of the Dean and Chapter to the Bishop's Charge* (Rochester 1984), pp. 13–17.

44 cf. Chapter 5, pp. 74–5; Chapter 11, pp. 254–5.

45 Conway, pp. 13–22; J. H. Churchill and A. B. Webster, in Marcombe and Knighton, pp. 173, 178–81; Beeson, *passim*.

46 cf. Chapter 4, pp. 38, 39, 40–1.

47 cf. Chapter 4, pp. 47, 49–51.

48 cf. Chapter 5, pp. 69–70 and n. 124.

49 cf. Chapter 9, p. 217.

50 cf. Chapter 9, pp. 220–3.

51 cf. Chapter 5, pp. 68–9.

52 cf. n. 41 above.

53 cf. A. C. Benson, *The Life of Edward White Benson, sometime Archbishop of Canterbury* (London 1899), vol. i, pp. 346, 352.

54 cf. Chapter 6, p. 94; Chapter 12, p. 278.

55 cf. Chapter 6, pp. 103–4.

56 cf. Chapter 12, p. 280.

57 cf. Chapter 5, p. 72.

58 cf. Chapter 5, pp. 79–81; Chapter 9, pp. 223–5.

59 cf. Chapter 11, p. 255. Unfortunately, the committees at both Worcester and Winchester caused difficulties for the dean and chapter; cf. R. B. Lockett, 'George Gilbert Scott, The Joint Restoration Committee and the Refurnishing of Worcester Cathedral, 1863–1874', *TWAS*, 3rd series, vol. 6, 1978, pp. 7–30, and Win. CA, Great Screen boxes, Portal correspondence.

60 Conway, pp. 23–34; cf. Churchill and Webster, in Marcombe and Knighton, pp. 161–3, 173–4, 177–8.

61 cf. M. Hanna and T. Marris, *English Cathedrals and Tourism* (London 1979).

62 cf. Chapter 11, pp. 267–70.

63 cf. Chapter 11, pp. 259–67.

64 Conway, pp. 35–9; cf. Churchill and Webster, in Marcombe and Knighton, pp. 163–6; cf. also Chapter 7, pp. 115–16, 117–19, 137–9.

65 cf. Lockett, pp. 15–18, 23–4.

66 cf. Chapter 8, pp. 212–15.

67 cf. Chapter 7, pp. 157–8.

68 Conway, pp. 40–42.

69 E. W. Benson, *The Cathedral: Its Necessary Place in the Life and Work of the Church* (London 1878), pp. 147–9. In 1880 J. C. MacDonnell, Dean of Cashel, said that the principles on which the newer cathedrals had been founded were far from clear (*CCR* 1880, p. 397); E. W. Benson said that there were inherent difficulties in converting parish churches into cathedrals (PP 1883, xxi, pp. 88–9); and the general confusion surrounding this question is illustrated by Canon Huntingford's suggestion in 1900 that Winchester Cathedral should be made into the leading parish church of the city on the grounds that the cathedral system was 'somewhat of an anachronism in these days of religious revival and earnest parochial work' (Bishop Davidson's visitation Mss., Win. CA).

70 cf. Chapter 10, pp. 232–41.

71 *Guardian*, 1891, p. 1548.

BIBLIOGRAPHY

MANUSCRIPT SOURCES

Bodleian Library, Oxford
Christ Church miscellaneous papers
Dean Burgon's papers

Bristol Capitular Records (Bristol City Record Office)
Chapter Minute Books 1800–1, 1818–1900 (these are the equivalent of the Act Books in other cathedrals)
Bye-laws, rules and orders of the dean and chapter 1855–84 (DC/A/7/3/4)
Capitular estates and other matters – letter books 1851–70, 1853–87 (DC/A/7/4/2–3)
Episcopal visitation papers 1849, 1885 (DC/A/7/8/1)
Duties of precentors in various cathedrals, 1892 (DC/A/13/5)
Papers re minor canons' wives, 1800 (DC/A/13/4)
Accounts for chapter dinners at local inns, 1776–1829 (DC/A/9/6/6)
Receipts for music purchased (DC/A/11/3/2)
Various letters and receipts (DC/A/11/1/1–2)
Receipts for copying music (DC/A/11/3/1)
Letters re consistory court (DC/A/6/11)
Rental accounts (DC/E/4/3)
Questions addressed by a Lambeth committee of eight deans and canons, 2 March 1872, with replies from Norwich Cathedral (DC/A/7/6/2)

Chichester Capitular Records – West Sussex County Record Office
Chapter Act Books 1800–76
Draft Acts 1874–1900
Vicars choral Act Books 1855–89
Cathedral Visitations Book (Cap.I/7/1)
Communar's accounts 1821–65 (Cap.I/23/6)
Treasurer's account book 1792–1870 (Cap.II/16/1)
Accounts, letters and precedents 1865–89; accounts and notes 1889–1934 (Cap.III/5/4)
Offertory Book 1867–84 (Cap.VI/2/1)
Weekly service sheets from 1888 (Cap.VI/4/1)
Canon Swainson's *Miscellanea*

Chichester Capitular Records – Chapter Clerk's Office, 5 East Pallant, Chichester
Chapter Act Books 1876–1900
Greater Chapter Minute Book 1876–1936
Chapter Minute Book 1891–1900

Church Commissioners
Files on Hereford Cathedral

Exeter Cathedral Library
Chapter Act Books 1800–1900
Calendar of archives compiled by Stuart Moore, 1873
Papers re organs and organists

Gloucester Capitular Records – Gloucester Cathedral Library
Chapter Act Books 1800–1900
Chapter Minute Book 1865–91
'Position, duties and emoluments of all persons connected with the Cathedral, made by
George Whitcombe, Chapter Clerk, 1863'

Gloucester Capitular Records – Gloucestershire County Record Office
Treasurer's accounts 1800–1900 (D 936 A/1/9–14)
Receiver's nominal ledger 1866–1900 (D 936 A 7/1–2)
Printed summaries of treasurer's and receiver's accounts (D 936 A/3)
The Dean's Book 1800–5
General estate correspondence 1842–9 (D 936/E/254)
Chapter clerk's letter books (D 936 C1/1–8)
Annual accounts of fines and fees 1801–25 (D 936 A/20)
Chapter clerk's correspondence (D 936 C2)
Letters and papers (capitular accounts) (D 936 C5)

Hereford Cathedral Library
Chapter Act Books 1800–1900
Vicars choral Act Books 1800–1900
Installation and enthronement papers: Ouseley, 1855 (HCA RSP/2/1)
                                    Leigh, 1894 (HCA RSD/1/4)
                                    Hampden, 1848 (HCA RSP/2)
                                    Dawes, 1850 (HCA RSD/1/4)
Details of lay clerks in various cathedrals (HCA 5071)
Letter from John Goss to editor of the *Hereford Times*, 31 March 1875 (HCA 5243)
Citation dated 12 May 1820 (HCA 5349)
Details of services and music, Advent, Christmas and Easter 1889, 1893; scheme for
week beginning 31 July 1892 (HCA 5818)
List of lay clerks from 1851 (HCA 5909)
Duplicate audit account 1798–1813 (HCA/5113)
W. Cooke, *Memorials of the Vicars Choral* (Ms.)
W. J. Rees, *A Memoir of the Life and Character of the late John Napleton* (Ms.) (HCA 6434)
Hebdomadary's book

Lambeth Palace Library
Tait papers
Benson papers

Norfolk County Record Office
Dean Pellew's papers
Dean Goulburn's papers
Dean Lefroy's papers

BIBLIOGRAPHY

Norwich Cathedral Library
Dean Goulburn's diary

Peterborough Cathedral Library
Chapter Act Books 1800–14

Peterborough Cathedral Chapter Office
Chapter Minutes 1878–1900

Salisbury Chapter Muniments (including records formerly kept at the DRO in Wren Hall)
Chapter Act Books 1800–1900
Vicars choral papers (Press III, Boxes 3,10,12b,28,29)
Chapter Minute Books 1877–1903
Bundle of papers re income of deans of old foundation cathedrals (Press II, Box 7)
Miscellaneous papers (Press V, Boxes 2 and 5)
Communars' accounts 1800–33
Masters of the fabric account book 1794–1810, 1828–52
Papers re Cathedral Commission 1854 (Press I, Box 39)

Wells Cathedral Library
Chapter Act Books 1800–1900
Chapter Minute Books 1831–1900
Vicars choral Act Books 1800–1900
Vicars choral Minute Books 1801–1900

Winchester Cathedral Library
Chapter Act Books 1800–1900
Cathedralia Winton – Minor canons 1860–1918
De Precentore 1863
Papers re choristers
Papers re enthronements
Papers re Ecclesiastical Commissioners
Treasurer's books 1794–1822, 1838–45, 1858–9
Greater chapter minutes 1892–1907
Bishop Davidson's visitation papers
Winchester Cathedral Chronicle No.1 (1873–91)
                              No.2 (1866–94)
                              No.3 (1895–1932)
                              No.4 (1800–65)
                              No.5 (1972)
D. King, 'Winchester Cathedral under Deans Rennell and Garnier', *Winchester Cathedral Chronicle*, 1972

Worcester Cathedral Library
Chapter Act Books 1800–1900
Treasurer's accounts 1800–1900
Receiver-general's accounts 1800–59
Volume of press cuttings

Restoration committee minutes and papers
'Record of some of the Principal Events Relating to the Cathedral of Worcester, the Dean and Chapter and their property'
Sacrist's accounts 1800–1900 (Add. Mss., 19–23)
Sermon and service registers 1879–1900 (Add. Mss., 31–3)
Visitors' Book 1872–4 (Add. Mss., 45)
'Summary of chief events in the history of Worcester Cathedral King's School, 1896–1917', by W. H. Chappell (Add. Mss., 55)
'Chapter Memoranda', by J. H. Hooper (Add. Mss., 71)
'The Honorary Canons of Worcester', by J. M. Wilson (Add. Mss., 96)
'Reminiscences of some of the Deans and Members of the Cathedral Church of Worcester', 1912 (Add. Mss., 104)
'Reminiscences of Worcester Cathedral before the Restoration of 1857' and 'Biographical Sketches of the Bishops, and Dean and Chapter' by John Randall, 1910 (Add. Mss., 128)
'Recollections', by James Smith, 1920 (Add. Mss., 137)
Reminiscences of Mrs Limoelan, 1921 (Add. Mss., 141)
Uncatalogued Mss.: Bundle of Precentor's Reports, 1869–1918
Bundle of memorials from the minor canons
Bundle of papers and reports about the voluntary choir
Bundle of documents about vergers
Bundle of documents about choir, minor canons, organists, lay clerks and choristers
Bundle of Sacrists' Reports
Bundle marked 'Corn rents – lay clerks'
Bundle marked 'Ecclesiastical Commissioners 1832'
Agenda and draft minutes of chapter meetings
Attendance book (lay clerks, minor canons and choristers), 1836–42

Worcester Cathedral Music Library
Catalogue of music books, 1771 (A/1/6 (5))
Service papers and schemes from 1890 (F.7.16)

York Minster Library
J. W. Knowles, 'Records of the Musicians and Musical Services in York Minster, with notes thereon', 5 vols, unpublished Mss. (Mss. Add., 157/1–5)
G. Weston Craig, 'The Organs of York Minster 1147–1960', unpublished ms. 1967

PUBLISHED WORKS AND DISSERTATIONS

Abbott, E., and Campbell, L., eds, *Letters of Benjamin Jowett* (London 1899).
Addleshaw, G. W. O., and Etchells, F., *The Architectural Setting of Anglican Worship* (London 1948).
Adelmann, D. L., 'The Contribution of Cambridge and the Ecclesiological (late Cambridge Camden) Society to the Revival of Anglican Choral Worship, 1839–62' (Cambridge Ph.D. thesis 1991).
Alford, F., *Life, Journals and Letters of Henry Alford, Dean of Canterbury* (London 1873).
Alford, H., 'The Church of the Future', *Contemporary Review*, vol. ix, 1868, pp. 161–78.
Alford, H., 'Cathedral Reform', *Contemporary Review*, vol. xii, 1869, pp. 38–49.
Alford, H., 'Cathedral Reform: A Supplement', *Contemporary Review*, vol. xii, 1869, pp. 360–9.
Andrews, C. B., ed., *The Torrington Diaries* (4 volumes, London 1934–8).
Armstrong, H. B. J., ed., *Armstrong's Norfolk Diary* (London 1963).

BIBLIOGRAPHY

Arnold, F., *Our Bishops and Deans* (2 volumes, London 1875).

Arnold, J., *Rochester Cathedral – Visitation 1984: Response of the Dean and Chapter to the Bishop's Charge* (Rochester 1984).

Arnold, R., *The Whiston Matter* (London 1961).

Arnold, T., *Principles of Church Reform* (London 1833).

Ashwell, A. R., and Wilberforce, R. G., *Life of The Right Reverend Samuel Wilberforce* (3 volumes, London 1881–3).

Aston, P., *The Music of York Minster* (London 1972).

Atkins, E. W., *The Elgar–Atkins Friendship* (Newton Abbot 1984).

Atkins, E. W., 'George Robertson Sinclair – A Festival Centenary and his influence on the Three Choirs 1891–1912', *Three Choirs Festival Programme*, 1991, pp. 27–31.

Aylmer, G. E. and Cant, R., eds, *A History of York Minster* (Oxford 1977).

Bagot, R., *A Charge delivered to the Clergy of the Diocese of Oxford* (Oxford 1838).

Bailey, D. S., *The Canonical Houses of Wells* (Gloucester 1982).

Baker, D., ed., 'Schism, Heresy and Religious Protest', *Studies in Church History*, vol. ix (Cambridge 1972).

Bannister, A. T., *The Cathedral Church of Hereford* (London 1924).

Bannister, A. T., ed., *The Register of John Stanbury, Bishop of Hereford 1453–1474* (Hereford 1918).

Barham, T. F., *The Creation of a Cathedral* (Falmouth 1976).

Barnes, R., *Report of the Case of the Queen v. The President and Chapter of the Cathedral Church of St Peter in Exeter* (London 1841).

Barrett, P. L. S., 'English Cathedral Choirs in the Nineteenth Century', *Journal of Ecclesiastical History*, vol. xxv, no. 1, January 1974, pp. 15–37.

Barrett, P. L. S., 'John Merewether, Dean of Hereford 1832–50', *The Friends of Hereford Cathedral Annual Report*, 1977, pp. 23–39.

Barrett, P. L. S., *The College of Vicars Choral at Hereford Cathedral* (Hereford 1980).

Barrett, P. L. S., 'Chichester Cathedral Choir in the Nineteenth Century', *Southern Cathedrals Festival Programme*, 1980, pp. 29–31.

Barrett, P. L. S., 'Hereford Cathedral in the Nineteenth Century', *The Friends of Hereford Cathedral Annual Report*, 1986, pp. 12–37.

Barrett, P. L. S., 'Philip Williams – The Acceptable Face of Pluralism', *Winchester Cathedral Record*, no. 57, 1988, pp. 13–26.

Barrett, P. L. S., 'English Cathedral Life in the Nineteenth Century' (Oxford BD thesis 1989).

Barringer, C., ed., *Norwich in the Nineteenth Century* (Norwich 1984).

Barrington-Baker, G., *Quam Dilecta! A Chorister's Recollections* (Oxford 1948).

Barry, H. B., *Thoughts on the Renovation of Cathedral Institutions* (London 1852).

Bates, F., *Reminiscences and Autobiography of a Musician in Retirement* (Norwich 1930).

Baylis, H., 'The Prebends in the Cathedral Church of Saints Mary and Chad in Lichfield', *South Staffordshire Archaeological and Historical Society*, vol. II , 1960–1, pp. 33–52.

Bazeley, W., ed., *Records of Gloucester Cathedral* (Gloucester 1882– 97).

Beadon, H. W., *The Cathedrals and the Diocese* (Gloucester 1880).

Beaumont, R. M., *The Chapter of Southwell Minster* (Nottingham 1956).

Beazeley, M., 'History of the Chapter Library of Canterbury Cathedral', *Transactions of the Bibliographical Society*, vol. viii, 1907, pp. 113–85.

Beckett, R. B., *John Constable and the Fishers* (London 1952).

Bedford, Duke of, *A Great Agricultural Estate* (London 1897).

Beeson, T. R., *Mission and Management in the Cathedral: A Sermon Preached before the University of Oxford* (privately published 1991).

Bell, A., 'The Letters of Sydney Smith', *Bulletin of the John Rylands Library*, vol. 59, no. 1, 1976–7, pp. 13–39.

445

Bell, A., *Sydney Smith* (Oxford 1980).

Bell, C. C., *The Story of York Minster* (London 1932).

Bennett, F. G., Codrington, R. H., and Deedes, C., *Statutes and Constitutions of the Cathedral Church of Chichester* (Chichester 1904).

Bennett, F. S. M., *On Cathedrals in the Meantime* (London 1928).

Bennett, F. S. M., *The Nature of a Cathedral* (Chester 1925).

Benson, A. C., *The Life of Edward White Benson, sometime Archbishop of Canterbury* (2 volumes, London 1899).

Benson, A. C., *The Trefoil* (London 1923).

Benson, A. C., and Esher, Viscount, *The Letters of Queen Victoria* (London 1907).

Benson, E. W., 'Cathedral Life and Cathedral Work', *Quarterly Review*, vol. cxxx, no. 259, January 1871, pp. 225–55.

Benson, E. W., *The Cathedral: Its Necessary Place in the Life and Work of the Church* (London 1878).

Benson, G., *An Account of the City and County of the City of York, from the Reformation to the year 1925, being a continuation of 'Later Medieval York' by G. Benson* (York 1925).

Beresford Hope, A. J. B., 'Cathedral Reform', *Christian Remembrancer*, vol. xxix, no. 88, 1855, pp. 332–68.

Beresford Hope, A. J. B., *The English Cathedral of the Nineteenth Century* (London 1861).

Beresford Hope, A. J. B., *Worship in the Church of England* (London 1874).

Best, G. F. A., *Temporal Pillars* (Cambridge 1964).

Beswick, C. E., 'Liddon of St Paul's' (Exeter University MA thesis 1974).

Bill, E. G. W., *A Catalogue of Manuscripts in Lambeth Palace Library* (Oxford 1972).

Bill, E. G. W., and Mason, J. F. A., *Christ Church and Reform 1850–1867* (Oxford 1970).

Binney, M., 'Hereford Cathedral Close', *Country Life*, vol. clxviii, no. 4336, 25 September 1980, pp. 1026–9.

Blomfield, A., *A Memoir of Charles James Blomfield* (2 volumes, London 1863).

Blomfield, C. J., *A Charge delivered to the Clergy of the Diocese of London* (London 1838).

Blore, G. H., *Thomas Rennell, Dean of Winchester 1805–1840* (Winchester 1952).

Boggis, R. J. E., *A History of the Diocese of Exeter* (Exeter 1922).

Botfield, B., *Notes on the Cathedral Libraries of England* (London 1849).

Boutflower, A., *Personal Reminiscences of Manchester Cathedral 1854–1912* (Leighton Buzzard 1913).

Bowen, D., *The Idea of the Victorian Church* (Montreal 1968).

Boyle, G. D., *The Recollections of The Very Rev. G. D. Boyle* (London 1895).

Bradshaw, H., and Wordsworth, C., *Statutes of Lincoln Cathedral* (3 volumes, Cambridge 1892–7).

Braley, E. F., *More Letters of Herbert Hensley Henson* (London 1954).

Brewer, A. H., *Memories of Choirs and Cloisters* (London 1931).

Bridge, A. E., 'Walter Kerr Hamilton: The Making of a Tractarian Bishop, 1808–1854' (Oxford M. Litt. thesis 1988).

Bridge, J. C., 'The Organists of Chester Cathedral', *Journal of the Architectural, Archaeological and Historical Society for the County and the City of Chester and North Wales*, n.s., vol. xix, pt 2 (Chester 1913), pp. 63–124.

Bridge, J. F., *A Westminster Pilgrim* (London 1919).

Briscoe, J. F., and Mackay, H. F. B., *A Tractarian at Work* (London 1932).

Brock, M., *The Great Reform Act* (London 1973).

Brose, O. J., *Church and Parliament* (Stanford, USA, 1959).

Brown, C. K. F., *A History of the English Clergy, 1800–1900* (London 1953).

Brown, H. M., *A Century for Cornwall – The Diocese of Truro 1877–1977* (Truro 1976).

Brown, H. M., *The Story of Truro Cathedral* (Penryn 1991).

Browne, E. H., *Bishops and Cathedrals – a letter to the Dean of Norwich on his 'suggestions to facilitate business at the second Lambeth Conference on the subject of cathedral reform'*

BIBLIOGRAPHY

(London 1872).

Browne, G. F., *The Recollections of a Bishop* (London 1915).

Bullock, F. W. B., *A History of Training for the Ministry of the Church of England and Wales from 1800 to 1874* (St Leonard's-on-Sea 1955).

Bumpus, J. S., *The Organists and Composers of St Paul's Cathedral* (London 1891).

Bumpus, J. S., *A History of English Cathedral Music, 1549–1899* (2 volumes, London 1908).

Bumpus, T. F., *The Cathedrals of England and Wales* (3 volumes, London 1905).

Burgon, J. W., *Dr Swainson and the Dean of Chichester: An Address, a Protest and a Correspondence* (Chichester 1878).

Burgon, J. W., *Chichester Cathedral: Suggestions submitted to the Cathedral Commissioners* (Chichester 1879).

Burgon, J. W., *Remarks of Dr Swainson's Two Letters addressed to the Canons, Dignitaries and Prebendaries of Chichester Cathedral* (Chichester 1879).

Burgon, J. W., *Canon Parrington's Defamatory Letter to the Primate concerning the Dean, with the Dean's Reply in Chapter* (Chichester 1880).

Burgon, J. W., *Lives of Twelve Good Men* (2 volumes, London 1888).

Burne, R. V. H., *Chester Cathedral* (London 1958).

Burrows, R., *Halsbury's Statutes of England*, vol. vii (London 1949).

Bussby, F., 'Winchester Cathedral: 1789–1840', *Winchester Cathedral Record*, no. 44, 1975, pp. 21–30.

Bussby, F., *Winchester Cathedral 1079–1979* (Southampton 1979, 2nd edn 1987).

Bussby, F., 'The Great Screen – part II', *Winchester Cathedral Record*, no. 48, 1979, pp. 12–15.

Butler, A. J., *Life and Letters of William John Butler* (London 1897).

Butler, G., *Statutes of Peterborough Cathedral* (Peterborough 1853).

Butler, P., ed., *Pusey Rediscovered* (London 1983).

Butler, S., *Thoughts on Church Dignities* (London 1833).

Canterbury, *The Case of the Minor Canons and Inferior Officers of the Cathedrals of the New Foundation, particularly with reference to Canterbury* (Canterbury 1839).

Carpenter, E., *A House of Kings* (London 1966).

Carpenter, S. C., *Church and People, 1789–1889* (London 1933).

Cathedrals Commission, *Report of the Cathedrals Commission appointed in pursuance of a resolution of the National Assembly of the Church of England* (CA 245) (London 1927).

Chadwick, W. O., *The Victorian Church* (2 volumes, London 1966, 1970).

Chadwick, W. O., *Edward King, Bishop of Lincoln 1885–1910* (Lincoln 1968).

Chadwick, W. O., *Church and Historical Endowment in the Victorian Age* (London 1986).

Chambers, J. D., and Mingay, G. E., *The Agricultural Revolution, 1750– 1880* (London 1966).

Chanter, J. F., *The Custos and College of the Vicars Choral of the Choir of the Cathedral Church of St Peter, Exeter* (Exeter 1933).

Chappell, M. P., *Dr S. S. Wesley: Portrait of a Victorian Musician* (Great Wakering 1977).

Charlton, P., *John Stainer and the Musical Life of Victorian Britain* (Newton Abbot 1984).

Cheshire, C., *Henry Scott Holland: Some Appreciations* (London 1919).

Chitty, S. E. R., *The Beast and the Monk* (London 1974).

Church, M. C., *Life and Letters of Dean Church* (London 1895).

Clapham, J. H., *An Economic History of Modern Britain* (3 volumes, 2nd edn, Cambridge 1950–2).

Clark, J. W., and Hughes, T. McK., *The Life and Letters of The Reverend Adam Sedgwick* (2 volumes, Cambridge 1890).

Clarke, W. K. L., *Chichester Cathedral: Its History and Art* (London 1957).

Clarke, W. K. L., *Chichester Cathedral in the Nineteenth Century* (Chichester Papers no. 14, Chichester 1959).

Close, F., *Memorials of Dean Close by 'One Who Knew Him'* (London 1885).

447

Close, F., *Cathedral Reform* (London 1864).

Close, F., *Thoughts on the Daily Choral Services in Carlisle Cathedral* (Carlisle 1865).

Cobb, G., *English Cathedrals: The Forgotten Centuries* (London 1980).

Cobbett, W., *Rural Rides* (Penguin edn, ed. G. Woodcock, London 1967).

Coghlan, P. V., 'Cathedral Worship in the Church of England 1815–1914' (Leicester University M. Phil. thesis 1984).

Colchester, L. S., 'The Victorian Restoration of Wells Cathedral Church (Barnard Ms.)', *Transactions of the Ancient Monuments Society*, n.s., vol. iv, 1956, pp. 79–94.

Colchester, L. S., ed., *Wells Cathedral: A History* (Shepton Mallet 1982).

Colchester, L. S., Bowers, R., and Crossland, A., *The Organs and Organists of Wells Cathedral* (Wells 1974).

Coldstream, N., and Draper, P., eds, *Mediaeval Art and Architecture at Wells and Glastonbury* (British Archaeological Association Conference Transactions 1978) (London 1981).

Cole, D., *The Work of Sir Gilbert Scott* (London 1980).

Compton, B., *Edward Meyrick Goulburn, Dean of Norwich* (London 1899).

Conway, O. C., *A Cathedral Pilgrimage* (privately published 1990).

Cope, G., ed., *Cathedral and Mission* (Birmingham 1969).

Copleston, W. J., *Memoir of Edward Copleston* (London 1851).

Cordingley, R. A., 'Cathedral Innovations: James Wyatt, Architect at Durham Cathedral 1795–1797', *Transactions of the Ancient Monuments Society*, n.s., vol. iii, 1955, pp. 31–55.

Cornish, F. W., *The English Church in the Nineteenth Century* (2 volumes, London 1910).

Cotton, V. E., *Liverpool Cathedral: The Official Handbook of the Cathedral Committee* (11th edn, Liverpool 1951).

Cowie, L. W., 'The Church of England since 1837', *The Victoria History of the Counties of England: A History of Wiltshire* (ed. R. B. Pugh and E. Crittall), vol. iii, 1956, pp. 57–86.

Cowie, L. W., 'Worship in the Minster', *The Victoria History of the Counties of England: A History of Yorkshire: The City of York* (ed. P. M. Tillott) (London 1961), pp. 343–57.

Cox, J. C., 'The Treatment of our Cathedral Churches in the Victorian Age', *Archaeological Journal*, vol. liv, 1897, pp. 239–74.

Coxe, A. C. (Cleveland), *Impressions of England* (2nd edn, New York, 1856).

Craze, M. R., *King's School, Worcester (1541–1971)* (Worcester 1972).

Creighton, L., *Life and Letters of Mandell Creighton* (2 volumes, London 1904).

Crook, P. M. J., *A History of the Pilgrims' School and earlier Winchester Choir Schools* (Chichester 1981).

Crook, P. M. J., 'Half-a-century of Choral Indiscipline: George Chard and his Choir, 1802–1849', *Southern Cathedrals Festival Programme*, 1981, pp. 11–13.

Crook, P. M. J, 'The "Gumble" Affair and the House of Thomas Ken', *Winchester Cathedral Record*, no. 52, 1983, pp. 5–16.

Crook, P. M. J., 'Fifty Years of Choral Misrule: George Chard and the Choristers of Winchester Cathedral', *Winchester Cathedral Record*, no. 56, 1987, pp. 30–6.

Crosby, B., *Durham Cathedral Choristers and their Masters* (Durham 1980).

Crosby, B., 'A Service Sheet from June 1680', *Musical Times*, June 1980, pp. 399–401.

Curtis, L. P., *Chichester Towers* (New Haven and London 1966).

Curtis, M. E., *Some Disputes between the City and the Cathedral Authorities of Exeter* (Manchester 1932).

Davidson, R. T., and Benham, W., *The Life of Archibald Campbell Tait, Archbishop of Canterbury* (2 volumes, London 1891).

Davies, G. C. B., *Henry Phillpotts, Bishop of Exeter, 1778–1869* (London 1954).

Davies, D. H. M., *Worship and Theology in England, vol. iv: From Newman to Martineau, 1850–1900* (Oxford 1962).

Davies, D. H. M., *Worship and Theology in England, vol. v: The Ecumenical Century, 1900–1965* (Princeton 1965).

BIBLIOGRAPHY

Davies, J. G., *The Secular Use of Church Buildings* (London 1968).

Denison, E., *A Charge delivered to the Clergy of the Diocese of Salisbury* (London 1842).

Dewar, G. A. B., *The Letters of Samuel Reynolds Hole* (London 1907).

Dewey, C., *The Passing of Barchester* (London 1991).

Dibdin, L. T., and Downing, S. E., *The Ecclesiastical Commission* (London 1919).

Dickson, W. E., *Fifty Years of Church Music* (Ely 1894).

Dickson, W. E., *The Relation of the Cathedral of Ely to the Diocese* (Ely 1879).

Digby, R. S. Wingfield, 'The Central Tower Saga', *Friends of Peterborough Cathedral Annual Report*, 1981, pp. 7–17.

Dobson, R. B., *Durham Priory, 1400–1450* (Cambridge 1973).

Dobson, R. B., 'English Monastic Cathedrals in the Fifteenth Century', *Transactions of the Royal Historical Society*, sixth series, vol. I (1991), pp. 151–72.

Donaldson, A. B., *The Bishopric of Truro* (London 1902).

Dorling, E. E., *Register of Old Choristers of Salisbury Cathedral, 1810–97* (London 1898).

Dorman, B. E., *The Story of Ely and its Cathedral* (Norwich 1945, new edn Ely 1980).

Duncan-Jones, A. S., *The Story of Chichester Cathedral* (London 1933).

Edwards, F. G., 'The Musical Associations of Salisbury Cathedral', *Musical Times*, February 1903, pp. 81–9.

Edwards, K., 'The Cathedral of Salisbury, 1075–1950', *The Victoria History of the Counties of England: A History of Wiltshire* (ed. R. B. Pugh and E. Crittall), vol. iii, 1956, pp. 156–210; reprinted as *Salisbury Cathedral: An Ecclesiastical History* (Trowbridge 1986).

Edwards, K., *The English Secular Cathedrals in the Middle Ages* (2nd edn, Manchester 1967).

Ellicott, C. J., *Our Cathedral Institutions – will they stand?* (Gloucester 1871).

Elliott-Binns, L. E., *Religion in the Victorian Era* (London 1936).

Elvey, M., *Life and Reminiscences of George J. Elvey* (London 1894).

Elvy, J. M., *Recollections of the Cathedral and Parish Church of Manchester* (Manchester 1913).

Engel, A. J., *From Clergyman to Don* (Oxford 1983).

Evans, J. H., *Churchman Militant* (London 1964).

Eward, S., *No Fine but a Glass of Wine: Cathedral Life in Gloucester in Stuart Times* (Wilton 1985).

Faculty Jurisdiction Commission Report (The Chichester Report), *The Continuing Care of Churches and Cathedrals* (London 1984).

Falkner, J. M., and Thompson, A. H., *The Statutes of the Cathedral Church of Durham* (Surtees Society, vol. cxliii, Durham 1929).

Farington, J., *The Farington Diary* (ed. J. Grieg, London 1922–8).

Farrar, R., *The Life of Frederic William Farrar, sometime Dean of Canterbury* (London 1904).

Fawcett, J., ed., *The Future of the Past* (London 1976).

Fawcett, J., 'Nineteenth Century Restoration of Peterborough Cathedral', *Friends of Peterborough Cathedral Annual Report*, 1978, pp. 15–22.

Fearon, W. A., *The Passing of Old Winchester* (Winchester 1924).

Fellowes, E. H., *English Cathedral Music from Edward VI to Edward VII* (London 1941, new edns 1970, 1973).

Fenwick, R. D., 'An Early Victorian Organist at Work: I – John Goss in Quire at St Paul's Cathedral, 1838–1860', *The Organ*, vol. 62, no. 245, July 1983, pp. 98–111; and 'II – The Latter Years of John Goss at St Paul's Cathedral, 1860–1872', ibid., vol. 64, no. 254, October 1985, pp. 146–65.

Ferguson, R. S., 'Consistory Courts and Consistory Places', *Archaeological Journal*, vol. lvi, June 1899, pp. 85–122.

Ferrey, B., *Recollections of A. N. Welby Pugin and his father, Augustus Pugin* (London 1861).

Ferriday, P., *Lord Grimthorpe, 1816–1905* (London 1957).

Finlayson, A. R. M., *The Life of Canon Fleming* (London 1909).

Fitzgerald, M. H., *The Story of Bristol Cathedral* (London 1936).

Fletcher, R. J., *A History of Bristol Cathedral* (London 1932).

Forwood, W. B., *The Liverpool Cathedral: The Story of its Foundation, 1885–1914* (Liverpool 1925).

Foster, M., *The Music of Salisbury Cathedral* (London 1974).

Fowler, J. T., *Life and Letters of John Bacchus Dykes* (London 1897).

Fowler, J. T., *Durham University, earlier foundations and present colleges* (London 1904).

Fremantle, W. H., *Recollections of Dean Fremantle* (London 1921).

Frere, W. H., *Visitation Articles and Injunctions of the Period of the Reformation*, vols I and III (London 1910).

Frere, W. H., and Kennedy, W. Mc., *Visitation Articles and Injunctions of the Period of the Reformation*, vol. II (London 1910).

Frost, W. A., *Early Recollections of St Paul's Cathedral* (London 1926).

Galilee, D., 'Pusey: A Forgotten Text?', *Theology*, vol. lxxviii, no. 658, April 1975, pp. 196–202.

Garnier, A. E., *The Chronicles of the Garniers of Hampshire* (Norwich 1900).

Gatens, W. J., *Victorian Cathedral Music in Theory and Practice* (Cambridge 1986).

Gedge, D., 'Maria Hackett: The Choristers' Friend', *The World of Church Music*, 1983, pp. 41–9.

Gedge, D., 'The Redoubtable Miss Hackett', *Musical Opinion*, vol. 108, no. 1297, December 1985, pp. 441–6; vol. 109, no. 1298, January 1986, pp. 11–14; vol. 109, no. 1299, February 1986, pp. 49–53.

Gedge, D., 'In Quires and Places (ii)', *Musical Opinion*, vol. 104, no. 1244, June 1981, pp. 323–8, 354.

Gedge, D., 'The Gentle Mr Goss', *Musical Opinion*, vol. 108, nos. 1288–90, February – August 1985, pp. 139–47, 202–8, 304–6.

Gedge, D., 'John Goss (1800–1880) of St Paul's', *English Church Music*, 1980, pp. 25–35.

Gee, H., ed., *The Statutes of Gloucester Cathedral* (London 1918).

Gibson, W., 'Continuity and Change: The Cathedral Chapter at Winchester in the Nineteenth Century', *Proceedings of the Hampshire Field Club and Archaeological Society*, vol. 45, November 1989, pp. 167–72.

Godfrey, R. A., 'Cathedral Virgers through the Centuries', *Winchester Cathedral Record*, no. 47, 1978, pp. 22–5.

Goodman, A. W., and Hutton, W. H., *The Statutes Governing the Cathedral Church of Winchester* (Oxford 1925).

Goodman, F. R., *The Diary of John Young* (London 1928).

Goodwin, H., *Charge delivered to the Clergy and Churchwardens of the Diocese of Carlisle* (Carlisle 1881).

Goulburn, E. M., *John William Burgon, Dean of Chichester* (2 volumes, London 1892).

Goulburn, E. M., *Suggestions to facilitate business at the Second Lambeth Conference on the subject of Cathedral Reform* (Oxford 1872).

Goulburn, E. M., *The Functions of Our Cathedrals* (Oxford and London 1869).

Goulburn, E. M., *Reasons for not signing 'Report of Her Majesty's Commissioners for Inquiring into the condition of Cathedral Churches in England and Wales upon the Cathedral Church of Norwich'*, PHPR, 4978.

Goulburn, E. M., *The Principles of the Cathedral System vindicated* (London 1870).

Gowland, T. S., 'Ripon Minster and its Precincts', *Yorkshire Archaeological Journal*, vol. xxxv, 1943, pp. 270–87.

Green, I. M., *The Re-establishment of the Church of England, 1660–1663* (Oxford 1978).

Greig, J., ed., *The Farington Diary* (London 1922–8).

Gretton, F. E., *Memory's Hark-back Through Half a Century, 1808–1858* (London 1889).

Hackett, M., 'Lord Henley and the Cathedral Service', *The Harmonicon*, 1833, pp. 56–8.

BIBLIOGRAPHY

Hackett, M., *A Brief Account of Cathedral and Collegiate Schools* (London 1825, 1827, 1860 and 1873).

Hackett, M., *Correspondence, Legal Proceedings and Evidences respecting the ancient Collegiate School attached to St Paul's Cathedral* (3rd edn, London 1832).

Hamilton, W. K., *Cathedral Reform: A Letter to the Members of His Diocese* (London, Oxford and Salisbury 1855).

Hanna, M. and Marris, T., *English Cathedrals and Tourism* (London 1979).

Hannah, I. C., 'The Prebendal School at Chichester', *Sussex Archaeological Collections*, vol. 54, 1911, pp. 1–5.

Hannah, I. C., 'The Vicars' Close and Adjacent Buildings at Chichester', *Sussex Archaeological Collections*, vol. 56, 1914, pp. 92- 109.

Hannah, I. C., 'Houses in the Close at Chichester', *Sussex Archaeological Collections*, vol. 68, 1927, pp. 133–58.

Hannam-Clark, F., *Memories of the College School, Gloucester* (Gloucester 1890).

Hare A., *The Story of my Life* (London 1900).

Harper, F. W., *What are the York Residentiary Canonries?* (Selby 1880).

Harrison, F., *York Minster* (London 1927).

Harrison, F., *Life in a Mediaeval College* (London 1952).

Henley, Lord, *A Plan of Church Reform* (4th edn, London 1832).

Hennell, M., *The Deans and Canons of Manchester Cathedral, 1840–1948* (Manchester 1990).

Henson, H. H., *Retrospect of an Unimportant Life* (3 volumes, London 1942).

Heseltine, W., *A Tenant's Statement of the conduct recently pursued towards him by the Dean and Chapter of Canterbury at the occasion of his renewing his lease* (2nd edn, London 1839).

Hewett, J. W., *A Brief History and Description of the Conventual and Cathedral Church of the Holy Trinity, Ely* (1848).

Hill, D. I., *Christ's Glorious Church* (London 1976).

Hill, J. W. F., *Georgian Lincoln* (Cambridge 1966).

Hill, J. W. F., *Victorian Lincoln* (London 1974).

Hillard, G. S., *Life, Letters and Journals of George Ticknor* (1876).

Hillsman, W. L., 'Trends and Aims in Anglican Music 1870–1906, in relation to developments in churchmanship' (Oxford D. Phil. thesis 1985).

Historic Manuscripts Commission Report xii, appendix part ix (1891).

Hole, S. R., *The Memories of Dean Hole* (London 1893).

Hole, S. R., *More Memories, being thoughts about England spoken in America* (London 1894).

Holland, H. S., *Personal Studies* (London 1905).

Holloway, R., ed., *The Anglican Tradition* (Oxford 1984).

Holtby, R. T., 'Carlisle Cathedral Library and Records', *Transactions of the Cumberland and Westmorland Antiquarian and Archaeological Society*, vol. 66, 1966, pp. 201–19.

Honeyman, H. L., and Wake, T., 'The Cathedral Church of St Nicholas, Newcastle upon Tyne', *Archaeologia Aeliana*, 4th series, vol. ix, 1932, pp. 96–193.

Horn, P. L. R., *The Changing Countryside in Victorian and Edwardian England and Wales* (London 1984).

Howitt, W., *Visits to Remarkable Places* (2 volumes, London 1840–2).

Howson, J. S., ed., *Essays on Cathedrals by Various Writers* (London 1872).

Hudson, H. A., 'The Christmas Lights at Manchester Cathedral', *Transactions of the Lancashire and Cheshire Antiquarian Society*, vol. xxix, 1912, pp. 1–18.

Hughes, E., 'The Bishops and Reform, 1831-3: Some Fresh Correspondence', *English Historical Review*, vol. lvi, 1941, pp. 459- 90.

Hughes, H. D., *A History of Durham Cathedral Library* (Durham 1925).

Humfrys, W. J., *Memories of Old Hereford* (Hereford n.d.).

Hunt, D., *Samuel Sebastian Wesley* (Bridgend 1990).

Hutton, W. H., ed., *The Autobiography of Robert Gregory* (London 1912).

Jacob, W. M., 'The diffusion of Tractarianism: Wells Theological College 1840–1849', *Southern History*, vol. v, 1983, pp. 189–209.

Jancey, E. M., 'Hereford Cathedral and the Parish of St John the Baptist', *Friends of Hereford Cathedral Annual Report*, 1984, pp. 21–7.

Jebb, J., *The Choral Service of the United Church of England and Ireland* (London 1843).

Jebb, J., *Three Lectures on the Cathedral Service of the Church of England* (Leeds 1845).

Jebb, J., *A Plea for what is left of the Cathedrals* (London 1852).

Jebb, J., and Phillott, H. W., *The Statutes of the Cathedral Church of Hereford* (Hereford 1882).

Jenkins, C., ed., *The Statutes of the Cathedral and Metropolitical Church of Christ, Canterbury* (Canterbury 1925).

Johnson, N. E., ed., *The Diary of Gathorne Hardy, later Lord Cranbrook, 1866–1892: Political Selections* (Oxford 1981).

Johnston, J. O., *Life and Letters of Henry Parry Liddon* (London 1904).

Jones, E. L., *Seasons and Prices* (London 1964).

Jones, S., Major, K., and Varley, J., *The Survey of Ancient Houses in Lincoln I: Priorygate to Pottergate* (Lincoln 1984).

Jones, W. H., *Canon or Prebendary: A Plea for the Non-residentiary Members of Cathedral Chapters* (Bath 1877).

Jones, W. H., *Fasti ecclesiae Sarisberiensis* (2 volumes, Salisbury 1879, 1881).

Joyce, F. W., *The Life of Rev. Sir F. A. G. Ouseley, Bart.* (London 1896).

Judd, A., 'The Office of Subdean', *Church Quarterly Review*, vol. 166, 1965, pp. 36–46.

Kaufmann, P., 'Reading Vogues at English Cathedral Libraries of the Eighteenth Century', *Bulletin of the New York Public Library*, vol. 67, 1963, pp. 643–72; vol. 68, 1964, pp. 48–64, 110–32, 191–202.

Kennedy, W. P. M., *Elizabethan Episcopal Administration* (3 volumes, London 1924).

Kaye, J., *A Letter to His Grace the Archbishop of Canterbury on the Recommendations of the Ecclesiastical Commission* (London 1838).

Ker, N. R., 'Cathedral Libraries', *Library History*, vol. 1., no. 2, Autumn 1967, pp. 38–45.

Kerr, J. S., *Improvers and Preservers: A dissertation on some aspects of Cathedral Restoration 1770–1830 and in particular on the Great Screen squabble of York Minster from 1829 to 1831* (York 1973).

Kilvert, F., *Kilvert's Diary 1870–1879* (one volume edn, ed. W. Plomer, London 1944, reprinted 1967).

Kirby, I. M., *Diocese of Gloucester: A Catalogue of the Records of the Dean and Chapter including the former St Peter's Abbey* (Gloucester 1967).

Kirby, I. M., *Diocese of Bristol: A Catalogue of the Records of the Bishop and Archdeacons and of the Dean and Chapter* (Bristol 1970).

Kirk-Smith, H., *William Thomson, Archbishop of York 1819–1890* (London 1958).

Kirwan, A. L., *The Music of Lincoln Cathedral* (London 1973).

Kitchin, G. W., *Edward Harold Browne* (London 1895).

Kitton, F. G., *Zechariah Buck* (London 1899).

Knowles, M. D., *The Monastic Order in England* (2nd edn, Cambridge 1966).

Knowles, M. D., *The Religious Orders in England* (3 volumes, Cambridge 1948, 1955, 1959).

Lake, K., ed., *Memorials of William Charles Lake* (London 1901).

Laud, W., *The Works of William Laud* (Oxford 1853).

Leak, A. S., 'What are Cathedral Chapters for?', *Theology*, vol. lxxxvi, no. 710, March 1983, pp. 106–13.

Leak, A. S., 'Conflict and Reform at York Minister in the Nineteenth Century' (Oxford B. D. thesis 1988).

Lear, F., 'Reminiscences of Eighty Years', *Salisbury Diocesan Gazette*, vol. 23, July 1910, pp. 121–3; August 1910, pp. 140–3; September 1910, pp. 158–61.

Leeds, H., *Life of Dean Lefroy* (Norwich 1909).

Leeds, H., *Norwich Cathedral Past and Present* (Norwich 1910).

Lefroy, W. C., *Echoes from the Choir of Norwich Cathedral* (London 1894).

Lega-Weekes, E., *Some Studies in the Topography of the Cathedral Close at Exeter* (Exeter 1915).

Lehmberg, S. E., *The Reformation of Cathedrals* (Princeton 1988).

Le Huray, P., *Music and the Reformation in England* (London 1967).

Leigh, J. W., *Other Days* (London 1921).

Lichfield Cathedral, *Report to the Dean and Chapter relative to the Restoration now in progress* (Lichfield 1860).

Lichfield Cathedral, *Order of Ceremonial and Services at the Enthronement of the Bishop and the Diocesan Foreign Missions Festival*, 11 July 1878.

Liddon, H. P., *Walter Kerr Hamilton, Bishop of Salisbury* (London 1869, reprinted from *The Guardian*, 18 August 1869).

Liddon, H. P., *Life of Edward Bouverie Pusey* (4 volumes, London 1893).

Lloyd, L. J., *The Library of Exeter Cathedral* (Exeter 1967).

Lloyd, R., *The Church of England 1900–1965* (London 1966).

Lockett, R. B., 'The Victorian Restoration of Worcester Cathedral', *Mediaeval Art and Architecture at Worcester Cathedral* (British Archaeological Association Conference Transactions for the year 1975, ed. G. Popper, 1978, pp. 161–85).

Lockett, R. B., 'George Gilbert Scott, the Joint Restoration Committee and the Refurnishing of Worcester Cathedral, 1863–1874', *Transactions of the Worcestershire Archaeological Society*, 3rd series, vol. 6, 1978, pp. 7–30.

Long, K. R., *The Music of the English Church* (London 1971, new edn, 1991).

McCann, T. J., *Restricted Grandeur: Impressions of Chichester 1586–1948* (Chichester 1974).

Mackreth, D. F., 'The Irvine Papers', *The Friends of Peterborough Cathedral Annual Report*, 1976, pp. 15–19.

Maddison, A. R., *A Short Account of the Vicars Choral, Poor Clerks, Organists and Choristers of Lincoln Cathedral* (London 1878).

Mahon, Lord, and Cardwell, E., eds, *Memoirs of Sir Robert Peel* (2 volumes, London 1856–7).

Major, K., *Minster Yard* (Lincoln 1974).

Makower, F., *The Constitutional History and Constitution of the Church of England* (London 1895).

Manning, H. E., *The Principle of the Ecclesiastical Commission examined in a letter to The Rt. Revd. The Lord Bishop of Chichester* (London 1838).

Manning, H. E., *The Preservation of Unendowed Canonries, a Letter* (London 1840).

Marcombe, D., and Knighton, C. S., *Close Encounters: English Cathedrals and Society since 1540* (Nottingham 1991).

Marindin, G. E., ed., *Letters of Frederic, Lord Blachford* (London 1896).

Marsh, P. T., *The Victorian Church in Decline* (London 1969).

Mason, A. J., *Memoir of George Howard Wilkinson* (2 volumes, London 1909).

Massingham, B., *Turn on the Fountains: A Life of Dean Hole* (London 1974).

Massingham, H. W., 'The Nationalisation of Cathedrals', *Contemporary Review*, vol. 60, no. 309, September 1891, pp. 362–71.

Mathieson, W. L., *English Church Reform 1815–1840* (London 1923).

Matthews, B., *The Music of Winchester Cathedral* (London 1974).

Matthews, B., *Samuel Sebastian Wesley 1810–1876: A Centenary Memoir* (Bournemouth 1976).

Matthews, W. R., and Atkins, W. M., *A History of St Paul's Cathedral and the men associated with it* (London 1957).

Meacham, S., *Lord Bishop: The Life of Samuel Wilberforce* (Harvard 1970).

Merewether, J., *A Statement of the Condition and Circumstances of the Cathedral Church of Hereford* (Hereford 1842).

Merewether, J., *Diary of a Dean* (London 1851).

Merivale, J. A., ed., *Autobiography of Dean Merivale* (London 1899).

Millard, J. E., *Historical Notices of the Office of Choristers* (London 1848).

Milman, A., *Henry Hart Milman* (London 1900).

Minchinton, W. E., ed., *Essays in Agrarian History* (2 volumes, Newton Abbot 1968).

Mingay, G. E., *Rural Life in Victorian England* (London 1977).

Mingay, G. E., ed., *The Victorian Countryside* (2 volumes, London 1981).

Mitchell, D. J., 'Hereford in the Age of Reform 1832–1856', *Transactions of the Woolhope Naturalists' Field Club*, vol. xliv, 1982, pp. 91–114.

Moberly, C. A. E., *Dulce Domum* (London 1911).

Moir, A. L., *The Deans of Hereford Cathedral Church* (Hereford 1968).

Monk, J. H., *A Charge to the Clergy of the Diocese of Gloucester and Bristol* (London 1838).

Moore, D. C., *The Politics of Deference* (Hassocks 1976).

Moore, J. Northrop, *Edward Elgar: A Creative Life* (Oxford 1984).

Moore, P. C., 'The Organisation and Development of Cathedral Worship in England, with special reference to choral services, from the Reformation to the nineteenth century' (Oxford D. Phil. thesis, 1954).

Moore, P. C., *Three Restorations of Ely Cathedral* (Ely 1973).

Morgan, F. C., and Morgan, P. E., *Hereford Cathedral Libraries and Muniments* (Hereford 1970).

Morgan, P. E., 'The Cathedral Close', *Friends of Hereford Cathedral Annual Report*, 1976, pp. 15–19.

Morgan, P. E., 'Hereford Cathedral in the 1680s', *Three Choirs Festival Programme 1985* (Hereford 1985), pp. 23–7.

Moxley, C. E., *Cathedral, College and Hospital* (Winchester 1986).

Moxley, C. E., 'Minores Canonici – Part I: Nicholas Westcombe', *Winchester Cathedral Record*, no. 58, 1989, pp. 24–33.

Moxley, C. E., 'Minores Canonici – Part II: Thomas Westcombe', *Winchester Cathedral Record*, no. 59, 1990, pp. 23–34.

Newsome, D., *The Parting of Friends* (London 1966).

Newton, R., *Victorian Exeter, 1837–1914* (Leicester 1968).

Noake, R., *The Monastery and Cathedral of Worcester* (London 1866).

Norris, J. P., *The Statutes of Bristol Cathedral* (Bristol 1870).

Ollerenshaw, N., *A History of the Prebendal School* (Chichester 1984).

Orme, N., *English Schools in the Middle Ages* (London 1973).

Orme, N., *The Minor Clergy of Exeter Cathedral, 1300–1548* (Exeter 1980).

Overton, J. H., and Wordsworth, E., *Christopher Wordsworth* (London 1888).

Owen, D. M., *The Library and Muniments of Ely Cathedral* (Ely 1973).

Owen, D. M., 'The Early Years of Cathedrals of the New Foundation', *Friends of Peterborough Cathedral Annual Report*, 1983, pp. 2–4.

Paget, S., *Henry Scott Holland* (London 1921).

Parker, C. S., ed., *Sir Robert Peel* (2 volumes, London 1891, 1899).

Peckham, W. D., 'The Vicars Choral of Chichester Cathedral', *Sussex Archaeological Collections*, vol. 78, no. xxxvii, 1937, pp. 126–59.

Peckham, W. D., 'Two Dukes and the Chichester Chapter', *Sussex Notes and Queries*, vol. xvii, no. 5, May 1970, pp. 146–52.

Pellew, G., *A Letter to Sir Robert Peel on the means of rendering Cathedral Churches most conducive to the efficiency of the Established Church* (London 1837).

Perry, P. J., *British Farming in the Great Depression 1870–1914* (Newton Abbot 1974).

Perry, P. J., ed., *British Agriculture 1875–1914* (London 1973).

Phillimore, R., *The Ecclesiastical Law of the Church of England* (2 volumes, 2nd edn ed. by W. G. F. Phillimore, London 1895).

Pigou, F., *Phases of My Life* (London 1898).

Pigou, F., *Odds and Ends* (London 1903).

Plumptre, E. H., *The Ideal of Cathedral Life* (London 1882).

Port, M. H., *Six Hundred New Churches* (London 1961).

Portal, M., *Our Cathedral* (Winchester 1886).

Prescott, J. E., *The Statutes of the Cathedral Church of Carlisle* (Carlisle 1879, new edn 1903).

Prestige, G. L., *St Paul's in its Glory, 1831–1911* (London 1955).

Proby, W. H., *Annals of the Low Church Party in England* (2 volumes, London 1888).

Prothero, G. W., *A Memoir of Henry Bradshaw* (London 1888).

Prothero, R. E., and Bradley, G. G., *The Life and Correspondence of Arthur Penrhyn Stanley* (2 volumes, London 1893).

Pullen, H. W., *The Real Work of a Cathedral and why it is not done* (London 1869).

Pullen, H. W., *Mediaeval Mummery in 1870* (Salisbury 1870).

Purey-Cust, A. P., *Organs and Organists of York Minster* (York 1899).

Pusey, E. B., *Remarks on the Prospective and Past Benefits of Cathedral Institutions in the Promotion of Sound Religious Knowledge occasioned by Lord Henley's Plan for their Abolition* (London 1833).

Pusey, E. B., *Form of Petition against the Disposition of Cathedral Properties in the Fourth Report* (Oxford 1836).

Pusey, E. B., 'The Royal and Parliamentary Ecclesiastical Commissions', *British Critic*, vol. 23, no. 46, April 1838, pp. 455–562.

Pyne, J. K., 'Wesleyana', *Musical Times*, 1 June 1899, pp. 376–81.

Quiney, A., *John Loughborough Pearson* (London 1979).

Ragg, L., *A Memoir of Edward Charles Wickham, Dean of Lincoln* (London 1911).

Rainbow, B., *The Choral Revival in the Anglican Church, 1839–1872* (London 1970).

Rainbow, B., 'Singing for Their Supper', *Musical Times*, April 1984, pp. 227–9.

Rainbow, B., 'John Jebb (1805–1886) and the Choral Service', *The World of Church Music 1986* (ed. L. Dakers) (Croydon 1986).

Raine, J., *A Memorial of the Honourable and Very Reverend Augustus Duncombe DD* (London and York 1880).

Raine, J., ed., *Statutes etc. of the Cathedral Church of York* (Leeds 1900).

Rawnsley, H. D., *Harvey Goodwin, Bishop of Carlisle* (London 1896).

Read, E. A., *A Checklist of Books, Catalogues and Periodical Articles relating to the Cathedral Libraries of England* (Oxford 1970).

Repton, J. A., *Norwich Cathedral at the end of the Eighteenth Century* (ed. S. R. Pierce) (Farnborough 1965).

Reynolds, H. E., 'Our Cathedral Libraries', *Transactions and Proceedings of the First Annual Meeting of the Library Association 1878* (London 1879), pp. 32–43 and appendix 1.

Reynolds, H. E., *Wells Cathedral: Its Foundation, Constitutional History and Statutes* (Leeds 1881).

Ridding, L., *George Ridding, Schoolmaster and Bishop* (London 1908).

Riley, J., *Tomorrow's Cathedral* (London 1978).

Robertson, D., *The King's School, Gloucester* (Chichester 1974).

Robertson, D. H., *Sarum Close* (London 1938, new edn 1970).

Roe, W. G., and Hutchings, A., *J. B. Dykes, Priest and Musician* (Durham 1976).

Routley, E., *The Musical Wesleys* (London 1968).

Royle, E., *The Victorian Church in York* (York 1983).

Runcie, R. A. K., *Cathedral and City* (London 1977).

Russell, G. W. E., *Edward King* (London 1912).

Russell, W., *St Paul's in the Early Nineteenth Century* (London 1920).

Salisbury Cathedral, *Bishop Hamilton's Memorial. Restoration of the Choir of Salisbury Cathedral. Proceedings of the Committee, with the Report by G. G. Scott* (Salisbury 1870).

Sandford, E. G., ed., *Memoirs of Archbishop Temple by Seven Friends* (2 volumes, London 1906).

Sandys, C., *The Memorial and Case of the Clerici-Laici or Lay-clerks of Canterbury Cathedral* (London 1848).

Say, R. D., *Visitation Charge delivered in the Cathedral of Rochester on 26 November 1984* (Rochester 1984).

Sayers, R. S., *A History of Economic Change in England, 1880–1939* (London 1967).

Scott, D., *The Music of St Paul's Cathedral* (London 1972).

Scott, G. G., 'The Restoration Question with reference to Cathedrals', *The Builder*, vol. xx, 1862, pp. 70–1.

Scott, G. G., *Personal and Professional Recollections* (London 1879).

Selwyn, G. A., *Are Cathedral Institutions Useless?* (London and Eton 1838).

Selwyn, W., *An Attempt to investigate the True Principles of Cathedral Reform* (London 1839).

Shaw, H. W., *The Three Choirs Festival* (Worcester 1954).

Shaw, H. W., *The Organists and Organs of Hereford Cathedral* (Hereford 1976, new edn 1988).

Shaw H. W., 'Samuel Sebastian Wesley', *English Church Music*, 1976, pp. 22–30.

Shaw, H. W., 'The Achievement of S. S. Wesley', *Musical Times*, April 1976, pp. 303–4.

Shaw, H. W., ed., *Sir Frederick Ouseley and St Michael's, Tenbury* (Birmingham 1988).

Shipley, O., ed., *The Church and the World* (London 1866).

Simpson, W. J. S., *Memoir of the Reverend W. Sparrow Simpson* (London 1899).

Simpson, W. S. (Sparrow), 'The Charter and Statutes of the College of Minor Canons in St Paul's Cathedral, London', *Archaeologia*, vol. xliii, 1871, pp. 165–200.

Simpson, W. S. (Sparrow), *Registrum Statutorum et Consuetudinum Ecclesiae Cathedralis Sancti Pauli Londinensis* (London 1873).

Simpson, W. S. (Sparrow), *A Calendar of the Ecclesiastical Dignitaries of St Paul's Cathedral, 1800–1877* (London 1877).

Simpson, W. S. (Sparrow), *A Year's Music at St Paul's Cathedral* (2nd report, London 1879).

Sinclair, W. M., *Memorials of St Paul's Cathedral* (London 1909).

Smith, B. A., *Dean Church* (London 1958).

Smith, L., *The Story of Ripon Minster* (Leeds 1914).

Smith, N. C., ed., *The Letters of Sydney Smith* (2 volumes, Oxford 1953).

Smith, P. L., ed., 'The Recollections of John Harding of his time as a chorister at Salisbury Cathedral, 1826–1832', *The Hatcher Review*, no. 10, summer 1980, pp. 3–22.

Smith, S., *First Letter to Archdeacon Singleton* (London 1837).

Smith, S., *Second Letter to Archdeacon Singleton* (London 1838).

Smith, S., *Third Letter to Archdeacon Singleton* (London 1839).

Soloway, R. A., *Prelates and People* (London 1969).

Southwell Minster, *Cathedral Church of the Blessed Virgin Mary of Southwell: Regulations* (Nottingham 1887).

Spry, J. H., *Some Observations on the Tendency of a Measure for the Future Regulation of Cathedral and Collegiate Bodies* (London 1838).

Srawley, J. H., *Michael Honywood, Dean of Lincoln (1660–81)* (Lincoln 1950).

Srawley, J. H., *The Origin and Growth of Cathedral Foundations as illustrated by the Cathedral Church of Lincoln* (Lincoln 1951, 3rd edn 1965).

Stacpoole, A., ed., *The Noble City of York* (York 1972).

Stapleton, H., *Tribute to Ely: Ely Theological College 1876–1964* (privately published 1980).

Steer, F. W., and Kirby, I. M., *Diocese of Chichester: A Catalogue of the Records of the Dean and Chapter, Vicars Choral, St Mary's Hospital, Colleges and Schools* (Chichester 1967).

Stephens, W. R. W., *Cathedral Chapters considered as Episcopal Councils: A Letter to The Right Reverend The Lord Bishop of Chichester* (London 1877).

Stephens, W. R. W., *Memorials of the South Saxon See and Cathedral Church of Chichester* (London 1876).

BIBLIOGRAPHY

Stephens, W. R. W., *The Life and Letters of Walter Farquhar Hook* (7th edn, London 1885).

Stephens, W. R. W., *A Memoir of Richard Durnford* (London 1899).

Stephenson, A. M. G., *Anglicanism and the Lambeth Conference* (London 1978).

Stewart, P., *Diocese of Salisbury: Guide to the Records of the Bishop, the Archdeacons of Salisbury and Wiltshire and other Archidiaconal and Peculiar Jurisdictions and to the Records from the Bishop of Bristol's Sub-registry for Dorset* (Wiltshire 1973).

Still, B., ed., *250 Years of the Three Choirs Festival* (Hereford 1977).

Strachey, L. and Fulford, R., eds., *The Greville Memoirs* (Cambridge 1938).

Stranks, C. J., *Dean Hook* (London 1954).

Stranks, C. J., *This Sumptuous Church* (London 1973).

Stuart, E., *Do Away with Deans: Cathedral Reform* (London 1869).

Summers, N., *A Prospect of Southwell* (Chichester 1974).

Sumner, W. L., *The Organ* (4th edn, London 1973).

Sutton, J., *A Short Account of Organs built in England from the Reign of King Charles the Second to the Present Time* (London 1847).

Swistead, J. H., ed., *Christ Church Cathedral School: Register of Choristers, Probationers, Masters, Precentors, Organists from 1837–1900* (Salisbury 1900).

Tait, A. C., 'Cathedral Reform', *Edinburgh Review*, vol. xcvii, January 1853, pp. 152–82.

Tait, A. C., *Some Thoughts on the Duties of the Established Church of England as a National Church* (London 1876).

Taylor, B. M., 'Angel Voices ever singing', *The Lady*, vol. clxxxx, no. 4911, 26 July 1979, pp. 132, 150.

Taylor, E., *The English Cathedral Service: Its Glory, Its Decline and Its Designed Extinction* (London 1845).

Temperley, N., *Jonathan Gray and Church Music in York, 1770–1840* (York 1977).

Temperley, N., *The Music of the English Parish Church* (2 volumes, Cambridge 1979).

Temperley, N., *The Athlone History of Music in Britain: Volume 5: The Romantic Age, 1800–1914* (London 1981).

Temple, W., *Life of Bishop Percival* (London 1921).

Thompson, A. H., *The Cathedral Churches of England* (London 1928).

Thompson, A. H., ed., *York Minster Historical Tracts 627–1927* (London 1927).

Thompson, F. M. L., *English Landed Society in the Nineteenth Century* (London 1963).

Thompson, H. L., *Henry George Liddell* (London 1899).

Tiller, J., *A Strategy for the Church's Ministry* (London 1983).

Trevelyan, G. M., *British History in the Nineteenth Century and After (1782–1919)* (2nd edn, London 1937).

Trevor, G., *Cathedral Reform* (Hull 1880).

Trollope, A., *Clergymen of the Church of England* (1866, new edn Leicester 1974).

Trueman, B., 'The Administration of Hereford Cathedral 1776–1786', *The Friends of Hereford Cathedral Annual Report*, 1976, pp. 26–36.

Truro Cathedral, *Order for the Consecration of the Cathedral Church of the Blessed Virgin Mary at Truro* (Truro 1887).

Tucker, H. W., *Memoir of the Life and Episcopate of George Augustus Selwyn* (2 volumes, London 1879).

Turner, B. Carpenter, *Winchester* (Southampton 1980).

Tyng, S. H., *Recollections of England* (London 1847).

Van Loo, G., *A Victorian Parson* (Upton-on-Severn 1989).

Verey, D., ed., *The Diary of a Cotswold Parson (F. E. Witts), 1783–1854* (Gloucester 1978).

Victorian Church Art, *Catalogue of an Exhibition at the Victoria and Albert Museum, London, 1971–2* (London 1971).

Walcott, M. E. C., *Cathedralia* (London 1865).

Walcott, M. E. C., *Traditions and Customs of Cathedrals* (London 1872).

Walcott, M. E. C., 'The Early Statutes of the Cathedral Church of the Holy Trinity,

Chichester, with observations on its constitution and history', *Archaeologia*, vol. xlv, 1880, pp. 143–234.

Walcott, M. E. C., 'The Arrangement of secular Cathedral Closes', *Associated Architectural Societies Reports and Papers*, vol. xv, 1879, pt I, pp. 70–8.

Watson, E. W., *Life of Bishop John Wordsworth* (London 1915).

Watson, E. W., *The Cathedral Church of Christ in Oxford* (London 1835).

Welander, D. C. St.V., *The History, Art and Architecture of Gloucester Cathedral* (Stroud 1991).

Welsh, P. J., 'Contemporary Views on the Proposals for the Alienation of Capitular Property in England (1832–1840)', *Journal of Ecclesiastical History*, vol. v, 1954, pp. 184–95.

Welsby, P. A., *Rochester Cathedral in the time of Charles Dickens* (Rochester 1976).

Wesley, S. S., *A Few Words on Cathedral Music* (ed. W. F. Westbrook and G. Spink) (London 1849, reprinted London 1965).

Wesley, S. S., *Reply to the Inquiries of the Cathedral Commissioners relative to the improvement in the Music of Divine Worship in Cathedrals* (London 1854).

West, J. E., *Cathedral Organists Past and Present* (London 1899).

Westcott, A., *Life and Letters of Brooke Foss Westcott* (2 volumes, London 1903).

Westcott, B. F., 'On Cathedral Work', *Macmillan's Magazine*, vol. xxi, 1869–70, pp. 246–51, 308–14.

Whiston, R., *Cathedral Trusts and their fulfilment* (3rd edn, London 1849).

Williamson, D. M., *Lincoln Muniments* (Lincoln 1956).

Willis, T. G., *Records of Chichester* (Chichester 1928).

Woodruff, C. E., 'Reminiscences of the Cathedral and its personnel seventy-five years ago', *Canterbury Cathedral Chronicle*, no. 39, September 1943, pp. 15–22.

Woodruff, C. E., and Cape, H. J., *Schola Regia Cantuariensis* (London 1908).

Woodruff, C. E., and Danks, W., *Memorials of the Cathedral and Priory of Christ in Canterbury* (London 1912).

Wordsworth, C., *The Ecclesiastical Commission and the Universities: Letter to a Friend* (London 1837).

Wordsworth, C., 'On English Cathedrals', *Miscellanies Literary and Religious*, III (London 1879), pp. 290–335.

Wordsworth, C., and Macleane, D., *Statutes and Customs of the Cathedral Church of the Blessed Virgin Mary at Salisbury* (London 1915).

Wordsworth, C., and Robertson, D. H., 'Salisbury Choristers: their endowments, boy-bishops, music teachers, and headmasters, with the history of the organ', *Wiltshire Archaeological and Natural History Magazine*, vol. clxviii, June 1938, pp. 201–31.

Wordsworth, E., *Memorials of Henry William Burrows* (London 1894).

Worlledge, A. J., *Letters of Bishop Gott* (London 1918).

Yeats-Edwards, P., *English Church Music: A Bibliography* (London 1975).

Young, P. M., 'George Robertson Sinclair, 1863–1917', *Three Choirs Festival Programme 1985* (Hereford 1985), pp. 28–32.

Anonymous Tracts and Booklets

Henry Parry Liddon, 1829–1929: A Centenary Memoir (London 1929).

Cathedral Bodies and what they cost (London n.d.).

'Cathedral Life and Cathedral Reform', *Contemporary Review*, pp. 488–513 (n.d.).

The Case of the Deans of the Old Cathedrals stated and examined (London n.d.).

Cathedral Wealth and Cathedral Work (London 1861).

Wells Cathedral Library (Wells 1974).

Hereford Cathedral, City and Neighbourhood (Hereford 1867).

Sacred Music for the People (November 1886).

BIBLIOGRAPHY

Periodicals

Archaeologia
British Critic
Chronicle of the Convocation of Canterbury
Church Congress Reports
Churchman
Church Times
Ecclesiologist
Gentleman's Magazine
Guardian
Hereford Times
Mirror
Mirror of Parliament
Musical Times
Parish Choir
Quarterly Musical Review
Quarterly Review
Saturday Review
Standard
The Times
and: Hansard's Parliamentary Debates

Parliamentary Papers

1835	xxii, 15	*Report of the Commissioners of Inquiry into the Ecclesiastical Revenues of England and Wales*
1835	xxii, 1	*First Report from the Commissioners appointed to consider the state of the Established Church, with reference to Ecclesiastical Duties and Revenues*
1836	xxxvi, 1	*Second Report from the Commissioners appointed to consider the state of the Established Church, with reference to Ecclesiastical Duties and Revenues*
1836	xxxvi, 47	*Third Report from the Commissioners appointed to consider the state of the Established Church, with reference to Ecclesiastical Duties and Revenues*
1836	xxxvi, 67	*Fourth Report from the Commissioners appointed to consider the state of the Established Church, with reference to Ecclesiastical Duties and Revenues*
1837	xli, 37 *and*	*Communications addressed to his Majesty's*
1837–8	xxxviii, 69	*Commissioners appointed to consider the state of the Established Church in England and Wales with reference to Ecclesiastical Revenues and Duties, and to the Ecclesiastical Commissioners of England, relating to the Union of the Bishopric of Sodor and Man with that of Carlisle. Communications made to the same Commissioners from Cathedrals and Collegiate Churches in England and Wales and from their several Chapters, Dignitaries, Members and Officers*
1839	vii, 239	*Report from the Select Committee appointed to inquire into the Mode of granting and renewing Leases of the Landed and other Property of the Bishops, Deans, and*

		according to the Use of the United Church of England and Ireland (The Royal Commission on Ritual): evidence of Dean Close and Dean Duncombe
1871	lv, 197f., 246–7	*Copies of suggestions drawn up by Cathedral bodies for the Improvement of Cathedral Establishments*
1876	lviii, 539	*Return of the Number of Lay Vicars or Clerks in each Cathedral or Collegiate Church, stating whether or not they form separate Corporations; also specifying the Maximum and Minimum number enjoined by the Statutes or Charters, with their present Number, Ages and Stipends, whether Statutable or Supplementary; also the number of required Attendances, and Number of Omissions of Duty, for the Year ending 25th March 1875; and, whether there are any, if so, how many, Paid Supernumeraries, and from what Source they are paid*
1876	lviii, 553, 657	*Return showing the Number of Churches (including Cathedrals) in every Diocese in England which have been built or restored at a cost exceeding £500 since the year 1840*
1882	xx, 13	*First Report on Condition of Cathedral Churches in England and Wales*
1883	xxi, 15	*Second Report on Condition of Cathedral Churches in England and Wales*
1884–5	xxi, 453	*Final Report on Condition of Cathedral Churches in England and Wales*

Separate reports on individual cathedrals:

1883	xxi,	41	Truro
		93	St Paul's
		135	Chester
		175	Bristol
		227	Wells
		299	Rochester
1884	xxii,	15	Ely
		57	Norwich
		99	Carlisle
		143	Christ Church, Oxford
		159	Worcester
		201	Hereford
		237	Canterbury
		279	Ripon
1884–5	xxi,	15, 287	Manchester
		19	Winchester
		57	Durham
		103	Salisbury
		145	Lichfield
		213	Gloucester
		249	Peterborough
		315	Exeter
		345	Chichester
		381	Lincoln
		453	York

INDEX

❋

462

Index

Index

465

Index

Index

Index